The Killing Season

A HISTORY OF THE INDONESIAN MASSACRES, 1965–66

Geoffrey B. Robinson

PRINCETON UNIVERSITY PRESS
PRINCETON & OXFORD

Published by Princeton University Press,
41 William Street, Princeton, New Jersey 08540

In the United Kingdom: Princeton University Press,
6 Oxford Street, Woodstock, Oxfordshire OX20 1TR

press.princeton.edu

Jacket image: Suspected PKI members detained by army and anti-communist militias near the base of Mount Merapi, Central Java, 1965. Courtesy of the Indonesian National Library (Perpustakaan Nasional Indonesia)

Library of Congress Cataloging-in-Publication Data

Names: Robinson, Geoffrey, 1957– author.
Title: The killing season : a history of the Indonesian massacres, 1965–66 / Geoffrey B. Robinson.
Description: Princeton : Princeton University Press, 2018. | Includes bibliographical references and index.
Identifiers: LCCN 2017039519 | ISBN 9780691161389 (hardcover ; alk. paper)
Subjects: LCSH: Political violence—Indonesia. | Political atrocities—Indonesia. | Political prisoners—Indonesia. | Indonesia—History—Coup d'?etat, 1965. | Indonesia—Politics and government—1966–1998.
Classification: LCC HN710.Z9 V568 2018 | DDC 303.609598—dc23
LC record available at https://lccn.loc.gov/2017039519

British Library Cataloging-in-Publication Data is available

This book has been composed in Miller

Printed on acid-free paper. ∞

Printed in the United States of America

10 9 8 7 6 5 4 3 2 1

For Lovisa and Sofia

CONTENTS

PREFACE

THE LAST TIME I SAW BUDIARDJO, we shared a meal at his favorite Chinese restaurant near Piccadilly Circus in London. He told me a little about the evening classes he was taking and his time as a political prisoner. But mostly we talked about the changes that were then unfolding in Indonesia and his hope that he might finally be able to go home after more than fifteen years. He looked weary, and as always the London cold was getting to him, but otherwise he seemed in good spirits. A few months later, I learned that he had died—ten thousand miles from home, an exile from the country he had served and whose independence he had fought for.

Budiardjo's experience was not unusual. In fact, in many ways, his is the story of millions of Indonesian nationalists and leftists, from all walks of life, who were caught up in the awful juggernaut of arbitrary detention, interrogation, torture, mass killing, and political exile that followed an alleged left-wing coup attempt on the morning of October 1, 1965. Blaming the attempt on the Indonesian Communist Party, the army organized a campaign of violence intended to destroy the party and its affiliates and to drive the popular left-nationalist President Sukarno from power. That campaign was aided and abetted by the United States and its allies. By the time the violence ended, an estimated half a million real or alleged Communists had been killed, and another million or so had been arbitrarily detained. Budiardjo was among them; imprisoned without charge or trial for fourteen years, on his release he fled the country of his birth. If I mention him here, then, it is not because his experience was exceptional but because it was so common, and to make the point that the story I tell in this book is about hundreds of thousands of real people, just like him—husbands and wives, friends and lovers, whose lives were torn apart by the violence and can never again be made whole.

When I first learned about these events and the complicity of foreign powers in them, I was sickened and outraged. Today, more than thirty years later, I am still sickened and outraged—all the more so because the crimes committed have been all but forgotten and those responsible have not yet been brought to account. Through these years, whatever else I have done, I have never managed to get these feelings to go away. That is probably the single most important reason I have written this book: to share what I know about these events in the hope that it will make some kind of a difference, at the very least by disturbing the unseemly silence that has surrounded them. I am not naive enough to believe that this act of writing will change the course of history or even make much of a dent in it. But if it moves even one person to act or speak out against these crimes, or think more deeply about their responsibilities as citizen or scholar, I will rest a little more easily.

It goes without saying that in writing this book, I have accumulated substantial debts of gratitude. I first began to study the events of 1965–66 while still a graduate student at Cornell University in the early 1980s. From the outset, I was encouraged by Professors George Kahin and Benedict Anderson, both of whom had been investigating the subject since 1965, and who continued to do so for many more years. I was also spurred on by Audrey Kahin, a historian of Indonesia who served for many years as the editor of Cornell's prestigious journal *Indonesia*. Over the better part of three decades, George, Ben, and Audrey generously shared with me their findings and interview notes along with the hundreds of primary documents they had unearthed in Indonesia and elsewhere. They also offered me their honest reactions to my ideas, while gently prodding me to get on with writing. As if that were not enough, the Kahins allowed me to live in their guesthouse for a year rent free in exchange for feeding and building a shed for their pet goat, Sybil.

For the Kahins and Ben, untangling the events of 1965–66 was never simply an academic exercise. It was a matter of giving voice to people who had been wrongfully killed and imprisoned, rectifying a grossly distorted and dangerous official history, and holding those responsible to account. Through them, I was introduced to a community of scholars who had devoted many years to the study of the 1965 "coup" and its aftermath, and who likewise generously shared their insights and findings with me. I am especially grateful to Gabriel Kolko, who in the late 1990s made available several thousand pages of declassified US government documents that he had collected over the years, and Ruth McVey, who during a memorable week at her beautiful farmhouse in Tuscany in 1996, opened her extraordinary archive to me. It is no exaggeration to say that without the generosity, guidance, and encouragement of these inspiring people, and without their example of serious but engaged historical scholarship, I could not—and probably would not—have written this book. If I have any regret, and I do, it is that my dear mentors and friends George and Ben died before I reached the end of the path on which they set me so many years ago.

I owe an equal debt of gratitude to the great many Indonesian friends and colleagues, some of them now gone, who have helped me over the years to make sense of the terrible events that are the subject of this book. For their insights, scholarly contributions, and friendship, I especially wish to thank: Ben Abel, Andi Achdian, George Aditjondro, Haris Azhar, Suwondo Budiardjo, Arief Budiman, Leila Chudori, Hendardi, Hilmar Farid, Jafar Siddiq Hamzah, Sindhunata Hargyono, Ariel Heryanto, Diyah Larasati, Liem Soei Liong, Dede Oetomo, Degung Santikarma, Kamala Soedjatmoko, Tony Supriatma, Julia Suryakusuma, Galuh Wandita, and Baskara Wardaya. I also want to thank the former political prisoners and human rights advocates in Indonesia whom I met or came to know in the course of my work as the head of Indonesia research at Amnesty International's headquarters in London in the late 1980s and early 1990s. Because of the sensitive subject matter of this book, most of them would not wish to be mentioned here by name; for the same reason, I have not cited them in what follows. But they include a good number of former political prisoners and their family members as well as the activists and lawyers who bravely defended them, and spoke out in the name of human rights and the rule of law at a time when it was uncommon and sometimes unsafe to do so. To say that these people and experiences inspired me to write would be the grossest understatement. They did not inspire me to write; they left me no choice.

Through these Indonesian friends and colleagues, I came to see a different—more intimate and distressing—dimension of the story of the so-called coup and subsequent violence. In interviews and private gatherings across the country, I listened in stunned silence to stories of neighbors hacked to death with machetes, fellow prisoners raped by soldiers or militia members, and parents separated from their loved ones for years or forever through the deliberate cruelty of the New Order regime. In London, I read hundreds of letters sent by former political detainees and prisoners still being held decades after their arrest, thanking Amnesty International for its efforts on their behalf or asking for help in getting back on their feet. In Jakarta and elsewhere, I met some of those former prisoners when they gathered in private to share their memories and offer support to one another. From them, I learned about the obnoxious system of surveillance and control that disrupted the lives of hundreds of thousands of former political detainees and their families. My work with Amnesty International and later the United Nations also gave me new insights into the workings of the New Order state more generally, most notably in Aceh and East Timor, where Indonesian army forces and militias carried out campaigns of violence startlingly similar to those that had been waged in 1965–66. Through those experiences, and the practical day-to-day work of human rights reporting and analysis, I came to appreciate just how profoundly the events of 1965–66 had shaped modern Indonesia, giving rise to an extreme intolerance of dissent, a broad militarization of state and society, and a tendency to meet opposition with extreme violence.

Beyond Indonesia, the list of friends and colleagues who have helped me at some stage through the slow germination of this book is also long. It includes academics, of course, but also journalists, writers, filmmakers, human rights activists, and friends who have inspired or sustained me in one way or another. With the certainty that I am leaving someone out, I wish to thank the following: Nanci Adler, Christine Bloch, Martin van Bruinessen, Carmel Budiardjo, Michael Buehler, Patrick Burgess, Amander Clark, Robert Cribb, Harold Crouch, Leslie Dwyer, Martijn Eickhoff, Jonathan Emont, Victoria Forbes Adam, Ross and Ardeth Francis, Anthony Goldstone, Hillary Goyal, Wolf Gruner, David and Maria Harris, Vannessa Hearman, Eva-Lotta Hedman, Anne Lot Hoek, David Jenkins, Sidney Jones, Anett Keller, Gerry van Klinken, Robert Lemelson, Alex Li, Bill Liddle, Henk Maier, Ian Martin, Mike McClintock, John McGlynn, Kate McGregor, Jens Meierhenrich, Jess Melvin, Joshua Oppenheimer, Landon Pearson, Nancy Lee Peluso, David Petrasek, Annie Pohlman, Tessel Pollman, Hume and Azucena Rogers, John Roosa, Sara Schonhardt, Henk Schulte Nordholt, Laurie Sears, Brad Simpson, Karel Steenbrink, Karen Strassler, Scott Straus, Eric Tagliacozzo, Gaye and Andrew Taylor, Uğur Üngör, Patrick Walsh, Jessica Wang, David Webster, Saskia Wieringa, and Juliana Wijaya. I especially wish to thank Douglas Kammen and Mary Zurbuchen as well as two anonymous reviewers, who read the entire manuscript with great care and made invaluable suggestions for its improvement. Sincere thanks as well to David Jenkins for sharing his wonderful photographs, George Dutton for much-needed help with maps, and John Sidel for helpful comments on the manuscript and stimulating conversations over the years—some of them quite useful!

Sincere thanks are also due to colleagues, staff members, and students at UCLA, my institutional home for the past twenty years. In their role as successive departmental chairs, Brenda Stevenson, Ned Alpers, David Myers, and Steve Aron accommodated my requests for time off from teaching to write this book. Other colleagues contributed in no small measure through their collegiality, reading suggestions, and thoughtful comments in the course of many conversations, formal and less so. Among them, I especially wish to thank: Jade Alburo, Robin Derby, George Dutton, Nikki Keddie, Robin Kelley, Vinay Lal, Kelly Lytle-Hernandez, Benjamin Madley, Bill Marotti, Michael Meranze, Michael Salman, and Peter Stacey. For their heroic efforts in making the Department of History a productive and congenial place to work, and keeping a sense of humor against all the odds, heartfelt thanks and appreciation to Bibi Dhillon, Diana Fonseca, Hadley Porter, and other members of the department's administrative staff. Last but not least, sincere thanks to many current and former graduate students in various disciplines whose own work and probing questions have kept me thinking in new ways about the issues raised in this book: Marie E. Berry, Sebastiaan Broere, Gustav Brown, Chao-yo Cheng, Kimberly Claire, Nicole Iturriaga, Viola Lasmana, Saskia Nauenberg, Rebekah Park, Awet Weldemichael, Maya Wester, Juliana Wilson, and Matthew Wright. Among these, a special note of thanks to Dahlia Setiyawan for her own important work on the events of 1965–66 in Surabaya, and her invaluable research and editorial assistance with this book. A tip of the hat, as well, to the excellent students in my undergraduate seminar on the History of Human Rights for their stimulating insights and comments as this book neared completion.

Needless to say, I am also extremely grateful to Brigitta van Rheinberg and Eric Weitz at Princeton University Press for encouraging me to write this book, and providing me with all manner of helpful advice and encouragement along the way. Amanda Peery and others at the press have also been models of collegiality and professionalism throughout. To all of them, my sincere thanks.

As for my family, no words can properly express the depth of my gratitude. They have nurtured me and lifted me up. Although my father is now gone, I thank him and my mother for opening my eyes to a wider world, encouraging me to think a little less about myself and a little more about others, and showing me through their example how to fight against prejudice and injustice. I also thank my wonderful siblings, Katharine, David, and Ann—and their loved ones—for their enduring kindness and support, even through their own trials and heartaches. Ever ready with a note of encouragement or word of advice, their confidence in me, though mysterious, has been a constant source of strength. Sincere thanks as well to all members of the extended Robinson and Stannow clans around the world who have so generously opened their homes and hearts to me.

Finally, to my wife Lovisa and our daughter Sofia, I can say only that my love and gratitude to you are without end. From the day we met in London more than twenty years ago, Lovisa has been a source of wonder and inspiration to me. A passionate advocate for the underdog, experienced and formidable human rights advocate, and expert editor with a keen eye for nonsense, it was she more than anyone else who insisted that I write this book and who, when I flagged, insisted that I keep going. She is also the love of my life and mother of our child, Sofia. Almost as passionate as her mother in her concern for fairness, Sofia has witnessed this book unfold over the past few years with a sense of genuine amazement that any assignment could possibly take so long to complete. At least as much as Lovisa and my editors, it is she who has insisted that I stick to the schedule, keep my promises, and finish my homework by the due date. And so as I write these words, I know she is looking on with a measure of pride that her dad has finally done what he said he would do.

NOTE ON SPELLING AND TRANSLATION

IN GRAPPLING WITH the problem of variation and change in Indonesian spellings, I have opted for simplicity and consistency while trying to maintain historical accuracy. I have spelled the names of people and institutions consistently throughout the book, generally using the simpler modern spellings rather than the older ones: *u* not *oe* (*Sukarno* not *Soekarno*); *j* not *dj* (*Jakarta* not *Djakarta*); *y* not *j* (*Yogyakarta* not *Jogjakarta*); and *c* not *tj* (*cerita* not *tjerita*). The main exceptions to this rule are in quotations from other sources as well as citations of authors and titles that use the old spellings. I have also retained the old spellings of the names of people who are best known by or continue to use those spellings. The arcane vocabulary of Indonesian politics presents special translation problems, for the literal meanings of the terms are often either uninformative or misleading. To minimize confusion, I have sometimes provided a gloss along with a literal translation. All the translations from Indonesian and other foreign languages are my own unless otherwise indicated.

ABBREVIATIONS AND FOREIGN TERMS

abangan	nominal Muslim, Java
ABRI	Angkatan Bersenjata Republik Indonesia (Armed Forces of the Republic of Indonesia)
aksi sepihak	unilateral actions by the PKI and affiliated organizations to implement land reform legislation
Ansor	Nahdlatul Ulama-affiliated youth organization
Bakin	Badan Koordinasi Intelijens Negara (State Intelligence Coordinating Body)
Bakorstanas	Badan Koordinasi Bantuan Pemantapan Stabilitas Nasional (Agency for the Coordination of Support for the Development of National Stability)
Banser	Barisan Ansor Serbaguna (Ansor Multipurpose Brigade)
Baperki	Badan Permusyawaratan Kewarganegaraan Indonesia (Deliberative Association for Indonesian Citizenship)
Biro Khusus	Special Bureau
Brimob	Brigade Mobil (Mobile Brigade)
BTI	Barisan Tani Indonesia (Indonesian Peasants' Front)
CGMI	Consentrasi Gerakan Mahasiswa Indonesia (Unified Movement of Indonesian University Students)
Dewan Jendral	Council of Generals
Dewan Revolusi	Revolutionary Council
DPR	Dewan Perwakilan Rakyat (People's Representative Assembly)
Dwikora	Dwikomando Rakyat (People's Double Command: to crush Malaysia and defend the Revolution)
ELSAM	Lembaga Studi dan Advokasi Masyarakat (Institute for Policy Research and Advocacy)
ET	Eks-Tapol (former political detainee)
G30S	Gerakan 30 September (September 30th Movement)
Gerwani	Gerakan Wanita Indonesia (Indonesian Women's Movement)
Gestapu	Gerakan September Tiga Puluh (army acronym for September 30th Movement)
Gestok	Gerakan Satu Oktober (October 1st Movement)
GMNI	Gerakan Mahasiswa Nasional Indonesia (Indonesian National University Students' Movement)
Hanra	Pertahanan Rakyat (People's Defense)
Hansip	Pertahanan Sipil (Civil Defense)
HMI	Himpunan Mahasiswa Islam (Islamic University Students' Association)
HSI	Himpunan Sarjana Indonesia (Indonesian University Graduates' Association)

IPKI	Ikatan Pendukung Kemerdekaan Indonesia (League of Upholders of Indonesian Freedom)
IPPI	Ikatan Pemuda dan Pelajar Indonesia (League of Indonesian Youth and High School Students)
IPT 1965	International People's Tribunal on 1965
KAMI	Kesatuan Aksi Mahasiswa Indonesia (Indonesian University Students' Action Front)
KAP-Gestapu	Komando Aksi Pengganyangan Gerakan September Tiga Puluh (Action Command to Crush Gestapu)
KAPPI	Kesatuan Aksi Pemuda Pelajar Indonesia (Indonesian Youth and Student Action Front)
KASI	Kesatuan Aksi Sarjana Indonesia (Indonesian University Graduates' Action Front)
KKPK	Koalisi Keadilan Pengungkapan Keadilan (Coalition for Justice and Truth)
Kodam	Komando Daerah Militer (Regional Military Command)
Kodim	Komando Distrik Militer (District Military Command)
Komnas HAM	Komisi Nasional Hak Asasi Manusia (National Commission on Human Rights)
Komnas Perempuan	Komisi Nasional Anti Kekerasan terhadap Perempuan (National Commision on Violence against Women)
Konfrontasi	Confrontation (campaign to oppose the formation of Malaysia, 1963–66)
Kontras	Komisi untuk Orang Hilang dan Korban Tindak Kekerasan (Commission for the Disappeared and Victims of Violence)
Kopassus	Komando Pasukan Khusus (Special Forces Command)
Kopkamtib	Komando Operasi Pemulihan Keamanan dan Ketertiban (Operations Command to Restore Security and Order)
Koramil	Komando Rayon Militer (Local Military Command)
Korem	Komando Resor Militer (Sub-regional Military Command)
Kostrad	Komando Cadangan Strategis Angkatan Darat (Army Strategic Reserve Command)
KOTI	Komando Operasi Tertinggi (Supreme Operations Command)
LEKRA	Lembaga Kebudayaan Rakyat (People's Cultural Institute)
Mahmillub	Mahkamah Militer Luar Biasa (Extraordinary Military Tribunal)
Masyumi	Majelis Syuro Muslimin Indonesia (Consultative Council of Indonesian Muslims)
MPRS	Majelis Permusyawaratan Rakyat Sementara (Provisional People's Consultative Assembly)
Nasakom	Nasionalisme, Agama, Komunisme (Nationalism, Religion, Communism)
Nefos	New Emerging Forces
Nekolim	Neokolonialisme, Kolonialisme, Imperialisme (Neocolonialism, Colonialism, Imperialism)

NU	Nahdlatul Ulama (Council of Islamic Scholars)
Oldefos	Old Established Forces
Operasi Trisula	Trisula Operation
Opsus	Operasi Khusus (Special Operations)
Pancasila	Five Principles (Indonesian national philosophy)
Panglima	senior military commander
Pangdam	Panglima Daerah Militer (Regional Military Commander)
Parkindo	Partai Kristen Indonesia (Indonesian Christian Party)
Partai Katolik	Catholic Party
Partindo	Partai Indonesia (Indonesia Party)
PDI	Partai Demokrasi Indonesia (Indonesian Democratic Party)
pemuda	youth
Pemuda Demokrat	Democratic Youth
Pemuda Katolik	Catholic Youth
Pemuda Marhaen	Marhaenist Youth
Pemuda Pancasila	Pancasila Youth
Pemuda Rakyat	People's Youth
Pepelrada	Penguasa Pelaksanaan Dwikora Daerah (Regional Authority to Implement Dwikora)
Permak	Persatuan Masyarakat Anti-Komunis Jawa Barat (Anti-Communist People's Union of West Java)
Permesta	Piagam Perjuangan Semesta (Charter of Universal Struggle, a Sulawesi-based rebel movement)
Peta	Pembela Tanah Air (Defenders of the Fatherland)
PKI	Partai Komunis Indonesia (Indonesian Communist Party)
PNI	Partai Nasional Indonesia (Indonesian Nationalist Party)
PRRI	Pemerintah Revolusioner Republik Indonesia (Revolutionary Government of the Republic of Indonesia)
PSI	Partai Sosialis Indonesia (Indonesian Socialist Party)
RPKAD	Resimen Para Komando Angkatan Darat (Army Paracommando Regiment)
RTM	Rumah Tahanan Militer (Military Detention Center)
santri	devout Muslim; also student at an Islamic school
SARBUPRI	Sarekat Buruh Perkebunan Republik Indonesia (Plantation Workers' Union of the Republic of Indonesia)
Sekber 1965	Sekretariat Bersama 1965 (Joint Secretariat for 1965)
Seskoad	Sekolah Staf dan Komando Angkatan Darat (Army Staff and Command College)
SOBSI	Sentral Organisasi Buruh Seluruh Indonesia (Central Organization of Indonesian Workers)
SOKSI	Sentral Organisasi Karyawan Sosialis Indonesia (Central Organization of Indonesian Socialist Employees)
Supersemar	Surat Perintah Sebelas Maret (Order of March 11, 1966)
Syarikat	Masyarakat Santri untuk Advokasi Rakyat (Pious Muslim Community for People's Advocacy)

Tameng Marhaenis	Marhaenist Shield
tapol	tahanan politik (political detainee)
Tapol	A UK-based human rights organization
TNI	Tentara Nasional Indonesia (Indonesian National Army)
YPKP	Yayasan Penelitian Korban Pembunuhan 1965–66 (Research Institute on the Victims of the 1965 Killings)

THE KILLING SEASON

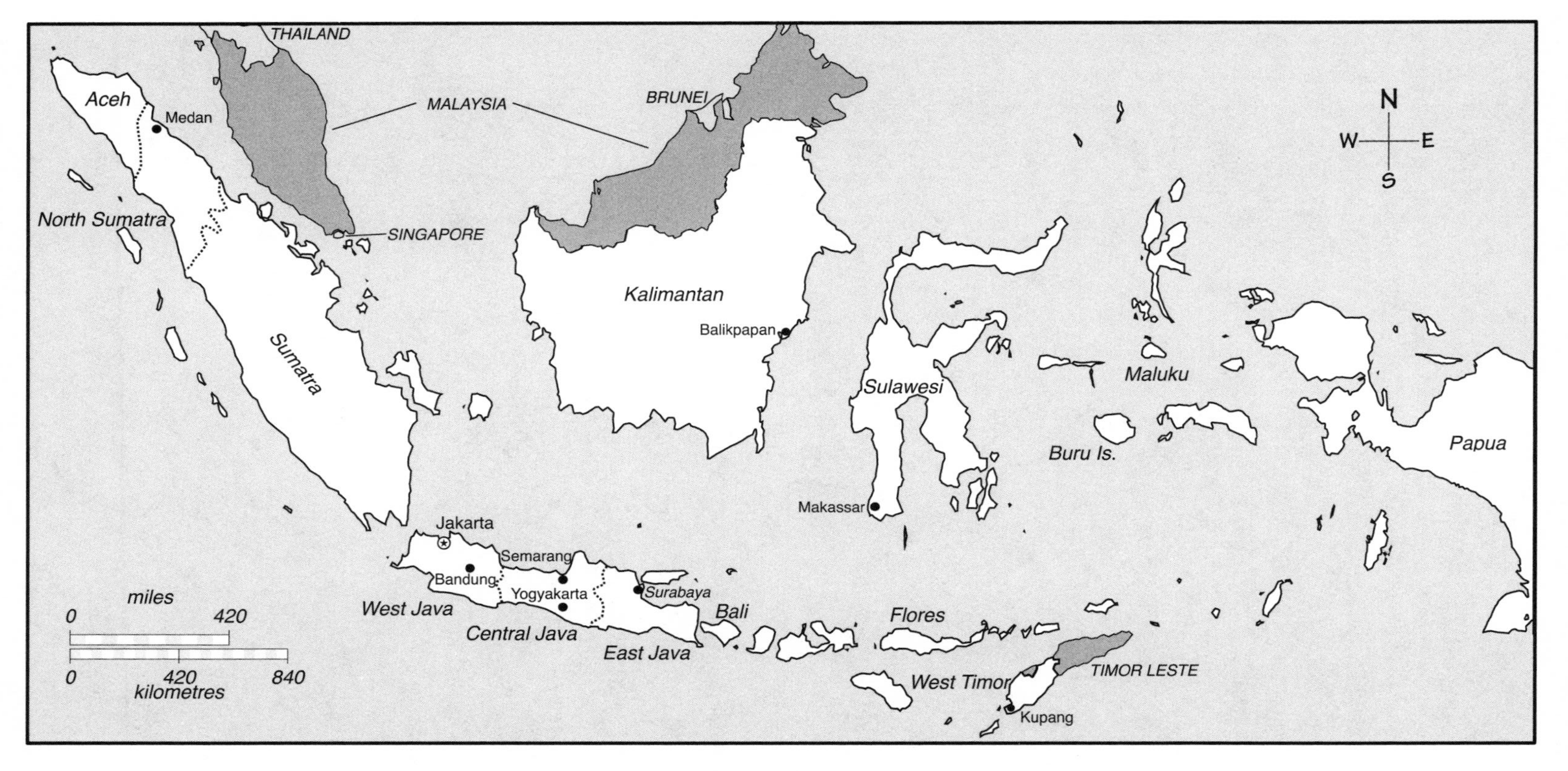

Map of Indonesia

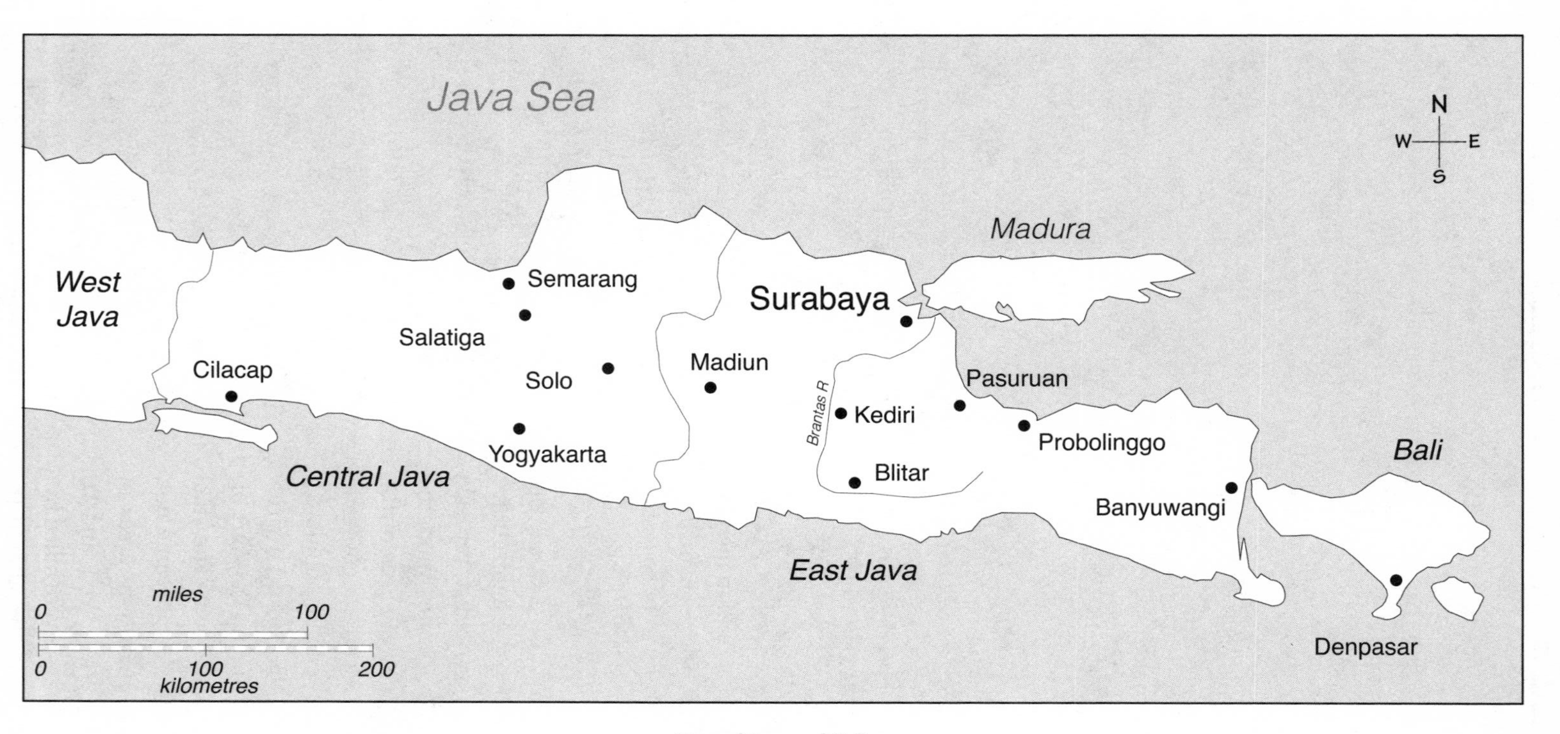

Map of Java and Bali

CHAPTER ONE

Introduction

I have never concealed from you my belief that a little shooting would be an essential preliminary to effective change in Indonesia; but it makes me sad to think that they have begun with the wrong people.

—SIR ANDREW GILCHRIST, BRITISH AMBASSADOR TO INDONESIA, OCTOBER 5, 1965

IN A LITTLE OVER SIX MONTHS, from late 1965 to mid-1966, an estimated half a million members of the Indonesian Communist Party (Partai Komunis Indonesia, or PKI) and its affiliated organizations were killed.[1] Another million or so were detained without charge, some for more than thirty years, and many of them were subjected to torture and other inhumane treatment. Few, if any, of the victims were armed, and almost all those killed and detained belonged to what were at the time lawful political and social organizations. This was not a civil war. It was one of the largest and swiftest, yet least examined instances of mass killing and incarceration in the twentieth century.

The consequences of the violence were far-reaching. In less than a year, the largest nongoverning Communist party in the world was crushed, and the country's popular left-nationalist president, Sukarno, was swept aside. In their place, a virulently anticommunist army leadership seized power, signaling the start of more than three decades of military-backed authoritarian rule. The state that emerged from the carnage, known as the New Order, became notorious for its systematic violation of human rights, especially in areas outside the heartland, including East Timor (Timor Leste), Aceh, and West Papua, where hundreds of thousands of people died or were killed by government forces over the next few decades. The violence also altered the country's political and social landscape in

FIGURE 1.1. Suspected PKI member arrested by soldiers in Jakarta, November 1965. (Rory Dell/Camera Press/Redux Pictures)

fundamental ways, leaving a legacy of hypermilitarism along with an extreme intolerance of dissent that stymied critical thought and opposition, especially on the Left. Perhaps most important, the events of 1965–66 destroyed the lives of many millions of people who were officially stigmatized because of their familial or other associations with those arbitrarily killed or detained. Even now, more than fifty years later—and some twenty years after the country began its transition to democracy—Indonesian society bears deep scars from those events.

In its sweep and speed, and its profound political and social implications, the violence of 1965–66 was comparable to some of the most notorious campaigns of mass killing and imprisonment of the postwar period, including those that occurred in Bosnia, Cambodia, and Rwanda, and it far surpassed other campaigns that have become iconic symbols of authoritarian violence in Latin America, such as those in Argentina and Chile. "In terms of the numbers killed," the Central Intelligence Agency (CIA) wrote in 1968, "the anti-PKI massacres in Indonesia rank as one of the worst mass murders of the 20th century, along with the Soviet purges of the 1930s, the Nazi mass murders of the Second World War, and the Maoist bloodbath of the early 1950s."[2] And while there is still no consensus on the matter, some scholars have described the Indonesian violence as genocide.[3] Yet half a century later, this violence remains virtually unknown internationally. Thus, the World History Project website entry for the year 1965 includes the fact that "Kellogg's Apple Jacks Cereal First Appears," but fails to mention the killing of half a million people in Indonesia.[4]

Even inside the country, the events of 1965–66 are still poorly understood, having only recently become the focus of serious discussion by historians, human rights activists, and the media. The massive production of testimony, memoir, truth telling, and forensic investigation—to say nothing of reconciliation, memorialization, and justice—that has followed virtually every genocide in the twentieth century has scarcely begun in Indonesia. Moreover, in contrast to most of the great mass killings of the past century, these crimes have never been punished or even properly investigated, and there have been no serious calls for any such action by international bodies or states. In this respect, Indonesia is arguably closer to the Soviet Union, China, and the United States than to any other country.

This book aims to disturb the troubling silence. Its first aspiration is to clarify some basic historical questions: How many people were killed and detained? Who were the victims, and how did they die? Who were the perpetrators, and what motivated them? What happened to the hundreds of thousands who were detained and their families? These basic questions—testament to the significant gaps in our knowledge—need to be answered as a matter of urgency, especially as the number of reliable witnesses and participants declines with every passing year. The book also explores a number of deeper analytic puzzles elaborated below. Most important, it asks the following questions: How and why did this extraordinary violence happen? What have been the consequences of the violence for Indonesian society? And why has so little been said or done about it in the intervening years?

With a few exceptions, scholars have viewed the events of 1965–66 as distinctively Indonesian, explicable mainly in terms of Indonesian culture, society, and politics. The implication has been that the dynamics at play are somehow unique and not comparable to other cases. While there is certainly much that is distinctive about the Indonesian case, my sense is that it shares many features with other instances of mass killing and detention, and that a more broadly comparative approach would be productive, both for understanding Indonesia's experience and enriching the general debate on such questions. And so while focusing substantively on Indonesia, this book also seeks to engage wider debates about the dynamic of mass killing and incarceration, about the long-term legacies of silence and inaction in the aftermath of violence, and about the history of human rights. To that end it asks: Under what conditions are mass killing and incarceration most likely to occur? Why are some such serious crimes remembered, condemned, and punished, while others are forgotten and left unpunished? What are the political, social, and moral ramifications of such acts and silence—for victims, for perpetrators, and for a society as a whole? My expectation is that a close examination of the mass violence of 1965–66 in Indonesia will provide insights into all these questions.

The Story in Brief

The immediate trigger—by some accounts, the pretext—for the violence came on October 1, 1965. Early that morning, six senior Indonesian Army generals and one lieutenant were detained and then killed by a group of lower-ranking officers belonging to a group called the September 30th Movement (Gerakan 30 September, or G30S). The movement claimed that it had acted to prevent a planned coup d'état by a CIA-backed "Council of Generals" and that it remained loyal to President Sukarno. Ignoring those claims, the surviving army leadership, led by Major General Suharto, insisted that the movement had been masterminded by the PKI, and began a campaign aimed at destroying the party and forcing President Sukarno, whom they regarded as too sympathetic to the PKI, from power. By mid-1966 Sukarno's authority had been gravely diminished, the army had effectively seized power, the PKI and all leftist organizations had been decimated, and Marxist-Leninist teachings had been formally banned.

The army leadership used a variety of strategies—political, judicial, and military—in its assault on the Left. Within days of the alleged coup attempt, for example, it set in motion a sophisticated propaganda campaign blaming the PKI for killing the generals, accusing it of attempting to seize power by force, and calling on the population to assist the army in crushing the traitors "down to the very roots." The most important strategy by far, however, was a campaign of violence that entailed outright killing as well as mass detention, ill treatment, torture, and rape. There were distinctive patterns to that violence that when taken together, point strongly to the army leadership's central role in its planning and implementation.

There were broad commonalities, for instance, in the manner of arrest, interrogation, and execution. Most victims were first arrested without warrant by the army, police, or local paramilitaries, and many were subjected to harsh treatment and torture while under interrogation. Following interrogation, they were sorted into three broad categories based on their alleged degree of involvement in the September 30th Movement and leftist organizations. After screening, some detainees were released, some remained in detention, and some were selected for killing. Those targeted for killing were typically transported to execution sites by military vehicle, or handed over to local vigilante and paramilitary groups. Bound and gagged, they were then lined up and shot at the edge of mass graves, or hacked to pieces with machetes and knives. Their remains were often thrown down wells, or into rivers, lakes, or irrigation ditches; few received proper burials. Many were subjected to sexual abuse and violence before and after their killing; men were castrated, and women had their vaginas and breasts sliced or pierced with knives. Corpses, heads, and other body parts were displayed on roads as well as in markets and other public places.

There were also clear patterns in the identity of those arrested and killed. In marked contrast to many other cases of mass killing and genocide, the victims in Indonesia were not targeted because of their ethnicity, nationality, or religion. On the contrary, with only occasional exceptions, they were selected for arrest and killing primarily on the basis of their real or alleged political affiliations. Moreover, while those killed and imprisoned included a number of high-ranking PKI officials, the vast majority were ordinary people—peasants, plantation workers, day laborers, schoolteachers, artists, dancers, writers, and civil servants—with no knowledge of or involvement in the events of October 1. In other words, the attack on the PKI and its allies was not based on the presumption of actual complicity in a crime but rather on the logic of *associative* guilt and the need for *collective* retribution.

The perpetrators also shared crucial commonalities. While arrests and executions were frequently committed by the army and police, many were carried out by armed civilians and militias affiliated with political parties on the Right. In such cases, one or more individuals were selected as special executioners—sometimes referred to as *algojo*. The involvement of such local figures and groups has led some observers to conclude that the violence was the product of spontaneous "horizontal" conflicts among different social and religious groups. As I will elaborate below, that view ignores—and perhaps deliberately obscures—the fact that such groups and individuals almost always acted with the support and encouragement of army authorities. In the absence of army organization, training, logistical assistance, authorization, and encouragement, those groups would never have committed acts of violence of such great scope or duration.

Despite these broad similarities, there were significant variations in the pattern of the killing. Geographically, they were most concentrated

FIGURE 1.2. PKI members and sympathizers detained by the army in Bali, ca. December 1965. (National Library of Indonesia)

in the populous provinces of Central and East Java, on the island of Bali, in Aceh and North Sumatra, and in parts of East Nusa Tenggara. By contrast, they were relatively limited in the capital city of Jakarta, the province of West Java, and much of Sulawesi and Maluku. The timing of the killing was also distinctive. It began in Aceh in early October, and spread to Central Java in late October and to East Java and North Sumatra in early November. In December 1965, a full two months after the alleged coup attempt, the violence finally started in Bali, where an estimated eighty thousand people were killed in a few months. Meanwhile, on the largely Catholic island of Flores toward the eastern end of the archipelago, it did not begin until February of the following year. The violence started to slow significantly in March 1966, shortly after the army seized power, but continued intermittently in some parts of the country through 1968.[5] As discussed below, one of the enduring questions about the violence has been how to explain these variations.

There was also significant variation in the levels of political detention in different parts of the country, and in the relative levels of detention and killing. For example, it appears that long-term detention was greatest where the levels of mass killing were lowest, such as in Jakarta, West Java, and parts of Sulawesi. The reverse was also true: where the killing was most intense, as in Bali, Aceh, and East Java, the overall levels of long-term detention were relatively low. In other words, long-term political detention and mass killing seem to have been inversely related. One possible explanation for that pattern is that the military authorities in different regions adopted different strategies for implementing an overall order to destroy the Left. In some areas they opted for a strategy of mass incarceration, while in others they chose mass killing.[6]

Acute political and social tensions were a critical part of the story, too. Some of these tensions were shaped by the Cold War, which fueled and accentuated a bitter split between the Left and Right inside the country. On the Left was the popular and powerful PKI that had roots dating to the early twentieth century. After an impressive fourth-place finish in the 1955 national elections—the last national elections before the alleged coup—the party grew dramatically in size and influence over the next decade. By 1965, it had an estimated 3.5 million members, and 20 million more in affiliated mass organizations—for women, youth, peasants, plantation workers, cultural workers, and other groups. Arguably the most powerful and popular political party at the time, it also had the ear of President Sukarno, increasingly friendly ties with Beijing, and even some support inside the Indonesian armed forces, especially in the air force.

Ranged against the PKI were most of the Indonesian Army and a number of secular and religious parties. The most important and powerful of these were the Council of Islamic Scholars (Nahdlatul Ulama, or NU) and the right wing of the secular Indonesian Nationalist Party (Partai Nasional Indonesia, or PNI). While these groups differed on many issues, they shared a deep hostility to the PKI. Like the PKI, moreover, the parties on the Right all had affiliated popular organizations that were routinely mobilized for mass rallies and street demonstrations—as well as armed militia groups that played a central role in the violence of 1965–66. In short, by 1965, Indonesia was deeply divided, largely along a left-right (or more precisely, communist-anticommunist) axis, and politics was increasingly being played out on the streets by rival mass organizations and their armed counterparts.

These internal divisions were exacerbated by the wider international conflict and heated rhetoric of the Cold War. Although it was an early proponent of nonalignment, by the early 1960s Indonesia was shifting markedly—and in the view of Western states, dangerously—to the left. Between 1963 and 1965, for example, President Sukarno sought increasingly cordial relations with Beijing, launched blistering attacks on US intervention in Vietnam, withdrew from the United Nations, and began a major military and political campaign—called Confrontation (Konfrontasi)—against the new state of Malaysia, which Sukarno claimed had been created by the United Kingdom and other imperialist powers to encircle and weaken Indonesia. For all these reasons, the United States, the United Kingdom, and their allies saw Indonesia as a major problem. Indeed, by summer 1965, US and British officials were convinced that Indonesia was set to fall to the Communists. As CIA director W. F. Raborn wrote to President Lyndon Johnson in late July 1965, "Indonesia is well embarked on a course that will make it a communist nation in the reasonably near future, unless the trend is reversed."[7]

Such anxieties were not new. From the late 1940s onward, the US government had worked assiduously to undermine the PKI, and weaken or remove President Sukarno. It did so, for example, by covertly supporting anticommunist political parties in Indonesia's 1955 national elections, through a covert CIA operation supplying arms and money to antigovernment rebels in 1957–58, and when that operation failed, through a program of military assistance and training designed to bolster the political position of the army at the expense of both Sukarno and the PKI. Under the circumstances, it is perhaps not surprising that the United States and its allies welcomed the army's campaign against the Left and Sukarno after October 1965. Nor should it come as a great surprise that these and others major powers eagerly assisted the army in that campaign and its seizure of power.

Capturing the heady mood of optimism of the period, *Time* magazine described the decimation of the PKI and the rise of the army as "the West's best news for years in Asia," and a *New York Times* story on the subject was headlined "A Gleam of Light in Asia."[8] The reason for these jubilant assessments is not hard to discern. In the context of the Cold War and against the looming backdrop of the war in Vietnam, the mass killing and arrest of hundreds of thousands of people was a small price to pay for the destruction of one of the world's largest and most successful Communist parties. Thus, after noting that "at least 300,000 Indonesians were killed" in the violence, a US State Department postmortem from 1966 concluded that "all in all, the change in Indonesia's policies has been a major 'break' in the Southeast Asian situation, and a vivid example to many other nations of nationalist forces rising to beat back a Communist threat."[9]

Over the next few decades, the United States and its allies remained stalwart supporters of Major General Suharto's New Order regime, lavishing it with economic and military assistance, and loyally defending it in the face of domestic and international criticism of its abysmal human rights record. The US government also went to extraordinary lengths to disguise its own role in the violence. In 1968, the CIA wrote and published an account of the alleged coup, *Indonesia—1965: The Coup That Backfired*, which largely embraced the dubious army version of events. Likewise, a succession of former US government officials, including Ambassador Marshall Green as well as the Jakarta CIA station chief, Hugh Tovar, and his agency colleagues J. Foster Collins and John T. Pizzicaro, published memoirs and articles that sought to divert attention from any possible US role, while questioning the integrity and political loyalties of scholars who disagreed with them.[10]

Although the mass killings subsided in mid-1966, the campaign against the Left continued—most notably in the program of arbitrary mass detention. Of the estimated one million people detained following the alleged coup attempt, only a few thousand were ever charged with a crime, and they were sentenced in conspicuously unfair show trials. The rest were held without charge in appalling conditions—some of them in forced labor camps and penal colonies—with no idea when or whether they might ever be released. While many of those detained were released after a few months or years in custody, a fair number were subsequently rearrested, and some thirty thousand uncharged political detainees remained in prisons or work camps until the late 1970s. In the face of unusual pressure from a newly credible transnational human rights movement and the administration of US president Jimmy Carter, Indonesia finally released most of the remaining detainees in 1979. Even after their release, however, former detainees and their families continued to be subjected to egregious restrictions on their civil, economic, and political freedoms, and suffer an officially fostered social stigma. In addition, over the years hundreds of political prisoners who had been sentenced in show trials were executed or died in custody, while dozens remained in prison until President Suharto finally stepped down in May 1998.

Suharto's resignation in the face of widespread protests stimulated lively demands for investigation into the events of 1965–66, a reassessment of the history of the period, apologies and compensation to the victims, and reconciliation and justice. In the intervening years there has been some progress on all those fronts. In 1999, then-president Abdurahman Wahid, a former head of the NU, apologized for that organization's role in the killings and called for a revocation of the New Order law banning the PKI. In 2004, a bill was passed establishing a Truth and Reconciliation Commission, and in 2012 the country's National Human Rights Commission issued a detailed report on the violence of 1965–66, calling on the attorney general to conduct further investigations and bring charges against those deemed responsible. Unfortunately, these and many other initiatives have been met with angry resistance from members of the government, retired army officers, and civil society groups, and the most promising—including all the items mentioned above—have either failed to materialize or been rolled back. The backlash has made it clear that the New Order's dogmatic approach to the question of 1965 remains deeply entrenched not only in the Indonesian state but also in society as a whole. The same is true of the various mythologies that were the product of the army's anti-PKI propaganda campaign. Meanwhile, Western and other states that abetted the violence of 1965–66, and roundly supported the New Order regime, have remained predictably silent about their role or the need to remedy those crimes so many years later. As a result, the prospects for truth, justice, and reconciliation in Indonesia remain elusive, more than fifty years after the violence began.

Explanations and Puzzles

Those who have examined the events of 1965–66 in depth have offered a wide range of explanations for them, focusing variously on psychological and sociopsychological dynamics, cultural and religious divisions, socioeconomic conflicts, army planning, and international meddling. Indeed, the available scholarship on these events is now so rich that it is possible to draw on it to develop a more comprehensive account of the violence and its legacies.[11] That scholarship is discussed in some depth in later chapters, but it may be helpful to outline here some of the main contributions, while also highlighting questions and puzzles that remain unanswered.

Many accounts of the Indonesian violence, both scholarly and popular, emphasize the personal and psychological motivations of the perpetrators.[12] Like Christopher Browning in his seminal study of the "ordinary men" of a German reserve police battalion and Alexander Hinton in his work on the Cambodian genocide, they stress factors like peer pressure, fear, compliance with authority, and cultural norms in motivating participation and acquiescence.[13] Such motives were undoubtedly important in Indonesia; it would otherwise be difficult to explain why so many people took part in the violence. They may also help to explain the extraordinary societal silence that followed the violence; few were prepared to risk speaking out against it. But as we know from other cases, and as the Indonesian experience confirms, such personal motivations alone cannot account for the onset and trajectory of mass violence. Crucial as personal motivations are in understanding those dynamics, they are necessarily shaped by other structural conditions, especially at the national and international levels.

Other accounts seek to explain the violence of 1965–66 by reference to ostensibly distinctive features of Indonesian cultural and religious life. The most persistent of these interpretations suggests that the killings were rooted in exotic cultural patterns like "running amok." An article in *Time* magazine from mid-1966 was typical: "Amok is a Javanese word, and it describes what happened at the collapse of the Communist coup. In a national explosion of pent-up hatred, Indonesia embarked on an orgy of slaughter that took more lives than the U.S. has lost in all wars in this century."[14] This sort of explanation is favored by Indonesian officials and their closest allies, but it is generally not taken seriously by scholars—or at least it shouldn't be.[15] Apart from its problematic cultural reductionism and the way it fudges the vital question of responsibility, it does not account for even the most rudimentary facts of the case. Perhaps most obviously, it offers no explanation for the program of mass arbitrary detention that lasted more than a decade; by definition, a program of detention that extends across a vast country and lasts for years cannot be the product of spontaneous or pent-up rage. Nor does it offer any plausible explanation for the long years of silence and impunity that followed the mass detention and killing.

More sophisticated analyses stress the importance of deeply rooted cultural and religious differences—for instance, between more pious (*santri*) and less pious (*abangan*) Muslims in Java—in laying the foundations for the violence.[16] Such accounts provide insight into the kinds of grievances that may have driven enmity and conflict in certain areas, and help to explain why some of the language and symbolism of the violence varied as it did from one place to the next. At the same time, like most accounts that locate the origins of genocide in long-standing conflicts and tensions, they do not really explain why such tensions should have suddenly escalated to mass killing when and where they did. If the differences between the groups were so bitter and intractable, why had they not led to more than a few isolated instances of violence before the alleged October coup? Why was there such a long delay before the onset of violence in some of the most conflict-ridden areas? And why did comparable tensions elsewhere in the country not also result in mass killings?

Some authors locate the root of the violence mainly in the socioeconomic conditions that gave rise to bitter conflicts among Indonesians in different parts of the country.[17] Such tensions do appear to correlate with observed patterns of violence, with some of the worst violence occurring in Central Java, East Java, and Bali, where the conflict over land (and land reform) had been most intense in the years before the alleged coup, and the plantation belt of North Sumatra, where tensions between labor and capital had reached a critical peak in 1965. Still, like analyses that seek to explain mass killings by reference to deeply rooted cultural and religious tensions, those based on underlying socioeconomic conflict fail to explain why such tensions should have escalated to the point of mass killing and incarceration. Nor do they offer a satisfactory account of the distinctive temporal patterns of the violence.

A handful of scholars have argued that the mass killing should be understood as the result of planning and coordination by army and political leaders. Jess Melvin has recently made that case for Aceh on the basis of a rare trove of Indonesian Army documents, and I have elsewhere made the argument for Bali.[18] Other scholars, including Douglas Kammen, John Roosa, and Robert Cribb, have likewise stressed that earlier studies overstated the importance of local social and cultural conditions, while underplaying the role of the army in fomenting and organizing the violence.[19] Others, however, have resisted this assertion, mainly on the grounds that significant geographic and temporal variations in the violence make it impossible to generalize. While accepting that the army may have played a significant role in some areas, they point to the variations as evidence that in other areas, horizontal social and cultural conflicts were the primary drivers of violence.[20] As elaborated below, my own view is that this latter interpretation is mistaken—and that the marked temporal and geographic variations actually point to a wider national pattern.

Finally, a number of authors have contended that the killings were mainly the result of a conspiracy, masterminded by foreign intelligence agencies like the CIA and the United Kingdom's Secret Intelligence Service (MI6), in coordination with a handful of Indonesian Army figures like Generals Suharto and Abdul Haris Nasution.[21] While there is no doubt that foreign agencies encouraged the army to act against the PKI and Sukarno before the supposed coup, and facilitated the violence after it (arguments I will discuss in some detail in this book), there are reasons to doubt that the entire affair was the result of a foreign conspiracy. Perhaps most important, that scenario probably attributes too much importance to a handful of CIA and MI6 operatives of doubtful competence, while ignoring the ample motives and capacities of Indonesian actors, chief among them the Indonesian Army leadership. As such, it perpetuates a simplistic, neocolonial narrative in which crucial political changes in the non-Western world, whether good or bad, are routinely attributed to the influence of the United States and other powerful outside actors. In any case, as I will elaborate later, the most careful studies on the subject do not support the claim of international conspiracy.

These explanations clearly offer important insights, and without them we could scarcely begin to make sense of the violence that followed the alleged coup. Still, as I have suggested, they leave some key questions unanswered: What accounts for the distinctive geographic and temporal patterns and variations in the violence? That is, why was it concentrated in certain regions—Bali, Aceh, Central Java, East Java, North Sumatra, and parts of East Nusa Tenggara—and why did it begin and end at markedly different times in different parts of the country? Why, despite those variations, did the violence take broadly similar forms across the country? Why, for instance, did vigilantes or death squads everywhere play such a central role, why did the violence so often seem to pit one social, cultural, or religious group against another, and why were methods like disappearance, bodily mutilation, corpse display, and sexual violence so common? How and why did deeply rooted cultural, religious, and socioeconomic tensions escalate to mass killing and incarceration? What was the relationship between the mass killing and program of mass detention? Who was ultimately responsible for the violence? What role, if any, did foreign powers play in it? And finally, what have been the consequences of the violence for Indonesian society, and why has so little been said or done about it over the past fifty years?

Wider Perspectives

In answering these questions, I have found it fruitful to think of Indonesia's experience in a comparative way, by contemplating the events and legacies of 1965–66 in light of the wider literatures on genocide, mass violence, human rights, and the Cold War. Considering the near absence of Indonesia from much of that literature, moreover, it seems to me that the Indonesian example might also help to refine and enrich those discussions.

A number of insights from the wider literature are especially germane to the Indonesian case. Among the most significant is the argument that genocide and mass killing are inherently political acts, initiated by actors (people but also institutions) with political motives and objectives. That is to say, genocides do not simply happen—they are not the "natural" by-product of socioeconomic or cultural conflicts—but instead are the result of deliberate and conscious acts by political and military leaders. This insight, compellingly argued by Benjamin Valentino, Scott Straus, Helen Fein, and others, usefully shifts the focus away from purely psychological and social dynamics that explain popular participation and acquiescence in mass killing, to the intentional political acts of those in positions of authority who set mass killings in motion, and provide the encouragement and means through which they can be carried out.[22] That shift helps to train our attention on the structural conditions that permit mass killings to happen, and the vital question of legal and political *responsibility* for such acts.

A related observation is that the capacities and character of states and state institutions are vital in creating the conditions for, and carrying out, programs of mass killing and incarceration. State capacity in the fields of logistics, propaganda, administration, and control over the means and organization of violence arguably mark the difference between isolated outbreaks of violence and sustained, geographically dispersed programs of mass killing and incarceration.

Although it may seem self-evident, among the most important of these is the existence of institutions—such as armies, police forces, paramilitaries, and militias—with the logistical wherewithal and inclination to organize and carry out systematic violence.[23] A critical feature of such bodies is what I call their "institutional culture," shorthand for their internal norms and patterns of behavior, which depending on their historical experience and training, may be more or less violent. An important dimension of an institution's culture is its "repertoire of violence," by which I mean the routines of violence learned and employed by all of those associated with the institution.[24] I believe that such institutional cultures and repertoires help to account for certain distinctive patterns of mass violence that are not easily explained by reference to personal psychology or peer pressure.

The wider literature also points to the importance of ideology in fueling genocide and mass violence. Eric Weitz has argued, for example, that a unique conjuncture of mass politics, ideas of racial purity, and revolutionary utopian ideologies fueled four of the twentieth century's worst genocides.[25] Other scholars have similarly highlighted the significance of ideologies rooted in racism, nationalism, and modernity—together with fears of an existential threat to the state—in explaining the onset and dynamics of genocide.[26] While the importance of state ideology can scarcely be denied, the Indonesian case raises some doubt about the significance of revolutionary utopianism and racial purity as the key elements in the equation. The ideology of Indonesia's New Order could hardly be characterized as utopian or revolutionary, and it was not in any obvious way rooted in ideas of racial purity. The existential threat to the nation imagined by the army leadership and its allies did not come from a particular racial or ethnic group but rather from a political group and ideology—the PKI and communism. And the remedy lay not in racial purification or even revolutionary transformation but simply the excision of the offending political category through execution, incarceration, reeducation, repression, and propaganda. Thus, if any ideology can be said to have driven the mass violence in 1965–66—and the later violence in Aceh, East Timor, Papua, and elsewhere—it was an ideology of strident, even hysterical anticommunism and militarism, informed by a narrative that portrayed the Left as an existential threat to the state and nation.

Another insight from the literature on genocide is that local conditions—along with the relationship between local and national actors—influence the trajectory of mass violence and genocide in significant ways. As Straus has argued, for example, local actors play a crucial role in implementing the plans and orders initiated by national leaders by identifying, detaining, categorizing, and killing designated enemies.[27] Mass violence may accelerate or slow depending on the willingness and ability of those local allies to carry out national plans, and the capacity of national leaders to mobilize and manage local allies and networks. Meanwhile, local socioeconomic and political conditions matter because they shape what kinds of tensions—for instance, land, political office, wages, or religion—become politically salient, and supply the language, symbols, and relevant collective memories through which such conflicts may be escalated or restrained.

Existing studies also point to language and visual representation as crucial in setting the stage for genocide and other kinds of mass violence.[28] Depictions of a targeted group as less than human, threatening, treacherous, immoral, or sexually depraved—together with explicit or implicit incitement to violence against members of the group—effectively serve to place it, in Fein's apt phrase, "outside the universe of obligation of the perpetrator," and make mass violence far more likely.[29] Whether in the context of mass rallies, print and electronic media, religious edicts, works of art, or carefully devised propaganda and psywar campaigns, pejorative representations of a target group help to create frameworks within which acts of violence against it are seen as justifiable, legitimate, and even necessary. The association between language and violence appears to be especially strong where the negative portrayals resonate with preexisting perceptions of the group, and where they are voiced or clearly condoned by powerful military, political, or religious figures. By removing the moral restraints on violent action, such representations help to forge the social consensus or at least popular compliance that is an essential component of mass violence.

Turning to a wider canvas, several scholars have made the case that genocide and other kinds of atrocities tend to emerge in the context of war, offering a variety of explanations for that connection.[30] Some have argued, for example, that the experience of modern war results in a general brutalization of both soldiers and society at large, and the emergence of a culture of violence that makes the turn to mass violence more likely. Others have stressed the way in which the binary "us versus them" mentality of war, together with the fear of an existential threat to the nation, lays the rhetorical and political groundwork for mass violence and killing. While recognizing the importance of war in the logic of genocide, historians of international human rights have taken a somewhat broader view, showing how international legal regimes, normative environments, and transnational networks can serve both to facilitate and to constrain mass violence.[31] These contributions show, in other words, that war is only one of many ways in which international actors and context can contribute to genocide and mass violence. In addition to explaining why genocides may happen, moreover, they offer clues as to how they may be prevented, ended, or remedied once the violence has ceased.

Likewise, historians of the Cold War have highlighted the many ways, short of all-out war, in which powerful states have historically helped to create the conditions for mass violence. Crucially, the best of this scholarship does not claim that Cold War calculations determined the course of events in other countries in a linear fashion, or that the military coups, wars, and rebellions of those years were solely the product of foreign conspiracy.[32] They show instead that the overthrow of neutralist or leftist leaders, and the rise of military regimes and violence that often followed, were shaped by a complex array of local interests and by the interplay of those interests with regional and international objectives and developments.[33] These findings suggest that there is a need for caution in attributing outbreaks of mass violence directly to foreign states and covert agencies. Still, as Greg Grandin has argued so powerfully for Guatemala, Cold War logic and interventions did have real, sometimes-grievous consequences for governments and populations in these years. That was certainly the case in Indonesia, where foreign intervention formed a crucial element of the wider context within which politics took shape in the years before and after 1965.

Finally, genocide scholars have underscored the pivotal role of historical processes, events, and contingencies in understanding the onset, dynamics, and end of genocide and mass violence.[34] They show, for example, how historical experiences, particularly as they are recalled in collective and official memory, may either encourage or constrain mass violence. They also argue that genocides and mass killings unfold in response to historically specific and changing conditions on the ground. This historically contingent and process-driven understanding of genocides is vital in explaining their geographic and temporal variations as well as how they end. One might add that historical memory along with official histories can have an especially profound effect on the ways in which mass violence is remembered, memorialized, and remedied. Where those responsible for the violence remain in power, they are in a strong position to write its history, and thus to construct a social memory that diverts blame, obscures responsibility, and obstructs all efforts at redress.

A New Account

Based on these insights and building on the rich body of existing work by Indonesia scholars outlined earlier, I want to suggest here a new approach that addresses many of the questions posed above—and accounts for the variations and particularities of the Indonesian case—while also making possible its comparison to other instances of mass killing and detention. That approach entails three broad claims, each of which is spelled out briefly below and which together form the basis for the discussion in the remainder of this book.

THE ARMY

My first claim is that the violence of 1965–66—its patterns and variations—cannot be properly understood without recognizing the pivotal role of the army leadership in provoking, facilitating, and organizing it. I do not mean that the army single-handedly carried out all the killings or acted alone; that was not the case. It faced pressure from a variety of social, religious, and political groups for "firm action" against the Left, and the success of its campaign depended on the often-willing collaboration of a great many Indonesians. What I am arguing, rather, is that the resort to mass killing and detention was neither inevitable nor spontaneous, but was encouraged, facilitated, directed, and shaped by the army's leadership. In other words, without the army leadership, those pressures—and

FIGURE 1.3. Army officer briefs soldiers and local militia members about the campaign against the PKI in a village in Central Java, ca.1965. (National Library of Indonesia)

the personal, socioeconomic, religious, and cultural tensions that fueled them—would never have resulted in mass killing or incarceration on such a wide scale, and would not have been followed by five decades of silence and inaction.

The army's decisive role had five crucial dimensions. First, in the immediate aftermath of the alleged coup attempt, the army developed and disseminated a discourse of existential threat to the nation that provoked and valorized acts of violence against real and alleged leftists. Through a carefully crafted media and propaganda campaign, it demonized and dehumanized the PKI and its affiliates, and called for them to be "destroyed down to the very roots." In doing so, the army leadership gave license to the party's enemies to do the same, and provided an essential ingredient in transforming underlying tensions and conflict into actual violence.

Second, the army leadership took a series of decisions and gave orders to detain, transport, categorize, register, interrogate, and prosecute vast numbers of people. To implement those decisions, it had to build and manage a network of local allies, and then sustain that network over an extended period of time. In the absence of such central planning, and without the army's unique organizational and logistical reach, the mass violence could not have extended to so many different areas of the country and could not have been sustained for so long. The army's central role also helps to explain the distinctive features of that campaign; disappearance, bodily mutilation, corpse display, sexual violence, and torture were elements of the army's repertoire of violence, shaped by its institutional culture.

Third, to carry out its plans, the army leadership mobilized an extensive network of civilian militia groups—like the NU's Banser and PNI's Pemuda Marhaen—and encouraged them to do the essential groundwork for the campaign of mass violence, such as identification, detention, transportation, and killing. While it is true that some groups occasionally acted without explicit army sanction, notably in East Java, such instances were localized and limited. In the vast majority of cases, militia forces operated with the full knowledge, and usually under orders from, local or regional army commanders. As a consequence, they were deeply influenced by the army's institutional culture, and the violence they committed drew on the army's standard repertoire. It was through these officially sanctioned militia groups, moreover, that long-standing tensions were transformed into mass violence, that violence was sustained for long periods over wide stretches of the country, and that so many people became complicit in the crimes committed.

Fourth, while the army alone had the unique organizational and logistical capacity to implement this plan, its capacity was not unlimited. In some areas, it was unable to mobilize local allies or even met resistance from local authorities, thereby delaying or derailing the implementation of the plan. In Bali, for instance, the central army leadership met resistance from the governor and regional military commander, resulting in a two-month delay in the onset of killings. By contrast, in Aceh, where the local civilian and army leadership were united in their support of the central army command's plan, the violence began almost immediately. Thus, the army leadership's uneven capacity to mobilize local allies helps to explain both the geographic and temporal variations in the violence.

Finally, by virtue of seizing power, the army leadership was able to write and disseminate its own history of the violence while silencing alternative versions. The army used various methods to do that, including public rituals, show trials, popular education, films, and other propaganda that evoked the "latent threat of Communism" and reminded potential critics of the dire consequences of being labeled a leftist. The result has been a profoundly misleading, but also remarkably resilient, account that has been crucial in enforcing the more than fifty years of silence and inaction that has followed the violence.

INTERNATIONAL CONTEXT

My second principal claim is that the actions of powerful foreign states—especially the United States and the United Kingdom—together with aspects of the international context were instrumental in facilitating and encouraging the army's campaign of mass violence in 1965–66. I am not suggesting that the United States or other foreign powers plotted the supposed coup or violence in advance. The evidence does not support such a claim. But I think it can be shown that in the absence of support from powerful states and in a different international context, the army's program of mass killings and incarceration would not have happened. An account that highlights the international context, and the acts and omissions of powerful states, also explains better than most others how the army got away with it, and why there has been such deafening silence and inaction over the five decades since it ended.

This claim is based on five main observations. First, contrary to blanket denials that the United States and its allies played any role in toppling Sukarno and destroying the PKI, there is now abundant evidence that they did. In fact, for more than a decade before the alleged coup, the United States and other Western powers worked assiduously to undermine Sukarno and the PKI through the provision of covert assistance to anticommunist parties and military backing to anti-Sukarno rebels. After 1958, moreover, they encouraged anticommunist elements in the army to act forcefully against the PKI and to play a leading role in politics by providing them with increased military assistance as well as secret assurances that they would support such a move. And in the final year before the supposed coup, the United States and its allies carried out a covert campaign designed to tarnish the reputation of the PKI and Sukarno, and supply a pretext for the army to act against them.

Second, the available evidence shows unequivocally that in the weeks and months after the alleged coup, the United States and United Kingdom encouraged and facilitated the violence that followed. They did this through a covert campaign of disinformation and propaganda designed to further "blacken the name" of the PKI, a policy of deliberate silence in the face of what they knew to be widespread army-instigated violence against civilians, and the provision of covert economic, military, and logistical assistance to the army leadership. These interventions, set in motion within days of the purported coup, provided vital assurance to Suharto and his allies that they could move against the PKI without fear of criticism, and buttressed the army's violent campaign at a critical juncture.

Third, the violence was crucially shaped by the broad international political context and more specifically the Cold War. As noted above, that context dominated the Indonesian political scene and helped to create the highly polarized left-right division that was arguably a precondition for mass violence. The Cold War was also essential in influencing the substance and style of Indonesia's international relations, especially after 1963, driving it ever closer to China while alienating it from the United States and other Western powers as well as the Soviet Union. It was Sukarno's drift to the left, after all, that led the United States, the United Kingdom, and their allies to view Indonesia as a major problem, and therefore to support the army leadership's move against the PKI and Sukarno, regardless of the cost in human lives. And it was Indonesia's (and the PKI's) decision to side with China after the Sino-Soviet split that led the Soviet Union to do so little to protect the PKI once the killing began.

Fourth, I think it can be shown that the violence was facilitated by the prevailing weakness at the time of international norms, institutions, and networks related to human rights. Perhaps most important was the near absence in 1965–66 of the transnational human rights and civil society networks that from the mid-1970s began to play an important part in efforts to prevent or stop mass violence. In the absence of such networks, the United Nations took no notice of the violence, most states expressed satisfaction or said nothing at all, and the mass media largely parroted official views. By contrast, the rapidly growing credibility of international human rights organizations and discourse in the 1970s, and the brief conjuncture of that new authority with the administration of US president Carter, help to explain the anomalous success of the campaign on behalf of Indonesia's political prisoners leading to the release of most by the end of 1979.

Finally, powerful international actors facilitated the Indonesian Army's work of rewriting the history of the violence. Through their economic, political, and military support for the regime that came to power in the wake of the killings of 1965–66, and their almost-total silence about them ever since, Western governments have helped to ensure that the official version of events prevailed, and have prevented the proper investigation and prosecution of what, by any measure, were among the worst crimes of the twentieth century. These conditions have also meant that unlike the survivors of some genocides—most notably the Holocaust—the survivors of 1965–66 have had neither the opportunity nor power to generate world attention about those events in the half century since they happened.

HISTORICAL CONDITIONS

Lastly, this account highlights the role of historical conditions and antecedents in understanding the dynamics of the mass violence of 1965–66. More specifically, I argue that in addition to the underlying cultural, religious, and socioeconomic tensions that shaped the violence, five crucial historical conditions related to Indonesian political life made the mass killings in Indonesia much more likely to happen. They did so by influencing political ideas and conflicts, shaping key political institutions and structures, and providing the basis for politically powerful historical reconstructions and memories.

The first of these conditions was a colonial and anticolonial history that made bitter ideological differences between the Left and Right a key fault line of Indonesian politics after independence. Notwithstanding its enormous linguistic, cultural, and religious diversity, by the 1920s Indonesia's anticolonial politics had begun to crystallize as much along ideological lines as on the basis of ethnic or cultural identities. Within that political constellation, the Left was unusually strong, and the PKI held an especially prominent position. The position of the Left was repeatedly challenged, however, not only by those who favored colonial rule but also by those who saw it as antithetical to Islam, and some who believed it represented a threat to national unity and stability. Those lines of tension survived into the postindependence period and laid the foundations for the deepening left-right conflicts that culminated in 1965.

The second condition was the emergence of a perception within the army and the political Right more generally that the PKI represented an existential threat to army unity and to the nation. That perception dated back at least to September 1948, when an armed group supported by the PKI, sought to establish an autonomous political command around the provincial town of Madiun in East Java. Alarmed by this apparent threat to their authority, the army and the national (Republican) leadership acted quickly to crush the movement, detaining and executing its principal leaders. From that point onward, the army and its allies on the right portrayed the events in Madiun as an armed rebellion by the PKI, and evidence of the party's essentially treacherous inclinations. As such, they became a rallying point for the goal of suppressing the PKI, especially after October 1, 1965, when the army and its allies repeatedly invoked the memory of Madiun as a reason to crush the PKI once and for all.

The third crucial historical condition for the violence was a process of state formation in the context of war and revolution that gave rise to a conservative and politically powerful army along with a highly militarized state after independence. If the idea of an Indonesian "nation" had already been articulated in the 1920s, the sinews of a new Indonesian state only began to form in the course of Indonesia's wartime occupation by Japan (1942–45) and in the four-year fight for independence from the Dutch known as the National Revolution (1945–49). Notwithstanding certain outward concerns with democracy and human rights, and a nominally civilian leadership, the state that emerged during these years was underpinned by a national army whose commitment to civilian rule and democracy was superficial at best. In the postindependence period, the army repeatedly asserted its right to be directly involved in political life, and with the president's declaration of martial law in 1957, it secured both substantial political and economic power that it was reluctant to relinquish. Over the same period, the state itself became increasingly militarized, both in style and substance.

The fourth condition was the early development of an army doctrine and practice of mobilizing civilian militia forces to combat domestic enemies. Influenced by the Japanese occupation forces with whom its members had trained during the wartime occupation, and in response to the challenges of fighting returning Dutch and Allied forces on Indonesian territory after 1945, the army relied to a great extent on the support of local populations and their "struggle organizations" known as *lasykar*. That strategy was eventually formalized into a doctrine of "total people's defense," which in essence called for the mobilization of local militias to fight domestic and foreign enemies. The strategy was used to considerable effect not only against the Dutch and their allies but also against domestic groups that in the army's view, threatened its preeminence or the nation. The strategy as well as the particular tactics and repertoires that were used in that campaign were employed again after independence, and formed an essential foundation for the mobilization of militia groups to detain and kill leftists after October 1, 1965.

The final condition was the consolidation by the early 1960s of a politics notable for its militancy and high levels of mass mobilization. That condition was accelerated by the polarizing logic of the Cold War, the compelling but sometimes-bellicose language of Sukarno's anticolonial nationalism, and the often-obnoxious behavior of the United States and other powerful states both in Indonesia and elsewhere. US support for regional rebellions in the late 1950s and its armed intervention in Vietnam were especially provocative; British support for the newly formed state of Malaysia over Sukarno's objections did nothing to relieve tensions.

On the other side, increasingly strong ties with China in these years encouraged militancy on the left, while heightening anxieties on the right. Together, these factors accentuated existing left-right divisions inside Indonesia, and a growing sense of crisis in which rumor, suspicion, and hostility flourished, providing a crucial backdrop and stimulus for mass political violence.

In short, the account presented here, and elaborated in the rest of the book, stresses the critical role of the army leadership, the influence of international actors and context, and the impact of historical conditions in shaping both the mass violence and the long silence that followed. In making these arguments, I do not mean that personal motives, social psychology, cultural and religious tensions, and socioeconomic conflicts were unimportant in generating mass violence—only that their significance was always shaped and circumscribed in decisive ways by the broader historical and political context.

Similarly, in stressing here certain "structural" conditions for the violence of 1965–66, and referring to the intentional acts of the army leadership, I do not mean to suggest that the mass killing and incarceration were preordained, or planned from start to finish. On the contrary, it is worth emphasizing that the violence emerged and changed in response to conditions on the ground. That is to say, this account leaves room for contingency and mere happenstance as essential parts of the explanation. The most important of these contingencies, though certainly not the only one, was the alleged coup of October 1, 1965, itself. Whoever the architects of that action were, the killing of the six generals provided a crucial opportunity for the army and its allies to move forcefully against the Left. In the absence of that event, and without the army leadership's decision to turn it to its political advantage, one cannot say with any certainty that the political tensions in Indonesia, profound as they were, would ever have resulted in violence on such a massive scale.

CHAPTER TWO

Preconditions

Revolution is only truly Revolution if it is continuous struggle. Not just an external struggle against an enemy, but an inner struggle, fighting and subduing all negative aspects which hinder or do damage to the course of the Revolution. In this light Revolution is . . . a mighty symphony of victory over the enemy and over oneself.

—PRESIDENT SUKARNO, INDEPENDENCE DAY SPEECH, AUGUST 17, 1957

IT IS COMMONPLACE to invoke Indonesia's history in explaining the mass violence of 1965–66, and there is no doubt that the violence was in some way informed by historical experience. There is less agreement about what sort of history matters, and in what ways history and the violence of 1965–66 were connected. Official Indonesian accounts, for example, focus almost exclusively on the history of the PKI's alleged treachery, highlighting its armed uprisings against the colonial authorities in 1926 and the fledgling Republic in 1948, and its supposed plans to seize power again in October 1965, as though this depiction were sufficient to explain the violence that followed the alleged coup. By contrast, many popular and some scholarly narratives implicitly locate the origins of the violence in a timeless "Indonesian" past, from which exotic cultural patterns, like running amok, deference to authority, and religious fanaticism, emerged fully formed to shape and guide the actions of those who killed and were killed. Neither of these portraits provides a satisfactory account of the historical forces that gave rise to the violence of 1965–66.

This chapter offers a different perspective, emphasizing the historical forces, actors, and contingencies that I think were most important in facilitating and shaping the violence of 1965–66. It begins with a brief look at Indonesia's colonial history, before tracing the emergence of leftist and nationalist movements in the early twentieth century, the Japanese occupation from 1942 to 1945, the struggle against Dutch rule that culminated in independence in 1949, and the first tumultuous decade and a half of independence. It then examines in more detail each of the principal political actors that emerged in the postindependence period and the tensions that developed among them. The last section provides a description of the final year before the alleged coup when these tensions came to a head, and shows how a number of key decisions and events helped to create the preconditions for the events of October 1, 1965, and violence that followed.

Through this account, the chapter underscores five aspects of Indonesia's modern history that appear to have been especially important in facilitating mass violence against the Left: a colonial and revolutionary experience that fueled acute ideological difference, and gave rise to widely divergent and conflicting historical narratives; an early perception within the army and among some Muslims that the PKI represented an existential threat to the nation; a process of state formation that entailed the development of a powerful, centralized, and politically conservative army with a strong stake in the status quo; the development within that army of an institutional culture, repertoire, and doctrine that supplied the template for the violent suppression of its domestic enemies; and a postcolonial politics characterized by mass political mobilization, militancy, and polarization.

Colonialism and Revolution

The country we call Indonesia today, a vast archipelago stretching some three thousand miles and encompassing hundreds of different linguistic groups, is a relatively recent invention; its modern geographic contours were the product of Dutch colonial rule over territory that had not previously been a single political entity.[1] That is not to say that the archipelago was a blank slate before the arrival of Europeans. On the contrary, these islands—Java, Sumatra, Bali, Sulawesi, Borneo, and hundreds of others—and the waters that link them were the site of impressive civilizations and vast trading networks dating from the early centuries of the Common Era. These included the great Hindu-Buddhist trading empire of Srivijaya, based in today's Sumatra, and the kingdom of Majapahit, whose influence covered most of Java and Bali, and extended to southern Borneo, Sumatra, and the islands of today's eastern Indonesia.

Important and impressive as these civilizations were, none was known nor can correctly be described as "Indonesia." That name, and the national idea that lay at its heart, did not emerge until the early decades of the twentieth century, when a handful of (mainly Dutch-educated) natives formed the first nationalist movements to articulate the idea that despite their many differences, all the disparate peoples of the Indies shared a single predicament, identity, and destiny.[2] That was also the moment when a regional trade and administrative language, Malay, was renamed and pressed into service as the new national language—Bahasa Indonesia. Like the idea of a unified national entity called Indonesia, the choice of that language, rather than one of the hundreds of local languages or indeed Dutch, was politically significant. It underscored the broader principle of the nationalist movement that no particular ethnic or religious group—no matter how large, economically dominant, or sophisticated—would dominate or define the nation, and that Indonesia would only succeed on the principle of unity and a civic as opposed to ethnically based citizenship.

COLONIAL AND ANTICOLONIAL LEGACIES

That ideal, while sometimes contested or dishonored, informed political debate for a century. Despite Indonesia's enormous ethnic and linguistic diversity, and notwithstanding some inevitable tensions, ethnicity and religion did not define Indonesia's political debate or national identity. That is to say, in marked contrast to the situation in many other colonial and postcolonial states—and the United States—race, ethnicity, and religion have not been the main fault lines of Indonesian political life. Instead, the principal debates and disagreements have been ideological or philosophical: What kind of anticolonial struggle should we wage? What kind of nation will this be? In accordance with what political ideology should we construct our new state and nation?

Indeed, in the 1920s and 1930s, the secular nationalist position that eventually came to dominate the debate was only one of many political visions articulated. Apart from those that sought the maintenance of colonial rule in some form, the main contenders included various manifestations of Islamism along with both revolutionary and moderate leftist positions. Sukarno, an early advocate of unitary Indonesian nationalism, aspired to draw these together into a single movement by insisting that nationalism, religion, and communism were not fundamentally incompatible but rather equally vital aspects of one struggle.[3] That idea, which

FIGURE 2.1. Sukarno (holding book) with colleagues and lawyers in front of the colonial courthouse, Bandung, ca. 1926. (Leiden University Library)

was later expressed by Sukarno in the acronym Nasakom (Nasionalisme, Agama, Komunisme, or Nationalism, Religion, Communism), became a crucial element of the nationalist struggle, but also a point of bitter contention in the years afterward, right up until the alleged coup of 1965. Yet both the bitterness and the attempts to overcome it only serve to underscore that the central debates, the key fault lines, primarily concerned ideology and political vision, and not identity claims based on ethnicity, race, or religion.

Colonial rule also gave rise to, or exacerbated, political and social tensions in the archipelago, both between colonizers and colonized and among the native peoples of the Indies. These included conflicts among rival claimants to aristocratic or other privileges, who then mobilized local populations against their rivals, often with the help of Dutch officials and military forces. Other tensions were rooted in class conflict, such as between disgruntled peasants and their landlords, or agricultural laborers and plantation owners, who were frequently backed by the Dutch. And some were conflicts over religious and cultural beliefs or practices, with

Dutch authorities often supporting ostensibly "traditional" prerogatives against the claims by modernizers and nationalists.[4]

Other features of the colonial period that had lasting consequences for Indonesia were the routine use of native auxiliaries to put down rebellions, and the practice of sending critics and opponents into internal exile. Commanded by Dutch officers, native forces comprised the vast bulk of the colonial armies that fought anticolonial rebel movements from Aceh to Bali in the late nineteenth and early twentieth century. In effect, native soliders dominated the colonial armed forces, and were then deployed, under Dutch command, to kill and detain other natives. That left deep scars, and arguably influenced the strategy and tactics used by Indonesia's armed forces in the revolution and period after independence. Likewise, Indonesian authorities later adopted the Dutch colonial approach to dealing with the leaders of rebel movements and other opponents, sending them into exile in remote parts of the archipelago, such as Boven Digul on the island of Papua. It was to such penal colonies that the Dutch sent the leaders of the 1926 PKI uprising and nationalist figures, like Sukarno, in the 1930s.

The brief Japanese wartime occupation (1942–45) also had important consequences for Indonesia's political development, encouraging the rapid spread of nationalist ideas, quickening the pace of mass political mobilization, and in Anderson's words, giving Indonesians "their first taste of a militarized state with a militaristic ideology."[5] In addition to facilitating the activities of older nationalist figures like Sukarno, Japanese authorities drew young people into mass political organizations in unprecedented numbers, and encouraged them to participate in a variety of military and paramilitary bodies.[6] Those organizations fostered a sense of militancy and fighting spirit among the country's youths, and became a breeding ground for the many youth-centered paramilitary units—known as *lasykar* and struggle organizations—that played a central role in the Indonesian National Revolution after the Japanese defeat in August 1945. The most important of those organizations was a native auxiliary force known as Defenders of the Fatherland (Pembela Tanah Air, or Peta) established by the Japanese in late 1943 in the face of Allied military advances. Significantly, Peta provided the bulk of the officers for the Indonesian Army from late 1945 through to the late 1970s, among them General Suharto.[7]

Crucially, Japanese occupation authorities also introduced to Indonesia's nationalist fighters—and through them, to its national army—some of the more notorious techniques and practices employed by its fighting

FIGURE 2.2. Indonesian nationalists parade before Japanese military authorities in Jakarta, ca. 1942–45. (Leiden University Library)

forces, including torture, harsh treatment, arbitrary imprisonment, and collective punishment.[8] Indeed, many of the specific techniques of torture and punishment used by Indonesian forces in 1965–66—including mock execution, immersion in fetid water, sexual assault, burning with lighted cigarettes, and electrocution using army field generators—appear to have been borrowed directly from Japanese wartime practice. Likewise, in their form as well as the system of inmate control and punishment they employed, the highly militarized prison camps used to detain political prisoners after 1965 bear a striking resemblance to the POW camps established by Japanese forces in Indonesia between 1942 and 1945.[9] In other words, the Japanese occupation appears to have influenced the institutional culture of the Indonesian National Army (Tentara Nasional Indonesia, or TNI) and its repertoires of violence.

INDONESIAN NATIONAL REVOLUTION

The Indonesian National Revolution (1945–49) was especially important in establishing the main contours of Indonesia's postcolonial state, leaving an indelible imprint on its institutions and founding narratives, and forever shaping the main fault lines of political conflict.[10] Although it was a complex affair defying easy characterization, the revolution was mainly a war of national resistance precipitated by the Dutch attempt to return to their former colony at the end of World War II. Indonesian nationalists who had declared independence on August 17, 1945, just days after the Japanese surrender but months before the Dutch and their allies were in a position to return, resisted that attempt.

By the time Allied troops landed, in November 1945, Indonesian nationalists—especially the secular nationalist Republicans led by Sukarno and his colleagues who had declared independence—were in no mood to relinquish their newfound freedom. The Dutch, for their part, were adamant that the Indies belonged to them, and that the Republicans represented a handful of radicals and "terrorists" who had no credibility because they had collaborated with the Japanese during the war. That charge was made especially against Sukarno, who had indeed worked with the Japanese in the furtherance of his nationalist objectives. The arrival of Dutch and Allied forces led to bitter and protracted fighting, which continued on and off until late 1949, when under pressure from the United Nations and United States, the Dutch finally accepted Indonesia's independence. Notably, that external pressure on the Dutch only began in earnest after Republican authorities crushed the leftist uprising in Madiun in September 1948, thereby establishing in US government eyes their anticommunist bona fides.

The military dimension of the revolution shaped Indonesian Army norms and practices—its institutional culture and repertoire—in significant ways.[11] Angered by the apparent collaboration of Indonesian nationalists with the Japanese, and embittered by their own appalling experiences in Japanese POW camps, Dutch forces employed methods that at the time some called "Nazi tactics" and have more recently been described as war crimes.[12] Perhaps mimicking the methods of their former enemies, they detained thousands of suspected supporters of independence without charge or trial, tortured detainees as punishment or to obtain information, and burned entire villages in retribution. Dutch colonial forces also carried out mass executions in villages thought to be supporting Republican rebels, disposing of the corpses in nearby rivers and irrigation canals just as Indonesian death squads would do with their Communist victims twenty years later.[13]

On the other side, Indonesian nationalist forces often adopted techniques that their opponents described as "terrorist" and that today would be considered grave violations of human rights. Fueled by the militancy and fighting spirit they had imbibed from the Japanese, and probably borrowing methods they had seen those forces use during the occupation, they too burned villages whose residents they suspected of supporting the other side, tortured detainees to obtain information, and sometimes killed suspected collaborators in their custody. These methods became part of the institutional repertoire and culture of the Indonesian armed forces after independence in 1949, and remained in place when the army began its campaign against the Left in late 1965.

The Indonesian National Revolution also had long-lasting consequences for army doctrine and structure.[14] It was the seedbed of the doctrine of "total people's defense," according to which the army would rely on close cooperation with the civilian population to combat internal rebellion and subversion. That notion lay at the heart of the strategy of mobilizing civilians as vigilantes and paramilitaries in the years after independence. The revolution also gave rise to the idea that Indonesia should have a "territorial army," with armed units permanently stationed in every province, regency, district, and village, again with a focus on combating the threat of internal unrest and subversion. Finally, over the course of the revolution, the army became ever more centralized and ideologically homogeneous, as it assimilated independent struggle organizations into its central command, and sought to purge both leftist and Islamist units—such as Pesindo and Hizbullah—that threatened its authority.[15] All these aspects of Indonesian Army doctrine and structure facilitated, and were arguably crucial preconditions for, the mass killing and incarceration of 1965–66.

Of course, the revolution was much more than a military contest between Indonesian and Dutch forces, and its ramifications extended beyond the military realm. At stake as well were fundamental questions about who should lead the fight (Republicans, federalists, Islamists, communists, or socialists), how the struggle should be conducted (through military or diplomatic means, from above or below), and what form the new nation-state should take (secular, unitarist, federal, or Islamic). The manner in which these debates were resolved, or left unresolved, affected the character of the postcolonial state and the configuration of political forces that emerged in the postindependence period. They also reinforced the politics of bitter ideological conflict that was a second precondition for the mass violence of 1965–66.

The impact of the revolution on the postcolonial state was perhaps most clearly evident in the constitution that was promulgated in the first heady days after the declaration of independence. Sensing the need for swift action and obvious arguments in favor of strong centralized rule, the small group that gathered to draw up the constitution in August 1945 devised a basic document that placed substantial authority in the president's office and envisioned a unitary—that is to say, nonfederal—Republican government. But this vision of a secular, authoritarian, and unitary state was by no means the only option on the table. The other possibilities advanced included a socialist but noncommunist state with democratic institutions modeled on those of the West, a communist state modeled on Joseph Stalin's Soviet Union, a federal state in which different regional governments would be granted substantial autonomy, and a theocratic state in which some version of Islamic law would be the law of the land. Each of these positions had its strong proponents who jockeyed constantly for influence and power in the constellation of forces leading the fight for independence, and who recalled their victories and losses with some clarity and bitterness in the years after independence.

The earliest challenge came from the Islamist position, which demanded at the time of the declaration of independence that the constitution should include the provision that Islamic law would prevail for the vast majority of Indonesian citizens who were Muslim. That demand, articulated in a document known as the Jakarta Charter, was narrowly—and according to its proponents, unfairly—rejected in favor of a secular state in which all religions would have an equal footing.[16] That defeat did not put an end to the Islamist challenge. On the contrary, by 1948, a rebel movement known as Darul Islam had emerged that demanded the formation of an Islamic state. Darul Islam, and its armed counterpart, Tentara Islam Indonesia, found strong support in some parts of the country—notably in West Java and Aceh, but also in South Sulawesi and South Kalimantan—and represented a continuing threat to the Republic until it was finally defeated in the early 1960s.[17] The campaign against Darul Islam represented a significant deepening of central army power both within and beyond Java, and the rebellion itself left a legacy of deep mistrust of Islamism among secular nationalists and within the army. The long military campaign against Darul Islam also provided an opportunity for the army to develop its counterinsurgency strategies and tactics, including the notorious "fence of legs" tactic, in which villagers were mobilized to flush out rebels by forming a human chain around presumed base areas. Such tactics eerily foreshadowed and arguably provided the blueprint for the army's campaign to crush the PKI after 1965.

A second significant challenge came from parties of the Left, which by 1948 found themselves increasingly at odds with the Republican leadership, especially its conservative Masyumi supporters. Convinced of the need for genuine social revolution rather than merely national liberation and threatened by the plan to "rationalize" the armed forces, parties of the Left came to adopt positions critical of the Republican leadership. Criticism turned to open opposition in mid-1948 shortly after the return to Indonesia of a prewar PKI figure named Musso, who regrouped the Left under a newly radicalized PKI leadership. It was against that backdrop, in mid-September 1948, that leftist officials and military units in the provincial town of Madiun, East Java, clashed with Republican forces and declared the establishment of a "National Front Government."[18] Although the uprising in Madiun appears to have been a local affair that caught the national PKI leadership by surprise, Republican leaders and foreign governments quickly accused the PKI of staging a coup as part of a broader Soviet plot to overthrow nationalist governments throughout the region. Masyumi leaders joined in by calling for a holy war against the atheistic PKI and mobilizing their paramilitary forces, the Hizbullah and Sabilillah, to assist the army. Over the next several weeks, Republican troops conducted raids throughout the area, ranging as far as Wonogiri (Central Java) to the west and Kediri (East Java) to the east. In the course of those operations, they arrested some thirty-five thousand PKI members and killed many—sometimes in grisly mass executions—including Musso and at least a dozen other top PKI leaders.[19]

While the number killed in Madiun was relatively small and most of the PKI detainees were soon released, the affair dramatically deepened the divide between the PKI and both the army and Masyumi. In that and other ways, too, Madiun helped to lay the foundation for the violence of 1965. In its campaign to crush the PKI in Madiun, for example, the army employed methods that presaged those used in 1965–66, including summary execution (see figures 5.2 and 5.3), and imprisonment without charge or trial. As in the case of Darul Islam, the army mobilized local paramilitaries to assist it in identifying, detaining, and killing suspects. The affair also gave rise to widely divergent and politically charged historical narratives that informed and inflamed political debate right through 1965. On the one hand, the PKI and its allies insisted that Madiun was the result of a "provocation" designed by the Republic and its imperialist allies to entrap the party and annihilate it.[20] Meanwhile, its opponents—particularly Masyumi—viewed Madiun as a clear example of the PKI's treachery and a warning that as a willing servant of foreign interests, it could never be trusted.[21] Indeed, in the immediate aftermath of the alleged October 1965 coup, the opponents of the PKI seized on that version of the history of Madiun as evidence of the party's disloyalty and subversive intentions.

Calling the failed 1965 coup a "second Madiun" and blaming it on the PKI, they insisted that this time the party had to be crushed completely, lest it rise again.[22]

The position that survived and emerged victorious from these various struggles was the secular, nationalist model articulated by Sukarno and the Republican movement. That model, and the compromises it sought to embrace, was articulated in the national ideology or philosophy known as Pancasila (Five Principles), penned by Sukarno in June 1945.[23] And it was Sukarno himself who emerged from the revolution as national hero, president, and indispensable mediator between competing political forces. Within that constellation, the army played a significant role; it was far stronger, more centralized, and more homogeneous ideologically than it had been in 1945. By contrast, both the Left and Islamist forces emerged from the revolution weakened and politically compromised. But they had not disappeared, and their proponents looked to the period of independence as an opportunity to expand their power and roll back their defeats.

LIBERAL AND GUIDED DEMOCRACY, 1950–65

The negotiated settlement that led to the transfer of sovereignty in December 1949 provided an opening for educated, internationally oriented Indonesians to replace the authoritarian 1945 presidential constitution with one that was more consistent with liberal, postwar norms. The new "liberal" constitution embraced principles that had recently been enshrined in the Universal Declaration of Human Rights (1948), including freedom of speech and assembly, established a form of multiparty parliamentary democracy, and relegated the presidency to a far less powerful position. Against that backdrop, dozens of political parties emerged, and party competition for office and followers intensified.

Observers praised the first national parliamentary elections, held in 1955, as a remarkable achievement in a country that had so recently emerged from years of colonial rule, war, and revolution.[24] More to the point, the elections revealed the strength of four main parties—the PNI, Masyumi, NU, and PKI—and marked the demise of previously influential parties, like the Indonesian Socialist Party (Partai Sosialis Indonesia, or PSI) (see table 1). The elections thereby forced a significant realignment of politics; henceforth, cabinets and other political bodies had to take account of the actual electoral strength of the parties, giving both the PKI and its main opponents unprecedented power.

Table 1. Results of the 1955 Parliamentary Elections: The Big Four Parties

Party	Seats	% of Vote
PNI	57	22.3
Masyumi	57	20.9
NU	45	18.4
PKI	39	16.4

The elections of 1955 also led to the formation of a Constituent Assembly, which was entrusted with drafting a new constitution to replace the interim one enacted in 1950. Differences on key issues proved difficult to resolve, however, and by late 1957 the assembly had not completed its work. Meanwhile, two other developments—regional elections and regional rebellions—further exacerbated political tensions. Regional elections in parts of Java in 1957 and 1958 revealed that the PKI had grown even stronger in the years since the national elections; in fact, the party won the contests for mayor and other offices in several localities.[25] These rapid gains caused serious alarm among parties of the Right and within parts of the armed forces that were nervous about the PKI.

At about the same time, the country was rocked by regional rebellions on the outer islands: the PRRI (Pemerintah Revolusioner Republik Indonesia, or Revolutionary Government of the Republic of Indonesia) rebellion in Sumatra and the Permesta (Piagam Perjuangan Semesta, or Charter of Universal Struggle) rebellion in Sulawesi.[26] Although neither rebellion demanded independence, both sought fundamental changes in the relationship with Jakarta—pushing for a more equitable distribution of wealth, revenues, and power between the center and regions outside Java. In both cases, too, the rebels included regional military commanders, and had the support of the PSI and Masyumi—and the US government, as discussed in chapter 4.

The rebellions provided the rationale for a series of decisions that strengthened the position of the army and the presidency, and changed Indonesia's course in fundamental ways. In March 1957, at the urging of the army leadership, Sukarno declared martial law, thereby giving the military new and sweeping powers over economic and political life. Under martial law, many recently nationalized industries—including foreign-owned plantations, oil fields, and refineries—ended up in the hands of the army officers and units.[27] That shift deepened the army's economic and political stake in the status quo, and substantially altered the balance of power between the army and PKI.

Then, in 1959, Sukarno called for an end to "liberal" democracy and a return to the 1945 presidential constitution. Declaring that parliamentary democracy was a foreign import ill suited to Indonesia's traditions, he announced the establishment of a new system called "Guided Democracy," which he said was better suited to Indonesian culture.[28] That move was welcomed by the army leadership as well as more conservative civilian figures, who judged that the parliamentary system had been a source of political instability, and moreover, had worked to the advantage of the PKI and other parties of the Left.[29] By guaranteeing military representation alongside political parties in all major legislative and executive bodies—by restoring the 1945 constitution that enshrined the principle of appointive representation by "functional group"—Guided Democracy strengthened the army's position and stake in political life. It also marked the end of parliamentary democracy in Indonesia for some four decades.

At least initially, Guided Democracy seemed to offer an answer to the divisiveness and paralysis of the parliamentary system, in large part because it played to Sukarno's considerable political talents. In rallying the population behind the demand that the vast territory of Irian Jaya—kept by the Dutch under the terms of the 1949 independence agreement—be returned to Indonesia, for instance, Sukarno appeared to have struck on a formula that would unite the population behind a common goal. Political parties and mass organizations of all stripes organized huge rallies and demonstrations, endorsing Sukarno's passionate nationalist rhetoric. But when the Irian dispute was settled in Indonesia's favor in 1962, the magic began to wear off, and Sukarno's subsequent attempts to find a national cause that would unite the country proved unsuccessful.[30] One of those efforts was the Confrontation campaign he set in motion in September 1963 in response to the creation of Malaysia out of the remnants of the British colonies on the Malay peninsula and northern Borneo. Far from uniting the country, the campaign to "Crush Malaysia" arguably helped to create an atmosphere in which politics became increasingly polarized, the PKI become more militant, and the army became ever more determined to prevent its political rise.[31]

In short, while it strengthened the president and army, and sought to weaken the parties by dispensing with elections, Guided Democracy did not in any sense signal the end of contentious politics. On the contrary, in the absence of elections, politics increasingly took place in the streets, as parties of the Left and Right sought to demonstrate their power—and win the president's ear—through the mobilization of ever-larger crowds and the performance of mass rallies and demonstrations. In that way, huge numbers of people from all walks of life, including youths, women, workers, peasants, artists, and writers, became directly involved in politics and the sometimes-bitter conflicts that ensued.[32] The language and tone of these demonstrations mimicked the president's increasingly nationalist and anti-imperialist declarations. The effect was that even parties of the Right framed their demands in the language of the revolution, declaring that their goal was to fight "Neo-colonialism, Colonialism, and Imperialism" (Nekolim), that they supported the "New Emerging Forces" (Nefos), that Sukarno was the beloved "Mouthpiece of the People," and that they were stalwart defenders of Pancasila, Nasakom, and so on. This climate of mass mobilization and the often-bellicose language of revolution that was part of it accelerated in the final years of the Old Order.

The Key Players

The escalation of mass politics after 1959 marked the onset of another of the main preconditions for the violence that followed the events of October 1. 1965. Alongside a deeply politicized and increasingly powerful army with a strong stake in the status quo, the bitter political divide between parties of the Left and Right, and the tradition of mobilizing civilians into militia groups to fight internal enemies, the new mass politics laid the essential structural foundations for the alleged coup and the violence that followed. Beyond these general features of Indonesian political life, the actions of key players coupled with the unpredictable unfolding of events in the final year before the alleged coup served to heighten tensions and make violence more likely.

SUKARNO

At the center of the system of Guided Democracy was President Sukarno, a pivotal figure in Indonesia's modern history and the story of the alleged October 1965 coup.[33] Although seen by his critics as a demagogue, womanizer, and dangerous leftist, inside Indonesia Sukarno was and to some extent still is widely regarded as a national hero. Jailed by the Dutch colonial authorities in 1929 for his leadership of the secular nationalist movement, he was a courageous, intelligent, and charismatic symbol of anticolonial resistance.[34]

FIGURE 2.3. President Sukarno of Indonesia, ca. 1951.
(Leiden University Library)

Sukarno was also a wily political operator, who used his considerable political skill to forge a successful nationalist coalition from an extraordinarily diverse and contentious set of ideological, regional, and political groups. Though his brand of nationalism contained a powerful anti-imperialist and anticapitalist strain, he was not a communist, nor ever a member of the PKI. Indeed, his support for leftist regimes notwithstanding, his ideological positions could more accurately be described as populist than communist; there was certainly little in his programs and policies that one could reasonably associate with Marxism-Leninism. He rejected the notion of the proletariat and the very idea of class analysis, and coined instead a concept of the little man—Marhaen—and a somewhat-amorphous ideology that he called "Marhaenism," a term later appropriated by the PNI.

More than anything else, Sukarno was a passionate defender of the idea of national unity—a concept that he and his contemporaries contrasted emphatically with the despised "federalism" that Dutch colonial authorities had attempted to use to defuse the strength of the anticolonial Republican movement. His most famously ambitious concepts, Pancasila and Nasakom, were both attempts at synthesis—to bring together in a single whole seemingly disparate and even contradictory impulses, beliefs, ideas, and political tendencies.[35] Nasakom, as we have seen, was an acronym for Nationalism, Religion, and Communism, while Pancasila sought to combine modern, secular notions of social justice and humanitarianism, with older, religious ideas like a belief in one god.

For more than a decade after independence, Sukarno also played the role of essential political mediator and unifier, carefully balancing the demands of the two most powerful political groupings in the country—the army and the PKI. Over time, however, he moved perceptibly to the left, lending his support to various PKI initiatives and adopting a more aggressively anti-imperialist posture abroad. That trend accelerated in the final two years before the alleged October coup, as Sukarno repeatedly denounced "communistophobia" at home and "Nekolim" abroad.[36]

After 1963, for example, Sukarno launched blistering attacks against the United States and United Kingdom, and encouraged or at least tolerated physical attacks on their properties and diplomatic installations. As relations with the West soured, Indonesia drew ever closer to China. Indeed, by 1965, China was probably Indonesia's closest and most reliable ally, and official missions between the two countries were frequent. In January 1965, Indonesia withdrew from the United Nations on the grounds that it was dominated by imperialist and neocolonial powers, and had voted to admit Malaysia as a member, and in May Sukarno addressed a huge rally on the occasion of the PKI's forty-fifth anniversary. Then, in his August 17 Independence Day speech, written with the help of key PKI figures, he announced, "We are now fostering an anti-imperialist axis—the Jakarta-Phnom Penh-Hanoi-Peking-Pyongyang axis."[37] In short, in the final year before the alleged coup of October 1, the PKI and its allies could feel confident that they had the support of the president, while the army and its allies on the Right had reason to worry about the direction the president and country were heading.

THE PKI

Another key player was the PKI. The oldest Communist party in Asia—formed in 1920, it was older even than China's—and by 1965, it was also the largest nonruling Communist party in the world.[38] In 1963, it claimed

FIGURE 2.4. PKI chair Aidit speaks at a party rally, September 1955. (Howard Sochurek / Getty Images)

to have some 3.5 million card-carrying members and another 20 million who belonged to affiliated organizations.[39] More remarkable still, it was a legal party with no armed wing and no plan for revolution. By some accounts, discussed below, the party's adoption of the "parliamentary road" was a strategic blunder and major reason for its sudden demise after October 1965.[40] But in the short term, that approach had brought the PKI to the very threshold of power through peaceful means. As such, it seemed to represent a novel strategy for leftist success at the height of the Cold War.

The PKI had not always followed the parliamentary path. In November 1926, with the Indies still firmly under Dutch control, it had launched an armed insurrection that it hoped would precipitate a crisis that would in turn bring an end to colonial rule. Instead, Dutch forces quickly crushed the uprising, and the party was banned; some thirteen thousand party members were arrested, and more than eight hundred were sent to a penal colony in Boven Digul in the remote eastern reaches of the archipelago.[41] The party emerged again during the Indonesian National Revolution, and as described earlier, supported another failed uprising, in the town of Madiun, East Java, in September 1948. That uprising too was crushed, this time by Indonesia's own army—a bitter confrontation that continued to resonate in Indonesian politics twenty years later.

Despite these repeated setbacks to its organization and reputation, the PKI emerged yet again shortly after independence. Soon, the party's older leaders were replaced by a new generation that committed it to the lawful, parliamentary path to power. The key figures were Aidit, Lukman, and Njoto—all in their twenties or early thirties—who formed the core of a new politburo in January 1951.[42] Although the PKI was more or less excluded from high political office for several years thereafter, its new strategy appeared to pay off handsomely in Indonesia's first national elections in 1955, when as noted earlier, it surprised political observers by placing fourth in a crowded field.

That strong showing provided the PKI with previously unheard of political influence and opened the possibility that the party might come to power through parliamentary means. The party's further success in the regional elections of 1957–58 made that possibility appear even greater. It was partly for that reason that the army and parties of the Right supported the idea of martial law in 1957, and the replacement of liberal democracy with Sukarno's Guided Democracy in 1959. But the shift away from electoral politics and toward the politics of mobilization did nothing to weaken the party's popularity. Indeed, the PKI proved to be exceptionally adept in the work of mass mobilization.

The PKI's success and popularity was partly due to its organizational effectiveness—but there were other factors at work, too.[43] For one thing, it had a reputation for being the least corrupt of all the major parties. It also articulated and fought for policies like land reform, higher wages, price controls, and union rights that were attractive to a substantial number of people. Moreover, despite its internationalist tendencies and connections, it consistently supported Sukarno's ardently nationalist positions—on Irian Jaya, Confrontation, nationalization, and against Nekolim powers. In short, it was a popular party with an organizational capacity and message well suited to the times and to the politics of Guided Democracy. Even the party's enemies recognized its strengths. As the executive secretary to the US National Security Council (NSC), James Lay, wrote in December 1960, the PKI "is relatively well-organized, well-financed and well led. It is unique among Indonesian political parties in its discipline, unity of purpose and command of the techniques of political action. It controls the labor movement, it has shown electoral strength, and it refrains from illegal actions, and so is in a strong psychological position."[44]

The party's popularity together with its growing militancy, especially after 1963, caused considerable alarm within the army and among parties of the Right. On a wide range of issues, from foreign policy to land reform to control of the armed forces, they saw the party as a genuine threat to their interests. They also worried that with Sukarno's evident backing, the PKI might soon take on a more central role in the political leadership of the country.

Despite its many short-term advantages, moreover, the party's strategy carried significant risks. For one thing, its apparent commitment to a peaceful, nonrevolutionary path after 1951 sometimes constrained its ability to articulate and advance the interests of the very working classes in whose name it was mobilized. That led, in turn, to diminishing esprit de corps and loss of internal control over its mass base, as seen famously in the "unilateral action" (*aksi sepihak*) campaigns in which the base in some areas moved much more forcefully on land reform than the leadership desired. In addition, the party's ever-greater reliance on Sukarno's patronage and protection left it vulnerable to any change in his position, whether as a result of ill health or political calculation.[45] Finally and perhaps most critically, the commitment to a peaceful strategy left the party's huge membership exposed to physical attack by its enemies, most especially by the army.

THE ARMY

Though less adept at mobilization politics than the PKI, the army was nevertheless a key player in the political constellation of Guided Democracy, and its power grew substantially in the years preceding the alleged coup of October 1965. Its influence stemmed, in part, from the fact that it controlled all or most of the guns, but also from the substantial political and economic power it had gained under martial law.[46] A crucial element of that power stemmed from another fact: the many foreign-owned plantations and other properties nationalized at this time were handed over to the military. Its political power and geographic reach also grew substantially as a result of a string of successful military operations, including those against the regional rebellions in Sulawesi and Sumatra as well as the Darul Islam rebellions in Aceh and West Java, and in support of the campaigns to win back Irian Jaya and crush Malaysia.[47] Lastly, as discussed in more detail in chapter 4, the army's power grew during these years as a result of its access to foreign military assistance. Foreign aid allowed the army to upgrade and modernize essential equipment, and perhaps just as important, gave the central command access to largesse that could be used to strengthen patronage networks and consolidate its authority.

As a result of all these developments, by the early 1960s the army was stronger, more centralized, and more ideologically homogeneous than ever before. Moreover, both in theory and practice, its focus was almost exclusively on combating domestic subversion rather than external threats. The army's power and its preoccupation with internal enemies were further reinforced by certain aspects of its structure and doctrine that dated back to the revolutionary period, but had been developed and refined in the period after independence.[48] These included the army's "territorial structure," which in practice meant that centrally commanded troops were stationed in every city, town, and village throughout the country, and the doctrine of total people's defense, according to which the civilian population could be mobilized as auxiliary militia forces to fight internal enemies under army command. Building on these principles, by 1965 the army had established a network of auxiliary forces, known as Hansip (Pertahanan Sipil, or Civilian Defense) and Hanra (Pertahanan Rakyat, or People's Defense), which spanned the country and had the potential to mobilize quickly hundreds of thousands of civilians under army command. Also critical was the doctrine of "dual function" (*dwi-fungsi*), first articulated in the 1950s, which dictated that beyond its role in national defense, the army had a legitimate part to play in economic, social, and political affairs.[49] That doctrine had an important influence on the army's role and self-image, and provided an essential foundation for its intervention in 1965 and after. Taken together, these elements of army doctrine and structure supplied critical infrastructure and models for the campaign against the PKI after 1965.

Powerful as it was, the Indonesian military under Guided Democracy was not a politically unified institution. While the army leadership was generally suspicious of or antagonistic to the PKI, and genuinely feared its potential to seize political power, most officers were also loyal to Sukarno and broadly sympathetic to his nationalist and anticolonial views. Moreover, some officers and enlisted men—notably in Central Java, East Java, Bali, and North Sumatra—went even further in supporting not only

Sukarno but also the PKI.[50] Sympathy for Sukarno's left-nationalist positions was strongest in the air force, whose commander, Air Vice-Marshal Omar Dhani, often took positions that placed him in conflict with the army.[51] There was also a powerful suspicion within the army of radical Islam stemming from its experience dealing with armed Darul Islam rebels from the late 1940s onward.[52]

The lack of political unity within the armed forces was partly the result of deliberate PKI efforts. Since the mid-1950s, and indeed even earlier, the party had sought to win recruits, or at least gain the sympathy of officers and enlisted men in the army and other armed services. That was the main purpose of the party's secretive "Special Bureau" (Biro Khusus), which is said to have played a role in planning the September 30th Movement.[53] But the disunity was also the natural outcome of a general weakness of state institutions in the years after independence—a weakness that left most of those institutions open to splits based on personal rivalries as well as divisions rooted in political influence, material interest, and ideology.[54] The disunity within the armed services in turn shaped the conflict that precipitated the alleged coup and violence that followed it.

OTHER ANTICOMMUNIST PARTIES

Ranged against the PKI in the mobilization politics of Guided Democracy were several religious and secular parties with more conservative orientations. The most important of these were the NU, Masyumi, and right wing of the PNI.[55] Alone and in combination, these parties competed with the PKI for the president's ear, and jockeyed for political positions in legislative and executive offices. In the absence of elections, their primary means of doing so was through the mobilization of mass rallies and demonstrations, palace intrigue, and the politically oriented press.

One of the oldest and largest religious associations in the country, the NU eschewed direct party politics for many years.[56] In the 1955 elections, however, it ran as a political party and won 18.4 percent of the popular vote, with most of its support in the heavily populated provinces of East and Central Java. That support gave it a strong voice in parliament along with the sometimes-grudging respect of Sukarno and his allies. A "traditionalist" Muslim party, the NU followed the leadership of respected rural Islamic teachers (*kiai*), but did not advocate an Islamic state. Nevertheless, through the 1950s and increasingly in the early 1960s, it adopted an openly hostile posture toward the PKI, accusing it, for instance, of being antireligious and atheistic. The party was also deeply critical of the PKI and BTI's (Barisan Tani Indonesia, or Indonesian Peasants' Front) support for land reform—and the so-called aksi sepihak (unilateral actions)—which not coincidentally, frequently targeted land owned by NU and other Islamic figures. Like the PKI and other political parties in these years, the NU mobilized a variety of mass organizations to demonstrate its political power and press its demands. Among these were two paramilitary youth organizations—Ansor and Banser (Barisan Ansor Serbaguna, or Ansor Multipurpose Brigade)—that often clashed with the PKI's youth group, Pemuda Rakyat, and would later play a central part in the mass killing of PKI members and other leftists after October 1965, especially in East and Central Java.

The second most influential religious party was Masyumi.[57] A "modernist" Islamic party with an educated, westernized leadership and support base that extended well beyond the heartland of Java, Masyumi was staunchly anticommunist. Indeed, the tensions between Masyumi and the PKI dated back to the Indonesian National Revolution, and had come to a head over the Madiun affair. Largely because of its strong opposition to the PKI, Masyumi had been favored by US officials at that time, and received covert financial and strategic support from the US government in the 1955 elections.[58] That aid helped it to win 20.9 percent of the vote (and fifty-seven seats), making it the second most popular party in the elections. Despite its strong showing in the polls, Masyumi was dissatisfied with its political position—and what its leaders saw as an imbalance of power between Jakarta and the Outer Islands. For these and other reasons some party leaders, together with leaders of the anticommunist PSI, lent their support to the regional rebellions of the late 1950s. That move seriously damaged the nationalist credentials of both parties and led, eventually, to their banning. Despite their parties' formal dissolution, though, Masyumi and PSI figures continued to work behind the scenes, as critics of Sukarno and the PKI. In addition, the Masyumi-affiliated Islamic University Students' Association (Himpunan Mahasiswa Islam, or HMI) continued to operate aboveground.[59] Both parties and the HMI were frequent targets of PKI criticism before October 1965, and all were centrally involved in the attempt to crush the PKI and sideline Sukarno in the immediate aftermath of the alleged coup.

After the PKI, the most important of the secular political parties was the PNI, which traced its roots back to the 1920s.[60] With its long history and solid nationalist credentials, the PNI had made a strong showing in both the 1955 national elections and regional elections that followed. Yet it was plagued by problems of corruption; though not alone in this regard, PNI members had a reputation for using official positions to benefit themselves and party members. An internal split between the party's left and right wings also weakened it—with the two factions competing for leadership positions, both nationally and at the local level. While the left wing was broadly supportive of Sukarno's anti-imperialist and anticapitalist positions, and was therefore open to cooperation with the PKI on some issues, its right wing was more conservative, deeply worried about too close an association with the PKI, and more inclined to cooperate with the army. Like the PKI and NU, by the early 1960s the PNI had mobilized a large number of mass organizations that carried out demonstrations and rallies in support of the party's objectives. These included the Marhaenist Youth (Pemuda Marhaen), which played an active role in the mass killings after October 1965.

The Year of Living Dangerously

The tensions among these political actors, together with the broad historical forces that framed postindependence political life—mass politics, bitter ideological conflict, deep military involvement in politics, and the mobilization of civilian paramilitaries—came to a head in the final year before the alleged October 1965 coup. The year saw a significant rise in PKI militancy, a marked leftward shift in Sukarno's position on a range of contentious issues, and a concomitant heightening of tensions between the PKI and the army leadership. It also brought worrying reminders of Sukarno's mortality, isolated but significant physical clashes between political groups, and rumors of foreign meddling in Indonesian affairs. While it was by no means inevitable that the result would be mass killings and detentions, these trends and events unquestionably contributed to that outcome.[61]

As though he were already conscious of what was to follow, Sukarno coined his August 1964 Independence Day speech "The Year of Living Dangerously." Over the next year, the PKI began to push for greater influence in government and adopted a number of increasingly militant positions that set the army leadership on edge. The most immediately threatening to the army was a proposal to create a "Fifth Force" by arming as many as twenty-one million peasants and workers.[62] PKI chair Aidit first floated the idea in January 1965, shortly after Foreign Minister Subandrio returned from an official mission to Beijing.[63] On that trip, China's Foreign Minister Chou En-lai had reportedly proposed the idea and offered to supply a hundred thousand light arms for the new force. For his part,

Sukarno appeared noncommittal but did not dismiss the idea outright, thereby raising alarm among army leaders.

Reactions to the Fifth Force proposal were mixed. The idea was supported by the air force, whose commander, Dhani, it will be recalled, tended to side with Sukarno and the Left against the other services. Meanwhile, the army, navy, and police leaderships worried that the plan would undermine their near monopoly on the means of force, placing arms in the hands of millions of their most implacable enemies. On the other hand, they knew that direct opposition to the idea would lay them open to charges of being insufficiently dedicated to the Confrontation campaign and perhaps even counterrevolutionary. Accordingly, they did what they often did in the politics of Guided Democracy, which was to feign support for the proposal while undermining it in practice.[64]

The army adopted a similar posture toward a second PKI initiative advanced in early 1965. Building on Sukarno's concept of Nasakom, which was by then widely invoked by all sides to demonstrate their loyalty to the president and justify their preferred political positions, the PKI proposed that there should be "Nasakomization in all fields," including the military. What that meant, in practice, was that the armed services would have to accept the insertion of "advisory teams" representing the three main streams of political life—nationalism, religion, and communism—within their command structures. The proposal would have given the PKI an unprecedented opportunity to influence the political thinking and direction of the armed forces. Once again, the air force leadership embraced the proposal while army leaders viewed it with alarm. As they had done with the Fifth Force idea, the army leaders pledged their support for "the spirit" of Nasakom in all fields while making it clear that they would never accept the proposal in practice. Through these experiences, some army leaders gained a new determination to resist PKI advances, even if that meant conflict with Sukarno.[65]

In early 1965, rumors began to circulate that an army Council of Generals was plotting to overthrow Sukarno, with the assistance of foreign intelligence agencies. Despite denials by army leaders and foreign diplomats, the rumors did not go away, and a document surfaced in May that appeared to show that the British and US governments were plotting some kind of clandestine action together with Indonesian Army officers. The document, which came to be known as the "Gilchrist Letter," was a draft message from the ambassador, Sir Andrew Gilchrist, to the British Foreign Office.[66] The most inflammatory passage in the letter referred to plans for "action" in concert with "our local army friends." While the army and most foreign embassies insisted that the letter was a forgery, Subandrio, Sukarno, and the PKI seized on it as evidence of covert, imperialist meddling in Indonesian affairs.

Sukarno responded by summoning military service commanders to his palace, where he asked General Yani, the army commander, whether his officers had been in contact with the British and US embassies. Yani reportedly admitted that Generals Parman and Sukendro had been, and that senior army officers occasionally got together at Yani's house to "let off steam." He denied, however, that there was a Council of Generals or any plot to overthrow Sukarno.[67] Despite these denials, Sukarno, together with Subandrio and the PKI, continued to insist that there was indeed a Council of Generals, and that the threat of an army coup was real. By the PKI's own account, that belief lay at the heart of its strategic planning over the next few months, and encouraged at least some in the party's leadership to step up efforts to work with more progressive military officers to prevent or forestall the army's planned coup.

Beyond the backroom deals and rumors of Jakarta politics, 1965 was also marked by mounting political tensions in the countryside and on the streets of towns and cities across the country. Riding a wave of anti-imperialist feeling, in January and February 1965, PKI-affiliated unions spearheaded the takeover of US and British properties and plantations, provoking angry reactions from the army and anticommunist parties. In February, for example, the PKI-affiliated Plantation Workers' Union of the Republic of Indonesia (Sarekat Buruh Perkebunan Republik Indonesia, or SARBUPRI) tried to seize plantations in North Sumatra owned by the US Rubber Company. Far from repudiating their actions Sukarno told US Rubber and Goodyear executives that the government was taking temporary administrative control over foreign rubber estates. He also endorsed the idea of a takeover of other Western properties, causing alarm among executives of the foreign oil companies, Caltex, Stanvac, and Shell Oil.[68]

Elsewhere, the PKI and BTI campaign to implement land reform through unilateral land seizures (aksi sepihak) led to conflicts with the NU, PNI, and their respective mass organizations.[69] In some cases, notably in East Java, Bali, and North Sumatra where the PNI and NU mobilized their mass organizations to resist land reform, those conflicts occasionally resulted in physical clashes and casualties.[70] Although the actual number of people killed or injured in those incidents was quite small, the clashes fueled antagonism between the groups, and formed a crucial backdrop to and precondition for the mass violence that followed the alleged October

1965 coup. A violent incident in May 1965 at the Bandar Betsy plantation in Simalungun in North Sumatra was a case in point. There, a retired army warrant officer had been killed while trying to force BTI members off plantation land that they claimed.[71] His death became a rallying point for the army and parties on the right in their campaign against the PKI after October 1965.

Likewise in towns and cities, mass demonstrations and rallies grew increasingly frequent and angry, and sometimes turned violent. Although all parties made sure to invoke the approved language and symbols of the revolution—declaring their support for Sukarno and Nasakom, firmly opposing Nekolim, calling for the destruction of Malaysia, and so on—the differences among opposing groups were abundantly clear. On the left, demonstrators demanded an end to the US bombing in Vietnam, accused Western powers of interfering in Indonesian politics, called for the "retooling" of anticommunist figures including cabinet ministers, denounced communistophobia and corrupt "capitalist bureaucrats," and called for the banning of various political groupings, including the HMI. Meanwhile, on the right, demonstrators and the anticommunist press denounced the PKI's atheism, accused the BTI of "terrorizing" the population through its aksi sepihak campaigns, warned that the revolution was drifting off course, and insinuated that the PKI and Sukarno had become puppets of China.

All these tensions were further accentuated by a rapidly deteriorating economic situation.[72] As a result of rampant inflation, the price of rice rose quickly, while wages and salaries for civil servants, teachers, and soldiers remained stagnant or declined. The dramatically falling value of the Indonesian currency, the rupiah, also meant that imported goods were beyond the reach of all but a tiny handful of wealthy or well-connected people. Apart from making life difficult for wage and salary earners as well as most urban dwellers, these conditions fueled corruption among government and military officials and politicians, and contributed to a general sense of uncertainty and anxiety. Against that backdrop, the PKI campaigns against corruption, and in favor of price controls, collective bargaining rights, and wage increases, were naturally popular with large sectors of the population. No wonder, then, that so many teachers, civil servants, university professors, writers, and even some soldiers began to lend their support to the PKI and its affiliated organizations.

While all these tensions were important preconditions for the alleged October coup and violence that followed, a crucial turning point came in early August 1965. On August 4, less than two weeks before he was scheduled to deliver his customary Independence Day speech, Sukarno collapsed and vomited while receiving an official delegation. Rumors of his illness spread quickly, and though the details were hard to confirm, they suggested that he might not have long to live. Inevitably that news generated anxiety, and set the different political parties and figures to planning for the eventuality of his death. The news was especially alarming to the PKI and its allies, who feared that "Sukarno's death or incapacitation ... would put the party in a position where it was virtually defenseless."[73] Worried that they might suddenly lose their key political patron—their defender against the army and parties of the Right—they started to consider how best to prepare for Sukarno's demise. Meanwhile, the army leadership understood that Sukarno's death, or even incapacitation, might present an opportunity for them to seize power or at least arrest what they viewed as the country's alarming drift to the left.

The result was a dramatic escalation in political tensions between the main contenders for power—the army and the PKI—and the initiation of serious planning on both sides for a post-Sukarno scenario. "During the following month," Harold Crouch writes, "the political atmosphere became extremely tense. With the president's health in doubt and rumors of coups in the air, the armed forces were preparing for a massive celebration of Armed Forces Day on 5 October to match the PKI's huge anniversary celebrations of the previous May. As some twenty thousand troops concentrated in Jakarta there was a feeling that 'something might happen.' "[74]

Early in the morning on October 1, 1965, it did.

CHAPTER THREE

Pretext

Power-mad generals and officers who have neglected the lot of their men and who above the accumulated sufferings of their men have lived in luxury, led a gay life, insulted our women and wasted government funds, must be kicked out of the Army and punished accordingly.

—LIEUTENANT COLONEL UNTUNG, SEPTEMBER 30TH MOVEMENT

IN THE EARLY MORNING HOURS of October 1, 1965, six of Indonesia's top generals were kidnapped from their homes in Jakarta by small teams of army soldiers.[1] Three of the generals resisted their captors and were shot on the spot before being taken to the Halim Perdanakusuma Air Force Base on the city's outskirts; three others were taken alive to the same place, where they too were either stabbed or shot to death.[2] A seventh general, Nasution, managed to escape but was injured, while his adjutant was killed. All seven bodies were dumped down a dried-up well in a rubber grove called Lubang Buaya (Crocodile Hole), and covered with dirt and leaves.

Shocking as these events were, it was neither obvious nor inevitable that they would lead to mass violence. Indeed, the crisis of that day might well have been resolved with relatively little bloodshed through the arrest and prosecution of the direct perpetrators of the killings and their commanders, and the deft intervention of the president. The fact that the operation instead led to killing and detention on an unprecedented scale has given it an importance that it would not otherwise have warranted. As a consequence, competing interpretations of those events—especially the question of who was behind the September 30th Movement that carried them out, and what their motives were—have been the focus of contentious scholarly and political debate for some five decades.

In some ways, that debate may seem like a distraction from the events that followed, particularly the mass killing and incarceration of hundreds of thousands of people. That violence was so reprehensible and so much more consequential than the events of October 1 that the question of who was responsible for the September 30th Movement hardly seems relevant. And yet the debate about the movement is important because it takes us to the heart of the matter: whether the army and those who supported its campaign to vilify, imprison, torture, and kill PKI members and other leftists did so on the back of a lie. After weighing the evidence, I think it is clear that they did, and that they did so quite deliberately. This chapter lays the foundation for that case in two parts. It opens with an account of the events of October 1 and their aftermath, based on the few historical facts that are not in dispute.[3] It then outlines the various competing accounts of the movement, highlighting the implausibility and inconsistency of the official version, but also looking critically at the alternatives. Later chapters explore the ways in which the official narrative laid down at this time was propagated and exploited to provide a pretext for the move against the PKI and Sukarno—including the mass killing and incarceration—and the army's seizure of power.

The September 30th Movement

The group responsible for the abduction and killing of the generals called itself the September 30th Movement, and was led by Lt. Col. Untung, a battalion commander of the Presidential Guard.[4] As the abductions were taking place, troops loyal to the movement seized control of key installations in Jakarta, including the Presidential Palace and national radio station, Radio Republic Indonesia (RRI). At about 7:15 a.m., a statement by Untung was broadcast on RRI announcing that the movement had acted to safeguard the president and nation against a planned coup by the CIA-backed Council of Generals:[5]

> The Council of Generals is a subversive movement sponsored by the CIA and has been very active lately, especially since President Sukarno was seriously ill in the first week of August of this year. Their hope that President Sukarno would die of his illness has not materialized. Therefore, in order to attain its goal the Council of Generals had planned to conduct a show of force (*machtvertoon*) on Armed Forces Day, October 5 this year, by bringing troops from East, Central and West Java. With this large concentration of military power

> the Council of Generals had even planned to carry out a counter-revolutionary coup.[6]

The statement said that President Sukarno was safe and under the movement's protection, and announced plans to establish a "Revolutionary Council" (Dewan Revolusi) to uphold the principles of the revolution. Significantly, it stressed that the movement was an internal army affair, "directed against the Council of Generals which has stained the name of the Army and harbored evil designs against the Republic of Indonesia and President Sukarno." It also decried their luxurious and corrupt lifestyles, neglect of subordinates, and womanizing.[7] On hearing of the morning's events, President Sukarno went first to the Presidential Palace and then to Halim air base. Informed that the generals had been killed, he ordered the action to stop, but for some time made no public statement about it.

Meanwhile, within hours of the movement's first radio broadcast, other army units began to mobilize to crush it. The leader of that effort was General Suharto—the man who would eventually replace Sukarno as president. Though he was commander of the army's Strategic Reserve Command (Komando Strategis Angkatan Darat, or Kostrad), Suharto had mysteriously not been targeted, and therefore was free to seize command of the army and mobilize troops against the movement. His path was also cleared by the death of the generals, especially Army Commander General Yani, and by General Nasution's temporary removal from the scene due to an injury he suffered while escaping his would-be captors.

In the midafternoon, the movement's leaders made a series of announcements whose mixed messages further heightened tensions. On the one hand, Decree No. 1 reiterated that the movement was "entirely confined within the body of the army to put an end to arbitrary actions of Generals who were members of the Council of Generals" and their henchmen.[8] On the other hand, it declared that all power would henceforth be transferred to the newly formed Revolutionary Council and Sukarno's existing cabinet would be decommissioned. Thus, in contrast to the earlier announcement that spoke of protecting the president, the later decrees left the impression that the movement was acting against the president or at least without his full approval. That impression was reinforced by President Sukarno's own silence.

For that reason, and as a result of General Suharto's efforts, support for the movement quickly began to unravel. By about 6:00 p.m. on October 1, most of its forces in Jakarta had surrendered or fled, and troops loyal to Suharto had complete control of the city. In effect, the movement had faltered less than a day after it began. Shortly thereafter, the army commander for Jakarta, General Umar Wirahadikusuma, closed down most major media outlets with the notable exception of two army-controlled papers, *Angkatan Bersendjata* and *Berita Yudha*. Later that evening, Suharto took to the airwaves to announce that the movement was "counterrevolutionary" and the president was safe, but that he, Suharto, had assumed leadership of the army. He also issued what amounted to an ultimatum, saying that Sukarno must leave Halim and the military units there must surrender by the following morning, or he would send troops to remove them.

At the air base, the situation was tense and confused. Over the course of the day, several key figures had gathered there, including President Sukarno, air force commander Dhani, PKI chair Aidit, and a number of presidential advisers. Of these, only Dhani had come out in favor of the movement, while Sukarno, Aidit, and the others had remained silent.[9] Also present were the remaining units of the movement forces, and members of the PKI-affiliated women's group, Gerwani (Gerakan Wanita Indonesia), and youth group, Pemuda Rakyat, some of whom had taken part in the actions against the generals. With Suharto's evening announcement and ultimatum to those supporting the movement, decisions had to be made. By the following morning, October 2, most of the remaining forces at Halim had melted away or been detained, and all the key figures had left the air base—Sukarno to the presidential residence in Bogor some fifty miles from Jakarta, and Dhani, Aidit, and Untung to Central Java.

SUKARNO ON THE DEFENSIVE

The next few days saw the beginning of the erosion of President Sukarno's authority and an assertion of power by the army under General Suharto. At a meeting with military commanders and close aides on October 2, the president reiterated that he had named General Pranoto Reksosamudro to replace the deceased General Yani as army commander. Suharto, who had declared the day before that he was taking over from Yani, resisted the president's decision. Faced with the prospect of noncooperation from one of the army's most senior officers, Sukarno relented, granting Suharto authority to "restore security and order."

In the early morning of October 3, Sukarno finally took to the airwaves to reassure the country that he was safe and in command, and call for calm.[10] But his reassurances were quickly outpaced by events on the ground. Less than twenty-four hours after his national radio broadcast, the bodies of the dead generals were discovered in the old well near Halim, and on the morning of October 4 they were exhumed. General Suharto was on hand to witness the exhumation. Against that grim backdrop, he spoke about the treachery and barbarity of those who had murdered the generals, and for the first time suggested the complicity of Gerwani and Pemuda Rakyat volunteers as well as the air force in the killings. A phalanx of soldiers, photographers, and journalists were present to record the exhumation and Suharto's remarks, which were later broadcast nationwide in print and electronic media.

The grisly images that appeared in the army-controlled print and television media, together with General Suharto's inflammatory speech, set the stage for the military procession and funeral the next morning, October 5. Accompanied by soldiers and heavy military equipment, the bodies of the dead generals were carried through the streets of Jakarta to the Kalibata Heroes' Cemetery. The procession was carefully designed as a display of military strength and unity; it also marked a turning point in the campaign to vilify the Left. At the gravesite, Nasution, whose young daughter had been gravely wounded in his attempted kidnapping and was then still fighting for her life in the hospital, gave an emotional speech in which he described the generals as "National Heroes," and repeatedly referred to the treachery and brutality of those who had killed them.[11] The combined effect of the propaganda and military ceremony was electric; crowds began to gather demanding vengeance against those who had killed the generals and the banning of all organizations connected to the movement. Soon, those angry demands descended into violence, with crowds ransacking and burning Pemuda Rakyat and PKI offices and homes.[12]

In an effort to stem the tide of vengeance and violence against the Left, and assert his own authority, the president called a cabinet meeting in Bogor on October 6. Invoking the spirit of the revolution and warning of the dangers of being duped by imperialists, he pleaded with ministers and military officers to remain calm, and await his "political solution" to the crisis. Yet once again, Suharto and his allies resisted the president's authority, and extracted from him still-greater latitude to restore security and order. On October 10, with Sukarno's permission, Suharto established the Operations Command to Restore Security and Order (Komando Operasi Pemulihan Keamanan dan Ketertiban, or Kopkamtib), the powerful extraconstitutional body that would become the principal institutional basis for the army's campaign against the Left and assertion of army dom-

FIGURE 3.1. Remains of the PKI headquarters in Jakarta, attacked and burned on October 8, 1965. The banner reads, "Death to the Generals' Kidnappers." (Bettman/Getty Images)

inance over the next three decades. A week later, on October 16, Suharto was officially sworn in as army commander, paving the way for the eradication of the Left and the army's eventual seizure of political power.

A mere two weeks after the events of October 1, then, the situation in Jakarta was roughly as follows. The September 30th Movement had been crushed militarily, and leadership of the army had been taken over by Suharto and those loyal to him. Formally, Sukarno remained in power, but Suharto held substantial de facto authority. The army also controlled the print and electronic media, and had begun to use it to great effect in spreading its version of events. Some mass organizations affiliated with the PKI, specifically Pemuda Rakyat and Gerwani, had been accused of involvement in the killing of the generals, and its members were being attacked and their houses and offices destroyed. Meanwhile, the PKI leadership was in disarray; some of its leaders had fled to Central Java while others were in hiding or had been arrested or killed.

Despite these dramatic developments, the move against Sukarno and the Left was neither simple nor swift. Indeed, it took another six months before the army and its allies were able to seize power, and a further year before Sukarno was finally removed from office and Suharto named acting president. One reason for the delay was that the president was still enormously popular in much of the country. The army and its allies could not afford to act precipitously, like staging a coup d'état or arresting the president, as such a move could easily lead to charges of treachery and thus backfire. Instead, they needed gradually to undermine Sukarno's legitimacy and authority so that his final removal would appear natural and lawful. Their principal strategy for doing so was first to insinuate and eventually allege openly that Sukarno was somehow involved in the movement, or at least had given it his blessing. That strategy was pursued systematically over the next several months—through the press, orchestrated mass demonstrations, and political trials—culminating with a formal demand that the president answer charges of complicity in the supposed coup attempt.

Complicating these moves against Sukarno was the fact that he, and many others besides, simply did not accept that the PKI was responsible for the movement. According to one of Nasution's top aides, as late as January 1966, "not everyone was convinced the PKI was responsible; or whether it was an internal army affair. The army was in the corner actually and it was a sensitive situation. We had to convince people that there was no Council of Generals.... We played the tape recorded confessions of Untung but he [Sukarno] was not convinced."[13]

A second reason the move against the Left took some time was that in parts of the country there was considerable support for the September 30th Movement. The greatest challenge lay in Central Java, where some key army units and commanders had supported the movement, and managed to hold their ground longer than the movement's leaders in Jakarta.[14] Even after those officers were detained or killed, a rough balance of political forces remained in Central Java for almost three weeks. As discussed later, it was only when Suharto ordered the deployment of the crack Army Paracommando Regiment (Resimen Para Komando Angkatan Darat, or RPKAD) to the province that the balance began to shift and the violence against the Left started in earnest.

A third obstacle to a swift move against Sukarno and the Left was the fact that notwithstanding Suharto's insistence to the contrary, there was considerable disunity within the army itself as well as between the army and other services, notably the air force. As discussed below, that disunity was arguably the condition that led to the movement's action in the first place, and was a problem that had to be solved before the army could move confidently against its enemies. Suharto also knew that there was some sympathy for the PKI within the army and civil service, and had to develop a plan to address that problem. The army leadership ultimately did that by undertaking a systematic purge of all officers, soldiers, and civil servants who had shown any signs of supporting the movement, or were judged to be sympathetic to Sukarno or any party of the Left.

SUHARTO'S "CREEPING COUP"

For all these reasons, the six-month period from October 1965 through March 1966 was characterized by a tense standoff between the president and his allies on the Left, and General Suharto and his allies. On one side, President Sukarno sought to use his popularity and the authority of his office to protect the PKI and its affiliated organizations from violent attack, and defend his key advisers, notably Subandrio, Oei Tjoe Tat, and Dhani, against allegations of involvement in the G30S. He called repeatedly for calm and unity lest "neocolonialist" forces exploit the situation, denounced the spreading violence, and urged the population to await a political solution.[15] The president also refused to use the army-created term Gestapu (Gerakan September Tiga Puluh) to describe the movement, insisting that it should be known as the October 1st Movement (Gerakan Satu Oktober, or Gestok).

On the other side, Suharto used a variety of strategies to erode Sukarno's authority and create the conditions for an attack on the Left. Among the most important of these was a sophisticated media and propaganda campaign, described in detail in chapter 6, which encouraged attacks against the PKI and its affiliates, and portrayed the army as the heroic guarantor of order and national salvation. The campaign was made possible by the army's closure of almost all Jakarta media outlets on the evening of October 1 and its invocation of national security to justify strict controls on all media thereafter. Popular fury against the PKI was stoked, for example, by media reports—which later turned out to be false—that the generals had been castrated and their eyes gouged out by women belonging to Gerwani, who had danced naked around them, cackling like witches, in the early morning light of October 1.[16] Within hours of the appearance of these false reports, large crowds began to form in Jakarta and throughout the country, first calling for the banning of the PKI, then ransacking the party's offices, and eventually attacking and killing PKI members themselves.

Suharto and his fellow officers in the high command also achieved their political objectives by authorizing and mobilizing mass political action in the form of demonstrations, petitions, and public statements demanding the banning of the PKI and its affiliates, the ouster of Sukarno and his allies, and firm action against those responsible for killing the generals. Such orchestrated mass actions had long been a mainstay of political life under Guided Democracy, and the army now used the old model to good effect. With army guidance, these demands came together in early 1966 in the form of the People's Three Demands (Tri Tuntutan Rakyat, or Tritura): banning the PKI, purging the cabinet of all Gestapu and PKI elements, and lowering the price of basic necessities. Suharto and the army readily acceded to these demands on the pretext that the demonstrations, rallies, and petitions were spontaneous expressions of the popular will. In reality, both the demands and the mode of their expression were discussed and coordinated by the army and its civilian allies.

In pursuing this strategy, the army had enthusiastic civilian allies, many of them drawn from Indonesia's educated middle classes. Among the most important were the leaders of the NU, which with the banning of Masyumi and the split within the PNI, had become the largest and most powerful political party in the country. In the weeks and months after October 1, the NU vice chair, Z. E. Subchan, emerged as a key figure, simultaneously spearheading his party's attack on the PKI and Sukarno. The army's campaign also had the support of the Partai Katolik (Catholic Party) and influential Catholic figures, such as the stridently anticommunist Father Josephus (Joop) Beek, whose close ties to military intelligence were well known.[17] Crucial backing also came from high school and university students, many of whom apparently believed that in opposing Sukarno and the PKI, they were striking a blow against authoritarianism and economic collapse. Grouped into various action commands—such as KAMI (Kesatuan Aksi Mahasiswa Indonesia, or Indonesian University Students' Action Front) and KAPPI (Kesatuan Aksi Pemuda Pelajar Indonesia, or Indonesian Youth and Student Action Front)—they took part in relatively peaceful street demonstrations, but more ominously, coordinated "sweeping actions" to identify and arrest suspected leftists. Finally, the campaign had the energetic backing of a broad spectrum of "liberal" intellectuals and cultural figures. These included a cohort of Western-educated economists, often referred to as the "Berkeley Mafia," who worked with the army to end what they saw as Sukarno's disastrous left-nationalist economic policies and open the country to foreign investment. They also included a number of prominent journalists and writers—like the novelist Mochtar Lubis—who in the final years of the Old Order had become outspoken critics of the country's shift to the left and LEKRA (Lembaga Kebudayaan Rakyat, or People's Cultural Institute), the PKI-affliliated cultural association. Taken together, this middle-class coalition gave to the army campaign an aura of civilian respectability that it would otherwise have lacked and made its drive to annihilate the Left far more effective.

Another important element of Suharto's strategy to destroy the Left—which likewise aimed to give it a veneer of legitimacy—was the creation of new pseudolegal bodies with the power to purge, detain, interrogate, and imprison anyone deemed to be involved in the movement, or considered to represent a threat to security and order. The most powerful body by far was Kopkamtib. With its sweeping power to do whatever necessary to restore security and order, it was beyond any effective control by political or judicial institutions, including the president and Supreme Court. In the weeks and months after its creation, Kopkamtib along with its regional and local commands became the key channels through which the "cleansing" and "annihilation" of the PKI and its allies were carried out. Orders issued by Suharto in the name of Kopkamtib were the basis for action by regional and local military and police commands. And they provided both essential guidance and justification for the statements and actions of anticommunist political and religious leaders.

A related element of the army leadership's strategy was the formation of a quasilegal judicial apparatus to generate evidence and publicity against Sukarno and his allies, which could be used either to justify their arrest or undermine their authority, or both. The key institutions in this apparatus were the Extraordinary Military Tribunals (Mahkamah Militer Luar Biasa, or Mahmillub) in which the most important political show trials were held for both civilian and military suspects. The Mahmillub, and every other element of the apparatus, were under the ultimate authority of Suharto in his capacity as commander of Kopkamtib. In addition to those directly involved in the movement, like Untung, key figures like Subandrio and Dhani were brought to trial before these courts, starting in early 1966. The clear purpose of these political trials was to implicate Sukarno's closest allies and inflict irreparable political damage on Sukarno himself, and in so doing pave the way for the complete eradication of the Left.[18]

By far the most important and grimly efficacious element of the army strategy was the systematic campaign of violence set in motion in early October 1965. That campaign, as elaborated more fully in later chapters, entailed both mass killing and mass incarceration as well as ill treatment, torture, rape, unfair political trials, and enslavement. Directed primarily against members of the PKI and its affiliated organizations, in some places it also targeted supporters of Sukarno, members of the PNI and

FIGURE 3.2. Anticommunist youths join the army's search for PKI leader Aidit on Mount Merapi, Central Java, November 1965. (Bettman/Getty Images)

Baperki (Badan Permusyawaratan Kewarganegaraan Indonesia, or Deliberative Association for Indonesian Citizenship), and even military personnel deemed to have leftist tendencies. The worst of the violence occurred in Aceh, Bali, Central Java, East Java, and North Sumatra—all but Aceh areas with strong and active PKI memberships. Most of the killing took place in the six-month period between October 1965 and March 1966, but the campaign of violence did not stop entirely at that point. Suspected leftists and Sukarnoists continued to be subjected to arbitrary arrest and detention well into 1968. In 1967–68, the army conducted two major military operations against what it described as PKI holdouts, one of them in the vicinity of Blitar, East Java, and a second in West Kalimantan.[19] In addition, political trials of those accused of involvement in the alleged coup continued for several years, with some still taking place in the late 1970s.

SUPERSEMAR

In the power contest between Suharto and Sukarno—and between the Right and Left more generally—March 1966 marked a critical turning point. With the PKI in disarray, hundreds of thousands of leftists in detention, on the run, or dead, and Sukarno weakened by the loss of his key advisers and insinuations of his association with the movement, the army emerged as the most powerful political force in the country. It remained now to formalize the change under the guise of an ostensibly constitutional transfer of authority. The pivotal moment in that process came on March 11, 1966, when in disputed circumstances, President Sukarno apparently signed an order granting executive authority to General Suharto, thereby signaling the end of his own authority in all but name and providing the crucial "legal" foundation for the army's seizure of power.

That order, commonly known as Supersemar—the Indonesian acronym for Surat Perintah Sebelas Maret, or Order of March 11—has been the subject of intense debate and controversy inside Indonesia. While supporters of the New Order have pointed to Supersemar as clear evidence that the transfer of authority was lawful, critics have insisted that it was a fig leaf for a disguised coup d'état. Some have claimed that the order was a forgery, while others have said that the army officers who presented the letter for Sukarno's signature explicitly or implicitly threatened the president with violence. They have noted, for example, that Sukarno was presented with the letter while heavily armed army units loyal to Suharto surrounded the Presidential Palace. Still others have suggested that the order may never have existed, or if it did, it was never signed—a claim that gained some credibility when government authorities were later unable to locate the original doucument.

Whatever the truth of the matter, the Order of March 11 definitively marked the end of Sukarno's authority, the demise of the Left, and the rise of the army as the dominant political force in the country. It paved the way for the purge of all Sukarnoists and leftists from the Provisional People's Consultative Assembly (Majelis Permusyawaratan Rakyat Sementara, or MPRS) as well as the June 1966 MPRS session in which Sukarno was called on to account for the G30S and his role in it. This was effectively an impeachment, the outcome of which was a foregone conclusion. Thereafter, despite occasional attempts to assert his authority, Sukarno was to play only a ceremonial role until March 1967, when he was officially stripped of the presidency by the MPRS, banned from political life, and placed under house arrest. He died three years later, on June 21, 1970. The Order of March 11 also smoothed the way for the passage on June 5, 1966, by the MPRS of Resolution No. XXV, which banned the dissemination of Marxism-Leninism and Communism, and outlawed the PKI and dozens of other organizations of the Left.[20] Despite its dubious legality, that resolution became the essential legal foundation and justification for the repression of the Left for half a century. Finally, it cleared a path for Suharto to become president through an ostensibly constitutional process. In March 1967, a thoroughly purged and compliant MPRS declared Suharto to be acting president, and in 1968 it elected him president—a position he held for another three decades.

A Matter of Interpretation

If there is now some consensus about the broad outlines of what happened on October 1, 1965, and in the months that followed, there is no such agreement on who was responsible for the movement and what their precise objectives were. More than fifty years later, there are at least six different accounts of those questions. Most rely on circumstantial evidence, a balance of probability, and a rather-limited and still-contested trail of documentary evidence. One might therefore conclude that it is impossible to know which account comes closest to the truth. But the problem is not quite as vexing as that. Some accounts are inherently more convincing than others. What follows is an attempt to outline the main interpretations, and assess their strengths and shortcomings.

THE PKI AS "MASTERMIND"

The official Indonesian government version of these events blames the killing of the six generals wholly on the PKI, claiming that those killings were part of a brazen attempt by the party to seize state power.[21] While acknowledging that some army officers were involved in the movement, the official version insists that they were mere dupes and that the PKI leadership masterminded the alleged coup attempt. In this version, General Suharto and his allies appear as national saviors for stopping a PKI power grab, and the mass killing and arrest of PKI members—if they are mentioned at all—are portrayed as the regrettable, but inevitable, consequence of spontaneous popular anger and outrage at the party's treacherous deeds. The official version also insinuates that the PKI acted at the behest of the People's Republic of China and its Communist party, while denying or obscuring any possible involvement by Western states.[22]

A more complex version of the official narrative highlights the role of the PKI's Special Bureau, a secret body that communicated with and sought to influence active-duty military personnel, and of its purported leader—a mysterious character named Sjam. While skeptics have suggested that Sjam might have been an "agent provocateur" whose role was to draw the PKI into a catastrophic plot that could then be used as a pretext to crack down on the Left, the army has insisted that he worked only for the PKI and was tasked with drawing army officers into a PKI plot.

There are a number of problems with the official account. For one thing, it does not offer a plausible *motive* for a PKI attempt to stage a coup. As described in chapter 2, by mid-1965 the PKI had achieved almost-unimagined political success through its strategy of lawful political activity and its close association with President Sukarno. Under the circumstances, one needs to ask why the PKI would have risked all it had gained by trying to seize power. And why especially it would have opted for a strategy of armed insurrection—a strategy it had explicitly eschewed for fifteen years and for which it was utterly unprepared—when such a move would almost certainly have provoked an angry and violent reaction from the army. Speaking to State Department officials in the Philippines in March 1965, the US ambassador to Indonesia, Howard Jones, expressed doubts that the PKI had any motive to seize power: "The PKI is doing too well through its present tactics of cooperation with Sukarno. Unless the PKI leadership is rasher than I think they are they will not give the army the clear-cut kind of challenge which could galvanize effective reaction."[23] Indeed, the group that stood to gain the most from a military coup—and had the wherewithal to do so—was not the PKI but rather the army itself, or at least some part of it.

These and other improbabilities were highlighted by foreign observers at the time, including embassies that had an interest in blaming the PKI. In an internal analysis of the alleged coup dated October 19, 1965, for example, British ambassador Gilchrist concluded, "It seems best to discount any theory which establishes the PKI as having plotted a major uprising or bid for power on the 1st of October, with Untung and his men as their shock troops. The unreadiness of the PKI and the general incompetence of the proceedings ... are far from characteristic of communist plots."[24] Likewise, in November 1965, US colonel George Benson, who had been stationed in Jakarta and had close ties to senior Indonesian Army officers, told Benedict Anderson that it was "out of the question that the PKI had any real hand in it."[25] As George Kahin noted in 1971, it was hard to see how "it was to the interest of either [the PKI or Sukarno] to risk killing the army officers and thereby providing a provocation which would make it easier for the army to strike back forcefully."[26]

A second set of problems concerns the matter of evidence. Here, the official version is on even shakier ground. For one thing, the abductions and killings of October 1 were clearly carried out not by PKI members but by regular soldiers under the command of uniformed army officers. Moreover, the movement leaders in Jakarta were backed by some twenty-five hundred troops, while those in Central Java had the support of a number of regular army commands and units. While it is true that members of PKI-affiliated organizations—Pemuda Rakyat and Gerwani—were at Halim air base, and some took part in the actions against the generals, their numbers and roles pale in comparison to the numbers and firepower of the army troops acting on behalf of the movement.

The few bits of documentary "evidence" that have been produced to support the official version are also of questionable veracity. The most important of these was an editorial printed in the PKI's national daily, *Harian Rakyat*, on October 2, expressing support for the September 30th Movement. That editorial turned out to be the sole piece of documentary evidence available to the army to implicate the PKI in the supposed coup. As such, the matter of its authenticity and authorship are crucial. On both fronts, troubling questions remain. Why, for example, would the official organ of the Communist party decide to publish an editorial supporting a coup attempt that had already failed? Why, moreover, would the PKI's paper have been permitted to publish one last self-incriminating editorial on a day when all other national media outlets in Jakarta were in army hands or had been closed down? That is all the more suspicious considering that on the morning of October 1, the editors of other newspapers were explicitly advised by the army not to publish anything about the movement.[27] One of those was the Islamic newspaper, *Suara Islam*, whose editors later revealed that at 11:00 a.m. on the day of the alleged coup, two army officers (one a lieutenant colonel) had come to their offices to tell them not to publish the story they had already written and sent to the printer. As one of the editors explained to Kahin in 1967: "So we pulled the story back from the printing plant and did not publish it. But as you can see we came very close to doing so." Why did no obliging army officer drop by the *Harian Rakyat* office that day to tell *them* not to publish? At a minimum, then, the available evidence suggests that the army leadership deliberately lured the editors at *Harian Rakyat* into publishing an editorial on the movement while explicitly warning others not to do so. Another possibility is that the incriminating editorial was not written by the PKI leadership at all but rather by someone with an interest in creating documentary evidence of the PKI's guilt, and with it a pretext for an aggressive campaign to destroy the party once and for all. As Anderson has noted, "The CIA report suggests that [the *Harian Rakyat* editorial] must have been composed beforehand. Perhaps it was, but not necessarily by the Party leadership."[28]

Other evidence offered in support of the official version includes testimonies and confessions extracted from prisoners under torture or extreme duress. Even if one sets aside the obvious ethical and legal concerns about using such confessions as proof, questions remain about their reliability. Bearing in mind the circumstances under which such confessions were extracted, it is likely that some, if not all, of them were actually prepared by intelligence officers and interrogators for signature by the detainees. The alleged confession of the party chair, Aidit, is a case in point. According to army information, he admitted his own and the PKI's responsibility for the movement in a statement written while he was in army custody. We have no way of verifying that claim, however, because he was shot dead by his army captor(s) immediately afterward.[29]

Serious questions also surround the testimonies of two key military conspirators, Lt. Colonel Untung and Colonel Abdul Latief, on which the official account relies heavily. Transcripts of their interrogations, selectively cited by the army in November 1965, purport to show that the two had taken orders from the PKI. But both men later contradicted those official interrogation reports when they stood for trial.[30] There are similar doubts about the testimony of Njono, a member of the PKI Politburo arrested on October 3, 1965, whose alleged confession of the party's responsibility was made public by the Army Information Center in early December 1965. His confession contains basic factual errors about the composition of the Politburo that no party leader could possibly have made and outlines a conspiracy scenario that would have required several party leaders to be in Indonesia when in fact they were abroad.[31] Expressing doubt that Njono could have been the author of this incriminating confession, Anderson and McVey wrote in 1966 that "it seems more likely ... that at least the portion concerning the Politburo discussions was presented ready-made for him to sign."[32]

The only legally "admissible" evidence of high-level PKI responsibility for the movement was the courtroom testimony of the mysterious figure Sjam. At the 1967 show trial of Politburo member Sudisman, Sjam claimed that he was the leader of the party's Special Bureau and had coordinated the movement on Aidit's orders. As noted above, however, serious doubt remains about Sjam's assertions. It is puzzling, for instance, that someone who admitted to playing such a central role in the movement remained at large for so long, when so many others were quickly rounded up, interrogated, and killed. Furthermore, although Sjam was eventually imprisoned, tried, and sentenced to death, fellow inmates noted that he had unusually cordial relations with army and prison officials, was never ill treated, and sometimes took part in the interrogation of other prisoners.[33] These and other oddities have led some observers to conclude that while he was undoubtedly a close confidant of Aidit, Sjam may also have been working for the army.[34] Given the secretive nature of Sjam's role and links to the party, the only person who could ever have contradicted his testimony was Aidit, whom the army had already killed. At a minimum, skeptics suggest, he may have reached a deal with his captors to provide incriminating testimony against the PKI in exchange for lenient treatment. As a high-ranking government official told an interviewer in 1979, "When the government discovers evidence of something, Sjam will readily confirm or deny it. [We] now consult him on everything concerning the PKI and the G30S."[35]

Finally, the suggestion that the PKI acted at the behest or influence of China or its Communist party is almost certainly untrue. At the time, the British ambassador wrote that "there are rumours implicating the Chinese People's Republic, but these do not amount to much.... I suspect that the extent of Chinese involvement was approximately the same as that of the PKI—foreknowledge, some support, but no direct control."[36] Recent scholarship on the subject has largely borne out that assessment, even while confirming that the PKI leadership discussed political strategy with China's highest leaders.[37] Similarly, the official insistence that Western powers played no role whatsoever is contradicted by the available evidence, as outlined in some detail in chapters 4 and 7.

THE "CORNELL PAPER"

An alternative account, first articulated in 1966 by Anderson and McVey of Cornell University, argues that the September 30th Movement was more or less what it claimed to be: a move by a group of disgruntled middle-ranking army officers against an army high command they viewed as corrupt, disloyal to the president, and in the CIA's pocket. According to their *Preliminary Analysis*, Untung and his colleagues acted out of a sincerely held belief that the army high command, in collusion with the CIA, had set up the Council of Generals that was planning to stage a military coup on October 5, Armed Forces Day.[38]

This account, later called the Cornell Paper, was based on a close reading of the movement's own announcements, and analysis of existing tensions and divisions within the army. It highlighted, for example, the many ways in which the movement's statements and actions reflected the concerns of lower- and middle-ranking officers. Noting that the key officers involved in the movement were all from Central Java, Anderson and McVey also argued that their actions were shaped by certain cultural norms and attitudes that distinguished them from the high-living, corrupt Jakarta generals whom they targeted.

Their argument raised serious questions about the official account of the alleged October coup. What possible motive could the PKI have had for making such a move when it was doing so well politically? Why would a party that had achieved success through a strategy of peaceful mobilization suddenly change course and stage an armed uprising, especially when it had no armed wing? And if indeed the party did organize the putsch, why did it not take even the most rudimentary precautions against failure—like securing the support of the president and mobilizing its huge popular membership? In posing these questions and insisting that the alleged coup was mainly an internal army affair, Anderson and McVey exposed a dimension of the story that the army clearly wished to keep under wraps. In doing so, they ignited an angry polemic that has lasted until today and resulted in their being banned from Indonesia for some three decades. Indeed, it was in response to the Cornell Paper that Colonel Suwarto, the former head of Indonesia's Army Staff and Command College (Sekolah Staf dan Komando Angkatan Darat, or Seskoad), and General Suharto commissioned two authors to write the army's second official account of the G30S in 1967.[39]

In the fifty years since the Cornell account was written, legitimate questions have been raised about it. For one thing, it seems to go out of its way to dismiss any evidence of possible PKI involvement in the movement. The presence of Gerwani and Pemuda Rakyat volunteers at Halim, sympathy shown for the movement by some Pemuda Rakyat units, and close cooperation between certain army officers and PKI officials in Central Java may not demonstrate PKI responsibility for planning the October 1 action. They do, however, suggest a degree of sympathy for and some measure of cooperation with it. Moreover, as discussed below, more recent scholarship has argued that PKI chair Aidit was indeed directly involved in planning the movement, even if he did not share those plans with other members of the Politiburo or Central Committee. By insisting that the PKI and its affiliates were not connected to or supportive of the movement in any way, Anderson and McVey appear to be protesting too much.

These shortcomings notwithstanding, the central thesis of the Cornell Paper remains compelling. Whatever might yet be revealed about the role of some PKI leaders in the plot, there is no doubt at all that army officers and soldiers played key roles both in its planning and execution, in Jakarta and elsewhere. Any explanation that obscures or denies the role of military officers and soldiers—and underplays the existence of tensions within the army in triggering the action—is simply misleading and must be regarded as a deliberate deception.

SUKARNO—THE DEVIOUS DALANG?

A third interpretation lays responsibility for the alleged coup at the feet of President Sukarno, describing him as a "devious dalang" or shadow puppet master. According to this account, Sukarno either initiated the kidnapping of the generals himself or was aware that some kind of plot against them was in the works, and allowed it to proceed in the expectation that it would be to his political advantage.

The claim of Sukarno's involvement was originally developed by the army and its allies in late 1965 and early 1966, as part of the concerted effort to undermine his legitimacy and ease him from power. The campaign drew on a vast array of state resources, including the intelligence apparatus and quasi-judicial bodies established by Suharto after October 1, and led eventually to something like an impeachment trial by the MPRS.[40] Antonie Dake, a writer with close ties to the Suharto regime, later made essentially the same case in a book titled *The Sukarno File*.[41] More recently, the argument has been advanced by Salim Haji Said, an expert on the Indonesian military who in 1965 worked as a journalist with the army newspaper *Angkatan Bersendjata*.[42]

In one version of this scenario, Sukarno devised the plan to kidnap, but not kill, General Yani and replace him with a more pliable figure. After all, the use of abduction to force political action had some precedent in Indonesia. Sukarno himself had been abducted (along with Hatta) on August 16, 1945, by militant nationalist youths who insisted that the leaders should immediately declare independence and lead a revolt against the Japanese. They were soon released, unharmed but chastened, and declared independence the following day. Given that history, proponents of this theory suggest, Sukarno might have seen the kidnapping of Yani and the others as a way of dealing with politically troublesome opponents. But when the plan devolved into the killing of the six generals, Sukarno sought to distance himself from it.[43] In an interview in 1976, a former deputy prime minister in Sukarno's last cabinet, Johannes Leimena, told Kahin that he did not believe Sukarno had ordered or expected the generals to be killed: "He would not have agreed to such a course—such violence and brutality."[44]

The main evidence offered of Sukarno's involvement in the alleged coup are his actions and movements before and immediately after the abductions began. His accusers claimed, for example, that the president met with Untung sometime in August, ostensibly to discuss plans for the kidnapping, and that he had signed an order removing Yani as army commander on September 30, 1965. They also noted that Sukarno elected to be driven to Halim air base early on the morning of October 1, and remained there until late that evening when it was clear that the movement had failed. While Sukarno insisted that he had gone to the air base, together with several other high-ranking officials, to ensure that he would have a quick route to safety in the event of a worsening crisis, his accusers argued that his presence at Halim was proof of his collusion with the movement.

Sukarno's statements about the movement were likewise cited as evidence of his involvement in the plot. For instance, his reported comment that the events of October 1 were a "ripple in the ocean of the Indonesian revolution" and his refusal to call those events a "coup" were seen by his accusers as demonstrating sympathy for the movement and insufficient remorse over the death of the six generals. Likewise, his repeated calls for calm, his refusal to ban the PKI, his protection of Foreign Minister Subandrio and other leftists in the cabinet, and his insistence that all parties show restraint and await a political solution were characterized as evidence of his involvement in and support for the supposed coup attempt.

One serious problem with these arguments is that they rely heavily on evidence that is either suspect or open to plausible alternative interpretation. Thus, for example, key pieces of evidence concerning Sukarno's intentions and movements—including his alleged August meeting with Untung and September 30 order to replace Yani as army commander—are based on the testimony of Bambang Widjanarko, who stated that he was tortured while in military custody.[45] Given what we know about the ill treatment of suspects at this time and the fabrication of confessions made in custody, we must at least be skeptical about the veracity of that testimony. That is all the more true in view of the extreme importance that Suharto and his allies placed on finding evidence to weaken Sukarno at this time. The evidence amassed in the course of their investigations was frankly tendentious and far from definitive.

But even if we set aside those doubts and accept Widjanarko's testimony at face value, the evidence would still not offer a prima facie case of Sukarno's complicity in the movement for the simple reason that the explanations the president offered for his movements were at least as plausible as those advanced by his accusers. Likewise, his appeals for calm and an end to violence might as easily be seen as the voice of reason and political statesmanship as evidence of treason.[46]

SUHARTO—THE MISSING LINK?

A fourth theory points the finger at General Suharto as the mastermind—the "missing link" in the plot.[47] In this scenario, Suharto was a pivotal figure in a coup that was "designed to fail"—a deliberate provocation intended to supply a pretext for the army to take sweeping punitive action against the PKI and Sukarno. As one might expect, there is no conclusive documentary material to support this interpretation, but the circumstantial evidence is sufficient to raise serious questions about Suharto's role.

First, there is the curious fact that Suharto—the commander of the army's elite Strategic Reserve Command (Kostrad) and an officer who routinely filled in for Yani in his absence—was not targeted by the movement, leaving him free to use his troops and authority to crush the movement within hours of its start. The proponents of this theory argue that only rank incompetence or deliberate design could explain this apparent oversight, and that deliberate design is the more plausible explanation. Why else would such a powerful figure be left untouched?

One answer to that puzzle lies in the fact that the main military plotters—Untung and Latief—had long-standing personal and professional ties to Suharto, and had reason to believe that he would support their initiative.[48] Suharto had been Untung's commander during the Indonesian National Revolution and in the West Irian (Trikora) campaign. In April 1964, he had traveled to Central Java to attend Untung's wedding. Latief had also served under Suharto during the revolution and was a close friend of the Suharto family. On the basis of those strong ties, Untung and Latief apparently believed not only that Suharto was no threat to their plan but that he was a likely ally, too. As Latief wrote in his trial defense statement in 1978, "I was firmly convinced that if anybody could be considered loyal to the leadership of President Sukarno, it was he. I knew him already from Yogyakarta and I truly did know who 'Bapak' General Suharto was."[49]

A second and related answer to the puzzle is that Suharto may well have had foreknowledge of the movement's plans. The main evidence to that effect was the curious meeting between Latief and Suharto on the evening of September 30, just hours before the movement was set in motion.[50] There is no dispute that the two met in the main military hospital in Jakarta, where Suharto's youngest son was being treated for scald burns suffered a few days earlier. But the purpose of that meeting remains a subject of dispute. When asked about the meeting, Suharto maintained that Latief had come to the hospital either to kill him or to confirm that he was too preoccupied with his son to interfere with the plot. Latief, however, insisted that he had gone to the hospital to inform Suharto of the movement's plan to preempt a planned coup by the Council of Generals, so as "to be able to appeal to him at any time for support."[51] In other words, while Suharto claimed that he had no prior knowledge of the movement's plans and in fact had narrowly escaped being one of its victims, Latief said that Suharto knew of the movement's plans in advance but did nothing to stop them. These conflicting accounts may never be fully resolved, but at a minimum, the meeting between Suharto and Latief on the night before the generals were kidnaped and killed raises serious questions about the extent of Suharto's foreknowledge of the plot.

A third piece of evidence suggestive of Suharto's involvement in a plot that was designed to fail is that he was known to be a rival of at least one of the targeted generals, Yani, and to have harbored a deep grudge against another, Nasution, who had once disciplined him for corruption.[52] The removal of the six generals of the high command would have ensured that Suharto's main rivals were gone, leaving him as the highest-ranking army officer in the country. Apart from any interest that he may have had in crushing the Left, then, Suharto may have seen the plot as a chance to advance his own career.

In short, the available evidence arguably points at least as strongly to Suharto as one of the plotters of the movement, as it does to either the PKI or Sukarno. Even if one does not accept the claim that Suharto orchestrated the plot, there is at least a reasonable suspicion that he knew of the plans in advance and perhaps gave the impression of supporting them, but then at the critical hour turned against the plot, and used it as a pretext to crush the PKI and Sukarno. That approach would have fit well with the underlying political logic of the period. In late 1965, the PKI had the ear of President Sukarno, who was still enormously popular. Under those circumstances, no group—no matter how powerful—would have dared to move directly against the PKI. By blaming the movement on the PKI, Suharto and his allies would have had exactly the pretext they needed to crack down on the party and seize power on behalf of the army.

A FOREIGN PLOT?

A variation on the provocation thesis is the theory that the action of October 1 was the product of a covert operation devised by foreign intelligences agencies—especially the CIA and MI6—in collaboration with Indonesian allies, designed to provide a pretext for anticommunist forces to crush the PKI and ease Sukarno from power. Sukarno himself first made this claim when he blamed the movement on "deviation of the leadership of the PKI, the machinations of neo-colonialist forces, and the criminal conspiracies of certain individuals."[53] But foreign scholars, most notably Peter Dale Scott, and some Indonesian observers have further elaborated this case.[54]

Needless to say, the claim of US involvement has been hotly debated.[55] On the one hand, US government officials strongly deny that the United States had anything at all to do with the alleged coup. Echoing the official line, the US ambassador at the time, Marshall Green, wrote in his memoirs that "the events of October 1, 1965, came as a complete surprise to us."[56] Likewise, Suharto insisted that "the operation to destroy the PKI was totally and successfully done by Indonesians alone.... There was not one grain of aid from the CIA."[57] Given the terrible loss of life that followed these events and the great importance of Suharto's anticommunist New Order regime to US interests in the region, it is easy to understand why both the US and Indonesian governments have stuck by this story so steadfastly. And yet as discussed in detail in chapters 4 and 7, the documentary and circumstantial evidence that has so far been unearthed makes it clear that the United States and its allies shared both direct and indirect responsibility for the events of October 1, 1965 and for the violence that followed.

The first piece in the probability puzzle is the fact that for more than a decade before the alleged coup, secret US national security documents explicitly endorsed the use of "all feasible covert means and all feasible overt means," including armed force, "to prevent Indonesia ... from falling under Communist control."[58] These were more than simply words on a page; in 1957–58, the United States had acted in accordance with this mandate by actively supporting armed rebellions against the Indonesian government.[59] US support for those rebellions, moreover, involved the supply of military hardware and ammunition, and the provision of US pilots and military advisers to those whose avowed purpose was to overthrow the Indonesian government.

Given the overriding concern about the spread of communism, US perceptions of the communist threat in Indonesia are also relevant. Here again, the evidence supports the probability of US intervention. Available documents make it clear that by 1965, the US government was convinced that Indonesia was sliding inexorably toward communism. As noted earlier, in mid-1965, CIA director Raborn wrote to President Johnson that "Indonesia is well embarked on a course that will make it a communist nation in the reasonably near future, unless the trend is reversed."[60] If the US government was prepared to intervene militarily in 1957–58, when the threat of communism was relatively slight, it is hard to believe that it did not plan to intervene in some way in 1965, when that threat was perceived to be so much greater. The probability that the United States did so is further strengthened if we consider what it was doing elsewhere in the region at this time. After all, 1965 was the year that the Johnson administration began its major escalation of the war in Vietnam, with intensive bombing of the north and deployment of tens of thousands of US ground troops in the south. If the United States was prepared to go to war to stop communism in Vietnam, we must assume that it contemplated some kind of action in Indonesia.

Significantly, we also know from declassified documents that right up until 1965, the US government was encouraging elements in the Indonesian military to take strong action against the PKI and Sukarno. One approach suggested was to provide assurances to "friends" in the Indonesian Army that the United States and its allies would provide support as well as remain silent if the army were to move against the PKI. And despite heavy censorship, the available US documents show that by 1965, US officials had already identified Suharto as one of these army friends—the handful of staunch anticommunist military officers who might be counted on to act against the PKI.

Perhaps most chillingly, one of the US strategies proposed for defeating the PKI was almost identical to what actually happened in 1965: the PKI should be accused of an act of treachery, which would then provide a pretext for massive army retaliation. The perfect mechanism for setting such a chain of events in motion would be an act of provocation—in the form of a rumor or document purporting to show plans for a right-wing coup—that would lead the PKI and other progressive forces to take rash action that could be construed as treacherous and threatening to national security. The beauty of such a plan was that it could be accomplished with relatively few resources and little or no trace of foreign involvement. All that would be required would be some quiet cash, some help with producing the necessary documents, and secret assurances of support to reliable friends. Viewed in that light, the Gilchrist Letter of early 1965 and rumors of coup plans by a CIA-backed Council of Generals may take on a new meaning.[61]

Could the rumors and documents, and perhaps even the murder of the generals, have been products of an ingenious CIA and MI6 operation designed to provoke or justify an army backlash?[62] It is certainly possible, but it needs to be stressed that the evidence for that case remains largely circumstantial and there are reasons to doubt that the entire affair was the result of a foreign conspiracy. Nevertheless, as discussed in some detail in later chapters, there is abundant evidence that the United States and its allies played a critical role in encouraging the army to act against the PKI and Sukarno in 1965, and facilitating the mass violence that followed.

A JOINT ENTERPRISE

The most recent interpretation of these events, by the historian John Roosa, takes issue with aspects of all these accounts. Drawing on new evidence, Roosa argues that the action of October 1 was a flawed scheme planned jointly by a handful of progressive army officers and PKI leader Aidit, through the intermediary of the mysterious figure Sjam.[63] The action was not designed to fail by Suharto, as Wertheim and others have argued, but collapsed as a result of poor planning, botched implementation, and Suharto's swift countermeasures. It was facilitated, furthermore, by the United States and other foreign governments that had been encouraging army leaders for some time before 1965 to plan for an eventual takeover. While acknowledging a role for Aidit, Roosa's account emphatically refutes official claims that the PKI Politburo or Central Committee planned the movement, and stresses that the party membership as a whole had nothing whatsoever to do with it. That the Indonesian authorities understood Roosa's book to be a direct challenge to their own account was confirmed by the attorney general's decision in 2009 to ban it.[64]

In this interpretation, the plotters' original intention was to abduct the six generals in order to preempt what they sincerely believed to be a planned coup by the army high command. In detaining the generals but not killing them, the plotters would have been acting in line with a time-honored tradition of abduction in Indonesian politics. Provided it received the endorsement of the president, which the plotters clearly expected it would, such a move would prevent an expected army coup while also opening the way for a further leftward movement in national politics. In the event, the murder of the generals, rather than simply their arrest, made it impossible for Sukarno to endorse the movement's action and led to its swift collapse.

In suggesting that both Aidit and Sjam were involved in planning the movement, Roosa challenges the contention that it was exclusively an internal army affair. At the same time, in contending that Aidit did not share those plans with the PKI Politiburo or Central Committee—and demonstrating that those plans were developed jointly with progressive officers—he distinguishes his argument from the army's, which seeks to implicate the entire PKI leadership and party, and insists that the PKI was the sole mastermind.[65] Indeed, if there is a central culprit, in Roosa's view, it is not the party or the army but rather Sjam: "Sjam, the middle-man between the military officers and the Party leaders, unwittingly bamboozled both sides, dragging them both into an action that neither had properly planned."[66]

Roosa's account also offers a plausible understanding of Suharto's role, explaining why he was not targeted in the alleged coup attempt, and how he was able to respond so quickly and effectively once it began. He thinks it unlikely that Suharto planned the action himself and rejects the suggestion that the action was designed to fail. On the other hand, he argues that it was quite likely that—because of his friendship with both Latief and Untung, and perhaps also through his own Kostrad intelligence sources—Suharto knew of their plans in advance. That advance knowledge would explain how he was able to move so quickly on the morning of October 1. It is worth noting in this regard that if Suharto did have some foreknowledge of the action against the generals, but failed to report or take any action to prevent it, he would be guilty by his regime's own standards of "direct involvement" in the movement. And that would have been enough to have him jailed for many years, with or without a trial.[67]

Finally, Roosa maintains that the swiftness and efficiency of Suharto's move against the PKI and Sukarno in early October—before the army had any clear evidence of PKI responsibility—stemmed from the fact that the army, with the encouragement of the United States and its allies, already had a plan to go after the PKI and Sukarno as soon as it had a pretext:

> From the morning of October 1 Suharto knew that the movement had the potential to serve as the longed-for pretext for bringing the army

to power. The rapidity by which the army blamed the PKI, organized anticommunist civilian groups, and orchestrated a propaganda campaign suggests preparation. The generals had done contingency planning. The post-movement behavior of the army cannot be explained as a series of purely improvised responses.[68]

Roosa's account has many merits. But like the other theories discussed here, it leaves some questions unanswered. One lingering problem concerns the matter of motive. Even if one accepts Roosa's suggestion that the original plan was to kidnap rather than kill the generals, it is still not apparent why Aidit would have taken such provocative action. Was he really so politically careless that he would have risked the party's strongly favorable position on such a gamble? The question of motive comes into even sharper focus when one recalls the serious doubts, mentioned earlier, about the identity and role of Sjam. Bearing in mind the special treatment he received from the authorities after the movement collapsed and his apparent eagerness to testify to whatever the army wished to hear, one must ask who Sjam was working for. That question is all the more important in light of the crucial role Roosa ascribes to him in orchestrating the movement. If the answer leads back to the army—or some part of it, like Kostrad's intelligence unit—then theories suggesting that the movement was a deliberate provocation by the army and its allies once again appear plausible. Of course, none of these questions undermines Roosa's crucial assertion that the rank and file of the PKI knew nothing about the movement's plan, and Suharto and his allies used the events of October 1 as a pretext to destroy the party and seize power.

To sum up, while there is reasonable consensus about what happened on the morning of October 1, 1965, and in following weeks and months, major differences remain about who led the movement, why they took the actions they did, and what their historical and political significance was. By some accounts, the seemingly endless debate about the origins and nature of the movement has threatened to distract attention from the much more consequential events that followed: the killing of half a million people, mass incarceration of more than a million others, and the complete annihilation of the Left. It is certainly true that the mass violence of 1965–66 was vastly more important than the killing of six generals. It is also true that none of the competing interpretations of the movement—including the official one—can possibly explain, much less justify, the mass killing and incarceration of 1965–66 that followed.

And yet that does not mean the debate over interpretation is irrelevant to the question of violence. That debate has remained salient, in part, because the different interpretations render the events that followed—especially the mass violence against the Left—more or less reprehensible. If the official account has sought to justify the violence and exonerate those responsible for it, many of the alternatives make it clear that the violence was not only unlawful but also completely unjustifiable. More important still, the question of interpretation matters because the propagation of a particular narrative—the official one—was intrinsically linked to the mass violence that followed.

Put differently, the mass violence of 1965–66 was the product of a particular *interpretation* of the movement that blamed the killing of the generals on the PKI, and portrayed the party as guilty of murder and treachery. That narrative both provoked and sought to justify acts of extreme violence. It also served to justify the army's seizure of power in the short term, while in the longer term providing the founding mythology for the New Order regime and its nominally democratic successor.

CHAPTER FOUR

Cold War

A premature PKI coup may be the most helpful solution for the West—provided the coup failed.

—BRITISH FOREIGN OFFICE NOTE ON A REPORT ABOUT INDONESIA, DECEMBER 1964

The events of October 1, 1965, came as a complete surprise to us.

—MARSHALL GREEN, US AMBASSADOR TO INDONESIA

The G30S was a "communist coup arranged by the Peking regime as part of its concept of world revolution."

—*ANGKATAN BERSENDJATA*, ARMY NEWSPAPER

ONE OF THE MOST ENDURING and contentious questions about the alleged coup of October 1, 1965, is the degree to which it was the product of foreign influence or interference. One possibility is that the United States and its allies, working with key army officers, designed the action to fail as a way to justify a crackdown on the PKI and ease Sukarno from power.[1] Another is that the United States and its allies had nothing whatsoever to do with the alleged coup, and were in fact caught completely off guard by it.[2] A third claim, favored by the army and some foreign observers, is that the movement was the product of Chinese government interference in Indonesia's domestic affairs.[3] The truth probably lies somewhere in between these positions. Although important parts of the official record remain closed, there is to date no definitive evidence that the United States or its allies planned the affair in advance. In any case, that scenario arguably overestimates the competence of a small group of CIA operatives, and ignores the ample motives and capacity of local actors, especially within the Indonesian Army high command. Nor is there any evidence that the supposed coup was masterminded by Beijing.

But to say that the action of October 1, 1965 was not orchestrated by foreign powers does not mean that they played no role in bringing it about. On the contrary, there is now plenty of evidence that they did. That case has two elements. First, the wider international context, in particular the rhetoric and logic of the Cold War and anticolonial nationalism, affected the contours of Indonesian politics, making it more militant and polarized. That general atmosphere, together with the actions of major powers elsewhere in the region and beyond, contributed to political conditions inside Indonesia in which a seizure of power by the army was much more likely to occur. In creating this atmosphere of polarization and crisis, several major powers played some part, including China.[4] Yet it was overwhelmingly the United States, the United Kingdom, and their closest allies that played the central roles.

Second, in addition to such "unintended" or indirect effects, major governments—but again, especially the United States, the United Kingdom, and their closest allies—pursued policies that aimed deliberately to undermine the PKI and President Sukarno, and to see them replaced by a coalition of antileftist forces, chief among them the army. More specifically, plans set in motion as early as 1958 sought to create conditions that would encourage the army to act forcefully against the PKI. To that end, the United States and its allies provided military assistance, secret assurances, and financial support to antileftist elements in the army leadership, and encouraged them to take action against the PKI and Sukarno. They also pursued a covert campaign designed to tarnish the reputation of the PKI and Sukarno, and to supply a pretext for the army to act against them. By contrast, while China also sought to influence the political equation in Indonesia, its actual impact on the course of events was limited, and there is no evidence at all to support the claim that it encouraged the PKI to seize power or was involved in planning the alleged coup of October 1.

International Context

In March 1965, the United States launched a massive bombing campaign against North Vietnam, dubbed Operation Rolling Thunder, and a few months later tens of thousands of US ground troops began combat operations in South Vietnam. The intervention in Vietnam represented the culmination of several broader trends in international affairs that had been unfolding since the end of the Second World War and profoundly shaped the contours of Indonesian politics during that period. Chief among those trends were the onset and acceleration of the Cold War, the rise of a powerful anticolonial nationalism in many of the newly independent states of Asia and Africa, and a pattern of overt and covert interference in the affairs of those states by foreign powers. This wider context served in various ways to heighten political militancy and polarization inside Indonesia, and to lend a new legitimacy to the use of force in politics—creating the perfect preconditions for a showdown, a military seizure of power, and widespread violence.

COLD WAR, ANTICOLONIALISM, AND COVERT OPERATIONS

The decade and a half that preceded the alleged coup attempt of 1965 was among the most polarizing and bellicose of the Cold War. The divisive rhetoric and politics of the period were given an added dimension following the Sino-Soviet split of 1961, after which China became an increasingly important player in Asia. Indeed, like Fidel Castro's Cuba in Latin America, Mao Tse-tung's China became a beacon for leftists and revolutionaries across the region.[5] While the Soviet Union continued to provide economic and military assistance to various governments through the early 1960s, it was China and its allies whose positions on nuclear war, economic development, and revolution became ever more influential. That inevitably moved Indonesian politics to the left, while at the same time breathing new life into long-standing suspicions on the Right about Chinese intentions. Far from being cold, moreover, in much of the world at this time the Cold War was decidedly hot, and entailed a rapid expansion in the use of paramilitary forces, the practice of torture, and extrajudicial killings. That was especially true in Asia, where Cold War calculations and military interventions, covert and overt, contributed to protracted and bloody conflicts in Burma, Cambodia, China, Korea, Laos, Malaysia, the Philippines, and Vietnam. Taken together, these features of the Cold War served to exacerbate and give shape to long-standing political tensions beween the Left and Right inside Indonesia, and set the stage for the violent showdown of October 1965.

Equally crucial was the rise of a powerful anticolonial nationalism, especially in the newly independent states of Asia and Africa. Leaders like Jawaharlal Nehru of India, Gamal Nasser of Egypt, and Kwame Nkrumah of Ghana openly challenged Western hegemony and imperialism, and sought a middle path between the two superpowers in the form of the nonaligned movement. President Sukarno was a leading figure in that group, and hosted its first major gathering, the 1955 Asian-African Conference in Bandung.[6] Although Washington and its allies tended to see the nonaligned movement as a Trojan horse for the advance of communism, and nonaligned leaders did not hesitate to accept military and economic assistance from major powers on both sides, the commitment to nonalignment and national self-sufficiency was genuine, and shaped Indonesian political life in significant ways. Most important, it guided Sukarno's interactions with neighboring countries, influenced his attitude toward the United States and its allies, and was a key source of his popularity with a broad cross section of the Indonesian people.

As these observations suggest, Indonesian politics during these years were also shaped by the actions of the United States and other Western powers elsewhere in the world—and particularly by their persistent efforts to undermine leftist and neutralist leaders, and replace them with figures more amenable to US political and economic interests. The most notorious examples of that pattern included the overthrow of Prime Minister Mohammad Mosaddeq of Iran in 1953, the ouster of Guatemalan president Jacobo Arbenz in 1954, and the failed attempt to overthrow Castro by means of an invasion by paramilitary forces at the Bay of Pigs in 1961. Less well-known though still important examples included US support for the arrest and subsequent murder of Congo prime minister Patrice Lumumba in 1960–61, CIA efforts to ensure the defeat of the socialist candidate Salvador Allende in Chile's 1964 elections, and the US role in creating the conditions for the military coup in Bolivia that removed the civilian president Victor Paz Estenssoro from office in late 1964.[7] The landing of twenty thousand US Marines in the Dominican Republic in April 1965 to prevent the return to power of Juan Bosch further fueled perceptions that Western powers were intent on subverting regimes of the Left. These developments along with the broader pattern of foreign intervention of which they were seen to be a part highlighted differences among Indonesians about the intentions of Western powers, and contributed to a growing political conflict between Indonesia and the West.

Those effects were further accentuated by the actions of Western powers much closer to home, in Southeast Asia, where a pattern of interference was already well established by 1965.[8] The best-known case, of course, was the direct US military intervention in Vietnam, but that was hardly the only instance of Western meddling in the region. In the aftermath of the Second World War, most of the European powers had sought to restore their colonial rule in the region, often by force of arms. France fought for eight years (1946–54) to take back Vietnam, Cambodia, and Laos, while the Dutch war to prevent Indonesian independence lasted four years (1945–49). Moreover, although the United States granted the Philippines its independence in July 1946, both there and elsewhere in the region, it began almost immediately to organize covert campaigns to destroy leftist and neutralist movements, most notably in Burma, Cambodia, Laos, and Vietnam. The CIA's "Secret War" in Laos, set in motion by the Kennedy administration in 1962, was only the best known of those campaigns. Meanwhile, the United Kingdom returned to its former colony of Malaya after the war, granting the country independence only in 1957. During those years, and for some time afterward, it led a brutal counterinsurgency campaign against the Malayan Communist Party. Then in 1963, it backed the amalgamation of former British territories on the Malay Peninsula and the island of Borneo into a single nation-state, to be called Malaysia—an initiative that Sukarno viewed as an imperialist plot to "encircle" Indonesia.[9]

These interventions, in the region and beyond, became lightning rods for Indonesian critics of imperial overreach and accentuated existing conflicts in Indonesian political life. Alongside the polarizing dynamics of the Cold War and the rise of a powerful new anticolonial nationalism, they formed a crucial element of the wider context within which politics took shape in the years before 1965.

THE "COMMUNIST MENACE" IN INDONESIA

The Cold War also shaped the attitudes and policies of major powers toward Indonesia. A clear example of that dynamic came in late 1948, in the town of Madiun, East Java, where, it will be recalled, an uprising by leftist forces was crushed by Indonesia's own Republican Army.[10] In the context of the early Cold War, some observers immediately saw in Madiun the long hand of Soviet interference and dubbed the uprising an attempted Communist coup. Although there is little evidence to support that view, it was widely accepted by US officials at the time. The willingness of the Republican leadership to crush the movement was therefore seen as a sign of its strong anticommunist credentials and reason enough for the United States to lend it support in its quest for independence against the Dutch. But the anxiety about Communist intentions lingered after independence.

The seriousness with which the United States continued to view the possibility of a Communist takeover in Indonesia was made clear in an

NSC policy statement of November 1953 (NSC 171/1), which described the principal objective of US policy as being "to prevent Indonesia from passing into the Communist orbit."[11] Likewise, a statement on US policy toward the "Far East" from December 1954 (NSC 5429/5) included the following paragraph:

> In order to preserve the territorial and political integrity of the area, the United States should . . . (e) Employ all feasible covert means, and all feasible overt means including, in accordance with constitutional processes, the use of armed force if necessary and appropriate, to prevent Indonesia or vital parts thereof from falling under Communist control by overt attack, subversion, economic domination, or other means; concerting overt actions with the other ANZUS nations.[12]

Over the next decade, Washington and its allies saw cause for ever-increasing concern in Indonesia with regard to the issue of communist domination. Through much of the 1950s, that concern focused on the possible influence of the Soviet Union, which was providing substantial amounts of economic and military assistance in the hope of extending its sphere of influence in the region. Moves toward détente between the USSR and the United States did nothing to ease Western concerns over the "communist menace" in Indonesia. Indeed after 1963, the year of China's refusal to sign the Nuclear Test Ban Treaty, US decision makers evinced a growing anxiety about the region-wide implications of Chinese power. A 1964 NSC document, for example, mentioned the likelihood of a communist Indonesia tipping the balance toward communism in Malaysia and then on through mainland Southeast Asia.[13]

The unmistakable signs of growing cooperation between Indonesia and China and their respective Communist parties further heightened such worries.[14] Starting in late 1964, China's leadership took a number of initiatives that were aimed at bolstering Sukarno's leftist positions at home and abroad, and supporting the PKI in its struggle against the army and its allies. At a meeting with Indonesian foreign minister Subandrio in January 1965, for example, Chou expressed strong support for the idea of a Fifth Force of armed workers and peasants. Later, Chou and other high Chinese officials offered to supply Indonesia with a hundred thousand light arms, and began negotiations with Dhani for an initial transfer of some twenty-five thousand weapons to the air force. At about the same time, China also offered to provide Indonesia with expertise in developing a nuclear weapon, and by October 1965 a number of secret meetings had taken place to set that program in motion. Finally, from late 1964 through

1965, Chinese doctors sent by Beijing provided medical care to President Sukarno, who had come to mistrust the Western doctors he had previously consulted. For its part, China saw Indonesia as an increasingly important player in the region. It was impressed by the size and strength of the PKI, and pleased to have Sukarno in the anti-imperialist camp.

Leaving aside for the moment the question of whether, or to what extent, these Chinese initiatives actually led to the alleged October coup and subsequent violence, there can be no doubt that just as the United States and its allies encouraged the Indonesian Army and political Right, so China and its allies, like Albania and North Korea, encouraged the Indonesian Left and Sukarno. In that sense at least, China and its allies arguably played a role in creating the conditions in which both the supposed coup and violence were more likely to happen.

Although the struggle between "Communism" and the "Free World" was a driving force during these years, in their dealings with Indonesia, foreign governments were not motivated solely by ideological concerns. Of equal importance were the imperatives of maintaining control over essential natural resources, securing markets, and protecting the interests of private capital. With its roughly eighty million inhabitants (in 1953), Indonesia was the largest country in the region after China and regarded as a political linchpin. Economically, it represented a fantastic trove of minerals and resources, including tin, petroleum, and natural rubber. Strategically, the Indonesian archipelago, which lies astride the sea-lanes linking the Pacific and Indian Oceans, was (and still is) regarded as vital to military and commercial communications in Asia and the Pacific. As the NSC wrote in 1953,

> Indonesia is strategically important to the United States and the rest of the free world as a vast archipelago which commands the approaches between the Pacific and Indian Oceans and between Asia and Australia, is inhabited by 80,000,000 people, and is a producer of rubber, tin, and petroleum. The loss of Indonesia to Communist control would have serious security implications for the United States and the rest of the free world.[15]

These political, economic, and strategic interests added a further dimension—and urgency—to foreign competition over Indonesia. The United States and United Kingdom were worried that Sukarno's shift to the left represented a direct threat to private investment, especially in the areas of oil and rubber, while China seemed poised to supplant the West as a major beneficiary of Indonesia's vast natural resources and export markets. Those fears came to a head in early 1965, as Indonesian trade unions and others began to demand the expropriation of UK and US properties, including oil facilities and plantations. The affected companies included major players like Mobil, Caltex, Stanvac, and Goodyear, all of which had good access to key decision makers in Washington.[16] Moreover, as historian Brad Simpson has convincingly argued, the United States and its allies were anxious to ensure Indonesia's full integration into a liberal international political and economic order over which they presided, and to prevent the success of a nationalist or leftist economic experiment that would erode Western hegemony.[17] For all these reasons, in the years preceding the alleged coup attempt, the United States, the United Kingdom, and their allies saw Indonesia—and particularly Sukarno and the PKI—as a major problem.

POLARIZATION, RADICALISM, AND MILITANCY

Whatever their deeper motives and interests, the policies pursued by major foreign powers in the years before the alleged coup—and the Cold War rhetoric they typically employed in justifying those policies—helped to shape political differences and tensions inside Indonesia in a way that accentuated Left versus Right conflict, and increased political polarization, radicalism, and militancy.[18]

The actions of the United States and its allies, for example, confirmed Sukarno's worst suspicions about the imperialist objectives of the West. His criticism of the United States and United Kingdom grew decidedly more vitriolic after the formation of Malaysia in 1963. The United Kingdom was an obvious target because it was seen as having created Malaysia as an imperialist bastion to encircle and threaten Indonesia. Anti-British sentiment reached a high point in September 1963, when an angry crowd burned and ransacked the British Embassy, while Indonesian security forces looked on. The United States was seen as complicit in the neoimperialist plot because despite its public claims of neutrality, it clearly took the British and Malaysian side, and insisted on an end to Confrontation as a condition for US aid. Other indications of US collusion with Malaysia and the United Kingdom gave Sukarno and most Indonesians obvious reasons to wonder about the sincerity of US expressions of neutrality. It was in this context that in March 1964, before a large crowd, Sukarno famously said, "America—Go to hell with your aid!"

FIGURE 4.1. President Sukarno addresses a May Day rally in Jakarta, 1965. The panel above the crowd depicts "Workers of the World" striking a blow against their enemies. (Bettman/Getty Images)

US intervention in Vietnam as well as elsewhere in Indochina was another major irritant and provided ample evidence of its imperialist intent. In a June 1965 memo to McGeorge Bundy on the side effects of US actions in Vietnam, James Thomson accurately summarized the problem: "There is little to say on this sad subject except that our Vietnam operations have been a propaganda god-send to the powerful forces in Indonesia that seek to bring their country under Communist control."[19] Sukarno's criticism predated the United States' deployment of ground troops in Vietnam in mid-1965. In early August 1964, for instance, he offended US sensibilities by recognizing the government of North Vietnam and breaking ties with Saigon.[20] And in a feisty Independence Day speech on August 17, 1964, he denounced US policy in Vietnam and Malaysia. His remarks effectively threw open the floodgate, and anti-US attacks became central to the logic of domestic Indonesian politics.

In April 1965, President Johnson sent a personal emissary, Ambassador Elsworth Bunker, to Jakarta in a last-ditch attempt to smooth deteriorating relations between the two countries. The mission failed, in large part because Bunker was unable to promise a significant change in US foreign policy. According to notes on one of their meetings, Sukarno explained to Bunker that US actions in Malaysia and throughout the Afro-

Asian world were "burning, irritating obstacles" to good US-Indonesian relations.[21] Apparent US duplicity on the question of Confrontation together with strong Chinese support for the campaign made the resort to radical mass mobilization politics all the more appealing as an alternative to a successful resolution of the issue in Indonesia's favor. But that approach also exacerbated tensions, polarization, and militancy, paving the way for crisis.

Over the next several months, anti-US sentiment reached unprecedented heights. In July, Sukarno lectured the United States on Malaysia and Vietnam at the credentials ceremony for the new US ambassador, Marshall Green. July and August saw in quick succession an angry demonstration outside Green's official residence, an attack on the US Consulate in Medan, and another on the US Consulate in Surabaya. Then in his August 17 Independence Day speech, Sukarno launched a blistering attack on the United States and other neocolonial powers. While the anti-US rhetoric kept some political challengers at bay, it also had the effect of more seriously polarizing the domestic political scene.[22]

On the Indonesian Right, Western states' actions in the region and beyond were understood as evidence of Western resolve to stop communism. In that way, the US and British posture elsewhere may have emboldened the army and its allies to move against Sukarno and the PKI in 1965. That is certainly what the United States hoped for. In a March 3, 1965, telegram to the Department of State, for example, the US Embassy's Country Team wrote: "Over longer run we believe military and other actions which show clear evidence US determination hold fast in nearby Free World areas such as South Vietnam, Thailand, Malaysia and Philippines, will have salutary effect on Indo[nesian] behavior."[23]

Confrontation was also the source of serious tensions between Sukarno and the army—and those tensions led to a critical congruence of interest between the army and both the United States and the United Kingdom. Although army leaders had originally supported the Confrontation campaign, they soon began to see it as a liability on several counts. For one thing, they became uncomfortable with the political opportunities it provided to the Left, especially the PKI, which backed the campaign.[24] They also saw it as a dangerous drain on military resources away from the center of PKI power on Java.[25] Finally, they viewed Confrontation as a long-term threat to their chief sources of modern weaponry and military aid—the United States and the USSR. The fact that the campaign was strongly supported by China was small consolation as up to that point, China's military assistance to Indonesia had been negligible, and the motives of its leaders were suspect. As a consequence, the army high command "carried out a series of maneuvers designed to obstruct the effective implementation of the policy."[26]

The Right also saw Sukarno's improving ties with China as a boon to the domestic power of the PKI and the army's service rivals, such as the air force. While Sukarno received high-level Chinese delegations, and Air Marshal Dhani negotiated small arms contracts with Beijing, the army sensed that its own supplies of aid from the United States and USSR were being placed in jeopardy. China's support for the idea of a Fifth Force and its offer to help Sukarno build a nuclear weapon caused further alarm. For these as well as more purely ideological reasons, the army began to protest Sukarno's overtures to China, and to claim that the policies of the PKI and Sukarno were mere dictates from Beijing. While insisting that it was in no way beholden to any foreign power, moves like these placed the army clearly on the side of the United States and its allies in the struggle against communism.

US Meddling

Beyond the indirect consequences of their actions elsewhere, in the decade before 1965, foreign powers pursued policies that aimed deliberately to influence the course of Indonesian politics. Although China and to a lesser extent the USSR played some role, the most consequential and fully documented interventions by far were those pursued by the United States. The United States' meddling started at least ten years before the alleged coup. By seeing what the United States was prepared to do to stop the spread of communism in the ten years before 1965, we get a much clearer sense of what role it might have played in the events of October 1. A review of those efforts from 1955 and onward, then, provides a sense of their long-term trajectory as well as a foretaste of the thinking behind them and the methods employed.

COVERT OPERATIONS, 1955–58

One of the more common forms of US interference in Indonesian political life in the decade before the alleged coup was the provision of "information" and organizational assistance designed to give Indonesians "a clear understanding of the international communist menace."[27] And of course, such assistance was supplemented with quiet cash. The first clear instance of such meddling came in the run-up to Indonesia's first national elections in 1955. US officials were confident that the two strongly anticommunist parties—the Islamic party Masyumi and the PSI—would come out on top and that the PKI would "suffer a relative loss of position."[28] In an effort to hasten that outcome, the United States provided covert funding, technical assistance, and political advice to Masyumi and the PSI.

An Operations Coordinating Board Progress Report from January 1955 referred explicitly to US assistance in propaganda efforts designed to improve Masyumi's electoral prospects and weaken the appeal of the PKI:

> As Masjumi has become more actively and openly anticommunist the party is showing increased willingness to seek assistance from USIS [United States Information Service]. The post has made available films and pamphlets for Masjumi meetings, it supplies party publications with anticommunist feature material, furnishes background information to party leaders, and is assisting Masjumi in the publication of strongly anticommunist books.[29]

US efforts to influence the elections went well beyond the provision of anticommunist information. According to Joseph Smith, a former CIA official who worked on Indonesia in the 1950s, $1 million was made available to Masyumi in advance of the elections.[30] Similarly, Hugh Cumming, the US ambassador to Indonesia at the time, "recalled that on a trip to Washington in December 1954 he was told that covert operations of some sort were about to begin in Indonesia."[31] The timing of that trip suggests that the operation in question probably involved covert financial and propaganda support to Masyumi. The covert tie with Masyumi was confirmed in an April 1957 memo to the assistant secretary of state that noted, "US contacts, particularly in the covert field, have in the past been principally with the Masjumi."[32] The United States also had close ties with leading figures in the PSI and seems likely to have provided that party with support in the elections as well.

In the event, US efforts to influence the 1955 vote proved unsuccessful. Masyumi, which had been widely predicted to win the election, polled a surprisingly low 20.9 percent of the popular vote, while the PSI received just 2 percent.[33] Meanwhile, the PKI and PNI received unprecedented levels of support, together winning almost 40 percent of the vote. Masyumi's poor showing and the PKI's surprising success provoked alarm within the Eisenhower administration.[34] US anxiety was further heightened when the PKI made even more dramatic gains in the regional elections held in 1957. At that stage, the United States began to intervene more energetically, using both overt and covert means to undermine the PKI and destabilize

President Sukarno. Notably, in these operations it continued to rely on leading figures in Masyumi and the PSI, while also seeking ever closer ties with elements of Indonesia's military.

US efforts to undermine Sukarno during these years took a variety of forms, most of them drawn from a repertoire of "dirty tricks" that were being used with some frequency elsewhere. A 1975 Senate committee reported, for example, that it had "received some evidence of CIA involvement in plans to assassinate President Sukarno" and a suitable agent had been identified.[35] The CIA also concocted a plan to produce a pornographic film and still photos purporting to show Sukarno in bed with a Russian airline hostess. Once completed, the film and photos were to be sent anonymously to news outlets in other countries, alongside reports suggesting that Sukarno was being seduced or blackmailed by the Soviets. Commenting on the plan in his memoir, a CIA officer involved wrote, "We had, as a matter of fact, considerable success with this theme. It appeared in the press around the world."[36]

The most dramatic and consequential of US interventions, however, came in 1957–58, when the Eisenhower administration undertook to provide covert funds, military equipment, and air support to two rebel groups (PRRI and Permesta) that were then fighting the Sukarno government from base areas in Sumatra and Sulawesi.[37] Led by disgruntled military officers, the rebellions also had significant support from influential figures associated with Masyumi and the PSI. Although the rebels did not seek to overthrow the government, Washington officials saw in the rebellions an opportunity to weaken Sukarno, strengthen the main anticommunist political parties, and forestall a feared Communist takeover.

Thus, an ad hoc interdepartmental committee on Indonesia concluded in late 1957 that the United States should "strengthen the determination, will and cohesion of the anticommunist forces in the outer islands" so that they could serve as a "rallying point if the Communists should take over Java."[38] The Joint Chiefs of Staff went even further, arguing that additional *covert* military support of the rebels was necessary in order to prevent a Communist victory, not just in Indonesia, but also throughout the region and all the way to "the Moslem Middle East." In an April 1958 memorandum to the secretary of defense, the chiefs made that somewhat-exaggerated case:

> Present restrictions do not permit sufficient timely US aid to the dissidents to ensure victory. Defeat of the dissidents would almost certainly lead to communist domination in Indonesia. Such a turn of events would

> cause a serious reaction in Malaya and Thailand, probable trouble in Laos and possible trouble in Cambodia. It could result in the disappearance of SEATO as a viable pact and an extension of communist influence in the Moslem Middle East. Consequently, if communist domination is to be prevented, action must be taken, including overt measures as required, to ensure the success of the dissidents or the suppression of the pro-communist elements of the Sukarno government.[39]

Although US assistance prolonged the conflict and made it more bloody, the rebels were eventually defeated. Worse still from the US perspective, the substantial US financial and military support for the rebellions—long suspected by Sukarno—was proven beyond a doubt in May 1958 when the pilot of a B-26 aircraft shot down by Indonesian forces turned out to be an American named Allen Lawrence Pope. US claims that Pope was a freelancer were quickly revealed to be nothing more than a weak cover for a covert military operation in support of the rebels, run by the CIA.[40] That revelation, presented at a news conference in Indonesia, came less than a month after President Dwight Eisenhower had insisted that the United States was playing no role whatsoever in the conflict. "Our policy," he had declared, "is one of careful neutrality and proper deportment all the way through so as not to be taking sides where it is none of our business."[41]

Unsurprisingly, Sukarno and the Left made the most of this fact—as well as the discovery of US military equipment in Sumatra—to discredit the rebels and all those who had supported them, including leading figures in Masyumi and the PSI. Convinced that they were continuing to plot against him even after the defeat of the rebellions, Sukarno eventually banned both political parties and jailed some of their most prominent leaders. Meanwhile, US support for the rebels led to a dramatic souring of US-Indonesian relations, and left Sukarno with a deep and well-founded mistrust of US intentions. As General Yani told US Embassy officials in June 1965, "[The United States is the] only nation since independence that has openly supported a rebellion. This the President will never forget and it is something that makes it very easy for anti-American charges to receive a sympathetic ear at [the] Palace."[42]

MILITARY ASSISTANCE, 1958–65

With the collapse of the regional rebellions in 1958, the United States embarked on a new strategy, though with the same objective in mind: to weaken Sukarno and destroy the PKI. Rather than seeking to dismember the country, a strategy that had not only failed but had also threatened to strengthen Sukarno and the PKI, it began instead to build ties with the Indonesian Army. Portraying the army as the only reliable anticommunist force in the country, US policy makers sought to encourage it to play a more direct role in politics, to see itself as a viable alternative to the country's civilian leadership, and more specifically, to act forcefully together with civilian allies to remove or replace Sukarno and the PKI.[43] It pursued that strategy through a program of military aid and training that was deliberately divisive in intent.

The underlying idea behind the aid program was to accentuate political divisions and conflict inside the country, with a view to provoking a conflict from which the army could be almost certain to emerge victorious. In effect, a succession of US administrations consciously provided support to one side of the deepening political struggle, while simultaneously alienating and withdrawing support from the other. In so doing, they helped to foster a political environment in which the military had encouragement and a strong motivation to act.

Military aid had been rather limited through most of the 1950s. In fact, from 1951 to 1954, the United States provided Indonesia no military assistance whatsoever.[44] And when the decision was finally taken to supply some aid, the amounts were rather small. In June 1955, for example, President Eisenhower approved the disbursement of $200,000 under the Mutual Security Act of 1954 "for the purpose of providing assistance to Indonesia for a training program in police administration and the procurement of police communications equipment."[45] But the absence of substantial military aid in these years was not the result of official indifference. It was based on the judgment that it would be unwise to negotiate any military aid agreement with a government that was influenced by or as yet insufficiently opposed to communism.

That view changed significantly in 1958. The shift was partly the result of a realization—especially after the regional elections—that Sukarno and the PKI were becoming more powerful, not less so. It also stemmed from a belated concern that the USSR had been providing Indonesia with vastly more military assistance than the United States or its allies—an imbalance that was bound to influence the political equation. A memorandum from the navy to the Joint Chiefs of Staff in March 1958, for instance, warned that aid from the Soviets "might well lead to Indonesia's early domination by the Bloc."[46]

Accordingly, the United States began to ramp up its military aid program, although it made sure to channel that aid selectively to the army and police, but not to other forces. The army was targeted for aid not for any reason to do with national defense but rather because it was considered the most reliable *political* ally and bulwark against the PKI. Thus, a 1958 memo from the Joint Chiefs of Staff to the secretary of defense noted that aid to the army was begun in earnest on the estimate that

> (1) The Indonesian Army is the only non-communist force in Indonesia with the capability of obstructing the progress of the PKI toward domination of the country; and (2) given some encouragement in the form of US aid, Indonesian Army Chief of Staff Nasution will carry out his "plan" for control of the communists.[47]

As it happened, the army was also strongly antidemocratic—a posture that suited US interests well, mainly because US officials were convinced that free elections would benefit the PKI. Hence, in a January 1959 memorandum to the president recommending the doubling of military aid to Indonesia, the Department of State highlighted for praise a number of "measured but significant steps to circumscribe Communist activities" that had been taken by the army:

> The most important step in this regard has been the postponement of the general election scheduled for September 1959 in which the Communists were expected to score heavy gains. This postponement of election offers Indonesia a period of relative political stability in which to develop an effective government as a demonstrable alternative to the Communists' program and provides the United States and the free world with an excellent opportunity to greatly reduce if not eliminate the danger of a Communist takeover.[48]

Whether the army was solely responsible for this dubious achievement is open to debate. It was certainly not alone in seeking an end to electoral politics in Indonesia in the late 1950s.[49] Nevertheless, the active support of US policy makers for those who wished to put an end to elections was unmistakable. So was the logic of US policy. To the extent that elections seemed likely to produce victories for parties or coalitions favorable to the United States, they were to be championed. But as soon as there was a likelihood that the wrong side might win, elections were to be opposed.

Although the dollar value of US military aid after 1958 was still relatively small, especially when compared to massive Soviet aid, the focus on army training at US Army Service Schools was considered to be highly cost-effective.[50] As internal memorandums repeatedly stressed, the programs helped to develop a politically valuable "personal association between US and Indonesian military personnel."[51] In an April 1964 letter to General Nasution, US general Maxwell Taylor stressed the great importance of those personal ties and hope that they might continue:

> The special relationship that has grown up between officers of the armed services of our two countries in recent years has been a source of gratification to me and to my colleagues on the Joint Staff. . . . When we look beyond the issues of the moment to our mutual longer range objectives in Southeast Asia, I think it is clear that continued cooperation between us is important to the national interest of both Indonesia and the United States.[52]

The military training programs—undertaken by some twenty-eight hundred army officers in the period from 1950 to 1965—were also deemed valuable for encouraging anticommunist sentiments among the army's officer corps. A 1960 NSC report, for example, noted that the Military Aid Program had "bolstered the determination of non-communist and anti-communist elements in Indonesia to counter the Communist influence."[53] Perhaps significantly, five of the six generals killed on the morning of October 1, 1965, had undergone military training in the United States.

Another focus of US assistance to the army was the Civic Action program set in motion in 1962, modeled on programs that had been tried with some success in the Philippines, South Korea, and South Vietnam.[54] The idea of Civic Action, through which the army would take the lead in projects considered helpful to the local population—including public works, agriculture, and health—was not new for the Indonesian Army. Since the Indonesian National Revolution, it had been involved in social and economic activities down to the village level—an approach formalized in its doctrines of "Territorial Warfare" and "Dwifungsi." But the plan now had strong US backing and became a pet project of General Nasution, who worked closely with the US special adviser on Civic Action, Colonel Benson, between 1962 and 1965.[55]

While it was overtly aimed at fostering rural development, Civic Action was also a useful cover for covert action aimed at weakening the PKI. Declassified US government documents reveal, for example, that Civic Action was part of a plan approved by the Special Group—the secret NSC committee responsible for coordinating covert government operations. Minutes from a December 1961 meeting of that committee, though still partially censored, give a clear sense of the nature and dimensions of the program. For instance, they show that an undisclosed sum was allocated in fiscal year 1962 "to support civic action and anticommunist activities to be executed through [Indonesian] [*less than one line of source text not declassified*] instrumentalities." They also reveal that an undisclosed sum was allocated for fiscal years 1962 and 1963 "to assist [*less than one line of source text not declassified*] in covert training of selected personnel and civilians, who will be placed in key positions in the [*less than one line of source text not declassified*] civic action program."[56] In short, covert action and Civic Action programs were closely interwoven, and both were part of a wider plan designed to undermine the PKI.

US aid and training programs also helped to foster close personal ties between Indonesian Army officers and US officials. These eventually laid the foundation for a network of influence linking the army leadership, selected academics (Indonesian and American), and US government officials, including CIA operatives.[57] One such personal connection was forged between Guy Pauker, a political scientist at the RAND Corporation, and Colonel Suwarto, a PSI-leaning officer who was the head of the Army Staff and Command College.[58] With Pauker's encouragement, Suwarto came to embrace the idea that the army was the most reliable sociopolitical institution in the country, and taught officers that the army should prepare itself for a position of political and economic leadership—a role described as its civic mission.[59] It was through Suwarto as well that a number of US-trained economists—many of them educated at the University of California at Berkeley—were invited to lead seminars at Seskoad. This group, sometimes referred to as the Berkeley Mafia, eventually formed a network linking the anticommunist army leadership with modernizing economic technocrats.[60]

Significantly, one of the officers at Seskoad during these critical years was Suharto, then a colonel. It was at Seskoad, in the early 1960s, that Suharto became involved in the formation of the doctrine of Territorial Warfare and the army's policy of civic mission.[61] And it was there that he grew close to the network of officers and US-trained economists who would form the core of his kitchen cabinet after October 1965. During these years, Suharto's network also came to include a number of businesspeople and officers who served as intermediaries between large foreign corporations and the army. Such connections flourished after the declaration of martial law in 1957, as the army gained control over major economic enterprises and royalties from foreign corporations began to flow directly into army coffers.[62]

In 1961, US officials sought further adjustments in the aid program to make it more flexible and politically useful. In a top secret telegram to the

Department of State, US ambassador Jones recommended removing the political restrictions on military aid with a view to strengthening the confidence in the United States by the Indonesian Army, preventing a Soviet monopoly on conspicuous military equipment, and supplying modern, complex weapons systems to develop the need for a larger US training presence. These changes, Jones argued, were "based on recognition of [the] fact [that the] fundamental purpose in providing aid is political; namely strengthening anticommunist military leadership." More specifically, Jones contended that the US should "supply equipment strongly desired by Nasution, Yani and staff" in order to "improve leverage within the Indonesian Armed Forces."[63]

If Jones's memo highlighted the degree to which US decisions about military aid were based on political considerations, his reference to preventing a Soviet monopoly on conspicuous military equipment highlighted a worrying development. In 1960, Nikita Khrushchev had granted Indonesia $100 million in military aid, the first of several major disbursements over the next five years. By one estimate, between 1960 and 1965 Indonesia received roughly $1.1 billion in military aid from the Soviet Union, vastly outstripping US contributions. As a consequence, by 1965 some 90 percent of air force equipment and 80 percent of navy equipment was from the USSR.[64]

Despite these developments, in fall 1963 Congress passed the new Foreign Assistance Act, which restricted military and economic aid to Indonesia. And as tensions between Indonesia and the United States escalated further in 1964, there was pressure from Congress and the US media for even further restrictions. The Tower Amendment of August 1964, for example, called for an end to all aid to Indonesia.[65] Yet to those inside who understood that the real purpose of military assistance programs was political, it was far from obvious that a complete cut would best serve US interests. To do so would be to throw away any hope of influencing the political balance in Indonesia. Thus, a memo from Secretary of State Dean Rusk to the president, dated July 17, 1964, stressed that US military aid "is not helping Indonesia militarily. It is, however, permitting us to maintain some contact with key elements in Indonesia which are interested in and capable of resisting Communist takeover. We think this is of vital importance to the entire Free World."[66]

To avoid problems with Congress and the media, the Johnson administration publicly agreed to the cut while privately sustaining aid to its allies in the army. In a summary of proposed cuts, from August 1964, Rusk reported to the president that "our programs are now at the point where they maintain valuable ties with key Indonesian groups but do not bolster Sukarno or his Malaysia policy."[67]

The aid cuts that were ultimately made were the most visible as well as those most likely to undercut Sukarno's Confrontation campaign. But key programs considered beneficial to maintaining ties with the army were kept in place, notably the Military Training Program. In a memo to the president, Assistant Secretary of State for Far Eastern Affairs William Bundy made a now-familiar argument for maintaining that program: "We have felt that it is an important link to the Indonesian military and this long-term asset value is still considerable."[68] Also retained was the Civic Action program, Nasution's pet project, which was a useful cover for covert action against the PKI, as well as technical assistance for the national police "to preserve US influence in this important power center."[69]

The guiding logic behind US aid strategy at this time was summarized by National Security Adviser McGeorge Bundy in a memo to the president in late August 1964:

> The very fact that we are on a slippery slope makes it all the more important not to burn our bridges to Indonesia: (1) with Vietnam and Laos already on our Southeast Asia plate, we can ill afford a major crisis with Indonesia too just now; (2) we ought to keep a few links, however tenuous, to the Indo military, still the chief hope of blocking a communist takeover; (3) . . . we want to keep dangling the prospects of renewed aid; and (4) we do not want to be the ones who trigger a major attack on US investments there.[70]

Despite these precautions, the passage of the Tower Amendment in mid-August 1964 gave rise to massive anti-US demonstrations in Indonesia. On August 16, the day after Congress approved the amendment, the *New York Times* reported that the Thomas Jefferson Library of USIS in Yogyakarta had been seized by a "shouting crowd of young Indonesians," who claimed that the building was "now official property of the Indonesian people."[71] Against the background of this increasing militancy and polarization in Indonesian politics, the differential and discretionary distribution of US aid and support in the direction of anticommunist forces might have helped—in Ambassador Jones's phrase—to "tip the balance" in favor of those already possessed of a capacity and will to act against the PKI. In any case, that was the clear intention of US policy. The critical question was whether and how such a move might be undertaken.

Provocation

With the dramatic worsening of relations in 1964–65, and clear indications of Sukarno's increasingly close alignment with China, US and British officials viewed the situation in Indonesia with ever-greater alarm. The violent attacks on US and British properties, attempted seizures of foreign-owned plantations and petroleum facilities, vitriolic anti-US speeches, and mass demonstrations all gave the United States and United Kingdom more immediate and vital reasons to fight back.[72] At the same time, they recognized that any overt display of support for their noncommunist allies would be disastrous. And so while outwardly maintaining a posture of noninterference and even disinterest, their prescriptions for action became commensurately more desperate and covert. From late 1964, they effectively abandoned the normal tools of diplomatic relations and contemplated instead a variety of unconventional methods, including covert action and psywar. Over the same period, China's leaders undertook a number of initiatives that may have emboldened Sukarno and the PKI to confront the army, thereby accentuating tensions inside Indonesia.

EXTRAORDINARY MEASURES

A series of internal memorandums from late 1964 through mid-1965 provide insight into the growing anxiety of US officials and a glimpse of the courses of action that were being contemplated in the nine months before the alleged coup. A State Department memorandum of December 1964 concerning the upcoming visit of British prime minister Harold Wilson to Washington advised the president to say that "the US and Great Britain must be prepared to engage in full military battle" against Indonesia.[73] In January 1965, a CIA memorandum stated flatly, "The interests of the US and of Sukarno now conflict in nearly every quarter."[74] The same document argued that the chances of PKI success would only improve with time, making prompt and preemptive action by the army all the more urgent. It ended with the ominous assessment that "the momentum and direction which [Sukarno] has imparted to present trends are sweeping him along toward the eventual possibilities of war with the UK and the US, domination by communist China, or takeover of Indonesia by the PKI." At a meeting of the NSC's secret 303 Committee—successor to the Special Group—in early March, a CIA official urged the development of "a larger design or master plan to arrest the Indonesian march into the Chinese camp," noting that the loss of a nation of 105 million would "make victory in Vietnam of little meaning."[75] In a telephone conversation with McGeorge Bundy on March 15, George Ball said that developments in Indonesia were "moving very rapidly in the wrong direction" and "in the long political term it [Indonesia] may be more important to us than South Vietnam."[76] A top secret June 1965 memorandum from the assistant secretary of defense to McGeorge Bundy referred to Sukarno's regime as "a menace of notable dimension."[77] Then, as noted above, in a draft letter dated July 20, CIA director Raborn advised the president that "Indonesia is well embarked on a course that will make it a communist nation in the reasonably near future, unless the trend is reversed."[78] A few weeks later, in mid-August, Undersecretary of State Ball and National Security Adviser Bundy agreed that there should be a meeting "to alert the President to the seriousness of the situation in which the Communists may take over Indonesia"—a development that Ball said "would be the biggest thing since the fall of China."[79]

Thus in the months leading up to October 1965, there was consensus at the highest levels of the US government on the need to take new and resolute measures to deal with a country whose "slide to communism" would gravely damage the position of the United States in the rest of Asia and possibly worldwide. In the midst of these deliberations, Ambassador Jones—who was now seen as a Sukarno apologist and ineffective—was replaced by the hard-hitting Green, who by all accounts arrived in Jakarta with a new game plan.[80] Against this backdrop, the United States and United Kingdom looked to their friends in the army and among anticommunist civilians for indications that they would be prepared to confront Sukarno and the PKI. When they discovered a reluctance to act forcefully, they discussed how best to prod their local allies into action—and to create the conditions for a showdown with Sukarno and the PKI.

One of the earliest ideas, proposed by the CIA in a secret cable from September 1964, was the formation of an anticommunist coalition combining reliable army and civilian elements.[81] The cable noted that such a coalition would have an especially good chance of gaining power in a succession struggle and judged that its success "would rebound to America's advantage." It also made clear the agency's preference for having reliable army figures at the center of the coalition, noting that "the presence of additional military figures in a successor government (i.e. those whose current attitudes we can assess) would tend to reinforce that advantage (to the US)." More specifically, the CIA named those army officers it considered to be "friendly" and "on the good side" of Confrontation and Communism. They were "Generals Nasution, Suharto, Sudirman, Adjie, Sarbani [words deleted], and in a middle category, less staunchly anti-communist at the present time. . . . Generals Yani and Parman, and Admiral Martadinata." Thus, despite later US claims that he was an unknown figure, by September 1964 at the latest, Suharto was on the CIA's radar as a friendly general, thought to be on the good side on both Confrontation and Communism.

US officials also identified at this time key civilian and religious organizations as likely collaborators in the fight against the PKI, and began to channel assistance and advice to them. These included the powerful NU, the large Islamic party whose members were later among the principal perpetrators of the violence, especially in its base area of East Java where the killing was intense and widespread.[82] Those identified by the CIA as potential assets also included a number of political insiders, like Third Deputy Prime Minister Chaerul Saleh and Trade Minister Adam Malik.[83] According to a former CIA official who had been posted in Jakarta, Malik had been close to the agency since the early 1960s.[84] It was probably no coincidence that at about this time, Saleh and Malik were key figures in two strongly anti-PKI political organizations—the Body to Promote Sukarnoism (BPS) and the Murba Party—both of which were later banned amid allegations that the CIA had backed them.[85]

CREATING THE CONDITIONS

Beyond identifying potential friends and coalitions, the United States and its allies contemplated how to create the conditions for a showdown that the army could win. One proposal was to provide the army leadership with reassurances that Western states would not interfere should the army move forcefully against the PKI. US ambassador Bell in Kuala Lumpur suggested that strategy to his counterpart in Jakarta. In a telegram dated January 9, 1965, Bell pointed out that in the context of Confrontation, anti-PKI elements in the army might be hesitant to act against the PKI out of fear of reprisals by British, US, and Malaysian forces. Bell's proposal was to quietly assure army leaders that they would be given a free hand to move against the PKI:

> Is there any way we could reach completely reliable Indonesian military with assurances that GOM [Government of Malaysia] and Commonwealth would refrain from interference, at least until it becomes apparent [that the] PKI [is] going to come out on top[?] . . . Our policy

> has depended on the Army for some time. If we can give them this sort of shot in the arm, they might have more inclination to act.[86]

Just two weeks later, the US Embassy in Jakarta reported encouraging signs of "receptiveness" within the army high command to the idea of a military takeover before Sukarno stepped down. In a revealing (but partially censored) secret telegram to the Department of State, dated January 21, 1965, Jones reported on a meeting between an "excellent" source and General Parman, the head of army intelligence. According to the telegram, Parman had indicated that there was "strong sentiment" within the "top military command" for a "takeover of government" prior to Sukarno's demise and that "specific plans" for such a coup were being developed. Moreover, as described in the telegram, the army leadership realized that no coup targeting Sukarno directly could ever succeed, so it was suggested that "the coup would be handled in such a way as to preserve Sukarno's leadership intact" but to leave him with a fait accompli.[87] That was a fair description of what actually happened on October 1, 1965.

In March 1965, the NSC's secret 303 Committee also turned its attention to the Indonesian crisis and, more specifically, to the United States' covert action program in the country. A memorandum prepared for that meeting revealed that since summer 1964, the State Department and another agency—whose identity remains classified but was most likely the CIA—had been developing "an operational plan for political action in Indonesia." The main aim of the plan was to reduce the influence of the PKI and "Red China," and bolster anticommunist forces, by exploiting factionalism within the PKI, emphasizing traditional Indonesian distrust of China, and portraying the PKI "as an instrument of Red Chinese imperialism."[88]

Parts of that plan had already been implemented. "Through secure mechanisms," the memorandum noted, "some funds have been given to key personalities to bolster their ability and their resolve to continue their anticommunist activities which essentially are in the U.S. direction." Beyond secret financial support for anticommunist individuals and groups, the new plan envisaged a range of psywar activities, discussed in greater detail below. Although the amount of funding and their source remain classified, the 303 Committee approved the proposed covert action program, with immediate effect, on March 4, 1965.

One month later, Ambassador Bunker visited Indonesia on behalf of President Johnson. Although ostensibly intended as a last effort to bring

Sukarno on board, the visit provided an ideal opportunity to meet with opposition figures and to discuss contingency plans.[89] In the "general conclusions" to his April 1965 report to the president, Bunker outlined what was by then the prevailing US position: to *create the conditions* in which anticommunist forces, led by the army and its anticommunist allies, would take forceful action against the PKI and Sukarno. Thus, point twelve of the general conclusions to his report read as follows: "US policy should be directed toward creating conditions which will give the elements of potential strength the most favorable conditions for confrontation." Elsewhere in the document, the "elements of potential strength" were explicitly listed as: "a) The military, especially the army; b) Moderate moslem [*sic*] political organizations; c) Other moderate political elements now inactive."[90]

Taken together, we have here clear evidence that in the year before the purported coup of October 1965, US (and probably also Malaysian and British) officials were seriously contemplating—and indeed starting to implement—strategies designed to encourage the army and its civilian allies to act against the PKI, without leaving US or other foreign fingerprints. While the momentum of anti-Americanism and the general radicalization of politics at this juncture limited the effectiveness of normal foreign policy tools, the extreme polarization and near balance between opposing political forces provided the United States and its allies with a unique opportunity to have Indonesians fight what was, at least in part, the United States' war. By mid-1965, the army high command appeared to be on exactly the same page. At a meeting in July 1965, Yani reportedly told Benson, the US Civic Action adviser to the Indonesian Army, "We have the guns, and we have kept the guns out of their [the Communists'] hands. So if there's a clash, we'll wipe them out."[91]

PSYWAR AND BLACK OPS

Finally, in the years leading up to the alleged coup, the United States and United Kingdom sought to influence the political balance in Indonesia through a program of psywar and black operations. These operations were designed to tarnish the name of the PKI and Sukarno, and—importantly—to provoke political conflict between them and anticommunist elements. Indeed, declassified US government documents from this period reveal that provoking a showdown with the PKI was not simply a by-product of US policy in Indonesia but rather its very *intention*. A crucial focus of that campaign was the creation of conditions that would provide a pretext for a forceful move by the army against the Left. That strategy was not new, but in the crisis atmosphere of early 1965, it was revived and implemented with renewed vigor.

Eerily foreshadowing the events of October 1, 1965, a National Security Council policy document of December 1960 said the US should "give priority treatment to programs which offer opportunities to isolate the PKI, to drive it into positions of open confrontation with the Indonesian government, thereby creating grounds for repressive measures, politically justifiable in terms of the Indonesian national self-interest."[92] One month later, in January 1961, US officials began to discuss "psywar operations" more explicitly. In a top secret telegram to the Department of State, dated January 26, 1961—just days after President Kennedy's inauguration—Ambassador Jones recommended that the United States should prepare for a "possible major psychological war campaign coordinating covert and overt resources, when proper climate can be developed."[93] It is probably no coincidence that the US covert operation in Indonesia, conducted under the cover of the Civic Action program, commenced less than one year later.

Psywar operations reached a new level of intensity and sophistication after 1963, as the United States, United Kingdom, and Malaysia began to work together to weaken Sukarno and the PKI in the context of the Confrontation campaign announced by Subandrio in January of that year.[94] For the British and Malaysians, psywar plans were part of a wider covert operation, undertaken with the support of Australia and New Zealand, aimed at undermining Sukarno and even, in some scenarios, provoking the break up of the country.[95] In addition to providing weapons, military training, and funds to a variety of anti-Indonesian rebel groups, British and Malaysian officials at the highest levels authorized and developed guidelines for a psychological warfare campaign designed to "aid and encourage dissident movements inside Indonesia."[96] That campaign entailed, among other elements, clandestine radio broadcasts denouncing Communism, and advocating greater autonomy or independence for areas outside Java.

By early 1965, however, the British started to worry that support for secessionist movements would interfere with the army's capacity to resist the PKI and so adjusted their plans accordingly. Thus, in a March 1965 memorandum approved by senior ministers of Britain's new Labour government, the Joint Action Committee advised that

> in the long run effective support for dissident movements in Indonesia may be counter-productive in that it might impair the capacity of the

> Army to resist the PKI ... [and] therefore [Britain should] attempt, by covert means, to make it clear to the Indonesian Army that any support for dissidents is no more than a tactical response to "confrontation."[97]

These plans dovetailed neatly with the strategy of Indonesian Army officers who were growing impatient with Confrontation.[98] Two of the more significant elements of that army strategy began in mid-1964, and involved Major General Suharto and his close associates, Lieutenant Colonel Ali Murtopo, Colonel Yoga Sugama, and Major L. B. Murdani, all of whom had backgrounds in army intelligence. Through them, and with assistance from figures who had been involved in the 1958 rebellions, the army arranged a series of secret meetings with Malaysian officials at which a covert strategy of mutual avoidance of hostilities was planned.[99] In addition, Suharto took advantage of his position as deputy commander of the multiservice command for the Confrontation campaign—known as Kolaga (Komando Mandala Siaga)—to ensure that the forces on the front line with Malaysia were kept below strength and underequipped.[100] Both strategies were clearly designed to subvert Sukarno's policy, and in so doing, undermine him and the PKI. In this, the interests of Suharto and his close associates coincided with those of the United Kingdom, Malaysia, and United States, and the covert actions they undertook achieved exactly what those powers wanted. Moreover, the position of Suharto and his colleagues as avowed critics of Confrontation, and their involvement in these covert operations, laid a solid foundation for future army collaboration with those governments.

Intriguingly, the plans discussed by UK and US officials in the final year before the alleged coup attempt looked much like what happened on October 1, 1965. The crux of the covert strategy was provocation: the PKI should be provoked into making an aggressive move that would both spur and justify a harsh reaction by the army. The ideal scenario, discussed with some frequency by US, British, and other diplomats beginning in late 1964, was more or less precisely what the NSC had proposed in 1960: a "premature PKI coup" that would trigger a forceful response by the army and justify the destruction of the PKI in the name of the Indonesian "national interest."

In the September 1964 intelligence memorandum on US-Indonesian relations mentioned above, the CIA offered a first draft of that strategy. Outlining the circumstances favorable to an anticommunist victory, the report made two crucial points. First, it said that the chances for success

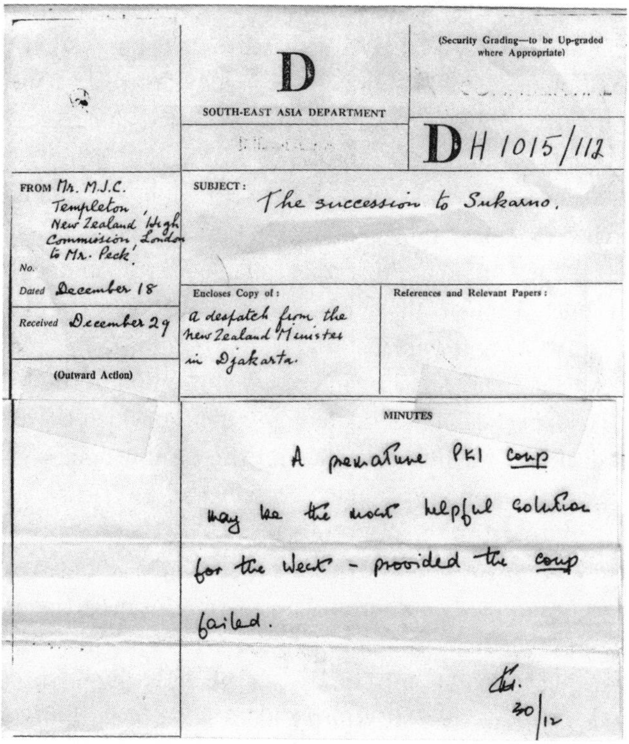

(Security Grading—to be Up-graded where Appropriate)

D

SOUTH-EAST ASIA DEPARTMENT

DH 1015/112

FROM Mr. M.J.C. Templeton, New Zealand High Commission, London to Mr. Peck.

No.

Dated December 18

Received December 29

(Outward Action)

SUBJECT: The succession to Sukarno.

Encloses Copy of: a despatch from the New Zealand Minister in Djakarta.

References and Relevant Papers:

MINUTES

A premature PKI coup may be the most helpful solution for the West – provided the coup failed.

30/12

FIGURE 4.2. British Foreign Office note on a December 1964 report about Indonesia reads: "A premature PKI coup may be the most helpful solution for the West—provided the coup failed." (UK National Archive)

would be greatest in a succession struggle of some kind, and second, that the army would be more likely to respond forcefully if the PKI were to take some provocative action: "An abrupt or aggressive move on the latter's [PKI's] part would surely evoke Army reaction."[101] In March 1965, Jones echoed and endorsed the idea, telling a closed meeting of State Department officials in the Philippines, "From our viewpoint, of course, an unsuccessful coup attempt by the PKI might be the most effective development to start a reversal of political trends in Indonesia."[102]

The idea of provoking a premature Communist coup also began to circulate among Commonwealth governments at this time, alongside plans to expand covert operations in Indonesia. In a memo dated November 27, 1964, the assistant secretary of state in the British Foreign Office, Edward Peck, wrote that "there might therefore be much to be said for encouraging a premature PKI coup during Sukarno's lifetime."[103] Responding to a December 1964 report on Indonesia prepared by New Zealand, another British official commented that "A premature PKI coup may be the most helpful solution for the West—provided the coup failed."[104] Shortly thereafter, in January 1965, the British moved to expand their covert operations by creating the position of director of political warfare against Indonesia within the Information and Research Department in Singapore.[105]

A March 4, 1965, telegram from the US Embassy to the Department of State stressed the limited options still available for responding to anti-US actions. It concluded that "the only effective retaliation we have is in [the] military field," but argued against that course mainly on the grounds that it would damage the credibility and political position of the Indonesian Army.[106] That conclusion highlighted the extent to which US hands were bound in dealing with Indonesia. Under the circumstances, a resort to covert methods was an undeniable necessity and, as far as the available evidence demonstrates, the preferred approach. As it happens, a covert action plan was already in place. In early March 1965, as noted earlier, the NSC's 303 Committee had approved a program for covert operations in Indonesia. Notably, that program included "covert liaison with and support for existing anticommunist groups, particularly among the [*less than one line of source text not declassified*], black letter operations, media operations, including possibly black radio, and political action within existing Indonesian institutions and organizations."[107]

In light of this evidence—and given standard practice for covert psywar operations—it is a virtual certainty that the operation launched at this time included the placement of untrue or provocative stories in Indonesian and foreign publications, the spreading of rumors regarding the intentions of various parties, and the dissemination of forged documents—all with the aim of developing a climate of heightened antagonism conducive to a forceful move against the Left. The ideal end point of such manipulation, as envisioned in US and UK planning, would be the provocation of Communists into taking compromising actions—ideally in the form of a failed "coup" attempt—thereby providing a pretext for their repression by the army.[108]

Against this background, a number of documents and rumors that began to circulate in late 1964 and early 1965 take on new meaning. The first document of significance was a letter from Pakistan's ambassador to Paris, J. A. Rahim, to his foreign minister, Zulfikar Ali Bhutto.[109] In the letter, dated December 1964, Ambassador Rahim reported on a conversation he had recently had with a Dutch intelligence officer attached to the North Atlantic Treaty Organization (NATO). The officer had told Rahim that Western intelligence agencies were organizing a "premature communist coup" in Indonesia. The coup "would be foredoomed to fail," but would provide the Indonesian Army with "a legitimate and welcome opportunity ... to crush the communists and make Soekarno a prisoner of the Army's goodwill." Indonesia, the NATO officer had concluded, "was ready to fall into the Western lap like a rotten apple." This account lends credence to the suggestion that starting in late 1964, Western governments were colluding with elements in the army to create a scenario in which the army would be in a position to act forcefully against the PKI and Sukarno.[110]

Late 1964 brought additional indications that some kind of Western psywar operation was under way. In December 1964, Chaerul Saleh—who it will be recalled had been named by the CIA in September as a good bet, and was a key figure in the anti-PKI Murba Party and BPS—began flashing about a document he claimed was a PKI plan to seize power. The PKI and Sukarno dismissed the document as a forgery, partly because it seemed so clearly designed to incriminate the PKI and partly because its language was so far from that used in most PKI documents.[111] Given the timing, so soon after Western agencies had started to discuss the creation of conditions for a succession crisis and plans for a premature Communist coup, it seems possible and even likely that the document was produced by (or at the suggestion of) Western intelligence agencies. It would have been a relatively simple and cost-effective way to create an atmosphere of political threat from the Left, which might in turn prompt a forceful army reaction.

Then in early 1965, rumors began to circulate that a Council of Generals had been set up with CIA backing and had started planning some kind of coup. When confronted by Sukarno on the matter, Yani insisted that the story was untrue, but admitted that he had formed a "brain trust" of senior officers to discuss matters of promotion.[112] The US defense attaché, Colonel Willis Ethel, who was close to Yani, later confirmed that the army had formed an "advisory group" to develop contingency plans for an army takeover in the event of Sukarno's death or PKI seizure of power.[113] Whether the story of the Council of Generals was true or not, it proved to be a crucial factor in the events that unfolded over the next few months. At a minimum, it gave rise to urgent discussions within the PKI and among progressive military officers about how best to forestall such a coup. At least some on the left and those loyal to Sukarno took the threat of a generals' coup seriously enough to make plans to preempt it.[114] That was, after all, the declared purpose of the September 30th Movement. In that sense, the rumor of a coup followed the psywar script perfectly, provoking the Left to act and, as the NSC had prescribed in 1960, "creating grounds for repressive measures, politically justifiable in terms of the Indonesian national self-interest."[115]

In May, Indonesian intelligence officials claimed to have discovered a letter from the British ambassador to Indonesia, Gilchrist, which appeared to provide evidence of Western plotting. The letter, on British Embassy letterhead, reportedly contained the following passage: "It would be as well to emphasize once more to our local army friends that the strictest caution, discipline and coordination are essential to the success of the enterprise."[116] The letter sent shock waves through the Presidential Palace and army high command. In a secret speech to regional commanders on May 27, Yani reported that Sukarno had summoned him and other armed service chiefs the previous day, and that the president had demanded to know who these "army friends" were.[117] British and US officials insisted that the letter was a forgery, and suggested that it had been concocted by Subandrio's intelligence agency to strike a blow at the British and his own domestic enemies. That might be true. But considering the timing and context, it is at least as likely that the letter was prepared by the British or Americans, either as a genuine communication with army friends, or a psywar trick designed to provoke the kind of careless action by the PKI that Western powers and the army saw as their best hope.[118] If the Gilchrist Letter turned out to be a British or CIA forgery deliberately planted to provoke the PKI and Sukarno to act, we would have convincing evidence that the plans proposed by the CIA and other US agencies since 1960 were actually being implemented.

In the final weeks before the alleged October 1 coup, the rumor of a planned coup by a CIA-backed Council of Generals, to be staged on or before Armed Forces Day (October 5, 1965), was widespread—so widespread, in fact, that there is reason to suspect that its dissemination was also a deliberate provocation. Such a rumor, in the tense, precariously balanced political atmosphere of September 1965, would have had enough credibility, according to Crouch, to have provoked some kind of preemptive action from pro-Sukarno, pro-PKI, and anti–high command forces.[119] At the very least, it would have given these groups reason to consider supporting, if not initiating, a preemptive or retaliatory action. It is significant, then, that the forces that were in some way involved in the September 30th Movement reflected precisely such an anti–Council of Generals orientation rather than a pro-PKI one.

In sum, forged documents, rumors, or other methods of spreading (mis)information, both on the eve of the alleged October coup and for many months before, may have been crucial in provoking an open act of violence against the alleged Council of Generals—an act that could then be used, in the NSC's proposed scenario, as a spur and pretext for forceful army action against the PKI. Although it cannot yet be definitively proven, there is good reason to believe that these rumors and documents were part of a deliberate effort to provoke the PKI into joining forces with the plotters of a preemptive coup. At any rate, the documents, together with the evidence of CIA and government proposals for dealing with the Communist threat, lend credence to an interpretation that includes deliberate US and other foreign efforts to provoke an open struggle between the Left and Right on the assumption that in an armed showdown, the Right would win.[120]

THE CHINA FACTOR

None of this should be taken to mean that the United States and its allies were alone in seeking to influence the course of political events in Indonesia. Through its program of substantial military aid, for example, the Soviet Union was clearly trying to win Indonesia as a regional ally, and it seems to have succeeded, at the very least, in driving a wedge between the air force and army. As noted earlier, moreover, in the final year before the alleged coup, China's state and party leaders took a number of initiatives that influenced Indonesian politics and no doubt were intended to do so. China's offer to supply Indonesia with a hundred thousand small arms, support for the Fifth Force idea, embrace of Sukarno's anti-imperialist foreign policy including Confrontation, and willingness to assist Indonesia in developing nuclear weapons capability plainly bolstered the Left, and probably emboldened the PKI and Sukarno to confront the army more directly in the year before the alleged coup.

At the same time, caution is warranted in assessing the significance of these moves in explaining the events of October 1, 1965 and the subsequent violence. For one thing, a careful examination of Chinese government records indicates that the twenty-five thousand small weapons that had been promised to the air force some time in July 1965 had not yet been shipped by the last week of September, and so could not have been used by the movement on the morning of October 1.[121] Under the circumstances, army claims that Chinese weapons had been found in the possession of Pemuda Rakyat members and other leftists must be treated with considerable skepticism. Indeed, there is every reason to suspect that those allegations were part of the propaganda campaign, devised by the army with help from the United States and United Kingdom, to tarnish the name of the PKI by, among other things, portraying it as a servant of Beijing.[122] Likewise, the plan to share nuclear expertise and technology was disrupted by the events of October 1, and so never came to fruition. Reviewing the Chinese documentary record, the scholar who has examined it most carefully, Taomo Zhou, has concluded, "Beijing's actual influence on political developments in 1965 was very limited."[123]

Caution is also in order in assessing the evidence of China's involvement in planning or masterminding the September 30th Movement. Zhou provides some important clues on that question, but no smoking gun. The documentary record appears to show that by early August 1965, Aidit or the party had devised a plan that bore similarities to the events that unfolded early on October 1. In a meeting with Mao and other senior Chinese officials in Beijing on August 5, 1965, Aidit reportedly described the plan as follows:

> In the first scenario, we plan to establish a military committee. The majority of that committee would be left wing, but it should also include some middle elements. In this way, we could confuse our enemies. Our enemies would be uncertain about the nature of this committee, and therefore the military commanders who are sympathetic to the right wing will not oppose us immediately. If we show our red flag right away, they will oppose us right away. The head of this military committee would be an underground member of our party, but he would identify himself as [being] neutral. This military committee should not last for too long. Otherwise, good people will turn [into] bad people. After it has been established, we need to arm the workers and peasants in a timely fashion.[124]

Zhou takes this passage to mean that Aidit was centrally involved in planning the September 30th Movement and shared those plans with Mao. While that is a possibility and is consistent with Roosa's claims regarding Aidit's role, it is not the only way the passage can be read. Given the serious concerns about Sukarno's health at exactly this time—he collapsed and vomited on August 4, 1965—it is at least as likely that Aidit was spelling out for Mao what the PKI might do in the event that Sukarno became gravely ill or died. There is nothing in the passage, moreover, that indicates that such a plan is already in place, or indeed that the PKI had any intention of setting it in motion while Sukarno was still alive and in good health. Just as important, neither this document nor any other that has come to light provides any support at all for Indonesian

Army claims that China masterminded the movement, or had any hand in planning it. Indeed, after examining and weighing the available evidence, Zhou concludes categorically that contrary to army claims, "Mao was not 'the architect of the coup.'"[125]

Foreign covert intervention in the internal affairs of states is easy to speculate on, but difficult to prove. And so it is in the case of foreign involvement in the alleged coup of October 1, 1965. Yet if it is not possible to prove that the action was the product of a foreign covert operation, it is clear that foreign states and the wider international context contributed substantially to that outcome. Moreover, it is beyond dispute that the US government and its allies wanted very much to make such a contribution. These are, I think, sufficient grounds for us to be deeply skeptical of US and British claims of noninvolvement, and Indonesian Army claims of sole PKI responsibility under Chinese direction. I am not suggesting that the alleged coup attempt of October 1965 was planned and carried out by foreign operatives with a view to toppling Sukarno and wiping out the PKI. I am arguing rather that both indirectly and by intention, the policies and actions of major foreign powers helped to bring about that result. More specifically, I am suggesting that US, British, and Chinese foreign policy influenced domestic Indonesian politics in ways that ultimately made a military coup and violent conflict between the Left and Right much more likely to occur.

Three related dynamics were at play. First, although not the only factor motivating the behavior of states, the general atmosphere of the Cold War had an important influence on Indonesian politics in the years leading up to 1965. It affected the language and style of politics, moving it in an ever more polarized, militant, and bellicose direction. That atmosphere was not by any means solely the result of the sometimes-hysterical anticommunism of Western powers. China and its allies, and to some extent the USSR, were also responsible. The growing militancy of the Left in Indonesia was not sui generis, after all, but part of a wider, global movement that had reached something of an apex in 1965. In addition to the general atmosphere of militancy, the Cold War context reinforced and accentuated existing ideological divisions inside Indonesia, sometimes recasting them as conflicts between the Left and Right, or driving a wedge between what might otherwise have been reconcilable positions.

Second, through a number of specific actions and interventions in Asia and elsewhere, the US and British governments further exacerbated the left-right polarization and radicalization of Indonesian politics. Among other factors, the British creation of Malaysia in 1963 and United States support for it, and US bombing runs over North Vietnam and deployment of ground troops in South Vietnam in 1965, were influential in fueling Sukarno's vitriolic assaults on US imperialism and increasing the credibility of those charges among the Indonesian population generally. At the same time, China's evident support for the PKI along with the leftward shift in Sukarno's domestic and foreign policy alarmed the army leadership and parties of the Indonesian Right, leading to further polarization between them and the PKI. It was at a crisis point in this polarization between the army and PKI-Sukarno alliance that the alleged coup attempt occurred.

Third, in addition to the indirect effects of their actions, US and British policy makers sought deliberately to undermine and weaken the Sukarno government and to destroy the PKI. They did so in a variety of ways over at least a decade. In 1955, the US government sought to influence the outcome of the first national elections by providing financial and other covert aid to anticommunist parties. A few years later, it supplied direct military and financial support to armed rebels in the hope that they would overthrow Sukarno and defeat the PKI. Later, it placed its bets on the Indonesian Army, providing substantial military training and aid in the hope that it would serve as an ally in the United States' bid to destroy the PKI and remove Sukarno from power. At heart, all these moves were designed to exploit and exacerbate internal political divisions *with the intention* of bringing about the demise of the established government and its partners.

On top of the various measures taken by the State and Defense Departments to maintain US support for and influence in the army, the CIA and its British counterparts played a direct role in encouraging the army to destroy the PKI and seize political power. In what appears to have been a coordinated initiative, starting in 1964, US and British officials set in motion a covert psywar campaign that was explicitly designed to tarnish the name of the PKI and Sukarno, and more important, to provide a pretext for the army to act forcefully against them, in "the national interest." Under the circumstances, it is difficult to take seriously the categorical claim of former CIA director William Colby that "we had nothing to do with the coup."[126]

It is perhaps worth stressing that the significance of all these contextual factors and courses of action depended on their capacity for accentuating domestic political cleavages, and encouraging forces of sufficient intrinsic strength to take political action consistent with those objectives.

We know that by 1965, there were strong domestic forces, especially in the army high command, whose interests were congruent with, if not always identical to, those of the United States and its allies. And on the basis of the evidence presented here, we can be certain that those powers did what they could to provide such forces with a convenient opportunity to act and assurances that they might do so with impunity. By contrast, there is as yet no evidence to support army claims that China had a direct hand in orchestrating or planning the September 30th Movement as part of a strategy of world revolution.

CHAPTER FIVE

Mass Killing

Members and sympathizers of the PKI who were to be murdered had their hands tied. Then an Ansor gang, accompanied and protected by an Army unit . . . took them to the killing places, the village of Sentong and the Botanic Gardens (Kebun Raya) in Purwodadi. Holes had already been prepared in these places. The victims were taken one by one up to the holes; nooses were put around their necks and then tightened until the victims collapsed. Then they were beaten with iron rods and other hard implements. After the victims had died, their heads were cut off. Dozens of people were killed like this in Sentong and about a thousand in the Botanic Gardens. Banana trees were planted over the graves.

—ANONYMOUS, "ADDITIONAL DATA ON COUNTER-REVOLUTIONARY CRUELTY IN INDONESIA"

THE CAMPAIGN OF VIOLENCE against the PKI and its allies began just days after the alleged coup, and by mid-1966, an estimated half a million people had been killed. In a 1968 report, the CIA described those events as "one of the ghastliest and most concentrated bloodlettings of current times."[1] Half a century later, there is still uncertainty and disagreement about even the most basic facts of those killings. There are also serious misconceptions about their nature and underlying logic. In the absence of any systematic official record of the killings, the task of reconstructing those events entails the careful excavation of a variety of accounts, including the testimonies and memoirs of both witnesses and perpetrators, declassified documents of foreign governments, and internal reports and official statements by military officials.[2] This chapter, the first of two concentrating on the killings, draws on such sources to address two related sets of questions. First, with a view to clarifying what happened and

FIGURE 5.1. Member of the anticommunist Pemuda Marhaen militia holding a machete, Bali, ca. 1965. (National Library of Indonesia)

dispelling at least some of the more persistent misconceptions, it asks, How many people were killed? Who were the victims? How, where, and when did they die? And who killed them? It then examines some of the arguments that have been advanced to explain the killings, focusing on those that stress underlying cultural, religious, and socioeconomic tensions. The chapter concludes with reflections on the merits of those explanations while posing a number of questions that they leave unanswered.

Patterns

Fifty years of official obfuscation, societal fear, and international indifference have helped to fuel some serious misconceptions about the killings in Indonesia, not to mention significant gaps in our knowledge of what happened. If we are to have any chance of understanding these events and thinking about them in a comparative way, these uncertainties need to be clarified and the misconceptions corrected.

HOW MANY WERE KILLED?

How many people were killed in the immediate aftermath of the alleged coup? The estimates range from 78,500 to 3 million.[3] That broad range is partly the result of how quickly the killings were carried out along with the fact that the bodies of victims were dumped in countless unmarked graves across the country. Perhaps more important, it reflects the reality that those responsible remained in power for some three decades, rendering impossible any serious investigation into the extent of the killings. As discussed elsewhere, it is also a consequence of the posture of deliberate silence and indifference adopted by Western states, international organizations, and the media with regard to the killing of communists at the height of the Cold War.

Not surprisingly, the question of numbers has been part of a sometimes-bitter polemic between the critics of the New Order and its apologists, with critics generally citing higher figures and apologists typically (though not always) insisting on lower ones. Some among the latter group have even seized on the uncertainty over numbers to question whether there was any mass killing at all. Notwithstanding the CIA assessment cited above, for example, a former CIA official who was posted to Jakarta at the time has referred to "the myth of the massacre," and others agency officials have claimed that the numbers have been wildly inflated.[4] And while the Indonesian authorities have never categorically denied that mass killings took place, they have routinely obscured rather than illuminated the numbers killed. Indeed, from the outset, they have sought to focus attention almost exclusively on the killing of the six generals, making these the centerpiece of an elaborate official history that glorifies the military, while relegating the mass killing of leftists to a mere footnote. One looks in vain in official accounts for any serious discussion or reckoning of the numbers killed beyond the generals. An official history of the "coup" attempt and its aftermath published in 1968, for instance, devotes only two paragraphs in a book of over two hundred pages to the killings, and offers no idea of their extent or causes. Tensions, the authors write, "finally exploded into communal clashes resulting in bloodbaths in certain areas of Indonesia."[5]

Despite these obstacles, a broad scholarly consensus has emerged in recent years that the number killed was somewhere around 500,000. That figure is consistent with the internal estimates of major Western embassies, which concluded in late February 1966 that a suggested figure of 400,000 was "a very serious under-estimate" and that the true figure might be as high as 1 million.[6] It is also consistent with estimates given by senior Indonesian military officers at the time, including an armed forces officer who cited it in a briefing for Western military attachés in January 1966.[7] Significantly, the figure of 500,000 dead is *lower* than the numbers cited by other senior Indonesian officials, including the powerful Kopkamtib chief of staff Admiral Sudomo, who in an October 1976 interview on Dutch television said that "*more* than half a million people were killed following the attempted coup."[8] Moreover, it is less than half the figure of 1.2 million killed cited by one of General Suharto's confidants, Jan Walendouw, in a meeting at the US State Department in September 1966.[9]

In other words, the figure of 500,000 killed is not a rhetorical fantasy of the Indonesian Army's critics but an estimate equal to or lower than those provided by its own officials and allies. If anything, the figure of 500,000 dead must be regarded as a conservative estimate, at least until more thorough investigations and documentary evidence prove otherwise.

WHO WERE THE VICTIMS?

A common misconception about the killings is that they were driven primarily by ethnic or racial hostility, and that many or most of the victims were ethnic Chinese.[10] Popular accounts and some scholarly ones also suggest that many of those killed were the victims of private vendettas—over thwarted love, business deals gone awry, or family feuds.[11] Without question, some were killed for such reasons. In Jakarta, and other large cities like Medan, Semarang, and Surabaya, a good many Chinese Indonesians were beaten and detained in the aftermath of the supposed coup, some were tried and sentenced to long prison terms, and some were killed.[12] The chaotic atmosphere after October 1 undoubtedly also provided an ideal opportunity for the settling of private scores. The central characters in Joshua Oppenheimer's film *The Act of Killing*, for example, proudly describe how after the alleged coup, they roamed through the city of Medan killing all the Chinese they could find, including the father of a young woman who had rejected one of their amorous advances.[13]

But what is really striking about the Indonesian killings is that the vast majority of victims were targeted *not* because of their ethnicity or for personal reasons but rather because of their *political* beliefs, activities, and associations.[14] The victims were overwhelmingly leaders and members of the PKI and its affiliated organizations, especially Pemuda Rakyat,

Gerwani, the BTI, the Unified Movement of Indonesian University Students (Consentrasi Gerakan Mahasiswa Indonesia, or CGMI), LEKRA, the Indonesian University Graduates' Association (Himpunan Sarjana Indonesia, or HSI), and the League of Indonesian Youth and High School Students (Ikatan Pemuda dan Pelajar Indonesia, or IPPI). Even those Chinese Indonesians who were killed after October 1965 seem to have been targeted not because of their ethnicity per se, or at least not *only* because of their ethnicity, but instead because of their involvement in one or another of the left-leaning or Sukarnoist political parties or associations—like Baperki and the Indonesia Party (Partai Indonesia, or Partindo)—that had been accused of involvement in the alleged coup.[15]

Perhaps unsurprisingly, senior national leaders of the PKI were among those targeted: Aidit, Lukman, Njoto, and Sakirman, for example, were all shot dead under mysterious circumstances after being detained by the military.[16] Of these, somewhat more is known about Aidit's killing than the others. He was summarily executed by the army after allegedly confessing his own and the PKI's responsibility for the coup attempt. An official army history describes his killing as follows:

> Aidit was then interrogated and made his confession in the presence of witnesses. His confession included the statement: "I alone bear responsibility for the G30S affair, which failed and was supported by other PKI members and by the PKI's mass organizations. As is already known, I worked out a plan to assemble communist forces in Central Java . . ." After the interrogation, and after Aidit had signed his confession, Colonel Yasir Hadibroto took him out of the city by jeep. They turned off the main road at Boyolali and came to a dry well in the middle of a banana grove. There Aidit was shot dead. His body was thrown into the well and covered with banana tree trunks.[17]

The murder of Aidit and other PKI leaders notwithstanding, most of those killed in 1965–66 were not major political figures. They were overwhelmingly poor or lower-middle-class people—farmers, plantation laborers, factory workers, schoolteachers, students, artists, dancers, and civil servants—living in rural villages and plantations, or in ramshackle *kampungs* on the outskirts of provincial cities and towns. They were not, by any stretch, people with direct knowledge of or involvement in the events of October 1. On the contrary, they were targeted because they, or a family member or close friend, had joined the PKI or one of its many affiliated organizations, all of which were both legal and popular at the time. Writing about Kediri, East Java, Ken Young captures this sense of ordinary people being caught up in the violence simply because of those affiliations: "With great suddenness, their cause was lost, and they were to die not only for what they had done or believed in, but simply because they could be labeled 'PKI.' To have the wrong friends, to wear such a label was to warrant summary execution."[18] In short, the vast majority of those killed were not targeted for anything they had actually done, and certainly not for any criminal act, but rather for their membership in lawful political and social organizations.

HOW WERE THEY KILLED?

The enormous numbers of people killed in just a few months might lead one to suppose that the killing relied on modern technologies of destruction, such as high-powered firearms, aerial bombardments, gas chambers, or chemical weapons. But that was not the case. Indeed, like most mass killings of the late twentieth century, Indonesia's were carried out with the most rudimentary implements, and without resort to sophisticated technologies beyond the radio, gun, and motor vehicle. The closest parallel, then, is not Germany but Rwanda or Cambodia. While some were killed with automatic weapons or other firearms, the vast majority were felled with knives, sickles, machetes, swords, ice picks, bamboo spears, iron rods, and other everyday implements. And while some died in military or police detention centers, most died in isolated killing fields—in plantations, ravines, and rice fields, or on beaches and riverbanks—in thousands of rural villages dotted across the archipelago.

At the same time, with few exceptions, the killings were neither random nor spontaneous. On the contrary, virtually all accounts—in widely varying locales—point to a high degree of organization in the identification and execution of suspects as well as the disposal of their remains. They also make it clear that the victims were, in most cases, detainees—that is to say, the killings were summary executions. As Roosa writes, "For all the diversity in the anti-communist killings one finds a remarkable consistency across the provinces in the practice of disappearing people who had already been taken captive."[19] Suspects were often rounded up at night—sometimes on the basis of lists prepared by army interrogators, anticommunist organizations, or helpful foreign embassies—then bound and blindfolded before being transported in trucks to killing sites. There, they would frequently be made to line up in front of large pits, beside a

FIGURE 5.2. Captive PKI members executed by a Republican soldier with bayonet in Magetan, near Madiun, East Java, 1948. (Leiden University Library)

riverbank, or at the edge of a ravine. Then they would be shot, clubbed with heavy objects, or hacked to death, and their bodies tumbled into the open holes or the nearby ravine or waterway.

The fact that most of those killed were detainees, and that the killings were effectively summary executions, is confirmed by the testimony of witnesses and perpetrators from across the country. In November 1965, a British military officer, K. L. Charney, provided the following account from East Java on the basis of information he had received from an Indonesian Army officer:

> PKI men and women are being executed in very large numbers. [*Word deleted*] says he knows the Chief Interrogator (he told me some really ghastly details not repeated here) who also takes part in executions. Apparently the victims, toughs whom no rehabilitation would ever change, are given a knife and invited to kill themselves. Most refuse and are

FIGURE 5.3. PKI captives lie dead in trench after being executed by a Republican soldier in Magetan, near Madiun, East Java, 1948. (Leiden University Library)

> then told to turn round and are shot in the back. When [*word deleted*] asked how he could bring himself to take part in the executions he replied that if he [*word deleted*] had seen and heard what he had he would consider it a duty to exterminate what he called "less than animals."[20]

Reporting on his study trip through East Java in February 1966, the Swedish ambassador, Harald Edelstam, likewise reported an account of systematic executions in the vicinity of Pasuruan, East Java:

> Two English textile engineers, who are helping the Indonesians build a spinning factory in Pasuruan 40 km south of Surabaya, described having been invited during the Christmas period to witness how the communists in Pasuruan were executed. A third of the factory construction workers, all members of the communist party, were killed on this occasion. They had been pre-selected by the military, which had relied on the membership rosters of the local communist party.[21]

An eyewitness described a mass killing by soldiers just outside Solo, in Central Java, in early December 1965:

> On the way home to Karanganyar from Solo when we went over the Bengawan river, I saw lots of people who were bound and tied up.... I thought to myself, what is going on here.... I was confused. Then, after some discussion between the prisoners and the army there ... suddenly the prisoners were shot. As they were shot, their bodies fell directly—plonk—into the Bengawan Solo river. The location was just under the railway bridge.[22]

In mid-1966, the head of the Goodyear rubber plantation near Medan, North Sumatra, told the Swedish ambassador what had happened to the hundreds of plantation workers who had been detained: "Every Saturday night, a couple of trucks arrived and took away a hundred or so [people] to the nearby bridge by a fast-flowing river close to the plantation headquarters. They were killed with jungle knives on the bridge and their bodies were thrown into the river."[23]

That account is consistent with a description provided by the former leader of a village death squad in the vicinity of the Snake River in North Sumatra: "Every night we would load our quota onto a truck and drive to Snake River. The truck would stop there. We'd pull our prisoners off the truck and drag them 100 meters downstream. Some screamed. Some cried. Some begged for mercy. We beat them on the truck so they couldn't run away once we got there."[24]

An eyewitness from Lhokseumawe, Aceh, offered a smiliar account of the systematic execution of prisoners there:

> The PKI prisoners who had been arrested and held in the jail, they were taken in the middle of the night and taken to Meunasah Lhok [30 kilometers west along the coast from Lhokseumawe]. Later there would be a few people from the community [civilians] that had been chosen by Koramil to become executioners (*algojo*).... After they were killed, a hole would be dug to put the bodies in.[25]

The testimony of a small farmer who witnessed three days of mass killings in West Timor, several hundreds of miles to the east, likewise highlights their systematic character:

> Prisoners were thrown onto the ground "like a sack of rice, some landing on their heads, some on their buttocks." Curious bystanders were

> ordered to grab each one—four to a prisoner.... As soldiers called out numbers, one by one the prisoners were stood up on the edge of the hole [which had been dug earlier], and shot in the back of the head, upon which they toppled into the hole.[26]

That account is consistent with the testimony of a police officer who took part in the execution of PKI detainees in West Timor:

> The prisoners were ordered to dig their own graves during the day. The shooting usually took place at night. Before they were taken to the execution site, they were beaten black and blue, then their hands were bound and they were ordered onto a truck. When they got to the execution site, they were blindfolded and ordered to stand with their backs to the grave, facing the firing squad. Then they were shot. If some were still alive after being shot, they would be bayoneted. Then they were pushed into the hole. The members of the firing squads were given quotas. There was one quota for army and one for police.[27]

Apart from the systematic quality of the killings, accounts by perpetrators and eyewitnesses often underscore their shocking brutality. A former death squad member from North Sumatra offered the following summary of the many ways his group killed detainees: "We shoved wood in their anuses until they died.... We crushed their necks with wood. We hung them. We strangled them with wire. We cut off their heads. We ran them over with our cars. We were allowed to do it. And the proof is, we murdered people and we were never punished."[28]

A death squad leader from the same area provided the following account of his execution of one detainee: "My men were afraid of blood so I choked him like this. His tongue came out. You asked! I ripped him open. His intestines spilled out."[29] A perpetrator's account of the killing of Suwoto, a PKI leader in Turen, Malang, likewise captured the immediacy and brutality of the killings: "Suwoto ran. He was chased. And with a single hack from a broad-bladed knife (machete), his back was torn open. The cut went through to his chest. Suwoto fell to the ground. His body convulsed. And then he was dead. Suwoto's corpse was left there on the road."[30]

As if to underscore the fact that those killed were less than human, and perhaps also to sow confusion and uncertainty about the fate of detainees, the remains of the dead seldom, if ever, received a proper burial. Most were dumped down dry wells, thrown out to sea, tossed into rivers, ravines, and irrigation canals, or buried in mass graves. A Western journalist reporting from Bali at the time of the killings, for example, heard of a beach in the district of Klungkung where fifteen hundred people were supposedly buried. Another journalist reported that in the district of Jembrana in Bali, many thousands of corpses had been dumped in mass graves or into the sea.[31]

In one of the most notorious cases, the Brantas River in East Java was said to have become clogged with dead bodies, some of them floating freely, some tied to bamboo stakes, and others piled up on rafts.[32] A resident of the area who had hidden out near the river in fear for his life after the alleged coup later described the scene: "In November [1965] the rains came. The river ran muddy and fast with weeds, leaves, human limbs, and headless corpses."[33] Another witness, not affiliated with the PKI, provided more details of the grisly scene:

> Usually the corpses were no longer recognizable as human. Headless. Stomachs torn open. The smell was unbelievable. To make sure they didn't sink, the carcasses were deliberately tied to, or impaled on, bamboo stakes. And the departure of corpses from the Kediri region down the Brantas achieved its golden age when bodies were stacked together on rafts over which the PKI banner proudly flew.[34]

As these accounts make clear, those killed were often decapitated or dismembered. Indeed, the beheading and dismemberment of captives appears in the accounts of both witnesses and perpetrators from across the country. So too do stories of headless corpses and body parts being left in public places. Reporting on a conversation with Ross Taylor, who was employed at a spinning factory in East Java, a British Embassy official wrote in mid-December 1965,

> About a fortnight ago, Taylor was taking an early morning walk by the side of a stream which flows by his house in the compound when he was horrified to see three headless corpses, one of them female, floating in the stream. A little way on, half a dozen heads were neatly arranged on the parapet of a small bridge, and still further along a group of small children were, with bamboo poles, helping another few headless corpses down the stream. Another member of the team, riding home on his scooter after an evening with a friend, was shocked when his headlamp picked out a head "decorating" one of the kilometre stones at the side of the road, some distance from the compound.[35]

An account from Banyuwangi, East Java, painted a similar picture:

> Victims were strangled with nooses around their necks. The bodies were then placed in a sitting position under trees along the main road. In some cases, the victims were beheaded, the body being left in the middle of the road and the head taken elsewhere. The killings took place along the roads and the river banks, and bodies were buried in mass graves.[36]

Likewise, recounting the summary execution of several PKI members in Kediri in mid-October 1965, a member of a local vigilante group described another member's skill with a broad sword (*kelewang*): "Every time the right hand that was holding the sword struck, a PKI head would be sliced off and fall to the ground."[37] An eyewitness later wrote about the summary execution and decapitation of an elderly schoolteacher, Pak Mukdar, by Ansor members: "With his hands still tied, his neck was hacked by Rejo, the [Ansor] youth from Wiyung. He finished off the unconscious, weak old man.... His head was removed and put in the sack. Then they dragged his body to the river and tossed it in. It washed away slowly in front of me."[38]

Dismemberment and decapitation also figure prominently in reports about the killings in Bali. Describing the murder of a BTI official by the victim's friend on a beach in Klungkung, the journalist Don Moser wrote, "Then Ali took his *parang*—a short sword-like knife used for chopping in the fields—and cut off his friend's left ear, then his right ear, then his nose. Finally, he raised his parang high and chopped his friend's head off."[39]

A plantation manager in North Sumatra told a US consular official in Medan that "at least 100 headless corpses [had been] left on his estate in recent weeks."[40] And an eyewitness from Aceh recalled seeing the head of a man named Rauf "being stuck on a pole and attached to the front of a jeep ... [and] paraded around town.... There were people on top of the car, military, all of them.... It was a big procession.... My child followed, parading around the town. I saw this with my own eyes.... A head on top of a car. Ya Allah Subhanallah."[41]

The public display of corpses, heads, and other body parts was almost certainly intended to sow terror.[42] The story of a former executioner from North Sumatra is instructive. He told the filmmaker Oppenheimer, "Once I brought a woman's head into a Chinese shop. The Chinese screamed." Asked why he had done so, the man said, "So they'd be scared."[43] The same objective, to sow terror, was almost certainly the reason the authorities sometimes arranged public executions. One especially gruesome case was the public mutilation and burning to death of a local PKI official in the town of Ende, East Nusa Tenggara. Gerry van Klinken describes the scene as follows:

> The military arrested him and put a poster up at the central monument advertising the place and time of his execution. This was carried out in daylight by Muslim activists belonging to Ansor. Along the way to Tanjung ... he was slashed with razors and dragged along the ground. Barely alive, he faced the flames in silence, watched by a large crowd.[44]

Women were not spared, particularly if they were real or alleged members of Gerwani or another PKI-affiliated organization. Some were raped and mutilated with knives or sickles before being killed. An account by a Banser commander in Kediri, East Java, for example, described the murder of a Gerwani member by men in his unit: "Among the Gerwani leaders who were detained, there was one very beautiful woman named Jamsiah. As it happened, she was very tenacious in her belief that the PKI was best in every way. In the end, Jamsiah was picked up and taken to Sumberbage forest in Gadungan. She resisted, but her body was cut in two by Banser."[45]

An account from the district of Blitar, East Java, recounts the rape and killing of another Gerwani woman: "Japik, a leading figure in the local branch of Gerwani and a member of the PGRI Non Vaksentral was killed along with her husband Djumadi.... They had been married only thirty-five days. She was raped many times and her body was then slit open from her breasts to her vulva. This was done by an Ansor gang."[46]

An account from the regency of Malang, East Java, described a similar fate that befell a woman PKI member:

> Oerip Kalsum, a woman who was lurah of the village of Dengkol in Singosari, was a member of the PKI. Before being killed, she was ordered to take all her clothes off. Her body and her honour [*kehormatannya*] were then subjected to fire. She was then tied up, taken to the village of Sentong in Lawang, where a noose was put around her neck and she was hacked to death.[47]

As these examples suggest, sexualized violence was a significant feature of many killings. Women suffered especially shocking violence, but men were also subjected to abuse. In acts that seemed to mimic the false allegations about the mistreatment of the six generals, for instance, some men were castrated. An anonymous account compiled sometime in the 1970s provided the following description of acts of violence committed in the area of Banyuwangi, East Java, in late 1965 and early 1966:

> In many cases, women were killed by being stabbed through the vagina with long knives until their stomachs were pierced. Their heads and breasts were then cut off and hung on display in guard huts along the road. . . . Male victims had their penises cut off and these too were hung up on guard posts. The heads of Pemuda Rakyat members were cut off and placed on bamboo stakes along the roadside or hung from trees.[48]

Another account from East Java, by Pipit Rochijat, portrayed a similarly gruesome scene in a red-light district near Kediri, East Java: "Once the purge of Communist elements got underway, clients stopped coming [to the brothels] for sexual satisfaction. The reason: most clients—and prostitutes—were too freightened, for, hanging up in front of the houses, there were a lot of male Communist genitals—like bananas hung out for sale."[49]

Some men who played an active role in the killings in North Sumatra have more recently provided similar accounts of their treatment of the women and men in their custody. Two former members of a death squad described, for example, how they had castrated a young man named Ramli, as they reenacted the scene of his execution on the bank of the Snake River: "We cut Ramli again and again, and stabbed him like this until he looked dead. Then, we pushed him in the river. He clung to the tree roots begging, 'Help me!' So we fished him out, and killed him by cutting off his penis."[50]

These awful accounts are not reproduced here merely to shock and repel but rather because they supply important clues about the nature and pattern of the killings in 1965–66. They make it clear, for example, that the killings were neither random nor spontaneous. On the contrary, they clearly entailed a significant measure of planning and organization. Far from being driven by emotion or popular anger, these were carefully organized summary executions. These accounts also highlight striking commonalities in the methods and techniques employed by perpetrators in widely dispersed locales—including deliberate brutality, decapitation, mutilation, corpse display, and sexualized violence. As such, they point to a distinctive and common repertoire of violence shared by the groups responsible for the killing across the country—a repertoire that seems to have been deliberately designed to terrorize leftists and the wider population. These patterns provide some crucial clues about the identity of the perpetrators and their motivations.

WHO KILLED THEM?

Like the victims, the perpetrators of these killings were not defined primarily by their ethnicity or religion but rather by their political and institutional affiliations as well as their ideological positions. Indeed, what is most striking about these killings—and what distinguishes the Indonesian case from many other instances of mass killing—is that the perpetrators and their victims were almost always of the same ethnic and religious group. Thus, Javanese Muslims killed Javanese Muslims, Balinese Hindus killed Balinese Hindus, Protestant Bataks killed Protestant Bataks, Florenese Catholics killed Florenese Catholics, and so on. In fact, the killers and their victims were not only from the same broad ethnic and religious group; they were often from the same village, the same neighborhood, and sometimes even the same family. Thus, with some exceptions (including the attacks against Chinese Indonesians), the perpetrators were not distinguished from their victims by virtue of ethnicity, race, or religion.

The centrality of the perpetrators' political and ideological, as opposed to religious or ethnic, identity needs to be underscored in part because it distinguishes the Indonesian case from so many cases of mass killing, but also because so much of the scholarship on Indonesia has focused on the role of Islam in the killings. Islamic leaders, symbols, and rhetoric are frequently given credit for igniting and driving the killing. It is certainly true that the majority of killings were committed by Muslims, and Islamic symbols and ideas were used to incite and justify violence, yet that is hardly surprising in a country that is roughly 85 percent Muslim. The more important point is that adherents of all major religions—notably Catholics, Protestants, and Hindus—joined in the killing, and deployed religious symbols and authority to incite or justify the violence. It is also noteworthy, as discussed elsewhere, that in the deeply Islamic province of West Java, there were relatively few killings. These patterns suggest strongly that contrary to most of the prevailing wisdom, Islam was not the driving force behind the killings—though religious symbolism and identity, broadly speaking, were undoubtedly contributing factors.

Regardless of their ethnicity or religious affiliation, and even beyond their shared political and ideological orientation, what virtually all perpetrators had in common was membership in a military, paramilitary, or vigilante organization.[51] That is to say, those who killed were either soldiers, members of a civil defense organization, or belonged to one of the many anticommunist militia groups and student associations that were mobilized in the campaign to crush the G30S and PKI. Those institutional associations, and the social psychological influences of such ties, arguably shaped the attitudes and actions of those who killed. Indeed, I think it is likely that members of these groups came to accept and embrace a distinctive institutional culture that valorized extreme violence, and learned to carry out specific kinds of violent acts from the group's repertoire. In this regard, the killers in Indonesia probably did not differ greatly from members of the German Reserve Police Battalion described in Christopher Browning's *Ordinary Men*.[52] In both cases, a combination of group dynamics, pressure of authority, and fear led otherwise-ordinary people to do things they might not otherwise have done.

But the significance of military and paramilitary institutions in the killings of 1965–66 was not limited to the realm of social psychology and group dynamics. Arguably more important was the fact that the killings were, for the most part, initiated and organized by the army. Contrary to official claims that the violence of 1965–66 was a spontaneous consequence of popular anger at the PKI, and against the received wisdom that the killings were driven mainly by local tensions and led by local people of violence, the preponderance of evidence—noted in the accounts above and detailed in chapter 6—points to the army as the chief instigator and organizer of the violence.

Within the military, certain units were significantly more active and engaged in killings than others. The most notorious unit was the RPKAD, a crack special forces unit that played a direct role in the killings, especially in Central Java and Bali.[53] But many other army units also took part, acting independently to arrest, interrogate, and kill alleged Communists. Units from the police, marines, and navy were somewhat less involved. Air force units, because of their real or presumed leftist sympathies and purported involvement in the September 30th Movement, were kept out of the action and so played almost no role in the killings.

Among the vigilante groups, those most actively involved were the militarized youth groups linked to one or another anticommunist political party or religious organization. These included the NU's Ansor and Banser, PNI's Pemuda Demokrat and Pemuda Marhaen (known in Bali as Tameng Marhaenis), IPKI's (Ikatan Pendukung Kemerdekaan Indonesia, or League of Upholders of Indonesian Freedom) Pemuda Pancasila

(Pancasila Youth), and Partai Katolik's Pemuda Katolik (Catholic Youth). Also active in some areas were a variety of religiously oriented student movements, including the Masyumi-affiliated HMI, the Union of Catholic University Students, and the Indonesian Christian Student Movement. These organizations sometimes acted independently, organizing mass rallies, signing petitions, destroying homes and offices, and beating up alleged leftists. When it came to killing, however, they seldom acted alone. Although there were some exceptions, they almost always killed at the behest of the army.

WHERE AND WHEN WERE THEY KILLED?

While there appear to have been killings in virtually every corner of the country, they were most concentrated in the densely populated provinces of Central Java, East Java, and Bali, and also in Aceh, North Sumatra, and parts of East Nusa Tenggara.[54] Mass killings were significantly less concentrated in certain areas, including the capital Jakarta and the province of West Java.[55] There was also variation in the timing, with the earliest killings beginning in some areas within a few days of the alleged coup, while in other areas they were delayed for several weeks and even months. Significantly, whenever it had started, the mass killing stopped almost like clockwork after several weeks. And while the worst of the killing was over by mid-1966, in some parts of the country the violence continued intermittently into 1968.[56]

By all accounts, the mass killings began first in the province of Aceh, at the far northern tip of Sumatra, within a few days of the supposed coup attempt, and then stopped suddenly in November 1965, leaving some 10,000 people dead.[57] In neighboring North Sumatra, despite serious tensions and some violence, mass killings did not start until early November 1965, at which point they spread quickly in the city of Medan, and through the province's many agricultural estates and plantations. By March 1966, at least 40,000 people, and perhaps twice that many, had died there.[58] In the densely populated province of Central Java, mass killings began around the third week of October and continued until mid-1966. Although there is no certainty about the number killed there, the estimate of 140,000 is widely accepted.[59] In neighboring East Java, systematic violence accelerated dramatically in early November, with especially high concentrations in the towns of Kediri, Blitar, and Pasuruan, and a cluster of rural regencies in the northeastern coastal region of the province.[60] The killings subsided there in December and had largely ended in mid-

1966, by which time an estimated 180,000 had died.[61] In early December 1965, a full two months after the alleged coup attempt, the killings began on the island of Bali, where some 80,000 people, of a total population of just over a million, were killed in the space of about three months.[62] The killings began even later in other areas. For example, in the province of East Nusa Tenggara at the far eastern end of the archipelago, there were no killings to speak of until mid-February 1966, and they ended in mid-March 1966 after as many as 6,000 alleged Communists had been killed.[63]

The broad geographic spread of the violence clearly suggests that it was not rooted in purely local conflicts or personal animosities but instead in some larger, national dynamic. At the same time, the distinctive geographic distribution of the killing—especially its concentration in Aceh, Bali, Central Java, East Java, North Sumatra, and East Nusa Tenggara, and its near absence in Jakarta and West Java—requires some kind of explanation. If the driving force was a national-level directive, command, or dynamic, why did the killing happen in some areas and not others? In other words, how can we explain the distinctive spatial pattern?

Likewise, the temporal distribution in the killings—the fact that they began almost immediately in some areas, but only after delays of weeks or months in others—raises questions about causation. How can we explain that pattern of variation? At the very least, the long delays suggest that the violence was not spontaneous but instead depended on some external stimulus, and forces us to think harder about its proximate causes. In particular, we need to ask what it was that caused local tensions to escalate into mass killings.

Explaining the Killings

Over the past fifty years or so, government officials, journalists, and scholars have tried in different ways to answer at least some of these questions. Many have sought to explain the killings by reference to certain deeply rooted cultural, religious, and socioeconomic features and conflicts in Indonesian society.[64] Those who adopt such approaches often speak of underlying causes and long-standing conflicts that "explode" or "erupt" into mass killings. While such analyses seldom provide a completely satisfactory account of genocide or other forms of mass violence, they can form some part of the explanation. With that caveat in mind, I want to look briefly at the main arguments of this kind that have been made for the case of Indonesia.

PERSONAL AND GROUP PSYCHOLOGY

Many popular and literary accounts of the 1965–66 killings focus on the personal and psychological motivations of the perpetrators—the soldiers, militia members, vigilantes, and gangsters who detained, tortured, and killed—and the bystanders whose indifference or inaction helped to fuel the violence. These accounts highlight factors like peer pressure, fear, compliance with authority, cultural norms, revenge, and the opportunity to settle scores in motivating participation and acquiescence.

The pressure to conform, even to the point of killing, is a central theme in autobiographical and nominally fictional accounts by the perpetrators in 1965–66. In one such account, a short story titled "Death" written soon after the killings, the protagonist describes the agonizing difficulty he faced in resisting the social pressure to conform and the urgings of a military official. And indeed, he did not resist but instead took part in the cold-blooded killing of his village neighbors, including a friend named Baidi.[65] Waiting for the detainees, bound and blindfolded, to be unloaded from military trucks and taken to their place of execution, he reflects on his involvement:

> I regretted having come. The military commandant of the city lived in our sub-district. We were on good terms; he insisted that I come. "It'll be good experience, friend." I could still have refused, but several of my friends had been on other nights and I felt left out. Ali had insisted, I was frightened but wanted to go. Now I was in agony. It was even worse when Tuhri, one of my companions, came and told me that Baidi was on the other truck.

In memoirs and testimonies, many former perpetrators also cite their obligation to follow orders and a fear of the consequences if they failed to do so as key reasons for their participation. A small-town police officer from West Timor, for example, explained his involvement as follows: "Soeharto ordered us to kill those communists. The local police chief passed that order on to us. At that time, no one dared question the truth of the story. Even to utter a word of comfort to the victims was seen to be sympathizing with the communists and you could be killed for it."[66]

For some perpetrators, such considerations were mixed with the notion that they were helping to "defend the state." In Oppenheimer's film *The Look of Silence*, the uncle of a young man killed in 1965 explained to a relative that although he was guarding the prison where the boy was held and knew what was going to happen to him, he could not intervene because his militia group was following army orders. "Komando Aksi was under army command, and so was I. I was ordered to guard the prison and so I did.... I did it to defend the state." Pressed to explain why he had not at least asked his superiors not to kill his nephew, he replied, "If I refused, I'd be accused too. Better just to follow orders."[67]

Many people must have become caught up in the killings for such reasons—because they were pressured by those in positions of authority, were fearful, believed that they were serving the state, or did not want to stand out from their peers.[68] Once they were part of a military unit or militia group, and the expectation of extreme violence was made clear, it is not difficult to imagine how hard it would have been not to go along with it. That is surely one of the clearest conclusions of Browning's study of Reserve Police Battalion 101 as well as Hinton's analysis of low-level Khmer Rouge executioners in *Why Did You Kill?*

At the same time, many must also have joined in the killings for the same reasons young people everywhere join gangs and armies—for the excitement, the chance to prove one's toughness, the opportunity to step away from the everyday, and to have a measure of power otherwise impossible. That is the strong impression one gains from Oppenheimer's *The Act of Killing* and *The Look of Silence*. In both films, we learn about the killings through the grisly recollections and reenactments of a handful of low-level gangsters from the Medan area. As far as one can tell from their accounts, they were driven mainly by feelings of revenge toward people who had slighted them, and an intoxicating cocktail of unconstrained power and sexualized violence. As a former member of the militia group Pemuda Pancasila later boasted, "If they were pretty, I'd rape them all. Especially back then, when there was no law ... when we were the law.... Especially if you get one who's only 14 years old. I'd say it's going to be hell for you, but heaven on earth for me."[69]

Such motives were undoubtedly at play in the Indonesian killings; without them it is difficult to see how mass violence could have happened. And yet as we also know from the wider literature—and as the accounts of killing outlined above make abundantly clear—such personal motivations were never decisive to the onset and overall trajectory of the violence. In every instance, they were contingent on and shaped by other forces, social, economic, and political, particularly at the national and international levels.

MASSACRE AS CULTURE

Other accounts suggest that the killings can best be understood in terms of certain essential features of Indonesian character, culture, and religion. One especially resilient variant of that claim suggests that the killings reflected Indonesia's "amok culture." Indonesians, this argument goes, are prone to sudden, inexplicable, and irrational outbursts of violence—running amok—in the course of which they lash out indiscriminately, killing everyone around them. According to such accounts, the killings of 1965–66 were simply a case of amok on a grand scale. As noted earlier, this sort of explanation has long been favored by Indonesian officials and their allies, and appears in many popular accounts.[70] A *New York Times* story from April 1966, for instance, offered the following description: "Indonesians are gentle and instinctively polite, but hidden behind their smiles is that strange Malay streak, that inner, frenzied bloodlust which has given to other languages one of their few Malay words: 'amok.' This time, the entire nation ran amok."[71]

Combining such Orientalist fantasies with evocations of an unruly peasant mob, *Le Figaro* informed its readers in mid-1966 that in Indonesia, the population had run amok—"that strange, murderous fever which befalls at times the Malays and the Javanese. And half a million of them perished under the cries of the peasants let loose."[72] And in December 1966, a US Embassy report concluded that the mass killings had "stemmed from fear, from a desire to settle old scores, and from a kind of mass running amuck [*sic*] as much as from any hatred of Communism per se."[73]

There is a certain appeal to this kind of argument; it may appear to explain how people who are otherwise "gentle" and "docile" could commit acts of such terrible brutality. But there are reasons for skepticism. Beyond the obvious problem of its simplistic cultural reductionism—its implication that all Indonesians are the same, and their actions are explicable only in terms of an exotic and unchanging culture—the amok assertion fails to account for even the most basic facts of the violence. For example, it does not explain why the killings happened when and where they did. Nor does it explain why those targeted were overwhelmingly leftists. Perhaps more to the point, it ignores the fact that historically at least, amok has always been a form of ritual suicide because other members of the community or government authorities generally killed "amokkers."[74] That certainly never happened in the killings of 1965–66. On the contrary, as noted above, those killers worked closely with the authorities and have never been punished for their deeds. Perhaps most important, it cannot possibly explain the systematic quality of the violence, its wide geographic spread, or its long duration.

A closely related claim, favored by Indonesian authorities and their apologists, is that the killings were a spontaneous reaction to the disruptive and threatening behavior of the PKI and its affiliates. Answering the question why "these people of grace and charm" had embarked on "so frenzied a massacre" in Bali, for example, the journalist John Hughes wrote in 1967, "Obviously the catalyst was the sudden boiling over of resentment toward the Communists, who had been busy beneath the placid surface of Bali but had made the serious mistake of deriding and attempting to undermine not only the island's religious values but its deep-seated cultural traditions as well."[75] Similarly, in a 1972 report, the military governor of East Nusa Tenggara claimed that killings began in the city of Kupang when "the emotions of the people ... and their zeal to crush the G30S/PKI spontaneously reached a peak."[76] Likewise, a former death squad commander from North Sumatra who later served for many years as speaker of the regional legislature claimed that "the mass killings were the spontaneous action of the people. The people hated communism."[77]

The same theme recurs in a number of studies by US scholars and officials published since 1966. A 1968 article by Pauker (who, it will be recalled, was a close confidant of the Seskoad commander, Suwarto) is a case in point. Drawing on the work of Clifford Geertz, he claimed that the "local custom" in Java—and, he implied, in Bali too—was to "do all things quietly, subtly, politely, and communally—even starve." By acting in "stark contrast with local custom," he argued, the PKI and BTI in Java and Bali

> made themselves not just enemies of the more prosperous elements in the village ... but enemies of the community as a whole, whose ancient ways they were disrupting. These considerations, more than genuinely ideological controversies, may have been the decisive factor behind the killings, which were as widespread in Bali ... as in East and Central Java.[78]

In a memoir published in 1990, the US ambassador to Indonesia at the time of the alleged coup, Green, made virtually the same argument. Summarizing most of the familiar myths about the "harmonious" nature of both Javanese and Balinese society, Green laid responsibility for the massacre squarely on those who were its victims. "In the last analysis," he wrote,

> the bloodbath visited on Indonesia can be largely attributed to the fact that communism, with its atheism and talk of class warfare, was

> abhorrent to the way of life of rural Indonesia, especially in Java and Bali, whose cultures place great stress on tolerance, social harmony, mutual assistance ... and resolving controversy through talking issues out in order to achieve an acceptable consensus solution.[79]

A related contention, most commonly found in accounts of the killing in Bali, is that the violence was motivated by mysterious religiocultural passions, and more specifically, that it was a form of ritual "exorcism" or "purification." In a typical passage, Moser wrote in 1966, "From the very beginning the political upheaval had an air of irrationality about it, a touch of madness even. Nowhere but on these weird and lovely islands ... could affairs have erupted so unpredictably, so violently, tinged not only with fanaticism but with blood-lust and something like witchcraft."[80] Overcome by their religious passions, this argument has it, Balinese and Javanese exploded spontaneously into a wild and "frenzied" purge of Communists. Likewise stressing the alleged spontaneity and unpredictability of the violence, Hughes writes that Bali continued its way of life until December 1965, when suddenly it "erupted in a frenzy of savagery worse than Java's."[81]

There is just enough truth in this sort of interpretation to make it seem plausible. It is possible that many Balinese and Javanese did understand the campaign against the PKI in terms of the need to exorcise evil or purge atheists. Yet there is also much that is misleading in this view. For if the cultural and religious passion of Indonesians can help us to understand the intensity of the violence once it started, it cannot plausibly explain how the idea of physically annihilating the PKI members developed, why it started when it did, and why it took the particular forms that it did. Moreover, as the outline of the killings above makes abundantly apparent, they were not spontaneous but systematic; they were not the product of uncontrolled emotions but rather of planning. As Melvin writes of Aceh, "There is simply no support in either the documentary evidence or oral testimony from the province that the killings were the result of spontaneous, popular and religiously motivated violence."[82]

In short, the fact that massive violence could somehow be justified or portrayed in terms of religious beliefs or cultural analogues may have contributed to the dynamic of the killing. But the physical annihilation of the PKI was not simply or even primarily the unavoidable consequence of spontaneous, religious, and cultural impulses. As I will argue later, they were rather the products of political processes in which human agency—in particular, the cynical political calculations of the army high command—played a central part.

RELIGIOUS AND ETHNIC TENSIONS

Clearly, arguments that locate the dynamic of the killings in simplified notions of Indonesian character and culture must be treated with deep skepticism. But that does not mean cultural and religious conflicts were of no consequence. The killings in each locality seem to have followed in some measure the broad lines of conflicts over religious belief and practice, and to have been framed in their language and symbols. To make sense of the pattern of killing, then, we need to have some idea what those conflicts were.

One pattern much discussed in the literature locates the dynamic of violence and killing, at least in Central and East Java, in marked differences within the Muslim community. The chief tensions were between those Muslims who saw themselves as more pious (*santri*) and those they regarded as less devout (*abangan*) because their religious observances blended Islam with a variety of pre-Islamic, Javanist beliefs and practices.[83] A key marker of the santri community was the respected position of the Islamic teacher, or kiai, who provided direction to the community on a wide range of matters. It was the kiai, for example, who typically presided over the traditional Islamic boarding school, the *pesantren* (or *pondok*) at which young boys learned to recite the Quran and receive life lessons. By contrast, Islamic practice in abangan communities coexisted comfortably with older Hindu and animist practices like ancestor worship and black magic. People who were adept at such practices were said to be spiritually powerful (*sakti*). The leaders of abangan communities were unlikely to be Islamic scholars, and few of their children enrolled in pesantren. In these and myriad other ways, the two communities were distinct, and indeed there was between them a degree of mutual mistrust, even fear, with a fairly long history.

These were important cultural and religious distinctions, but on their own they were not enough to ignite mass killings.[84] What arguably made their differences more combustible was the way in which they came to stand in for and overlap with political as well as class identities in the increasingly fractious and polarized politics of late Guided Democracy. By the early 1960s, the so-called santri-abangan cleavage had come to overlap significantly, though of course not perfectly, with differences in social class and political affiliation. Santri communities were more likely to be led by wealthy landowners and to be supporters of conservative religious parties like the NU. By contrast, abangan communities were likely to be poorer, with greater numbers of landless and tenant farmers. They were also more likely to be affiliated with the PKI or the left wing of the PNI. Given this overlap, religious and cultural tensions came increasingly to be expressed in political terms, while political rivalries came to be framed as conflicts over religious identity and practice.[85] The NU and smaller Islamic parties, for example, routinely accused PKI members of being atheists or practitioners of black magic, while the PKI denounced the NU and other conservative parties as corruptors, exploiters, and religious fanatics.

The existence of such tensions goes some way toward explaining the intense hostility toward the PKI that was expressed by the NU and other religious parties in the weeks and months after the events of October 1965, at least in some parts of Java.[86] The overlap of religious and political identities—and the prior political mobilization of both communities—may well have fueled hostility and violence, in part by providing the language, symbols, and leadership through which it could be fomented. It helps to explain, say, why NU and Ansor members in East Java set off to attack PKI members shouting "Allahu Akbar!" and why santri youths "demanded the dissolution of the PKI, and that the death of each general be paid for with those of 100,000 Communists." As Rochijat wrote of the situation in late 1965, "In an atmosphere of crisis suffused with so much hatred for the PKI, everything became permissible. After all, wasn't it everyone's responsibility to fight the *kafir*?"[87] It is less clear that it was these tensions alone that led to the violence.[88] The shift from underlying conflict to mass killing is seldom so simple or automatic.

In other areas, different kinds of religious and cultural tensions were at work. In Bali, for instance, where the vast majority of the population practiced a distinctive variant of Hinduism, there were simmering tensions between those who saw themselves as more devout and those they regarded as heretical, atheist, or at a minimum, irreligious. The tension had roots in long-standing conflicts over caste, but also over the degree to which different communities accepted the more formalized and hierarchical version of Hinduism advocated by the self-appointed arbiters of the religion.[89]

But again this was not simply a matter of religious difference. As in Java, religious conflict in Bali overlapped in significant ways with social status and political affiliation. Those who regarded themselves as arbiters of religious rectitude were more often than not people of high caste (*triwangsa*), members of one of the island's aristocratic families, with significant landed wealth. They tended to side with parties of the Right, especially the right wing of the PNI and PSI, as did a substantial number of poorer people who regarded them as indispensable patrons. They also tended to resist the PKI's aggressive efforts to implement national land reform laws. Those less inclined to follow the lead of the religious conservatives and feudal families, who favored land reform, or who remained loyal to Sukarno and his local protégé Governor Anak Agung Bagus Suteja, more often sided with parties of the Left, especially the PKI and Partindo.

As in Java, such overlapping identities meant that political and social differences were often expressed in the language of religion and culture and in debates over "tradition"—increasingly so as national political life became more polarized in the early 1960s. Thus, for example, the more conservative supporters of the PNI accused PKI followers of being atheists and threatening Balinese cultural traditions. Those on the left, by contrast, accused their opponents of clinging to Bali's feudal past, and standing in the way of economic and social progress. The overlap between political and religious identities, and the infusion of religious claim and counterclaim into the debate, unquestionably made political debate more vitriolic. And that certainly provided a strong rhetorical foundation on which conservatives could attack the PKI after the supposed coup. But as in Java, these tensions alone cannot explain mass killings on such a scale.

In yet other cases, the conflicts had ethnic overtones. The clearest example was a long-standing, if fluctuating, hostility toward ethnic Chinese, some of whom were attacked and killed after the alleged October coup. That hostility, which had roots dating back several hundred years, was sometimes expressed as intolerance of Chinese cultural practices—for instance, speaking Chinese, eating with chopsticks, reading Chinese-language newspapers, and living in separate areas of town. Such hostility had an economic dimension as well. Whatever the reality in any particular case, Chinese Indonesians were widely perceived to be wealthy. Yet as noted above, these tensions also had a crucial political dimension, especially in the polarized climate of the early 1960s. All too often, conservative political leaders and the army deliberately highlighted the alleged cultural, social, and economic distinctiveness of Chinese Indonesians, leading to resentment, hostility, and sometimes violence.[90] Meanwhile, because the PKI and other parties of the Left had a record of defending their interests, many Chinese Indonesians joined or supported them.

Such tensions were especially pronounced in the months immediately preceding and following the events of October 1. Worried by Sukarno's increasingly close ties with China, and the PKI's close relationship with its Communist party, anticommunists of all stripes began to question whether Chinese Indonesians could be trusted to remain loyal to Indonesia. Rumors began to circulate of Chinese Indonesians working as spies for China and the party, and bankrolling the PKI. And so when the alleged coup attempt happened, antipathy toward ethnic Chinese reached a fever pitch. Many in the army, moreover, shared that antipathy and suspicion, and thus fanned the flames or, at a minimum, declined to intervene when crowds attacked Chinese. It was against this backdrop that some ethnic Chinese were killed in the aftermath of the alleged coup, notably in Medan, where as many as a hundred may have been killed on a single day in December 1965 and in Aceh, where many were killed and some ten thousand were expelled in May 1966.[91] And yet as mentioned above, these killings were an exception. On the whole, ethnic Chinese were not the main targets, and those who were killed were more often than not members or leaders of one of the leftist parties or associations like Baperki.[92]

In short, underlying religious and ethnic tensions point to some of the grievances that may have driven enmity and conflict in certain areas, and may help to explain why the language and symbolism of the violence varied as it did from one area to the next. At the same time, like most accounts that locate the origins of genocide in long-standing conflicts and tensions, those that stress underlying religious and ethnic tensions do not really explain why and how those tensions escalated to mass killing when and where they did. If the differences between groups were so bitter and intractable, why had they not led to more than a few isolated instances of violence before the events of October 1? Why was there such a long delay before the onset of violence in some of the most affected areas? And why did comparable tensions elsewhere in the country not also result in mass killings?

SOCIOECONOMIC CONFLICTS

Some scholars highlight the role of socioeconomic conflicts—most notably conflicts over land and working conditions—in driving the violence and killings after the alleged coup.[93] Such conflicts appear to have been important in shaping the pattern of violence, especially its geographic distribution, but also in defining both its perpetrators and victims.

Conflicts over land, for example, were especially intense in the densely populated provinces of Bali, Central Java, and East Java—precisely the provinces that saw the most concentrated killings in 1965–66. Those tensions were dramatically heightened after national land reform legislation was introduced in the early 1960s. While the PKI and more specifically its peasant league, the BTI, were energetic in seeking the implementation of the reform, the PNI, NU, Partai Katolik, and their affiliated peasant organizations either dragged their feet or actively opposed the reform. Tensions were accentuated by the BTI's unilateral land seizures known as aksi sepihak, which led to some isolated physical clashes between opposing sides before October 1965. It appears that some of the worst violence after the alleged coup occurred where land reform had been most successfully implemented or at least where it had been most bitterly contested, including, for example, Boyolali in Central Java, Kediri in East Java, and parts of Bali.[94] At the same time, it would be a mistake to imagine that the mass killing in these areas stemmed naturally or inevitably from conflicts over land. For while such conflicts were nothing new, the violence was. The critical question is how and to what extent the preexisting conflicts over land became the basis for widespread killings.

The same may be said for conflicts between labor and management. Such conflicts were increasingly common in the larger urban centers and port cities, like Jakarta, Surabaya, and Medan, where left-wing trade unions, under the umbrella of the PKI-affiliated Central Organization of Indonesian Workers (Sentral Organisasi Buruh Seluruh Indonesia, or SOBSI), had become active in demanding better conditions for their members. They were also common in areas with a high concentration of commercial estates and state-run plantations—chiefly rubber, palm oil, sugar, and tobacco—where PKI-affiliated unions such as the SARBUPRI had achieved considerable success in mobilizing agricultural laborers to demand better treatment and even rights to the land they worked.[95]

All these efforts placed workers and organizers on a collision course with factory and plantation owners and managers. It was no coincidence that most of the latter were either active in or affiliated with parties of the Right, like the PNI, NU, and the banned Masyumi. After the imposition of martial law in 1957, moreover, many of those factory and plantation managers were military officers, as nationalized plantations and industries were placed under military control. That shift gave the army a direct economic stake in those enterprises, and inevitably hardened its attitude and position with regard to left-wing unions.[96] It also inspired the army to establish its own trade union group, the Central Organization of Indonesian Socialist Employees (Sentral Organisasi Karyawan Sosialis Indonesia, or SOKSI) as a counterweight to SOBSI and SARBUPRI. In some areas, too, the army began to train and arm militant youth groups and the anticommunist unions, leading to isolated physical clashes with left-leaning unions. In short, by October 1965, the unions had fought bitterly for several years, perhaps creating the conditions for the violence that followed.[97]

In sum, socioeconomic conflicts do appear to correlate with observed patterns of mass violence in 1965–66, with the worst violence occurring in Central Java, East Java, and Bali, where conflict over land was most intense, and in the plantation belt of North Sumatra, where tensions between labor and capital had reached a critical peak in 1965. Here again, however, it needs to be stressed that with only one or two exceptions, these conflicts over conditions of work, and the tensions between left- and right-wing unions, had not resulted in widespread acts of violence before October 1965. Thus, like analyses that explain mass violence by reference to deeply rooted religious and ethnic tensions, those based on such socioeconomic conflicts fail to explain why such conflicts should have suddenly escalated to the point of mass killings. Nor do they offer a satisfactory explanation for the distinctive temporal variations in the killings. The key question, then, is how and why those tensions, bitter as they may have been, escalated into widespread violence when and where they did.

In short, some of the existing explanations of the killings are clearly more persuasive than others. Analyses rooted in ostensibly immutable features of Indonesian character and culture are largely unconvincing. Nor is it plausible that the killings represented a wholly spontaneous eruption of popular anger against the PKI, as Indonesian authorities and some popular accounts have claimed. Arguments focusing on long-standing tensions—religious, political, and socioeconomic—appear to provide more useful insights into the logic of the killings. For example, they offer at least partial explanations for the distinctive spatial distribution of the violence in the sense that there appears to be some correlation between the worst mass killings and the deepest conflicts. They may also help to explain the bitterness and mutual suspicion that seems to have fueled the killings in many areas. Importantly, they offer some understanding of the language and symbolism of the violence even as it varied from place to place.

And yet approaches that focus on underlying causes and long-standing tensions still leave critical questions unanswered. How and why did cultural, religious, political, and socioeconomic tensions escalate into mass killings in some areas but not in others? Why did the killings begin and end at markedly different times in different parts of the country? Why, despite such geographic and temporal variations, did the mass killings nevertheless take broadly similar forms across the country? Why, for example, did vigilantes or death squads everywhere play such a central role, and why were methods like summary execution, bodily mutilation, corpse display, and sexual violence so common? Perhaps most significant, approaches that locate the roots of violence in deep underlying causes tend to divert attention from more immediate political processes and human agency. In that way, they serve to obscure rather than enhance our understanding of the patterns of violence and leave unanswered the crucial question of responsibility.

CHAPTER SIX

The Army's Role

Dear listeners, it is clear that the actions [of the September 30th Movement] were counter-revolutionary and must be destroyed down to the very roots. We have no doubt that with the full assistance of the progressive and revolutionary population, the counter-revolutionary September 30th Movement will be crushed to bits.

—MAJOR GENERAL SUHARTO, RADIO ADDRESS, OCTOBER 1, 1965

WHO, THEN, was responsible for the mass killings of 1965–66? To put the matter simply, it was the army. In making that claim, I do not mean to suggest that the army acted alone. In fact, it worked closely with a variety of local groups and actors who had their own reasons for taking action against the PKI and its allies. Nor am I claiming that cultural, religious, and socioeconomic factors were of no importance; clearly they were. They provided real and imagined reasons for grievance against the PKI and its affiliates as well as some of the language and symbolism through which those grievances were expressed. Nor, finally, do I mean that powerful international actors like the United States and United Kingdom played no role in facilitating or fomenting the violence; unquestionably they did. My point, rather, is that—whatever underlying religious, cultural, and socioeconomic conflicts may have existed in October 1965, however willing civilians were to join the fray, and no matter how permissive the international context may have been—the mass killings of 1965–66 were neither inevitable nor spontaneous. On the contrary, the evidence is now clear that the killings were deliberately encouraged, facilitated, directed, and shaped by the army's leadership.[1] In other words, without army leadership, the events of October 1, 1965 would not have resulted in what some authors have called genocide.

This chapter develops that argument in several parts. It shows first how the temporal and geographic variations in the pattern of mass killing corresponded closely to the varied political postures and capacities of army commanders in a given locale, and how the army's logistical assets facilitated the killings. That close correlation strongly suggests that all other considerations aside, the posture and capacity of the army leadership in a given area was a critical factor in triggering and sustaining the mass killings. Next, it outlines how the army encouraged and carried out mass killings by mobilizing civilian youth groups and death squads, and encouraging them to identify, detain, and kill members of the PKI and their allies. The close relationship between the army and these groups belies the common claim that the killers acted spontaneously on the basis of religious or other deeply rooted impulses. Third, the chapter describes how the army provoked and legitimized mass killings by launching a sophisticated media and propaganda campaign that blamed the PKI for the kidnap and murder of the generals, and called for the party and its affiliates to be physically annihilated. Fourth, it shows how a variety of religious and political leaders embraced and replicated the army's polarizing and retributive language and propaganda, adding their considerable authority to the campaign of violence. Finally, it draws on this evidence to address the critical question of responsibility.

Temporal and Spatial Variation

Within a few days of the kidnap and murder of the generals on October 1, the new army leadership under Major General Suharto set out to crush both the September 30th Movement and the PKI and its affiliated organizations. It carried out that intention in a number of ways, none of them more important than the use of overwhelming armed force against the alleged perpetrators and hundreds of thousands of unarmed civilians. Without the army's resort to armed force, and without access to its substantial logistical assets, the mass killings could not and would not have happened.

ARMY POSTURE AND CAPACITY

Perhaps the clearest evidence of the army's central role in the killings is the uncanny relationship between the political disposition and capacity of army commanders in a given area and the timing and intensity of the violence there. This pattern makes clear that far from being a spontaneous popular reaction to the treachery of the PKI, as the Suharto regime and its successors have always insisted, the killings were set in motion by the army leadership itself. It also suggests strongly that the marked geographic and temporal variations in the pattern of killings did not stem directly or inevitably from long-standing religious, cultural, and socioeconomic tensions in a given locale but rather from the capacity of army commanders in each area to fuel and mobilize those tensions with a view to destroying the Left.[2] Their ability to do so was contingent on a number of other factors, including the willingness of civilian political and religious leaders to work with them, the degree of cooperation or resistance they encountered within their own ranks, and their success in mobilizing anticommunist vigilante groups in support of their cause.

The close connection between the posture and capacity of army commanders and the killings in a given area is discernible in three distinct patterns. First, where the regional military command was united and had sufficient troops at its disposal, the killings were either swift and extensive, as in Aceh, or limited, as in West Java. In Aceh, for example, the scene of the first mass killings, the military commander, Brigadier General Ishak Djuarsa, and his direct superior, Lieutenant General Ahmad Mokoginta, were united in their opposition to Sukarno and the PKI, and had ample troops loyal to them. They immediately embarked on an operation to "annihilate" the movement and the PKI, and carried it out with singular speed and efficiency. Thus, contrary to the conventional wisdom that the violence in Aceh was a kind of "holy war" driven by the anger of its deeply religious Muslim population, the available evidence now makes clear that the killings were part of a deliberate army operation to destroy the PKI.[3]

Meanwhile, in West Java, the regional military command under Brigadier General Ibrahim Adjie was also unified and had sufficient troops available. And yet West Java saw relatively few killings. The decisive difference was that Adjie decided *against* the strategy of mass killing, preferring a program of mass arrest.[4] Though an ardent anticommunist, Adjie had a deep personal loyalty to Sukarno and, unlike many of his fellow officers, he followed Sukarno's admonition not to resort to violence against the PKI.[5] No doubt he was also reluctant to arm and empower Muslim villagers and militias so soon after defeating the troublesome Darul Islam rebellion in the province. Adjie explained his approach to the British military attaché and another British Embassy official in the course of a conversation in early February 1966. According to their account,

> Adjie commented that it was not always necessary for blood to show. His tactics had been to put the leaders of the PKI in concentration camps, work on the masses to prove how the leaders had deceived them, and then let the leaders out.... Adjie was critical of the different tactics employed in East Java. The kind of internecine war that had gone on had been wrong and had left many wounds open.[6]

Second, where the army command was politically divided, faced resistance, or did not have sufficient troops at its disposal—conditions that prevailed in many parts of the country—the mass killing was delayed for some time, but then accelerated dramatically when the balance of forces tipped in favor of the anticommunist position. In North Sumatra, for example, both the regional military commander, Brigadier General Darjatmo, and the governor, Ulung Sitepu, were sympathetic to the Left, and as many as 30 percent of troops were thought to have leftist sympathies.[7] The result was a tense stalemate with anticommunist forces that delayed the onset of mass killings for at least a month. Thus, notwithstanding the deep-seated socioeconomic and political conflicts in the province, the killings did not begin there until after October 29, when Brigadier General Sobiran, whom US officials described as "violently anticommunist," replaced Darjatmo.[8]

Similarly in Bali, where the regional military commander, Brigadier General Sjafiuddin, was a supporter of Sukarno and had the backing of the leftist governor, Suteja, mass killings were forestalled for a full two months, and began only after both Sjafiuddin and Suteja had been sidelined. Thereafter, the killings spread rapidly, resulting in the death of some eighty thousand people in a little over three months.[9] In East Java, too, where the regional military commander, Brigadier General Basoeki Rachmat, had limited troops at his disposal and not much confidence in their loyalty, mass killings did not begin in earnest until early November.[10] Moreover, when army leaders began to fear that conservative Muslims who had been mobilized to help with the killing were challenging army dominance, the violence was brought swiftly to a close.[11] Meanwhile, in Flores, where the subregional military commander, Lieutenant Colonel Soetarmadji, had been reluctant to support the anticommunist campaign, mass killings did not begin until February 1966, after he had been replaced by a more compliantly anticommunist officer.[12] In each of these cases, then, mass killings were delayed until the relevant army commander (and civilian officials) had been removed or replaced.

Third, in areas where there was no consensus within the military leadership or where loyalist troop strength was insufficient, the onset of mass killings coincided with or immediately followed the deployment of troops loyal to Suharto from outside the command area. The most notorious of those troops were from the elite para-commando regiment, the RPKAD. As I have argued elsewhere with respect to Bali, and others have demonstrated for Central Java, the violence in these contested areas coincided with the arrival of these elite mobile forces.[13] Units of the RPKAD were first deployed from Jakarta to Central Java, where some elements of the army had shown open support for the September 30th Movement. Arriving in the provincial capital, Semarang, on October 18, they quickly set about crushing all possible support for the movement and the PKI, and in the process gained a reputation for extraordinary brutality. Summarizing these actions, Jenkins and Kammen write, "In the months ahead, at the behest of Suharto, [the RPKAD commander] Sarwo Edhie was to instigate a reign of terror and mass murder in Central Java, crushing both the September 30th Movement and the PKI, and tipping the uncertain political balance decisively in the Army's favour."[14] With their task in Central Java accomplished, RPKAD troops apparently returned to Jakarta in late November.[15]

Finally, in early December, RPKAD troops arrived in Bali, where there had been almost no killings in the two months after the alleged coup. Within days of their arrival, the killings accelerated dramatically, and quickly reached levels comparable to or worse than the other areas. The conventional wisdom is that the violence in Bali spread spontaneously and became so "frenzied" that when crack troops arrived from Java in December, their main job was to stop it. In fact, virtually all the evidence indicates that RPKAD forces together with political party authorities orchestrated and incited the violence in Bali, as they did in Java and Aceh.[16]

GUNS, TRUCKS, AND HIT LISTS

Although the killings were largely carried out with simple weapons and did not rely on elaborate modern technologies, they required planning and logistical support. The army played a crucial role in providing both, often supplementing its own assets and capacity by mobilizing the local population and confiscating the property of private citizens. Without the army's logistical and organizational leadership, it is safe to say that the mass killings could not have happened, or at least would not have been nearly as swift and widespread as they were.

FIGURE 6.1. Detained members of the PKI-affiliated Pemuda Rakyat are transported in the back of a military vehicle under armed guard in Jakarta, October 10, 1965. (Bettman/Getty Images)

The army's logistical role took a number of forms. The first, and most obvious, was the provision of firearms to its own soldiers and militia allies. Firearms were not the only means used in killing—as we have seen, machetes, knives, bamboo spears, and swords were also common—but they were important in projecting the army's power. The display and use of high-powered firearms, for example, were a crucial aspect of the "show of force" strategy employed by the RPKAD and other army units. So too were armored personnel carriers and tanks. A US Embassy cable from November 1965 provided a glimpse of that strategy, gleaned from an official army account of the killing of nine Gerwani women in Central Java:

> Army info bureau also reported that Para-commandos (RPKAD) in armored vehicles entering city of Surakarta ... were blocked in village at outskirts by nine "witches" from PKI women's affiliate Gerwani, who insulted them and refused to let them pass. After asking them quietly to give way, and firing into the air, [RPKAD] para-commandos were "forced by their intransigence to terminate breathing of these nine Gerwani witches."[17]

Firearms were also important in lending authority to the local allies the army empowered to round up and kill PKI members. These included the civil defense units, known as Hansip and Hanra, which were mobilized down to the village level across the country. According to one recently discovered document, Hansip and Hanra units in North Aceh were provided with rifles and automatic weapons for the specific purpose of assisting in the campaign to "exterminate" the G30S.[18] Given the fact that Hansip and Hanra were part of a national civil defense apparatus, it is reasonable to assume that units in other parts of the country were also supplied with weapons. The army also gave weapons and training to selected members of the anticommunist vigilante groups it mobilized. According to one account from East Java, for example, the commander of the Sixteenth Infantry Brigade, Colonel Sam, "gave a Luger [pistol] to the Ansor chairman in Kediri and trained him how to shoot at Mount Kolotok, a small moumnain west of Kediri."[19] Similarly, a former student leader in Central Java has recounted how the army gave him and others arms and training and a "license to kill" Communists:

> I had a license to kill people who were proven involved in the PKI. Ten people were given FN pistols and trained in Kaliurang. The pistols were provided around November 1965.... I returned to Kostrad head office in Yogyakarta most often to secure bullets. With the pistol, I launched operations to find PKI sympathizers and leaders in Yogyakarta nearly every day, from [late] 1965 to mid-1966.[20]

Equally important were the trucks and other vehicles the army provided for the transport of soldiers, vigilante killers, and their victims. Accounts from virtually every part of the country describe the transportation of suspects, bound and tied, in open-backed military-type vehicles.[21] Many of the trucks belonged to the army itself, while others were commandeered from private citizens as part of the army campaign. Among the most vivid accounts is from Niko, a former detainee from West Timor:

> When the trucks stopped it was a terrible sound. The horns were the sound of death. When the trucks stopped it was like the instruments of death you hear on the radio. Even the geckos were quiet. The birds were still. The roosters stopped crowing.... When we heard that sound our hair would stand on end and we would experience the most terrible fear. Some of the prisoners would be loaded onto the trucks. We would wait for them to come back, but none of them ever did.... Anyone whose name was called quickly climbed up on the high tray of the truck. If they were not quick about it, they would be pushed from behind.[22]

In the town of Negara, Bali, eyewitnesses reported that dozens of army trucks, loaded with alleged Communists picked up from surrounding villages, formed a slow and orderly procession down the main street for several days. At a large warehouse, the prisoners were unloaded one by one, hands bound, and taken inside, where they were shot with automatic weapons. In the course of three days in December, an estimated six thousand were killed.[23] An article in Bali's local newspaper in the second week of December 1965 declared that "they don't even need to see the red beret [of the RPKAD], it is enough simply to hear the roar of the truck, and the hearts of the big-shot G-30-S types begin to beat wildly with fear."[24] A man who served on an army-organized night patrol in Aceh also remembered the trucks: "We were on the night watch [at that time].... I saw when they [those who had been held in detention] were brought on the back of a ... truck. When they were killed I didn't see.... [But] I knew that they were brought on trucks, one truck, two trucks. I [also] saw the graves."[25] Photographic and film images of the period likewise highlight the centrality of military vehicles in the implementation of the plan to crush the PKI.

Many accounts also mention the existence of lists on the basis of which victims were targeted for arrest or execution.[26] Reporting a conversation with Ross Taylor, an English engineer living in Pasuruan, East Java, a British Embassy official wrote in December 1965 that the engineer had given him "horrifying details of the purges that have been taking place at the Nebritext factory in the village of Pasuruan," where Taylor lived.

> The local army commander, [Taylor] told me, has a list of PKI figures in five categories. He has been given orders to kill those in the first three categories. So far, some 2,000 people have been killed in the environs, starting with those living nearest the main roads, and working outwards.... In the factory itself about 200 have been liquidated.[27]

In some cases, such lists were prepared by the army, and then passed along to vigilantes with orders to kill those named or to select those who should be killed. According to a Banser leader from Kediri, for example, "What usually happened was that Banser would receive a list of PKI detainees from the District Military Command headquarters (Kodim) with the instruction to choose who among the detainees should be executed. So, the killings were done in accordance with the law."[28] Likewise, a former vigilante group member from Aceh testified that "we only picked up people we knew were definitely PKI.... [W]e read their names on a list made up by the leadership."[29] And according to a former death squad commander in North Sumatra, "We exterminated communists for three months day and night.... We got lists of the prisoners we brought to Snake River. Every night I signed the list."[30]

In some cases, army authorities sought and secured the acquiescence of local religious and political party leaders in compiling as well as vetting death lists. An anonymous account from the town of Maumere, Flores, for instance, described a meeting at army headquarters in late February 1966, at which the leaders of political parties and social organizations were pressured to take part in deciding who among those detained should be "secured."

> One by one the names of the detainees was read out, the reason why they had been detained and the nature of their supposed offence. The atmosphere was edgy; it made the hairs on their necks stand up, because each of the military personnel in the room had his weapon in his hand. In this situation the parties and organizations one by one had to state clearly their attitude to the detainees whose names had been read out.... This night of 27 February 1966 was the moment that Catholic leaders started losing their grip, or to put it more strongly they had already abandoned Catholic principles.[31]

Similar lists were reportedly compiled by army intelligence officers in Kupang, West Timor, and likewise vetted by local political party representatives.[32]

Such procedures, and the lists themselves, leave no doubt that the killings were planned and premeditated, and not the result of a sudden frenzy. Indeed, those procedures and lists were almost certainly part of the system for "cleansing" political suspects that was set up by the army shortly after October 1. Under that system, suspects were placed by military officials in one of several broad categories according to their alleged degree of involvement in the September 30th Movement. The classification system was spelled out in a decree issued by General Suharto on President Sukarno's authority on November 15, and so had the force of law.[33]

Finally, the army provided the places of detention in which many suspects were held, and where some either died under torture or from which they were transported to a killing field.[34] In addition to small local jails and larger prisons, the detention sites included military camps and buildings as well as sports stadiums, warehouses, and private homes seized from their owners by the army. In some parts of the country, the army also established concentration and work camps to house the ever-expanding numbers of detainees. These logistical assets became an essential part of the infrastructure of mass killing.

Mobilizing the Population

Of course, the army did not act alone. On the contrary, because of lingering uncertainty about the loyalty and capacity of some military units and officers, and also to cover their tracks, the army leadership sought allies wherever it could find them. Chief among those allies were leaders of the ardently anticommunist political parties, like the NU, PNI, IPKI, and Partai Katolik along with their respective mass organizations. Crucially, the army also formed alliances with, and mobilized, a variety of armed vigilante groups and militia forces, deploying them in a coordinated campaign of violence against the Left.

MASS ORGANIZATIONS

Mass organizations had been actively involved in politics for some years before the events of October 1965, and were ripe for quick mobilization afterward.[35] That was especially true of the religious and political party youth organizations, which had been engaged in increasingly bitter and occasionally violent conflict with PKI-affiliated groups since at least 1963. It was to these groups that the army turned in its campaign against the PKI and its allies. What changed after October 1, 1965, was that the mass organizations began to work more closely and openly with the army than ever before—coordinating plans for demonstrations, declarations, and "sweeping" actions. With explicit and tacit army support, these mass organizations were mobilized to demand action against the "traitors" who had killed the generals, providing the army with a useful rationale for taking "firm action" against the PKI, on the grounds that "the people demand it." In the course of those actions, they committed acts of violence, including the destruction of homes and offices, looting, beating, and eventually, mass detention and killing.

The earliest expression of this new cooperation was an umbrella group of militant anticommunist mass organizations, known as KAP-Gestapu (Komando Aksi Pengganyangan Gerakan September Tiga Puluh, or Action Command to Crush the September 30th Movement). The participating mass organizations included those affiliated with the NU, IPKI,

FIGURE 6.2. Suspected PKI members detained by army and anticommunist militias near the base of Mount Merapi, Central Java, ca. 1965. (National Library of Indonesia)

and the Catholic Party, among others. Although ostensibly an independent civilian body, KAP-Gestapu was set up on the initiative of the army leadership just a few days after the alleged coup—with financial assistance later provided covertly by the US government—and effectively served as an anticommunist political action command for the army.[36] Once KAP-Gestapu had been established, many more coordinating bodies and "action fronts" were set up, in each case with the support of army authorities.

Among the most active of the new organizations were KAMI, KAPPI, and a parallel organization for college graduates, KASI (Kesatuan Aksi Sarjana Indonesia, or the Indonesian University Graduates' Action Front). In addition to these national bodies, army authorities established parallel organizations at the provincial and local levels.[37] Despite their benign middle-class names and appearance, these student action fronts played a crucial role in the campaign of violence against the Left in 1965–66. As a political insider confided to a researcher in late 1966, "The students were fanatical right wingers, used by the Army and [NU vice chair] Z.E. Subchan. One could never be sure whom they would 'arrest' and what would happen if they did. They were not a democratic but a fascistic phenomenon."[38]

The close cooperation between these organizations and the army was no secret. US Embassy officials spoke of the relationship between the students and army in the most natural way. A report on a meeting with one of the leaders of these groups, A. B. Nasution (no relation to General Nasution), noted that the reporting officer "has been impressed with Nasution's contacts both with the Army and with younger people in other branches of the Indonesian Government." A. B. Nasution, the report continued, "was one of the founders and editors of a new anticommunist weekly newspaper, *Djiwa Proklamasi*," and as KAMI stepped up its actions, Nasution "became the founder of a parallel cooperating organization of college graduates ... KASI which has subsequently become a significant pressure group working in close cooperation with both the Army and student groups."[39] In short, as the Indonesian foreign minister, Malik, told Ruth McVey in October 1966, "The students could move because they had relations with the army. The army let them know when and how much they were to move."[40]

MILITIAS AND DEATH SQUADS

Even more important in fueling the violence and killings, however, were the anticommunist militia groups that were mobilized after October 1. Most of these were directly affiliated with political parties—such as NU's Ansor and Banser, PNI's Pemuda Marhaen (also known as Tameng Marhaenis), and IPKI's Pemuda Pancasila. Other units, such as the Hansip and Hanra, were part of the existing civil defense apparatus. After October 1, all these groups became, in effect, anticommunist militias. It was to these groups, and their leaders, that the army turned to identify and locate local PKI leaders and members; it was they who surrounded the houses of alleged leftists at night, angrily demanded their arrest, destroyed their property, and burned their houses. And it was they who made up the squads that tracked down and detained alleged leftists, took them to sites of detention, and joined in killing them. There is no firm indication of how many joined these groups, but it must have been in the hundreds of thousands. According to a US Embassy cable from mid-November 1965, in the Solo area alone "the Army was training and equipping some 24 thousand Moslem youth for action against communists."[41] Likewise, the districts of East Aceh and North Aceh were each reported to have some 15,000 militia members.[42]

The relationship between these groups and the army has been the subject of much speculation and discussion over the years. Some observers have embraced or inadvertently lent credence to the official position that such groups acted on their own initiative, independently of the army, on the basis of long-standing local antipathies and conflicts.[43] A more common position is that while in some areas vigilante groups operated at the army's behest, in others they acted independently on the basis of local interests and conflicts.[44]

It is now clear that this consensus view was mistaken, and with rare exceptions, these militia groups and death squads operated under army direction and control. Although there was some variation from one region to the next, the basic pattern was the same wherever the mass killings took place. Militias were mobilized, armed, trained, and supported by the army, and more often than not, carried out the arrests and killings. That is not to say that the members of such groups were always simply following orders. Most had real motives for cooperating with the army, including fear, peer pressure, anger, and sincerely held religious or ideological beliefs. But that does not mean their involvement in mass killings was spontaneous or inevitable. Indeed in virtually every case, they engaged in killing only after being given the green light or being prodded to action by the army. A few examples from different parts of the country make this apparent.

In a report from early November 1965, a senior US Embassy official described the army's strategy as it had been explained to him by an Indonesian Army contact: "In Central Java Army (RPKAD) is training Moslem youth and supplying them with weapons and will keep them out in front against the PKI. Army will try to avoid as much as it can safely do so direct confrontation with the PKI."[45] And as the RPKAD commander, Sarwo Edhie, told a journalist, "We decided to encourage the anti-communist civilians to help with the job. In Solo we gathered together the youth, the nationalist groups, the religious organizations. We gave them two or three days' training, then sent them out to kill communists."[46] Internal army documents confirm, in somewhat more circuitous language, that the mobilization of the population to attack the PKI was a deliberate strategy. An army history of the campaign against the PKI in Central Java, for example, says,

> In order to defeat the PKI tactic of arousing the mass of its followers in a campaign of terror and disruption, the government itself mobilized the mass of the people. The RPKAD gave military training, including instruction in the use of weapons and techniques for securing villages,

> as part of a general programme of cooperation between the army and the people to crush the remnants of the G30S/PKI.[47]

A November 1965 report by the US consulate in Surabaya about the killings in Kediri and Pare, East Java, tells a similar story:

> American missionary from Baptist Hospital Kediri told us that 3,400 PKI activists were killed by Ansor with probable assistance from Marhaenist youths over period Nov 4–Nov 9.... Source also stated same [kind of] slaughter took place at Pare 30 kilometers northeast of Kediri; 300 Communists reported killed there.... Armed Forces did nothing to stop the slaughter and in fact apparently colluded with anti-PKI youths and perhaps instigated them. Col. Welly Soedjono, Commander for Madiun-Kediri area, reported by sources to have been in Kediri at time and to have told youth leaders that he [was] sure they could find more than 3,500 communists in Kediri if they really looked.[48]

Further evidence of the cooperation between the army and militias in East Java comes from the accounts of militia members and commanders themselves. A history of the Banser campaign to crush the PKI in East Java offers a rare glimpse into that world.[49] Three patterns stand out clearly. First, local Banser commanders repeatedly mention that their people received military training from elite army units, such as the Raiders, Brimob (Mobile Brigade), and RPKAD, and that this training gave them an important advantage in their efforts to crush the PKI. A commander in Banyuwangi, for instance, noted that Banser "quietly strengthened its forces by undertaking military training with RPKAD instructors."[50] Second, Banser leaders describe how local army units assisted Ansor and Banser in their attacks on PKI villages, often with deadly consequences. One account explained that "Banser operations to hunt the PKI were quietly backed by local military forces, while another stated bluntly that "the Army facilitated and supported the extermination of the PKI."[51] Finally, they describe how, at the end of October 1965, the army informed them that the arrest and killing of PKI could only be done with army permission.[52] Accordingly, Banser and Ansor units received formal written orders to arrest and kill PKI members. As one Ansor member from Turen, Malang, put it, "Orders to kill PKI members came from ABRI. The transfer of PKI detainees to Banser units was always accompanied by an official order (*surat perintah*)."[53] A Banser leader from Rengel District (Tuban) East Java, later told researchers, "We were called up whenever there was an execution scheduled. Usually it was at night after the [evening] prayer. There was a schedule, along with the name of the victims, that was transferred from the District Office to the District Military Command."[54]

The same basic pattern was reported from North Sumatra. As Ken Young writes, "The army encouraged local youth groups in the capital city (Medan) to murder their communist rivals. The youth squads here were Muslim, Catholic, and Pemuda Panca Sila."[55] According to US officials in Medan in December 1965, "Sumatra military officer reported that Army, while counseling public restraint, is actually encouraging Moslems to kill all PKI cadres, and that hundreds are being killed every day in North Sumatra."[56] A death squad commander responsible for many executions in the vicinity of the Snake River similarly described the army's behind-the-scenes role: "They waited at the road with the truck. They didn't come down here [to the riverbank].... They called this 'the people's struggle' so they kept their distance. If the Army was seen doing [the killing] the world would be angry."[57]

In Bali, too, the army worked closely with civilians and vigilante groups in carrying out the killings. The main vigilante group was the PNI-affiliated Tameng Marhaenis, but the NU's Ansor was also active on some parts of the island. Sometimes the army took the lead. According to Hughes, after the troops had arrived from Java, "the military and police got together with civilian authorities and made sure the right people were being executed. People were ... arrested and, usually, shot by the soldiers."[58] In other cases, the job of killing was delegated to villagers. Hughes writes that "sometimes villages were specifically assigned to purge themselves of their Communists. Then took place communal executions as the village gathered its Communists together and clubbed or knifed them to death."[59]

The evidence from Aceh points to a similar pattern and provides definitive proof that the main vigilante groups were officially sanctioned.[60] Those groups included the Front Pembela Panca Sila (Pancasila Defenders Front), formally established in Banda Aceh on October 6, 1965, and in West Aceh a few days later, and Pembela Rakyat (People's Defenders), formed in South Aceh in the first half of October.[61] As in Bali, the killings in Aceh were sometimes carried out by the army itself, and sometimes by the death squads operating under army supervision. In virtually every case, the killings began shortly after the regional military commander, Brigadier General Djuarsa, and other senior officials arrived in a district and exhorted the population to take action against the PKI.[62] John

Bowen recounts the aftermath of one such visit to Takengon, Aceh, in early October:

> On each evening for the next few weeks men and women were seized from their homes, taken to the [Takengon] jail, and then driven to secluded spots along the road to the north coast and executed.... The army carried out the killings but ordered boys and young men to join the arrests. "The government wanted us to be out in front, to give them a way out later on," said one subdistrict civil defense commander.[63]

In Kupang, West Timor, religious youth groups (Protestant, Catholic, and Muslim) coordinated closely with the chief of staff of the District Military Command, Major M. Noor, in conducting anticommunist sweeps. As van Klinken writes, these sweeping operations led inexorably to the detention and, in many cases, summary execution of alleged Communists: "The youths handed them over to the military in such numbers that the old colonial jail ran out of space and many were held in the Merdeka Football Stadium. From the beginning of January [1966] and peaking between February and April 1966, the military began taking them out at night to their executions."[64]

In short, the evidence now available from a wide range of locales suggests that with few exceptions, militia forces and vigilantes operated under explicit army control, especially when it came to killings. That case, long accepted for Central Java, is now strong for other parts of the country as well, including Aceh and Bali. That is significant because, according to the conventional wisdom, it was precisely in those areas (Aceh and Bali) that the local populations had clearly taken the initiative and "run amok," and that the army's role had been to stop the violence. It is now clear that that picture was untrue, and that the claims of popular and spontaneous violence were, in fact, deliberate lies concocted and spread by the very army officers who orchestrated the killings.

Language and Propaganda

The idea of killing members of the PKI and the Left did not emerge spontaneously. On the contrary, it was encouraged and facilitated by the army leadership through the use of language calculated to create an atmosphere of hostility and fear in which killing anyone associated with the PKI appeared not only morally justifiable but also a patriotic and religious duty.[65] That language spread rapidly across the archipelago, partly through the army-controlled newspapers and television, but also through radio as well as countless mass rallies, demonstrations, ceremonies, declarations, sermons, and face-to-face meetings. In the resulting atmosphere of anticommunist hysteria, existing conflicts over politics, religion, culture, and land were easily ignited.[66]

"DOWN TO THE VERY ROOTS"

Several aspects of this official language and propaganda were especially important in fomenting violence against the PKI. First, it was extraordinarily bellicose. To some extent, this may be understood as a continuation of the combative style and tone of political life under Sukarno's Guided Democracy. After all, under that system political parties on all sides had been in the habit of denouncing their enemies in highly aggressive language—calling for Malaysia to be "crushed," capitalist bureaucrats to be "retooled," and the US ambassador to be "strung up." And yet even by those standards, the army's language after October 1, 1965, was shocking. High-ranking army officers, including Major General Suharto, declared early on that the September 30th Movement and the PKI must be "smashed," "crushed," "buried," "annihilated," "wiped out," "exterminated," and "destroyed down to the very roots." And like so many campaigns that have led to genocide, the actions against the culprits were repeatedly described as "cleansing" operations and "sweeping."

In a national radio broadcast on RRI at 10:10 p.m. on October 1, 1965, Suharto first used the phrases that would be repeated many thousands of times over the coming months and years, and employed as justification for violence against the PKI. "Dear listeners," Suharto said, "It is clear that the actions [of the September 30th Movement] were counter-revolutionary and must be destroyed down to the very roots. We have no doubt that with the full assistance of the progressive and revolutionary population, the counter-revolutionary September 30th Movement will be crushed to bits."[67]

Almost immediately, military and religious figures across the country began to mimic the army leadership's violent and exclusionary language. In a speech broadcast from Medan at midnight on October 1, Lt. General Mokoginta declared that "in order to safeguard the State/Nation and the revolution, it is ordered that all members of the Armed Forces resolutely and completely annihilate this counter-revolution and all acts of treason down to the roots."[68] An official statement from Aceh's executive council, dated October 4, went even further, declaring, "It is mandatory for the People to assist every attempt to completely annihilate the counter-revolutionary September 30th Movement along with its lackeys."[69] At a mass rally in Jakarta the same day, the NU vice chair, Z. E. Subchan, read out a statement on behalf of an anticommunist umbrella group, which stated, in part, "We call upon all political parties and mass organizations ... to assist the Armed Forces in destroying the 'counter-revolutionary September 30th Movement' down to its roots, and we are ready together with the Armed Forces ... to defend and safeguard the Pantjasila State ... to the last drop of our blood."[70]

The same day, October 4, General Suharto used the occasion of the exhumation of the generals' decomposing bodies to point the finger of responsibility for their deaths directly at the PKI and its affiliates. [71] One day later, the NU's governing board followed the army's lead, naming the PKI and its affiliates as the culprits, and warning that "every counter-revolutionary movement must immediately be eliminated down to its very roots."[72] In Bali, a PNI-affiliated youth group called on all members to "provide concrete assistance to the Armed Forces in annihilating the G-30-S."[73] And at a mass rally in November 1965, the newly appointed anticommunist bupati of Gianyar told a crowd of some hundred thousand that "those who are not prepared to repent and who remain obstinate must be cut down to the very roots."[74] Speaking to members of a student action front in Jakarta on November 12, 1965, General Nasution said that "the PKI has clearly betrayed the state and nation ... and therefore we are obliged and duty bound to wipe them from the soil of Indonesia."[75] Later, warning against the revival of the PKI in North Sumatra, Lt. General Mokoginta told an audience, "We will be condemned by our children if the counter-revolutionary Gestapu were to occur again. In order to prevent that the PKI must be buried as deep as possible so that it cannot rise again from its grave to haunt the people."[76]

TRAITORS AND WHORES

The army propaganda campaign also sought to cast the movement and the PKI as barbaric, inhuman, morally base, and evil. In his remarks on the occasion of the generals' exhumation, broadcast nationwide on state radio and television on October 4, Suharto specifically implicated Gerwani and Pemuda Rakyat in the "barbaric actions" (*tindakan-tindakan jang biadab*) against the generals. The text of his speech appeared in army-controlled newspapers the following day alongside grisly photographs of the decomposing bodies of the slain generals. The funeral procession and ceremony for the generals, which took place on October 5, and the death of Nasution's young daughter the following day, provided further opportunities to vilify the alleged perpetrators.

In this heated atmosphere, the army coined the term "Gestapu" to describe the September 30th Movement. The term was clearly intended to equate the movement with the "Gestapo" (the Nazi Secret State Police), and invoke its connotations of arbitrary power and evil.[77] Indeed, in a briefing to newspaper editors on October 7, 1965, the chief of the Army Information Center, Brigadier General Subroto, explicitly alluded to that historical comparison, describing the September 30th Movement as a "Gestapo-like terror."[78] Recognizing the dangerous political ramifications of the term and the devious objectives of those who coined it, President Sukarno insisted on using the term "Gestok." But the term Gestapu prevailed.[79]

In other ways as well, the army's language routinely portrayed members of the PKI and its affiliates as beings outside the bounds of civilized, moral society—describing them as "traitors," "devils," "child murderers," "atheists," "whores," "terrorists," and "animals." On October 14, the editors of the army newspaper *Angkatan Bersendjata* wrote that "there are no words which can be found to describe how low and lacking in decency were the terroristic actions of the Gestapu in savagely murdering Army officers."[80] In a pattern seen in so many genocides, then, the army portrayed the movement and the PKI, in Helen Fein's apt phrase, as "outside the universe of obligation of the perpetrator."[81] In doing so, the army facilitated and encouraged acts of violence against them.

As the references to devils and atheists attest, moreover, the army's propaganda invoked powerful religious norms and symbols. In his speech by the generals' graveside on October 5, General Nasution spoke of how the army had been insulted (*dihina*) and slandered (*difitnah*), and called on Allah to provide guidance.[82] In the following days, the army-controlled press was thick with references to the "holy" task of the army and its allies in destroying the PKI. On October 8, for example, the army newspaper *Angkatan Bersendjata* called for holy war: "The sword cannot be met by the Koran ... but must be met by the sword. The Koran itself says that whoever opposes you should be opposed as they oppose you."[83] And on October 14, the same paper editorialized, "God is with us because we are on the path that is right and that He has set for us."[84] Army leaders outside the capital conveyed the same message. In North Sumatra, General Mokoginta addressed the newly formed North Sumatra Muslim Joint Committee, "urging his audience to extend their organization down to the district and even village level in order to 'undertake an Islamic offensive' against the PKI."[85]

In no case, perhaps, were the intentions of this official vilification so evident and consequences so grave as in the demonization of Gerwani, the women's organization loosely affiliated with the PKI. In the days and weeks after the movement fizzled, army propagandists and their allies circulated a story that the six generals had been sexually assaulted and mutilated before they were killed on the morning of October 1.[86] The story, reported in the army-controlled press and then endlessly repeated, described in lurid detail how members of Gerwani had danced naked around the generals, before castrating them with razor blades and gouging their eyes out with ice picks.[87] Apart from casting the Gerwani women as inhuman witches, the story powerfully evoked male anxieties about castration. Moreover, as Saskia Wieringa has convincingly argued, it played on the particular anxieties of conservative Indonesian men, for whom the ostensibly uncontrolled sexuality of Gerwani women—not to mention their autonomy and lively political engagement—represented an unacceptable threat to their patriarchal position and worldview.[88]

Before long, similar stories began to appear in places outside Jakarta. In Bali, officials claimed that their interrogation of a senior Gerwani figure had revealed that members of the organization had been instructed to "sell" themselves to soldiers in order to obtain weapons for the PKI, and having done so, to murder and castrate the men they had seduced. As the local paper dutifully reported, "It is clear from these revelations how base and depraved PKI plans were. After scraping as much profit as possible from their shameless sexual activities, Gerwani members were supposed to murder and at the same time cut off the genitals of their victims."[89] Such stories were plainly intended to make Gerwani members, and the PKI generally, appear to be not merely political traitors but also immoral, debauched, and inhuman.[90]

In all these ways, the story seemed calculated to stir up deep hatred and fear of Gerwani, and thereby to provide both a powerful motivation and justification for acts of violence against its members. The problem is that the story was false. Official autopsies performed on the generals confirmed that they had not been tortured or mutilated—a crucial fact that President Sukarno tried in vain to impress on the population.[91] More troubling still, given the existence of those autopsies, it is certain that the top army officials up to and including Suharto *knew at the time* that the story was false. The only possible conclusion to be drawn from these facts is that the army leadership deliberately concocted and disseminated the false story to impugn Gerwani and to incite violence against its members.

DOCUMENTS, GRAVES, AND WEAPONS

Meanwhile, the army had commenced "sweeping actions" that provided further opportunities for provocation and violence. In practice, "sweeping" meant raiding the offices and homes of PKI members, and either beating or detaining them. In the course of those raids, the army and its civilian allies claimed to have discovered documents detailing PKI plans to annihilate anticommunists. These discoveries were breathlessly reported in the army-controlled press and on the radio, where they were held up as evidence that the PKI had indeed been behind the movement, and had planned to destroy its enemies and seize state power.[92]

Soon enough, military and political authorities across the country began to report similar discoveries, and to highlight them in mass rallies, sermons, and declarations. In November, authorities in Bali claimed to have found documents implicating the local PKI, including a list of army personnel allegedly involved in an underground PKI.[93] Likewise, in dozens of speeches made in towns across Central Java, RPKAD commander Sarwo Edhie "announced the discovery of documents which, he claimed, revealed communist plans to massacre members of the 'nationalist' and 'religious' groups."[94] And in Aceh, the head of the National Front claimed to have received an anonymous letter from the PKI with the ominous warning, "We will have revenge on Islamic Youth."[95] Curiously, as far as we know, none of these documents was ever introduced as evidence in the political trials of PKI leaders or members.

The army and its allies also reported the discovery of large holes, which they alleged had been dug by the PKI and Pemuda Rakyat to serve as mass graves for their victims. As in the case of the documents, reports of large holes soon began to appear around the country, and the story quickly spread that they had been dug by the PKI to bury those they planned to kill.[96] Army authorities also claimed to have found the weapons that were to be used.[97] The weapons included firearms, supposedly of Chinese provenance, as well as knives, sickles, machetes, and ice picks. Although all but the firearms were everyday tools that would be found in almost any home at the time, the army and its allies portrayed them in the most sinister possible light. Ice picks, they said, were to be used by the PKI to gouge out the eyes of their victims, just as Gerwani had allegedly gouged out the eyes of the generals.

Whatever the truth of these claims about documents, killings, grave-like holes, and weapons—and there is good reason to doubt them—army leaders, politicians, and religious authorities seized on them to spread the message that in light of the PKI's evil plans, there was no choice but to "kill or be killed."[98] That message was repeated in hundreds of speeches, meetings, and mass rallies, and through countless face-to-face conversations across the country. It is hard to believe that such language—especially coming from people in positions of some authority—would not have incited or at least given license to real acts of violence, including killing. Indeed, most perpetrator accounts of the killings emphasize these discoveries as the reason that they had no choice but to crush the PKI.

MEDIA WAR AND PSYWAR

As these examples make clear, a crucial avenue for the dissemination of the army's inflammatory language and propaganda were the mass media, which at the time meant printed newspapers, radio, and for a select few, television. The media had been a vital political battleground long before October 1965, with most newspapers being closely affiliated with one or another political party or institution. The national press agency, Antara, as well as the state-run radio and television bodies (RRI and TVRI) were in theory nonpartisan, yet they too had become the focus of intense political fights for control.[99] It was hardly surprising, then, that the movement leaders had first seized the national radio station, or that one of Suharto's first moves against them had been to seize it back. It was likewise natural that within twenty-four hours of the movement's first actions, the army had closed down virtually all the country's newspapers, except those it owned or controlled.

The papers that were allowed to remain open, *Angkatan Bersendjata* and *Berita Yudha*, were controlled by the army. Before long, the army permitted other papers to publish, but always under the strictest control and "guidance" from the army information office. According to one prominent newspaper editor, he and others "were told in early October that the Army was starting a campaign against the PKI and anyone printing information critical of that campaign would be considered an ally of the PKI. No neutrality was permitted."[100] In practice, then, the papers that were permitted to publish were either run by the army or, like the notoriously anticommunist daily, *Api Pancasila*, and the NU's *Duta Masjarakat*, closely parroted official army statements. The main message was that the PKI was guilty of treason. As the British ambassador reported to London on October 19, 1965, "Certainly the press and radio which since the 2nd of October had been entirely in army hands has kept up a steady supply of reports and articles pointing up the guilt of the PKI."[101] That was the context in which, oddly, the PKI's national daily, *Harian Rakyat*, was permitted to publish one final issue containing an editorial expressing support for the September 30th Movement. As noted earlier, that October 2 editorial turned out to be the sole piece of documentary evidence available to the army to implicate the PKI in the alleged coup.

In its effort to destroy the PKI and the Left, the army also adopted a psychological warfare strategy that almost certainly accentuated tensions and increased the likelihood of violence, including killing. In parts of the country thought to be sympathetic to the PKI and its affiliates, the army deployed psychological warfare teams, known in some areas as Tim Penerangan Operasi Mental (Operation Mental Information Teams), and in others as Tim Komando Operasi Mental (Operation Mental Command Teams) or Tim Indoktrinasi (Indoctrination Teams).[102] In Bali, these teams went from village to village spreading the army's deadly message of nonneutrality: one could either be against the PKI or for it, but there was no middle ground. As one newspaper described the message, "It was stressed that there are only two possible alternatives; to be on the side of the G-30-S or to stand behind the government in crushing the G-30-S. There is no such thing as a neutral position."[103]

Army officers stressed that declarations of loyalty were not enough. At an official ceremony just days before the mass killings began in Bali, the district military commander in Kerambitan told his audience that the army needed "concrete evidence of ex-PKI members' loyalty to the Republic of Indonesia and to Pancasila, because making a written statement is very easy; what matters most is real proof."[104] Likewise, in a series of mass rallies across Aceh in October, the regional military commander, Brigadier General Ishak Djuarsa, exhorted the population to kill PKI members or risk punishment. As one eyewitness from Takengon recalled, Djuarsa told a crowd, "I will destroy them to their roots! If in the [village] you find members of the PKI, but do not kill them, it will be you who we punish!"[105] That kind of language, coupled with a natural impulse for self-preservation, compelled not only the genuinely neutral but also even former PKI members to join in the attack on the PKI.

In all likelihood, these psywar operations were conducted under the auspices of the powerful Kopkamtib that had been established by Suharto on October 10, 1965, and was under his direct command. From the outset, Suharto had interpreted Kopkamtib's mandate broadly to encompass both military and political domains, and in December a presidential decree specified that it had the power to "restore the authority of the Government by means of *physical-military and mental operations*."[106] An army order outlining the strategy for crushing the PKI explicitly mentioned the use of psychological warfare: "The G30S/PKI should be given no opportunity to consolidate. It should be pushed back systematically by all means, including psy-war."[107]

Beyond its barely concealed threat of and incitement to violence, what is most striking about this language is how much it sounds like the rhetoric of a country at war. The entire political field was reduced to a battle between good and evil, between loyalists and traitors, between the nation and its enemies. Here again, one can perhaps see the rhetorical imprint of Guided Democracy and the Cold War. But that is not the whole story. What made this different, in both degree and kind, was that the language of war was now being articulated by the army—that is, by the institution that had a near monopoly on the means of force and was trained in the use of violence—and was being directed at hundreds of thousands of unarmed civilians. That was an altogether-different matter than a ragtag group of students angrily denouncing their political enemies while waving hand-drawn placards. When an army declares war, especially against its own civilian population, the stakes are much higher—and the results are inevitably more catastrophic.

Religious Allies

The army was not alone in employing the language of demonization, fear, and war, or provoking violence. That language was eagerly embraced and recycled by religious leaders, political party officials, and other anticommunist groups. When used by religious leaders it was especially powerful and provocative, and must have been persuasive to many.

Leading the charge was the NU, which had worked assiduously to push for strong action against the PKI from the outset. On October 5, it had called for the banning of the party and its affiliates, and had instructed its branch committees to actively campaign for that objective. On October 7, the party's newspaper, *Duta Masjarakat*, gave voice to a bellicose and provocative anticommunism that invoked God while echoing the army's propaganda: "Let us safeguard the revolution and help the Armed Forces in their holy task of destroying the so-called September 30th Movement ... and always pray to God that our correct struggle will have His help and blessing."[108]

On October 8, a large crowd made up mainly of Muslim youth organizations staged a rally, after which it attacked the national PKI headquarters, looting it and setting it alight. Within a few days, Muslim political and religious leaders across the country began to describe the September 30th Movement and PKI using religious imagery and language that was certain to spur their followers to action as well as violence. Those who had killed the generals, the statements said, were not merely traitors but also "atheists" and "infidels" whose vile actions demanded a firm response by Muslims. Islam was a religion of peace, they said, but when people had acted against it and against God, there could be no mercy shown. What was required was jihad against the infidel.

These themes resonated powerfully in East Java, the center of the NU's strength, and parts of Central Java. Respected Muslim figures, such as the venerated Islamic teachers known as kiai, encouraged young men to join the campaign against the PKI, and provided those who did so with "spiritual guidance."[109] When those young men set off to raid a PKI village, they would shout "God is Great!"[110] The alleged atheism of the PKI was frequently invoked as a justification for killing its members in the most brutal fashion. Kiai Abdul Ghofur Mustaqim, of Pesantren PETA in Tulungagung, East Java, gave the following account:

> I once witnessed a pesantren [Islamic boarding school] student aged 14 who got hold of a PKI member who was disguised as a cigarette vendor. The student knew that the PKI member had often insulted religion/Islam in the past. And so, as soon as he had got hold of the guy, he slit his throat with a knife so that his head almost came off. The student was covered in blood.[111]

Spiritual guidance and prayer were also invoked to explain and legitimize such killings. Recounting the story of a mass killing of PKI members in Kediri in which none of his men had suffered any injury, a Banser commander later commented, "Perhaps as a result of the spiritual training they had received from the kiai, not a single one of the Banser members was wounded or killed."[112] In another story, a kiai explained how he had used the power of Islam to help his students defeat and kill spiritually powerful (*sakti*) PKI members who had used "black magic" to make themselves invulnerable: "To defeat someone like that, I supplied my students with lengths of rotan that had been blessed. Praise be to Allah, with those lengths of rotan the 'sakti' PKI members were defeated and then killed."[113]

The accounts of many former killers give a clear sense of the importance of religious sanction in motivating their actions and justifying them after the fact. A former member of an Islamic boarding school who took part in killings in Kediri and Probolinggo, East Java, explained that he saw the killings "as a personal religious obligation ... because if the PKI had won, Islam would have been destroyed. Moreover, my parents and the kiai gave their approval."[114] An Ansor member from Tempeh District, East Java, recalled attending meetings organized by NU leaders before Ansor and Banser members went out to conduct killings. At these meetings, he noted, "the religious figures said murdering PKI members was a form of *jihad*, that 'if they were not killed first, then we would be killed.'"[115] A Banser member from Sumbersuko District, East Java, who admitted to killing many PKI prisoners later recalled that when doing so, he thought of the words of an NU religious scholar, who had said, "A person is not a real Muslim if he does not want to exterminate PKI members."[116] And a former Banser leader from Rengel District, East Java, explained, "I felt this conflict with the PKI was not just over ideological difference, but was a holy war. . . . They had attacked our faith."[117]

But it was not only Muslim clerics and party leaders who employed religious language and symbols to encourage and legitimize killing. Leading Hindu, Protestant, and Catholic figures spread similar messages. Religious authorities in Bali, including Brahmana priests (*pedanda*), lay priests (*pemangku*), and soothsayers (*balian*) were in a position to stoke a sense of outrage against the PKI, contributing to the violence. Sometimes out of genuine religious conviction, yet often for narrow political reasons, religious leaders justified the killing of Communists on the grounds that the PKI was "antireligious." Donald Kirk quotes a priest as saying, "Our religion teaches us not to kill or hurt . . . but we felt we had to crush whoever tried to disgrace God."[118] Religious symbols and sanction were used in other ways as well. A former political prisoner from Bali recalled that members of the PKI and its mass organizations in his village had been summoned to the main temple, where they were made to swear an oath: "I curse the deeds of the Communist Party and I no longer want to be a member." Rather than being spared, however, that oath was then used as "proof" of their guilt, and as the basis for targeting them for detention and execution.[119]

The political parties in Bali, in particular the PNI, also fostered the idea that the campaign against the PKI was a holy war.[120] According to a PNI-Bali member writing in 1967, "The killing of PKI members and sympathizers was not seen by the killers themselves as a criminal deed or a political act. If one asks a Balinese what made him join in the killing, the answer will always be the same: the fulfillment of a *religious* obligation to purify the land."[121] But that idea did not spring naturally from Bali-Hindu theology; it was an interpretation concocted and disseminated by religious and political leaders. Thus, for example, the educated, high-caste figure who would later become Bali's governor, Dr. Ida Bagus Oka, told a rally in Bali, "There can be no doubt that the enemies of our revolution are also the cruelest enemies of religion, and must be eliminated and destroyed down to the roots."[122]

Christian religious leaders also helped to fan the flames of fear and hatred. Reporting on a visit to Makassar in April 1966, Sweden's Ambassador Edelstam related the following story about his encounter with the Protestant bishop there, whom he described as "a sympathetic Indonesian about 35 years old."

> His congregation in Makassar included about 10,000 people and I was invited to participate in a service.... They sang the psalms with enthusiasm but the emphasis of the service was the hour-long sermon. I heard the preacher frequently mention the words communist and kill, which led me to ask the bishop after the service whether it wouldn't have been more in line with the Christian faith to speak of reconciliation, forgiveness, and peace. He responded, a bit embarrassed, that nowadays it was standard practice in all sermons and public speeches to condemn communism and, he added, "there are no communists left in this part of the country anyway."[123]

On the predominantly Catholic island of Flores, church leaders not only failed to protect parishioners from arrest and killing but also used their considerable religious authority aggressively to praise the army's campaign against the PKI and encourage Catholics to take part in it. In a pastoral letter written from Rome in early December 1965, the archbishop of Ende, Gabriel Manek, lavished praise on the army for defeating Communism and called on all Catholics to help the government to "cleanse" the land.

> Praise and thanks without end to the Omnipresent, Almighty God who has defeated the cruel aim of the communists. Abundant praise and thanks for the vigilance of our armed forces who have saved our motherland from such a terrible disaster.... Praise and thanks that God did not permit our Catholic religion throughout the country to be handed over to the enemies of the country and of religion.... In whichever Catholic organization you are involved, we implore you to give as much assistance as possible to our Government, help to the utmost of your ability to cleanse our land from the enemies of the revolution, from elements that betray the country with their 30th September Movement (G30S). In requesting such, I urge you to give assistance

> everywhere with the greatest generosity and in our own Catholic way. In supporting the act of cleansing, let us continue to uphold the principle of humaneness and the Catholic principle of love.[124]

Two months later, the Catholic Party and Catholic Youth organization in the area eagerly joined the army in conducting a cleansing campaign in which some two thousand alleged Communists were killed in about six weeks. In the midst of that killing spree, the archbishop issued a second letter to the religious and clergy of the diocese, in which he once again praised both God and the army for rooting out and destroying the "serpent's poison," and told Catholics that it was their obligation to support the cleansing and "extermination":

> From the event of last year we can conclude, with heartfelt thanks, that God's love for our nation and country is overwhelming.... Apart from that, whether we like it or not, we have to focus our attention on the cleansing action which is presently being carried out and is reaching its climax. We thank God that the serpent's poison, which had spread widely in the body of society, is now being rooted out and destroyed. This extermination, by a nation that was threatened by dangerous elements, is nothing more than our obligation to make ourselves secure.[125]

In short, the manipulation of cultural and religious symbols by political and religious leaders was crucial to the dynamic of the killing. For while the PKI was in some respects iconoclastic, it was not self-evidently or officially atheistic, nor had its members actually committed any crime. These ideas about the PKI's nature and culpability had to be, and were, nourished as the foundation for collective action. Moreover, the idea that the PKI's alleged guilt would best be resolved by mass murder did not emerge naturally from the precepts of Islam, Hinduism, Protestantism, or Catholicism but instead originated with the Indonesian army leadership. All these ideas were consciously disseminated with the assistance of political party and religious leaders eager to see the demise of the PKI at any cost.

Far from being a spontaneous popular reaction to the treachery of the PKI, as the New Order regime and its successors have always insisted, the mass killings of 1965–66 were set in motion by the army itself. It was the army leadership, under Major General Suharto, that introduced the idea that the political crisis of October should and could be resolved through resort to violence, and provided the means through which that intention was achieved. It was the army whose territorial and elite paracommando units took the lead in conducting cleansing campaigns in which members of the PKI and its affiliates were detained, beaten, and killed. It was the army that provided the essential logistical matériel and organizational backbone for those operations. It was the army that mobilized, trained, and armed tens (and perhaps hundreds) of thousands of young people to serve in the militia groups and death squads that detained and killed Communists across the country. It was the army that led the campaign of vilification that portrayed the PKI and its members as atheists, traitors, devils, barbarians, whores, and terrorists, thereby providing both motive and justification for the killing of many thousands of civilians who had committed no crime. It was the army that made sophisticated and unscrupulous use of the mass media to achieve these ends, and in all likelihood, to create false documentary evidence of the PKI's guilt. And it was the army that deployed the language of war, deliberately creating an atmosphere in which there was only friend and foe, but in which violence was to be used only by those with weapons, against those with none.

The army had allies in this effort, of course, none more enthusiastic than the anticommunist religious and political leaders who fanned the flames of hatred and violence by allusions to long-standing religious and cultural differences. As argued in the next chapter, the violence was also fueled by the wider international context of the Cold War and the acts and omissions of key foreign powers. But without the army's orchestrated campaign to cast the PKI as evil, without the conscious decision to effect its physical annihilation, and without the mobilization of the army's considerable organizational and logistical capacity to carry out that decision, it is unlikely that any of those long-standing tensions or external influences would ever have given rise to violence of such staggering breadth and brutality.

CHAPTER SEVEN

"A Gleam of Light in Asia"

> *The Indonesian business is developing in a way that looks encouraging. The Moslems have burned the PKI headquarters in Djakarta last night and they seem to be moving against the Communists around the country.... For the first time, the Army is disobeying Sukarno. If that continues and the PKI is cleaned up... we will have a new day in Indonesia.*
>
> —GEORGE BALL, US UNDERSECRETARY OF STATE, OCTOBER 8, 1965

THE US AND OTHER WESTERN STATES have steadfastly denied any responsibility for the terrible violence that followed the alleged coup of October 1, 1965. That violence, they have maintained, was the product of domestic political forces over which outside powers had little, if any, influence.[1] That claim is untrue. There is now clear evidence that in the crucial six months after the alleged coup, Western powers encouraged the army to move forcefully against the Left, facilitated widespread violence including mass killings, and helped to consolidate the political power of the army. In doing so, they helped to bring about the political and physical destruction of the PKI and its affiliates, the removal of Sukarno and his closest associates from political power, their replacement by an army elite led by General Suharto, and a seismic shift in Indonesia's foreign policy toward the West and the capitalist model it advocated.[2] As Australian prime minister Harold Holt joked in a speech to the Australian-American Association in New York City in July 1966, "With 500,000 to 1 million communist sympathizers knocked off, I think it is safe to assume a reorientation has taken place."[3]

The central players in this drama were the United States and United Kingdom, but key allies, including Australia, Germany, and New Zealand,

and regional partners, most notably Malaysia, Thailand, and Japan, ably supported them. While some foreign officials harbored doubts about the culpability of the PKI, and privately discussed the extent and brutality of the killings, few governments expressed any opposition to the violence or army's seizure of power. Moreover, despite the Cold War context, even the Soviet Union and its bloc members adopted a position of passivity and silence with respect to the violence, and quickly adjusted to the new military regime. Only China and on a much smaller scale Sweden expressed any real concern about the violence or criticism of the army takeover.

The concerted campaign by foreign powers had three principal elements. The first was a pattern of secret assurances to the army leadership of political support and noninterference in Indonesia's internal affairs. These assurances were intended to encourage the army to act forcefully against the Left and amounted to a green light for the violence that ensued. The second was a sophisticated psychological warfare campaign designed to tarnish the PKI and Sukarno, and stir up opposition to them both inside Indonesia and abroad. Set in motion within a few days of the supposed coup, that operation spread inflammatory and misleading information, much of it based on army propaganda, which encouraged widespread violence and silenced critical or skeptical voices. The third element of the campaign was a carefully calibrated program of material assistance to the army in the form of rice, cotton, communications equipment, medical supplies, cash, and possibly weapons, thereby facilitating and effectively rewarding the army's campaign against the PKI and Sukarno. In all these ways, Western powers—but most especially the United States and the United Kingdom—share responsibility for what today we would call crimes against humanity.

Encouraging the Army

Western officials sensed quickly that the failed "coup" of October 1 offered an ideal opportunity to destroy the PKI and ease Sukarno from power, and they were determined that the opportunity should be exploited. To that end, they readily embraced the army's plan to pin the blame for the killing of the generals on the PKI and use that questionable claim as a pretext for an all-out assault on the left. At the same time, they realized that any overt expression of support for the army on their part would be counterproductive, and so decided early on that any assistance would have to be clandestine.

With that in mind, they sought out and maintained secret contacts with army leaders and other anticommunist groups, while avoiding all but the most cursory contact with President Sukarno and his cabinet. They also coordinated closely with their allies to provide secret assurances of support and noninterference to the army while it "dealt with" the PKI. In all these efforts, the governments involved exhibited a bland indifference to the credible and mounting reports of massive arrests, sweeps, and killings. In fact, Western support for the army solidified as it demonstrated its "resolve" through such campaigns.

ASSURANCES AND SILENCE

In the days and weeks after the alleged coup, senior US officials reported with enthusiasm on the unfolding campaign against the PKI and its affiliates.[4] In a phone call on October 8, 1965, for example, Undersecretary of State Ball told the vice president that

> the Indonesian business is developing in a way that looks encouraging. The Moslems have burned the PKI headquarters in Djakarta last night and they seem to be moving against the Communists around the country.... For the first time, the Army is disobeying Sukarno. If that continues and the PKI is cleaned up ... we will have a new day in Indonesia.[5]

If US officials had any concern at this stage, it was that their Indonesian Army friends might not act quickly or forcefully enough against the PKI and Sukarno. In a memorandum to the White House, dated October 5, the CIA noted that "the US Embassy in Djakarta estimates that the Indonesian Army must now act quickly if it is to exploit its opportunity to move against the PKI."[6] And after noting that the Indonesian Army had published gruesome photos of the dead generals in all newspapers, the Johnson administration's Indonesian Working Group commented, "The major question is whether the Army will capitalize on the feelings aroused by the death of its generals and move to a showdown with the PKI."[7] Two days later, on October 7, the CIA wrote, "The US Embassy comments that there is danger the Army may settle for action against those directly involved in the murder of the Generals and permit Sukarno to get much of his power back."[8] In other words, embassy officials favored broad, arbitrary attacks against PKI members rather than targeted police action against those who might actually have been guilty of a crime. The CIA

FIGURE 7.1. Generals Nasution (left) and Suharto at a gathering in September 1966. (New York Times/Camera Press/Redux Pictures)

conveyed that message to the highest authorities, including President Johnson, and as far as one can tell from the documentary record, it was never challenged or contradicted.

To ensure that the opportunity to crush the PKI and drive Sukarno from power would not be squandered, the United States acted to assure the army leadership of its support and encourage it to act more forcefully. To that end, almost immediately after the supposed coup, US officials sought out and maintained close contacts with key anti-Sukarno officers. Beyond the goal of gathering information about army plans, the main purpose of these contacts was to provide reassurances of US political, economic, and military support. Ambassador Green cabled Washington to propose that he "indicate clearly to key people in Army such as Nasution and Suharto our desire to be of assistance where we can."[9]

The central problem was how to support the army without appearing to be doing so. The problem was twofold: if the army were seen to be backed by the United States and its allies, it would be an easy target for criticism from Sukarno and the Left generally, and such criticism could greatly weaken the army's political position and popular legitimacy. In addition, the army leadership had to consider the powerful residue of support for Sukarno (and the PKI) within its own ranks and among its officer corps. Any sign that Suharto and Nasution were working with outside powers to undermine Sukarno or even the PKI might easily lead to a backlash within the army, to a revival of Sukarno's position, or to their displacement by other officers.

These considerations led to the early conclusion that to be of maximum benefit to the army, any support from the United States (and its allies) would have to be covert. On October 14, 1965, the US Embassy outlined the logic of that position:

> Main reason we must move cautiously is that we will handicap Army if our support shows, at least as long as Sukarno is head of state and government.... In this context anything we can do for Army will obviously have to be of very discreet or covert nature. Within those limitations and on case by case basis, I believe we can: (A) do kindly things which express our true nature.... (B) Do things which will help Indonesia as a whole where we can channel such help indirectly as in case of Title III PL480 food for welfare organizations.... (C) Find way to reassure Army of our sympathy when they are uncertain, as with their concern over Confrontation.... (D) *Help Army by keeping our mouths shut here and elsewhere.*[10]

In short, the apparent absence of foreign involvement was a deliberate illusion. Far from precluding the provision of assistance and support to the army and its allies, the policy of silence simply dictated that support would be provided on a strictly clandestine basis. As the State Department wrote in mid-1966, "Until late March, our major policy on developments in Indonesia was silence.... This policy remains generally sound, particularly in light of the wholesale killings that have accompanied the transition.... While continuing this public position, we have throughout made it privately clear that we are ready at the right time to begin making limited material contributions to help the new leaders get established."[11] It was against the backdrop of such silence that the army was able to conduct its campaign of violence against the Left without fear of criticism or challenge.

Beyond general expressions of support and a policy of deliberate silence, the United States and its allies also discussed what more might be done to encourage the army to act forcefully against the Left and Sukarno. Just two weeks after the alleged coup, the United States and United Kingdom settled on a joint strategy. The plan was to provide Generals Suharto and Nasution with secret assurances that the two countries would do nothing to interfere while the army undertook the "necessary task" of dealing with the PKI.

The plan was proposed by British ambassador Gilchrist less than a week after the alleged coup and was quickly embraced by the United Kingdom's Office of the Political Advisor to the Commander in Chief for the Far East, in Singapore. In a cable to the Foreign Office, the political adviser's office agreed that "we should get word to the generals that we shall not attack them whilst they are chasing the PKI" in order to "ensure that the Army is not distracted from what we consider to be a necessary task."[12] These deliberations laid the basis for a crucial joint US-UK intervention just two weeks after the alleged coup. An October 13 cable from the Department of State to the US Embassy in London outlined the plan:

> 1. You will have been briefed [*words deleted*] on subject assurances to Indonesians about our and UK intention not to attack them or otherwise take advantage of Army-PKI fight. 2. Department (Berger) today reviewed subject with British Embassy (Trench) pointing out that we believe most effective step would be to give Indonesians quiet but official reassurance in general terms re our intentions ... and handed him following language which we would pass to Indonesians through appropriate channels.... "[W]e wish to assure you that we have no intention of interfering in Indonesian affairs, directly or indirectly. Second, we have good reason to believe that none of our allies intend any offensive actions against Indonesia."[13]

In a follow-up cable to the US Embassy in Jakarta, the State Department noted that the language of the message had been approved with minor amendments, saying, "You may pass via [US military attaché Colonel Ethel] who may make clear message originates [from] Washington but should not present [it] in writing. In view [of] its importance, you may wish to reiterate it to Nasution and other military leaders through other secure channels if available."[14] The next day, the embassy reported with evident satisfaction that

> Colonel Ethel conveyed to Nasution's aide today our oral message.... Aide took it down on a piece of paper and said he would give it to Nasution within the hour. He commented to effect that this was just what was needed by way of assurances that we (the Army) weren't going to be hit from all angles as we moved to straighten things out here.[15]

As the Americans and British surely understood and intended, this confidential promise of noninterference—delivered directly to General Nasution—represented a crucial reassurance to the army that it had the political support of two powerful states. It constituted, in effect, a bright green light for the army to continue and even accelerate its campaign of violence against the Left.

CONDONING VIOLENCE

By late October 1965, Western officials began to express greater confidence in the army's resolve in destroying the PKI. That confidence appeared to grow in November as it became apparent that a major campaign of violence was under way, though there was concern that the army might not be willing to finish the job by removing Sukarno. When the army finally seized power in mid-March 1966, Western officials lavished praise on Suharto for his skill in bringing about a victory by "moderate forces." At no point during these critical six months (or after) did any Western government utter a word of criticism of the individuals and institutions responsible for the killings on the back of which Suharto had engineered his takeover. On the contrary, at every opportunity they condoned and encouraged it.

In a cable to the State Department, dated October 20—two days after the RPKAD began its reign of terror in Central Java—Ambassador Green reported that the army was "working hard at destroying PKI and I, for one, have increasing respect for its determination and organization in carrying out this crucial assignment."[16] A week later, on October 28, the embassy approvingly reported that "to date Army has done far better than expected. It has gone ahead with attacks on PKI despite well-known and frequently expressed wish of President that these attacks stop. In general, we believe top Army leadership prepared to continue go against President's wishes in order to make real clean up of Communists and their allies (including Subandrio)."[17]

By November, Western embassy reports were referring to "killings on a very wide scale," "slaughter," and "massacres," and accurately describing the army's key role in this violence. But embassy officials went out of their way to stress that their governments supported the army's repressive actions. Thus, at the end of a report outlining systematic army-backed purges, arrests, and killings in Central Java, the US Embassy's deputy chief of mission (Francis J. Galbraith) wrote that he had "made clear [to a senior army officer] that Embassy and USG generally sympathetic with and admiring of what Army doing."[18] That report was copied to the White House, the CIA, the National Security Agency, and the USIS, and there is no record of any objection to the position it conveyed.

By early 1966, Western officials were fully aware of the extraordinary scale of the violence. In January, Canadian authorities were informed by the respected Indonesian ambassador in Ottawa that as many as 500,000 people had likely been killed by that date.[19] In mid-February, the British and Australian Embassies concluded that the number killed might be significantly higher than 400,000. That conclusion was reported in a confidential cable to the Foreign Office, dated February 23, 1966, by British ambassador Gilchrist.[20] It was based on the account he had received from the Swedish ambassador, Edelstam, who had recently returned from a tour of Central and East Java with the Swedish head of Ericsson-Indonesia and his Indonesian wife. "The Ambassador and I had discussed the killings before he left," Gilchrist wrote, "and he had found my suggested figure of 400,000 dead quite incredible. His enquiries have led him to consider it a very serious under-estimate." Gilchrist shared this information with US ambassador Green, who then cabled Washington, explaining, "British Ambassador informed me that as a result of calculations by his Embassy as well as Australians, a total of about 400,000 killed as a result of the Sept 30 Affair had been agreed ... but that Swedish Ambassador determined figure of 400,000 for country 'far too conservative.'"[21] Western embassy officials also knew that the killings were being committed "either by the army directly or ... strong-arm groups ... acting with army support," they were being committed "in circumstances of great brutality," and they must be arousing "widespread bitterness and disappointment."[22] Under the circumstances, it is striking that—with the sole exception of the Swedish ambassador—those officials voiced no protest and expressed no concern about the killings.

A short time later, moreover, these same officials were praising Suharto's March 11 move against Sukarno as "constitutional" and "bloodless," as though it were quite unrelated to the violence that preceded it and was still going on in some parts of the country. In a cable to the Foreign Office dated March 18, 1966, for example, Gilchrist offered high praise for Suharto's achievement. Concurring with a colleague's comment that Suharto had "the courage of Patton and the intelligence of Montgomery," he said without apparent irony that the general's seizure of power "must be one of the most sweeping, yet skillfully and constitutionally engineered purges of government in a world where violence and lawlessness in the change of governments has become all too familiar."[23] Likewise, in a political assessment written in early April 1966, US Embassy official Edward Masters avoided any mention of the violence. Instead, he wrote that "moderate political forces" had succeeded in ousting Sukarno in "a circuitous, peculiarly Javanese fashion which has cost few casualties and has preserved national unity."[24]

The indifference of Western powers—and the violence they thereby condoned and abetted—was also facilitated by the silence of key international organizations, most notably the United Nations. One possible reason for that silence was the fact that Indonesia had angrily withdrawn from the organization in January 1965, thereby dampening any enthusiasm its members and deliberative bodies may have had for raising concerns. Another, and more likely, reason was that Western states and their regional allies saw no advantage in raising questions at the United Nations about developments they regarded as broadly favorable to their interests. Whether by design or inattention, the United Nations' silence in the face of the antileftist violence of 1965–66 arguably expanded the moral and political space within which that violence was able and likely to spread. That effect was exacerbated by the absence in 1965 of anything approaching the powerful international human rights organizations and networks that had emerged by the late 1970s and 1980s. For example, while Amnesty International had been founded in 1963, it was another ten years before it gained the traction and reputation, let alone the basic research capacity, to take on human rights crises in more than a handful of well-known trouble spots.

SKEPTICS AND CRITICS

It is worth highlighting that acquiescence, covert support, and silence were not in any sense the only possible responses to the army's seizure of power and one-sided violence that ensued. Indeed, not all states or organizations were so easily convinced of PKI responsibility for the apparent coup attempt. Nor was there unanimity that widespread violence was the appropriate response to the crisis or that army rule represented the best possible outcome. Dutch, Australian, and even some British officials, for instance, expressed skepticism about the PKI's culpability and army's reliability, while Sweden's ambassador voiced serious concern about the campaign of violence against the Left. There was some muted criticism from the Soviet Union. But the strongest public criticism came from China, which condemned attacks on the PKI and its affiliates, and on Chinese nationals, while extending a welcome mat to Indonesian leftists seeking refuge from the violence.[25]

Among the first to express doubts about army claims of PKI responsibility and the wisdom of backing the army as a solution were Dutch government officials. According to a British cable of October 7, the Dutch representative to NATO thought it was "unlikely that the Communist Party had instigated the coup."[26] A Dutch official (Rookmaker) in The Hague told the British ambassador there that he doubted that the PKI or Sukarno were behind the supposed coup, and expressed strong reservations about the Indonesian Army leadership: "Rookmaker has emphasised to me," the ambassador wrote, "that it would be a grave mistake to regard the generals as knights in shining armour who have only to suppress Communism for all to be well. Several of them are notoriously corrupt and poor material for popular leadership."[27]

Somewhat surprisingly, perhaps, Australia's Department of External Affairs also expressed early doubts about the culpability of the PKI and Sukarno in the killing of the generals. In an October 14 cable to its High Commission in London, the department noted that while Sukarno probably had some prior knowledge of the plot, we "doubt whether he would have condoned murder." The department also expressed caution in attributing to the PKI a central role in the apparent coup: "PKI personnel certainly participated in the events of 1st October but it is unlikely that the Party was directing the operation. It appears to have been ready to exploit a situation of which it was aware but which was not its creation."[28]

Even some British officials were skeptical of US enthusiasm for getting immediately into bed with the army—mainly because of continued concern over Indonesia's Confrontation with Malaysia. An exchange among officials in London, for example, revealed anxiety about the prospect of a regime that would come to power with strong US economic and military backing. "It is undeniable that a strong military regime would be preferable to a communist regime. However, a strong military regime which had not called off Confrontation with Malaysia would be very awkward for us, possibly even worse than Sukarno's regime before the coup."[29] And in a letter to a member of its NATO delegation, the Foreign Office spelled out its disagreement with the US view that the situation in Indonesia was almost entirely domestic: "Unfortunately, some Americans tend to have their eyes so focused on the internal struggle for power that they are brushing aside the significance of Confrontation." The Foreign Office suggested that the official should tell his NATO colleagues "that attitudes towards Confrontation continue to be our acid test for discriminating between one Indonesian faction and another."[30]

There was also pushback from neutralist middle powers, most notably Swedish ambassador Edelstam, who shook Jakarta's easy diplomatic consensus by traveling through Java, North Sumatra, and Sulawesi in the first half of 1966 to investigate the killings for himself; no other ambassador had done anything remotely like that.[31] Apart from his stunning conclusion that the figure of 400,000 killed was a serious underestimate, the ambassador's reports stand in stark contrast to those of other embassies in their clear expression of concern and even revulsion at the behavior of the Indonesian Army. In one report dated May 13, 1966, for example, he explicitly compared the events in Indonesia to scenes from Nazi Germany. "The circumstances," he wrote, "are reminiscent of the persecution of the Jews in the 1930s in Nazi Germany and of the Greek minority in Istanbul between 1955 and 1965."[32]

The Soviet Union and its bloc partners did not immediately respond to the events of October 1 or the repression of leftists that followed.[33] In part, that hesitation was a product of the Sino-Soviet rift that led the Soviets to judge that under Chinese influence, the PKI and Sukarno had indeed been behind the apparent coup attempt and, in some sense, had got what they deserved for being so undisciplined.[34] In part, too, it reflected a concern that the wrong move might jeopardize the repayment of a debt on the order of $1 billion and drive the country closer to the West.[35] Eventually, however, Soviet officials did condemn the killings. By one account, for example, the Soviet ambassador in Jakarta complained to General Nasution about the persecution of leftists. And when the massacres began in earnest in November 1965, the Soviet foreign minister, Anastas Mikoyan, reportedly expressed official concern about the repression, referring to it as "white terror."[36] Despite such criticism, the Soviet Union and its allies ultimately sought accommodation with the new military regime.

Perhaps not surprisingly, the most pointed criticism of the army's moves after October 1 came from the People's Republic of China. Jakarta diplomats noted, for instance, that Chinese officials did not lower their embassy's flag to half-mast on the day of the generals' funeral. Official Chinese protests and denunciations became more vocal after demonstrators began to turn against Chinese institutions and individuals, resulting in the burning of a Chinese university and an assault on the headquarters of the Chinese commercial counselor by security forces in mid-October.[37] China lodged an official protest against that attack, charging that it had been carried out by "Indonesian troops" that had struck a commercial attaché and searched their premises for documents. The note demanded an apology, punishment for the "culprits and their instigators," and a guarantee against similar incidents in the future.[38] Over the next few weeks, Radio Peking and the *People's Daily* issued an ever-growing number of "vitriolic protests, demands and evaluations of events in Indonesia."[39] And in late

October, the *People's Daily* reportedly described the September 30th Movement as having acted "against a subversive movement engineered by the CIA."[40] Chinese criticism reached new heights in early 1966 following an attack on the Chinese Embassy by anticommunist students and the army. The Indonesian Army responded by accusing China of "Yellow Neo-Imperialism."[41] Although China's protests tended to focus on Indonesia's treatment of its own nationals or Chinese Indonesians, it provided a place of refuge for some forty-five hundred Indonesian leftists who were stranded in China or sought protection there after October 1.[42] In 1967, the two countries severed diplomatic relations.

Finally, although they received scant notice in the mainstream media, there were significant protests and campaigns by international organizations and movements—or as Katharine McGregor has called them, "communities of resistance." These included the Afro Asian People's Solidarity Organization, which included some Indonesian leftists stranded in exile after 1965; a network of Dutch socialist women with strong ties to Indonesia; the Dutch-based Indonesia Committee; the International Labour Organization (ILO); and Amnesty International.[43] With the exception of Amnesty International, these organizations were connected to international socialist networks, and their critiques tended to reflect the political and economic preoccupations of the Left rather than highlighting violations of human rights broadly speaking. In a similar vein, the leftist international media voiced criticism not only of the mass killing and detention but also the new regime's economic policies and political directions. The French Communist daily *L'Humanité*, for instance, spoke out consistently against the army's politics and in defense of the Indonesian Left.[44] For a variety of reasons, however, these critical voices were drowned out by the steady drumbeat of support for the army, and never really stood a chance of slowing or reversing the relentless move against the Left.

Psywar

One reason the critics and skeptics were not easily heard was that information about the alleged coup and the violence was deliberately skewed by a sophisticated international propaganda and psywar operation organized by British and US government agencies and their Indonesian Army friends. The campaign, set in motion within just a few days of the events of October 1, was explicitly designed to "blacken" the PKI and Sukarno, strengthen the political position of the army, and hasten Sukarno's removal. Through that campaign, British and US authorities and their allies—including Australia, Germany, Malaysia, and others—effectively encouraged widespread violence amounting to crimes against humanity, while dampening international sympathy for or action on behalf of its victims.

"BLACKEN THE PKI"

Although there was serious doubt, even among Western states, about what had happened on October 1 and who was responsible for it, British and US officials wasted no time in seizing the opportunity to turn the tide against the PKI and Sukarno.[45] An October 5 memorandum from the United Kingdom's Office of the Political Advisor to the Commander in Chief for the Far East to the Foreign Office spelled out the thinking and strategy with admirable clarity:

> It is not in our interests to see the PKI recovering its influence and preparing itself for the day when it will be strong enough to seize power. I submit that we should not miss the present opportunity to use the situation to our advantage. . . . I recommend that we should have no hesitation in doing what we can surreptitiously to blacken the PKI in the eyes of the army and the people of Indonesia. . . . The C-in-C has addressed himself to the Chief of the Defence Staff on this subject.[46]

In its reply of October 6, the Foreign Office fully endorsed the proposal for "unattributable propaganda or psy-war activities which would contribute to weakening the PKI permanently," and offered a number of concrete suggestions for "suitable propaganda themes." These included "PKI brutality in murdering Generals and Nasution's daughter; Chinese interference in particular arms shipments; PKI subverting Indonesia as agents of foreign Communists; fact that Aidit and other prominent Communists went to ground; the virtual kidnapping of Sukarno by Untung and PKI; etc., etc." The same memo underscored the need for great caution and secrecy in conducting the operation, and provided the following specific guidance:

> We want to act quickly while Indonesians are still off balance, but treatment will need to be subtle, e.g.:
>
> (a) all activities should be strictly unattributable;
> (b) British participation or cooperation should be carefully concealed;
> (c) we should cooperate as closely as possible with the Malaysians;

(d) material should preferably appear to originate from Pakistan or the Philippines;

(e) overt Malaysian, and British, attitude should be one of strict non-interference.[47]

At precisely the same time, US officials were hatching almost identical psywar plans. A cable from the embassy to Washington dated October 3, for example, advised that Voice of America (VOA) reporting on the apparent coup attempt should "stick to the facts for now," but at the same time focus on PKI and air force responsibility: "Factual information indicating PKI [role] in Sept 30 movement and involvement leadership Air Force, particularly Omar Dani, might be usefully worked into general content of broadcast if it can be done subtly. Might be especially effective if used in third country broadcasts for background briefing press."[48]

Behind the scenes, US and British officials had begun to coordinate their propaganda plans.[49] On October 5, an officer with the US Embassy in London shared with his British counterparts several cables from the US Embassy in Jakarta "updating the situation and suggesting publicity guidance" for the VOA, USIS, and other agencies.[50] Those telegrams offered clear direction to US agencies to stress the PKI's alleged role in the alleged coup and emphasize its brutality, while at the same time playing down any signs of splits within the military. Following army cues, they also suggested stirring up memories of the 1948 Madiun uprising. One cable, for example, advised that

> fast moving events require immediate [repeat] immediate treatment. For now, play up communist participation, go easy on mention Sukarno and Army–Air Force differences and repeatedly emphasize horrible mutilation of Army Generals, shock of Indonesian people and brutality exhibited by those involved in the coup. References to similar brutalities by PKI at Madiun in 1948 may be usefully insinuated.[51]

As events on the ground unfolded, the focus of the US and British psywar campaign expanded. PKI culpability and brutality remained the dominant themes, but these were now supplemented with reporting and commentary on the alleged (but never proven) role of China in the supposed coup and its connection with the PKI. This focus provided an opportunity to tarnish both the PKI and China, and at the same time score propaganda points against North Vietnam. In a cable dated October 11, 1965, for example, the US Embassy suggested that broadcasts inside Indonesia should insinuate a Chinese role in the events of October 1: "For

Indonesia, we should claim Chicoms were trying to gain control and end Indo independence, using PKI and other elements under their influence, even some at highest level of GOI." For non-Indonesia broadcasts, the embassy recommended a focus on the purported Chinese strategy of violence and terrorism, commenting that the PKI had followed this strategy with disastrous consequences.[52]

What is striking about these efforts to link China to the September 30th Movement and PKI culpability is that US officials themselves had doubts about the veracity of the claim of a Chinese role, and lacked even the most rudimentary evidence to support it. Summarizing a detailed analysis of the alleged coup attempt, for instance, the US Embassy in Jakarta admitted in late October 1965 that China's involvement had not been proven: "There [is] circumstantial evidence that Peking aware of or perhaps even had hand in plot but this not established."[53]

At about the same time, the US consulate in Hong Kong expressed strong doubt about the allegations of Chinese involvement in the alleged coup, noting that those allegations were based solely on circumstantial evidence and were being circulated by elements with an obvious political agenda. The consulate also pointed out that any evidence that the United States was spreading this story was likely to undermine its credibility. Despite these reservations, the consulate's cable concluded with recommendations on how best to spread the unfounded allegations of China's role in the plot: "In sum, for the time being, at least, believe best means of spreading idea of Chicom complicity are first, to let events and statements in Indonesia tell their own story; second, continuation covert propaganda; third, conversations in other countries as emerging evidence of Indonesian and local circumstances permit."[54]

USING ARMY MEDIA

Western diplomats understood well that in the days following the purported coup, print and broadcast media had become crucial fields in the political struggle. They also knew that the army had a clear advantage in that war. The army's most obvious advantage, as discussed in an earlier chapter, was that within two days of the alleged coup, it had closed down all opposition media outlets and exercised almost complete control over those that remained open.

As the US Embassy wrote on October 5, "*Antara* news service and all newspapers have been suspended with the exception of two army newspapers which publish with an increasingly anti-communist tone. Radio

Indonesia, the main source of news for the population as a whole, is tightly controlled by the army."[55] Describing the army's dominant political position a few days later, the embassy remarked, "Additional asset is the fact that Army controls information media.... [It is] taking effective stand against 30 Sept Movement and its supporters (PKI).... Army continues exercise tight rein over press. *Indonesian Daily Mail* appeared on streets today listing Army Information Director Soeghandi as Chief Editor."[56] US officials were aware that the news coverage provided by the army-controlled press was highly sensationalistic and deliberately provocative.[57] As the CIA wrote in a memo on its covert operations in Indonesia, the army leadership had already "instituted psychological warfare mechanisms, control of media prerequisite to influencing public opinion and have harassed or halted Communist output."[58]

It was against this background—and with this knowledge—that the US government decided to use Indonesian media stories and army press briefings as the sources for its own stories and guidance to the media.[59] On October 6, the State Department wrote,

> We plan and are already carrying out VOA and information program based on citation Indonesian sources and official statements without at this stage injecting US editorializing. At least in present situation we believe ample such material pointing finger at PKI and playing up brutality of September 30 rebels is available from Radio Djakarta and Indo press, but we will look at situation again if in coming days or weeks these sources dry up. Similar cover will be given by VOA to Indonesian situation in key broadcasts other than to Indonesia.[60]

This was a disingenuous move, deliberately calculated to facilitate the dissemination of scurrilous and inflammatory army propaganda, while maintaining the pretext of simply reporting "the facts" without "editorializing." As an official in the British Embassy in Washington said at the time, "The sort of thing which interests the Americans is the line being taken in the two army newspapers attempting to link the PKI with the 30th September coup, to work up emotions about the dead generals, demand the banning of the PKI Youth Wing and so on."[61]

Notwithstanding their condescending comment about the kinds of stories the Americans liked, the British used precisely the same strategy, as revealed in an October 13 Commonwealth Relations Office telegram to the British High Commission in Canberra. After repeating the psywar guidelines spelled out in the October 6 Foreign Office cable cited above, the telegram added the following instruction on the use of army-controlled media: "We are seeking to put these ideas across to Indonesians by means of overt broadcasting from BBC, Radio Malaysia, etc., drawing on the often helpful output of Djakarta Radio, Army newspapers, etc., particularly while Indonesia's own communications media are partially inoperative."[62]

An exchange between the British Embassy in Jakarta and the Foreign Office in late November provided evidence of a broad willingness among British officials to employ army propaganda. It revealed, for example, that Gilchrist's account of the alleged mutilation of the generals was taken directly from an army-controlled paper, the *Daily Mail*. Mimicking the sensational prose of the army press, moreover, Gilchrist added the following commentary: "It was during the previous hour [on October 1, 1965], or perhaps rather less, that the revolting mutilations with knives and scissors had taken place."[63] Foreign Office officials then repeated the story without caveat, despite the valid denials by President Sukarno, among others. One official (Tonkin) commented that "the atrocity story will be included in SEAMU's output, in spite of Sukarno's denial on 12 December, that the Generals were mutilated." Officers of several departments then duly signed the document.[64]

There is also evidence that US and other Western officials willingly adjusted their own coverage in accordance with direct and indirect Indonesian Army requests. In a cable dated October 7, 1965, for instance, the US Embassy wrote,

> Have indirect request from Indo Army not [repeat] not to unduly emphasize that Army is seeking revenge against Communists. Army feels it has hands full restoring order and stability without creating impression it going to massacre Communists.... This does not mean that we should let up on the PKI or soft pedal our efforts to associate Communists with the Sept 30 Movement. These should be stressed. It does mean that we should go easy on any speculation or inference that there will be an Army vendetta against all Communists and should avoid pinning anticommunist label on Army.[65]

Australian and German officials showed a similar willingness to influence their own country's media coverage in response to the Indonesian Army's needs and preferences, and on the basis of its propaganda.[66] Richard Tanter writes, for example, that the Australian Department of External Affairs "worked systematically to ensure that RA [Radio Australia] coverage of events in Indonesia conformed to its guidelines," and notes that "at the height of the killings, the Indonesian army requested the assistance of the Department to ensure that RA reported on Indonesian politics in army's preferred manner."[67] Likewise, Bernd Schaefer reports that in the aftermath of the alleged coup, the German Embassy in Jakarta "helped to orchestrate West German press coverage via the German news agency DPA correspondent Ulrich Grundinski." In addition to providing Grundinski with embassy facilities to prepare and transmit his reports, Schaefer notes, embassy officials ensured that he had access to all army-supplied information.[68]

Indonesian Army officers also made direct requests for propaganda assistance from friendly regional governments. One of the key figures in those approaches was Brigadier General Sukendro, a former army intelligence officer and minister of state, and the only member of General Yani's brain trust not to have been killed on October 1.[69] At a meeting with a Malaysian Foreign Ministry official in early November, 1965, Sukendro spelled out army plans to tarnish the PKI and undermine the foreign minister, Subandrio. To that end, he requested Malaysian government assistance in the "character, political assassination [of] Subandrio. Sukendro to supply background information." Sukendro also made a specific request for treatment by the official Suara Malaysia radio: "Sukarno should not be attacked but PKI atrocities [and] 30 Sept coup emphasized.... Tape recorded statements [of] Untung and others re 30 Sept coup which were furnished [to] GOM will not be broadcast [by] Suara Malaysia until [Indonesian] Army gives green light."[70]

Given the clear evidence that Western governments initiated covert psywar and propaganda operations within days of the October 1 action, and that the operations focused on the print and broadcast media, it is not unreasonable to think that their agents were also involved in a covert psywar campaign inside Indonesia itself. Suspicion has centered on the media blitz that was set in motion in the weeks and months after the alleged coup, as described in chapter 6. Anderson has argued, for instance, that the coordination and sophistication of that operation was beyond the capability of a disorganized Army Information Bureau, raising the possibility of foreign, especially CIA and MI6, involvement in coordinating and funding the domestic media campaign.[71]

One of the more suspicious media events of the period was the sudden emergence of the sensationalist anti-PKI newspaper *Api* only days after the alleged coup and its disappearance after the population had been provoked to violence. The suspicion that the paper was part of a psywar operation with international links is deepened by the fact that it was owned and published by the former army intelligence officer Sukendro.[72] Perhaps more germane to the question of his possible involvement in a psywar operation, in the post-October 1 period Sukendro served as a key point of contact between the army and a range of foreign governments, traveling widely through Asia and Europe to secure economic and military aid and support. Given his role as owner and publisher of *Api*, moreover, and his requests for Malaysian propaganda assistance in tarnishing the PKI and Subandrio, it is more than likely that those discussions and negotiations also encompassed psywar media strategy and planning.

FRIENDLY JOURNALISTS

A further element of the international psywar campaign was the cultivation of "friendly" foreign correspondents and journalists by various Western governments. As an October 13 cable to the British Embassy in Canberra explained, UK government officials were doing what they could to stimulate "helpful" media commentary. "We are giving background guidance to Press with a view particularly of stimulating helpful comment as widely as possible, especially in non-aligned countries. And we are trying to get the right matter into newspapers which are read in Indonesia, e.g., *Straits Times*." The telegram then asked that Australian and New Zealand authorities be informed of these plans and invited to cooperate in the propaganda effort. "We should be grateful for their views," the cable says, "and any cooperation which they may feel able to offer in these short term propaganda activities." Finally, the telegram alluded to more covert activities to be discussed through different channels: "We are also considering more surreptitious activities, of which we will tell the Australians through other channels."[73] The Australians were eager to cooperate in the propaganda effort. In October or November 1965, an Australian Embassy official, Richard Woolcott, proudly cabled Canberra to report that "we are now in a position to influence the content of leaders in practically all major metropolitan newspapers."[74]

Without a doubt, the US government was doing the same thing—providing briefings, access, and encouragement to sympathetic journalists in the expectation that they would spread helpful stories about the events in Indonesia. On October 4, in a telephone conversation with the influential, Pulitzer Prize–winning *New York Times* columnist and associate editor James Reston, Undersecretary of State Ball offered up a preferred story line, saying that "he did not know whether he wanted this attributed to the Administration but anybody could say on his own that the PKI ... was behind this and Sukarno was trying to play his tactic to restore his balance and bring PKI in." Ball added that "this is a very critical time for the Army—if the Army does move they have [the] strength to wipe the earth with the PKI and if they don't, they may not have another chance."[75] A staunch supporter of US government policy in Vietnam and reliably anticommunist, Reston responded, "Everyone is entitled to hate someone and he [Sukarno] is my man.... [W]e can do without him." Perhaps unsurprisingly, a Reston article that later described the annihilation of the PKI and ouster of Sukarno was titled "A Gleam of Light in Asia."[76]

In February 1966, the embassy expressed concern that the United States was missing a chance to convey the facts and implications of what was happening in Indonesia. To remedy the situation, it proposed calling on reliable US journalists and giving them background briefings based on recent embassy reporting, so that they could spread the word through the US and world media. Two journalists mentioned in the cable were Jerry King of the *New York Times* and Ted Stannard of UPI, "both seasoned, discreet correspondents known to Embassy."[77] Other journalists no doubt also received briefings from the embassy and Indonesian Army, with the result that few offered accounts that departed in any significant respect from the official line. Indeed, most US journalists repeated the hyperbolic stories of the army-controlled press without critical comment, even though those reports were known at the time to be of dubious validity. Brian May writes, for example, that one Western correspondent "reported that the bodies [of the generals] had been decapitated and dismembered. But photographs provided by the Army showed no dismemberment; and Brig. Gen Sugandhi who saw the bodies when they were retrieved, said there was none."[78]

Economic and Military Assistance

Alongside secret political assurances and psywar operations, the US government and its allies began almost immediately after October 1 to provide the army leadership with covert material assistance, in the form of communications equipment, large quantities of rice, cotton, medical supplies, cash, logistical support, and possibly weapons.[79] And when the army finally seized power through the ostensibly "bloodless" coup of March 11, 1966, and Confrontation was ended later that year, the aid floodgates opened, and various states rushed in to supply unprecedented levels of economic and military assistance.[80] Although it was ultimately less important, it is worth noting that the Soviet Union and its allies continued to provide economic and military aid to Indonesia throughout this period, threatening to stop it only if Indonesia's new rulers should refuse to pay their debts.[81]

While in dollar terms the amount of aid in the first six months after October 1 was relatively small, it was carefully calibrated to ensure the maximum political benefit to the army while weakening or destroying its rivals. The documentary record makes it clear, for example, that an exception to the generally cautious posture on aid was explicitly made for any assistance that might bring about or encourage the destruction of the PKI and its allies. It is also noteworthy that the flow of material aid to the army and its allies continued, and even increased, as the campaign of violence accelerated and Western governments learned more about it in November–December 1965. On December 3, for instance, Ambassador Green called for the quick provision of emergency rice through covert channels to "tip the balance" in favor of the "friendly" forces now positioning for power.[82] It is difficult to escape the conclusion that the wholesale physical annihilation of the Left in the six months after the alleged coup was seen as evidence that the army was on the right path and was encouraged.

THE POLITICAL LOGIC OF AID

Discussion among Western officials about possible aid to the army began almost immediately after the alleged October coup. From the outset those talks weighed the potential value of aid against the political dangers that public knowledge of such aid might pose for the "good guys." In a top secret cable to the Foreign Office, dated October 11, 1965, British ambassador Gilchrist noted that notwithstanding remaining doubts about the culpability of the PKI and Sukarno, his Australian and US counterparts in Jakarta shared a desire to back the army to help them crush the PKI. "I may add," Gilchrist wrote, "that my Australian colleague seems equally anxious with the Americans to consolidate the position of the Generals by meeting their main deficiencies—money and rice. The aim—to enable them to settle with the Communists once and for all."[83]

By the third week of October, the US government's policy on short-term aid to Indonesia had been more or less worked out. A State Department memo, dated October 22, made it clear that targeted material aid would be provided to the army, that to avoid political problems for both parties it would have to be covert, and that it would be responsive to expressed army needs:

> In view of foregoing, we assume Indos will want to avoid anything looking like overt GOI turn toward US. For short run our assistance to them would probably have to be on covert or semi-covert basis related specific, small, ad hoc needs. We quite willing go along with this. In addition showing Indos we will not take advantage of difficult internal situation to intervene, we recognize probable need for passage of time to allow cooling off period.... If real PKI insurgency situation develops we would, of course, try to meet Army needs as expressed to us by Army.[84]

The US Embassy in Jakarta concurred with the state department's assessment, stressing that the purpose of the aid should be to bolster the political position of the army against its rivals. It advised that "small amounts of carefully placed assistance [be] given without publicity [*words deleted*] to strengthen the hands of those we want to see win in the current mortal struggle for political power." Thus, if the embassy were asked for such aid, "a one-shot secret USG contribution might be considered [*lines deleted*]. I suggest the department now explore the availability of funds for this purpose in order to prepare for prompt reply [to] any such request and also explore how this operation could be done."[85]

As this and later cables show, the primary purpose of US aid was political; it was intended to help the army consolidate its political position, and simultaneously destroy the PKI and undermine Sukarno. The point was underscored in an embassy cable of November 19, 1965, which discussed plans for aid to Indonesia in advance of planned talks in Bangkok: "Above all," the cable stressed, "we should not provide assistance that will redound to benefit of Sukarno." Then, after spelling out the need for caution in providing any substantial overt aid to the army until its political intentions were clear, it added the caveat that aid to assist the army in crushing the PKI would not be constrained by such considerations: "Carefully placed assistance which will help Army cope with PKI actions [is] different."[86]

Central to all these discussions on aid was rice. As the essential staple food for much of Indonesia, and a key element of the pay packet of both civil servants and army personnel, rice was understood to be vital in helping the army to consolidate its political position. Just over a week after the supposed coup, the State Department wrote to the embassy in Jakarta:

"We['re] interested being in [a] position to assist Indonesian Army in making rice available to meet urgent needs." To that end, the department asked the embassy for estimates of rice stocks and supplies—for the general population and for distribution to civil servants and the armed forces. "In latter connection, your judgment as to whether for near-term, in order to give Army some credit, Army could distribute GOI stocks and publicize distribution in way which would not require large quantities and yet score some points for them."[87]

It was probably no coincidence that just a few days later, there was a sudden drop in the price of rice in Indonesia. According to a story in the NU newspaper *Duta Mayarakat*, the price had fallen because the army had discovered PKI warehouses filled with hoarded rice, which the army was now releasing onto the market.[88] That was a politically valuable spin; in one stroke, it maligned the PKI and scored points for the army. The story also concealed the fact that new rice had been shipped covertly to the army, from friendly countries like Thailand and Japan, with US assistance.[89] As the US Embassy reported on October 21, the "price of rice which was up to 2,000 Rupiahs per liter was down to 900 last Saturday due to releases of rice from local storage and rice seized on PKI premises. Army enabled to make these releases due to impending arrival of some 70,000 tons of rice from Thailand."[90] And as the embassy noted in a separate message, the army's move "forced the price down to pre-coup levels, and the explanation in the kampongs is that once Suharto was put in charge, the rice flowed."[91] The covert food aid strategy was working.

MILITARY SUPPORT

The events of October 1, 1965 also triggered a significant change in the policy of the United States and its allies with respect to military assistance—and the objectives of that aid were again almost entirely political.[92] Within days, US officials began to provide covert military and logistical support to the army, in the form of portable communications equipment, medical supplies, and possibly weapons and ammunition. Though relatively modest in dollar terms, this aid was carefully targeted to lend support and encouragement to the army, especially to Generals Nasution and Suharto, in their campaign against the PKI and Sukarno. In September 1966, by which time "the Army had isolated Sukarno and formally ended Confrontation with Malaysia," a formal military assistance program was resumed, supplying critical backing to army leaders and shielding them from accountability for the violence through which they had come to power.[93]

In response to a request just a few days after the alleged coup attempt, for example, the US Embassy provided General Nasution with the portable communications equipment he had requested. Shortly thereafter, Nasution's senior aide told the US military attaché, Colonel Ethel, that Nasution had "expressed great appreciation for portable communications equipment."[94] In mid-November, the Department of State cabled the embassy to report that "we have just received [a] request for simple communication equipment to enable Army leaders to stay in touch with one another, and [the] matter [is] now under consideration."[95]

US officials saw the provision of modern communications equipment to the army as having both operational and political value. Operationally, such equipment would help army leaders to coordinate their actions in the "delicately balanced struggle" against the PKI and Sukarno. It also made it possible for US intelligence agencies to monitor those operations, giving the United States a picture of army attacks on the PKI.[96] Politically, it would send a strong message of US support and trust in the army that would pay dividends in the months and years ahead. Commenting on the political benefits of providing even limited quantities of such equipment, Ambassador Green wrote, "I am naturally anxious to see that the Army gets equipment best suited their needs. Suggest 303 Committee give this early reconsideration."[97]

US government officials also considered the political advantages and dangers of providing more substantial military and logistical assistance to the army. Three weeks after the alleged coup, the Department of State suggested that the United States might assist the army in transporting troops from the Outer Islands to Java to bolster anticommunist forces there. Embassy officials in Jakarta argued against the idea, however, on the grounds that it would be impossible to keep it a secret and evidence of US involvement would hurt rather than help the army.[98] Nevertheless, US officials continued to support the idea of targeted, covert, military assistance to the army.

In considering such aid, officials made it clear that its central purpose was to maintain "important channels of influence" with army leaders, to "fortify their confidence" that they could be the main actors in saving Indonesia from chaos, and to reassure them that they had "some real friends." Official thinking on the logic of military assistance to the army was spelled out in a State Department cable dated October 29, 1965:

> The Indonesian Army leaders' close service-to-service relations with our military provide important channels of influence. . . . The next few

> days, weeks or months may offer unprecedented opportunities for us to begin to influence people and events, as the military begin to understand problems and dilemmas in which they find themselves.... We should try to fortify their confidence that Indonesia can be saved from chaos, and that Army is the main instrument for saving it.... We should get across that Indonesia and Army have real friends who are ready to help.[99]

The same document referred explicitly to the possible provision of lethal military assistance, noting that "small arms and equipment may be needed to deal with the PKI." Responding to this cable, the embassy remarked, "We agree with general conclusions of Dept's analysis." On the specific subject of arms, it added, "We have already commented on possible need for small arms in another message. It is conceivable that Soviets might supply such items, even while Army is attacking PKI, if Moscow believes this is best way to keep Chicoms out."[100] In a later message, the department noted that it expected it might receive a request from the army for small arms, and that such a request "would involve wider and deeper considerations."[101]

In early November 1965, in response to a request from Sukendro, discussions turned suddenly to the possibility of providing the army with "medical supplies."[102] Some observers have concluded that the terms "medicines" and "medical supplies" in the documentary record were code words for "weapons" and "ammunition."[103] That possibility is explored below. But it is worth stressing that even if the subject of the cables was nothing more than medical supplies, the provision of such aid to the army would have had real political, logistical, and psychological significance. It would have sent a clear signal to the army leadership that the United States supported what they were doing, and would have freed up scarce army resources for use against the PKI.

Exchanges among US officials on the subject of medical supplies make apparent the eagerness of US officials to be of service to the Indonesian Army. In a telegram to the Department of State dated November 4, 1965, the embassy urged a "sympathetic response" to a request for such supplies made by Sukendro on behalf of Suharto and Nasution:

> Army is doing a first-class job here of moving against communists, and by all current indications is the emerging authority in Indonesia.... It is against this background that I believe we should give sympathetic response to Sukendro's request for medicines. This is precisely the kind of item with which we can symbolize to new authority our desire to help.[104]

A second cable, sent on November 5, underscored the perceived importance of the supply of this aid to both US and Indonesian Army officials, and the US government's eagerness to assist. That cable also raises questions about whether the terms medical supplies and medicine might actually refer to something more lethal. The cable, which was passed through the White House, reads in part,

> DCM saw source ... afternoon Nov 5 and carried out instructions.... Source was pleased. He said quantities of vitamins are particularly needed to keep soldiers ... as strong as possible. DCM emphasized that before we could go much further we would have to know a great deal more ... about direction of Army's thinking on political future of Indonesia.[105]

Several aspects of this cable lend credence to suggestions that the subject under discussion might not have been medical supplies at all. For one thing, the great importance attached to the provision of "vitamins" in keeping soldiers "as strong as possible" seems puzzling, as does the deliberate omission of the source's name. Were vitamins really so vital to the Indonesian Army and was their provision really so sensitive that the name of the source could not be mentioned even in a secret cable? It also seems strange that a plan to supply the Indonesian Army with vitamins should have to be passed by the White House for approval. Few cables made their way from Jakarta to the president's desk. Why was this one an exception? Finally, the comment that the US government would "need to know a great deal more" about the army's political thinking before "going further" seems odd, if indeed the subject of the conversation was nothing more than the provision of medical supplies and vitamins.

Whatever the terms medicines, vitamins, and medical supplies actually referred to, their covert delivery to the army was quickily approved by the 303 Committee—the secret NSC committee responsible for coordinating covert government operations—prompting the embassy to write, "Greatly appreciate Deptel 576 authorizing supply of medicines. Believe this is sound investment, defensible on all counts, which in time will yield dividends."[106]

LOGISTICS AND QUIET CASH

Beyond such material aid, there is evidence that US officials provided vital logistical assistance and quiet cash to the army leadership and its allies at the height of the violence. As noted earlier, a journalist reported in 1990 that a US Embassy official in Jakarta, Robert Martens, had supplied the Indonesian Army with lists containing the names of thousands of PKI officials in the months after the alleged coup attempt. According to the journalist Kathy Kadane, "As many as 5,000 names were furnished over a period of months to the Army there, and the Americans later checked off the names of those who had been killed or captured."[107] Despite Martens's later denials of any such intent, these actions almost certainly aided in the death or detention of many innocent people. They also sent a powerful political message that the US government agreed with and supported the army's campaign against the PKI, even as that campaign took its terrible toll in human lives.

US authorities also provided financial assistance to ostensibly civilian groups formed by the army and directly involved in the violence against the PKI as well as other leftists. In early December 1965, for instance, by which time the extent and nature of the violence against the Left was well known to US and other officials, the Department of State authorized a payment of fifty million rupiah to KAP-Gestapu, the stridently anticommunist action front established by the army in early October to crush the September 30th Movement and PKI. In a secret (Roger Channel) cable to Assistant Secretary of State for Far Eastern Affairs William Bundy, Ambassador Green spelled out the plan and logic of the cash transfer as follows:

> This is to confirm my earlier concurrence that we provide Malik with fifty million rupiahs requested by him for the activities of the Kap-Gestapu movement [*1.5 lines of source text not declassified*]. The Kap-Gestapu activities to date have been important factor in the army's program, and judging from the results, I would say highly successful. This army-inspired but civilian-staffed action group is still carrying burden of current repressive efforts targeted against PKI.... The chances of detection or subsequent revelation of our support in this instance are as minimal as any black bag operation can be [*2 lines of source text not declassified*].[108]

In light of this evidence, it is interesting to note that a US Embassy cable of January 20, 1966, reported persistent rumors that the US government, and specifically Green, had been orchestrating anti-Sukarno and anti-PKI protests. Those stories noted that Green was an expert in mobilizing youth demonstrations to overthrow undesirable governments and referred to his "success" in doing that on his previous posting in South Korea.[109] The same cable referred to information received from an "Api

Group source" about Sukarno and Subandrio allegations that the student demonstrations were being orchestrated by "Nekolim."[110] Though the allegations were dismissed out of hand by US officials, the documentary record of Green's support for funding KAP-Gestapu suggests that they were not far off the mark.

Although official documents declassified to date offer no further cases of such "black bag operations," it is reasonable to assume that other individuals and organizations also received some financial assistance.[111] Likely candidates for some quiet cash would have included reliably anticommunist figures and embassy contacts like the Minister of Plantations and Catholic Party chair Frans Seda, Api group figure Darmawan Moenaf, various Masyumi leaders, members of anticommunist action fronts like A. B. Nasution, and an assortment of NU leaders and associates including its vice chair, Z. E. Subchan.[112] Finally, though there is still no definitive documentary record to prove it, it seems likely that some financial aid flowed directly but covertly to individual army officers, including Suharto. As part of a request for material assistance, in November 1965, General Nasution's aide hinted broadly to Green that while Subandrio still had access to government resources and funds, the army's access was limited and that Suharto was "especially short of financing."[113]

AID AND VIOLENCE

One of the more disturbing patterns in the disbursement of economic and military aid in this period was that assistance increased in tandem with evidence of army-supported violence. Indeed, the connection between the provision of aid and political reliability of the army was a recurring motif in diplomatic communications of this period. But the destruction of the PKI was only one part of the picture. Western governments also wanted the army to get rid of Sukarno, and reorient the Indonesian economy toward a free market that they dominated and would benefit foreign capital. The adoption of an expansive aid program remained conditional on the army's willingness to meet that expectation.[114]

In a January 1966 cable to the US Embassy, the State Department clarified that while continuing targeted covert assistance to the army, a more substantial and overt aid program would have to wait until it was clear that "Indo moderates really can and intend to take charge."[115] With Suharto's seizure of power in mid-March 1966, that political condition was at least partially met and the aid began to flow. In the view of US policy makers, the provision of aid at that juncture would have far-reaching political benefits. As the Department of State noted in a cable to the US Embassy in Kuala Lumpur on March 29, 1966, "We believe emergency-type assistance of food and fibers can help to reinforce present non-Communist leaders and thus serve interests of Free World."[116]

Accordingly, at a high-level meeting in Washington in late March 1966, US secretary of state Rusk informed the British ambassador that the United States would be sending fifty thousand tons of rice to Indonesia.[117] An internal State Department memo also noted that arrangements were under way to sell Indonesia seventy-five thousand tons of cotton on generous terms and that the United States was providing quiet support for other kinds of economic assistance including debt rescheduling.[118] In early April, Japan announced plans to provide Indonesia with $30 million in rice and cotton.[119] And in May 1966, the British followed suit, supplying Indonesian authorities with a bilateral aid injection of £1 million.[120] Later that month, Indonesia's new ambassador to Washington met State Department officials to discuss plans for long-term multilateral assistance and debt rescheduling as well as interim bilateral aid. The ambassador told State Department officials that Indonesia's total debt was $2.5 billion—more than they could possibly pay—and that it was therefore hoping for substantial economic assistance, principally from the United States, Germany, Japan, the Netherlands, and the United Kingdom.[121]

In July 1966, Green expressed his enthusiasm about the positive turn of events: "I venture that nowhere in the world in recent years has there been a more dramatic reversal of communist/chicom fortunes than in Indonesia this past year." On that basis, he proposed a wide range of new forms of assistance, including military training, educational exchanges, and "economic aid, including 100,000 bales of cotton, up to 500,000 tons of rice."[122] In August, Green reportedly promised Suharto $500 million in bilateral aid, and in September an individual bearing a letter from Estates Minister Seda requested $50 million of that amount immediately to cover Indonesia's debt to the International Monetary Fund (IMF). During a visit to Washington in September by Foreign Minister Malik, the US government committed to provide Indonesia a further 50,000 tons of rice and 150,000 bales of cotton on generous terms.[123] At about the same time, Green held talks with an Indonesian official, whose name is deleted from the record, about a "short-term assistance package for Indonesia." According to Green's account of the meeting, the unnamed official had discussed the "US offer" with Suharto and reported that "Suharto was appreciative and encouraged by our support which would help move things forward along the stabilization front."[124]

Meanwhile, friendly governments had begun to meet with Indonesian Army officials and technocrats to plan for economic recovery. Those plans encompassed a major program of debt rescheduling, long-term economic and military aid commitments, and the relaxation of restrictions on foreign investment. In 1967, these efforts came together in the form of a new multilateral consortium known as the Inter-Governmental Group on Indonesia, which channeled hundreds of millions of dollars of aid and investment to Indonesia.[125] From the perspective of the World Bank, the IMF, Indonesian leaders, and friendly governments, this multilateral economic assistance program provided the essential foundation for Indonesia's economic recovery and modernization. But the massive flow of aid and foreign investment starting in mid-1966 also had critical political consequences—bolstering the new army regime and whitewashing the massive campaign of violence through which it came to power.

Suharto's seizure of power in mid-March 1966 also triggered a significant increase in military aid, without regard to the army's responsibility for the death and arbitrary imprisonment of hundreds of thousands of civilians. In a memo of October 27, 1966—that is, just months after the worst of the violence had subsided—the US Embassy urged the resumption "soonest" of a full military assistance program. The embassy proposed that among other items, the aid program should encompass "selective non-combat items to help improve morale within the Army and strengthen position of General Suharto and his colleagues."[126] As with economic assistance, the decision to resume military aid was based overwhelmingly on a political calculation: that a regime dominated by the army was the best possible outcome for the United States, and every effort should be made to consolidate its political position.

In short, Western states were not innocent bystanders to unfolding domestic political events following the alleged coup, as so often claimed. On the contrary, starting almost immediately after October 1, the United States, the United Kingdom, and several of their allies set in motion a coordinated campaign to assist the army in the political and physical destruction of the PKI and its affiliates, the removal of Sukarno and his closest associates from political power, their replacement by an army elite led by Suharto, and the engineering of a seismic shift in Indonesia's foreign policy toward the West. They did this through backdoor political reassurances to army leaders, a policy of official silence in the face of mounting violence, a sophisticated international propaganda offensive, and the covert provision of material assistance to the army and its allies. In all these ways, they helped to ensure that the campaign against the Left would continue unabated and its victims would ultimately number in the hundreds of thousands.

CHAPTER EIGHT

Mass Incarceration

The whole household lies sleeping peacefully.
Suddenly they are woken, startled and shaken,
By pounding at the door, the thud of boots.
The nickel-plated pistol points, accusing,
Commanding
Squat down there in that corner
Just in your underpants.
How this scene stays in my memory,
Ambushed as dawn breaks.

—SUDISMAN, PKI GENERAL SECRETARY, "ANALYSIS OF RESPONSIBILITY"

BEYOND THE HALF A MILLION PEOPLE killed in the aftermath of the alleged October coup attempt, many hundreds of thousands were caught up in a juggernaut of arbitrary detention, interrogation, torture, forced labor, and long-term imprisonment carried out at the behest of the Indonesian Army. Like the killings, most of the mass detentions occurred in the six-month period following the alleged coup, but there were further waves of arrest between late 1966 and 1968, and sporadic detentions continued well into the 1970s. A small fraction of those detained were charged and tried for their alleged involvement in the supposed coup attempt. Some of those tried were executed while others died in custody many years later; a few remaining prisoners were finally released shortly after General Suharto stepped down in 1998. The vast majority of detainees, however, were never tried; instead, they were held in appalling conditions and legal limbo for months or years, before finally being released without explanation, apology, or compensation. Even after their release, those who had been detained and also their families were subjected to all manner of restrictions, both formal and informal, justified on the specious grounds of having once been arrested or for their alleged involvement in the September 30th Movement.

This chapter, the first of two on the subject, examines the campaign of mass incarceration with a view to understanding why and how it occurred, how it was related to the mass killings of the same period, and what its consequences were for those detained. It argues, in brief, that the campaign had three defining features: it was a highly organized program that entailed detailed planning and coordination at the national level; it was initiated and carried out by the army leadership and more specifically Suharto; and in its logic, rationale, and implementation, it bore striking similarities to campaigns of mass internment in other authoritarian contexts, most notably the Japanese occupation during the Second World War. The chapter also contends that mass incarceration and mass killing were integrally related in two ways: first, in the sense that most of those eventually killed were first detained, and second, that rates of long-term imprisonment were lower where the rates of killing were highest.[1] Finally, it makes the case that in its rationale, discourse, methods, and organization—in almost every respect—the campaign of mass incarceration was emblematic of the Suharto regime's hypermilitarism and obsession with "order."

The chapter develops these arguments in three parts. It begins by addressing some basic factual questions about the mass detentions, asking, How many people were detained, who were they, who detained them, and how were they treated? It then examines more closely key patterns in the program of long-term imprisonment, including the categorization of prisoners, the conditions of their detention, and the relationship between imprisonment and killing. Finally, the chapter takes a close look at the case of Buru Island, the penal colony where some ten thousand detainees were held without charge or trial, and subjected to forced labor from 1969 to 1979.

Detention, Interrogation, and Torture

For at least a decade after the alleged coup attempt of October 1, 1965, Indonesia had one of the largest populations of political detainees anywhere in the world—comparable to those in the Soviet Union and China, fascist Spain and Portugal, and the authoritarian regimes of Latin America.

Scattered across the archipelago in cramped colonial era prisons, army lockups, secret detention centers, and forced labor camps, hundreds of thousands of men, and a smaller but significant number of women, passed their days not knowing when, if ever, they might be released. If there were any doubt that the assault on the Left and Sukarno that followed the events of October 1 was a deliberate campaign coordinated by the army leadership, the basic facts and patterns of this program of mass incarceration must surely lay them to rest.

PATTERNS OF DETENTION

As in the case of those killed, there are no precise figures for the number of people detained after October 1, 1965. Indeed, the campaign of detention was so widespread and so swift that even the Indonesian authorities directly responsible for it had no clear idea exactly how many people were held at any time. As the attorney general said in a 1971 press conference, it was impossible to give an exact number of political detainees because that figure "was like a floating rate, like the yen vis-à-vis the dollar: every day it changes."[2] The question of numbers is further complicated by the fact that many detainees were killed either in custody or after being "loaned out" by the authorities, with no record left either of their detention or death.

The estimates of people interned range from a minimum of 106,000 to a maximum of about 3 million.[3] The figure of 106,000 is certainly too low, considering that key Indonesian military authorities seeking to *underplay* the problem in the mid-1970s said that the number of detainees was between 600,000 and 750,000.[4] The higher figure of 3 million is not impossible, but there is little hard evidence to support it. A more reasonable figure would appear to be about 1 million, as suggested by Amnesty International in 1977.[5] While somewhat higher than numbers reported by Indonesian authorities at the time, 1 million is actually lower than numbers cited by officials in the 1980s and 1990s. In 1985, for example, a senior official in the Ministry of Home Affairs announced that some 1.7 million "coup participants"—more than 1.4 million of whom were former category C prisoners—would have to be reregistered prior to the 1987 national elections.[6] And in the mid-1990s, the number of people reportedly denied certain political and civil rights because of their status as former political prisoners was said to be 1.4 million.[7]

Those detained came from all walks of life, from the highest government and political party officials to the lowliest peasant farmer. The best-known detainees were key figures in Sukarno's government such as Sub-

FIGURE 8.1. Political prisoners under armed guard at Tangerang prison near Jakarta, ca. December 1965. (Bettman / Getty Images)

andrio and Oei Tjoe Tat, leading PKI figures like Sudisman and Njono, and high-ranking military officers like Omar Dhani, Supardjo, Latief, and Untung. Most of these figures were charged and tried between 1966 and 1976; all were found guilty, and sentenced to long prison terms or in some cases death.[8] The campaign of detention also targeted leading intellectuals and cultural figures, including well-known writers like Pramoedya Ananta Toer as well as journalists, civil servants, artists, dancers, puppet masters, teachers, and musicians. Army authorities were evidently especially worried about such people because of their presumed potential for influencing the less-educated segments of the population in which the army had little faith.[9]

But the vast majority of those interned were neither important political leaders nor leading cultural figures; they were ordinary people—peasants, tenant farmers, plantation workers, street vendors, and others—who were detained solely because of their real or alleged membership in or association with a party of the Left, or one of the dozens of organizations that were deemed to be leftist in orientation. Despite the fact that all these had been lawful political and social organizations at the time of the alleged October coup—and remained that way until they were formally banned in 1966—mere membership in these organizations was considered sufficient grounds for arrest after October 1965.

In addition to those detained for their political activities and associations, some were held for less obviously political reasons—victims of mistaken identity and personal score settling.[10] Such cases were not the norm, however, and should not be taken as evidence that the campaign of detention was somehow random or spontaneous. On the contrary, as described below, everything about the detentions points to the fact that they were the product of official policy. That policy created a permissive environment in which score settling could happen. In that sense, Indonesia's experience does not differ significantly from other instances of mass incarceration, like those in Stalin's Soviet Union, Mao's China, Franco's Spain, or the military regimes in Argentina and Chile.

Arrests were often carried out by uniformed soldiers or police operating on orders from a commanding officer. In many cases, though, soldiers and police worked with militia groups and vigilantes associated with one or another anticommunist party or religious organization. As explored in earlier chapters, these included the formally constituted militia groups known as Hansip and Hanra, politically affiliated youth groups like the PNI's Pemuda Marhaen as well as the NU's Banser and Ansor, and IPKI's Pemuda Pancasila. By all accounts, the involvement of such militia groups was quite deliberate. As we have seen, from the outset the highest army authorities—including Suharto himself—called explicitly on the general population to assist in the army's work of cutting the September 30th Movement down to the very roots.

The involvement of the population in the campaign of mass detention served a number of related purposes. For one thing, it helped to create the illusion that the actions against the movement and the PKI were the result of spontaneous popular anger against traitors. That was a claim military authorities would routinely use when challenged on the matter of responsibility. The mobilization of local militias also helped to ensure that responsibility for the unlawful arrests would not rest solely with the army officers who were instigating them but would be widely shared. Not only did that approach expedite the effort to destroy the Left, it also limited the likelihood of a widespread popular backlash against the army. With so many people involved in the campaign, with the web of complicity cast so widely, the chances of blowback were substantially diminished.

As in other cases of mass detention, the campaign in Indonesia was facilitated by the willingness of some detainees to work as informers and interrogators for their captors.[11] Whether out of fear, or as a result of torture or other kinds of physical or psychological duress, some PKI members and leaders were "turned" while in detention and became instruments in the army campaign.[12] By most accounts, for example, PKI general secretary Sudisman was finally captured on December 6, 1966, after a member of the PKI's Central Committee betrayed him. Indeed, according to Sudisman, the member in question actually accompanied the soldiers to the place where he was hiding.[13]

Beyond these general observations, arrests followed a number of recognizable patterns. With rare exception, suspects were detained without a warrant, and picked up off the street without warning or in their homes in the middle of the night. In some cases, soldiers would ask a suspect to come with them to provide "clarification," giving no indication that they were in fact being arrested. In many cases, especially in rural areas, suspects were detained by militia members, and marched off to the nearest police or army detachment for processing.[14] In still other cases, the arrest would start with some kind of threat or assault on the suspect by local militia members or vigilantes. Soldiers and police would then appear and take the suspect away under the guise of "protecting" them from the angry crowd. The arrest of the author Pramoedya Ananta Toer on October 13, 1965, was fairly typical of this pattern:

> At 10:30 p.m., Pramoedya was jarred from his work by the sound of voices. Looking out the window he saw a crowd had gathered outside his gate. Most of the people were wearing masks. They demanded to be allowed in. Having gathered stones from the nearby construction site, the mob began to pelt the house, breaking windows and shattering doors, threatening to burn the author's home to the ground, with him in it.... Suddenly, there was a round of automatic gunfire. The crowd fell back slightly from the gate. Four or five police officers and soldiers emerged from the lane. The crowd parted as they walked toward the gate. "We're here to take you to safety," one of the soldiers said to Pramoedya. "Gather up the things you'll need."[15]

In virtually all documented cases, arrests were carried out with considerable brutality, even when those detained were relatively old and offered no resistance. Detainees were often beaten, and sometimes tied up and blindfolded, before being marched off or loaded onto a military vehicle for transport to a detention center. Witnesses described the 1966 arrest of the Partindo secretary-general, Adisumarto, a man in his sixties, as follows: "He was beaten till his face was all swollen and bleeding. He tried to protest against this arrest without warrant, but that only made matters worse and at last he was dragged off to the waiting jeep and driven to the political prison camp. His wife and daughter both had to witness the horrible spectacle."[16] The story of Rahim Marhab, arrested with his relatives in a village in Central Sulawesi in November 1965, was also typical:

> While I was firing bricks at the factory ... a mob of about 300 people from the village of Pelawa arrived. They captured me, my older brother Hajasa, my uncle Harati and my cousin Agi. Suddenly, they started beating us with pieces of blackwood, beating my entire body except for the soles of my feet and toes. They hit my head until it bled. After I passed out twice, we were taken to the Parigi district police station.[17]

Arrest was frequently accompanied by the destruction of the suspect's personal property. Sumiyarsi, a pediatrician and member of the HSI, has described how at the time of her arrest in 1965, everything was destroyed, including her family's "books, music collection, photo albums, letters and private papers, valuable documents and so on."[18] Likewise, the soldiers and vigilantes who came to arrest Pramoedya targeted his books and manuscripts for destruction, throwing them into a pile in the yard and setting them alight.[19] The wanton destruction of such materials suggests that the aim was not to find and preserve evidence of wrongdoing but simply to punish and demoralize alleged traitors. The parallels with the destruction of property of supposed "enemies of the people" during the Stalinist purges of the late 1930s are quite striking.[20]

Of course, some property was seized rather than destroyed; notably, many documents were taken from the offices and homes of PKI officials in the course of army raids. Army officials then used some of those documents in preparing the official narrative of PKI guilt. Beyond such documents, those conducting raids often seized property, including money, wristwatches, jewelry, motorcycles, automobiles, houses, and commercial buildings. These seizures were a straightforward case of looting by soldiers and vigilantes, with the evident approval of their commanders. Apart from providing the army with valuable assets—some of which were used in the campaign of detention and killing—granting soldiers and militia members permission to loot improved their morale, at least in the short term.

INTERROGATION AND TORTURE

If they were not immediately killed, detainees were transported—usually by truck but sometimes by boat or train—to one of the many jails and detention centers for preliminary interrogation. Some were taken to nearby military posts, while others were brought to one of the informal facilities the army had established in the days after October 1. Many of these interrogation sites were commercial and residential buildings that had been seized by army authorities. These included the notorious two-story building on Jalan Gandhi in Medan where many detainees were tortured and killed by army authorities, and a nondescript building on Jalan Gunung Sahari II in Jakarta, where an infamous military unit known as Tim Operasi Kalong extracted confessions from hundreds of detainees. Without any signs or markings to indicate their purpose, these places were in effect secret detention centers. Although no formal records exist of their numbers and locations, the testimony of former prisoners and human rights organizations suggests that at least one secret facility existed in virtually every town across the archipelago, and that large cities like Jakarta, Surabaya, Bandung, and Medan had several.[21]

Interrogation was generally carried out by army or police personnel. Interrogators operated under various mandates, but principally on orders from the powerful state security agency Kopkamtib established in mid-October 1965.[22] Those conducting interrogations acted within the context of officially sanctioned anticommunism, as described earlier, in which all leftists were assumed to have committed heinous crimes that placed them outside the bounds of civilized humanity. As a consequence, interrogations did not follow anything close to normal legal procedure. Detainees were provided no legal counsel, there was neither a right to silence nor a presumption of innocence, and there was no process for appealing the decisions of arresting authorities. In short, the gloves were off.

The initial interrogation process entailed routine data gathering; the detainee's name, date of birth, address, party affiliation, and so on, were entered in wide, bound ledger books or dutifully typed in triplicate by military staff. At some point, however, the focus shifted to the detainee's real or alleged involvement in organizations or activities that had been declared subversive. That stage of interrogation could be a prolonged affair, especially for important figures. Sudisman claimed, for example, that he was interrogated "14 times over a period of 18 days for no less than 70 hours and filling 152 pages of pre-trial statements."[23]

A common feature of interrogations, especially in the period immediately after detention, was torture and other kinds of ill treatment.[24] Torture took a variety of forms, including severe beatings with lengths of wood, electric cable, and other materials; crushing toes or feet under the legs of tables or chairs; breaking fingers and pulling out fingernails; electric shocks; and burning with cigarettes and molten rubber. Some detainees were forced to watch or listen to other prisoners, including their children or spouses, being tortured.[25] In her memoir, Sumiyarsi tells the story of a young man beaten by interrogators while she was in the room:

> The two toughs immediately began to beat him with their clubs. They beat his right shoulder and his left, his neck, his throat, and his head, again and again, and then his chest and his back, paying no attention as the young man screamed and begged for mercy, all the while trying to protect himself with his arms. There was blood everywhere. His face began to swell up, turning black and blue, but the beating continued. Then the young man stopped reacting, and the [commanding officer] Major Johan was completely silent, like a robot.[26]

Carmel Budiardjo related a similar story told to her by a fellow detainee, SOBSI activist Sri Ambar, who had been present when a young activist was beaten to death under interrogation:

> She was in the room when they started flogging him. They aimed at his back and neck, the most vulnerable parts of the body.... The flogging grew in intensity and Sri tried not to watch. She stared at a piece of paper in front of her, trying to concentrate on anything but the atrocity going on in her presence. But when she heard him fall, she turned around to see what had happened. He was lying prostrate on the floor; thick white foam was oozing out of his mouth. When she rushed over to him, the torturers did nothing to hold her back.... A few moments later, the boy was dead.[27]

Prisoners, both men and women, also suffered various kinds of sexual violence.[28] Some were given electric shocks to their genitals.[29] Others were forced to have sex while their interrogators looked on shouting abuse and obscenities. Some women were made to strip naked, and were subjected to forced touching and rape by their interrogators.[30] The account of a woman arrested on suspicion of being a Gerwani member in Central Java is fairly typical: "I was beaten and stripped naked. My pubic hair and the hair on my head was burnt. All I could do was scream and call upon the name of God.... I was once made to sit in the lap of a male prisoner. While naked, I was held and ordered to kiss the penises of all the officers interrogating me."[31]

According to one account by a fellow detainee, several teenage girls accused of taking part in the alleged torture and killing of the generals at Halim air base were groped and raped by their army captors. Later, still in custody, they were filmed while being made to reenact the lascivious

FIGURE 8.2. Women political detainees pray in Plantungan prison camp, Central Java, 1977. (David Jenkins)

dance they had supposedly performed while at Halim.[32] Sexual exploitation by military and prison officials was also common. Some prison and military officials took advantage of their positions of authority to rape female prisoners, or sell them as prostitutes outside the prison walls.[33]

As in most other cases of political imprisonment, torture was frequently used to obtain information that could be used to track down and arrest more suspects. Prisoners were pressed, for instance, to reveal the names and whereabouts of other party members, or information about their party's plans, networks, and intentions. Torture was also used to coerce confessions for use in political trials and public campaigns. In fact, confessions and interrogation statements were virtually the only evidence introduced in the political trials; for example, the confessions of several young women about the alleged actions of Gerwani members at Lubang Buaya became the basis of the army's grotesque but effective psywar campaign.[34] Like their counterparts in Pol Pot's Cambodia and Franco's Spain,

Indonesian interrogators seemed to care less about the actual facts than in securing evidence to support a preexisting narrative of guilt.

Beyond such instrumental aims, the torture of Indonesian detainees had a number of other purposes. As in other campaigns of mass incarceration, one goal was to humiliate, terrorize, and turn the detainee. To be clear, such torture had no judicial purpose; it was aimed solely at punishing a prisoner for their presumed treachery or political beliefs. Thus, for example, one detainee told the story of two leftist journalists (Suroto and Walujo) who were made to undergo a painful and humiliating ritual in military detention: "First the soldiers smashed a large number of beer bottles on the floor. When the sharp fragments had been evenly spread, they made the two men crawl over them on their hands and knees. With their clothes torn to shreds and bleeding profusely, they had to cry '*Hidup Sukarno!*' (Long Live Sukarno!) all the time in a loud voice."[35]

Torture was sometimes also driven by the perceived need by lower-ranking or politically suspect soldiers and officials to demonstrate their reliability to superior officers. A similar need may also explain the unusual brutality of prisoners who became informants and interrogators for their captors. Desperate to save themselves, they sometimes tried to prove their value to their captors by turning against and abusing their former colleagues with exceptional brutality.[36]

Long-Term Imprisonment

If the basic facts of preliminary detention provide strong indications that the mass incarceration after October 1965 was encouraged and facilitated by the army, the patterns of longer-term imprisonment leave no room for doubt that the program was centrally designed and orchestrated by the army high command. Three aspects of that program are especially revealing. First, the system of categorizing political prisoners, set in motion within weeks of the alleged coup, was devised by the army leadership, and implemented through the army chain of command and under its authority. Second, the conditions under which political detainees were held (and the conditions of their release) clearly reflected the political motives and interests of the army leadership, and paid scant attention to norms of justice or due process. Third, regional variations in the intensity of mass detentions, like variations in the pattern of killings, appear to be linked directly to the postures, interests, and strategies of regional army authorities.

CATEGORIZING PRISONERS

After preliminary interrogation, detainees were placed by military officials in one of three broad categories (A, B, and C) according to their alleged degree of involvement in the September 30th Movement.[37] Category A detainees were those said to have been "clearly directly involved" in the movement, either because they participated in it, took part in planning it, or knew of the plan but did not report it to the authorities. Category B detainees were those said to be "clearly indirectly involved" in the movement. That category targeted leading figures of the PKI and its many affiliated organizations, and anyone who had allegedly expressed approval of the movement or had opposed efforts to suppress it. As a practical matter, category B encompassed leading leftist figures for whom there was no evidence of their actual involvement in the alleged coup. As Attorney General Sugih Arto explained in 1971, "Then there are the B prisoners. We know for certain they are traitors, that they are ideologically conscious, but there is not enough evidence to bring them to court."[38] Category C detainees were those "who may reasonably be assumed to have been directly or indirectly involved" in the "coup."[39] More specifically, category C covered PKI sympathizers and members of PKI-affiliated mass organizations. It also included people who had allegedly been "involved" in the 1948 Madiun uprising and did not immediately oppose the alleged 1965 coup. This system of categorization was first spelled out as a guide for arresting and processing suspects on November 15, 1965, in a decree issued by General Suharto on President Sukarno's authority.[40] That decree was later amended and reissued several times under Suharto's authority, but the basic system of categorization was left intact.[41]

Several things are immediately striking about this system. For one thing, it affirmed that mere membership in or sympathy for the PKI or one of its affiliates were sufficient grounds to be detained. It did so, moreover, several months *before* those organizations had been banned formally, making membership in or sympathy for a lawful organization a reason for imprisonment. Second, the system of categorization was based on a conception of guilt that rested not on the actions of the accused but on their affiliations and *presumed* ideas, attitudes, and intentions. Third, it introduced the fuzzy distinction between "direct" and "indirect" involvement, as though these terms and categories were somehow self-evident. Indeed, the language of the edict was so vague that it gave the impression of having been drafted in great haste. But the vagueness was probably quite deliberate, and provided the army leadership with virtually unlimited power to detain anyone and to hold or release them at will.[42] Finally and perhaps most important, the Kopkamtib decrees and the system of prisoner categorization they created underscore the point that the mass political incarceration was a deliberate, centralized, and coordinated campaign, and not in any way the product of spontaneous anger or popular emotions run wild.[43]

Of the estimated one million people interned after October 1, the vast majority were designated as category C detainees—those who "may reasonably be assumed to have been directly or indirectly involved" in the movement by virtue of their political affiliation or presumed sympathies. As noted above, this group included hundreds of thousands of people who had been members of various mass organizations associated with the PKI. Few, if any, of this group would have had any knowledge of, let alone involvement in, the events of October 1, 1965. A smaller number, perhaps thirty thousand, were designated as category B detainees—people deemed to have been "clearly indirectly involved" in the movement by virtue of their leadership positions in left-wing organizations, but for whom there was insufficient evidence to bring any charges.[44] This group included, for instance, local and regional officers of the targeted groups on the Left, leading cultural figures, and some military officers and civilian government officials deemed to have leftist or Sukarnoist sympathies. As discussed below, some ten thousand category B detainees were eventually transported to the prison island of Buru, where they remained without charge or trial for up to a decade. A much smaller number, probably a few thousand, were designated as category A detainees—those deemed to be "clearly directly involved" in planning and carrying out the supposed coup, or failing to report it to the authorities. They included well-known political party figures, Sukarno loyalists, and senior military officers implicated in the alleged coup plot. Many category A prisoners, but not all, were eventually charged and sentenced in political show trials between early 1966 and 1976.[45]

PRISON CONDITIONS

Regardless of their category, detainees were subjected to conditions of imprisonment that amounted to serious ill treatment, and many prisoners became sick or died.[46] Although prison conditions varied, and some detainees were treated reasonably well, most experienced extreme overcrowding, dangerously inadequate nutrition, lack of basic amenities, unsanitary conditions, and little or no medical care. Worse still, detainees lived in constant fear of being "loaned out" (*dibon*) by prison authorities—that is, removed from their cell and taken away to an undisclosed location, often to be killed. Finally, detainees suffered psychological and emotional problems, in part stemming from their isolation from family and friends, and uncertainty about their fate, but also from heavy-handed programs of ideological indoctrination that a senior Kopkamtib officer explained were aimed at "readjusting the mental condition" of detainees.[47]

The arrest of hundreds of thousands of people in a matter of months meant that places of detention were chronically overcrowded. It was not uncommon for several detainees to be housed in cells that had been built, in many cases by Dutch colonial authorities, to house one or two prisoners. At Kopkamtib's notorious Kalong detention center in Jakarta, five detainees typically shared a cell measuring 2.5 by 3 meters; at a lockup in Bandung, six detainees slept in a cell measuring 3 by 4 meters; at Maesa prison in Central Sulawesi, twenty prisoners were crammed into a cell of the same size; and one detainee describes sharing a cell of 1.5 by 2.5 meters with eight others.[48]

The food provided by military authorities was inadequate—a problem compounded in many cases by corruption.[49] Even where budgets were sufficient to feed the huge influx of detainees, food was often stolen or sold by prison authorities before it ever reached the prisoners. If they were lucky, prisoners received some rice and a bit of salt fish or soybean cake twice a day. More commonly, they were given a small amount of corn, cassava, or other root crop with a piece of salt or salt fish once a day. To stay reasonably healthy, prisoners had to supplement their diets by getting food from family or friends on the outside. But even that option was impossible for those who were detained far from their homes, for those who had no family, or whose families were too poor or frightened to make the journey to the detention center. In such cases, prisoners supplemented their diets by eating rats, lizards, snakes, insects, and any other forms of protein they could find.[50] The consequences of such food shortages were predictable. As Pramoedya wrote to his daughter from prison,

> You've probably never witnessed the abnormal physical movements or the odd mental manifestations of a person whose body weight is less than fifty percent what it should be. The man's eyes bulge from their sockets; yet his vision is blurred. His skin is cracked and dry, and when he moves his joints are stiff like those of King Kong in the silent film.

> When he walks he looks around himself, his head bobbing slowly and uncertainly, but his stare is blank and uncertain. Such a sight was a common one during the Japanese occupation and now today is a common one again among Indonesia's political prisoners.[51]

Detainees were also deprived of basic amenities. Cells typically had no beds, mattresses, or pillows, no chairs or tables, and no nets to protect them from malarial mosquitoes. Most detainees slept on the concrete floor, or if they were lucky, on a woven mat provided by a family member or friend on the outside. Basic toiletries like soap and toothpaste were seldom provided, and so had to be obtained from the outside, or through barter with other prisoners or guards. Worse still, the overcrowded cells often had no running water and toilets. Prisoners in such cells had no choice but to defecate in buckets and plastic bags, or on the floor. Pramoedya wrote about his place of detention in 1969: "When we entered the barracks that had been assigned to us at Karang Tengah Prison on Nusa Kambangan, we had found there ... a hill of human shit. In each barracks it had been the same: a petrified mound of shit starting from just inside the door and continuing all the way to the latrine."[52]

Under these conditions, it was hardly surprising that many detainees became seriously ill and some died. By the late 1970s, Amnesty International concluded that tuberculosis had become "endemic" among Indonesia's political prisoners, and that in the worst prisons, "more than half of the prisoner population" was affected.[53] The situation was further exacerbated by the lack of proper medical care in most detention facilities. Few, if any, employed full-time medical staff, more often relying on occasional visits by an itinerant doctor or nurse. In the absence of medical staff, prisoners relied on the expertise of fellow inmates, some of whom were experienced doctors and nurses.[54] Others took up the study of traditional medical practices, such as acupuncture and reflexology, as a way to offer some relief to themselves and their prison mates. Even those facilities that did have a nurse or doctor on site usually suffered from a chronic shortage of medicines. And so prisoners were once again left to their own devices, forced to obtain medicines from the outside or corrupt prison officials. After suffering severe bronchitis for several months in Salemba prison, Suwondo Budiardjo was finally able to obtain medicine from the outside. After his release, he wrote, "Without the help of my family, other detainees, and good-hearted people from Amnesty International, church groups, and others many of us, including myself, would certainly have died in Salemba."[55]

FIGURE 8.3. Political detainees at Sumber-Rejo prison camp, East Kalimantan, 1977. (David Jenkins)

In addition to these burdensome conditions, some prisoners were required to perform forced labor.[56] Indeed, certain detention centers were effectively organized and run as work camps, providing unremunerated labor for government construction projects, manufacturing operations, and agricultural production. The most notorious of these was the prison island of Buru, examined below, but it was hardly the only one. Among others, the Mocong Loe camp in South Sulawesi, the Ameroro and Nanga-Nanga camps in Central Sulawesi, and the Kemaro Island camp in South Sumatra were effectively penal colonies for category A and B prisoners.[57] Likewise, in Salemba prison in Jakarta, Tangerang prison just outside the city, and the Nusa Kambangan prison complex off the south coast of Java, political prisoners were required to work on prison farms and other unremunerated projects.[58] In many cases, too, camp authorities compelled detainees to perform "corvée labor" for their personal benefit, such as building, gardening, and cleaning.

Appalling as these physical conditions were, the memoirs and testimonies of detainees suggest that for some at least, the most debilitating aspects of their detention were psychological and emotional. Time and again, their accounts return to feelings of anger, frustration, and resentment at being treated as less than human, as mere animals, deprived of the most basic requirements of human dignity and the possibility to act as part of a community. Thus, for example, Tan Swie Ling writes that "throughout the period of their detention, G30S political prisoners were never treated like fellow human beings."[59] Similarly, in her memoir, Sumiyarsi stresses, "It was as though we were not regarded as human beings at all, but as nothing more than pieces of salt fish or lengths of wood."[60]

In an account of his visit to the Sumber-Rejo prison camp in East Kalimantan in 1977, the journalist David Jenkins described the mood as "one of resignation and smouldering resentment." At the time, the camp was home to 525 category B prisoners—470 men and 55 women—most of whom had already been held without charge or trial for twelve years. After so long in captivity, Jenkins wrote, the detainees had mixed feelings about their situation, but there was no mistaking their anger or resolve.

> On the one hand, they act like men who recognize the futility of outward opposition.... On the other hand, they are plainly bitter about their long detention. When the guards are not present, they seethe with indignation about the conditions in the camp.... What comes through most forcefully at Sumber-Rejo is the pride and dignity of the detainees; the stubborn resolve written on so many of their faces.... No one at Sunber-Rejo looked cowed or submissive—there were no model prisoners trotted out, as in other camps, to abjectly defend the Pancasila way of life.[61]

Among the most alarming aspects of political imprisonment after October 1965 was the practice of "loaning out" detainees. Mentioned in virtually all memoirs of former detainees, the term described a practice in which authorities would remove a detainee from their cell—frequently in the middle of the night—and take them to an undisclosed location from which they might never return. Loaning out, a classic example of the army's Orwellian doublespeak, could mean a prisoner was being transferred to another detention center, called for interrogation, or sent to perform corvée labor. But it was also a common preliminary to execution. That was certainly the understanding of political detainees who witnessed the practice firsthand.[62]

Detainees also suffered from the terrible uncertainty that was a direct result of the arbitrary nature of their incarceration.[63] Because all but a few were being held without charge or trial—and because the reasons for their detention were never explained—they had no way of knowing how long they might be in detention or if they would ever be released. During a political trial in 1975, the courageous human rights lawyer Yap Thiam Hien cited the plea of one political detainee: "We are like leaves on a tree, just waiting to fall to earth and become one with it. Help us get our freedom back, to rejoin our unprotected families. Help us at the very least to be brought to trial so that this soul-destroying uncertainty can end."[64]

Equally disturbing to many political detainees was the program of ideological indoctrination they were required to endure while in detention. The program aimed at "cleansing" the detainees of their old ideas—including Communism, atheism, and Old Order thinking—and replacing these with "healthy" ideas based on belief in God and the army's version of Pancasila.[65] Explaining the rationale of the program in 1977, a senior Kopkamtib officer said, "We have to be sure that we have changed their minds to Pancasila minds."[66] As though echoing Michel Foucault, army authorities responsible for implementing the program spoke of the prisoners as suffering mental illness and themselves as doctors who could "cure" them. One former detainee recalls an army captain at Salemba prison telling the detainees who had been gathered for an indoctrination session, "I treat you like people who are suffering mental illness because you have been infected by Old Order and atheist thoughts, and I am like the doctor who is going to make you all well again."[67] As Jenkins's observations about the detainees at Sumber-Rejo suggests, the army cure was not always effective.

In the mid-1970s, Indonesian Army and government authorities took these ideas a step further through the psychological testing of political detainees. Among the inmates assessed were more than four hundred women at Plantungan women's prison in Central Java. Toward the end of 1975, a group of some twenty-five academics from various disciplines—accompanied by the armed forces psychologist, Professor Major General Sumitro—arrived at the prison to do their work.[68] Inmates were gathered on the first day to complete lengthy psychological questionnaires and undergo interviews for a period of several hours; the next day, they were brought together to hear the academics offer their conclusions about their mental health. The academics' assessments were overwhelmingly positive; they marveled at how well the inmates had adjusted to their "new environment" and suggested that their excellent mental health was the result of "strong religious faith." Jenkins, who visited Plantungan prison in 1977, offered a somewhat-different interpretation:

> Here, as elsewhere, intense psychological pressure is exerted on detainees to make them conform to the norms of "Pancasila society." The result, in some cases, is that women who were once of an independent

> disposition had been turned into apologists for a way of life they once deplored; frail shells whispering intensely about the gratitude they feel for a Government which has deprived them of their liberty for more than a decade.[69]

Notably, senior Dutch psychologists and social scientists were instrumental in setting up the program of psychological testing. Preliminary research indicates that the psychological assessments of political detainees were part of a formal collaboration between several Indonesian and Dutch universities known as the KUN-2 Project.[70] Under the terms of that project, Dutch academics assisted their Indonesian partners in designing the psychological testing of political prisoners. According to Dutch media reports from the late 1970s, the aim of the project was to investigate the level of "communist-ness" of the detainees.[71] Thus, apart from revealing the army's cynical deployment of "scientific" expertise for political purposes, the program suggested the disturbing possibility of complicity on the part of medical professionals and academics, Indonesian and foreign, in the army's program of arbitrary political imprisonment and thought reform. That possibility underscores the observation of historian Petteri Pietikainen that "in authoritarian states, psychiatry and all other sciences, especially if they [do] research on humans, [are] easily drawn into the trajectory of politics, power and intrigue."[72]

TO KILL OR DETAIN?

Broad similarities notwithstanding, patterns of imprisonment varied by locale; in some areas—notably Jakarta, West Java, Sulawesi, and Buru—a great many people remained in detention, while in others—Aceh, Bali, and East Java—the number of long-term prisoners was relatively small. More significant perhaps, there appears to have been an inverse relationship between the levels of long-term detention and mass killing: where the number of long-term detainees was relatively high, the number of killings was low, and vice versa.[73] As such, the areas with the greatest concentrations of long-term detainees were those with relatively lower levels of killing: Jakarta, West Java, North and South Sulawesi, and the prison island of Buru. By contrast, the areas with relatively low levels of long-term incarceration had high levels of killing: Aceh, Bali, and East Java. Indeed, Aceh and Bali seem to have had few detainees after about 1967.[74]

As in the case of killings, it appears that rates of long-term incarceration were shaped in part by the postures and strategies of different regional military commanders. Although the order to destroy the movement and the PKI clearly came from the central army leadership, regional military commanders had some autonomy in deciding how to achieve that objective.[75] The regional commanders in certain areas evidently favored a policy of killing while others adopted a strategy of mass incarceration. Thus, the regional military command in Aceh opted to kill rather than detain alleged supporters of the movement, or to be more precise, opted to kill detainees rather than holding them for the long term. By contrast, the regional military command in West Java adopted a strategy of mass detention with relatively little killing.[76] Such differences in strategy may help to explain variations in other regions and other national contexts as well.

Second, the pattern of incarceration seems to have been shaped by logistical considerations, like the facilities and resources available to the authorities in different areas. The detention and processing of vast numbers of detainees was both time-consuming and expensive. Entirely new bureaucratic systems had to be set up and funded in order to process and keep track of the prisoners. Some regional and local commands were better placed—and perhaps more inclined—to create those systems than others. Thus, where regional and local commanders had fewer facilities and resources—such as prisons, jails, barracks, warehouses, interrogators, clerks, food, and gasoline—or preferred not to use those resources for detention purposes, the rates of incarceration tended to be somewhat lower. The grim corollary to that pattern was that more of those who might have been kept in detention were killed instead. Simply stated, where the logistics of detention became difficult—either because of a shortage of available space, or because it was too costly to house and feed large numbers of detainees—the result appears to have been an increased resort to killing.

That pattern has been observed in a number of different locales. Yenling Tsai and Douglas Kammen have observed, for instance, that the large number of detainees initially held in rural North Sumatra was a strain on the army budget, which in turn may have led to more killing: "There were ... persistent rumours that the budget allocated for detention centers was insufficient and so the Army intended to kill many of the prisoners, perhaps even sending them to Aceh for execution."[77] Likewise, in a February 1966 cable to the Foreign Office concerning the pattern of killings, British ambassador Gilchrist wrote,

> In Jakarta, of course, there have been no mass killings. A large number—possibly thousands—were rounded up in the early days and thrown into prison or, when the prisons were full, taken to one of the

> small islands offshore. It seems likely that some of these people have been killed if only because (as in Medan) the problems of feeding them were so burdensome.[78]

Similar dynamics were at work in parts of Java as well. In Banyuwangi, East Java, for example, the army was reportedly unable or unwilling to hold all those who had been arrested. As a result, many were sent back to the NU's paramilitary Banser units to be killed. According to a former Banser leader, "Every night, the District Military Command (Kodim) sent us dozens of PKI members with orders to kill them."[79] Likewise, in late November 1965, the US Embassy reported that in Central Java, there were large numbers of detainees who the military had no desire or ability to feed and house. The solution there, as elsewhere, was "for military personnel to 'move' detainees at night and en route hand them over to designated civilian death squads."[80] Two years later, in the context of a sweep against alleged Communists in the area of Purwodadi, Central Java, the district military commander reportedly told an Indonesian journalist, "If we arrested everyone who was PKI ... we would not know what to do with them. We do not have space to detain them."[81] There too, hundreds of political detainees were killed.

Finally, there seem to have been fewer killings where army authorities appropriated or exploited detainee labor for government projects or personal gain, once again suggesting an inverse relationship between longer-term detention and mass killing. Thus, for example, in South Sulawesi and Central Sulawesi where the exploitation of political detainee labor was common, the levels of killing were relatively low. The clearest case of the relationship, however, was the forced labor camp on Buru Island, where some ten thousand category B detainees spent up to ten years. As the writer and former Buru inmate Pramoedya remarked several years after his release, "The people who went to Buru were the people who were spared from execution."[82]

Buru: Prison Island

In 1969, some twenty-five hundred category B political detainees were secretly transported by train and then ship from their prisons in Java to the tiny island of Buru, in the far eastern reaches of Indonesia's vast archipelago. There, with only the most basic tools and materials, and under constant guard by heavily armed soldiers, they began to build the barracks, roads, staff headquarters, fences, and guardhouses of what would eventually become one of the largest and most notorious concentration camps in Asia.[83]

Over the next few years, this first group was joined by successive waves of category B detainees, until by 1975 the total number held on Buru Island was at least ten thousand.[84] Except for the hundreds who died there due to starvation, suicide, and disease, all these prisoners remained on Buru until the late 1970s. The last of the prisoners were finally returned to Java in late 1979, a full ten years after the first boatload had arrived. None of those held in the camp were ever charged with a crime. Nor was any plausible reason ever given for their eventual release.

When Indonesian Army authorities acknowledged the existence of the camp in late 1969, they insisted that it was not a concentration camp. It was, they said, a resettlement project that would provide "settlers" the chance to be productive citizens, developing a remote part of the country, while at the same time undergoing political "rehabilitation." Formally coordinated by the prosecutor general, Buru was in reality a penal colony run and controlled by the army, and more specifically the powerful Kopkamtib.[85] Everything about Buru—from the geographic layout of its barracks and yards, to the treatment of the so-called settlers, and the language used to rationalize it—bore the army's distinctive imprint. That military ethos was made apparent in one of President Suharto's first public comments about Buru in December 1969: "Some elements of the foreign press have tried to discredit Buru as an Indonesian version of [the Dutch colonial place of exile] Boven Digul or a concentration camp. They forget that in history, war always brings risks for the losing side."[86] The detainees, then, were seen as the defeated enemies in a war.

Indeed, while some observers and former prisoners sought to draw parallels between Buru and the places of exile to which the Dutch colonial authorities had sent their most troublesome political opponents, Buru was actually quite different and, in reality, worse. The more fitting comparison was with the POW camps that the Japanese military authorities had set up in Indonesia and elsewhere during the Second World War.[87] As in those camps, the inmates on Buru were made to work under military guard from morning to night, building barracks and staff quarters, roads and walkways, and turning dense jungle and grasslands into farmland. Like the POWs in the Japanese camps, the Buru internees received only the barest ration of food, which they had to supplement to stay alive; slept in barracks with virtually no amenities; suffered illness for which they received no medical care; and lived in constant fear of punishment for the slightest infraction or perceived offense against the rules or a particular commander. And like those in the Japanese camps, Buru's detainees were subjected to a constant barrage of political messages and instructions ostensibly aimed at their ideological improvement and reeducation, but that in reality, led only to frustration and despair. The main differences between the two were that the prisoners on Buru suffered these conditions and indignities for up to ten years, rather than the three and a half years that prisoners remained in the Japanese camps, and they suffered not under an occupying power but instead at the hands of their "own" security forces.

The same basic conditions of detention that existed elsewhere in the country were also common on Buru.[88] But in addition, those held on Buru experienced further ill treatment and indignities, including forced labor.[89] Using only the most rudimentary tools, like sickles, axes, and hoes, inmates cleared dense forests and grasslands to make the roads and pathways that would connect the different units of the camp. They spent months and years turning grasslands and dense forests into irrigated rice paddies. They constructed the officers' houses, the camp buildings, and the very barracks in which they and future inmates would eventually live. To make matters worse, the crops and other products of their labor were routinely expropriated by camp officials, either for their own consumption or resale at the market in the small town of Namlea.

Such labor always took place under armed guard, and so under the constant threat of punishment. One of the more striking aspects of these punishments, beyond their simple brutality and unfairness, was the degree to which they replicated the highly militarized style of the POW camp. Exhausted and undernourished prisoners who had infringed a rule or offended a guard were made to drop and do one hundred push-ups, stand at attention for hours in the rain or blazing sun, or walk repeatedly around the yard in a squatting position with their hands behind their head.[90] Through sheer lack of imagination, it seems, the army punished the detainees using its limited repertoire, learned from the period of the Japanese occupation.

The products of prisoner labor, including rice and other food, were ostensibly to be used to feed the prisoners themselves. And it is true that in time, the food that prisoners produced did provide an essential supplement to the meager rations supplied by the camp authorities. Nevertheless, the search for adequate food was a constant preoccupation. As Pramoedya writes, "Eating snakes was common. Some of the men ate wood worms, too, disposing of the head first and then eating the fatty lower part of the body, sometimes raw. Dogs, too, found their way into our stomachs."[91]

PSYCHOLOGICAL BURDENS

Beyond the physical demands faced by the prisoners on Buru, and in some ways far exceeding them in seriousness, were the enormous psychological and emotional burdens to which their incarceration gave rise. Among the most common themes in the accounts of Buru prisoners is silence. Former prisoners lament, for example, that their past contributions to the nation were either ignored or forgotten, that they were not permitted to speak or write about anything meaningful, and that they were forbidden to read newspapers, listen to the radio, or read books other than religious texts. Writers were denied pen and paper, and when they were allowed to write, there was always the possibility that their writings would be confiscated or destroyed. Thus, after Pramoedya had filled nine tablets with notes for a novel about the early years of the nationalist movement, the camp authorities confiscated them all and never returned them.[92]

Another common refrain in the memoirs of Buru prisoners, as of other political detainees, was the indignity of being treated as less than human: as a beast, a thing, or an automaton. This denial of prisoners' humanity is revealed in many forms—in the recurrent statements that the food they were given was not fit for human consumption, that they were cut off from the families they loved and from the social ties that made them human. In an echo of Hannah Arendt, ex-prisoner Setiawan writes that political detainees were not recognized as "political beings" but only as "biological animals"; they were known by their numbers and not their names.[93] Similarly, Pramoedya writes that the years of being treated like animals robbed political detainees of their self-confidence, dignity, and sense of personhood.[94]

Of the psychological burdens borne by prisoners on Buru, as for those detained without charge elsewhere, unquestionably one of the greatest was uncertainty—uncertainty about their own future, but also the fate of their families and loved ones.[95] Having never been charged, tried, or sentenced, prisoners had no idea how long they might have to remain on the island, and the authorities, perhaps deliberately, provided no clarification on the matter. Some detainees simply gave up hope, and assuming the worst, sank into despair or mental illness; perhaps inevitably, some committed suicide.[96] Others hung on to vague rumors picked up from prisoners who may have worked in the camp commander's house, or listened for clues on the radio that one or two prisoners managed to keep hidden in their barracks. And while they wondered if they would ever be released, they worried about and longed for their families back on Java. For apart from being physically separated from them for years, most prisoners were not even able to communicate with their families by post. In theory, prisoners were permitted to send one postcard home per month, but in reality few of those cards ever reached their destinations.[97]

As if all this were not enough, the Buru prisoners were subjected to a heavy-handed program of indoctrination and reeducation that was euphemistically known as the "Mental Guidance" program, coordinated by a "Headquarters Mental Guidance Officer." The explicit purpose of this program was to get all prisoners to renounce their "Communist ideology," adopt and practice one of the state's recognized religions, and embrace the army's version of the national ideology, Pancasila. As the attorney general said in October 1972, "If an individual has fulfilled the condition of being a genuine Pantja Silaist, he can naturally come back from Buru."[98]

There were several obvious problems with this plan. The first was that it assumed that all the prisoners on Buru were Communists when in reality many were not. As the detainee Setiawan reportedly told an International Committee of the Red Cross (ICRC) delegation to Buru in the 1970s, "Actually not all of us are communists. We're just people despised by the regime."[99] The second problem was that as nationalists and Sukarno loyalists, the vast majority of prisoners were already ardent supporters of Pancasila. Indeed, there were among them many who had helped to defend Pancasila when it had come under attack at various times before 1965. For those prisoners as well as countless other Indonesians, there was no contradiction between being a leftist, a Sukarnoist, or even a Communist and believing in Pancasila. The purported conflict was one of the army's own making—a conflict born of political expediency and a limited grasp of the country's political history. What prisoners objected to was that they who actually knew a good deal about Pancasila, and had long embraced it, should have to receive lectures about it from army officers who not only had a poor grasp of its meaning but who were now misrepresenting it. Emblematic of the problem was the minister of information, a military officer, who in an interview for a Dutch documentary film about the political prisoners was himself unable to remember the five main tenets of Pancasila.[100]

Detainees found some relief from these burdens in the occasional opportunities provided by camp authorities for cultural activities, sports, and religious worship. In their memoirs, some former detainees write with fondness about the musical and theatrical performances they were allowed to undertake, about their exploits on the dirt soccer field and volleyball court, and their sense of communion in church or mosque.[101] One of the most cherished memories, though, was of gathering in Pramoedya's hut in the evenings to listen as he spun a rich tale about the early years of Indonesia's national awakening at the turn of the twentieth century. That story, an oral history built up and reshaped by suggestions from a group of disheveled political exiles, formed the basis for Pramoedya's masterwork of historical fiction, a tetralogy appropriately named *The Buru Quartet*. Published shortly after Pramoedya's release from Buru, the first two volumes were instant best sellers; one year later, the attorney general banned them on the spurious grounds that they contained Communist teachings.[102]

INTERNATIONAL CONNECTIONS

In spite of its isolated location and the absence of meaningful government information about it, the story of Buru eventually began to make its way to other parts of Indonesia and beyond. The first accounts came in letters from prisoners that had somehow been smuggled back to Java, where they were circulated among friends and sympathizers, and sometimes shared with human rights organizations. As the news spread and human rights organizations began to express alarm, the Indonesian authorities sought to reassure both domestic and international audiences that there was nothing sinister about the prison island.

In 1971–72, the authorities permitted a number of Indonesian and foreign journalists to visit Buru to see for themselves. One of the first to go and report on the situation there was the Indonesian journalist Marcel Beding, who visited Buru in late 1971. His article, published in the national daily *Kompas*, sounded a surprisingly critical tone, asking,

> How long have they to stay there [in Buru]? They themselves are asking this question. Their families are asking this question and I myself join in asking it. And the answer is as dark as the sky above Unit 2 on that December afternoon in 1971. . . . They are all lonely men. They are all lonely while laboring from morning to sunset. They are also troubled by the feeling of uncertainty about the future and about their loved ones far across the sea, parents, wives, children, relatives.[103]

The accounts of most foreign journalists and human rights organizations were similarly critical, providing a grim picture of the reality of life for the Buru detainees, and expressing doubt about the wisdom and legality of their detention without charge or trial. Commenting on the regime of forced labor, a foreign journalist who visited Buru in December 1971 wrote in *Newsweek* that "for those with no previous farming experience, and for the older men and intellectuals, the grueling manual labor is sheer punishment."[104]

Irritated by the tone and content of these press reports, the army declared the island off limits to journalists and tourists for the next five years. During that period, the only visitors to the camp were military authorities—including Kopkamtib commander General Sumitro—occasional ICRC delegations, some missionaries, a few handpicked journalists, and a team of psychologists. Prisoner accounts of these visits offer intriguing glimpses into the attitudes and behaviors of the Indonesian authorities, and confirmation—if any were needed—that the Buru prison camp, like the entire program of political incarceration, was a project of the army's central leadership.

For much of the 1970s, the only meaningful contact Buru's detainees had with the outside world was through the brief visits of small ICRC delegations.[105] Preparation for these visits was feverish on the part of both the detainees and the authorities. Detainees strategized about how to outwit the camp authorities in order to pass sensitive information to the delegation. One strategy was to appoint a detainee who could speak a European language, like French or German, to communicate with the ICRC representative. The assumption, probably correct, was that the soldiers supervising these interactions would not understand what was being said. Another, more dangerous approach was to prepare written reports to be passed on secretly to a member of the delegation in the course of their inspections. Meanwhile, army authorities anxiously prepared for the visits by ordering a cleanup of the camp and warning detainees not to say anything that could be construed as criticism. They also managed to limit the duration of the visits to one or two days, and to prevent the ICRC delegates from speaking at any length with the detainees; about fifteen minutes for each of a handful of detainees was about the norm.[106]

During one visit in 1973 or 1974, a detainee managed to pass a handwritten report about the conditions on Buru to the delegates while carrying their bags to the boat. Unfortunately, news of the report made its way to the camp commander and led to an angry response. As one detainee recalled,

> The day after the visitors left, there was an extraordinary roll call for all inmates. The Commander, shrieking, demanded to know which prisoner had given a letter in English to the Swiss visitors.... The letter was unsigned but described the prisoners' real situation, saying it was

> nothing like what they had seen because everything had been staged. While waiting for the confession, all the prisoners were left standing in the rain. Because no one confessed, the chief guard threatened to use brand new technology to find the culprit—a lie detector.[107]

Despite these difficult conditions, the ICRC was able to gain a fairly accurate sense of the camp conditions. And although in keeping with its standard protocols, the ICRC promised not to make its findings public, it was nevertheless able to insist on some changes. After one visit, for instance, Pramoedya and others were provided with paper and pens and permitted to write again. Moreover, through its informal contacts with other human rights organizations like Amnesty International, the ICRC was able to convey in a general sense its impressions of the conditions in the camp; those communications gave other organizations the confidence to pursue their own reporting and campaigning.

Other visitors to Buru included a delegation of government-approved academics, most of them psychologists, and a handful of Indonesian journalists, who spent a few days there in mid-October 1973.[108] Led by Fuad Hasan, a professor of psychology (and later minster of education), the "Inter-University Psychology Team" was made up of several professors from the well-regarded University of Indonesia and Gadjah Mada University. Ostensibly sent to assess the psychological welfare of the detainees, the team was clearly operating under an army mandate; indeed, Kopkamtib commander Sumitro and other senior army officers accompanied the team. As in the case of the psychologists who studied the detainees in Plantungan women's prison in 1975, these academics had, perhaps unwittingly, begun to serve as a "scientific" arm of the army and the New Order state. Likewise, the journalists who accompanied them had become tools of the regime's propaganda campaign to dodge or derail growing criticism of its program of arbitrary political imprisonment.

Pramoedya's account of the visit suggests, moreover, that in their interviews with detainees, the psychologists may have breeched basic codes of medical confidentiality and independence. Rather than assessing the mental health of detainees, for example, they questioned them about their political beliefs, asking what they thought about the September 30th Movement and the killing of the generals, and what kind of political system they preferred. Over the next few days, the prisoners underwent a battery of written psychological tests, followed by further group interviews with the psychologists, journalists, and senior army officers, including Sumitro. In these interviews, the detainees were once again asked about their political opinions and religious beliefs. One journalist asked whether Pramoedya had "found God" during his time in detention, while another asked whether prison had been of spiritual value. The meeting concluded with a fatuous speech by General Sumitro, who with journalists eagerly taking notes, urged the detainees not to give up hope.

In the course of his twelve-year imprisonment without charge or trial, one Indonesian political detainee asked the authorities, "Why don't you take me to court?" They told him, he said later, that it was a political matter, "and in political matters black becomes white and white becomes black."[109] That remark captured neatly a crucial dimension of the program of mass incarceration that was set in motion after October 1, 1965: its underlying motivation was not judicial but purely political. What the remark left unsaid, perhaps intentionally, was precisely what that political objective was and who was driving it. The evidence presented here leaves no room for doubt that the main objective of the campaign was to destroy the PKI and Indonesian Left, and that the principal force behind that move was the army leadership under Suharto.

Beyond that general conclusion, several features of the campaign are worth highlighting. First, the vast scale and systematic quality of the mass incarceration—including the common patterns of detention and ill treatment found across the country, the elaborate system of prisoner classification, and the heavy reliance on executive orders and decrees—make clear that it was centrally planned and coordinated, and belie any suggestion of spontaneity or randomness. Second, the methodology and logistics of incarceration—the routine brutality of the arresting officers, the common practice of torture and sexual violence during interrogation, and the resort to highly militarized routines, punishments, and rationales—point unequivocally to the army as the institution responsible and to wartime Japan as a model for the army's program. Third, the geographic variations in the pattern of incarceration, like the spatial variations in the intensity of mass killings, appear to have been related to the postures, interests, and strategies of regional and local military authorities in implementing national-level directives. Taken together, these characteristics illuminate a defining feature of the program of detention and the wider campaign of violence of which it formed a part: that in its organization, language, methods, and leadership, it was the product of a deep and entrenched militarism.

CHAPTER NINE

Release, Restrict, Discipline, and Punish

We are all aware that screening is a means for the government to discipline and purge the state apparatus of communist elements and latent communist threats in particular, as well as from extremist activities in general. It has a very strategic place in the effort to create a state which is clean and carries authority.

—GENERAL TRY SUTRISNO, ARMED FORCES COMMANDER, 1990

THE PROGRAM OF MASS DETENTION, torture, forced labor, and show trial continued for more than a decade, but by the end of 1979, all but a few dozen category A prisoners had been released. Given the massive scale of the program, and the New Order's insistence that it was vital to national security, the decision to curtail it demands further scrutiny. Why did the regime eventually decide to release all but a handful of its political detainees in the late 1970s? Did the releases signify fundamental changes in the character of the regime? And what were the consequences for former prisoners, their families, and Indonesian society as a whole?

This chapter argues that the decision to release most political detainees was the result of a major international campaign undertaken by human rights organizations in the mid-1970s. That campaign succeeded in large part because it coincided with significant changes in global norms and attitudes pertaining to human rights as well as the position of the US government, and came at a time when Indonesia was vulnerable to outside economic pressures. The chapter makes clear, however, that there was powerful resistance to the idea of releasing these prisoners—and an insistence on the continued need to protect the body politic from the "latent danger of Communism"—particularly on the part of the army leadership. As a consequence, even after prisoners were released, they and their families continued to suffer egregious restrictions, formal and informal, on every aspect of their lives. The formal restrictions continued until the end of the New Order in 1998, but the deep social and psychological legacies have lasted much longer.

Finally, the chapter makes the case that the onerous restrictions on released prisoners were part of a more general obsession on the part of the New Order regime with creating and maintaining order, discipline, and stability. That obsession was manifest in an extraordinary program of ideological screening, surveillance, and control that not only survived but intensified after the releases of 1979, and in a system of state propaganda and censorship through which the regime's militarist preoccupations became deeply embedded in Indonesian social and political life.

Release

For some time after October 1965, international reactions to Indonesia's program of arbitrary detention were predictably muted. Although Western embassies reported on the arrests to their home governments, none expressed any public or private objections to them, or inquired into the fate of the many tens of thousands who were being detained. In fact, for at least ten years, the most significant critiques came not from any government or intergovernmental body but from a handful of foreign scholars and nongovernmental organizations (NGOs), and occasionally, detainees themselves. The same was true of the political show trials. When they began in early 1966, a number of Western embassies sent staff to monitor and report on them. As the trials continued, though, fewer and fewer embassy officials attended, and by 1967, only a small number bothered to show up at all. Recalling the trial of PKI general secretary Sudisman in July 1967, which he attended with Australian political scientist Herbert Feith, Anderson later wrote that "after the first day of the trial, embassy officials apparently got tired of attending or perhaps they were busy with other matters. Herb was also quite busy, and so for the final days of the trial until Sudisman was sentenced to death, I was the only foreigner still there."[1]

THE CAMPAIGN FOR INDONESIA'S PRISONERS

That picture remained more or less unchanged until the early 1970s, when a handful of international human rights organizations—notably Amnesty International, the International Commission of Jurists, Tapol, and some church groups—began to campaign energetically on behalf of Indonesia's political prisoners. Unlike earlier advocacy efforts, these adopted a deliberately nonideological posture, arguing that the vast majority of Indonesia's political detainees were being held for their peaceful political beliefs, and must be given a fair trial or freed without condition. Embracing a style of human rights campaigning that would soon become the norm, they made their arguments in the public sphere, using demonstrations and the media not only to "name and shame" the Indonesian authorities but also to call on other governments to insist that Indonesia adhere to basic human rights norms.[2] These efforts culminated in a major Amnesty International campaign and report published in 1977, the same year the organization won the Nobel Peace Prize.

For various reasons, that campaign captured the attention of Western political and cultural elites in a way that the killings and detentions had not done a decade earlier. One reason was that it coincided with a growing awareness of the problem of political imprisonment in the Soviet Union and Eastern Europe along with the rise of an international human rights movement.[3] The fate of Indonesia's prisoners resonated powerfully with emerging international concerns focusing on freedom of expression, arbitrary detention, torture, and forced labor. The fact that a good number of Indonesia's political prisoners—or at least those in the news—were respected intellectuals and cultural figures made the problem understandable to educated, middle-class audiences in North America and Europe. Partly for these reasons, starting around 1973, the cause of Indonesia's prisoners began to be championed by selected Western states, notably the Netherlands, and world bodies such as the ILO.[4]

The campaign on behalf of Indonesia's political prisoners also received a boost from Carter's election in November 1976. Whatever might be said about the way his administration actually implemented his vision of a human rights–based foreign policy, President Carter opened the door to a set of demands and arguments grounded in human rights that could not easily be brushed aside.[5] The campaign also coincided with a period of political soul-searching in the United States. In the aftermath of Watergate and Vietnam, the US Congress—as well as many journalists, intellectuals, and cultural figures—were critically reexamining what were seen as the serious failures of US foreign policy in Southeast Asia and around the world. It was against that backdrop that in mid-1976, Congress held hearings on "The Question of Human Rights in Indonesia."[6]

Carter's presidency was influential well beyond Washington. Advocates for human rights inside Indonesia—and even political prisoners themselves—heard about his vision and grasped it as a weapon that could be used in their fight. In his memoir, one former political detainee on Buru recalled how the news of Carter's inaugural address in January 1977 had immediately spread throughout the camp, igniting hopeful rumors that their release could not be far off.[7] And in an open letter published in August 1977, a recently released political prisoner invoked Carter's new approach, saying, "This renewed call for the respect of human rights surely brings new hopes!"[8] In short, the mid-1970s were a time of unusual receptiveness to the messages that were at the heart of the prisoner campaign, and the NGOs made the most of it.

That is not to say that human rights campaigners were following the lead of government officials. On the contrary, the record is clear that human rights activists began their campaign years before most Western governments were on board, and both before and after Carter's inauguration, they faced resistance from disinterested or recalcitrant governments. An official human rights report on Indonesia prepared by the US Department of State in mid-1976 offers a revealing glimpse of the problem. Reviewing specific categories of rights articulated in the Universal Declaration of Human Rights, the report provided an accounting that borrowed directly from Indonesian Army propaganda and was wholly at odds with reality:

> Article 3: The right to life, liberty and security of persons is conditioned by the 1966 Emergency Powers Act. However, the Indonesian Government does not practice unlawful killings, and liberty and security of the person are generally observed.
>
> Article 5: Torture, cruel, inhuman or degrading treatment or punishment are not used by the Government as an instrument of policy nor officially tolerated by the Government.
>
> Article 8: Access to legal remedies can be difficult because of the complexity of several co-existing systems and understaffed and overcrowded courts.
>
> Article 9: Arbitrary arrests and detentions occur in Indonesia in cases involving national security. The continued detention of about 31,000 persons is based on the fear of the Indonesian leadership that

> if the communists are allowed to regroup Indonesia will again be plunged into disorder and an apprehension that feelings still exist against those detained which would cause disturbances if they returned to their homes.
>
> Article 11: Appropriate safeguards appear to be followed in criminal trials. Such procedures also appear to be followed in political trials. Under the 1966 Emergency Powers detainees need not be brought to trial.

The report also claimed that Indonesia's press was among the freest in Asia outside Japan, and—incredibly—that there were few limits on freedom of association. "Apart from the outlawing of the communist party," the department noted blandly, "there are no unusual limitations on freedom of association which apply to the general public."[9]

Notwithstanding the craven posture adopted by the State Department, by mid-1976 the campaign on behalf of Indonesia's political prisoners had begun to have an effect on the attitude of Western governments as well as international organizations, not to mention human rights organizations inside Indonesia itself. While naturally anxious to maintain close relations with Indonesian authorities, whom they still regarded as vital strategic and political allies, the United States and other powers started to raise questions about the fate of the prisoners, and even to suggest that the generous packages of economic and military aid they had provided since 1966 might be jeopardized by a failure to address the situation. In late 1976, for example, a delegation of US senators visited Jakarta to call on Suharto to resolve the prisoner problem or risk losing substantial US (and IMF and World Bank) aid. Over the same period, US deputy secretary of state for human rights Patricia Derian and other administration officials were pushing hard for their release, and likewise made it plain that US and other foreign aid hung in the balance.[10] As it happened, those initiatives came at a time when Indonesia was uniquely vulnerable to a decline in economic assistance. The state oil company, Pertamina, had virtually gone bankrupt in early 1975, revealing a potentially catastrophic vulnerability in the Indonesian economy and political system.[11]

OFFICIAL RESPONSE

It was clear from the outset that Indonesian Army authorities were extremely sensitive to outside opinions of their campaign to crush the PKI and sideline Sukarno. Their furious reaction to the unpublished paper of

Cornell University scholars Anderson and McVey, who took issue with the official version of the supposed coup, was a sign of just how much they worried. It was also telling that the first published official account of the alleged coup was written not in Indonesian but in English—a language that only a tiny fraction of Indonesians could read.[12] The preface to that account offers a fascinating glimpse into the reasons behind its publication. It reveals not only that the book was intended for a foreign audience but also that it was researched and written on instructions from the army leadership with the explicit aim of rebutting the claims of foreign critics:

> In the light of the existence of a campaign being waged in certain circles in Western countries against the New Order in Indonesia, posing the rebel's view of the [September 30] affair, the two authors were sent to the United States and the Netherlands, where they were able to observe the campaign from its very centers. It should be mentioned here that the "political guerilla" waged by certain Eastern Bloc countries were considered well-known enough; consequently the two authors were not sent to those countries as was planned earlier. By studying the hostile campaigns, the authors were able to rewrite their manuscript in order to cope with the issues posed by the articles of those circles.[13]

The preface to the book also affirmed that the army's preoccupation at the time was with foreign challenges to the official version of the supposed coup. While that question never went away entirely, by the early 1970s the army's attention had begun to shift to the subject of political prisoners. The reason, it seems clear, was that political prisoners were now the main focus of foreign criticism.

As external pressure mounted, Indonesian authorities responded in ways they hoped would satisfy their foreign critics.[14] In doing so, they offered up an ever-changing array of explanations, none of them convincing, for the continued detention of so many prisoners without charge or trial. The shifting justifications offered by those authorities provide important insights into the character of the regime and the thinking of its leaders, so are worth reviewing here briefly.

Their first attempt to justify the detention of so many political prisoners concentrated on the trials, emphasizing that they were conducted in accordance with Indonesia's 1945 Constitution and broadly accepted international human rights standards. As critics, both at home and abroad, began to point out the myriad problems with these claims—the most obvious being that the vast majority of prisoners had never been charged or tried, and that the trials did not, in any case, come close to meeting international standards of fairness—army strategists shifted gear.[15]

While never completely abandoning the dubious claims about legality and the rule of law, they began to argue as well that untried prisoners were being held out of concern for their own safety; such was the animosity toward them, the government said, that if they were released too soon, they might not be accepted by their communities and might even be subjected to physical violence.[16] In its statement to the ILO meeting in June 1976, for example, the Indonesian delegation claimed that "release of detainees if not carefully prepared may very well ... pose real and grave danger to the personal safety of the detainees themselves at the hands of members of their original communities who may not have forgotten the role these detainees played in the period of terror and intimidation prior [to] and during the abortive coup."[17]

A third sort of explanation, which may have been somewhat closer to the real reason, was that in the government's view, these untried prisoners represented a threat to national security and stability—commonly described as the latent danger of Communism.[18] Even if they had never been tried, and even if there was insufficient evidence to charge them with any crime, the authorities were sure that by virtue of their political beliefs and past associations, those detainees represented a mortal danger to the state and nation as well as the sacred ideology of Pancasila. Thus, in the preface to an official brochure about Buru, Attorney General Sugih Arto clarified that the prisoners sent there were people whom the authorities believed had played "an important role in planning, supervising and carrying out the 30 September/PKI Movement ... however we have not sufficient evidence to prosecute them further. We consider it still to be a danger to our security to return them to the community."[19]

The truth was that there was no evidence to support any of these explanations. By the mid-1970s, tens of thousands of category B and C prisoners had been released, but the government could not point to a single instance of violent attack against them.[20] Moreover, after the last whiff of PKI resistance had been utterly crushed in 1968—and arguably long before that—the threat of Communist subversion had been virtually nonexistent. Indeed, when asked specifically about these two claims in November 1976, a senior military officer, General Ali Murtopo, told Amnesty International's Secretary-General Martin Ennals that "communist subversion was not a serious threat to the Indonesian Government and that there had not been wide-scale reprisals against [released] political prisoners."[21]

Faced with these obvious problems, Indonesian government officials scrambled to find additional justifications for the continued arbitrary detention without trial of many thousands of political prisoners. Mounting international pressure, especially from Washington, also motivated the search for plausible explanations. As the International Commission of Jurists wrote in December 1976, "During 1976, there has been intensive pressure in the US Congress and elsewhere about political detainees in Indonesia."[22] Accordingly, Indonesian authorities began to offer a new explanation, quite different from the others, yet no more satisfactory.

The category B prisoners could not yet be released to society, officials now said, because in the tough economic conditions of the time, they would have difficulty finding jobs. Unemployment among former prisoners would in turn give rise to security threats. As Kopkamtib chief of staff Admiral Sudomo explained in December 1976, before category B prisoners could be released, "there must be sufficient employment opportunities for them, since unemployment would create fertile ground for all kinds of acts contrary to law, and this in itself would pose a threat to national security."[23] As a solution to this problem, army authorities proposed that category B prisoners would not return to their homes in Java and elsewhere but instead would be resettled to less populous and developed parts of the country—including Sumatra, Kalimantan, and Sulawesi—where they would form settler colonies, opening up new farmland. In other words, as Amnesty International and others pointed out, the authorities were effectively proposing an expansion of the Buru resettlement program—the creation of a network of penal colonies.[24]

It was against this backdrop that Amnesty International published its comprehensive report on Indonesia's prisoners, and launched a major media and publicity campaign calling for their release. The publication of that report in 1977 and the campaign launch, coming so soon after the start of Carter's presidency, signaled a turning point in the Indonesian government's efforts to justify its continued detention of political prisoners.

The government's initial reaction to the Amnesty International report was to dismiss it as a politically motivated hack job. Government and military officials suggested that Communists had hijacked Amnesty International, and that its report could therefore safely be ignored.[25] The idea that Amnesty International was a hotbed of Communism, and that its Indonesia research desk in London was staffed by PKI members and sympathizers, persisted throughout the New Order. At a meeting in Jakarta in 1993, the former foreign minister, Mochtar Kusumaatmadja, told me that Amnesty International's head of research for Indonesia was a card-carrying member of the PKI. As it happened, I held that post at the time, and so I took the opportunity to tell him that he was mistaken. The minister insisted that he was right, declaring that the person in question was someone much more important than me.

Eventually, the government recognized the need to respond more seriously to the evidence presented in the report. Accordingly, in January 1978, the Department of Foreign Affairs published a pamphlet—in English—that returned to the earlier claims about the rule of law, while also drawing on the other explanations. In doing so, the government revealed that an additional category (X) had been added to cover those political detainees still not processed a full thirteen years after the events of 1965, and confirmed, without apparent embarrassment, that category B prisoners were being held without trial because there was insufficient evidence to charge them with a crime. The pamphlet is worth quoting at length:

> The arrest and detention of those involved in the G30S/PKI never had as its purpose solely to safeguard the interest of society in public order and safety. On the contrary, their detention was equally directed towards preparing their cases for trial before the judicial courts in order for them to account for their violations of the law, or, as the case may be for their return to society, in accordance with their fundamental rights as members of that society.
>
> As a first step in implementation of this policy, it was necessary to determine to what degree a person was actually involved in the G30S/PKI affair, through a process of thorough investigation, involving meticulous screening and crosschecking of data on a national scale. Based on this process, which by its nature is a continuing one, four categories were established, namely:
>
> Category A: those who were clearly and directly involved as planners, leaders or executioners in the attempted coup, with sufficient evidence of their guilt so that their cases could be brought to the court of justice for trial . . .
>
> Category B: those for whom strong indications exists [*sic*] that they played similar roles to those of A-category detainees, especially in the preparations for the attempted coup. Owing to insufficient amount of evidence so far, they could not yet be brought to trial but neither could they be set free precipitately without endangering national security and stability and their own safety . . .

> Category C: those who were indirectly involved in the G30S/PKI and who, after investigation established them as neither belonging to the A-category or the B-category, could hence be returned to society . . .
>
> Category X: a temporary classification denoting those still being processed to determine whether they should be categorized as either A or B, or should be released.[26]

In addition to these ever-shifting justifications, Indonesian authorities also sought to evade criticism by throwing up a barrage of inaccurate, misleading, and constantly changing information about the numbers of prisoners in detention. The government apparently hoped that these numbers would reassure its foreign supporters and deflect the criticism of its opponents. But far from protecting the government, its cavalier approach to the numbers actually became a new focus of international criticism, drawing still more attention to the problem rather than diminishing it.[27]

At that stage, old allies stepped up in a last-ditch effort to defend the Indonesian position. In early 1978, for example, former US ambassador to Indonesia Francis J. Galbraith (who had been deputy chief of mission in the embassy at the time of the September 30th Movement) responded angrily to an article, "In Indonesian Prisons," in the *New York Review of Books* written by two Amnesty International staff members. In his letter, Galbraith not only repeated the government's dubious claims regarding the numbers but also sought to justify Indonesia's continued detention of political prisoners on the grounds that they were all "Communist cadres" and the government was "fighting a Communist insurgency."

> Indonesia and most of Indonesia's neighbors . . . are fighting Communist insurgencies, and have been doing so for years. Desperately trying to develop the country economically, the Suharto Government has understandably hesitated to turn loose the slightly more than 30,000 Communist cadres still detained (not 100,000 as alleged by Amnesty International) to fuel such an insurgency. The government has, however, released tens of thousands over the past few years and has announced its intention of releasing 10,000 more by the end of this year and 10,000 more in each of the following two years.[28]

Not only was Galbraith's central claim untrue—Indonesia was not fighting a Communist insurgency—his letter appeared to cast aside some of the most elementary tenets of human rights and the rule of law. As Ennals wrote in his reply to Galbraith,

> In conclusion, it is only fair to point out that there is a deep and terrifying logic underlying Mr. Galbraith's argument. He says "the Suharto Government has understandably hesitated to turn loose" those untried political prisoners because they posed the threat and reality of communist insurgency in Indonesia. It is the logic of arbitrary power to maintain that large numbers of people should be detained without trial and without evidence for many years. It is precisely in certain periods of a nation's history, when there is political polarization, that the safeguard for each and every person can only be found in the rule of law. Otherwise, if Mr. Galbraith will reflect a moment, he must realize that people can be treated in appalling and arbitrary ways out of mere suspicion or from guilt by association.[29]

In the face of such mounting international criticism, by mid-1978 the Indonesian authorities had come to accept that the category B prisoners would have to be released. Finally, by late 1979, more than fourteen years after the events in which they were alleged to have been involved, but for which they were never charged or tried, the last of those prisoners was released. Yet that did not mean their ordeal had come to an end.

Restrict

In their memoirs, letters, and occasional public statements, Indonesia's former political detainees sound a common theme: that despite their formal release, they were never freed. As a former Buru detainee wrote in his memoir, "I don't want to say we were 'freed' because the truth is that once we were back in Java we were not free at all."[30] Another referred to the condition of all former detainees as "the freedom of a person whose freedom is restricted, that is to say, not free."[31] At the height of the New Order, critics described the restrictions on former prisoners and their families as a system of collective punishment, comparable to the practice of old Javanese kings, Dutch colonial authorities, the Japanese occupation army, and European fascists.[32] The renowned Indonesian human rights lawyer Yap Thiam Hien referred to the restrictions as tantamount to "civil death."[33]

The first indications of the limited nature of detainees' freedom came at the moment of their release. Despite the fact that they had never been charged or tried, as a condition of release they were required to confess that they had belonged to a banned organization, to condemn the September 30th Movement, and to swear that they would be loyal to the state ideology, Pancasila.[34] Those conditions were only a foretaste of what was to come. As Kopkamtib Chief of Staff Sudomo clarified in December 1978, "After they are released and returned to society, they still have to assure the Government through concrete deeds that they consciously have discarded their communist ideology, and that they are faithful to the Pancasila ideology.... This adjustment is a social process in itself... which also requires supervision by the society in general as well as by the law enforcement agencies."[35]

Over some three decades, New Order authorities set in motion a bewildering array of policies and practices that profoundly affected—and sometimes destroyed—the lives of many thousands of former detainees along with untold numbers of their friends and relatives. These policies and practices touched on, and effectively restricted, virtually every aspect of their lives, from political expression and association to economic activity, to the most intimate details of family relations. As an internal army document from 1974 described it, the goal was to "cleanse all remnants of the G-30-S/PKI from the government, the military, and society," through the creation of "an integrated system of surveillance and control of former [political] detainees and prisoners that is both efficient and effective."[36] To the extent that the regime called on the general population to assist in implementing this system, it also cast a pall over the entire country, fostering a climate of fear, mutual suspicion, and anxiety about the very suggestion of critical historical inquiry and political debate.

POLITICAL RIGHTS

For one thing, the political rights of former political prisoners were explicitly restricted. Under the country's basic electoral law, security forces could deny the right to vote to anyone who was deemed "disloyal to the Constitution" or had disseminated Marxist-Leninist ideas. Presidential Decree 63 of 1985 authorized the review and scrutiny of former political detainees to determine if they should be permitted to vote.[37] That same year, as noted earlier, a senior official in the Ministry of Home Affairs announced that some 1.7 million accused of "involvement" in the September 30th Movement and PKI would be reviewed to determine whether they would be eligible to vote in the 1987 elections.[38] Even those who were permitted to vote did so in the shadow of official surveillance and pressure to support the government party, Golkar. The experience of Luh Sutari, a former political detainee from Bali, was far from unusual. "Every time there was an election," she later told an interviewer, "we had to attend a 'santiaji' or propaganda course, and we were ordered to join Golkar."[39]

The political rights of former detainees were restricted in other ways as well. For example, ex-tapols (*eks-tahanan politik*, or former political detainees) were required to undergo ideological screening before their nominations for political party membership were accepted. Those already serving as elected officials, but later discovered or alleged to have had some connection to the PKI, were subject to removal from office. Inevitably, too, allegations about an individual's past ties to the PKI or the September 30th Movement were sometimes used to attack or discredit certain political figures, especially those critical of the regime. In 1995, for example, three hundred members of the new Indonesian Democratic Party (Partai Demokrasi Indonesia, or PDI), were accused of having Communist ties.[40] Allegations of "involvement" in the PKI or the September 30th Movement were also a common means used to harass and limit labor organizing, student activism, and other kinds of political activity.[41]

Government and military officials also sought to limit the political rights and activities of former detainees by rearresting them on spurious grounds, making thinly veiled threats against them, or requiring them to undergo what was euphemistically called "guidance" (*pembinaan*) by army officials. These actions typically took place in the context of national elections or other significant political events. In the late 1960s and early 1970s, for example, recently released political prisoners in certain regions were sometimes rearrested to ensure security during presidential visits.[42] In 1972, the minister of home affairs warned released category C prisoners that if they were caught trying to revive Communism, they would be rearrested and placed in category B.[43] Responding to criticism of irregularities in the 1977 elections, President Suharto threatened that "critics of the election administration can be categorized either as members of the outlawed Communist party or members of illegal Muslim organizations."[44] And in 1994, the regional military commander for Greater Jakarta, General Hendropriyono, announced that the military would "carry out guidance activities toward all former prisoners" in advance of the important Asia Pacific Economic Cooperation meeting in Jakarta. The aim, he said, was to "guard against elements that might do things to embarrass the state and the nation."[45]

Under such circumstances, most ex-tapols chose to remain silent and avoid any involvement in political activity. One ex-tapol explained the logic of their silence: "If we had done even the slightest thing to attract public attention, we would have been accused of practicing communism or Sukarnoism."[46] Indeed, the decision to remain silent and the fear of being unmasked appear as constant refrains in the memoirs and testimonies of former detainees. Describing a visit to Jakarta in 1983 to help with the decorations for a parade, one former detainee from Central Java recounted, "I was terrified that my identity as an ex-political prisoner would be found out.... I kept away from the media so my identity would not be discovered. I just listened and kept my mouth shut."[47] Another, from Bali, explained that even in his own village, "I never talk about sensitive things. If I talk, I talk about general things, things that can be spoken about, and things that I know."[48]

SOCIAL AND ECONOMIC RIGHTS

Despite having been released and never found guilty of any crime, moreover, former tapols were required to report (*wajib lapor*) to various local authorities for years after their release, typically on a weekly or monthly basis.[49] Those who failed to show up, whether because of ill health or family obligations, were subject to discipline and punishment at the discretion of the relevant authority. And while there appeared to be no legal basis for the requirement, ex-tapols were typically required to obtain official permission to travel abroad. In late 1992, the coordinating minister for political and security affairs announced that some thirty-three thousand former PKI prisoners remained on a government blacklist restricting their travel out of the country. In addition, thousands of Indonesians —some but not all of them former members of the PKI and affiliated organizations—who were abroad in October 1965 were effectively prevented from returning home for at least three decades.[50] Although government officials said that the exiles would be permitted to return, they warned that those doing so should be prepared to face legal proceedings in connection with their past political activities and associations.

Former political prisoners were also required to obtain special permission each time they sought to renew their national identity card, obtain a loan, attend a class, or undertake any economic activity. Each reporting requirement created new opportunities for authorities to monitor, restrict, harass, and extort money from former detainees. Furthermore, because such requirements were not based in law but rather in a raft of obscure bureaucratic and military regulations of dubious legality, they varied widely from place to place and over time, inevitably adding uncertainty and anxiety to the already-precarious and disrupted lives of former prisoners.

Former political detainees were also prohibited from working in a wide range of "sensitive" occupations.[51] Without the explicit approval of government and military authorities, they could not work in the civil service or armed forces, nor in any "strategic industry"—including oil and gas production, mining, chemical manufacturing, electricity, sugar and rubber production, postal services, banking, and sea, rail, and air transport.[52] And depending on how the rules were interpreted, former political detainees could also be prohibited from serving on the boards of corporations and cooperatives, working as teachers, journalists, puppeteers, university professors, actors, priests, or lawyers—in short, any profession in which they would have been in a position to spread leftist ideas.[53] Barred from many fields of employment, they tried to make a living by establishing small-scale businesses, such as selling noodles and cakes, repairing bicycles, or tutoring.[54] But even here they faced serious obstacles. Obtaining a bank loan, for instance, was next to impossible because it required the approval of government officials. It also required property, which few former political prisoners had because their land and houses had often been confiscated at the time of their detention, and never returned.[55]

Among the more notorious mechanisms of official discrimination, and one that invited comparisons with Nazi Germany and South Africa's apartheid regime, was the requirement that the mandatory national identity cards of former political detainees bear the annotation "ET" for "Ekstapol." The policy, which was spelled out in a 1981 Ministry of Home Affairs regulation on "the Guidance and Monitoring of Former G30S/PKI Political Detainees and Prisoners," affected roughly a million people.[56] Quite apart from the inherent injustice of being labeled and stigmatized for crimes they had not committed, and for which they had never even been charged, the ET mark had potentially dire everyday consequences for those required to bear it. By ensuring that government authorities, potential employers, acquaintances, and prospective in-laws would all know of their "tainted" past, the ET mark impeded every aspect of life, from interactions with officialdom to the most intimate matters of personal relationships and family life. More than one critic compared the ET mark to the Star of David that Jews were required to wear under the Nazis.[57]

One of the most jarring and controversial aspects of these policies was that they affected not only people who had themselves been detained, however unjustly, for their political activities and beliefs but also their relatives, their children, and even their grandchildren.[58] In the term used by critics at the time, the New Order state treated affiliation with the PKI and the Left as an "inheritable sin" or "generational sin" (*dosa turunan*). The result was that young people who had perhaps not even been born at the time of the alleged coup, and may never have met their "unclean" parents, nevertheless lived with a powerful social stigma. That stigma inevitably took a heavy emotional toll and contributed to a variety of psychological problems.[59] For an untold number of ordinary citizens, it also meant the loss of employment, estrangement of friends and family, bullying, withdrawal from school, and difficulties in finding a life partner, as employers, friends, and potential in-laws feared any association with them. The solution for many former prisoners was to cut off all ties with their family, and to change or hide their true identity.[60]

Discipline and Punishment

At the heart of the restrictions on former prisoners were two features of the New Order state that profoundly affected Indonesian society at large. The first was a deeply intrusive system of ideological policing and mass surveillance, designed to root out, isolate, discipline, and punish anyone even remotely associated with or influenced by the PKI and other banned organizations.[61] The second was an elaborate system of propaganda and censorship likewise designed to maintain social order, discipline, and control. Both bear close scrutiny not only because of their dire consequences for many hundreds of thousands of Indonesians but also for what they reveal about the mind-set and inner workings of the Indonesian state. For while many of the restrictions and regulations were formally rescinded after the demise of the New Order in 1998, the toxic ideas and norms that underpinned them have persisted within the state and society at large.

MENTAL SCREENING

The system of ideological policing was established in the late 1960s with a set of regulations aimed at purging leftists from the armed forces and the civil service.[62] Over the next three decades, it was elaborated and intensified—in a dizzying array of presidential, ministerial, and military decrees and instructions—to encompass all members, or prospective members, of the country's huge civil service, armed forces, and "strategic" industries. By the 1980s, moreover, the state's ideological screening norms and protocols had been adopted by many private employers and service providers as well, effectively creating a vast dragnet of surveillance and ideological policing, enforced by state and quasi-state entities and by Indonesian society itself.

The ideological vetting process established soon after October 1, 1965 was referred to in internal documents as "mental screening" (*screening mental*) or "ideological mental screening" (*screening mental ideologis*). Those who passed the screening were given a certificate guaranteeing that they were "free from Communist influence" (*Surat Bebas G-30-S/PKI*), which in theory allowed them to live a normal life. In principle, such certificates were required only of a person seeking employment in the civil service, military, or a "stategic industry." In practice, by the early 1970s they were being requested of almost everyone for all manner of business, including routine matters like "applications to install a telephone, requests to see land titles in the government Land Office, or admissions to institutions of higher education." Indeed, these certificates were so broadly required that those who did not have one lived in what Justus M. van der Kroef has called "a kind of security limbo."[63]

Following the promulgation of new regulations in the early 1980s, the vetting process came to be known as the "clean environment" (*bersih lingkungan*) campaign, because the new system judged not only an individual's actions, words, and beliefs but also their wider familial and social environment.[64] As one of those decrees clarified, "The ideological mental screening includes an assessment of civil servants and prospective civil servants with regard to their environment which encompasses their personal identity and also that of their family as well as their broader environment, place of residence, and acquaintances."[65] Only those with a clean environment would survive the vetting.

The following questions, drawn from official screening questionnaires and interviews from the mid-1980s, give some sense of the process:[66]

1. Outline your family history (including your grandparents on both your mother's and father's sides, their religious beliefs, and their social condition).
2. If you are married, do the same for your wife's family history . . .
5. What is your opinion of Golkar [the governing party]? . . .
10. What is your opinion of P-4 [the official program of ideological indoctrination]?
11. What do you know about G-30-S? What is your opinion about that event?
12. Were any members of your family "involved" in G-30-S? If so, in what way?
13. What is Marxism/Leninism?

14. Communism is said to be a latent danger. Why?
15. What is your opinion of the New Order?
16. What do you think about protest actions with banners?
17. What is your opinion of Indonesian citizens who refuse to vote?
18. What do you think of [the armed forces'] Dual Function?

Following criticism of this system, in 1990 the vetting process was given the name "special review" (*penelitian khusus*, or *litsus*), and the term clean environment was phased out.[67] Apart from the name change, however, the system remained the same—with the same Orwellian mindset, the same obsession with loyalty and obedience, and the same broad notions of ideological guilt and impurity as the previous system. Like the earlier arrangements, special review was aimed at confronting the latent threat of Communism, disciplining and purging those connected in any way with the September 30th Movement or the PKI, and enforcing absolute loyalty and obedience to the state and its ideology.[68]

And while vetting was to be conducted by "litsus teams" established in each government department and agency, overall responsibility for the system was left in the hands of the powerful state security body that had replaced Kopkamtib in 1988, known as the Agency for the Coordination of Support for the Development of National Stability (Badan Koordinasi Bantuan Pemantapan Stabilitas Nasional, or Bakorstanas). The authoritarian rationale for the policy—its emphasis on discipline, order, and cleanliness—was spelled out clearly by the armed forces commander and head of Bakorstanas, General Try Sutrisno, at a meeting of officials on the date the policy was announced in 1990:

> We are all aware that screening is a means for the government to discipline and purge the state apparatus of communist elements and latent communist threats in particular, as well as from extremist activities in general. It has a very strategic place in the effort to create a state which is clean and carries authority. Consequently, we must try as hard as possible to ensure that such screening remains consistent in character, comprehensive, ongoing and firmly grounded in the law.[69]

A press release issued by Bakorstanas on the same date provided a further rationale for the policy: to guard against the "latent Communist threat," and specifically to prevent a "comeback" by the September 30th Movement and the PKI:

> Even though physically we have been able to put down these [PKI] uprisings, and by law the teaching of the PKI and other doctrines have

> been prohibited, as a political ideology communism has not yet been eradicated.... In fact, supporters of these doctrines have continued to engage in G30S/PKI activities and have made various illegal attempts at a comeback.... Thus we have to guard and sharpen our sense of alert against a latent communist threat. In connection with this, the concept of the involvement in G30S/PKI and other prohibited organizations has been defined in a broad sense to cover and prevent all current and future efforts to stage a comeback among what is left of G30S/PKI.[70]

In keeping with these objectives, the new policy articulated astonishingly broad parameters for identifying possible involvement in the September 30th Movement or the PKI and other banned organizations. "Basically," military authorities explained, "any person who has at any time, through speech, action, or writing, *expressed an attitude or belief* supportive of the PKI participants in G30S/PKI or the political convictions and strategies of the G30S/PKI incident can be said to be 'involved' in G30S."[71] To be clear, that meant that a person who had not been born in 1965, but who read a book, wrote an essay, or expressed an opinion that could be construed as sympathetic to the PKI, could be judged to have been "involved" in the purported coup attempt of 1965.

But the screening system did not stop there. Like the earlier system, litsus was meant to explore and judge the possible "negative" consequences of an individual's "interactions" with others in their "environment." As an official document clarified in 1990,

> Basically, all humans are affected by those with whom they interact in their environment. For this reason, a "special review" of each civil servant will be undertaken to check for interaction with persons involved in the G30S/PKI incident and with supporters of communism, as such interaction can influence a person's own attitudes, opinions and way of thinking such that an overall negative influence is effected on his/her sense of loyalty and obedience to Pancasila, the 1945 Constitution, State and Government.[72]

There were obvious problems with this arrangement. For one thing, it was vulnerable to gross abuse; employers and vetting committees could use the pretext of political unreliability to remove unwanted or troublesome employees, or create job openings for friends and family members.[73] Among its most pernicious aspects, however, was the fact that guilt was judged not only on the basis of a subject's actions or words—which would have been bad enough—and certainly not on the basis of any crime that had been committed, but rather on the basis of their presumed thoughts, ideas, and associations. It was, in effect, a form of collective punishment based on the tendentious pretext that political ideas were a form of viral infection, or perhaps a genetic problem, that could be passed on through bodily or social interaction.[74]

Despite the name changes, then, the rudiments of the ideological screening system remained the same. The goal was to discipline and purge the politically unreliable with a view to securing absolute obedience and loyalty to the state and its ideology. Under this system, state authorities were empowered to investigate hundreds of thousands of people for their possible connections to the PKI and other banned organizations. Those found to have such inclinations or connections could be, and were, denied all manner of political, social, and economic rights.[75] In short, this was an extrajudicial system designed to police and punish thought, comparable in its tone and hysterical anticommunism to McCarthyism in the United States, and in its broad reach to the ideological purges of China's Cultural Revolution.[76]

"THE LATENT THREAT OF COMMUNISM"

The second feature of the New Order regime that shaped the lives of former prisoners and Indonesian society as a whole was an intensive, long-term program of state-sponsored propaganda. Through that program, New Order authorities succeeded in popularizing and rendering hegemonic a profoundly misleading but remarkably resilient historical account of the events of 1965–66 while silencing alternative versions. From the outset, it portrayed the PKI as the party responsible for setting the violence in motion, and depicted the anticommunist violence as both heroic and necessary for national stability and security. The official narrative also cast the PKI as cruel and depraved, repeatedly evoked the "latent threat of Communism," and reminded any potential critics of the dire consequences of being labeled a leftist.

As Ariel Heryanto has argued, moreover, official conjuring of the specter of Communist cruelty and subversion penetrated deeply into popular culture, discouraging political opposition, and eliciting mass obedience and silence.[77] The steady drip-drip of falsehoods and elisions, developed during the New Order, had deep and lasting effects. Whether critics like it or not, a great many Indonesians actually believed (and still believe) these characterizations. As Anderson and McVey predicted more than fifty years ago, official demonization of the PKI has had deep and long-lasting consequences:

> On a long-term basis the "monster" explanation of PKI sponsorship of the affair has the advantage of firmly replanting the image with which the Indonesian Communists have been burdened since the Madiun Affair and which they had only partly succeeded in erasing. Whatever questions may later be asked, whatever counter-arguments produced, people who absorbed the view of the PKI which is now presented will not be able to think of the Communists later except as a group stained by atrocity and treason.[78]

One of the most important examples of New Order propaganda, whose effects are still felt today, was the lengthy film *Pengkhianatan Gerakan 30 September/PKI* (The Treachery of the September 30th Movement/ Indonesian Communist Party) that was compulsory annual viewing for all schoolchildren in the country from 1984 to 1998.[79] Through its graphic and violent representation of the alleged coup, the film introduced all the official tropes of PKI treachery and depravity, including the allegedly debauched behavior of Gerwani women, and left no room for doubt about the party's responsibility for the torture and killing of the six generals. The film's soundtrack wove the popular song *Genjer-Genjer* into the moments portraying the greatest acts of cruelty, creating an association between the song and the PKI's ostensible barbarism.

The intense and disturbing sensory experience of watching the film undoubtedly had a profound effect on those who viewed it; many children found the film extremely frightening, and some later experienced trauma and nightmares. Given the fact that the film was compulsory viewing for all schoolchildren—and required television programming every September 30—for fifteen years, the number of people affected may be conservatively estimated in the hundreds of millions. That conclusion is borne out by opinion polls carried out just after Suharto's resignation in 1998. A poll conducted by the respected national media outlets *Tempo* and *Kompas* in 1999 found that 97 percent of respondents had seen the film, and that 72 percent said it was their main source of information about the events of October 1, 1965. The following year, a *Kompas* survey found that 77 percent of respondents agreed with the characterization of Communists as "sadistic, atheistic, and immoral," while more than half agreed that Communists were comparable to murderers.[80]

For more than three decades, millions of Indonesian schoolchildren were also the target of relentless state propaganda through their nationally mandated lessons in history and civics. Throughout the New Order period, school textbooks and teachers' manuals presented only the official version of the supposed coup attempt, which contrasted the alleged cruelty, depravity, and treachery of the PKI with the heroism and sacrifice of the six generals—unfailingly described as "Revolutionary Heroes"—and the selfless courage of the army in saving the state and nation from ruin. While dwelling on the purported torture and killing of the six generals, the textbooks and manuals made no mention of the killing of half a million unarmed citizens or the incarceration of a million more.

Perhaps even more remarkably, this perverse official version of history is no relic of the past. On the contrary, years after Suharto was forced to step down and Indonesia began its transition to democracy, it continued to be taught in schools.[81] In a shocking scene from the documentary film *The Look of Silence*, shot several years after Suharto's resignation, an elementary school teacher relates to his class the story of the alleged coup attempt, as follows:

> Communists are cruel. Communists don't believe in God. To change the political system—the communists kidnapped six army generals. They sliced the generals' faces with razor blades. Would you like that? Imagine how painful it would be if your eyes were gouged out. Their eyes were ripped out! If you slaughter a chicken—and just rip its head off. . . . Wouldn't that be cruel? The communists were cruel so the government had to repress them. The communists were put in prison. Their children couldn't become government officials. Hey, you're the child of a communist! You're not allowed to work for the government. Hey, your grandfather was a communist! You're not allowed in the army! Hey, your grandmother was a communist! You can't join the police! [So, to be clear, if] you rebel against the state, you go to jail. So let's thank the heroes—who struggled to make our country a . . . democracy![82]

The New Order's version of history was also enforced through quasi-religious public rituals that glorified the military, and reinforced the negative and dehumanizing mythologies about the PKI. The most important of these was Sacred Pancasila Day (*Hari Kesaktian Pancasila*), held every year on the anniversary of the "coup" at the Sacred Pancasila Monument erected at the spot where the generals were killed. The ritual mourned the death of the generals while simultaneously erasing the memory of the

FIGURE 9.1. General Pramono Edhie Wibowo, then army chief of staff, reviews army weapons exhibition in Jakarta, October 2012. (Yamtomo Sardi/Stock Photo)

hundreds of thousands killed or detained, and warning of the ever-present danger of Communism.[83]

Notably, this and other anticommunist rituals continued long after the New Order ended, effectively keeping alive a set of ideas and tropes that dated back to the late 1960s. At the ceremony in 2011, for example, the army chief of staff, General Pramono Edhie Wibowo—son of the notorious RPKAD commander Sarwo Edhie Wibowo—told the country that vigilance must be maintained against Communists so that the G30S affair would never be repeated: "This event to recite the confession of the faith and a joint prayer organized by the Army in praying for our revolutionary heroes is not to prolong grudges, but we must understand that the [G30S] incident really did happen. We, as the successors of the nation must be vigilant, lest it be repeated."[84]

The authorities also sought to enforce silence and compliance through the continued imprisonment and occasional judicial execution of the remaining category A prisoners. Between 1985 and 1990, for example, twenty category A prisoners were killed by firing squad. Four of those, all of them members of the Presidential Guard, were executed on a single day in February 1990, more than two decades after their arrest. Another six, all former members of the PKI, were set to be killed the following month but their executions were postponed in the face of intense international criticism.[85] Meanwhile, at least two dozen elderly prisoners, some of them very ill, languished in prison through the 1990s.[86]

Silence and compliance was also maintained through official censorship. For most of the New Order, state censors vetted books, films, artworks, and the media for any mention of the events of 1965–66 that questioned the official narrative. They also banned the works of authors who had a previous association with the PKI or leftist organizations, even when they could not point to anything in the works themselves that could possibly be construed as support for or dissemination of Communist ideas. And they jailed those found to be in possession of or distributing those works.[87] News editors and publishers who pushed the limits received visits from state authorities, and were occasionally punished or their presses were closed down. Gradually, a kind of self-censorship became the norm among publishers, editors, and most authors.

RESISTANCE

Given these facts, it is easy to imagine that serious criticism and debate about the New Order's treatment of ex-tapols, and the violence of 1965–66 in general, dates from the era of reform and democracy that accompanied Suharto's resignation in May 1998. But that is not entirely the case. Indeed, against all odds, both foreign and Indonesian critics began to raise their voices within just a few months of the onset of the killings, and continued to do so through more than thirty years of authoritarian rule. We have seen, for instance, how scholars at Cornell University openly challenged the army's version of events as early as January 1966, stimulating a bitter debate with Indonesian authorities that lasted for decades. In 1976, one of those scholars, Anderson, concluded his scathing congressional testimony on human rights in Indonesia with this blunt assessment: "The problem lies not in individuals abusing their authority but with a government which has shown itself over a whole decade to be increasingly authoritarian, suspicious of its own citizens, and indifferent to the rights of the weak and vulnerable."[88] Likewise, from the early 1970s international human rights organizations like Amnesty International, Tapol, and the International Commission of Jurists were constant sources of criticism and discussion about those issues, and through their campaigning helped to bring about the release of tens of thousands of political prisoners.

Even inside Indonesia, there was criticism quite early on.[89] The defense speech of PKI general secretary Sudisman, who was eventually sentenced to death in 1967, is among the earliest and most eloquent critiques of the New Order's brutality.[90] The same year, the Indonesian student activist Soe Hok Gie, who would later die under mysterious circumstances, openly criticized the army's practice of detaining political opponents without charge or trial. These lonely voices of dissent were encouraged by a handful of courageous lawyers in private practice who sought to restrain the regime through appeals to the rule of law and the formation of fledgling human rights organizations like the Legal Aid Institute (Lembaga Bantuan Hukum). Moreover, in spite of heavy-handed army censorship of the press, there were always some Indonesian journalists and student activists doing what they could to shine a light on the violence. Even the strongly anticommunist former defense minister, General Nasution, voiced some criticism, saying in 1975 that political prisoners "should be released while taking into account the prosecution of committed crimes and security requirements.... A hysterical anticommunist reaction is not called for."[91]

Important as these early interventions were, criticism and debate about 1965–66 and the treatment of ex-tapols reached a new level in the 1990s, thanks partly to the efforts of an energetic generation of young activists who embraced transnational ideas of democracy and human rights, partly because of decay and disagreement within the New Order itself, and partly because of a more general shift in international norms with respect to human rights that followed the end of the Cold War. Against that backdrop, New Order authorities faced unprecedented domestic criticism, some of it from current or retired state officials, especially on the treatment of elderly political prisoners as well as ex-tapols and their families. That criticism provided an opening for prominent citizens and human rights groups to enter the debate, and increase the pressures for change.

In response to criticism of its restrictions on ex-tapols, senior New Order officials periodically indicated that some could be phased out. In mid-1993, a group of retired military officers called for the ET designation to be removed from national identity cards, asserting that it was outdated and not consistent with the rule of law in a modern society.[92] In December 1993, the armed forces commander, General Feisal Tanjung, told a parliamentary commission that the military had no objection to removing the ET designation from the identity cards of ex-tapols, but that it was up to the Ministry of Home Affairs to make the necessary changes.[93] And in 1995, with the approach of the fiftieth anniversary of Indonesia's declaration of independence, a number of prominent citizens called again for the ET identifier to be scrapped.[94] The president's adviser for state propaganda, H. Roeslan Abdulgani, called on the government to stop using the designation and grant clemency to former political detainees. "It is high time," he said, "that we, as a nation, forgive the sins of our own people."[95] Finally, in mid-1995, the government announced that the ET mark would be removed from national identity cards, and a handful of elderly political prisoners, including former Air Force Commander Omar Dhani, were released.[96]

While these were certainly positive developments, reactions were mixed with regret that they had taken so long, and skepticism that they would bring any meaningful change. Commenting on the proposed removal of the ET mark, one older ex-tapol, who had been detained for thirteen years without trial, said, "I'm too old for it to make any difference to my life.... If they had done it years ago, then most of us would have been young enough to still enjoy our lives." He also voiced an understandable skepticism that the policy change would significantly alter the attitude and behavior of government and military officials toward former political detainees. "The neighbours know who we are and they've been kind to us," he said, "but local officials are more wary, and psychologically I don't know whether this will bring about any change in their thinking."[97]

The reasons for that skepticism were not hard to discern. Even as the ET policy change was announced, and for many years afterward, high-ranking military officers continued to insist that Communism represented a latent danger, that ex-tapols needed to be controlled and monitored, and that the practice of ideological screening should continue. Just before the change in the ET policy was announced, for example, General Tanjung dismissed the idea of clemency for the aging PKI prisoners, saying, "We still foresee the danger if they are released." The speaker of the house, a former military officer, likewise urged caution: "Even though the prisoners are quite old, we have to keep in mind the latent danger of the PKI." Meanwhile, the minister of information, Harmoko, and senior military officials underscored that even while the ET stamp would now be removed, ex-political prisoners would continue to be monitored.[98]

To sum up, the regime's decision to release many thousands of untried political detainees in the late 1970s was, without question, the result of a coordinated transnational campaign led by human rights organizations and supported by some Western governments, especially the United States. The success of that campaign rested on an unusual and temporary coincidence of three factors: a shared inclination to act on the part of human rights NGOs, the US Congress, and White House; an international environment that was for a time conducive to appeals in the language of international human rights; and an Indonesian government that was uniquely vulnerable to real or threatened economic sanctions.

Yet if the New Order eventually succumbed to the combined pressure of human rights organizations and the US government, and released its untried political prisoners, it did not thereby cease its efforts to monitor and control the political actions and ideas of its enemies. On the contrary, in the aftermath of the releases, it imposed an increasingly elaborate system of restrictions on former political prisoners and their families that disrupted virtually every aspect of their lives and left lasting scars. Those restrictions, moreover, were symptomatic of a deeply seated obsession on the part of army leaders with imposing control, order, and discipline on what they saw as a dangerously unruly population. That obsession was manifest in the heavy-handed systems of thought control, surveillance, policing, propaganda, and censorship that became the hallmarks of the regime and of Indonesian society under the New Order. Those systems not only imposed heavy burdens on former political detainees and their families but also stymied and distorted normal political discourse and social interaction in society at large.

On the other hand, there was always some resistance to these policies and systems, and as the regime started to fracture in the 1990s, that resistance began to grow. Both tendencies—the impulse to silence, cleanse, and control along with the desire to speak, discuss, and be free—found expression in the heady period of political reform leading up to and following General Suharto's resignation in May 1998.

CHAPTER TEN

Truth and Justice?

So, now that my childen are beginning to have their own lives, I have begun to think, why should I remain silent? I have begun to think about the people whose fate was like mine, those people who were cast aside as I was. I decided to start talking about the lies that have led this country down the wrong path. I want to do this so that the evil done by my people to their own people will not happen again in times to come.

—"AGATHA SUMARNI," FORMER POLITICAL DETAINEE

IN MARCH 2001, a ceremony was organized for the reburial of the remains of some twenty people killed in the violence of 1965–66. A victims' group had exhumed the bodies from a mass grave in the district of Wonosobo, Central Java, and the plan was to rebury them in a multifaith ceremony in Kaloran near Temanggung.[1] With the remains arranged in coffins, the mourners prepared to set out for the local cemetery. But before they could begin, a crowd attacked them, seizing the coffins, breaking them open, and scattering the remains. Declaring that Communists could not be buried in their cemetery, the attackers called on local authorities to disband the victims' group in order to prevent the revival of Communism in the area. Local police authorities did nothing to prevent the attack or stop it once it had started. Nor were any of the attackers detained or charged with a crime. By contrast, the principal organizer of the ceremony, a former political prisoner, was forced into hiding while the remaining families and supporters were warned not to attempt anything of the sort again. The attack served its purpose: the threat of violence inhibited any further exhumations and reburials in the area for more than a decade.

President Suharto's resignation in May 1998 amid widespread demands for reform provided an unprecedented opportunity to reexamine the events of 1965–66. It stimulated calls for thorough investigations into the violence, for rewriting the history of those events, for the prosecution of those who had committed serious crimes, for apologies and compensation to the victims, and for reconciliation.[2] In the intervening years, some progress has been made on all those fronts. But as the story above suggests, for every step forward there has been at least one step back. Worse still, rather than gradually abating over time, there are indications that the intolerant and authoritarian mind-set that underpinned the New Order's approach to the question of 1965 remains deeply entrenched. So too are the dubious mythologies that were the product of the army's anti-PKI propaganda campaign. As a result, there is still a long way to go before the objectives of truth seeking, justice, and reconciliation that were articulated in 1998 are achieved.

This chapter explores the related problems of establishing a fair and truthful record of 1965–66 and securing justice for the victims of those events. It begins by recounting briefly the efforts that have been made since 1998 by Indonesian officials as well as historians, activists, survivors, artists, and journalists to excavate the past. It makes clear that in the first few years after Suharto's resignation, there was a significant new openness in both official and public attitudes toward the events of 1965–66, fueled in part by a general spirit of reform, and also by the availability of many new avenues for sharing information and political opinion. The chapter then contrasts these hopeful signs with the evidence of a serious backlash against the new openness, starting as early as 2000. It argues that the backlash has entailed a dogmatic refusal by state officials to countenance any meaningful initiatives in the arena of policy change, truth gathering, or justice, which in turn has enlivened and empowered resistance to reform by a variety of conservative religious and political groups.

One Step Forward

First the good news: since the end of the New Order, there have been a number of official initiatives to reexamine the violence of 1965–66, and address the unjust treatment of survivors and ex-detainees. Many of these initiatives were stimulated by a spirit of reform and a domestic human rights movement that had begun to gain momentum even before 1998. That movement, consisting largely of NGOs and student groups, but also supported by the National Commission on Human Rights (Komisi Nasional Hak Asasi Manusia, or Komnas HAM), provided the crucial legal and rhetorical framework for many of the positive changes introduced immediately after Suharto's fall.[3] The importance and credibility of human rights ideas and norms was evident, for example, in the language used by the many NGOs and other groups that emerged after 1998, and the enactment of new human rights laws in 1999 and 2000.[4]

OFFICIAL STATEMENTS AND ACTIONS

The new spirit of openness was given a significant boost by Abdurrahman Wahid, the former NU leader who became president in October 1999. Wahid stunned the country in March 2000 by apologizing for the NU's role in the mass killings of 1965–66 and urging citizens to "open up" the history of that period. These were not isolated initiatives. Shortly after his inauguration in 1999, for instance, Wahid had invited Pramoedya, the renowned author and former political prisoner whose works had been banned for more than thirty years, to meet at the Presidential Palace. And in a speech on International Human Rights Day (December 10, 1999), he had invited political exiles to return home, and then instructed his ministers to take steps to restore the rights of former political prisoners, detainees, and people in exile. In perhaps his boldest move, Wahid called for the revocation of MPRS Resolution No. XXV/1966, which banned the PKI and all Communist teachings, describing it as unconstitutional. In doing so, he openly challenged one of the most enduring legal and symbolic foundations of the New Order.[5] Even before becoming president, in early 1999 Wahid had broken with a long tradition of official denial with respect to 1965–66 by proposing the formation of an independent Truth Commission for National Reconciliation (Komisi Pencari Kebenaran untuk Rekonsiliasi, or KINKONAS). Although that proposal was never realized, a coalition of human rights activists and legislators continued to push the idea, and in 2004, a law establishing a Truth and Reconciliation Commission was passed.[6]

A similar spirit of reform and openness was evident at this time in the work of the Komnas HAM. Although it had been established in the early 1990s to deflect mounting international criticism of Indonesia's human rights record, by the late 1990s the Komnas HAM had developed a remarkable degree of independence.[7] In 2003, it began a wide-ranging investigation into the most serious human rights violations committed during the Suharto years, including the crimes of 1965–66.[8] Though that investigation focused only on the case of political detainees held on Buru Island, the resulting report represented a significant breakthrough and a challenge to decades of official silence on the subject.[9]

In an even more important milestone, in 2012 the Komnas HAM released a detailed report on all aspects of the 1965–66 violence and called on the attorney general to investigate further with a view to prosecuting those deemed responsible.[10] The Komnas HAM report was the first ever by an official Indonesian body to state clearly that the violence of 1965–66 amounted to "crimes against humanity" and to conclude that Indonesian military officers bore individual criminal responsibility. Although it recommended that the attorney general's office should conduct further investigations, it also proposed a nonjudicial remedy in the form of a Truth and Reconciliation Commission "to provide a sense of justice for victims and their families." These were bold suggestions, and they were warmly welcomed both by victims' groups and many in the wider human rights community.

The move toward reconciliation and openness appeared to gain further momentum in early 2012, when the mayor of Palu in Central Sulawesi issued a rare public apology to the victims of the 1965–66 violence—the first by a government official since President Wahid's in early 2000. The mayor also initiated a local program of reparations that included free health care, scholarships, and small business grants for survivors and their families.[11] While he stopped short of endorsing the prosecution of those responsible for the violence, and explicitly avoided offering an apology to the PKI, the mayor's public statements and program of reparations were seen as a sign of a shift in public attitudes toward 1965–66, and a model that might be followed by other public officials.

The election of a new president in July 2014 gave rise to hope among human rights activists that the momentum toward reconciliation and justice might be reinforced at the national level. During his campaign, the new president, Joko Widodo (commonly known as Jokowi), had promised to tackle long-standing human rights issues, including the thorny question of 1965–66. Because Jokowi was seen as a political outsider—neither a member of the Jakarta political elite nor a military man—there was an expectation that his administration would be willing to address the problem in an open and forthright way. That expectation was bolstered by his support for a 1965–66 victims' group during his time as mayor of Solo, and his reputation as an honest and forthright "man of the people."

In April 2016, the government took the unprecedented step of organizing a national symposium called Discussing the 1965 Tragedy.[12] Spearheaded by the Komnas HAM and the President's Advisory Council, the event brought together dozens of survivors, scholars, human rights activists, as well as military and government officials to hear testimony and to discuss both the violence and its legacies. There was cautious optimism that the symposium marked a significant shift in official attitudes toward the events of 1965–66 and the government might now finally "take further action to resolve the country's dark past."[13]

NGO INITIATIVES

As important as these official initiatives have been, the campaign to investigate the crimes of 1965–66, bring the perpetrators to justice, and seek reconciliation and healing in various forms has been spearheaded by national and local NGOs, sometimes in cooperation with international organizations.[14] But that campaign has also reflected significant differences in the underlying aims and philosophies of the organizations involved. Thus, where some of the older, national- and international-level NGOs have stressed the need to establish historical truth and justice as well as structural political and judicial reform, many of the newer and local-level NGOs have focused on reconciliation, healing, and addressing the immediate physical and emotional needs of survivors. To be sure, there is some overlap between the two approaches, but the distinction still captures a meaningful divide in the public discourse about 1965.

Many of the national-level NGOs whose work has focused on the search for historical truth and justice have their origins in the last decade of the Suharto years, when the language and ideals of human rights gained a new legitimacy among Indonesian activists. Some began, for example, as underground support groups for former political detainees, and later blossomed into activist organizations campaigning for the basic rights of survivors while still providing essential psychological and modest economic support. Among the most prominent of these groups is the Research Institute on the Victims of the 1965 Killings (Yayasan Penelitian Korban Pembunuhan 1965–66, or YPKP). Formed in 1999 by former political detainees, the YPKP describes its aims as "revealing truth and clarifying history," and "taking part in the effort to bring about justice, truth, prosperity, peace, democracy and human rights in Indonesia."[15]

Other national-level NGOs with a similar focus on human rights, historical truth, and justice include the Institute for Policy Research and Advocacy (Lembaga Studi dan Advokasi Masyarakat, or ELSAM), formed in the mid-1990s; the Commission for the Disappeared and Victims of Violence (Komisi untuk Orang Hilang dan Korban Tindak Kekerasan, or Kontras), formed at the height of the *reformasi* movement in 1998; and independent National Commission on Violence against Women (Komisi

Nasional Anti Kekerasan terhadap Perempuan, commonly known as Komnas Perempuan), also founded in 1998.[16] Two more recent national-level organizations active in this area have been the Coalition for Justice and Truth (Koalisi Keadilan Pengungkapan Keadilan, or KKPK), and Asia Justice and Rights (AJAR), a regional human rights organization based in Jakarta.[17] Each in their own way, and often together, these organizations have been persistent in their efforts to challenge official narratives of the events of 1965–66, demand justice for the victims and survivors, and advocate for fundamental structural changes that they believe would limit the chances of such crimes being committed in the future.

As in the past, Indonesian NGOs have continued to work closely with international human rights organizations to spread their messages more widely. Taking their lead from national NGOs, groups like Amnesty International, Human Rights Watch, Tapol, ETAN, Watch Indonesia, and others have campaigned energetically on the question of 1965, generally stressing the need for truth, justice, and accountability.[18] National and international activists have also collaborated closely in their campaigning and messaging.[19]Among the more important of those collaborations was the joint initiative to establish the International People's Tribunal on 1965 (IPT 1965).[20] Spearheaded by the Indonesian human rights activist and scholar Nursyahbani Katjasungkana, and supported by a broad transnational network of activists, lawyers, and survivors, IPT 1965 was held in The Hague over three days in November 2015. By its own account, the tribunal's mission was "to examine the evidence of [the crimes committed in 1965–66], develop an accurate historical and scientific record, and apply principles of international law to the collected evidence."[21] After hearing testimony and examining a raft of documentation, IPT 1965's panel of judges ruled that the violence amounted to crimes against humanity, including genocide.[22] Although the tribunal had no official juridical standing, it drew wide international attention to the problem of impunity for the crimes of 1965–66. Its organizers, moreover, aimed to present the tribunal's findings to the UN Human Rights Council and UN Office of the High Commissioner for Human Rights, with a recommendation that the United Nations take up the question of Indonesia's responsibility for crimes against humanity, including genocide.[23]

As crucial as these broader efforts have been, most national organizations have also begun to work toward more modest—but no less important—goals of ensuring the immediate emotional and material well-being of survivors along with the communities in which they live. Their shift in that direction is based in part on frustration with the glacial pace of reform and action at the national level, and in a realization that the needs of survivors call for more direct measures that entail healing, reconciliation, and reparation alongside the loftier but more distant goals of truth and justice. In late 2015, for example, the national organization ELSAM supported a community initiative to exhume a mass grave in a village in Bali and perform a proper religious ceremony for the deceased. The aim of the exhumation was not to gather evidence of a crime—for example, by conducting a forensic examination of the remains—but instead to fulfill what the village community saw as a religious obligation. Doing that work together as a community, ELSAM noted, "was far more important and meaningful than the approach of political elites who perpetuate the stigma against victims by forbidding discussion about the events of 1965."[24]

That broad shift in approach has been inspired by the dozens of small social, religious, and community groups that have been working at the local and district levels to address the needs and concerns of their communities with respect to 1965–66 and other issues. Among the more notable of these local initiatives has been the group Solidarity with the Victims of Human Rights Violations (Solidaritas Korban Pelanggaran Hak Asasi Manusia, or SKP-HAM).[25] Established in late 2004, it has painstakingly gathered the testimony of some twelve hundred victims of the violence of 1965–66 in the area of Palu in Central Sulawesi, while working to support victims and broaden public awareness of their plight. And it has achieved some notable successes. It was largely as a result of SKP-HAM's efforts, for example, that the mayor of Palu offered his 2012 apology to victims noted above and established a program of reparations. At the same time, the organization has all but abandoned any expectation that the perpetrators will ever be brought to justice. In an interview in 2013, the organization's founder and leader commented, "We know that human rights tribunals are unlikely. But a public apology like the one made by the mayor helped a lot."[26]

Another local nongovernmental initiative with a similar focus on reconciliation and reparation is the Joint Secretariat for 1965 (Sekretariat Bersama 1965, or Sekber 1965). Self-consciously apolitical, Sekber 1965 places priority on the material and emotional well-being of victims and their families, and on the work of reconciliation with former enemies. For that reason it does not engage in political advocacy—for instance, on matters of truth and justice—unless it is sure that such activities will not complicate the lives of its members. For similar reasons, the group does not support demands that the perpetrators be brought to justice. In its view, the legal system cannot be trusted to render justice, and in any case, the main perpetrators are all dead.[27] In short, like many local groups, Sekber 1965 concentrates squarely on reconciliation and reparations, rather than truth and justice. It is this group that earned the support of President Widodo when he served as mayor of Solo from 2005 to 2012.

A third significant example in this mold is an NGO called Pious Muslim Community for People's Advocacy (Masyarakat Santri untuk Advokasi Rakyat, or Syarikat). Although affiliated with the NU, the Islamic party whose members played a central role in the 1965–66 killings, Syarikat is dedicated to reexamining the history of the violence, and encouraging reconciliation between former members of the NU and the PKI.[28] As its program coordinator, Imam Aziz, told a researcher, "Syarikat has been investigating the massacres ... in order to start the reconciliation process. The process mostly involves the NU given that it was NU youth who perpetrated much of the violence."[29] But it has not advocated judicial remedies. Indeed, having concluded that judicial avenues for redress remain blocked by an unreformed government and a corrupt legal system, Syarikat has taken the view that the best solution is a restorative justice approach through community reconciliation at the local level. Such local-level restorative justice initiatives have become increasingly popular and common in recent years. By one 2013 estimate, they had already occurred "in tens of thousands of families and thousands of neighborhoods across Indonesia."[30]

CULTURAL INTERVENTIONS

The silence about 1965–66 has also begun to be broken by Indonesian journalists, academics, former prisoners, activists, schoolteachers, and artists working in a wide variety of formats and media. Through their interventions in the cultural sphere, they have started to challenge some of the more deeply rooted attitudes that developed and became hegemonic during the New Order. That is perhaps especially true of the work of younger artists who by using graphics, film, and music—and sharing these through various social media platforms—may ultimately have a greater impact on Indonesian society than interventions in conventional media like history books, newspapers, and memoirs that are consumed by a relatively small segment of the educated elite.[31]

Since 1998, Indonesian journalists and media outlets have taken advantage of the relaxation of government controls, and rapid expansion of the Internet and social media, to engage in much more open and serious investigations into the events of 1965–66. Major dailies, like *Kompas* and the *Jakarta Post*, have published stories and editorials that would never have been permitted under the New Order, and large circulation weekly magazines, like *Tempo*, *Editor*, and *D & R*, have published investigative reports, features, and interviews that challenge or raise questions about official narratives. In 2012, for example, *Tempo* published an explosive special edition about the events of 1965–66 titled "Executioners' Confessions," which included interviews with killers, survivors, and human rights advocates.[32]

Likewise, Indonesian scholars, who were so long silent about 1965–66, have also taken advantage of the new environment to conduct new research and explore hitherto-forbidden or at least delicate themes. Among the most prolific has been the historian Baskara Wardaya, who since 1998 has produced several books and edited volumes about the events of 1965–66 and their aftermath, and has spoken out at both domestic and international forums on the subject.[33] Also active in seeking a clearer understanding of the history and speaking publicly about past injustice has been the historian Asvi Warman Adam.[34] Meanwhile, a new generation of Indonesian scholars has begun to conduct serious historical research and analysis on the events of 1965–66. The most pioneering are those who have emerged out of a tradition of critical social history and anthropology, including Hilmar Farid, Ayu Ratih, and Degung Santikarma. Their work has not only added to our substantive understanding of 1965–66 but also significantly broadened the analytic focus of investigations.[35] The new group also includes US-trained scholars like Hermawan Sulistiyo and Iwan Gardono Sudjatmoko, both of whom produced PhD dissertations that shed new light on the mass killings, and Yosef Djakababa, whose doctoral dissertation explores the role of the September 30th Movement in the construction of New Order history.[36]

Perhaps even more impressive has been the surge of memoirs by former political detainees and other survivors. Dozens of such works have been published since 1998, most of them soon after Suharto fell, when the spirit of reformasi was still strong. They include the memoirs of prominent national political figures like former foreign minister Subandrio, and notable ex-tapols such as former Gerwani leader Ibu Sulami and the author Pramoedya.[37] The publication of Pramoedya's memoir in 1999, and his international book tour the same year, appear to have been important in opening up discussion of the tapol experience and giving others the courage to do the same.[38] As a result, in addition to the memoirs of major political actors, there are now many books written by less well-known fig-

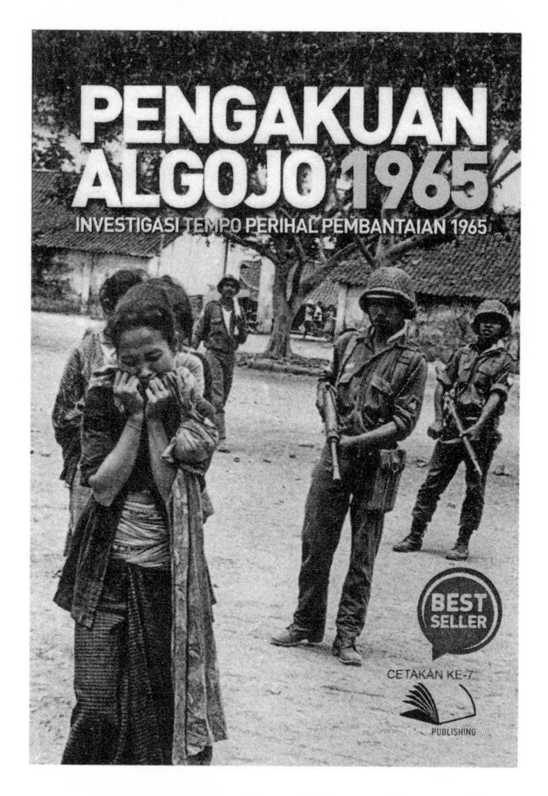

FIGURE 10.1. Cover of special issue of the weekly Indonesian magazine *Tempo* titled "Executioners' Confessions 1965," published in 2012. (Tempo)

ures and published by local printing houses around the country. These include accounts by people detained for their membership in leftist organizations as well as children of the killed or disappeared.[39] They also include memoirs and local histories written by, or in cooperation with, former perpetrators.[40] Another new genre to emerge in the past decade has been edited collections based on testimonies and oral histories from survivors, witnesses, and perpetrators.[41] These works, it seems, are indicative of a gradual democratization of the field of memoir—a development that holds promise for our understanding of the history of those years. They also appear to reflect a new willingness and even determination on the part of survivors to break decades of silence, both for themselves and others. As one former detainee put it more than three decades after her release,

> So, now that my childen are beginning to have their own lives, I have begun to think, why should I remain silent? I have begun to think

> about the people whose fate was like mine, those people who were cast aside as I was. I decided to start talking about the lies that have led this country down the wrong path. I want to do this so that the evil done by my people to their own people will not happen again in times to come.[42]

A similar, though still nascent, trend toward democratization and resistance is evident among Indonesian schoolteachers, especially teachers of history. Impatient with the one-sided accounts presented in officially approved textbooks and curricula, and frustrated by the obstacles to having those standards changed, some teachers have begun to use alternative materials and methods.[43] In one innovative program, sponsored by Komnas Perempuan and Syarikat, secondary school students interviewed female survivors of 1965–66 to produce a collaborative documentary film called *Putih Abu-Abu: Masa Lalu Perempuan*. In 2012, the head of the Indonesian History Teachers Association acknowledged that she herself used alternative texts and promoted outside learning through other sources.[44] And in 2016, a high school teacher in Riau said that she screened the Oppenheimer film, *The Look of Silence*, in her classroom and encouraged her students to explore the history of 1965 on the Internet. Her message to the authorities who sought to limit student learning about these events was blunt: "Don't deceive the people any more. The younger generation is not as stupid as you might think, because they can now find everything on the Internet."[45]

The past two decades have also seen a marked increase in the publication of fictional works in which the events of 1965–66 are critically portrayed or at least form an essential part of the story. Among the most notable of these have been the novels of two Indonesian women, Leila Chudori and Laksmi Pamuntjak.[46] Chudori's *Pulang* explores the personal ramifications of the events of 1965–66, focusing on a group of people who, because of their real or alleged associations with the Left, lived most of their lives as exiles in Paris.[47] Pamuntjak's novel *Amba* is essentially a love story set against the backdrop of the violence of 1965 in Central Java, and the mass incarceration and forced labor on Buru Island.[48] Through these intimate portraits and their nuanced representations of the historical context, both novels make it possible for readers to view the events of 1965 in new ways; in doing so, they effectively challenge the official narratives.[49] It is thus significant that both novels have been met with wide popular and critical acclaim, inside Indonesia and abroad.[50]

In addition to authors, artists working in a wide variety of styles and formats—including film, photography, music, and social media—have also played a vital role in creating a new awareness about the events of 1965–66 and challenging New Order orthodoxies, especially among the generation of Indonesians with no direct experience of that history.[51] These works are powerful not only because they reach new audiences but also because they use many of the same media formats, especially film and music, that New Order propagandists employed. In that sense, they are meeting the old narratives head-on and confronting them on familiar terrain. Some use these formats to give voice to long-suppressed themes, stories, and perspectives about 1965—notably those of former political prisoners and leftists. Others directly appropriate film footage and sound tracks from official propaganda works, and remix or reinterpret them to articulate new, more subversive narratives and possibilities. In one recent "video slam," for example, Indonesian video artists remixed the infamous government film *Pengkhianatan G30S/PKI* with the aim of demystifying, deconstructing, and subverting state propaganda—and opening the door to new understandings.[52]

Among the more novel interventions in this genre have been those produced by the 1965 Park Community (Komunitas Taman 65), a loose collective of young artists formed in 2005 around the site of a small memorial park to the victims of 1965 in Bali. Among other things, they have released a collection of essays and stories called *Against Forgetting: Stories of the 1965 Park Community* that contests the official account of 1965–66.[53] The group has also produced a collection of songs composed and sung by former political prisoners: *Prison Songs: Nyanyian Yang Dibungkam*.[54]

The recovery and performance of music associated with the Left has also been the focus of a number of other groups and artists. And no single piece of music has been more central to this revival than the once-popular folk song *Genjer-Genjer*, which dates to the period of the Japanese occupation, but was banned by the New Order because of its alleged association with the PKI.[55] The song, whose lyrics tell the story of a poor woman who gathers wild spinach to sell in the marketplace to feed her family, has become something of an anthem for the advocates of a historical reassessment of the violence of 1965–66 and justice on behalf of its victims. A quick search of YouTube reveals that alongside the original 1960s' recordings by Bing Slamet and Lilis Suryani, younger Indonesian artists have produced dozens of new versions of the song, including rap and reggae variants, and continue to perform it in all kinds of venues, formal and informal.[56] One of those artists is Tomi Simatupang, an Indonesian living in Germany who described his first encounter with the song as follows: "My life changed the day I walked into a screening of a film [*Gie*]. In that film was a song, a song with such a simple and haunting melody that it consumed my days thereafter. That song is called *Genjer-Genjer*." Captivated by the music, Simatupang spent the next five years researching and developing a documentary concert he called *Genjer-mania*, a collage of live music, archival footage, and homemade video about the song and the events of 1965–66.[57]

As this story suggests, film has also played a significant role in stimulating critical reflection on the events of 1965, particularly among younger Indonesians.[58] Although a number of foreign films about those events were produced during the New Order, they did not have anything like the influence inside Indonesia as the films that have appeared since Suharto's demise. Domestic films about 1965 include a handful of commercial features, such as *Sang Penari*, a love story set against the backdrop of the violence. In a significant departure from standard narratives, that film clearly depicts the role of the military and civilian militias in the killings, and is sympathetic to their victims. As such, Heryanto writes, it "poses the most politically critical stance to the official ideology so far."[59]

The vast majority of newer films, however, have been documentaries, both foreign and domestic. Among the more influential foreign documentaries have been *The Shadow Play* (2001), *Terlena: Breaking of a Nation* (2004), *The Women and the Generals* (2009), and *40 Years of Silence* (2009). Domestic documentary films about 1965–66 have been more numerous, although somewhat uneven in their quality and public impact. Many films have been produced by former political prisoners and NGOs sympathetic to their plight. The documentary film *Putih Abu-Abu: Masa Lalu Perempuan*, for example, was produced under the guidance of the NGO Syarikat and Komnas Perempuan.[60] Half a dozen short documentaries have also been produced by the Institute of Creative Humanity (Lembaga Kreatifitas Kemanusiaan, or LKK), a network of former political prisoners detained for their membership in LEKRA.[61] Although their distribution and public impact has been somewhat limited, these films are notable for giving voice to former political prisoners and challenging official narratives. Among the more influential of the domestic documentaries in recent years have been *Mass Grave* (2002), *Tjidurian 19* (2009), *Buru Island My Homeland* (2016), and *On the Origin of Fear* (2016).[62]

But the most influential films on the subject by far, both within Indonesia and abroad, have been those directed by Joshua Oppenheimer. His two documentaries, *The Act of Killing* and *The Look of Silence*, train an unblinking eye on the events of 1965–66. Both recount acts of the most staggering brutality: perpetrators slitting the throats, cutting off the heads, and drinking the blood of their victims. What is perhaps most shocking about the films, though, is what they reveal about the ramifications of those acts fifty years later—for these are films about the ways in which the violence, and the long silence that followed, destroyed the lives of those who lived through it and corrupted the society that emerged in its wake.[63] Among the most troubling signs of that legacy is the way the perpetrators remain free to tell their awful stories without fear of prosecution or reprimand. Yet it is equally troubling to see, in the *The Look of Silence*, how the events of fifty years ago continue to haunt the family of a young man named Ramli who was hacked to death by a military-backed militia group in 1965. As the film unfolds, we see Ramli's brother—a middle-aged optometrist named Adi—bravely confront those responsible for his brother's murder, asking them to accept responsibility or express remorse for their actions. He is met with denials, threats, and silence.

In part because of their disturbing subject matter, but also because of their unusual cinematic qualities, these films have generated lively debate inside Indonesia and a whole new level of awareness abroad. Indeed, the impact of the films has been so significant that some analysts have referred to it as the "Oppenheimer effect." Initially screened in secret, the Indonesian-language version of *The Act of Killing* was eventually watched by many thousands of Indonesians in public settings and online. Many viewers noted that the film contradicted everything they had learned in their history lessons and from their parents, and expressed incredulity and anger that they had been lied to by their government.[64] The second film, *The Look of Silence*, first screened in late 2014, was much more widely publicized than the first, and stimulated more public commentary and reaction. Predictably, state officials and anticommunist groups claimed that the film was Communist propaganda, and sought to prevent its screening or have it banned. Notwithstanding these efforts, most Indonesian reviewers thought the film should be required viewing and insisted that the authorities should be held responsible for the crimes that had been committed. Some measure of the film's impact—and the sense that it depicted something utterly new and courageous—may be gleaned from the fact that when the film's protagonist, Adi, appeared at screenings, he was greeted with long ovations.[65]

FIGURE 10.2. Theatrical poster for *The Look of Silence*, one of Oppenheimer's two pathbreaking films on the violence of 1965–66 and its legacies. (Drafthouse Films/Participant Media)

One Step Back

But not all the news has been positive. In fact, in virtually every sphere there has been strong, sometimes-ugly resistance to the initiatives just described. It is not an exaggeration to say that in spite of all the advances—and perhaps even because of them—Indonesia has experienced a powerful anticommunist backlash. That backlash is partly attributable to a set of norms and attitudes toward Communism and the PKI that remains deeply entrenched in Indonesian society as a whole. It has also been fueled by the statements and posturing of powerful state officials and politicians along with an underlying system of laws and regulations that date to the early years of the New Order.

NATIONAL AUTHORITIES

Although many of the executive decrees and regulations limiting the rights of former prisoners and PKI members were finally rescinded soon after President Suharto resigned in 1998, legislators left in place the fundamental legal foundation for restricting leftist ideas, organizations, and activities.[66] Chief among these was MPRS Resolution No. XXV of 1966, which, it will be recalled, prohibits the dissemination or advocacy of Communism and Marxism-Leninism and bans the PKI and all organizations or activities associated with those ideologies. Enacted by the MPRS shortly after it had been purged of all leftist and Sukarnoist elements, the law is intentionally vague and sweeping. It was designed by New Order planners as a catchall to restrict and punish dissent, particularly from the Left, and it has continued to serve that purpose for more than half a century.

Notwithstanding the spirit of reform that accompanied the end of Suharto's regime in Indonesia, the legislature's unwillingness to rescind that draconian law reveals just how deeply rooted anticommunist ideas and anxieties remain. Indeed, not only did the legislature not rescind the law but it also deepened the legal basis for repression by passing new antileftist legislation. The clearest example was Law No. 27 of 1999, which stipulated prison sentences of up to twenty years for disseminating or embracing "Communist-Marxist-Leninist" ideas, or expressing opposition to Pancasila.[67] Together, these laws have provided the legal basis and political rationale for much of the resistance to and backlash against leftist dissent, both official and societal.

The remarkable resilience of the anticommunist position has also been reflected in the reactions of state authorities and politicians to the various initiatives described earlier. The reaction to Wahid's move to open up discussion about 1965–66—especially his apology to the PKI victims of NU violence and his proposal to rescind MPRS Resolution No. XXV of 1966—was fast and furious; by some accounts, it was one reason he was drummed out of office in July 2001. Criticism came from religious leaders, parliamentarians, and military officers, while student organizations and anticommunist vigilante groups organized mass demonstrations against what they described as a dangerous attempt to revitalize Communism and the PKI.[68] Likewise, the law establishing a Truth and Reconciliation Commission that had passed in 2004 amid much rejoicing was soon challenged by a vocal anticommunist coalition and then revoked by the Constitutional Court in 2006.

The same fate befell the plans to change the treatment of the events of 1965 in the school curriculum. After a period during which national textbook standards were relaxed and revised to reflect the new spirit of openness, in 2006 the Ministry of Education ordered that all references to "G30S" must be changed to "G30S/PKI," the New Order's preferred term.[69] On the same principle, and under the pretext that they were disrupting public order, the attorney general ordered the withdrawal of all textbooks that departed from the official narrative.[70] Indeed, while the end of the New Order in 1998 brought a significant new measure of press freedom, the practice of official censorship did not stop. In 2009, for example, state officials banned a book about 1965 by the historian John Roosa, *Pretext for Mass Murder*.[71] The ban was eventually overturned in court, which suggested a degree of softening or at least fragmentation in official attitudes to the matter of censorship. Moreover, as Roosa has noted, the net result of the ban was that many more people read the book than would otherwise have done so. Despite these changes, the possibility of censorship remained even if its implementation appeared less coherent than it once did.[72]

Official reactions to the Komnas HAM's 2012 report were likewise overwhelmingly negative. Current and former army officers as well as prominent political and religious figures publicly criticized the report. At a meeting organized by military veterans and attended by the deputy speaker of the People's Representative Assembly as well as members of the Ulama's Council (Majelis Ulama) and representatives from the militia group Pemuda Pancasila, the report was criticized and flatly rejected on the grounds that it had not considered "the violence of the PKI."[73] Following the meeting, a delegation of former veterans and others met the president, General Susilo Bambang Yudhoyono, and urged him not to accept the report's recommendations or apologize to the PKI.[74] In August, the NU's leadership likewise rejected the report.[75] In the face of such opposition, the attorney general's office set the report aside, declaring that it was incomplete.[76] After taking part in a state ceremony to mark National Heroes' Day, the attorney general clarified that "in principle," the anti-communist violence did not "meet the requirement to be considered a gross violation of human rights."[77] According to Komnas HAM member Stanley Adi Prasetyo, these developments undermined expectations that 1965–66 might be dealt with in a serious way: "Looking at all of this, the public became pessimistic because it was as though the way ahead was becoming ever more narrow and twisted. Are we going to pass the resolution of these serious crimes on to our grandchildren?"[78]

Meanwhile, after some three years in office, President Jokowi had not fulfilled early hopes that his administration would make a real difference. In August 2015, for instance, he sidestepped demands for a comprehensive solution to the violence of 1965–66, encompassing truth and justice mechanisms, by proposing instead a Reconciliation Committee to review and dispose of past human rights crimes, including those committed in 1965–66. Speaking before the People's Consultative Assembly on August 14, 2015, Jokowi said, "The government wants there to be a national reconciliation so that future generations will not have to bear the burdens of history. Our children have to be free to face the wide future."[79] The director general of human rights in the Ministry of Justice and Human Rights reiterated that view, asserting in August 2015 that "past human rights violations should be addressed with reconciliation."[80] Likewise, the attorney general said such a committee would aim to resolve human rights violations through "non judicial means" in the spirit of reconciliation.[81]

It is worth noting here that although reconciliation is in principle a laudable goal, the idea has a checkered history in Indonesia. More often than not, the language of reconciliation has been used to evade calls for justice and truth telling. Indonesian authorities have also routinely expressed a preference for nonjudicial solutions on the grounds that these are more consistent with Indonesian "values" and less likely to "open old wounds." Rather than being proposed as part of a wider transitional justice process alongside justice and truth seeking, then, reconciliation and nonjudicial solutions have been proffered as stand-alone mechanisms—as alternatives rather than complements to truth seeking and judicial remedies. That was certainly the position adopted by the Indonesian authorities with regard to East Timor, where its forces committed crimes against humanity, including genocide, in the course of an illegal twenty-four-year occupation (1975–99). Using the fig leaf of reconciliation and restorative justice, Indonesian authorities successfully stymied and derailed what had begun in 1999 as serious international and domestic demands to bring those responsible to justice.[82] The result has been that some two decades later and in spite of overwhelming evidence of wrongdoing, not a single Indonesian military officer has been successfully prosecuted for the crimes committed in East Timor. Official calls for reconciliation and nonjudicial remedies in connection with the serious crimes committed in 1965–66 must be viewed in that light.

More specifically, that is the context in which President Widodo decided in July 2016 to appoint the notorious General Wiranto to the powerful post of coordinating minister for political, legal, and security affairs.

As armed forces commander in 1999, Wiranto had presided over the systematic violence in East Timor, as a result of which he was indicted for crimes against humanity.[83] A few months after his appointment in 2016, Wiranto reiterated the government's intention to resolve the matter of 1965–66 through a nonjudicial mechanism.[84] Wiranto made it clear, moreover, that the government considered the violence of 1965–66 to be legally justifiable, thereby making a nonjudicial mechanism not just the government's preferered approach but the only one possible: "When a judicial process is no longer an option," Wiranto said, "we should utilize what we have. We can resolve cases through deliberation and understanding."[85]

To that end, Wiranto announced in late 2016 that the government would establish a task force on 1965–66, comprised of representatives from state institutions, law enforcement agencies, and civil society.[86] While human rights advocates did not oppose the idea of reconciliation per se, they insisted that it could not be pursued in the absence of other initiatives, such as truth seeking, apology, justice, and rehabilitation.[87] The government, however, appeared adamant that reconciliation would stand on its own. As Wiranto explained in October 2016, the nonjudicial approach would adopt the principle "not to blame any parties, not to incite hate or vengeance, as well as justifying the government's decisions by law."[88]

In any case, official statements in recent years have made it abundantly clear that in the absence of serious mechanisms for truth telling and justice, even symbolic reconciliation will be almost impossible to achieve. Amid rumors that Jokowi might apologize to the victims of the 1965–66 violence in his 2015 Independence Day speech, for example, Islamic groups and senior military officers angrily insisted that there was no need to apologize to the PKI.[89] Speaking to journalists in August 2015, Minister of Defense General Ryamizard Ryacudu mocked the very idea that the state should apologize to the families of the PKI victims. "Excuse me," he said,

> but think about this logically. . . . Who was it who rebelled? Who was it who killed first? Who was it who murdered the Generals? On what grounds should we apologize to those who killed and rebelled against us? It's as if I got beaten up, black and blue, and then I apologized to the person who mugged me.[90]

To reinforce his point, the minister maintained that apologizing would be an admission of guilt and, in a familiar refrain, asserted that talking about the past would only cause trouble: "Enough, forget about it. Let's look to the future. Asking forgiveness means admitting we were wrong, which will lead to demands for compensation. And then what? It will never be finished.... Don't take all that we have achieved and make it dirty." Finally, invoking a common authoritarian trope of the nation as family, he compared PKI victims to children who ought to love and forgive their parents even if they had been treated badly: "So the PKI should love Indonesia. There is no need to harbor feelings of revenge. They need to think in a fresh way. If they are consumed by feelings of revenge, there will be no progress."[91]

Perhaps unsurprisingly, when he spoke on the subject at the annual commemoration of the slain generals on October 1, 2015, President Widodo pointedly declined to apologize. "Apologize to whom?" he asked. "Who should forgive whom when both sides claim to be victims?"[92] Human rights activists pointed out that in any case, apologies only make sense once one knows what happened. As one wrote, "Sorry can only be done based on a historical narrative of an injustice—the story of what happened.... A 'sorry' needs a truth. Even if the truth is bitter."[93]

On the matter of truth seeking, the government response to IPT 1965 in November 2015 and the national symposium on 1965 in April 2016 provided little grounds for optimism. High-ranking officials, including the vice president, Jusuf Kalla, the defense minister, Ryamizard Ryacudu, the coordinating minister for political, legal, and security affairs, Luhut B. Panjaitan, and the attorney general, Muhammad Prasetyo, criticized the tribunal for interfering in Indonesian affairs, stirred up bogus claims of neocolonialism, and suggested that Indonesians who took part in the proceedings were disloyal. And when the tribunal issued its verdict on genocide, the former Chief of Indonesia's Constitutional Court was quoted saying that the IPT 1965 had been "a joke."[94] Likewise, while the government earned praise for hosting the symposium on 1965 in April 2016, it was conspicuous that in his remarks to the gathering, Panjaitan refused to offer an apology to victims, downplayed the number killed, and challenged activists to find the alleged mass graves. Notably, the event was not followed by any meaningful initiative to compensate or apologize to victims, to end impunity for the crimes committed, or to enhance historical understanding of the violence. On the contrary, the April symposium led to an angry backlash. In June 2016, a group of retired generals organized an "anti-PKI" symposium that was addressed by various military figures, including Defense Minister Ryacudu as well as representatives from various conservative Islamic organizations. Predictably, the speakers warned against the revival of Communism, called on the PKI to "apologize" to the Indonesian people, and urged the public not to "reopen the past."[95]

LOCAL AUTHORITIES AND "THE COMMUNITY"

Regional and local authorities have also acted to prevent or silence the activities of artists, journalists, activists, and scholars. While some meetings and seminars on the subject of 1965–66 have been permitted and have proceeded smoothly, many others have either been prevented or closed down midstream. Such prohibitions have been especially common in the weeks surrounding the anniversary of the events of October 1. In almost every case, these interventions have been justified as enforcement of MPRS Resolution No. XXV of 1966 and Law No. 27 of 1999. In most cases, they have also been justified as a response to feelings of "discomfort" within the so-called community about "reopening old wounds," and the possible resurgence or comeback of the PKI. In a manner reminiscent of the anticommunist actions of 1965–66, moreover, the authorities have worked together with local anticommunist groups, if not by openly mobilizing them, then at least by acceding readily to their demands, or failing to intervene to stop or prevent their attacks on alleged Communists.

It is worth stressing that, more often than not, "the community" whose concerns are taken so seriously by police and military authorities in such cases have been the virulently anticommunist organizations that have become increasingly active in Indonesia since 1998. Many of these groups have direct historical and ideological ties to the anticommunist militia groups of the 1960s, or represent the interests and concerns of the military and police themselves. And despite the passage of more than five decades, including almost twenty years of reform and democracy, the language they employ to attack their enemies is immediately recognizable as that of the anticommunist propaganda that fanned the flames of mass killing in 1965–66, and sustained a climate of fear and hatred throughout the New Order period.

The community includes, for example, the HMI, which was so energetic in leading the campaign against the PKI and its affiliates in 1965–66. In the aftermath of a clash between students from two universities in Jakarta in September 2006, the HMI deployed the language and rhetoric used at that time and throughout the New Order. Claiming that the opposing university group had been holding pictures of the hammer and sickle, an HMI statement noted, "There are indications of communist inclinations among the [opposing] activists," and called on the authorities to take "firm action"—by arresting those students who "deliberately spread communism," arresting university officials who "protect the spread of communism," and calling on the Indonesian people "to be vigilant about the latent danger of communism on campus and its surroundings."[96]

As this case suggests, in the debate over 1965–66, students and scholars have not all lined up on the same side. Indeed, while there has been a broad shift toward more openness and critical inquiry on the question, there are scholars and university administrators who steadfastly oppose any talk of historical revision, justice, or reconciliation. One of these is Aminuddin Kasdi, a professor of history at Surabaya State University, former Ansor activist, and founder/member of the anticommunist Community of Indonesian Historians (Masyarakat Sejarawan Indonesia, or MSI).[97] Although Kasdi was already known for his stridently anticommunist views, few were prepared for his decision in September 2009 to conduct a public burning of leftist books, together with the Anti-Communist Front (Front Anti-Komunis), outside the headquarters of the respected regional newspaper *Jawa Pos*. And while the book burning caused some dismay among colleagues and students, it was notable that Kasdi was neither arrested for endangering public safety nor disciplined in any way by university authorities. Three years later, in September 2012, Kasdi stoked the flames of anticommunism again, in a seminar titled "Beware the Latent Danger of Communism in Indonesia" at the Muhammadiyah University Surabaya Faculty of Law.[98]

Another member of the concerned community that has benefited from official backing is the Anti-Communist Peoples' Union of West Java (Persatuan Masyarakat Anti-Komunis Jawa Barat, or Permak), an organization that counts among its supporters the notorious Islamic Defenders Front (Front Pembela Islam, or FPI), HMI, and Kasdi's MSI.[99] In April 2008, Permak issued a statement broadly condemning the National Human Rights Commission's decision to investigate the crimes committed in 1965–66. The statement was a catalog of the arguments routinely articulated by anticommunist groups, with heavy doses of New Order propaganda and fearmongering thrown in for good measure. It claimed, for example, that the crushing of the PKI had been a "spontaneous reaction of the people to the one-sided actions of the PKI," that the campaign of violence had been a legal "police action" needed to "uphold the law and defend the Unitary State of the Republic of Indonesia," and that the political situation in 1965 had been "like a war," in which "whoever had power would crush his enemy." Based on these assertions, Permak concluded that moves to revisit the G30S/PKI were "ahistorical and could endanger the cohesiveness of the Indonesian nation and state" by "disrupting a society that is relatively harmonious and has already forgotten the past." An investigation, it argued, would "open old wounds" for no good reason. It was far better, Permak insisted, "to close the book on the dark history of a bygone era and look to the future." Finally, in language reminiscent of the 1960s and the New Order, it called on the government "to cleanse Komnas HAM of the defenders of the ex-PKI and New Style Communists who are now seeking ways to rise up again and stage a comeback."[100]

The Komnas HAM plan to investigate the events of 1965–66 was also the subject of an angry rebuke by the Communications Forum of Military and Police Veterans (Forum Komunikasi Purnawirawan TNI-POLRI) issued in April 2008. The statement contended, among other things, that in taking up the issue of 1965–66, Komnas HAM was diverging from its original purpose; that what security forces did in 1965–66 was nothing more than their duty to the state, and "was in keeping with positive law and . . . did not constitute grave violations of human rights." The statement also criticized "some members" of the Komnas HAM along with "certain NGOs" for "using laws and regulations in an arrogant and provocative way" that could "disrupt the unity and harmony of the nation and undermine the spirit and morale of the armed forces now and in the future." Accordingly, it rejected the Komnas HAM's plan to investigate the events of 1965–66, supported security force veterans who refused to testify before the commission, called for the commission's leadership to be changed as soon as possible, and urged that it "stop being used as a stick to beat our own nation."[101]

Anticommunist groups also took it upon themselves to track down all indications of what they considered to be a resurgent Communism and report these to the authorities. In 2009, for instance, the Indonesian National Patriot Movement (Gerakan Nasional Patriot Indonesia, or GNPI) wrote to the national chief of police urging the immediate arrest of the leader of an organization of ex-tapols on the grounds that the organization had tried to "spread communist ideas" at a meeting in one of their homes.[102] The group in question was the YPKP, the lawfully registered victims' support group described above. In its letter, the GNPI recounted how some of its members had reported the meeting to local officials and police, who had then intervened to break it up.[103] Then, invoking various decrees and laws banning the dissemination of Communist teachings—including, of course, MPRS Resolution No. XXV of 1966 and Law No. 27

of 1999—it called on the chief of police to outlaw the YPKP and arrest its leader.

Such anticommunist posturing has continued unabated in recent years. In November 2015, for instance, a member of the Prosperous Justice Party said that Indonesians who had taken part in IPT 1965 were traitors for "defending" the PKI and called for them to be prosecuted: "The PKI were rebels, how can they be defended? You can say [that those who took part in the IPT] have resisted the state by acting in violation of the 1966 ban on communism."[104] And in April 2016, a nongovernmental group called the Pancasila Front denounced the national symposium on 1965 on the familiar grounds that it would "open old wounds," and was contrary to Pancasila, the 1945 Constitution, and MPRS Resolution XXV of 1966. Claiming that 85 to 90 percent of the participants were supporters of the PKI, the group warned that the symposium would "rejuvenate communist ideology [and] force the government to apologize for the atrocities [against] PKI members."[105]

THE CULTURAL SPHERE

Cultural and artistic productions related to 1965–66 have been a particularly strong focus of resistance and criticism. Oppenheimer's films, discussed above, have been common targets of anticommunist disruptions, and in response to expressions of concern by "the community," many showings have been canceled. In most instances, militant Islamist groups like the Islamic Defenders Front or anticommunist militia groups like Pemuda Pancasila have spearheaded the disruptions.[106] But as in 1965–66, the public role of these groups has often obscured the complicity of state officials who have responded to the concerns of these groups by ordering the films not to be shown.[107] In 2014, for example, the Film Censorship Institute banned public screenings of *The Look of Silence* on the grounds that "it would lead viewers to sympathize with the PKI and communism."[108]

Long before the Oppenheimer films became the subject of debate, however, Indonesian films related to 1965 were already major focal points of political contention. In 2008, for example, in the face of protests by so-called community members in Central Java, the production of a feature film was brought to a halt. The film, *Lastri*, told the love story of a man and woman persecuted after October 1965 because of their membership in left-wing organizations (Gerwani and CGMI). Although the director had reportedly received permission from the national police to shoot the film, "local communities" had protested and forced the shooting to be stopped.[109] Summarizing the reasons for those protests, a group called the Anti-Communist Coalition of Indonesia (Koalisi Masyarakat Anti Komunis Indonesia) stressed that the film was based on the testimony of former Gerwani members and was a deliberate attempt to "distort history." Then, repeating the old army-generated myth of Gerwani depravity, the coalition wrote, "The history of Gerwani at that time was that some of them were prostitutes and there are many witnesses who state that [Gerwani members] were believers in free sex. The cruelty of Gerwani in torturing the Generals at Lubang Buaya demonstrates clearly how base their morality and sense of humanity was." In short, the Anti-Communist Coalition said, the film should not be produced because it was a work of "propaganda and provocation," which should it ever be screened, would give rise to national instability by provoking new social conflicts and "opening up old wounds."[110]

The same patterns have been evident in recent years. Indeed, far from fading away, the backlash against the PKI and the Left appeared to accelerate after Widodo became president, suggesting that it may have been fueled by political opposition and opportunism. In July 2015, for instance, members of Pemuda Pancasila together with local police went to the home of a poet and activist, Kelana, in Kendal, Central Java, to investigate what they said were his unlawful and provocative efforts to spread Communist teachings. More specifically, they claimed that he had uploaded photographs of a performance he had given onto a Facebook page under the rubric "PKI Awakening Day" and accused him of having materials related to the song *Genjer-Genjer* on his walls. Invoking MPRS Resolution No. XXV of 1966, the militia members demanded that Kelana remove all "communist attributes" from the Facebook page and his house, and urged the police to arrest him.[111]

In August 2015, a planned meeting of the survivors' group YPKP was canceled after organizers received death threats from Islamist groups, and "advice" from intelligence officers and police that they should not go ahead. The meeting, planned for August 7–8 in the Central Javanese city of Salatiga, was to have been attended by representatives of Komnas HAM, Komnas Perempuan, and the Minister of Justice and Human Rights. But anticommunist groups insisted that the meeting was a front for Communist activities, and spread a story on Facebook that the YPKP had put up hammer-and-sickle flags and banners around the town. The head of YPKP, Bedjo Untung, described those allegations as false and a provocation. He also said that the threats had come from the Islamic Defenders Front and Islamic Defenders Guard (Garda Pembela Islam, or GPI), which "use the words of jihad and say that [spilling] the blood of former political prisoners is halal."[112]

As always, the situation became even more contentious around the anniversary of the alleged coup. In October 2015, police authorities in Sumatra, Java, and Bali intervened to stop a variety of peaceful activities commemorating or discussing the events of 1965–66. In the city of Salatiga, a group of university students was questioned in mid-October in connection with the publication of a magazine (*Lentera*) that examined the events of 1965–66 in the city. Although none of the students was formally charged, they were ordered to burn all copies of the magazine. Police claimed that it was not they but instead university authorities who had called for the magazines to be burned. The student editor of the magazine, however, said that they first received negative comments on the magazine from the police, military, and mayor, and that the protests culminated in their interrogation by police, who ordered all copies of the magazine to be burned.[113]

In October 2015, authorities in West Sumatra detained, deported, and blacklisted a Swedish Indonesian man, Tom Ilias, who had tried to visit a gravesite where his father was supposedly buried alongside other victims of the 1965–66 killings. Ilias was one of many thousands of Indonesians working or studying abroad in 1965 who were prevented from returning home. Stateless for many years, he was finally given Swedish citizenship in the early 1980s. When he returned to Sumatra in 2015, local authorities accused him and those traveling with him of making a film about cruelty against the PKI—a charge they denied. According to a friend who was with him,

> Tom Ilias was making a personal pilgrimage, possibly to see the graves of his father and mother for the last time. . . . His father's grave is one of the mass graves documented by Komnas HAM's investigations of the 1965 killings. And now Tom's spirit has died because his deportation resulted in him being blacklisted. He can never return to Indonesia again.

The district police chief acknowledged that Ilias and his group had been detained, but claimed that "we were only trying to save them from being mobbed by the villagers," who the officer claimed were displeased that people were filming a documentary about the 1965 killings.[114]

Just a few days later, police in Bali intervened to prohibit three panel discussions and a film screening related to 1965–66 at an international writers festival in the town of Ubud.[115] Explaining the decision, the Gianyar district police chief predictably pointed to MPRS Resolution No. XXV of 1966. Like almost all state officials, he also alluded to the interests of the community and the need to avoid opening old wounds. "This is for the benefit of the people," he said. "The spirit of the festival is not to discuss things that would just open old wounds."[116] Commenting on the ban, a leading Indonesian author, Eka Kurniawan, who was to appear on one of the banned panels, said, "Recently a new wave of anti-communism seems to have been revived, even when communism barely exists in Indonesia. If censoring ideas is tolerated, it will continue until it reaches its peak: eliminating the lives of men considered different."[117]

This pattern of disruption, in which law enforcement officials intervene in the name of security and the "concerned community" to prevent cultural events related to 1965, has continued since then. In March 2016, for example, the Islamic Defenders Front threatened to disrupt a screening of the film *Buru Island My Homeland* at the Goethe Institute in Jakarta. After meeting with police, the hosts opted to cancel the event.[118] That was only one of many instances in which films about 1965 have been disrupted. Indeed, according to a report from late 2016, restrictions on freedom of expression had increased in Indonesia the previous year, with most restrictions taking the form of the disruption or banning of film screenings and seminars. And of the films banned, most were on the subject of 1965.[119]

Of course, silence and inaction on the matter of 1965–66 has not been exclusively a product of state propaganda, official censorship, and deeply rooted anticommunism. It has also stemmed from a range of societal pressures and personal choices. Writing in 2002, Mary Zurbuchen referred perceptively to the pervasive "suppression of personal memory," noting that the memories of victims, witnesses, and perpetrators alike had been held, and were still being held, "in cautious silence."[120] Silence, both enforced and chosen, has certainly been a preoccupation of former prisoners. Silence is preferable to speech, it seems, because words cannot adequately express their feelings and because to speak as a former prisoner is still dangerous. More recently, Heryanto has suggested that the silence may stem from simple indifference, especially on the part of many younger Indonesians, for whom the events of 1965–66 appear distant and of no intrinsic interest.[121]

There is also reason to believe that the path of silence has been chosen by many people who were directly or indirectly involved in the killings and arrests, whether as perpetrators or bystanders. Given the army's strategy of mobilizing the population to carry out the violence in 1965–66, the numbers of people in that category must be enormous, conservatively in the hundreds of thousands. Whether out of a sense of guilt, a desire to forget, or less likely, a fear of prosecution, such people have preferred to remain silent. This suggests that popular involvement in mass killing may be associated with postviolence silence and inaction. Mass mobilization to carry out a campaign of violence—for example, through civilian militias—may prove to be a serious barrier to later demands for truth and justice.

In short, while there have been signs since 1998 of a new openness and courage in revisiting the history of 1965–66, and some modest progress in assisting victims, the resistance to such efforts has not gone away. Indeed, there is some reason to think that the opposition has become more hostile precisely as the challenges to old orthodoxies have grown. It seems clear, moreover, that while anticommunist actions are often being carried out by local social and religious groups, in doing so they are acting in accordance with long-established norms and traditions of official anticommunism, and their actions are facilitated and even encouraged by state authorities, by politicians, and by restrictive laws. On the side of reformers, the record of the past several years indicates that the center of gravity has moved away from an earlier reliance on the state to fix the problem, and toward more grassroots and locally based experiments and solutions. While such local solutions appear promising, they are also more vulnerable to disruption from local anticommunist groups and alliances. If this assessment is correct, the way ahead promises to be difficult and fraught with conflict.

CHAPTER ELEVEN

Violence, Legacies, Silence

Yes, the dead do speak, but in their own way and in their own time. Buchenwald, Ravensbruck, Dachau, Auschwitz, and all the other human slaughterhouses, even those in Indonesia, cannot silence the dead.

—PRAMOEDYA ANANTA TOER, *THE MUTE'S SOLILOQUY*

THE VIOLENCE OF 1965–66 destroyed millions of lives and altered the course of Indonesian history. More than fifty years later, the violence has been largely forgotten outside Indonesia, and fundamental historical and analytic questions about it remain unanswered. In the preceding pages, I have tried to tell the story of the violence in a way that captures some of its complexity while also providing answers to those unanswered questions. My hope is that in doing so, I have contributed in some way to the efforts being made by others, especially inside Indonesia, to disturb the silence that has for too long surrounded these events. It remains now to draw together the main threads of the story and argument, and to suggest some of their broader implications. I want to do that by returning to the three central questions I posed at the outset: How can we explain the violence? What have been its consequences? And why has so little been said or done about it in the past half century? While focusing on the Indonesian story, I also want to point to some ways in which that experience might inform our general understanding of the logic of mass killing and incarceration, the legacies of such violence, and the ways in which it is dealt with over time.

Violence

How can we explain the mass violence of 1965–66 in Indonesia? To put the matter simply, I have argued here that rather than arising naturally from deeply rooted cultural, religious, and social tensions, the violence was organized by the army, facilitated by powerful states and international conditions, and made more likely by certain distinctive features of Indonesia's modern political history. Preexisting conflicts helped to shape and fuel the violence in various ways, but they did not do so spontaneously. Without army leadership, and without the help of powerful states and an enabling international environment, those conflicts would never have given rise to violence of such extraordinary scope and intensity.

The focus on the army leadership explains certain patterns and variations in the violence that have long perplexed observers. It provides an explanation, for example, of how social and economic tensions were transformed into mass violence, why the violence took such similar forms across the country, why militia groups everywhere played such a prominent role, and where the distinctive language of the violence came from. Importantly, the emphasis on the army's role also helps to explain the significant geographic and temporal variations in both killings and long-term detention. More than anything else, those variations reflected the political postures, strategies, and capacities of different regional commanders as they sought to implement central directives. But variations also reflected the fact that in carrying out its campaign, the army relied on a network of local and regional intermediaries, some of them more reliable than others, and exploited existing socioeconomic, religious, and political tensions that varied from one locale to the next. In that sense, variations in the geographic distribution and timing of the violence reflected the different ways in which central army plans were interpolated through these different networks and local conditions.

Both the central role of the army and the coordinated nature of the campaign were highlighted by certain features of the mass detentions that began shortly after October 1, 1965. First, the common methodology of incarceration across widely different locales—especially the routine use of torture and sexual violence during interrogation, and the resort to highly militarized punishments—point to the army as the institution responsible. Second, the vast scale and systematic quality of the detentions—most notably, the elaborate systems of prisoner classification and transportation—make it clear that it was centrally planned and coordinated, rather than spontaneous or random. Finally, the geographic variations in the levels of incarceration appear to have been related to the postures, capacities, and strategies of regional and local military authorities in implementing national-level directives.

As opposed to being two distinct processes, I have also argued here that the mass killings and detentions were closely related aspects of a single army-led campaign against the Left. The close relationship between killing and detention was evident in a number of patterns. One disturbing pattern was that many and perhaps most of those who were killed had first been detained, before being removed from their places of detention and executed. Equally disturbing and revealing is the evidence—admittedly, still incomplete—that the level of killing was greatest where the rate of long-term detention was lowest. The inverse relationship between killing and long-term detention suggests that some army authorities used killing as an alternative to detention. Taken together, these characteristics underscore a defining feature of the program of detention: that like the wider campaign of violence of which it formed an integral part, it was deliberately organized and carried out by the army.

Further evidence that the violence was part of a coordinated army campaign against the political Left emerged, paradoxically, after its most obvious manifestations had ended. With the release of most political detainees in the late 1970s, overt violence was transformed into a coordinated program to repress, control, and discipline former detainees, and to cleanse both state and society of leftists and other political undesirables. That program directly affected roughly one million former detainees, but also their families, friends, and associates, creating a kind of deep chill—or what Andrew Nathan, referring to North Korea and other authoritarian states, has called "an anxious conformity"—in political and social relations that lasted for more than three decades.[1] While some elements of that apparatus of repression and control were dismantled following the resignation of President Suharto in 1998, many of the authoritarian ideas and attitudes—and even the basic laws—that informed and underpinned it remained, and appeared to have established deep roots in Indonesian society as a whole.

The army's campaign of violence against the Left was facilitated and encouraged by powerful foreign states—especially the United States and the United Kingdom—and shaped in significant ways by the wider international context. That is not to say foreign powers plotted the supposed coup or the violence in advance, although that remains a possibility. Rather, in a variety of ways—through the timely provision of economic and military aid, covert propaganda and psywar campaigns, and through a policy of deliberate silence—the United States and its allies helped to create the political conditions in which an army seizure of power was more likely to occur, and encouraged the army and its allies to pursue their campaign of violence against the Left. That is to say, the United States and its allies aided and abetted crimes against humanity, possibly including genocide.

In addition to the intentional actions and omissions of powerful states, certain aspects of the wider international context—notably the Cold War, the rise of a militant anticolonial nationalism, and the weakness of human rights norms and networks—contributed to the same outcomes. The Cold War context encouraged mass violence both because of its deeply polarizing political logic and language, and because it engendered a lack of empathy for victims of violence who were understood to be Communists. Anticolonial nationalists like Sukarno embraced a militant style of politics that valorized bellicose language, thereby further heightening the tensions. In that context, international human rights norms gained little traction, and the protests of largely leftist transnational solidarity networks were drowned out. On the other hand, as I have argued here, shifting international norms in the late 1970s, especially with respect to state violence and human rights, together with a newly influential transnational human rights network and a decline in militant anticolonial nationionalism, appear to have been important in temporarily constraining Indonesia to adjust its policy with respect to leftist political detainees.

Finally, I have suggested here that five broad historical conditions made the mass killing and incarceration in Indonesia much more likely to happen, and help to explain their distinctive patterns. First, the country's colonial and revolutionary history made ideological differences between the Left and Right a key fault line of Indonesian politics, and formed the basis for divergent historical narratives and memories, especially on the part of the army, the PKI, and certain Muslim parties. Second, serious conflicts dating to the revolutionary period gave rise to a perception within the army and among some Muslims that the PKI represented a threat to the nation, and fueled a deep mutual suspicion and hostility. Third, the process of state formation during and immediately after the revolution led to the emergence of a politically powerful and conservative army with a strong stake in the status quo. Fourth, the development within the army of an institutional culture, repertoire, and doctrine that borrowed from both Japanese and Dutch colonial forces and revolutionary experiences made the violent suppression of its domestic enemies far more likely, while also shaping the means by which that was achieved. And lastly, the emergence after independence of a politics notable for its militancy, polarization, and mass mobilization laid the foundations for widespread popular participation in the army's campaign of violence.

Beyond these specific conclusions, the Indonesian case highlights a number of more general observations about the conditions in which mass killing and incarceration are most likely to occur. Perhaps the most important observation is that mass violence is not in any sense the natural or inevitable consequence of ancient cultural proclivities, deep-seated religious differences, underlying socioeconomic conditions, or even political conflicts. It is rather the product of historically specific acts and omissions by people in positions of political and social power. In other words, no matter how deeply rooted they may be, underlying biases, tensions, conflicts, and hatreds do not lead automatically or inevitably to mass violence. The turn to mass killing and incarceration requires something more than enmity or conflict; it requires an agent who articulates the idea that conflict can and should be resolved through violence, and an institution with the inclination and capacity to do so. The obvious candidates are armies, police forces, militia groups, and revolutionary movements, whose institutional norms and doctrines portray violence as legitimate and effective in achieving political ends, and have the logistical and organizational wherewithal to carry it out. It is these institutions, I think, that serve as crucial vectors or accelerators in translating enmity and conflict into mass violence, including genocide.

How they do so depends a great deal on their internal institutional dynamics. Over time, such institutions develop what I have referred to here as distinctive "institutional cultures," which may be more or less violent, and identify specific threats to their own existence and power. Such institutions also develop what I have called "repertoires of violence," which are essentially routines of violence learned by those associated with the institution. Through a variety of processes—including socialization, indoctrination, command authority, and peer pressure—the members of institutions come to embrace these institutional cultures, and to enact their repertoires in ways that can both accelerate violence and give it a distinctive character. In the Indonesian case, for example, such institutional cultures and repertoires arguably gave rise to certain common features of the violence—such as the use of specific techniques of torture, the decapitation and castration of victims, the public display of corpses and body parts, and the disposal of dead bodies in wells, irrigation ditches, and rivers. Such behaviors and patterns are not easily explained by reference to personal psychology, happenstance, or deeply rooted social or cultural tensions. Nor, indeed, are they likely to be the product of written orders or commands.

At the same time, the Indonesian case underscores the critical significance of regional and local actors and conditions in the logic and dynamic of mass violence. As Straus and others have observed, even where violence is centrally ordered, its implementation invariably depends on such "mesolevel" actors and conditions. If they are enthusiastic allies of the central command, with both the will and capacity to carry out its directives, mass violence will be facilitated or accelerated. By contrast, where important regional and local actors are resistant to central directives, or lack the organizational and logistical capacity to carry it out, mass violence is likely to be slowed, at least until those conditions change. The point is that even in the most centralized and authoritarian political systems, such mesolevel actors always have some measure of autonomy, and the exercise of that autonomy can help to account for important geographic and temporal variations in the observed patterns of violence. That was certainly the case in Indonesia, where the intensity and character of violence varied in accordance with the different political postures and capacities of regional and local military commanders and their civilian allies.

The Indonesian example also confirms a long-standing judgment that genocide and mass killing are provoked and facilitated by language that dehumanizes target groups—portraying them, say, as atheists, traitors, animals, barbarians, whores, or terrorists. As Fein and others have contended, public discourse, narratives, and visual representations that effectively exclude the target group from the perpetrator's moral community make the move from conflict to mass violence far more likely. In that process, moreover, the mass media play a crucial role, especially where technology, political power, or force of arms permit one side to control or monopolize them, to the near exclusion of alternative voices. One additional insight from the Indonesian case is that the power of such narratives and representations to accelerate violence depends far less on their inherent plausibility or truthfulness than on the perceived authority of their author or speaker. Depending on the context, that might be an army officer, a political leader, or a religious authority, though with the onset of violence, one can surmise that the authority of military figures increases commensurately.

To these largely domestic processes, the Indonesian case suggests a number of ways in which international actors and context can contribute to or constrain the dynamic of genocide and mass violence generally. To put the matter most simply, genocide and mass killing are facilitated by a range of international actions (and omissions) that strengthen the perpetrators of those crimes vis-à-vis their victims, including arms transfers, propaganda and psywar operations, military intervention, nonlethal aid, inaction, and deliberate silence. Perhaps less obviously, as noted above, genocide and mass killing can be facilitated by prevailing international norms that construe violence as legitimate in achieving certain political or moral ends. That category undoubtedly includes utopian and revolutionary ideologies, but the Indonesian example suggests that other norms, including "national security," "law and order," and "development," may also be invoked in ways that facilitate or justify extreme violence by the state.

If these conclusions tend to confirm what we know about the most studied cases of genocide and mass violence—notably the Holocaust as well as the Armenian and Rwandan genocides—there are at least three features of Indonesia's experience that arguably distinguish it from those cases and may point in new directions. For one thing, in contrast to the iconic genocides, the victims in Indonesia were not defined primarily by their ethnicity, race, or religion but instead by their political identity; that is, they were all leftists. Then, too, the mass killing and detention did not take place in the context of war, either international or civil, as has been true of so many genocides, but in a time of relative peace. And third, the regime that carried out the campaign—Suharto's New Order—was decidedly not driven by a utopian vision, as were so many other genocidal regimes, including Hitler's Germany, Stalin's Soviet Union, Mao's China, and Pol Pot's Cambodia.

These differences pose a challenge to some existing theories of genocide and mass violence—or at least suggest ways in which they might be refined. For instance, if the victims in Indonesia were defined primarily by their political identity, arguments that stress the ways in which ethnic, racial, or religious hatred give rise to mass violence must be broadened to account for targeting on the basis of political identity. What emerges is a picture, like the one I have sketched here for Indonesia, in which the intentional acts of state and particularly military authorities are far more important in generating mass violence than personal psychology, "primordial sentiment," age-old ethnic rivalries, religious hatreds, or socioeconomic conditions. Indonesia's experience also serves as a useful reminder that most, if not all, instances of mass political violence and genocide have a clear political dimension, and that the line between a political identity and ethnic, religious, or racial one is seldom, if ever, absolute. That is to say, even where the targets of violence are mainly defined in ethnic, racial, or religious terms, the intentions of those who target them in that way is almost always in some measure also political.[2]

Similarly, because the mass killing in Indonesia occurred outside the context of war, we need to consider the possibility that the supposed effects of war on genocide—such as brutalization, perceptions of threat, discourses of treachery, and the creation of an us versus them mentality—might equally arise in other contexts. The Indonesian case suggests that these effects can emerge not only during a conventional war but also in a time of intense yet largely nonviolent conflict over political ideas. Both contexts can evidently fuel claims of an existential threat to the nation, acute political polarization, mass mobilization, and discourses of treachery, all of which can encourage or accelerate mass violence. On the other hand, Indonesia's experience gives some reason to believe that international norms and legal regimes that challenge, subvert, or otherwise weaken such a binary rhetoric, whether in the name of human rights or some other principle, may serve to inhibit or even stop mass violence, including genocide.

Finally, to the extent that Suharto's New Order was not driven by a utopian vision, we need to consider the possibility that the underlying ideological force in genocide and mass killing is not necessarily utopianism, as Weitz has maintained, but something else. One possibility is that the common thread linking Hitler, Franco, Stalin, Mao, Pol Pot, and Suharto is a set of state norms, practices, and institutions that together may be described as militarism. Normatively, militarism entails a body of doctrine and discourse through which domestic opponents can readily be portrayed as enemies, or existential threats to the state, against whom the use or threat of great violence is warranted and even required. As a matter of practice, militarism provides the actual routines and repertoires of violence through which state leaders respond to such perceived threats via resort to force. Institutionally, militarism affords the structures and organizational capacity that are essential to carrying out any plan to commit violence on a wide scale over an extended period of time. In short, militarism supplies the critical normative, doctrinal, and organizational building blocks for the performance of mass violence against a population.

Legacies

What have been the consequences and legacies of the Indonesian violence of 1965–66? Most obviously, it left at least half a million people dead, and shattered the lives of many more. For more than three decades after their release, some one million former political detainees and their families suffered egregious restrictions—formal and informal—on their political, social, and economic rights and freedoms. In the name of "order and stability," they were subjected to official restrictions on their right to vote, prohibited from working in a wide range of "sensitive occupations," and subjected to a noxious regime of surveillance and control that hampered all aspects of their lives. Many also suffered social stigma as a consequence of their real or alleged involvement with the PKI or the alleged coup. Moreover, for the families and friends of those killed, the events of 1965–66 frequently meant the destruction of family life, the loss of a spouse, father, mother, beloved uncle, aunt, niece, or grandparent. Even after those missing family members returned, the damage could not easily be undone; spouses had often remarried or moved away, and children did not know their parents, or having heard the official accounts of PKI brutality and treachery, wanted nothing to do with them. The long-term psychological and social consequences of such treatment and experience, enforced by both state authority and societal norms over many decades, are almost impossible to fathom.

Although much less is known about it, and I have not described it here in any detail, the violence of 1965–66 also appears to have had deep and lasting psychological consequences for those who took part in it, whether as perpetrators or bystanders.[3] The tortured behavior of the perpetrators highlighted in Oppenheimer's films *The Act of Killing* and *The Look of Silence* are cases in point, but the same symptoms—such as nightmares, physical illness, psychological disturbance, domestic violence, and substance abuse—may be observed in the memoirs, fictionalized accounts, and testimonies of perpetrators and bystanders across the spectrum of such circumstances. In the course of an interview with community members in Bali in 1994, for example, I met two men who as young boys had been splattered by the flesh and blood of PKI members whose execution by the army they watched. When I asked the men if they wished to share their story with me, they first smiled broadly and then began to weep uncontrollably. Other accounts describe former killers who apparently lost their sanity, became uncontrollably violent, or suffered hallucinations of various kinds.

There has been a tendency among scholars and other observers to describe responses like these as signs of "trauma." While there may be merit in using such terminology—and I am certainly no expert on the subject—it is probably worth pointing out that most Indonesians who suffer symptoms of this kind do not portray them in such terms. Far more common are explanations rooted in beliefs about haunting, spirit possession, and religious imbalance or obligation. Likewise, the remedies for such disturbances often take culturally specific forms. For instance, when a former police officer from West Timor who had taken part in the killings began to behave erratically and beat his wife, the family decided that it was time for him to undergo a ritual to cool his blood. As his daughter later recounted, "He was led to the river, where he had to drink a few drops of blood from a butchered dog. They made the sign of the cross with the dog's blood on his forehead to cool down the hot blood in his body. That seemed not to be sufficient, so they approached a faith healer. My father told me later that only then he felt his peace of mind coming back to him."[4]

Looking beyond individual psychology, the events of 1965–66 also meant the silencing, whether by killing, imprisonment, or censorship, of an entire generation of writers, activists, and artists associated with the Left—a fact that has crippled, or at least profoundly altered, the course of Indonesian cultural and intellectual life. The victims of that persecution included some of the country's most highly regarded cultural figures. But the effects on Indonesia's political and cultural life have extended far beyond the consequences for a few high-profile intellectuals. The larger and more intractable problem is that an entire tradition of leftist thinking, writing, and political action that was so central to the construction of modern Indonesian political identity and culture since the 1920s has been decimated and rendered illegitimate. That process has robbed Indonesia of an appreciation of its own past, while weakening vital traditions of critical thinking and analysis. More immediately, it has compounded the already-substantial difficulty faced by Indonesians in critically analyzing the events of 1965–66.

By destroying the Left, moreover, the coalition that carried out the violence and distorted its history closed off a vital avenue of popular political expression and criticism. In doing so, it may well have redirected popular anger and dissatisfaction into other institutional forms, including the militant Islamism of groups like the Islamic Defenders Front, right-wing nationalist "youth groups" like Pemuda Pancasila, and populist political movements such as those of the notorious General Prabowo Subianto. As Heryanto, Ricklefs, and others have argued, the destruction of the Left after 1965–66 was the essential precondition for the process of Islamization that occurred during the final years of the New Order, and has continued ever since.[5] The destruction of the Left also ushered in the common use of thugs for hire, known as *preman*, by the political elite and, as Oppenheimer's films show so vividly, led to the entrenchment of the practice in both the state and society.[6] Far from eroding that tendency, the democratization and decentralization of political life since 1998 have helped to spawn new forms of political thuggery, including its Islamist variant. As one preman told a researcher, "Now, in the *reformasi* era, nationalism, defending the state ... and all that shit doesn't cut it any more. It's the groups that are about jihad and fighting vice [*maksiat*] that are the way to go."[7] These groups and the violent intolerance they espouse do not yet dominate Indonesian politics, but they do represent an ever-present threat to the country's traditions and public image of religious tolerance and civility.

For somewhat-different reasons, the mass violence of 1965–66 also led to a significant realignment of religious life and affiliation. Under official pressure, and out of fear of being accused of atheism, after 1965 many Indonesians abandoned their old, animist religious belief systems and adopted one of the five officially recognized faiths—Islam, Hinduism, Catholicism, Protestantism, and Buddhism. In most cases, that shift represented a significant loss for the adherents of those unrecognized belief systems, while doing little to enhance the vitality of the major religions. Indeed, by enforcing notions of religious orthodoxy, the New Order arguably paved the way for a pattern of discrimination, persecution, and violence against ostensibly heterodox groups, including Ahmadis, Seventh-Day Adventists, and adherents of the pre-Islamic belief system of Java known as Kejawen. Those patterns have not only survived the end of the New Order, they have arguably accelerated since then. Significantly, too, the clear complicity of the established religions in the violence of 1965–66 have made their leaders reluctant to examine that history in a meaningful way, let alone take measures to atone for their sins.

The events of 1965–66 have also had a profound impact on women and gender relations in Indonesia. As we have seen, women and girls, especially those affiliated with Gerwani, were targeted for killing and detention, and many were subjected to sexual violence by their attackers and jailers. Apart from being targeted, women and girls suffered trauma and discrimination as the mothers, wives, sisters, and daughters of the men killed or detained in the antileftist campaign. Through its physical and psychological assault on women, moreover, the New Order derailed a strong movement toward women's political and social empowerment that had roots in Indonesia's nationalist awakening in the early twentieth century. In its place, the regime imposed an outmoded patriarchal ideal of the docile, apolitical woman whose place was in the home. Like other legacies of the mass violence of 1965–66, that ideal has been challenged in the two decades since the end of the New Order.[8] But the outmoded ideal has not been overturned. It persists in a variety of forms, including the decisions of legislators and executive officials that either reinforce or ignore gender inequality and violence against women, and in persistent insinuations that women who are involved in political life are not behaving in accordance with Indonesian tradition.

More broadly, the violence of 1965–66 marked a critical turning point in the history of the Cold War, signaling the end of an unusual experiment in lawful political mobilization by parties of the Left in Southeast Asia along with the acceleration of a strategy of armed intervention against the Left in Vietnam, Cambodia, Laos, the Philippines, Thailand, and elsewhere. With the destruction of the PKI, the path of legal parliamentary competition for political power was decisively closed off to Communist parties, leaving only the routes of violent insurrection, conflict, and war. The decimation of the PKI also encouraged a misplaced optimism on the part of the United States and its allies that Communism could be defeated through resort to arms and alliances with fundamentally antidemocratic military regimes. Some observers have gone further, suggesting that the operation to destroy the PKI—especially the use of deliberate provocation, psywar tactics, and death squads—may have served as a template for covert anticommunist operations in other parts of the world. Scott has suggested, for instance, that the US role in the overthrow of Cambodia's Prince Norodom Sihanouk in 1970, and Chile's Allende in 1973 as well as its sponsorship of death squads in Central America from the 1960s onward may have been modeled on the purportedly successful Indonesia operation of 1965–66.[9]

Finally, the events of 1965–66 crystallized certain features of the Indonesian state, and shaped its approach to dissent and opposition for the next half century. After 1965, the regime routinely resorted to extreme violence—including extrajudicial killing, torture, and arbitrary detention—in dealing with its real or perceived opponents. Building on techniques and repertoires honed in 1965–66, it relied on the deployment of militias and paramilitary forces against real and alleged government opponents, especially in areas outside the Javanese heartland—in East Timor (Timor Leste), Aceh, and Papua. In those places and elsewhere, it killed and detained large numbers of its critics, and subjected detainees to the same kinds of torture and sexual violence that it had used against leftists after 1965. In the absence of any meaningful legal or political sanction against such abuses, a culture of violence and impunity became deeply entrenched in the army and its allied institutions.[10] Together, these features of the

FIGURE 11.1. Entrance to the Sumber-Rejo prison camp in East Kalimantan, 1977. The sign reads, "Attention: Gate Must Remain Closed and Locked." (David Jenkins)

New Order earned it a well-deserved reputation as a notorious abuser of human rights and resulted in the deaths of hundreds of thousands of people after 1966.[11] Even with the demise of the New Order in 1998, and the start of a process of democratization and decentralization, many of these features of the state survived.

Beyond these conclusions, the long-term consequences of violence in Indonesia may offer some insight into the boader question, What are the political, social, and moral ramifications of mass violence—for victims, perpetrators, and society as a whole? Indonesia's experience confirms much of what we know about the impact of mass killing and incarceration on victims and their loved ones. These effects encompass psychological distress, mental illness, the breakdown of family and other social ties, economic difficulty, social exclusion, and the denial of political rights. Perhaps less obviously, the Indonesian case tells us that the consequences of mass violence and silence may also be significant for perpetrators and bystanders. Especially for those who were directly involved in killing or torture, the long-term effects may include psychological distress and mental illness. Even those who simply witnessed such acts are likely to have suffered distress, particularly where enforced silence has offered no avenue for expressing remorse or asking forgiveness.

Indonesia's experience suggests as well that the effects of such violence and silence for society as a whole may be profound. To name only the most obvious ramifications, in the aftermath of mass violence one might expect to find the routine use of violence in response to alleged threats to the state, an institutional culture of impunity within the security services, a general militarization or brutalization of political and social life, heightened levels of sexual and domestic violence, and a lack of public trust in key state institutions. That has certainly been the case in many countries emerging from long periods of violence, such as Cambodia, Timor Leste, and South Africa, and has appropriately been the focus of much work in the area of transitional justice.

Although it would require much more research to draw any firm conclusions, it seems likely that all these problems would be significantly compounded in cases where alternative historical interpretations have been officially repressed, and where there has been no compensation, redress, memorializing, and justice for at least two generations. For if deep individual and social trauma along with political disfunction continue to plague societies that have embraced some or all these transitional justice mechanisms, it seems reasonable to assume that those problems would be even worse in societies that have not done so.

The critical question is whether such damage can ever be undone, especially after such a long delay, and what kinds of mechanisms might prove effective in achieving that goal. For many millions of people, the answer is obviously no—the damage cannot be undone. For those who have survived—and for a society as a whole—the answer is more complicated. Some appear to believe that an official apology would be enough, others view clarification of the historical record as the ultimate goal, and still others consider that nothing less than a full judicial process in which those most responsible are held accountable will suffice. This very diversity of views should make us wary of any simple solutions, particularly those that seek to impose a single value over and above all others. That is especially true of solutions that seek to supplant the goal of justice and punishment with the softer solution of reconciliation. Indeed, if there is any lesson to be learned from the Indonesian case, it is that while reconciliation is unquestionably a good thing and justice alone is never enough, there are strong reasons to doubt that reconciliation at the expense of justice will ever provide a satisfactory solution.

Silence

Given the profound and disturbing consequences of the violence of 1965–66, it is fair to ask why so little has been said or done about it over the past half century. But first, let me offer a disclaimer. To say that the Indonesian violence has been met with complete silence would be a disservice to those who have spoken out bravely against it. As we have seen, many have done so, including journalists, artists, teachers, writers, filmmakers, human rights activists, scholars, and even some politicians. And in spite of the serious obstacles they have faced, they have begun to challenge the dominant narrative in significant ways.

And yet in important respects, the characterization is true: notwithstanding the positive steps that have been taken to shake things up, serious restrictions, if not taboos, remain on the open discussion of the events of 1965–66. Just as crucial, despite the initiatives taken by citizens, Indonesian authorities have failed to pursue or have deliberately obstructed virtually every serious effort to address the violence. As of 2017, no truth commission had been established, no comprehensive effort to exhume the hundreds of mass graves dotted across the country had been made, no memorials had been constructed to honor the dead or other victims, no proper judicial investigations had been undertaken, no criminal charges had been brought against the alleged perpetrators, and no formal apology or reparations had been offered by the state. Meanwhile, the international community has declined to speak out against these events or even describe them as what they were: crimes against humanity. Instead, more than half a century after the events occurred, a pattern of denial, obstruction, and impunity prevails.

Indonesia's failure in this regard stands in contrast to the hard-won, if admittedly incomplete, progress made by a number of countries with similarly violent pasts—notably Argentina, Bosnia, Cambodia, Chile, Germany, Japan, Rwanda, South Africa, and Timor Leste. While their records are certainly far from perfect—and a great deal of work remains to be done—the authorities in all these countries have at least made some halting effort to come to grips with their violent pasts, to seek a shared understanding of that history through the formation of truth commissions, to bring at least some of the perpetrators to justice, to recognize and memorialize past crimes, and to provide some kind of reparations (or at least apology) to the victims of those crimes. Indeed, notwithstanding the valiant efforts of its civil society, Indonesia's poor performance on all these fronts arguably places it in the company of a handful of states notorious for their evasion of meaningful human rights action, including the People's Republic of China with respect to the Great Leap Forward and Cultural Revolution, the Soviet Union in regard to the great purges and collectivization campaign, and the United States in connection with its genocide against indigenous peoples as well as the bombing of Hiroshima and Nagasaki.

The question is why? Why, in spite of the brave efforts of civil society actors, is Indonesia in this undistinguished company? Why, almost half a century after the fact, have these crimes not been properly investigated, let alone punished? Why has there been no official apology, no credible attempt at reconciliation by the state, and no move toward reparations?

The simplest answer is that it is a matter of political power. In marked contrast to many regimes responsible for genocides or other crimes against humanity, General Suharto's New Order regime survived for more than thirty years. During that time, it used propaganda, (mis)education, public ritual, repression, and fear to silence critics and stymie serious demands for action. Moreover, because those responsible for the violence remained in power for so long, they were able to write the history of the violence and to recast Indonesian political and social life in ways that made any attempt to question the official version both dangerous and unlikely. In other words, like their Chinese, Russian, and US counterparts, their long-lasting grip on state power served to limit or derail efforts to achieve goals like truth and justice, which are at odds with the personal, political, and institutional interests of the perpetrators.

Perhaps more surprisingly, the ostensibly democratic regime that replaced the New Order after 1998 has employed many of the same techniques and mechanisms, with similarly chilling effects. Beyond the surviving statutory and legislative legacies of the late 1960s, which continue to form the legal basis for repressive action against the Left, what is most notable is the persistence of the old authoritarian mind-set that since 1965 has portrayed the PKI as a treacherous enemy that must be crushed, a subversive threat to the very existence of the nation and the state.

If it is true that virulently anticommunist and authoritarian views remain dominant within the Indonesian state, it follows that the impetus for meaningful change with regard to 1965–66 is unlikely to come from within that state. The dismal record of national institutions—the legislature, judiciary, presidency, and armed forces—to make meaningful progress on the issue since 1998 surely points to the same conclusion. And that is probably the reason why, in recent years, Indonesians who are genuinely concerned about human rights, including the question of 1965–66, have increasingly turned to grassroots strategies that circumvent or simply ignore state political actors and institutions. While necessarily more modest in scope and promising no quick fixes, those nonstate solutions have actually begun to bear some fruit—for example, in the form of local acts of reconciliation, apology, and compensation. But if in some sense it shows more promise, the strategy of incremental change from below is also inherently more difficult, especially so as an entire tradition of critical thinking and political action has been destroyed, or at least irreparably tainted.

The problem is further compounded by the fact that there is still a great deal of societal resistance, some of it quite ugly, to such initiatives. The reasons for that resistance are complex. In some cases, state authorities have fueled or facilitated what is portrayed as community anger. In others, opposition to the PKI and Left appears to be based on genuinely held religious and political beliefs. In such reactions, we can see the legacy of five decades of polarizing politics and language—a politics and language so long in the making that it has become hegemonic. Whatever one may think of the views themselves, and however outdated they may appear to critics and outsiders, legacies of that age and depth are not easy to erase. If this analysis is even partly correct, we can expect that the events of 1965–66 will continue to be the focus of deep and potentially violent confrontation for the foreseeable future. In the longer term, one can only hope that there will be a realization that some kind of reconciliation is necessary—and that it will not be achieved without openness to alternative truths and some form of justice.

Meanwhile, there are still further obstacles to the idea of truth telling, memorialization, and justice. One of those is that despite the best efforts of human rights advocates, public support for such initiatives remains limited, even among survivors. As Zurbuchen has noted, some survivors may simply "prefer not to articulate their sufferings and grievance, or share these with others."[12] Their reticence might also stem from the limited capacity of language and memory to express traumatic experience—a problem that Zurbuchen describes as "the impossibility of recovering or representing the past completely."[13] Heryanto offers the disheartening suggestion that the silence may simply reflect a lack of interest in the history of 1965–66, especially on the part of younger Indonesians. And of course the choice of silence may well be rooted in fear, still deeply embedded twenty years after the end of the New Order.

Like the violence itself, the silence and inaction with respect to 1965–66 has been the result of the enabling behavior of powerful states and certain features of the international environment. As we have seen, the New Order was eagerly assisted from the outset by the United States and other states that viewed the violence of 1965–66 as a small price to pay for the destruction of the Indonesian Left. That support took a variety of forms, including covert economic, propaganda, and political support before and during the violence, followed by massive infusions of economic and military assistance for decades afterward. The US government and its officials have also gone to great lengths to direct attention away from their involvement in the supposed coup and resulting violence, and to muddy the documentary record that might disprove that claim. Indeed, for most of the past fifty years, US officials have declined or deflected requests from scholars under the Freedom of Information Act to declassify relevant documentary materials bearing on the events of 1965–66, most notably CIA intelligence reports from and about Indonesia.[14] In a bizarre but revealing move, for example, in 2001 the Department of State sought to withdraw a volume of declassified documents from 1964–66 that had already been published and distributed to libraries.[15]

It perhaps goes without saying that for much of the past fifty years, the United States and its allies have neither initiated nor supported any serious program or process aimed at elucidating the truth, or seeking justice for the victims of 1965–66. The only significant exception to that rule came in the late 1970s, when the Carter administration pressured the government of Indonesia to release thousands of the political prisoners still held without charge more than a decade after the alleged coup. Significantly, that move came against the backdrop of a powerful international campaign on behalf of those prisoners. In the absence of that campaign, it is doubtful that the United States would have done anything at all.

In short, while primary responsibility for the silence and inaction with regard to the crimes of 1965–66 rests squarely with Indonesian authorities, the US government and other Western states share the blame. Through their economic, political, and military support for the regime that came to power in the wake of the crimes of 1965–66, and their almost-total silence about them ever since, they have helped to ensure that the official version of events prevailed, and have prevented the proper investigation and prosecution of what, by any measure, were among the worst crimes of the twentieth century.

In addition to the acts and omissions of states, the silence and inaction surrounding the events of 1965–66 and their aftermath have arguably been a function of two features of international human rights history and practice. The first of these is the fact that the 1948 UN Convention on the Prevention and Punishment of the Crime of Genocide defines the potential victims of genocide in such a way as to exclude political groups. According to Article II of the convention, genocide is any of a specified list of acts "committed with intent to destroy, in whole or in part, a national, ethnical, racial or religious group, as such."[16] In limiting the purview of genocide to national, ethnical, racial, or religious groups, the convention has arguably diminished the stigma attached to the mass killing of peoples on the basis of their political identity. That has, in turn, made appeals for international judicial or political action on their behalf less likely to succeed. Viewed from the other side, this is precisely the reason some scholars and advocates—most recently the jurists of IPT 1965—have sought to name the Indonesian violence as genocide. The expectation is that use of the term genocide will engender more sympathy for the victims while also improving the prospects of a serious political and judicial response. Whether it will do so in the case of Indonesia remains to be seen, but for now the chances appear remote.

A second aspect of human rights history that has contributed to the silence and inaction with respect to the events of 1965–66 was the relative weakness at that time of a transnational human rights and civil society network. The international human rights movement, which since the late 1970s has assiduously reported on almost every instance of mass violence around the globe, was still in its infancy in 1965–66, with the result that there was virtually no detailed reporting on the events in Indonesia. Despite the best efforts of international solidarity groups and some reporting by a fledgling Amnesty International, expressions of outrage were scarcely audible in that climate, and networks of influence were largely ineffective. Dissenting voices in the media were likewise rare. In that context, neither powerful states nor international bodies like the United Nations felt any pressure to voice concern about the crimes being committed, let alone take any action to stop or punish those responsible.

Thus, a case might be made that the states that have effectively escaped international censure for their great crimes—for example, China, Russia, the United States, and Indonesia—have managed to do so, at least in part, because the crimes in question were all committed years before human rights norms and networks achieved the critical weight and legitimacy they attained starting in the late 1970s. By contrast, most states whose crimes were committed during or after the rise of the human rights movement in the late 1970s—for example, Argentina, Cambodia, Chile, Guatemala, and Rwanda—have been characterized differently and judged in the increasingly hegemonic language of universal human rights. In other words, the timing of the crimes in question in relation to the position of human rights norms and networks may have been a crucial factor in the degree as well as nature of the criticism and response they encountered. The obvious outlier here is the Third Reich, whose crimes were indeed condemned and punished long before the late 1970s. On the other hand, its crimes were arguably so singular, and their condemnation so tied up with the postwar agenda and victory of Allied powers, that they may be regarded as an exception that proves the rule.

Thanks in part to a significant shift in prevailing international norms with respect to human rights since the late 1970s, the conspicuous silence of the New Order period has gradually been replaced by demands for some kind of accountability, truth telling, justice, and compensation for the victims of the violence in Indonesia. That was certainly one reason why Indonesia's genocidal campaign in East Timor was so roundly condemned, and how it was ultimately stopped in 1999. A genuinely transnational network now links Indonesian and international organizations, activists, scholars, and artists, facilitating the dissemination of information about the events of 1965–66 and underpinning campaigns on behalf of its victims. The substantial coverage these events have started to receive in the international media, and the attention being paid to them by a new generation of scholars, artists, and filmmakers, are all a testament to how much things have changed in the past twenty years. And yet as I have argued here, within Indonesia and beyond, resistance to any meaningful change—especially on the crucial questions of truth and justice—remains powerful, and is likely to remain that way for many years to come.

Given these experiences, the Indonesian case may offer some insight into the third broad question I posed at the outset: Why are some serious crimes remembered, condemned, and punished, while others are forgotten and left unpunished? The most important insight from Indonesia is simply that power matters. As long as those responsible for the violence remain in power, the processes of truth seeking, justice, reconciliation, compensation, and memorialization are not likely to happen. Even after the regime has been deposed, those processes will be difficult to set in motion. That is especially so if the regime has used its time in power to propagate a version of history that blames the victims, diverts attention from the question of responsibility, and threatens danger if any attempt is made to propose alternative histories or demand justice. In other words, the struggle over history, like the struggle to name and punish human rights violations, involves power. Indonesia's experience also suggests that silence and inaction may stem from the particularities of the international context—including the posture adopted by powerful states, prevailing international norms with regard to human rights, and the strength and disposition of transnational civil society networks. The Indonesian case highlights the disappointing fact that the first of these, the posture of powerful states, may be decisive, and that where those interests do not favor disclosure, international norms and civil society networks will be less consequential.

More positively, Indonesia's experience makes it clear that the power of states to control historical narrative, memory, and justice is never absolute. Even in the darkest years of the New Order—in spite of the threat and reality of violence, the pervasive fear, and the ideological policing—there were still those, both inside Indonesia and abroad, willing to challenge official narratives, to share or hold onto their memories, to bear witness to the experience of others, and to work for justice in some form. Since the collapse of the New Order in 1998, both the desire and the opportunity to do those things have grown, and it is a virtual certainty that they will continue to do so, despite the obstacles. There is a useful reminder in this experience that history is not preordained, and that questions of historical memory and justice are never fixed, but always open to interpretation and contestation. That is to say, even where powerful interests appear to make change impossible, where laws and societal norms seem to militate against justice, the acts of even a few people—including acts of conscience like bearing witness—can and often do make a difference.

All this begs the question of what, if anything, scholars and citizens should do in the case of Indonesia and others like it. One answer is that we should do nothing—on the familiar grounds that it is better not to open old wounds, that we have no business telling others how to deal with their own histories, and that scholars especially should not be involved in the subjects they seek to study. At the risk of breaching all these norms, I want to suggest instead that there are things we can and should do. First, at least as far as Indonesia is concerned, I think we should insist that our governments help to clarify the historical record by opening their archives from this period without restriction. More than fifty years after the fact, there can be no possible justification for keeping any of those documents secret. Second, I think we should demand that our governments encourage all credible judicial proceedings against those deemed responsible for the crimes committed, while also supporting serious initiatives in the direction of truth and reconciliation. Finally, I believe we should do whatever we can to disrupt the terrible silence and ignorance that has allowed these crimes and similar ones to go unnoticed and unpunished for more than half a century. My hope is that whatever other purpose this book serves, it might help in some way to achieve these ends. It is an improbable hope, I know, but it is surely better than doing nothing at all.

NOTES

Chapter One: Introduction

1. As detailed in chapter 5, there is uncertainty about the numbers, with estimates ranging from 78,500 to 3 million. There is a broad consensus among scholars, however, that something like half a million people were killed.

2. US Central Intelligence Agency, Directorate of Intelligence, *Indonesia—1965: The Coup That Backfired* (Washington, DC: CIA, 1968), 71.

3. That position has been argued, for example, in Robert Cribb, "Political Genocides in Postcolonial Asia," in *The Oxford Handbook of Genocide Studies*, ed. Donald Bloxham and A. Dirk Moses (Oxford: Oxford University Press, 2010), 445–65; Jess Melvin, "Mechanics of Mass Murder: How the Indonesian Military Initiated and Implemented the Indonesian Genocide—The Case of Aceh" (PhD diss., University of Melbourne, 2014). On the other hand, the term genocide has been eschewed by a number of other scholars, including Benedict Anderson and Douglas Kammen. It is also noteworthy that the chapter on Indonesia 1965–66 was excluded from a recent edition of one of the standard works on genocide, Samuel Totten and William S. Parsons, eds., *Century of Genocide: Critical Essays and Eyewitness Accounts*, 4th ed. (New York: Routledge, 2013).

4. See "What Happened in 1965," accessed May 23, 2017, http://worldhistoryproject.org/1965.

5. In 1967–68, the army conducted two significant military operations against alleged PKI holdouts—one of them in West Kalimantan, and a second in the environs of Purwodadi, Central Java, and Blitar, East Java.

6. These patterns reflect the current state of our knowledge, but should not be regarded as definitive. Much more research is needed—especially on areas outside the densely populated islands of Java and Bali—to establish the true geographic and temporal parameters of the violence as well as the nature of the relationship between killing and incarceration.

7. Draft Letter from CIA Director W. F. Raborn to the President, July 20, 1965, personal archive of George McT. Kahin [Kahin Papers], "Chronological File."

8. "Indonesia: Vengeance with a Smile," *Time*, July 15, 1966, 26; James Reston, "A Gleam of Light in Asia," *New York Times*, June 19, 1966.

9. US Department of State Report, "Indonesia," [May 1966?], US *Declassified Documents Catalog* [*DDC*], 1994, #3183. A State Department history likewise concluded in 1968 that "Indonesia's transition from a nation moving steadily toward Communist control to a responsible member of the free community is one of the major success stories of recent years." *Administrative History: State Department*, vol. 1, chapter 7, Section L—Indonesia [ND], *DDC*, 1994, #3184.

10. See, for example, the memoir of former US ambassador Marshall Green, *Indonesia: Crisis and Transformation, 1965–1968* (Washington, DC: Compass Press, 1990); article by former CIA Jakarta station chief Hugh Tovar, "The Indonesian Crisis

of 1965–1966: A Retrospective," *International Journal of Intelligence and Counterintelligence* 7, no. 3 (Fall 1994): 313–38; article by former CIA Jakarta officer John T. Pizzicaro, "The 30 September Movement in Indonesia," *Studies in Intelligence* 13 (Fall 1969): 97–111. Also see the tendentious attack on Indonesia scholars George McT. Kahin and Audrey Kahin by CIA officer J. Foster Collins and Hugh Tovar, "Sukarno's Apologists Write Again," *International Journal of Intelligence and Counterintelligence* 9, no. 3 (Fall 1996): 337–57.

11. Those contributions are too numerous to list here, but they include several excellent local and regional studies, a variety of general and thematic accounts, and a growing number of memoirs and testimonies by survivors and perpetrators of the violence. For a sampling of the recent scholarship, see Douglas Kammen and Katharine McGregor, eds., *The Contours of Mass Violence in Indonesia, 1965–68* (Singapore: NUS Press, 2012); Martijn Eickhoff, Gerry van Klinken, and Geoffrey Robinson, eds., *1965 Today: Living with the Indonesian Massacres*. Special Issue, *Journal of Genocide Research* 19, no. 3 (2017).

12. That is true, for example, of the compelling films by Joshua Oppenheimer: *The Act of Killing* (Drafthouse Films, 2013), DVD; *The Look of Silence* (Drafthouse Films, 2016), DVD. It is also true of many of the fictionalized accounts written by Indonesian authors. See, for example, Putu Oka Sukanta, "Leftover Soul," in *Silenced Voices: New Writing from Indonesia*, ed. Frank Stewart and John McGlynn (Honolulu: University of Hawaii Press, 2000), 214–23; Mohammad Sjoekoer, "Death," in *Gestapu: Indonesian Short Stories on the Abortive Coup of 30th September 1965*, ed. and trans. Harry Aveling (Honolulu: University of Hawaii Press, 1975), 23–26.

13. Christopher R. Browning, *Ordinary Men: Reserve Police Battalion 101 and the Final Solution in Poland* (New York: HarperCollins, 1993); Alexander L. Hinton, "Why Did You Kill? The Cambodian Genocide and the Dark Side of Face and Honor," *Journal of Asian Studies* 57, no. 1 (February 1998): 93–118.

14. "Indonesia: Vengeance with a Smile," 23.

15. See, for example, Green, *Indonesia*. For a detailed critique of this position, see Geoffrey Robinson, *The Dark Side of Paradise: Political Violence in Bali* (Ithaca, NY: Cornell University Press, 1995), especially 275–80.

16. Kenneth R. Young, "Local and National Influences in the Violence of 1965," in *The Indonesian Killings, 1965–1966: Studies from Java and Bali*, ed. Robert Cribb, no. 21 (Clayton, Victoria: Monash Papers on Southeast Asia, 1990), 63–100; Margot Lyon, *Bases of Conflict in Rural Java* (Berkeley, CA: Center for South and Southeast Asia Studies Research Monograph No. 3, 1970); Robert W. Hefner, *The Political Economy of Mountain Java: An Interpretive History* (Berkeley: University of California Press, 1990).

17. See, for example, Ann Laura Stoler, *Capitalism and Confrontation in Sumatra's Plantation Belt, 1870–1979* (New Haven, CT: Yale University Press, 1985); Robinson, *Dark Side of Paradise*.

18. Melvin, "Mechanics of Mass Murder"; Robinson, *Dark Side of Paradise*, especially chapters 11–12.

19. Kammen and McGregor, *Contours of Mass Violence*, 1–24; John Roosa, "The State of Knowledge about an Open Secret: Indonesia's Mass Disappearances of 1965–

66," *Journal of Asian Studies* 75, no. 2 (May 2016): 281–97; Cribb, "Political Genocides in Postcolonial Asia."

20. See, for example, Hermawan Sulistyo, "The Forgotten Years: The Missing History of Indonesia's Mass Slaughter" (PhD diss., Arizona State University, 1997); Christian Gerlach, *Extremely Violent Societies: Mass Violence in the Twentieth-Century World* (Cambridge: Cambridge University Press, 2010).

21. For the classic statement of that case, and still the most sophisticated and persuasive one, see Peter Dale Scott, "The United States and the Overthrow of Sukarno, 1965–1967," *Pacific Affairs* 58, no. 2 (Summer 1985): 239–64.

22. See Benjamin Valentino, *Final Solutions: Mass Killing and Genocide in the Twentieth Century* (Ithaca, NY: Cornell University Press, 2004); Scott Straus, *Making and Unmaking Nations: War, Leadership, and Genocide in Modern Africa* (Ithaca, NY: Cornell University Press, 2015); Helen Fein, *Accounting for Genocide: National Responses and Jewish Victimization during the Holocaust* (Chicago: University of Chicago Press, 1979).

23. A number of scholars have noted that state-funded paramilitary and militia groups are a common feature of genocides. See Straus, *Making and Unmaking Nations*; Michael Mann, *The Dark Side of Democracy: Explaining Ethnic Cleansing* (New York: Cambridge University Press, 2005).

24. See Geoffrey Robinson, *"If You Leave Us Here, We Will Die": How Genocide Was Stopped in East Timor* (Princeton, NJ: Princeton University Press, 2010).

25. Eric D. Weitz, *A Century of Genocide: Utopias of Race and Nation* (Princeton, NJ: Princeton University Press, 2003); Eric D. Weitz, "The Modernity of Genocides: War, Race, and Revolution in the Twentieth Century," in *The Specter of Genocide: Mass Murder in Historical Perspective*, ed. Robert Gellately and Ben Kiernan (Cambridge: Cambridge University Press, 2003), 53–74.

26. Ben Kiernan, "Twentieth Century Genocides: Underlying Ideological Themes from Armenia to East Timor," in *The Specter of Genocide: Mass Murder in Historical Perspective*, ed. Robert Gellately and Ben Kiernan (Cambridge: Cambridge University Press, 2003), 29–52; Jacques Sémelin, *Purify and Destroy: Political Uses of Massacres and Genocide* (New York: Columbia University Press, 2007); Mann, *Dark Side of Democracy*; Robert Melson, *Revolution and Genocide: On the Origins of the Armenian Genocide and the Holocaust* (Chicago: University of Chicago Press, 1992); Straus, *Making and Unmaking Nations*.

27. Straus notes that in the most studied cases of genocide—the Armenian genocide, the Holocaust, and Rwanda—"local actors are critical in the identification and sorting of target populations as well as in the infliction of violence against them." Straus, *Making and Unmaking Nations*, 131.

28. See, for example, Fein, *Accounting for Genocide*; Erwin Staub, *The Roots of Evil: The Origins of Genocide and Other Group Violence* (Cambridge: Cambridge University Press, 1989); René Lemarchand, *The Dynamics of Violence in Central Africa* (Philadelphia: University of Pennsylvania Press, 2009); Sara Lipton, *Dark Mirror: The Medieval Origins of Anti-Jewish Iconography* (New York: Metropolitan, 2014).

29. Helen Fein, "Revolutionary and Anti-Revolutionary Genocides: A Comparison of State Murders in Democratic Kampuchea, 1975–1979, and in Indonesia,

1965–1966," *Comparative Studies in Society and History* 35, no. 4 (October 1993), 799. See also Helen Fein, *Accounting for Genocide*, especially chapter 1; Helen Fein, "Genocide: A Sociological Perspective," *Current Sociology* 38 (Spring 1990): 1–126.

30. See, for example, Doris L. Bergen, *War and Genocide: A Concise History of the Holocaust* (Oxford: Rowman and Littlefield, 2003); Scott Straus, *The Order of Genocide: Race, Power, and War in Rwanda* (Ithaca, NY: Cornell University Press, 2006); Norman Naimark, *Stalin's Genocides* (Princeton, NJ: Princeton University Press, 2007); Manus Midlarsky, *The Killing Trap* (Cambridge: Cambridge University Press, 2005); John W. Dower, *War without Mercy: Race and Power in the Pacific War* (New York: Random House, 1986); Valentino, *Final Solutions*; Melson, *Revolution and Genocide*; Weitz, "Modernity of Genocides."

31. Margaret Keck and Kathryn Sikkink, *Activists beyond Borders: Advocacy Networks in International Politics* (Ithaca, NY: Cornell University Press, 1998); Patrice McMahon, *Taming Ethnic Hatred: Ethnic Cooperation and Transnational Networks in Eastern Europe* (Syracuse, NY: Syracuse University Press, 2007); Anja Jetschke, *Human Rights and State Security: Indonesia and the Philippines* (Philadelphia: University of Pennsylvania Press, 2011); Robinson, *"If You Leave Us Here, We Will Die."*

32. See, for example, Christopher E. Goscha and Christian Osterman, eds., *Connecting Histories: Decolonization and the Cold War in Southeast Asia, 1945–1962* (Stanford, CA: Stanford University Press, 2009). That case has also been made compellingly for Bolivia, Guatemala, and Chile, among others. See Thomas C. Field Jr., *From Development to Dictatorship: Bolivia and the Alliance for Progress in the Kennedy Era* (Ithaca, NY: Cornell University Press, 2014); Greg Grandin, *The Last Colonial Massacre: Latin America in the Cold War*, updated ed. (Chicago: University of Chicago Press, 2011); Tanya Harmer, *Allende's Chile and the Inter-American Cold War* (Chapel Hill: University of North Carolina Press, 2011).

33. In *From Development to Dictatorship*, Field has shown, for example, that the United States actually *opposed* the 1964 military coup in Bolivia, but that it nevertheless contributed directly to that outcome through its relentless support for a military-led modernization program under the auspices of the Alliance for Progress after 1961.

34. See, for example, Donald Bloxham, *The Final Solution: A Genocide* (Oxford: Oxford University Press, 2009); Christopher Browning and Jürgen Matthäus, *The Origins of the Final Solution: The Evolution of Nazi Jewish Policy, September 1939–1942* (Lincoln: University of Nebraska Press, 2004); Mann, *Dark Side of Democracy*; Straus, *Order of Genocide*; Valentino, *Final Solutions*; Uğur Üngör, "When Persecution Bleeds into Mass Murder: The Processive Nature of Genocide," *Genocide Studies and Prevention* 1, no. 2 (2006): 173–76.

Chapter Two: Preconditions

1. Although the European presence in the archipelago dated from the late sixteenth century, the colony that the Dutch called the Netherlands East Indies did not take its final form until the first decade of the twentieth century. The geographic boundaries established at that time became the boundaries of the Republic of Indonesia that declared its independence from the Dutch on August 17, 1945.

2. On the genesis and history of Indonesia's nationalist movement, see George McT. Kahin, *Nationalism and Revolution in Indonesia* (Ithaca, NY: Cornell University Press, 1952), 37–100.

3. Sukarno, *Nationalism, Islam, and Marxism*, trans. Karel H. Warouw and Peter D. Weldon (Ithaca, NY: Modern Indonesia Project, Southeast Asia Program, Cornell University, 1970). See also J. D. Legge, *Sukarno: A Political Biography* (Sydney: Allen and Unwin, 1990).

4. See Geoffrey Robinson, *The Dark Side of Paradise: Political Violence in Bali* (Ithaca, NY: Cornell University Press, 1995), chapters 2, 3, and 6.

5. Benedict Anderson, ed., *Violence and the State in Suharto's Indonesia* (Ithaca, NY: Cornell Southeast Asia Program, 2001), 11. On the political significance of the Japanese occupation, see Benedict R. O'G. Anderson, *Java in a Time of Revolution* (Ithaca, NY: Cornell University Press, 1972); Robinson, *Dark Side of Paradise*, chapter 4; Ruth McVey, "The Post-Revolutionary Transformation of the Indonesian Military," *Indonesia* 11 (April 1971): 133–42.

6. These included Peta (Defenders of the Fatherland), Heiho (Auxiliary Forces), Barisan Hizbullah (Forces of God), Seinendan (Youth Corps), Keibodan (Vigilance Corps), Jawa Hokokai (Java Service Association), and Barisan Pelopor (Vanguard Corps). See Anderson, *Java in a Time of Revolution*, 22–30.

7. On Peta, see Anderson, *Java in a Time of Revolution*, 22–25.

8. The Japanese wartime military regime "regularly practiced torture in private and executions in public, which brought about mass starvation, and sent hundreds of thousands to their deaths in forced labor gangs." Anderson, *Violence and the State in Suharto's Indonesia*, 9.

9. Anderson notes that the Dutch who did not manage to escape when the Japanese arrived "were sent to harsh detainment camps where their guards were usually Japanese-trained natives." Ibid., 11.

10. On the Indonesian National Revolution, see Kahin, *Nationalism and Revolution*; Anderson, *Java in a Time of Revolution*; Anthony Reid, *The Indonesian National Revolution* (Hawthorn, Victoria: Longman, 1974).

11. On the history of the Indonesian Army, see Harold Crouch, *The Army and Politics in Indonesia* (Ithaca, NY: Cornell University Press, 1978). See also Ulf Sundhaussen, *The Road to Power: Indonesian Military Politics, 1945–1967* (Kuala Lumpur: Oxford University Press, 1982); Geoffrey Robinson, "Indonesia—On a New Course?," in *Coercion and Governance: The Declining Political Role of the Military in Asia*, ed. Muthiah Alagappa (Stanford, CA: Stanford University Press, 2001), 226–56.

12. For example, a Swiss scholar who gained access to previously secret Dutch military archives has made such a case. See Rémy Limpach, "Business as Usual: Dutch Mass Violence in the Indonesian War of Independence," in *Colonial Counterinsurgency and Mass Violence: The Dutch Empire in Indonesia*, ed. Bart Luttikhuis and A. Dirk Moses (New York: Routledge, 2014), 64–90; *De Brandende Kampongs van General Spoor* (Amsterdam: Uitgeverij Boon, 2016).

13. See, for example, Anne-Lot Hoek, "Wij gaan het hier nog heel moeilijk krijgen," *NRC Weekend*, January 9–10, 2016; "Ook op Sumatra richtte Nederland en bloedbad aan," *NRC*, February 13, 2016; "Waarheidscommissie Indie is nodig," *NRC Weekend*, October 10, 2015; "Bloedbaden op Bali," *Vrij Nederland*, November 13, 2013.

14. On the evolution of army doctrine and structure, see Robinson, "Indonesia," 230–33. See also Ruth McVey, "The Post-Revolutionary Transformation of the Indonesian Military," *Indonesia* 11 (April 1971): 133–42; Crouch, *The Army and Politics in Indonesia*; and Sundhaussen, *The Road to Power.*

15. The army "rationalization" plan proposed by Vice President Mohammad Hatta and spearheaded by Colonel Nasution, then deputy commander of the army, aimed to reduce an armed force of some 800,000 regular and irregular troops to a disciplined army of about 160,000. Ruth Ann Swift, *Road to Madiun: The Indonesian Communist Uprising of 1948* (Ithaca, NY: Cornell Southeast Asia Program, 1989), 44.

16. On the origins of the Jakarta Charter in mid-1945, see Legge, *Sukarno*, 170–71.

17. On Darul Islam, see C. van Dijk, *Rebellion under the Banner of Islam: The Darul Islam in Indonesia* (The Hague: Martinus Nijhoff, 1981).

18. For the most complete account of the Madiun uprising, see Swift, *Road to Madiun*.

19. Musso was killed on October 31, 1948, while eleven other PKI leaders were killed in mid-December. Shortly after the Dutch broke the truce in December 1948, all but a few of those who had been detained were released and permitted to join the fight. Ibid., 80. Hamish McDonald writes that "By December the rebellion was smashed, its leaders executed; unknown thousands had been killed, and some 35,000 had been arrested by the government. Hamish McDonald, *Suharto's Indonesia* (Sydney: Fontana, 1981), 18.

20. See, for example, Mirajadi, "Tiga Tahun Provokasi Madiun," *Bintang Merah*, August–September 1951.

21. See, for example, the Masyumi-run newspaper *Abadi*, September 4, 1953. For an official government account of the Madiun affair, see Sekretariat Negara Republik Indonesia, *Gerakan 30 September: Pemberontakan Partai Komunis Indonesia. Latar Belakang, Aksi, dan Penumpasannya* (Jakarta: Sekretariat Negara Republik Indonesia, 1994), 17–23.

22. See, for example, Tim PBNU, *Benturan NU-PKI, 1948–1965* (Jakarta, 2013).

23. The five principles as Sukarno originally articulated them were nationalism, internationalism (and humanitarianism), democracy, social justice, and belief in God in the context of religious freedom. On the genesis of Pancasila, see Legge, *Sukarno*, 184–88.

24. See Herbert Feith, *The Indonesian Elections of 1955* (Ithaca, NY: Cornell Modern Indonesia Project, 1957).

25. For a comparison of the results of the 1955 and 1957 elections in selected provinces, see J. D. Legge, *Central Authority and Regional Autonomy in Indonesia: A Study in Local Administration, 1950–1960* (Ithaca, NY: Cornell University Press, 1961), 150.

26. On the regional rebellions, see George McT. Kahin and Audrey Kahin, *Subversion as Foreign Policy: The Secret Eisenhower and Dulles Debacle in Indonesia* (New York: New Press, 1995); Barbara Harvey, *Permesta: Half a Rebellion* (Ithaca, NY: Cornell Modern Indonesia Project, 1977).

27. Crouch, *Army and Politics*, 39; Daniel Lev, *The Transition to Guided Democracy: Indonesian Politics, 1957–1959* (Ithaca, NY: Cornell Modern Indonesia Project, 1966), 34, 69–70.

28. See Daniel Lev, *The Transition to Guided Democracy*; Herbert Feith, *The Decline of Constitutional Democracy in Indonesia* (Ithaca, NY: Cornell University Press, 1962).

29. A common complaint about the parliamentary system was that it produced weak and short-lived governments. Between December 1949 and March 1957, there were seven cabinets, none of them lasting more than two years. Feith, *Decline of Constitutional Democracy*, xvii–xix.

30. Crouch, *Army and Politics*, 45.

31. For this view of Confrontation, see ibid., 55–62. See also John Subritsky, *Confronting Sukarno: British, American, Australian, and New Zealand Diplomacy in the Malaysian-Indonesian Confrontation, 1961–1965* (New York: St. Martin's Press, 2000).

32. Anderson describes this process as "an accelerando of mass politics penetrating ever more widely down and across Indonesian society [such that] each of these parties [the PKI, PNI, and NU] claimed, with some justification, to be the core of a huge, organized, ideological 'family,' each about 20 million strong, which completed fiercely for influence in every sphere of life and on a round-the-clock basis." Benedict Anderson, "Old State, New Society: Indonesia's New Order in Comparative Historical Perspective," in *Language and Power: Exploring Political Cultures in Indonesia*, ed. Benedict Anderson (Ithaca, NY: Cornell University Press, 1990), 107.

33. On Sukarno's life and political thought, see Legge, *Sukarno*.

34. Sukarno was arrested in December 1929 and tried together with three others in 1930. He was released in December 1931, but rearrested in August 1933, remaining in detention until the onset of the war in 1942. Kahin, *Nationalism and Revolution*, 90–94. Sukarno's defense oration, "Indonesia Accuses!," prepared for his 1930 trial, became a classic statement of the anticolonial, nationalist position. See Sukarno, *"Indonesia Accuses!" Sukarno's Defense Oration in the Political Trial of 1930*, ed. and trans. Roger K. Paget (Kuala Lumpur: Oxford University Press, 1975).

35. See Benedict R. O'G. Anderson, "The Idea of Power in Javanese Culture," in *Culture and Politics in Indonesia*, ed. Claire Holt, Benedict R. Anderson, and James T. Siegel (Ithaca, NY: Cornell University Press, 1972), 1–69. See also Legge, *Sukarno*.

36. Crouch, *Army and Politics*, 68.

37. Cited in ibid., 67.

38. The PKI was established on May 23, 1920, while its forerunner, the Indies Social Democratic Union, had been formed in 1914. Kahin, *Nationalism and Revolution*, 74–75. China's Communist Party was established on July 1, 1921.

39. Rex Mortimer, *Indonesian Communism under Sukarno: Ideology and Politics, 1959–1965* (Ithaca, NY: Cornell University Press, 1974), 366. Mortimer provides the following membership figures, in millions: PKI (3.5), Pemuda Rakyat (3), SOBSI (3.5), BTI (9), Gerwani (3), LEKRA (5), and HIS (0.07). See also *Harian Rakyat*, May 14, 1965; Crouch, *Army and Politics*, 67.

40. See, for example, Sudisman, "Analysis of Responsibility: Defense Speech of Sudisman, General Secretary of the Indonesian Communist Party at His Trial before the Special Military Tribunal, Jakarta, 21 July 1967," trans. Benedict Anderson (Melbourne, Victoria: Works Co-operative, 1975); Olle Törnquist, *Dilemmas of Third World Communism: The Destruction of the PKI in Indonesia* (London: Zed Books, 1985).

41. Kahin, *Nationalism and Revolution*, 86. The uprising was set in motion on November 12, 1926, and sputtered on in some areas until early 1927, but it never involved more than a few thousand people. On the 1926 uprising and early history of the PKI, see Ruth McVey, *The Rise of Indonesian Communism* (Ithaca, NY: Cornell University Press, 1965).

42. The new generation of leaders had all been part of the new PKI Politburo set up under Musso's leadership in late August 1948. In 1951, Aidit was twenty-seven years old, Lukman was thirty-one, and Njoto was twenty-three. Swift, *Road to Madiun*, 56–57.

43. See Ruth McVey, "Nationalism, Revolution, and Organization in Indonesian Communism," in *Making Indonesia: Essays on Modern Indonesia in Honor of George McT. Kahin*, ed. Daniel Lev and Ruth McVey (Ithaca, NY: Cornell Southeast Asia Program, 1996), 96–117; Rex Mortimer, *The Indonesian Communist Party and Land Reform, 1954–1965* (Clayton, Victoria: Monash University Centre for Southeast Asian Studies, 1972); Mortimer, *Indonesian Communism*.

44. Memorandum from Executive Secretary of NSC, "US Policy on Indonesia," December 19, 1960, *Declassified Documents Catalog*, United States, 1982, #592.

45. In 1967, a senior figure in the anticommunist PSI told George Kahin that Aidit had allowed the PKI to become too dependent on Sukarno: "Partly this was due to Aidit's personality and in particular his vanity and his feudalistic outlook which inclined him to be overawed by and adulate Sukarno to a dangerous degree." George Kahin interview with senior PSI figure, June 14, 1967, Jakarta, Kahin Papers.

46. Martial law lasted from March 1957 to May 1963, but was then partially restored in September 1964, at the army's request. That ensured the continuation of substantial army power until the events of October 1965. Crouch, *Army and Politics*, 76, 33.

47. On the entrenchment of army power, see Lev, *Transition to Guided Democracy*. See also Crouch, *Army and Politics*, 47.

48. For a brief synopsis of Indonesian Army structure and doctrine, see Robinson, "Indonesia."

49. Originally articulated in 1958 as the doctrine of the "Middle Way" by army Chief of Staff Nasution, it was refined and formalized in April 1965 as the army doctrine of Tri Ubaya Sakti (Three Sacred Promises). Crouch, *Army and Politics*, 82; Robinson, "Indonesia," 232.

50. According to General Nasution's top aide, Aidit's captured diary listed a number of army intelligence officers in Central and East Java as PKI sympathziers. George Kahin interview with Lieutenant Colonel Henu Heli, June 13, 1967, Jakarta, Kahin Papers. Another informant told Kahin that in 1965, as many as 30 percent of the military representatives on the regonial leadership bodies in Central and East Java were pro-PKI. George Kahin interview with Sumarman, June 20, 1967, Jakarta, Kahin Papers. Likewise, army authorities in North Sumatra reportedly told US officials that up to 30 percent of troops in North Sumatra were sympathetic to the PKI. Douglas Kammen, personal communication, January 24, 2017.

51. For example: "While there is no evidence to show that Omar Dhani and other senior air force officers were ideologically committed to the PKI, their antagonism toward the army had placed them beside the PKI as supporters of the president

against the army leadership." Crouch, *Army and Politics*, 84. On the posture of the navy and police, see ibid., 84–85.

52. Ibid., 37.

53. On PKI efforts to recruit within armed forces and the formation of the Special Bureau, see ibid., 82–83.

54. One of the more important tensions within the army, for example, was based on a largely personal hostility between the army commander, General Yani, and the commander of the armed forces, General Nasution. On the lack of cohesion in the army and the armed forces, and the Yani-Nasution split, see ibid., 79–81.

55. There were several other parties on the right, of course, including the PSI, which was banned in 1960 along with Masyumi for supporting the regional rebellions; Murba, which was "frozen" in January 1965; and the Partai Katolik. But compared to the PNI, NU, and Masyumi, their roles were relatively minor.

56. On the NU, see Greg Fealy and Katharine McGregor, "East Java and the Role of Nahdlatul Ulama in the 1965–66 Anti-Communist Violence," in *The Contours of Mass Violence in Indonesia, 1965–68*, ed. Douglas Kammen and Katharine McGregor (Singapore: NUS Press, 2012), 104–30. See also Andrée Feillard, *NU vis-à-vis Negara: Pencarian Isi, Bentuk dan Makna* (Yogkakarta: LKiS, 1999).

57. Masyumi (Majelis Syuro Muslimin Indonesia, or Consultative Council of Indonesian Muslims) was originally formed by the Japanese occupation authorities in November 1943 to unify various elements of Islam in Indonesia. See Harry J. Benda, *Crescent and the Rising Sun: Indonesian Islam under the Japanese Occupation* (The Hague: W. van Hoeve, 1958).

58. On US support for Masyumi in the 1955 elections, see chapter 4.

59. On the HMI during these years, see M. Alfar Alfian, *HMI, 1963–1966: Menegakkan Pancasila di Tengah Prahara* (Jakarta: Kompas, 2013).

60. On the history of the PNI, see J. Eliseo Rocamora, "Nationalism in Search of an Ideology: Indonesia's Nationalist Party, 1946–1965" (PhD diss., Cornell University, 1974).

61. Crouch, *Army and Politics*, 42.

62. The figure of twenty-one million was the number of people who had reportedly volunteered to join the campaign to "Crush Malaysia." On the Fifth Force idea and debate around it, see ibid., 86–94.

63. Aidit reportedly suggested the idea to Sukarno in January 1965. See *Harian Rakyat*, January 15, 1965.

64. Crouch, *Army and Politics*, 91.

65. Ibid., 87–89.

66. On the Gilchrist Letter, see Brian May, *The Indonesian Tragedy* (London: Routledge and Kegan Paul, 1978), 125–26. An illegible copy of the letter and a transcript, dated March 24, 1965, are included in the official record of Foreign Minister Subandrio's 1966 trial. See *"Gerakan 30 September" Dihadapan Mahmillub, Perkara Dr. Subandrio, Vol. 1* (Jakarta: Pusat Pendidikan Kehakiman A.D., 1967), 102–3. The letter is discussed in more detail in chapter 4.

67. According to other accounts, General Yani told the president that a Council of Generals of sorts did exist, but that it was simply a forum for discussing personnel issues. Some observers have speculated that the whole idea of a Council of Generals

was a deliberate provocation, set in motion by the Kostrad intelligence officer Ali Murtopo to provide a pretext for Kostrad to strike against the PKI.

68. Bradley Simpson, "The United States and the International Dimension of the Killings in Indonesia," in *1965: Indonesia and the World, Indonesia dan Dunia*, ed. Bernd Schaefer and Baskara T. Wardaya, bilingual ed. (Jakarta: Gramedia Pustaka Utama, 2013), 54–55.

69. On the conflicts over land reform, see Mortimer, *Indonesian Communism*, chapter 7; Robinson, *Dark Side of Paradise*, 235–72.

70. Crouch, *Army and Politics*, 64. For a detailed account of the PKI position on land reform, see Mortimer, *Indonesian Communism*, 132–40.

71. For details of the Bandar Betsy incident, see Crouch, *Army and Politics*, 87–88.

72. Crouch writes that the "inflation of 119 percent in 1963 and 134 percent in 1964 was followed by a 50 percent rise between January and August of 1965. While prices continued to rise, exports fell and foreign governments became less willing to make new credits available. As the capacity to pay for imports declined, the president made a virtue of necessity by announcing the principle of *Berdikari* (Standing on Our Own Feet) as one of the Five Magic Charms of the Revolution and declared that imports of rice would be stopped in 1965 followed by imports of textiles in 1966.... Meanwhile, the government's capacity to raise revenues declined, and roads, railways, ports, and other infrastructure facilities fell into disrepair." Crouch, *Army and Politics*, 95–96. See also J.A.C. Mackie, *Problems of the Indonesian Inflation* (Ithaca, NY: Cornell Modern Indonesia Project, 1967).

73. Crouch, *Army and Politics*, 82.

74. Ibid., 96.

Chapter Three: Pretext

1. The main army units involved were the First Battalion of the Tjakrabirawa Regiment, Battalion 454 of the Diponegoro Command in Central Java, and Battalion 530 of the Brawijaya Command in East Java. Altogether, the movement controlled about twenty-five hundred troops.

2. Generals Yani, Pandjaitan, and Harjono were killed while being kidnapped; Generals Soeprapto, Parman, and Soetojo were killed later.

3. The account here draws mainly from a number of trusted sources, including Harold Crouch, *The Army and Politics in Indonesia* (Ithaca, NY: Cornell University Press, 1978); John Roosa, *Pretext for Mass Murder: The September 30th Movement and Suharto's Coup d'Etat in Indonesia* (Madison: University of Wisconsin Press, 2006); Douglas Kammen and Katharine McGregor, eds., *The Contours of Mass Violence in Indonesia, 1965–68* (Singapore: NUS Press, 2012). It also draws on a series of interviews with key figures conducted in the late 1960s and 1970s by Professor George McT. Kahin, notes from which were made available to the author. Personal archive of George McT. Kahin [Kahin Papers].

4. Untung was commander of the First Battalion of the Tjakrabirawa Regiment, the Presidential Guard. Other army officers centrally involved included Colonel Abdul Latief and Brigadier General Supardjo.

5. The events of October 1, 1965, are commonly described as a coup, failed coup, or abortive coup. Some observers have noted that such terms are misleading in the sense that they appear to accept the disputed premise that the September 30th Movement attempted to stage a coup d'état and obscure the fact that in the months after October 1, an actual coup occurred in which the army seized power. For these reasons, I refer to the events of October 1, 1965 as an alleged coup, a supposed coup, or a purported coup. Wherever possible, I refer to the group that led the actions of October 1, 1965 as the September 30th Movement.

6. "Initial Statement of Lieutenant Colonel Untung," reprinted in Benedict Anderson and Ruth McVey, *A Preliminary Analysis of the October 1, 1965 "Coup" in Indonesia* (Ithaca, NY: Cornell Modern Indonesia Project, 1971), 164–66.

7. It said, for example, that "power-mad Generals and officers who have neglected the lot of their men and who above the accumulated sufferings of their men have lived in luxury, led a gay life, insulted our women and wasted government funds, must be kicked out of the Army and punished accordingly." Ibid., 166.

8. "Decree No. 1 on the Establishment of the Indonesian Revolution Council," reprinted in Anderson and McVey, *A Preliminary Analysis*, 167–69. Likewise, Decision No. 2 effectively demoted all generals by declaring lieutenant colonel to be the highest-possible rank in the armed forces, and promoted all who supported the movement by one rank, and two ranks for those who played a direct role. "Decision No. 2 Concerning Demotion and Promotion of Rank," reprinted in Anderson and McVey, *A Preliminary Analysis*, 175–76.

9. Dhani had signed an order in support of the movement's action at 9:30 a.m. on October 1, 1965. For various reasons, however, the order was not broadcast on RRI until later that afternoon. For the text of the order, see Boerhan and Soebekti, *"Gerakan 30 September,"* 2nd ed. (Jakarta: Lembaga Pendidikan Ilmu Pengetahuan dan Kebudajaan Kosgoro, 1966), 83–84.

10. For the text of Sukarno's remarks, see ibid., 79–81.

11. For the text of Nasution's speech, see ibid., 97–100.

12. See, for example, *Angkatan Bersendjata*, October 9 and 14, 1965; *Duta Masyarakat*, October 13 and 15, 1965.

13. George Kahin interview with Colonel Henu Heli, June 13, 1967, Jakarta, Kahin Papers.

14. The key army figures who supported Untung's movement in Central Java were younger officers at the Semarang headquarters of the Diponegoro Division. They included Colonel Suherman, Colonel Marjono, and Lieutenant Colonel Usman Sastrodibroto. In Yogyakarta, movement troops killed two of their prisoners, Colonel Katamso Darmokusumo and Lieutenant Colonel Soegiono, but in Solo and Salatiga all prisoners were released unharmed. On the situation in Central Java at this time, see Anderson and McVey, *A Preliminary Analysis*, 89–101, 106–11, 115–18.

15. Kammen and McGregor write that during this period, "Sukarno continued to speak out against the blatant lies and the propaganda inciting civilians to exact revenge, and the pogroms." Kammen and McGregor, *Contours of Mass Violence*, 3.

16. In December 1965, Sukarno contested the allegations that the generals had been mutilated and cited the official autopsies to prove his case. But nobody paid any

attention. His appeals were dismissed as special pleading on behalf of the Left and as evidence of his lack of remorse at the death of the generals.

17. On Father Beek, see Made Supriatma, "Kamerad Dalam Keyakinan: Pater Joop Beek, SJ dan Jaringan BA Santamaria di Asia Tenggara," *Harian Indoprogress*, September 29, 2016.

18. Crouch writes that the trials were mainly aimed at "discrediting the President by proxy and demonstrating his lack of power to save his most loyal colleagues." Crouch, *Army and Politics*, 211. On the trials, see also Amnesty International, *Indonesia: An Amnesty International Report* (London: Amnesty International, 1977), 45–54.

19. The focus of the military operation in Blitar was a small group of PKI members who, in the wake of the mass killings, had sought to establish a stronghold in a cluster of villages known to be sympathetic. In 1967, portraying the group as dangerous armed rebels, the army conducted a full-scale military operation in the area known as Operasi Trisula that left hundreds dead. See Vannessa Hearman, "Dismantling the Fortress: East Java and the Transition to Suharto's New Order Regime" (PhD diss., University of Melbourne, 2012). The operation in West Kalimantan was directed against alleged Communists, most of them Chinese Indonesians. In that case, the army mobilized ethnic Dayak people, and playing on ethnic differences and rivalries, incited them to attack and kill the ethnic Chinese in their communities. See Jamie Davidson and Douglas Kammen, "Indonesia's Unknown War and the Lineages of Violence in West Kalimantan," *Indonesia* 73 (April 2002): 53–87.

20. Majelis Permusyawaratan Rakyat Sementara (MPRS) Republik Indonesia, *Ketetapan MPRS Republik Indonesia No: XXV/MPRS/1966 tentang Pembubaran Partai Komunis Indonesia, Pernjataan Sebagai Organisasi Terlarang Diseluruh Wilajah Republik Indonesia bagi Partai Komunis Indonesia dan Larangan Setiap Kegiatan Untuk Menjebarkan Paham atau Adjaran Komunis/Marxisme-Leninisme*, July 5, 1966.

21. Although this account began to emerge in sensationalized media reports within days of the purported coup attempt, its first systematic articulation was in an armed forces publication, Angkatan Bersendjata Republik Indonesia, *40 Hari Kegagalan G-30-S* (Jakarta: Staf Pertahanan Keamanan, 1966). A second official version, published in English in 1968, was Nugroho Notosusanto and Ismail Saleh, *The Coup Attempt of the "September 30 Movement" in Indonesia* (Jakarta: Pembimbing Massa, 1968). An official Indonesian-language account, the government's so-called white book, was finally published in 1994 as Sekretariat Negara Republik Indonesia, *Gerakan 30 September: Pemberontakan Partai Komunis Indonesia. Latar Belakang, Aksi, dan Penumpasannya* (Jakarta: Sekretariat Negara Republik Indonesia, 1994). Roosa argues that these accounts actually differ on three key questions: the nature of PKI responsibility, the nature of the movement, and how the movement was destroyed. See John Roosa, "The September 30th Movement: The Aporias of the Official Narratives," in *The Contours of Mass Violence in Indonesia, 1965–68*, ed. Douglas Kammen and Katharine McGregor (Singapore: NUS Press, 2012), 25–49.

22. This version bears a remarkable resemblance to the official CIA version published in 1968: US Central Intelligence Agency, Directorate of Intelligence, *Indonesia—1965: The Coup That Backfired* (Washington, DC: CIA, 1968). US officials also

favor this view. Francis Galbraith, who served as the deputy chief of mission in Jakarta at the time of alleged coup, and later as ambassador, told Kahin in 1971 that he was convinced that the PKI had played the major role in the actions of October 1. George Kahin, interview with Francis Galbraith, June 1, 1971, Jakarta, Kahin Papers.

23. Howard P. Jones, "American-Indonesian Relations," presentation at Chiefs of Mission Conference, Baguio, Philippines, Howard P. Jones Papers, box 21, Hoover Institution Archives, 12, cited in Roosa, *Pretext for Mass Murder*, 193.

24. British Embassy Jakarta (Gilchrist) to Foreign Office (Stewart), "Attempted Coup in Indonesia," October 19, 1965, DH 1015/215, FO 371/180320, National Archives of the United Kingdom [UKNA].

25. According to Anderson, Benson felt "sure that the PKI was cornered and backed into an impossible position once the coup had flopped." Benedict Anderson interview with Colonel George Benson, November 10, 1965, personal archive of Ruth T. McVey [McVey Papers], box 9, file 190.

26. George Kahin, interview with Francis Galbraith, June 1, 1971, Jakarta, Kahin Papers.

27. George Kahin interview with five top leaders of the HMI, June 18, 1967, Jakarta, Kahin Papers.

28. Benedict Anderson and Ruth McVey, "What Happened in Indonesia?" *New York Review of Books*, June 1, 1978.

29. Dinas Sejarah TNI-AD, "Crushing the G30S/PKI in Central Java," in *The Indonesian Killings, 1965–1966: Studies from Java and Bali*, ed. Robert Cribb, no. 21 (Clayton, Victoria: Monash Papers on Southeast Asia, 1990), 165.

30. Roosa, "September 30th Movement," 36.

31. For the text of Njono's alleged confessions and an extended commentary on it, see Anderson and McVey, *A Preliminary Analysis*, 211–17.

32. Ibid., 217.

33. Interview with Siauw Giok Tjan, June 14, 1979, McVey Papers, Biog box 2; interview with Supeno and Siauw Giok Tjan, June 16, 1979, McVey Papers, Biog box 2.

34. See, for example, W. F. Wertheim, "Whose Plot? New Light on the 1965 Events," *Journal of Contemporary Asia* 9, no. 2 (1979): 197–215. See also interview with Oei Tjoe Tat and Mas B, April 21, 1979, McVey Papers, box 8, file 169a.

35. Interview with SB, April 9, 1979, London, McVey Papers, file 169b.

36. British Embassy Jakarta (Gilchrist) to Foreign Office (Stewart), "Attempted Coup in Indonesia."

37. Taomo Zhou, "China and the Thirtieth of September Movement," *Indonesia* 98 (October 2014): 29–58. While Zhou suggests that Aidit told Mao Tse-tung of plans for the movement, the evidence she provides does not support that claim.

38. Thus they write: "The October 1st coup was essentially an internal Army affair, stemming from a small clique in the Diponegoro Division, which attempted to use both Soekarno and the PKI leadership for its own ends, and succeeded merely in irremediably damaging the moral and political authority of one, and causing the physical destruction of the other." Anderson and McVey, *A Preliminary Analysis*, 119.

39. Notosusanto and Saleh, *Coup Attempt*. On the history of the dispute between Cornell and the army, see Benedict R. O'G. Anderson, "Scholarship on Indonesia

and Raison d'État: Personal Experience," *Indonesia* 62 (October 1996): 1–18; Asvi Warman Adam, "Ben Anderson's Work on Indonesia Challenged Suharto's Military Rule," *Jakarta Globe,* December 18, 2015; George McT. Kahin, *Southeast Asia: A Testament* (New York: Routledge, 2003), chapter 8.

40. See the compilation of documents, including interrogation reports and Mahmillub testimony, prepared by Kopkamtib and submitted to the MPRS by General Suharto in January 1967: Departemen Angkatan Darat, Direktorat Kehakiman, Team Pemeriksa Pusat, "Laporan Team," Jakarta, January 19, 1967, Kahin Papers.

41. Antonie Dake, *The Sukarno File, 1965–1967: Chronology of a Defeat* (Leiden: Brill, 2006).

42. Salim Haji Said, *Gestapu 65: PKI, Aidit, Sukarno, dan Soeharto* (Jakarta: Mizan Publishers, 2015).

43. After the army had made its case through the media, quite a few local observers apparently believed that Sukarno had been involved in the plot to kidnap but not kill the generals. These included the following figures interviewed by George Kahin: five HMI leaders, June 18, 1967, Jakarta; the Sultan of Yogyakarta, June 12, 1967; a senior PSI figure, June 14, 1967; Sumarman, June 20, 1967, Kahin Papers.

44. George Kahin interview with Johannes Leimena, May 3, 1976, Jakarta, Kahin Papers.

45. For a scathing critique of Dake's uncritical reliance on Widjanarko's testimony, see the memoir of a former political detainee, Tan Swie Ling, *G30S 1965, Perang Dingin dan Kehancuran Nasionalisme: Pemikiran Cina Jelata Korban Orba* (Jakarta: Komunitas Bambu, 2010), 14–17.

46. Among those who have strongly disputed claims of Sukarno's complicity is Manai Sophiaan, a former Indonesian ambassador to Moscow (1964–67). His book, *Kehormatan Bagi Yang Berhak: Bung Karno Tidak Terlibat G30S/PKI* (Jakarta Yayasan Mencerdaskan Kehidupan Bangsa, 1994), caused a firestorm of protest when it was pubished.

47. W. F. Wertheim, "Suharto and the Untung Coup—the Missing Link," *Journal of Contemporary Asia* 1, no. 2 (Winter 1970): 50–57; Wertheim, "Whose Plot?" Suharto also appears to have been connected to some of the lower-ranking figures in the plot, including Lieutenants Dul Arief and Djahurup. Both were members of the Presidential Guard and were believed to be close to Colonel Ali Murtopo, Suharto's close confidant. Although further research is certainly needed to draw any conclusions, these connections at least raise the possibility that Murtopo and Suharto were involved in the plan to kidnap and kill the generals. See Adam, "Ben Anderson's Work on Indonesia."

48. For details of these ties, see Wertheim, "Whose Plot?"; Ruth McVey, "A Preliminary Excursion through the Small World of Lt. Col. Untung," unpublished manuscript, n.d.

49. Abdul Latief, *Pleidoi Kol. A. Latief, Soeharto Terlibat G30S* (Jakarta: Institut Studi Arus Informasi, 2000), 279.

50. For a fuller discussion of that meeting and its implications, see Wertheim, "Whose Plot?," 208–11. Latief had apparently also visited Suharto and his wife at their home in Jakarta two days before the alleged coup attempt to ask about the Council of Generals. On that occasion, according to Latief's account, Suharto told him that he

had recently received information about a planned coup by the Council of Generals. See Latief, *Pleidoi*, 277.

51. Ibid., 279.

52. As army commander, General Nasution had relieved Suharto of his command of the Central Java Diponegoro Division in October 1959. Hamish MacDonald, *Suharto's Indonesia* (Sydney: Fontana, 1980), 32.

53. Sukarno, "Nawaksara," cited in Kammen and McGregror, *Contours of Mass Violence*, 4.

54. Peter Dale Scott, "The United States and the Overthrow of Sukarno, 1965–1967," *Pacific Affairs* 58, no. 2 (Summer 1985): 239–64. In 1967, a senior PSI figure with close ties to the army told Kahin that the October 1 action had been a provocation, most likely orchestrated by British intelligence. Kahin interview with senior PSI figure, June 14, 1967, Kahin Papers.

55. For a critique of the Scott argument, see H. W. Brands, "The Limits of Manipulation: How the United States Didn't Topple Sukarno," *Journal of American History* 76 (December 1989): 785–808.

56. Marshall Green, *Indonesia: Crisis and Transformation 1965–1968* (Washington, DC: Compass Press, 1990), 63. See also B. Hugh Tovar, "The Indonesian Crisis of 1965–1966: A Retrospective," *International Journal of Intelligence and Counterintelligence* 7, no. 3 (Fall 1994): 313–38.

57. Cited in "CIA's Role in Anti-Communist Drive Denied," *Jakarta Post*, November 2, 1994.

58. NSC 5429/5, December 22, 1954, "Statement of Policy by the National Security Council on Current US Policy in the Far East," cited in US Department of State, *Foreign Relations of the United States* [*FRUS*], vol. 12, *East Asia and the Pacific (1952–54)*, part 1:1066.

59. George McT. Kahin and Audrey Kahin, *Subversion as Foreign Policy: The Secret Eisenhower and Dulles Debacle in Indonesia* (New York: New Press, 1995).

60. Draft Letter from CIA Director W. F. Raborn to the President, July 20, 1965, Kahin Papers, "Chronological File."

61. Though far more risky, the murder of the generals might also be understood as a deliberate act of provocation intended to get the army to act against the PKI and Left. Writing a few weeks after the apparent coup attempt, British ambassador Gilchrist observed that "the generals were forced to take action on the 1st of October by the most extreme provocation that could possibly have been given them." British Embassy Jakarta (Gilchrist) to Foreign Office (Stewart), "Attempted Coup in Indonesia."

62. Some Indonesian observers have stressed the likely involvement of agent provocateurs in setting the crisis in motion. A former PSI official, for example, noted in 1967 that the strange actions of the movement on October 1 seemed calculated to provoke a strong reaction from the army, and speculated that Sjam had served as an agent provocateur for MI6. George Kahin interview with senior PSI figure, June 14, 1967, Jakarta, Kahin Papers.

63. Roosa, *Pretext for Mass Murder*. The new evidence on which Roosa draws includes a document about the movement written by Brigadier General Supardjo sometime in 1966, a document written by Politburo member Iskandar Subekti while in prison, and an interview he conducted with PKI member Asep Suryaman. Crouch

suggested something similar many years ago: that the PKI leadership was at most a partner in a joint action with a group of the left-leaning military officers. See Harold Crouch, "Another Look at the Indonesian Coup," *Indonesia* 15 (April 1973): 1–20. See also Crouch, *Army and Politics*.

64. See Roosa, "September 30th Movement," 49.

65. Roosa, *Pretext for Mass Murder*, 201. Additional support for that argument lies in the fact that one of the six generals killed on October 1, Parman, was the brother of Politiburo member Sakirman. It seems unlikely that Sakirman knew of any plans to kill the generals.

66. Roosa, "September 30th Movement," 39. Some observers at the time thought that Aidit and perhaps Njoto may have taken this action as a way to force the party to a more radical path. That line of reasoning was based on signs that there was a split in the PKI between a pro-Beijing group (Aidit and Njoto) and pro-Moscow one (Jusuf Adjitorop and Lukman) with some remaining independent (Sakriman). George Kahin interview with General Kabul Arifin, Colonel Partono, and Kusnadi, May 16, 1967, Jakarta, Kahin Papers.

67. According to official regulations, those suspected of direct involvement in the movement, and defined as category A detainees, included all those who "planned, took part in planning, or knew about plans for the counter-revolutionary movement, but did not report it to the relevant authorities." See Presiden Republik Indonesia, *Instruksi Presiden/Pangti ABRI/KOTI No. 22/KOTI/1965—Kepada Kompartimen2/ Departemen2, Badan2/Lembaga2 Pemerintah—Untuk Laksanakan Penertiban/ Pembersihan Personil Sipil dari Oknum "Gerakan 30 September,"* signed on president's behalf by Soeharto (Kepala Staf Komado Operasi Tertinggi/Panglima Operasi Pemulihan Keamanan dan Ketertiban), November 15, 1965, printed in Boerhan and Soebekti, *"Gerakan 30 September,"* 239–48. For further discussion, see chapters 8 and 9 below.

68. Roosa, *Pretext for Mass Murder*, 221.

Chapter Four: Cold War

1. Peter Dale Scott, "The United States and the Overthrow of Sukarno, 1965–1967," *Pacific Affairs* 58, no. 2 (Summer 1985): 239–64; W. F. Wertheim, "Suharto and the Untung Coup—the Missing Link," *Journal of Contemporary Asia* 1, no. 2 (Winter 1970): 50–57.

2. Marshall Green, *Indonesia: Crisis and Transformation, 1965–1968* (Washington, DC: Compass Press, 1990); US Central Intelligence Agency, Directorate of Intelligence, *Indonesia—1965: The Coup That Backfired* (Washington: CIA, 1968); H. W. Brands, "The Limits of Manipulation: How the United States Didn't Topple Sukarno," *Journal of American History* 76 (December 1989): 785–808; B. Hugh Tovar, "The Indonesian Crisis of 1965–1966: A Retrospective," *International Journal of Intelligence and Counterintelligence* 7, no. 3 (Fall 1994): 313–38.

3. Among foreign observers who have alleged that China orchestrated the alleged coup is Victor Fic, *Anatomy of the Jakarta Coup: October 1, 1965* (New Delhi: Abhinay Publications, 2004).

4. See Bernd Schaefer and Baskara T. Wardaya, eds., *1965: Indonesia and the World, Indonesia dan Dunia*, bilingual ed. (Jakarta: Gramedia Pustaka Utama, 2013).

5. On Cuba's role in Latin America in these years, see Tanya Harmer, *Allende's Chile and the Inter-American Cold War* (Chapel Hill: University of North Carolina Press, 2011).

6. On the Bandung Conference, see George McT. Kahin, *The Asian-African Conference, Bandung, Indonesia* (Ithaca, NY: Cornell University Press, 1956).

7. On Guatemala, see Greg Grandin, *The Last Colonial Massacre: Latin America in the Cold War*, updated ed. (Chicago: University of Chicago Press, 2011). On Congo, see Stephen R. Weissman, "What Really Happened in Congo," *Foreign Affairs* 93, no. 4 (July–August 2014): 14–24. On Bolivia, see Thomas C. Field Jr., *From Development to Dictatorship: Bolivia and the Alliance for Progress in the Kennedy Era* (Ithaca: Cornell University Press, 2014). On the CIA's covert operations during these years, see Rhodri Jeffreys-Jones, *The CIA and American Democracy* (New Haven, CT: Yale University Press, 1989), 82–155.

8. For a useful summary of US interventions in Southeast Asia and elsewhere during the Eisenhower years, see George McT. Kahin and Audrey Kahin, *Subversion as Foreign Policy: The Secret Eisenhower and Dulles Debacle in Indonesia* (New York: New Press, 1995), 3–19.

9. Sukarno also objected to the plan on the grounds that it denied the peoples of Sabah and Sarawak in Borneo a say in determining their future.

10. Ruth Ann Swift, *The Road to Madiun: The Indonesian Communist Uprising of 1948* (Ithaca, NY: Cornell Southeast Asia Program, 1989).

11. NSC 171/1, "United States Objectives and Courses of Action with Respect to Indonesia," in US Department of State, *Foreign Relations of the United States* [*FRUS*], vol. 12, *East Asia and the Pacific (1952–54)*, part 2:398.

12. NSC 5429/5, "Statement of Policy by the National Security Council on Current US Policy in the Far East," in *FRUS*, vol. 12, part 1:1066.

13. National Security Action Memorandum 288, March 17, 1964, cited in Franz Schurmann, *The Logic of World Power: An Inquiry into the Origins, Currents, and Contradictions of World Politics* (New York: Random House, 1974), 450.

14. On China's relations with Indonesia during this period, see David Mozingo, *Sino-Indonesian Relations: An Overview, 1955–1965* (Santa Monica, CA: Rand Corporation, 1965). See also Taomo Zhou, "Ambivalent Alliance: Chinese Policy towards Indonesia, 1960–1965," *China Quarterly* 221 (March 2015): 208–28; Taomo Zhou, "China and the Thirtieth of September Movement," *Indonesia* 98 (October 2014): 29–58.

15. NSC 171/1, "United States Courses of Action with Respect to Indonesia," 396. See also Memorandum from Joint Chiefs of Staff to Secretary of Defense, February 28, 1958, US *Declassified Documents Catalog* [*DDC*], 1981, #313B.

16. In a telephone conversation on March 15, 1965, Undersecretary of State George Ball told National Security Adviser McGeorge Bundy that he was "very worried about Indonesia and that he had been having meetings yesterday and today with the oil companies." George W. Ball Papers, series 3, Seeley G. Mudd Manuscript Library, Princeton University [Mudd Library].

17. Bradley Simpson, *Economists with Guns: Authoritarian Development and U.S.-Indonesian Relations, 1960–1968* (Stanford, CA: Stanford University Press, 2008); Bradley Simpson, "The United States and the International Dimension of the Killings in Indonesia," in *1965: Indonesia and the World, Indonesia dan Dunia*, ed. Bernd Schaefer and Baskara T. Wardaya, bilingual ed. (Jakarta: Gramedia Pustaka Utama, 2013), 52.

18. As Crouch writes, "The domestic impact of foreign policy developments in 1964 and 1965 had reinforced the trends already set in motion by the PKI's new militancy." Harold Crouch, *The Army and Politics in Indonesia* (Ithaca, NY: Cornell University Press, 1978), 68.

19. James C. Thomson Jr. Memorandum for Mr. Bundy, June 11, 1965, National Security Council, NLK-77-95 #3. Personal archive of George McT. Kahin [Kahin Papers].

20. Franklin B. Weinstein, "The Uses of Foreign Policy in Indonesia" (PhD diss., Cornell University, 1972).

21. Embtel 2116 (part 2 of 3), US Embassy Jakarta to Department of State, April 5, 1965, Indonesia, vol. 4, Country file, NSF, box 247, Lyndon Baines Johnson Library [LBJ Library].

22. Weinstein, "Uses of Foreign Policy," 588.

23. Embtel 1735, US Embassy Jakarta to Department of State, March 4, 1965, Record Group [RG] 59, Central Files of the Department of State, 1964–66 [Central Files], POL INDO-US, US National Archives and Records Administration [NARA].

24. Ulf Sundhaussen, *The Road to Power: Indonesian Military Politics, 1945–1967* (Kuala Lumpur: Oxford University Press, 1982), 188.

25. Rudolf Mrázek, *The United States and the Indonesian Military, 1945–1966* (Prague: Czechoslovak Academy of Science, 1978), 2:152.

26. Crouch, *Army and Politics*, 73.

27. Progress Report on NSC 5518, "US Objectives and Courses of Action with Respect to Indonesia," April 3, 1957, *DDC*, 1982, #588. See also NSC 171/1, "United States Courses of Action with Respect to Indonesia," November 1953, *FRUS*, vol 12, part 2.

28. "If the general elections were held in the near future . . . it is probable that the Masjumi and Socialists would have the greatest strength and that the Communists would suffer a relative loss of position." NSC 171/1, "United States Objectives and Courses of Action with Respect to Indonesia," November 1953, 397.

29. Operations Coordinating Board, Progress Report on NSC 171/1, "United States Objectives and Courses of Action with Respect to Indonesia," January 12, 1955, 13; NSC Series, Policy Papers Subseries, box 8, NSC 171/1—Policy on Indonesia, Dwight D. Eisenhower Presidential Library.

30. Joseph B. Smith, *Portrait of a Cold Warrior* (New York: Putnam, 1976), 210–11, 215.

31. Kahin and Kahin. *Subversion as Foreign Policy*, 78.

32. Cited in ibid., 78n12.

33. Herbert Feith, *The Indonesian Elections of 1955* (Ithaca, NY: Cornell Modern Indonesia Project, 1957), 58.

34. The Kahins write: "Indonesia's first national elections, in 1955, brought the Eisenhower administration to focus on Indonesia's domestic politics with greater con-

cern. Although the Communist PKI emerged as only the fourth largest party, Washington regarded this development as ominous." Kahin and Kahin, *Subversion as Foreign Policy*, 79.

35. Select Committee to Study Governmental Operations with Respect to Intelligence Activities, US Senate, *Interim Report: Alleged Assassination Plots Involving Foreign Leaders*, November 20, 1975, 4.

36. Smith, *Portrait*, 238–40, 248. Sam Halpern, an official in the Far East Division of the CIA's Deputy Directorate of Plans, apparently hatched the idea. In an interview in 1990, Halpern said that the plan had backfired, but that papers in Mexico City, Bangkok, and the Philippines had covered the story. BBC interview with Sam Halpern, October 23, 1990, transcript in author's possession.

37. On the regional rebellions, see Kahin and Kahin, *Subversion as Foreign Policy*; Barbara Harvey, *Permesta: Half a Rebellion* (Ithaca, NY: Cornell Modern Indonesia Project, 1977).

38. "Special Report on Indonesia," prepared by the Ad Hoc Interdepartmental Committee on Indonesia for the NSC, September 3, 1957, *FRUS*, vol. 22, *Southeast Asia (1955–1957)*, 436–40.

39. Memorandum from the Joint Chiefs of Staff to the Secretary of Defense, April 8, 1958, *DDC*, 1982, #2385.

40. That operation used as many as twenty aircraft owned by Civil Air Transport, the CIA's front airline that was used for covert military operations throughout East and Southeast Asia during the 1950s and 1960s. Pope's aircraft was shot down on May 18, 1958. He was tried and sentenced to death in Indonesia, but in 1962 he was released and allowed to return to the United States.

41. David Wise and Thomas B. Ross, *The Invisible Government* (New York: Random House, 1964), 145. The government's mendacious claim of neutrality was accepted and repeated by the mainstream press. See *New York Times*, May 9, 1958.

42. Embtel 2650, US Embassy Jakarta to Department of State, June 7, 1965, RG 59, Central Files, DEF 6 INDON, NARA.

43. The idea that the military could act as an agent of "modernization" and "political stability" in what were then known as "underdeveloped" countries was not unique to the Indonesian context. It was part of a much wider trend, articulated by US-based social scientists in the late 1950s and 1960s, and endorsed by both the Eisenhower and Kennedy administrations. See Ron Robin, *The Making of the Cold War Enemy: Culture and Politics in the Military-Intellectual Complex* (Princeton, NJ: Princeton University Press, 2001).

44. By contrast, other countries in the region received substantial amounts. The countries of Indochina, for example, received military assistance totaling over $1.25 billion during the same period. Thailand received about $140 million, and the Philippines received about $114 million. For complete figures, see NSC, "Costs of Approved and Projected United States Economic and Military Programs in the Far East," *FRUS*, vol. 12, part 1:290–293.

45. Memorandum for the Director of the Foreign Operations Administration from the White House, June 16, 1955, *DDC*, 1992, #1557.

46. Memorandum for the Joint Chiefs of Staff from Department of the Navy, "Sino-Soviet Bloc Assistance to Indonesia," March 28, 1958, *DDC*, 1982, #2384.

47. Memorandum for the Secretary of Defense from the Joint Chiefs of Staff, "Aid for Indonesia," September 22, 1958, *DDC*, 1982, #2386.

48. Memorandum for the President from the Department of State, January 30, 1959, *DDC*, 1995, #0224.

49. See Daniel Lev, "On the Fall of the Parliamentary System," in *Democracy in Indonesia: 1950s and 1990s*, ed. David Bourchier and John Legge, no. 31 (Melbourne: Monash Papers on Southeast Asia, 1994), 39–42.

50. A 1961 Department of State memorandum to the president noted that US military aid to Indonesia began in earnest in 1958, and amounted to about $20 million per year up to 1961, for a total of $59.8 million by the start of fiscal year 1961. Over the same period, Sino-Soviet aid totaled about $1 billion. See Memorandum for the President from the Department of State, "The Sukarno Visit," April 20, 1961, *DDC*, 1981, #367A; Memorandum from Executive Secretary of NSC, "US Policy on Indonesia," December 19, 1960, *DDC*, 1982, #592.

51. See NSC 5429/5, *DDC*, 1982, #586; Memorandum for the Secretary of Defense, September 22, 1958, *DDC*, 1982, #2386. For a careful study of the impact of US military training during this period, see Bryan Evans III, "The Influence of the United States Army on the Development of the Indonesian Army (1954–1964)," *Indonesia* 47 (April 1989): 25–48.

52. Telegram (JCS 5747) from CJCS to US Embassy Jakarta, April 8, 1964, RG 59, Central Files, DEF 19 US-Indonesia, NARA.

53. OCB Report on Indonesia (NSC 5901), January 27, 1960, *DDC*, 1982, #590.

54. Starting in 1962, the program received guidance from the US Military Training Advisory Group (MILTAG), which was headed by Colonel Benson. Scott, "United States," 248, 255.

55. For a sympathetic account of Civic Action, see Guy Pauker, "Political Consequences of Rural Development Programs in Indonesia," *Pacific Affairs* 41, 3 (Fall 1968): 400–401.

56. "CIA Paper for the Special Group," December 11, 1961, and "Minutes of the Special Group," December 14, 1961, cited in "Memorandum Prepared for the 303 Committee," February 23, 1965, *FRUS*, vol. 26, *Indonesia; Malaysia-Singapore, Philippines (1964–66)*, 237n2.

57. On this network, see Scott, "United States," 246–51.

58. By some accounts, Pauker was also responsible for passing the Cornell Paper on to contacts in the Indonesian Army and other officials. Personal communication with George Kahin, May 1984, Ithaca, NY. See also "Points from Talks with Lance Castles," September 18–19, 1966, personal archive of Ruth T. McVey [McVey Papers], box 4, file 97, 1.

59. Suwarto was also an associate of Colonel Benson, the head of the US MILTAG office in Jakarta that provided guidance and support to the Civic Action program. Scott, "United States," 255.

60. David Ransom, "The Berkeley Mafia and the Indonesian Massacres," *Ramparts*, October 9, 1970; Hamish McDonald, *Suharto's Indonesia* (Sydney: Fontana, 1980), 68–86.

61. Sundhaussen, *Road to Power*, 188.

62. Among the key players in this network were the large US oil companies, Caltex and Stanvac, whose royalty payments were channeled through the army's oil company, Permina, headed by Suharto ally Ibnu Sutowo, and a second Indonesian oil company, Pertamin, headed by Chaerul Saleh. Another important player was the US aerospace giant Lockheed, which may have paid commissions in exchange for army contracts. Two figures identified as middlemen in those alleged arrangements were General Alamsjah, who joined Suharto's staff in 1960, and businessman Bob Hasan. Both later became close associates and business partners of General Suharto. Scott, "United States," 254–57.

63. Embtel 2536, US Embassy Jakarta to Department of State, March 7, 1961, *FRUS*, vol. 23, *Southeast Asia (1961–1963)*, doc. 152.

64. Zhou, "China and the Thirtieth September Movement," 41.

65. *New York Times*, August 14, 1964.

66. Memorandum for the President from Secretary of State Dean Rusk, "Your Meeting with Prime Minister Tunku Abdul Rahman," July 17, 1964, US Declassified Documents, accessed June 1, 2017, http://tinyurl.galegroup.com/tinyurl/47QSU4. In his memoir, Ambassador Jones wrote that by maintaining some assistance to the army and police, "we fortified them for a virtually inevitable showdown with the burgeoning PKI." Howard P. Jones, *Indonesia: The Possible Dream* (New York: Harcourt Brace Jovanovich, 1971), 324.

67. Memorandum for the President from Secretary of State Rusk, August 30, 1964, *FRUS*, vol. 26, attachment to doc. 67.

68. Memorandum for the President from Assistant Secretary of State William Bundy, August 27, 1964, Kahin Papers, "Jones File."

69. Ibid.

70. Memorandum for the President from Special Assistant for National Security McGeorge Bundy, August 31, 1964, *FRUS*, vol. 26, doc. 67.

71. *New York Times*, August 16, 1964.

72. For US reactions to these attacks, see *New York Times*, January 21 and 24, February 26, April 23, May 2, August 16, 18, and December 9, 1964; February 4, 19, 20, and 27, March 1, 17, 19, 20, 22, and 24, April 7, 18, and 29, May 22, July 19, August 1, 4, 8, 22, and 31, and September 15, 1965.

73. Memorandum for the President from the Department of State, "Harold Wilson Visit to Washington," December 5, 1964, *DDC*, 1978, #431A.

74. CIA, Office of National Estimates, Special Memorandum No. 4-65, "Principal Problems and Prospects in Indonesia," January 26, 1965, Indonesia, vol. III, Country file, NSF, box 247, LBJ Library.

75. "Memorandum Prepared for the 303 Committee," February 23, 1965, *FRUS*, vol. 26, 237n3.

76. George Ball Telephone Conversation (Telcon) with McGeorge Bundy, March 15, 1965, George W. Ball Papers, box 4, Indonesia (4/12/64–11/10/65), LBJ Library.

77. Memorandum for the National Security Adviser from the Assistant Secretary of Defense, Attached to Report on Military Assistance Reappraisal FY 1967–1971, Office of the Assistant Secretary of Defense, International Security Affairs, June 1965, *DDC*, 1981, #33A.

78. Draft Letter from CIA Director W. F. Raborn to the President, July 20, 1965, Kahin Papers, "Chronological File."

79. George Ball Telephone Conversation (Telcon) with McGeorge Bundy, August 16, 1965, George W. Ball Papers, Mudd Library.

80. Green had previously served as ambassador in South Korea and had been good friends with CIA officer William Colby since the early 1950s. On Green's appointment, see Memorandum from the President's Special Assistant for National Security (McGeorge Bundy) to President Johnson, June 30, 1965, *FRUS*, vol. 26, doc. 125.

81. CIA Intelligence Info Cable #TDCS-315-00846-64, "US-Indonesian Relations," September 19, 1964, *DDC*, 1981, #273B.

82. Ibid.

83. According to the September 1964 CIA document, "Politically-minded Army elements in the Nasution–Ruslan Abdulgani sector also think well of Saleh and Malik.... A coalition of forces along such lines is, by no means, unthinkable, and it would be powerful if present centrifugal tendencies could be overcome." Ibid.

84. In 1990, the former official told an interviewer, "Before he [Malik] left to go back to Moscow [where he served as Indonesian ambasssador from 1959 to 1962] I met him on agency authority, to tell him it was time to organize against communism.... He said he'd think about it.... The CIA jumped on it, and he became part of the organized resistance contingency plan." BBC interview with William (Bill) Ostlund, April 1990.

85. The BPS was established in September 1964, and banned on December 17, 1964. It was led by Malik and newspaper editor B. M. Diah, and supported by Saleh. The Murba Party was formed in 1948, and "frozen" on January 6, 1965. The party's leader in 1964 was Sukarni, while Malik and Saleh were key patrons. See Crouch, *Army and Politics*, 65; Rex Mortimer, *Indonesian Communism under Sukarno: Ideology and Politics, 1959–1965* (Ithaca, NY: Cornell University Press, 1974), 377; Coen Holtzappel, "The 30 September Movement: A Political Movement of the Armed Forces or an Intelligence Operation?," *Journal of Contemporary Asia* 9, no. 2 (1979): 238.

86. Embtel 836, US Embassy Kuala Lumpur to Department of State, January 9, 1965, Indonesia, vol. III, Country file, NSF, box 247, LBJ Library.

87. Embtel 1435, US Embassy Jakarta to Department of State, January 21, 1965, US Declassified Documents, accessed June 2, 2017, http://tinyurl.galegroup.com/tinyurl/44QB88.

88. "Progress Report on [*less than one line of source text not declassified*] Covert Action in Indonesia." See "Memorandum Prepared for the 303 Committee," February 23, 1965, *FRUS*, vol. 26, 234–37.

89. This secondary purpose of Bunker's visit was apparently referred to in the Gilchrist Letter. According to a US Embassy cable, in late May 1965 General Yani told a gathering of regional commanders that the letter said the "visit of personal envoy of President Johnson would give them sufficient time to discuss and prepare careful joint planning." Embtel 50, US Embassy Jakarta to Department of State, July 10, 1965, RG 59, Central Files, POL INDON-US, NARA.

90. Memorandum for the President, "Ambassador Bunker's Report on Indonesia," April 24, 1965, cited in Frederick Bunnell, "American 'Low Posture' Policy toward

Indonesia in the Months Leading up to the 1965 'Coup,'" *Indonesia* 50 (October 1990): 45.

91. Cited in Theodore Friend, *Indonesian Destinies* (Cambridge, MA: Harvard University Press, 2003), 102.

92. NSC 6023, "US Policy on Indonesia," December 19, 1960, *DDC*, 1982, #592.

93. Embtel 2154, US Embassy Jakarta to the Department of State, January 25, 1961, *FRUS*, vol. 23, doc. 143.

94. Commonwealth governments adopted a covert war approach in 1963 in response to Confrontation, with the aim of provoking "a prolonged struggle for power leading to civil war or anarchy." Simpson, "United States," 53.

95. For a careful account of these plans, see David Easter, "British and Malaysian Covert Support for Rebel Movements in Indonesia during the 'Confrontation,' 1963–1966," *Intelligence and National Security* 14, no. 4 (Winter 1999): 195–208.

96. Cited in ibid.

97. JA(65)9 (Final), cited in ibid.

98. As Crouch writes, "Thus during 1964 and 1965 the army leaders carried out a series of maneuvers designed to obstruct the effective implementation of the policy of confrontation." Crouch, *Army and Politics*, 73.

99. According to various accounts, some PSI and ex-PRRI/Permesta figures assisted in making contact with the Malaysians. They included Des Alwi, Daan Mogot, Welly Pesik, and Jan Walandouw. See Masashi Nishihara, *The Japanese and Sukarno's Indonesia: Tokyo-Jakarta Relations, 1951–1966* (Honolulu: University Press of Hawaii, 1976), 149; Crouch, *Army and Politics*, 74–75; Julius P. Pour, *Benny Moerdani: Profil Prajurit Negarawan* (Jakarta: Yayasan Kejuangan Sudirman, 1993), 323–43.

100. Suharto was appointed deputy commander of Kolaga on January 1, 1965. Roosa writes that "Suharto slowed down the deployments and kept the forces stationed near the Malaysian borders constantly understaffed and underequipped." John Roosa, *Pretext for Mass Murder: The September 30th Movement and Suharto's Coup d'Etat in Indonesia*, (Madison: University of Wisconsin Press, 2006), 187. See also Crouch, *Army and Politics*, 71–75.

101. CIA Intelligence Info Cable #TDCS-315-00846-64, "US-Indonesian Relations," September 19, 1964, *DDC*, 1981, #273B.

102. Howard P. Jones, "American-Indonesian Relations," presentation at Chiefs of Mission Conference, Baguio, Philippines, Howard P. Jones Papers, box 21, Hoover Institution Archives, 12, cited in Roosa, *Pretext for Mass Murder*, 193.

103. Cited in Roosa, *Pretext for Mass Murder*, 190.

104. British Foreign Office note on Mr. M.J.C. Templeton, New Zealand High Commission in London to Mr. Peck, "The Succession to Sukarno," December 18, 1964, FO 371/175251, UKNA. Interestingly, the original report from the New Zealand Legation in Jakarta also refers to the advantages of a premature PKI coup, noting that "an attempt of the PKI to seize power ... would seem to us to be in important respects beneficial to both Indonesia and ourselves." Report from the New Zealand Legation, Jakarta to Secretary of External Affairs, Wellington, "Sukarno and the Succession," December 1, 1964, FO371/175251, UKNA.

105. Simpson, "United States," 56.

106. Embtel 1735, US Embassy Jakarta to Department of State, March 4, 1965, RG 59, Central Files, POL INDO-US, NARA.

107. Memorandum Prepared for the 303 Committee, "Progress Report on [*less than one line of source text not declassified*] Covert Action in Indonesia," February 23, 1965, *FRUS*, vol. 26, 234–37.

108. NSC 6023, "US Policy on Indonesia," December 19, 1960, *DDC*, 1982, #592; Roosa, *Pretext for Mass Murder*, 193.

109. Neville Maxwell, a British scholar, discovered the document in the Pakistan Foreign Ministry archive. His unpublished letter of June 5, 1978, to the *New York Review of Books* describing the document's contents was later printed as Neville Maxell, "CIA Involvement in the 1965 Military Coup: New Evidence from Neville Maxwell," *Journal of Contemporary Asia* 9, no. 2 (1979): 251–52.

110. It is quite possible that the sharing of this information was part of a wider psywar operation. In that scenario, the Dutch NATO officer could have deliberately shared the inflammatory information with the Pakistani ambassador in the reasonable expectation that the information would then find its way to the Indonesians.

111. Ruth McVey, Letter to George McT. Kahin, Benedict Anderson, Herbert Feith, and Frederick Bunnell, July 4, 1978, McVey Papers, box 8, file 172. Mortimer cites *Harian Rakyat* (January 22, 1965) as claiming that the document was a forgery. Mortimer, *Indonesian Communism under Sukarno*, 367.

112. The brain trust reportedly included Generals Suprapto, Harjono, Parman, and Sukendro. US Central Intelligence Agency, Directorate of Intelligence, *Indonesia—1965: The Coup That Backfired* (Washington, DC: CIA, 1968), 191. Also involved in contingency planning was Suwarto, the former head of Seskoad, who was good friends with Pauker, had trained at Fort Leavenworth, and whom Colonel Ethel described as "really pro-US." David Ransom Interview with Col. Willis Ethel, n.d., McVey Papers, box 10, file 198, 5.

113. David Ransom Interview with Col. Willis Ethel, n.d., McVey Papers, box 10, file 198, 5. Similarly, when asked about the Council of Generals in November 1965, Benson said, "I think the general staff got together and talked about things they wouldn't write about, and were planning for the day that they would have to face up to the PKI." See "Record of a Telephone Conversation between Colonel George Benson, Ruth McVey, and Fred Bunnell on November 15, 1965," McVey Papers, box 9, file 190.

114. Politburo member Njono made that point clearly in testimony during the course of his 1966 trial. See *"Gerakan 30 September" Dihadapan Mahmillub, Perkara Njono* (Jakarta: Pusat Pendidikan Kehakiman A.D., 1966), 31–42. See also Crouch, *Army and Politics*, 133.

115. NSC 6023, "US Policy on Indonesia," December 19, 1960, *DDC*, 1982, #592. The view that the Council of Generals rumor was deliberately disseminated by the CIA and US Embassy was shared by some members of Malik's entourage in 1966. See Ruth McVey Interview with Adam Malik and Company, October 2, 1966, McVey Papers, box 2, file 31C, 8.

116. Cited in Brian May, *The Indonesian Tragedy* (London: Routledge and Kegan Paul, 1978), 125–26.

117. According to a US Embassy report about his speech, Yani told the regional commanders that he had admitted to Sukarno that there were members of the army who "are very critical especially in regard to political problems," and some of them "are sympathetic with Americans." Embtel 50, US Embassy Jakarta to Department of State, July 10, 1965, RG 59, Central Files, POL INDON-US, NARA.

118. Another possibility that warrants further research is that the Gilchrist Letter and rumors of a planned coup by the Council of Generals were creations of the Kostrad intelligence chief and Suharto ally, Colonel Murtopo.

119. Crouch, *Army and Politics*, 133.

120. The former CIA officer, Ralph McGehee, has suggested that after 1965, this strategy became something of a CIA trademark. Interview with Ralph McGehee, November 1983, Ithaca, NY.

121. Zhou, "China and the Thirtieth of September Movement," 40.

122. Scott notes, for example, that rumors about the smuggling of Chinese weapons to the PKI appear to have originated in vaguely sourced media stories first published in Bangkok, Hong Kong, and Kuala Lumpur. Such untraceabilty, he observes, was the "stylistic trademark" of the CIA's covert media operations. Scott, "United States," 260.

123. Zhou, "China and the Thirtieth of September Movement," 58.

124. "Chairman Mao Meets the Delegation of the PKI," *Chinese Communist Party Central Archives*, August 5, 1965, cited in Zhou, "China and the Thirtieth of September Movement," 51.

125. Zhou, "China and the Thirtieth of September Movement," 58.

126. Frederick Bunnell Interview with William Colby, August 1978, McVey Papers, box 10, file 198.

Chapter Five: Mass Killing

1. US Central Intelligence Agency, Directorate of Intelligence, *Indonesia—1965: The Coup That Backfired* (Washington, DC: CIA, 1968), 70.

2. In addition to older published sources and declassified foreign government documents, this account draws in particular on a number of recently published memoirs and testimonials by survivors and perpetrators, including Baskara T. Wardaya, ed., *Truth Will Out: Indonesian Accounts of the 1965 Mass Violence*, trans. Jennifer Lindsay (Clayton, Victoria: Monash University Publishing, 2013); Putu Oka Sukanta, ed., *Breaking the Silence: Survivors Speak about the 1965–66 Violence in Indonesia*, trans. Jennifer Lindsay (Clayton, Victoria: Monash University Publishing, 2014); Kurniawan et al., eds., *The Massacres: Coming to Terms with the Trauma of 1965* (Jakarta: Tempo, 2015); Mery Kolimon, Liliya Wetangterah, and Karen Campbell-Nelson, eds., *Forbidden Memories: Women's Experiences of 1965 in Eastern Indonesia*, trans. Jennifer Lindsay (Clayton, Victoria: Monash University Publishing, 2015). It also draws on the extraordinary testimonials of a number of perpetrators in two documentary films by Joshua Oppenheimer: *The Act of Killing* (Drafthouse Films, 2013) and *The Look of Silence* (Drafthouse Films, 2016).

3. An official Fact Finding Commission proposed the figure of 78,500, after having conducted its investigations over a period of ten days (December 27, 1965–January

6, 1966) while the killings were still going on. Komando Operasi Tertinggi (KOTI), *Fact Finding Commission Komando Operasi Tertinggi* (Jakarta, January 10, 1966). Its suggested figure is widely regarded as a significant underestimate; one of the commission's own members told Sukarno that the real number was several times higher. Oei Tjoe Tat, *Memoar Oei Tjoe Tat: Pembantu Presiden Sukarno*, ed. Pramoedya Ananta Toer and Stanley Adi Prasetyo (Jakarta: Hasta Mitra, 1995), 192. In 1989, Brigadier General Sarwo Edhie Wibowo, who played a direct role in the violence, suggested the figure of 3 million dead, but it is widely viewed as too high. The same is true of the figure of 2 million cited by a number of sources. For a review of the estimates, see Robert Cribb, ed., *The Indonesian Killings, 1965–1966: Studies from Java and Bali*, no. 21 (Clayton, Victoria: Monash Papers on Southeast Asia, 1990), 12.

4. Richard Howland, "The Lessons of the September 30 Affair," *Studies in Intelligence* 14 (Fall 1970): 26. See also Hugh Tovar, "The Indonesian Crisis of 1965–1966: A Retrospective," *International Journal of Intelligence and Counterintelligence* 7 no. 3 (Fall 1994): 313–38; J. Foster Collins and Hugh Tovar, "Sukarno's Apologists Write Again," *International Journal of Intelligence and Counterintelligence* 9, no. 3 (Fall 1996): 337–57.

5. Nugroho Notosusanto and Ismail Saleh, *The Coup Attempt of the "September 30 Movement" in Indonesia* (Jakarta: Pembimbing Massa, 1968), 77.

6. British Embassy (Gilchrist) to Foreign Office (de la Mare), February 23, 1966, FO 371/186028, National Archives of the United Kingdom [UKNA]. The Swedish Ambassador (Edelstam) offered the estimate of 1 million in February 1966. See Edelstam to Nilsson, "Utrotningen av kommunist-partiet i Indonesien," February 21, 1966, Utrikesdepartementets arkiv, Serie HP, Grupp 1, Mal XI, Politik: Allmänt Indonesien, 1965 maj–juli 1966, National Archives of Sweden, Riksarkivet [UA/HP 1/XI, Riksarkivet]. In a report from June 1966, the ambassador noted that the former German ambassador (Werz) had suggested even higher figures. See H. Edelstam to H. Bergström (Utrikesdepartementet), "Likvidering av kommunister på norra Sumatra, Indonesien," June 16, 1966, UA/HP 1/XI, Riksarkivet.

7. The officer was Colonel Stamboel. See letter from British Embassy (Murray) to Foreign Office (de la Mare), January 13, 1966, FO 371/186027, UKNA.

8. Amnesty International, *Indonesia: An Amnesty International Report* (London: Amnesty International Publications, 1977), 22. A 1966 Kopkamtib report on the killings reportedly concluded that the total number killed was about 1 million. Robert Cribb, "On Victims Statistics," in *The Massacres: Coming to Terms with the Trauma of 1965*, ed. Kurniawan et al. (Jakarta: Tempo, 2015), 133.

9. In his meeting at the State Department, Walendouw related "gory accounts of [the] execution of unreliable elements carried out personally by Colonel Murtopo. In Walendouw's words, 'anyone not believing in rule of law is shot.' Walendow put [the] total number of Communists liquidated at 1.2 million." Deptel 49647, Department of State to US Embassy Jakarta, September 19, 1966, Record Group [RG] 59, Central Files of the Department of State, 1964–66 [Central Files], POL 23-6 INDON, US National Archives and Records Administration [NARA].

10. For a careful discussion of this misconception, see Robert Cribb and Charles A. Coppel, "A Genocide that Never Was: Explaining the Myth of Anti-Chinese Massacres

in Indonesia, 1965–1966," *Journal of Genocide Research* 11, no. 4 (December 2009): 447–65.

11. Indonesian historian Hermawan Sulistiyo, for example, has suggested that in the years before and after 1965, ideology was a cover for personal conflicts and vendettas. See Hermawan Sulistiyo, "Mass Murder from 1965–1966: Vendetta and Jingoism," in *The Massacres: Coming to Terms with the Trauma of 1965*, ed. Kurniawan et al. (Jakarta: Tempo, 2015), 83–87.

12. See J.A.C. Mackie, "Anti-Chinese Outbreaks in Indonesia, 1959–1968," in *The Chinese in Indonesia: Five Essays*, ed. J.A.C. Mackie (Honolulu: University of Hawaii Press, 1976), 117–18. For North Sumatra, see Yen-ling Tsai and Douglas Kammen, "Anti-Communist Violence and the Ethnic Chinese in Medan, North Sumatra," in *The Contours of Mass Violence in Indonesia, 1965–68* ed. Douglas Kammen and Katharine McGregor (Singapore: NUS Press, 2012), 131–56. For Semarang, see Martijn Eickhof, Donny Danardono, Tjahjono Rahardjo, and Hotmauli Sidabalok, "The Memory Landscapes of '1965' in Semarang," in *1965 Today: Living with the Indonesian Massacres*, ed. Martijn Eickhoff, Gerry van Klinken, and Geoffrey Robinson, special issue, *Journal of Genocide Research* 19, no. 3 (2017). See also Wardaya, *Truth Will Out*, 121–24, 125–28.

13. Oppenheimer, *Act of Killing*.

14. Both Coppel and Mackie have concluded that ethnic Chinese were not victims of widespread killing in 1965–66. See Charles A. Coppel, *Indonesian Chinese in Crisis* (Kuala Lumpur: Oxford University Press, 1983); Mackie, "Anti-Chinese Outbreaks."

15. On the killings in North Sumatra, for instance, Tsai and Kammen write, "While several informants noted the murders of particular individuals, such as Tan Fhu Kiong, the secretary of the provincial Baperki branch and editor of the PKI daily *Harian Harapan*, no one recalled any systematic effort to arrest or kill ethnic Chinese." Tsai and Kammen, "Anti-Communist Violence," 142. The memoirs of several Chinese Indonesians targeted in 1965–66 reflect a similar pattern. See, for example, Tan Swie Ling, *G30S 1965, Perang Dingin dan Kehancuran Nasionalisme: Pemikiran Cina Jelata Korban Orba* (Jakarta: Komunitas Bambu, 2010); Djie Siang Lan (Lani Anggawati), *Di Dalam Derita Manusia Membaja*, 2nd ed. (Klaten: Wisma Sambodhi, 2004).

16. Aidit was shot on or about November 25, 1965, Njoto on about December 6, 1965, and Lukman on about April 30, 1966. Other high-level party officials killed included a senior PKI figure in Bali, I Gede Puger, who was summarily executed in December 1965. See John Roosa, "The State of Knowledge about an Open Secret: Indonesia's Mass Disappearances of 1965–66," *Journal of Asian Studies*, 75, no. 2 (May 2016): 281–97.

17. Dinas Sejarah TNI-AD, "Crushing the G30S/PKI in Central Java," in *The Indonesian Killings, 1965–1966: Studies from Java and Bali*, ed. Robert Cribb, no. 21 (Clayton, Victoria: Monash Papers on Southeast Asia, 1990), 165.

18. Kenneth R. Young, "Local and National Influences in the Violence of 1965," in *The Indonesian Killings, 1965–1966: Studies from Java and Bali*, ed. Robert Cribb, no. 21 (Clayton, Victoria: Monash Papers on Southeast Asia, 1990), 82.

19. Roosa, "State of Knowledge," 19. Jess Melvin points to a similar pattern in the context of Aceh. See Jess Melvin, "Mechanics of Mass Murder: How the Indonesian

Military Initiated and Implemented the Indonesian Genocide—The Case of Aceh" (PhD diss., University of Melbourne, 2014); Jess Melvin, "Documenting Genocide," *Inside Indonesia* 122 (October–December 2015).

20. Report by K. L. Charney, Group Captain, attached to UK Embassy Jakarta (Murray) to Foreign Office (Peck), November 25, 1965, FO 371/180325, UKNA.

21. H. Edelstam to Nilsson (Foreign Minister), "Utrotningen av kommunistpartiet i Indonesien," February 21, 1966, UA/HP 1/XI, Riksarkivet. The use of lists was widely reported. As a death squad commander in North Sumatra later testified, "We exterminated communists for three months, day and night. We'd take them two miles from here. We'd dig a hole and bury them alive. We got lists of the prisoners we brought to Snake River. Every night I signed the list." Oppenheimer, *Look of Silence* (0:49).

22. Wardaya, *Truth Will Out*, 127. For a smiliar account, involving a mass killing by soldiers on the banks of the Wedi River near Klaten, Central Java, see ibid., 57.

23. H. Edelstam to H. Bergström, "Likvidering av kommunister på norra Sumatra, Indonesien," June 16, 1966, UA/HP 1/XI, Riksarkivet. The transportation of prisoners to execution sites, usually in trucks, is commonly mentioned in the accounts of witnesses and perpetrators. According to an Indonesian journalist, an official in the area of Purwodadi, Central Java, told him, "When the prisoners had been collected, they took 75 away each night, in two lots. Later, this became less and they took away 75 prisoners every Saturday night." Maskun Iskandar, cited in Robert Cribb, "The Indonesian Massacres," in *Century of Genocide: Critical Essays and Eyewitness Accounts*, ed. Samuel Totten and William S. Parsons, 3rd ed. (New York: Routledge, 2009), 259.

24. Oppenheimer, *Look of Silence* (0:24 minutes).

25. Cited in Melvin, "Mechanics of Mass Murder," 188.

26. Gerry van Klinken, *The Making of Middle Indonesia: Middle Classes in Kupang Town, 1930s–1980s* (Leiden: Brill, 2014), 246–47.

27. "Beny: The Search for Healing," in Sukanta, *Breaking the Silence*, 27. For a similar account from Bali, see "Permadi: A Life in Painting," in Sukanta, *Breaking the Silence*, 133.

28. Oppenheimer, *Act of Killing* (2:05).

29. Oppenheimer, *Look of Silence* (0:02).

30. Agus Sunyoto, Miftahul Ulum, H. Abu Muslih, and Imam Kusnin Ahmad, *Banser Berjihad Menumpas PKI* (Tulungagung: Lembaga Kajian dan Pengembangan Pimpinan Wilayah Gerakan Pemuda Ansor Jawa Timur and Pesulukan Thoriqoh Agung Tulungagung, 1996), 129.

31. Geoffrey Robinson, *The Dark Side of Paradise: Political Violence in Bali* (Ithaca, NY: Cornell University Press, 1995), 301.

32. See Olle Törnquist, *Dilemmas of Third World Communism: The Destruction of the PKI in Indonesia (London: Zed Books*, 1985), 233–34; Sunyoto et al., *Banser Berjihad*, 153. See also Pipit Rochijat, "Am I PKI or Non-PKI?," trans. Benedict Anderson, *Indonesia* 40 (October 1985): 37–56.

33. Anonymous, "On the Banks of the Brantas," in Cribb, "Indonesian Massacres," 249.

34. Rochijat, "Am I PKI or Non-PKI?," 44.

35. Geoffrey Windle Memo on Situation in East Java, Appended to British Embassy (Cambridge) to Foreign Office (Tonkin), December 16, 1965, FO 371/180325, UKNA. A local resident likewise reported, "At one time, the road leading to Mount Kotok was decorated with PKI heads." Rochijat, "Am I PKI or Non-PKI?," 44.

36. Anonymous, "Additional Data on Counter-Revolutionary Cruelty in Indonesia, Especially in East Java," in *The Indonesian Killings, 1965–1966: Studies from Java and Bali*, ed. Robert Cribb, no. 21 (Clayton, Victoria: Monash Papers on Southeast Asia, 1990), 174. And according to an account from Pare, East Java, "The victims were taken off by truck and then set down in front of holes prepared in advance. Then their heads were lopped off with a Samurai [sword] that had been left behind by a Japanese soldier." Rochijat, "Am I PKI or Non-PKI?," 45.

37. Cited in Sunyoto et al., *Banser Berjihad*, 136.

38. The same author described the execution of an elderly bicycle repair person: "He cried, and because he couldn't keep quiet, they plugged up his mouth with a clump of earth. Rejo went into action, his machete cut through the neck of his victim, the one-eyed, powerless bicycle repairman. His head went into a sack." Anonymous, "On the Banks of the Brantas," 250–51.

39. Don Moser, cited in Robinson, *Dark Side of Paradise*, 299. Moser also reported on the fate of one of Bali's left-leaning district heads (*bupati*), who had been detained by the military and executed in custody. Later the same day, one of the soldiers involved was seen with a paper parcel containing the ears and fingers of the dead bupati.

40. Cited in Tsai and Kammen, "Anti-Communist Violence," 146.

41. Cited in Melvin, "Mechanics of Mass Murder," 153.

42. Cribb writes that the display of corpses and body parts "highlights the extent to which the killings were intended to create terror, as well as eliminating opponents." Cribb, "Indonesian Massacres," 248.

43. Oppenheiner, *Look of Silence* (1:20).

44. van Klinken, *Making of Middle Indonesia*, 243–44.

45. Cited in Sunyoto et al., *Banser Berjihad*, 155.

46. Anonymous, "Additional Data," 172.

47. Ibid., 171.

48. Ibid., 175. Former executioners from North Sumatra have likewise boasted of stabbing women in the stomach and cutting off their breasts. See Oppenheimer, *Look of Silence* (0:18, 0:37).

49. Rochijat, "Am I PKI or Non-PKI?," 44.

50. Oppenheimer, *Look of Silence* (0:59).

51. The testimonies of witnesses, survivors, and perpetrators alike concur on this crucial point. See, among others, the testimonies of perpetrators in Kurniawan et al., *Massacres*. See also the testimonies of witnesses, survivors, and some perpetrators in Wardaya, *Truth Will Out*; Sukanta, *Breaking the Silence*.

52. Christopher R. Browning, *Ordinary Men: Reserve Police Battalion 101 and the Final Solution in Poland* (New York: HarperCollins, 1993).

53. For a meticulous and revealing account of the role played by the RPKAD in the killings, see David Jenkins and Douglas Kammen, "The Army Para-Commando Regiment and the Reign of Terror in Central Java and Bali," in *The Contours of Mass*

Violence in Indonesia, 1965–68, ed. Douglas Kammen and Katharine McGregor (Singapore: NUS Press, 2012), 75–103.

54. There is still a great deal we do not know about these patterns—especially in areas beyond Java and Bali—but our understanding has been enhanced considerably by some excellent regional and local studies. On Central Java, see Margot Lyon, *Bases of Conflict in Rural Java* (Berkeley, CA: Center for South and Southeast Asia Studies. Research Monograph No. 3, 1970); Young, "Local and National Influences in the Violence of 1965"; Jenkins and Kammen, "Army Para-Commando Regiment." On East Java, see Robert W. Hefner, *The Political Economy of Mountain Java: An Interpretive History* (Berkeley: University of California Press, 1990); Greg Fealy and Katharine McGregor, "East Java and the Role of Nahdlatul Ulama in the 1965–66 Anti-Communist Violence," in *The Contours of Mass Violence in Indonesia, 1965–68*, ed. Douglas Kammen and Katharine McGregor (Singapore: NUS Press, 2012), 104–30; Hermawan Sulistyo, "The Forgotten Years: The Missing History of Indonesia's Mass Slaughter" (PhD diss., Arizona State University, 1997); Siddharth Chandra, "New Findings on the Indonesian Killings of 1965–66," *Journal of Asian Studies* 76, no. 4 (November 2017). On Surabaya, see Dahlia G. Setiyawan, "The Cold War in the City of Heroes: U.S.-Indonesian Relations and Anti-Communist Operations in Surabaya, 1963–1965" (PhD diss., University of California at Los Angeles, 2014); Robbie Peters, *Surabaya, 1945–2010: Neighbourhood, State, and Economy in Indonesia's City of Struggle* (Singapore: NUS Press, 2013). On Bali, see Geoffrey Robinson, *The Dark Side of Paradise: Political Violence in Bali* (Ithaca, NY: Cornell University Press, 1995); I Ngurah Suryawan, *Ladang Hitam di Pulau Dewata: Pembantaian Massal di Bali 1965* (Yogyakarta: Galangpress, 2007); Leslie Dwyer, "The Intimacy of Terror: Gender and the Violence of 1965–66 in Bali," *Intersections: Gender, History, and Culture in the Asian Context* 10 (August 2004). On Aceh, see Melvin, "Mechanics of Mass Murder." On North Sumatra, see Tsai and Kammen, "Anti-Communist Violence." On Eastern Indonesia, see Gerry van Klinken, *The Making of Middle Indonesia: Middle Classes in Kupang Town, 1930s–1980s* (Leiden: Brill, 2014); John M. Prior, "The Silent Scream of a Silenced History: Part One. The Maumere Massacre of 1966," *Exchange: Journal of Missiological and Ecumenical Research* 40, no. 2 (2011): 117–43; Steven Farram, "The PKI in West Timor and Nusa Tenggara Timur, 1965 and Beyond," *Bijdragen tot de Taal-, Land- en Volkenkunde* 166, no. 4 (2010): 381–403.

55. On West Java, see Nina Herlina, " 'Tata Sunda' Digonceng Konflik Sosial Politik," in *Malam Bencana 1965 Dalam Belitan Krisis Nasional: Bagian II, Konflik Lokal*, ed. Taufik Abdullah, Sukri Abdurrachman, and Restu Gunawan (Jakarta: Yayasan Pustaka Obor Indonesia, 2012), 51–78.

56. Killings flared up again in 1967–68 in the context of anticommunist army operations in Purwodadi, Central Java, and Blitar, East Java, but these were arguably part of a separate dynamic. On the army operations in Purwodadi, see Maskun Iskandar, "Purwodadi: Area of Death," in *The Indonesian Killings, 1965–1966: Studies from Java and Bali*, ed. Robert Cribb, no. 21 (Clayton, Victoria: Monash Papers on Southeast Asia, 1990), 203–13. On Blitar, see Vannessa Hearman, "Dismantling the Fortress: East Java and the Transition to Suharto's New Order Regime" (PhD diss., University of Melbourne, 2012).

57. Melvin, "Documenting Genocide." See also Melvin, "Mechanics of Mass Murder."

58. In March 1966, the British Consul in Medan suggested the estimate of forty thousand dead. Tsai and Kammen, "Anti-Communist Violence," 146. A few months later, the Swedish honorary consul in Medan (Nyberg) estimated that ninety thousand had been killed in North Sumatra and Aceh, while a Swedish missionary put the figure at two hundred thousand killed in North Sumatra alone. Edelstam to Bergström, "Likvidering av kommunister på norra Sumatra, Indonesien," June 16, 1966, UA/HP 1/XI, Riksarkivet. Ann Stoler suggests as many as a hundred thousand may have been killed there. Ann Laura Stoler, *Capitalism and Confrontation in Sumatra's Plantation Belt, 1870–1979* (New Haven, CT: Yale University Press, 1985).

59. Douglas Kammen and Faizah Zakaria, "Detention in Mass Violence: Policy and Practice in Indonesia, 1965–1968," *Critical Asian Studies* 44, no. 3 (2012): 452.

60. In his detailed demographic analysis of the killings in East Java, Chandra shows that the provincial towns of Kediri, Blitar, and Pasururn were most severely affected, and that six rural regencies in the northeast coastal area (Sidoardjo, Pamekasan, Panarukan, Sampang, Sumenep, and Surabaya) suffered higher than average losses. See Chandra, "New Findings on the Indonesian Killings of 1965–66." Perpetrator accounts suggest that there were also many killings in Banyuwangi, Tulungagung, and Malang. See Sunyoto et al., *Banser Berjihad*, 127.

61. According to an Australian Embassy cable of December 23, 1965, West German officials estimated that 70,000 had been killed in East Java by that date. See Jenkins and Kammen, "Army Para-Commando Regiment," 95. Kamen and Zakaria cite an overall figure of between 180,000 and 200,000 killed for East Java. Kamen and Zakaria, "Detention in Mass Violence," 452. Chandra concludes that the number killed in East Java was "likely in excess of 150,000" based on an estimated total population loss of 175,169. See Chandra, "New Findings on the Indonesian Killings of 1965–66."

62. For a discussion of the death toll on Bali, see Robinson, *Dark Side of Paradise*, 273.

63. Van Klinken proposed the figure of six thousand on the basis of the most recent testimonial and demographic evidence. See van Klinken, *Making of Middle Indonesia*, 249–50. See also John M. Prior, "The Silent Scream of a Silenced History"; Mery Kolimon, Liliya Wetangterah, and Karen Campbell-Nelson, ed., *Forbidden Memories: Women's Experiences of 1965 in Eastern Indonesia*, trans. Jennifer Lindsay (Clayton, Victoria: Monash University Publishing, 2015); Farram, "The PKI in West Timor and Nusa Tenggara Timur, 1965."

64. One scholar has argued, for example, that the violence of 1965–66 stemmed from the fact that Indonesia is an "extremely violent society." See Christian Gerlach, *Extremely Violent Societies: Mass Violence in the Twentieth-Century World* (Cambridge: Cambridge University Press, 2010).

65. Sjoekoer, "Death," 24.

66. Sukanta, *Breaking the Silence*, 26.

67. Oppenheimer, *Look of Silence* (1:08).

68. There are countless stories from across the country of people being pressured to join militia groups and death squads. A schoolteacher who took part in mass

executions in Aceh testified, "I didn't agree. I was just a teacher.... Oh, there were some that screamed, those PKI [people].... I helped out [at one of the killing sites]. I didn't want to. I saw some of them that copped it. Oh my god ... they were [decapitated].... [I]t bled." Cited in Melvin, "Mechanics of Mass Murder," 195.

69. Oppenheimer, *Act of Killing* (1:56)

70. One Indonesian author, for example, has written that thousands were killed in Aceh in 1965 "when the youth ran amok" and that they did so because "the teachings of communism are really in conflict with the beliefs of the people of Aceh as ardent believers in the teachings of Islam." Rusdi Sufi, *Pernak Pernik Sejarah Aceh* (Banda Aceh: Badan Arsip dan Perpustakaan Aceh, 2009), 183, 193, 194.

71. C. L. Sulzberger, "Mass Murders go on in Indonesia," *New York Times*, April 19, 1966.

72. *Le Figaro*, August 1966, cited in Heinz Schutte, "September 30, 1965, and Its Aftermath in the French Press," in *1965: Indonesia and the World*, ed. Bernd Schaefer and Baskara T. Wardaya, bilingual ed. (Jakarta: Gramedia Pustaka Utama, 2013), 124.

73. Airgram #A-263, US Embassy Jakarta to Department of State, December 26, 1966, US *Declassified Documents Catalog* [*DDC*], 1980, #85B.

74. Robert Cribb, "Genocide in Indonesia, 1965–1966," *Journal of Genocide Research* 3, no. 2 (2001): 219–39; John C. Spores, *Running Amok: An Historical Inquiry*, Southeast Asia Series, no. 82 (Athens, OH: Monographs in International Studies, 1988).

75. John Hughes, *Indonesian Upheaval* (New York: David McKay Co., Inc., 1967), 175.

76. Cited in van Klinken, *Making of Middle Indonesia*, 233.

77. Oppenheimer, *Look of Silence* (1:02). For additional examples, see the testimony of a retired military officer, "It Was Just Unavoidable Fallout," in Wardaya, *Truth Will Out*, 5–26. See also the testimony of a former Ansor member, "AM: 'We Never Buried the Bodies,'" in Kurniawan et al., *Massacres*, 26–29.

78. Guy Pauker, "Political Consequences of Rural Development Programs in Indonesia," *Pacific Affairs* 41, no. 3 (Fall 1968): 390.

79. Marshall Green, *Indonesia: Crisis and Transformation, 1965–1968* (Washington, DC: Compass Press, 1990), 59–60.

80. Don Moser, "Where the Rivers Ran Crimson from Butchery," *Life*, July 1, 1966, 26–27.

81. Hughes, *Indonesian Upheaval*, 175.

82. Melvin, "Mechanics of Mass Murder," 13.

83. Young writes of "the mutual alienation between those (often referred to as santri) who seek to conduct their lives strictly in conformity with what they take to be orthodox Islamic precepts and those (Javanists, often referred to by the santri as abangan) who blend Islam with pre-Islamic beliefs and practices." Young, "Local and National Influences," 65. On the history and practices of the abangan, see Niels Mulder, "Abangan Javanese Religious Thought and Practice," *Bijdragen tot de Taal-, Land- en Volkenkunde* 139 (1983): 260–67; Merle C. Ricklefs, "The Birth of the Abangan," *Bijdragen tot de Taal-, Land- en Volkenkunde* 162, no. 1 (2006): 35–55; Clifford Geertz, *The Religion of Java* (Glencoe, IL: Free Press, 1960).

84. As Robert Hefner has argued for the case of Pasuruan, the santri-abangan cleavage was not simply a matter of religious difference: "Whatever its very real religious dimensions, the conflict was not in any organizational sense exclusively or even primarily about religion." Cited in Young, "Local and National Influences," 88. See also Robert W. Hefner, *The Political Economy of Mountain Java.*

85. The idea of santri and abangan constituting distinctive, and often conflicting, cultural streams (*aliran*) in Javanese society has been the basis for much theorizing about Indonesian politics, and about the killings in Central and East Java in particular. See, for example, Robert R. Jay, *Religion and Politics in Rural Central Java* (New Haven, CT: Yale University Southeast Asia Studies Program, 1963); Lyon, *Bases of Conflict in Rural Java*; Hefner, *The Political Economy of Mountain Java;* Merle Ricklefs, *Islamisation and Its Opponents in Java: A Political, Social, Cultural, and Religious History, c. 1930 to the Present* (Honolulu: University of Hawaii Press, 2012).

86. It may also help to explain the geographic distribution of the killing within a given province. In his demographic analysis of the killings in East Java, for example, Chandra finds that losses were greatest in areas of NU strength, and least severe in PKI and PNI strongholds. See Chandra, "New Findings on the Indonesian Killings of 1965–66."

87. Rochijat, "Am I PKI or Non-PKI?," 43.

88. As Chandra acknowledges, "While there is a clear statistical association between the strength of support for NU and the killings, the methods used in this study-cannot establish causality between the two phenomena." Chandra, "New Findings on the Indonesian Killings of 1965–66."

89. On the history and politics of tensions over caste in Bali, see Robinson, *Dark Side of Paradise.*

90. There had been anti-Chinese riots in West Java as recently as May 1963. Tsai and Kammen, "Anti-Communist Violence," 137. Writing about the anti-Chinese violence in North Sumatra after October 1965, Kammen has observed that "at the moment the army first mobilized anti-Communist violence, or needed to remobilize it, the Chinese made a convenient first target: identifiable and nearby." Douglas Kammen, personal communication, January 24, 2017.

91. There may also have been serious anti-Chinese violence on the islands of Lombok and Sumbawa, but these cases have yet to be thoroughly researched.

92. See Tsai and Kammen, "Anti-Communist Violence," 142–46. Melvin argues that while most of the anti-Chinese violence in Aceh after October 1 was politically motivated, some of it was not. See Melvin, "Mechanics of Mass Murder," chapter 6.

93. On the significance of conflicts over land, for example, see Rex Mortimer, *Indonesian Communism under Sukarno: Ideology and Politics, 1959–1965* (Ithaca, NY: Cornell University Press, 1974). On the socioeconomic dimensions of conflict in Bali, see Robinson, *Dark Side of Paradise*, chapter 10.

94. Young notes that in Kediri, a center of killing, there had been serious conflicts over land, some of which had resulted in physical conflicts and casualties. Young, "Local and National Influences," 75. For Bali, see Robinson, *Dark Side of Paradise*, chapters 10–11.

95. Tsai and Kammen, "Anti-Communist Violence," 133; Stoler, *Capitalism and Confrontation.*

96. Daniel Lev, *Transition to Guided Democracy: Indonesian Politics, 1957–1959* (Ithaca, NY: Cornell Modern Indonesia Project, 1966).

97. Tsai and Kammen describe the mounting tensions in North Sumatra, and conclude that it was "a region with a strong PKI support base and a growing military-Muslim alliance waiting to strike back." Tsai and Kammen, "Anti-Communist Violence," 134. Likewise, Sunyoto highlights a number of deadly attacks by Banser units in plantation areas known to have been PKI and SARBUPRI strongholds, especially in Blitar and Kediri. Sunyoto et al., *Banser Berjihad*, 116–17. And according to US Embassy officials who spoke to army officer Kemal Idris, on hearing the news of the supposed coup, he had contacted Kostrad headquarters and was told "to divert his troops from entering Medan, and head them instead toward the rubber and other plantations nearby to begin rounding up and eliminating Communists. Idris estimated that he had 'secured'—i.e. killed or arrested—from 20–30 percent of the plantation workers in the first week of October alone." Airgram #A-82, US Embassy Jakarta to Department of State, August 17, 1966, RG 59, Central Files, POL 23-6 INDON, NARA. Although there is good reason to doubt that widespread killings took place as early as this report suggests, the report does highlight the army's perception that many plantation workers were Communists and needed to be "pacified."

Chapter Six: The Army's Role

1. That case has recently been made for Aceh by Jess Melvin on the basis of newly discovered Indonesian army documents. See Jess Melvin, "Mechanics of Mass Murder: How the Indonesian Military Initiated and Implemented the Indonesian Genocide—The Case of Aceh" (PhD diss., University of Melbourne, 2014). I have elsewhere made the argument for Bali in Geoffrey Robinson, *The Dark Side of Paradise: Political Violence in Bali* (Ithaca, NY: Cornell University Press, 1995). Other scholars, notably Douglas Kammen, Katharine McGregor, John Roosa, and Robert Cribb, have likewise stressed that earlier studies overstated the importance of local social and cultural conditions, while underplaying the role of the army in fomenting and organizing the violence. See Douglas Kammen and Katharine McGregor, eds., *The Contours of Mass Violence in Indonesia, 1965–68* (Singapore: NUS Press, 2012), 1–24; John Roosa, "The State of Knowledge about an Open Secret: Indonesia's Mass Disappearances of 1965–66," *Journal of Asian Studies* 75, no. 2 (2016): 281–97; Robert Cribb, "Political Genocides in Postcolonial Asia," in *The Oxford Handbook of Genocide Studies*, ed. Donald Bloxham and A. Dirk Moses (Oxford: Oxford University Press, 2010), 445–65.

2. For a related argument, see Douglas Kammen and Faizah Zakaria, "Detention in Mass Violence: Policy and Practice in Indonesia, 1965–1968," *Critical Asian Studies* 44, no. 3 (2012): 441–66. In explaining temporal and spatial variations in the violence, Kammen and Zakaria also consider the nature of political party competition—a factor that warrants further research but is not explored here.

3. For a presentation of that case and the supporting evidence, see Melvin, "Mechanics of Mass Murder." Melvin writes that the army leadership in Aceh launched "a swift and coordinated attack against the PKI from day one." As evidence, she cites a speech by Mokoginta at midnight on October 1, 1965, in which he ordered "that all

members of the Armed Forces resolutely and completely annihilate this counter-revolution and all acts of treason to the roots." She also cites two orders issued by Aceh's executive council on October 4, 1965. The first of those orders supported the plan to "completely annihilate" the September 30th Movement, while the second declared it "mandatory for the people to assist" in that effort. Ibid., 87, 97–98.

4. Kenneth R. Young, "Local and National Influences in the Violence of 1965," in *The Indonesian Killings, 1965–1966: Studies from Java and Bali*, ed. Robert Cribb, no. 21 (Clayton, Victoria: Monash Papers on Southeast Asia, 1990), 67.

5. In 1967, HMI leaders told Kahin that Adjie "was completely loyal to Sukarno and would not have moved against him." George Kahin interview with five HMI leaders, June 18, 1967, Jakarta, Personal archive of George McT' Kahin [Kahin Papers].

6. Adjie also recounted a visit he had received from "a party of politicians from the NU in Jakarta who after the coup had come to encourage him to get on with killing communists. He had berated them ... saying that the counter-coup was not a victory for them and that if he found them contravening the Pantjasila principles he would treat them as severely as he was treating the PKI." British Embassy Jakarta (Murray) to South East Asia Department, Foreign Office (Cable) February 10, 1966, DH 1015, FO 371/186028, National Archives of the United Kingdom [UKNA].

7. The estimate was reported by US officials in Embtel 1098, US Embassy Jakarta to Department of State, October 20, 1965, Record Group [RG] 59, 1964–66 [Central Files] POL 18 INDON, National Archives and Records Administration [NARA].

8. Cited in Yen-ling Tsai and Douglas Kammen, "Anti-Communist Violence and the Ethnic Chinese in Medan, North Sumatra," in *Contours of Mass Violence in Indonesia, 1965–68*, ed. Douglas Kammen and Katharine McGregor (Singapore: NUS Press, 2012), 141. Tsai and Kammen date the onset of the mass killings in North Sumatra to November 2, 1965.

9. There was some conflict in Bali in October and November, including physical clashes that resulted in a few casualties, but nothing like what happened in December. See Robinson, *The Dark Side of Paradise*, 286, 290–92.

10. Troop strength was limited in East Java because eight of the province's sixteen organic battalions were serving elsewhere at the time. David Jenkins and Douglas Kammen, "The Army Para-Commando Regiment and the Reign of Terror in Central Java and Bali," in *Contours of Mass Violence in Indonesia, 1965–68*, ed. Douglas Kammen and Katharine McGregor (Singapore: NUS Press, 2012).

11. In September 1966, a senior military officer told the US consulate in Surabaya that the "army considers rightists to be as much of a threat to short and long term security and welfare of country as leftists. Islamic state idea is as much to be feared as PKI and extreme Sukarnoists of PNI." Contel 45, US Consulate Surabaya to US Embassy Jakarta, September 13, 1966, RG 1964–66, 59, POL 15 INDON, NARA.

12. Soetarmadji was a protégé of Sjafiuddin and like him was slow to act against the PKI. Eventually he was arrested and replaced by Lieutenant Colonel Abdul Djalal, who lost no time in carrying out Suharto's orders. Gerry van Klinken, *The Making of Middle Indonesia: Middle Classes in Kupang Town, 1930s–1980s* (Leiden: Brill, 2014), 235–36. See also John M. Prior, "The Silent Scream of a Silenced History: Part One. The Maumere Massacre of 1966," *Exchange: Journal of Missiological and Ecumenical Research* 40, no. 2 (2011): 117–43; Steven Farram, "The PKI in West Timor

and Nusa Tenggara Timur, 1965 and Beyond," *Bijdragen tot de Taal-, Land- en Volkenkunde* 166, no. 4 (2010): 381–403.

13. On the pivotal role of the RPKAD in fomenting violence in Central Java and Bali, see Jenkins and Kammen, "Army Para-Commando Regiment."

14. Ibid., 80.

15. Two Central Java-based RPKAD battalions apparently remained in the province after the Jakarta-based battalion departed. Some accounts have suggested that RPKAD units moved on to neighboring East Java in November, where they joined troops loyal to Suharto, and a variety of armed youth groups and paramilitary forces, in crushing the PKI and its affiliates. Jenkins and Kammen, however, have raised doubts about that claim, suggesting that RPKAD forces did not go to East Java until June 1966. See ibid., 96, 98–99.

16. In my earlier work, I argued that the mass killing in Bali began only after the arrival of RPKAD forces in early December 1965. Jenkins and Kammen have since presented evidence that some killings occurred in Bali in the days just before those forces landed. There is no dispute, however, that the killings accelerated very dramatically after the deployment of these outside forces. See Robinson, *Dark Side of Paradise*, 295–97; Jenkins and Kammen, "Army Para-Commando Regiment."

17. Embtel 1360, US Embassy Jakarta to Department of State, November 6, 1965, RG 59, POL 23-9 INDON, NARA.

18. The document read, "Within the framework of the cleansing/extermination of the G30S, the membership of Hansip/Hanra in Sector IV North Aceh was given weapons by the Kosehkan North Aceh for this purpose." Cited in Melvin, "Mechanics of Mass Murder," 187.

19. Kurniawan et al., eds., *The Massacres: Coming to Terms with the Trauma of 1965* (Jakarta: Tempo, 2015), 12.

20. Ibid., 53.

21. For such references in East Java, see Vannessa Hearman, "Dismantling the Fortress: East Java and the Transition to Suharto's New Order Regime" (PhD diss., University of Melbourne, 2012), 105, 108, 116; Kurniawan et al., *Massacres*, 13–14, 17, 21, 25, 28, 31–32, 40. For Central Java, see Putu Oka Sukanta, ed., *Breaking the Silence: Survivors Speak about the 1965–66 Violence in Indonesia*, trans. Jennifer Lindsay (Clayton, Victoria: Monash University Publishing, 2014), 42, 133. For Aceh, see Melvin, "Mechanics of Mass Murder," 17, 155, 203. For Flores, see Kurniawan et al., *Massacres*, 71–72, 78–79. For North Sumatra, see Joshua Oppenheimer and Michael Uwemedimo, "Show of Force: A Cinema-Séance of Power and Violence in Sumatra's Plantation Belt," *Critical Quarterly* 54, no. 1 (April 2009): 84–110.

22. Sukanta, *Breaking the Silence*, 118.

23. Robinson, *Dark Side of Paradise*, 297–98. For further accounts on the use of trucks from Bali, see Sukanta, *Breaking the Silence*, 134; Kurniawan et al., *Massacres*, 63, 66–67, 69.

24. Cited in Robinson, *Dark Side of Paradise*, 298.

25. Cited in Melvin, "Mechanics of Mass Murder," 203.

26. For references to such lists in East Java, see Kurniawan et al., *Massacres*, 28, 37, 57. For Central Java, see Baskara T. Wardaya, ed., *Truth Will Out: Indonesian Accounts of the 1965 Mass Violence*, trans. Jennifer Lindsay (Clayton, Victoria:

Monash University Publishing, 2013), 30. For Bali, see, Kurniawan et al., *Massacres*, 65, 67, 69. For North Sumatra, see Joshua Oppenheimer, *The Look of Silence* (Drafthouse Films, 2016), DVD (0:49). For Flores, see van Klinken, *Making of Middle Indonesia*, 239–41; Kurniawan et al., *Massacres*, 73. For West Timor, see Sukanta, *Breaking the Silence*, 25.

27. Windle Memorandum, Appended to British Embassy Jakarta (Cambridge) to South East Asia Department, Foreign Office (Tonkin), December 16, 1965, DH 1015/335a, FO 371/180325, UKNA.

28. Rohim, cited in Agus Sunyoto, Miftahul Ulum, H. Abu Muslih, and Imam Kusnin Ahmad, *Banser Berjihad Menumpas PKI* (Tulungagung: Lembaga Kajian dan Pengembangan Pimpinan Wilayah Gerakan Pemuda Ansor Jawa Timur and Pesulukan Thoriqoh Agung Tulungagung, 1996), 156.

29. Cited in Melvin, "Mechanics of Mass Murder," 142.

30. Oppenheimer, *Look of Silence* (0:49).

31. Cited in van Klinken, *Making of Middle Indonesia*, 240–41.

32. Ibid., 239–40.

33. Presiden Republik Indonesia, Instruksi Presiden/Pangti ABRI/KOTI No. 22/KOTI/1965, 15 November 1965.

34. These detention sites and the treatment of prisoners held in them are dealt with in detail in chapter 8 below.

35. In North Sumatra, for example, army commanders were already mobilizing anticommunist groups before the alleged coup: "A devout Muslim, Mokoginta seconded Army personnel to the big estates, established pro-Muslim and pro-Army newspapers, cultivated militant youth groups by enlisting the services of local toughs and, in the context of Indonesia's policy of Confrontation with Malaysia, even began arming members of the Army's own unions." Tsai and Kammen, "Anti-Communist Violence," 134.

36. KAP-Gestapu was reportedly formed on the suggestion of Brigadier General Sutjipto, the head of the political section of the KOTI, and Kostrad officers encouraged its mass rallies. Harold Crouch, *Army and Politics in Indonesia* (Ithaca, NY: Cornell University Press, 1978), 141. In a secret cable from early December 1965, US ambassador Green spelled out the plan to channel secret cash to the group: "This is to confirm my earlier concurrence that we provide Malik with fifty million rupiahs requested by him for the activities of the KAP-Gestapu movement." Embtel 1628, US Embassy Jakarta to Department of State, December 2, 1965, US Department of State, *Foreign Relations of the United States* [*FRUS*], vol. 26, *Indonesia; Malaysia-Singapore, Philippines (1964–66)*, 379–80.

37. Shortly after arriving in Bali, for example, the RPKAD established the Coordinating Body of Action Fronts to Crush the Counterrevolutionary Gestapu (Badan Koordinasi Kesatuan Aksi Pengganjangan Kontrev Gestapu). See "Badan Koordinasi Kesatuan Aksi Pengganjangan Kontrev Gestapu," *Suara Indonesia* (Denpasar), December 10, 1965. Similar bodies were established in Kupang, West Timor, though with a slight delay. See van Klinken, *Making of Middle Indonesia*, 231–35.

38. Mansuruddin Bogok, an associate of the then foreign minister, Malik, made this comment. Adam Malik and Company Interview with Ruth McVey, October 2, 1966, New York, personal archive of Ruth T. McVey [McVey Papers], box 2, file 31c.

39. Airgram A-583, US Embassy Jakarta to Department of State, March 25, 1966, POL 2 INDON, NARA.

40. Adam Malik and Company Interview with Ruth McVey, October 2, 1966, New York, McVey Papers, box 2, file 31c.

41. Embtel 1435, US Embassy Jakarta to State Department, November 13, 1965, POL 23–9 INDON, NARA, cited in Jenkins and Kammen, "Army Para-Commando Regiment," 91–92n61.

42. East Aceh's Front Pembela Panca Sila claimed to have 15,000 members, and an official government document from late 1965 indicated that North Aceh had 14,182 members of Hansip and Hanra. See Melvin, "Mechanics of Mass Murder," 161, 186.

43. To those unfamiliar with the wider history, for example, Oppenheimer's first film about 1965–66, *The Act of Killing*, might leave the impression that the perpetrators were nothing more than local gangsters whose actions were unconnected to a wider army campaign. Oppenheimer's second film on the subject, *The Look of Silence*, corrects that impression, making it clear that the army delivered truckloads of detainees, blindfolded and hands tied, to local toughs who then killed them and dumped their bodies into the Snake River near Medan.

44. See, for example, Hermawan Sulistyo, "The Forgotten Years: The Missing History of Indonesia's Mass Slaughter" (PhD diss., Arizona State University, 1997); Christian Gerlach, *Extremely Violent Societies: Mass Violence in the Twentieth-Century World* (Cambridge: Cambridge University Press, 2010). While accepting that the army may have played a significant role in some areas, such authors point to the variations as evidence that in other areas, horizontal social and cultural conflicts were the primary drivers of violence. For a recent critique of that view, see Roosa, "State of Knowledge."

45. Embtel 1326, US Embassy Jakarta to Department of State, November 4, 1965, Indonesia, vol. 5, Country file, NSF, box 247, Lyndon Baines Johnson Library [LBJ Library]. And in a cable dated November 13, 1965, Ambassador Green reported that "from 50 to 100 PKI members are being killed every night in East and Central Java by civilian anti-Communist troops with blessing of the army." Cited in Jenkins and Kammen, "Army Para-Commando Regiment," 90.

46. Cited in Jenkins and Kammen, "Army Para-Commando Regiment," 88.

47. Dinas Sejarah TNI-AD, "Crushing the G30S/PKI in Central Java," in *The Indonesian Killings, 1965–1966: Studies from Java and Bali*, ed. Robert Cribb, no. 21 (Clayton, Victoria: Monash Papers on Southeast Asia, 1990), 166.

48. Contel 32, US Consulate Surabaya to US Embassy Jakarta, November 14, 1965, Indonesia, vol. 5, Country file, NSF, box 247, LBJ Library.

49. Sunyoto et al., *Banser Berjihad*, 89–136, 153–60.

50. See ibid., 124. For additional examples, see ibid., 101, 153, 157.

51. Ibid., 113, 153. See also ibid., 115, 121.

52. Ibid., 124.

53. Ibid., 159.

54. Cited in Kurniawan et al., *Massacres*, 37.

55. Young, "Local and National Influences," 93.

56. Cited in Tsai and Kammen, "Anti-Communist Violence," 141n40.

57. Oppenheimer, *Look of Silence* (0:59).

58. John Hughes, *Indonesian Upheaval* (New York: David McKay Co., Inc., 1967), 181.

59. Ibid., 180. On the army's role in coordinating the killings in Bali, see also Kurniawan et al., *Massacres*, 67, 69; Robinson, *Dark Side of Paradise*, chapter 11.

60. For most of this evidence, see Melvin, "Mechanics of Mass Murder," especially chapters 3–5.

61. Ibid., 104, 133.

62. "Eyewitness testimony reveals that Djuarsa used these meetings to call explicitly for local civilians to 'assist' the military by hunting down and killing members of the PKI, while warning those who did not participate . . . that they risked becoming targets of such violence themselves." Ibid., 133.

63. John Bowen, *Sumatran Politics and Poetics: Gayo History, 1900–1989* (New Haven, CT: Yale University Press, 1991), 119–20.

64. Van Klinken, *Making of Middle Indonesia*, 235.

65. Michael van Langenberg, "Gestapu and State Power in Indonesia," in *The Indonesian Killings, 1965-1966: Studies from Java and Bali*, ed. Robert Cribb, no. 21 (Clayton, Victoria: Monash Papers on Southeast Asia, 1990), 47; John Roosa, "The September 30th Movement: The Aporias of the Official Narratives," in *The Contours of Mass Violence in Indonesia, 1965–68*, ed. Douglas Kammen and Katharine McGregor (Singapore: NUS Press, 2012), 29.

66. Jenkins and Kammen write that Suharto and his fellow army officers went out of their way "to inflame communal tensions in what was already a deeply and dangerously polarized society, provoking pious Muslims (and, in some places, Hindus and Christians) to turn without mercy on their generally poorer, PKI-voting abangan (nominal Muslim) neighbours." Jenkins and Kammen, "Army Para-Commando Regiment," 91. See also van Klinken, *Making of Middle Indonesia*, 237–38.

67. For the text of Suharto's October 1 radio address, see Boerhan and Soebekti, *"Gerakan 30 September,"* 2nd ed. (Jakarta: Lembaga Pendidikan Ilmu Pengetahuan dan Kebudajaan Kosgoro, 1966), 77–79.

68. Cited in Melvin, "Mechanics of Mass Murder," 87.

69. Cited in ibid., 98.

70. Original text in *Berita Yudha*, October 5, 1965, reprinted in *Indonesia* 1 (April 1966): 203–4.

71. For the text of Suharto's remarks at Lubang Buaya on October 4, 1965 see Boerhan and Soebekti, *Gerakan 30 September*, pp. 87–88.

72. Pengurus Besar Partai NU, Jakarta, October 5, 1965, cited in Sunyoto et al., *Banser Berjihad*, 104–6.

73. Cited in Robinson, *Dark Side of Paradise*, 287n41. And at a mass rally on October 8, the PNI leader (I Gusti Putu Merta) called on President Sukarno to order Bali's Governor Suteja to "cleanse" the local government of all G30S elements. *Suara Indonesia* (Denpasar), November 2, 1965.

74. *Suara Indonesia* (Denpasar), November 11, 1965. Calls for the PKI to be "cut down to its roots" were also commonly heard in Kupang, West Timor. Van Klinken, *Making of Middle Indonesia*, 234.

75. Original text in *Berita Yudha*, November 12, 1965, translated and reproduced in *Indonesia* 1 (April 1966): 182–83.

76. British Embassy Jakarta (Cambridge) to South East Asia Department Foreign Office (Tonkin), December 23, 1965, DH 1015/349, FO 371/180325, UKNA.

77. The term first appeared in print in one of the army-controlled newspapers. "Inilah tjerita kebinatangan 'Gestapu,'" *Angkatan Bersendjata*, October 8, 1965. By most accounts, it was the brainchild of Brigadier General Sugandhi, the director of *Angkatan Bersendjata*. Van Langenberg, "Gestapu and State Power," 46.

78. CIA to White House Situation Room, "The Indonesian Situation." Report No. 21, October 7, 1965, Indonesia, vol. 5, Country file, NSF, box 247, LBJ Library.

79. On the origins and political meaning of the term "Gestok," see Kammen and McGregor, *The Contours*, 3–4.

80. *Angkatan Bersendjata*, October 14, 1965.

81. See Helen Fein, "Revolutionary and Anti-Revolutionary Genocides: A Comparison of State Murders in Democratic Kampuchea, 1975–1979, and in Indonesia, 1965–1966," *Comparative Studies in Society and History* 35, no. 4 (October 1993), 799.

82. Nasution's speech was broadcast on RRI on October 5, 1965, and reported by *Berita Yudha* on October 6. For the text of the speech, see Boerhan and Soebekti, *"Gerakan 30 September,"* 87–88. Nasution returned with some frequency to the themes of slander and treachery. In an infamous speech to an HMI gathering on March 12, 1966, he reportedly declared that "slander is more savage than murder!" That night, twenty-one political detainees were reportedly removed from their cells in Wirogunan prison and killed. Hersri Setiawan, *Aku Eks Tapol* (Yogyakarta: Galang Press, 2003), 182.

83. *Angkatan Bersendjata*, October 8, 1965.

84. *Angkatan Bersendjata*, October 14, 1965.

85. Tsai and Kammen, "Anti-Communist Violence," 143.

86. The first sensational version of the Gerwani story appeared in *Berita Yudha*, October 11, 1965. The story also appeared in publications of the official Army Information Bureau. See Pusat Penerangan Angkatan Darat Republik Indonesia, *Fakta2 Persoalan Sekitar Gerakan 30 September* (Jakarta: Penerbitan Chusus nos. 1, 2, and 3, October–December 1965).

87. For an early retelling of the story, which refers to the events at Crocodile Hole as a "death party," see Boerhan and Soebekti, *"Gerakan 30 September,"* 95–97. The story continued to be repeated many years later. See, for example, Sunyoto et al., *Banser Berjihad*, 99. It was also faithfully reproduced in a 1967 NBC documentary, *Indonesia: The Troubled Victory*.

88. Saskia Wieringa, *Sexual Politics in Indonesia* (New York: Palgrave, 2002).

89. "Pengakuan Seorang Ketua Gerwani. Diperintahkan Mendjual Diri Kepada Anggota ABRI," *Suara Indonesia* (Denpasar), November 5, 1965.

90. Another sensational story that started to circulate in the army-controlled media in October claimed that the wife and seven children of a Central Java–based army officer, Colonel Katamso, had been killed by the PKI and chopped into little pieces. Like the Gerwani story, this one turned out to be a deliberate fabrication, evidently designed by the army to stir up fear and anxiety. See Benedict Anderson and Ruth McVey, *Preliminary Analysis of the October 1, 1965 "Coup" in Indonesia* (Ithaca, NY: Cornell Modern Indonesia Project, 1971), 114n6.

91. In December 1965, Sukarno cited the official autopsies to prove his case, but nobody paid attention. See Anderson and McVey, *Preliminary Analysis*, 49n8. For a definitive debunking of these allegations, based on an analysis of the official autopsies, see Benedict R. O'G. Anderson, "How Did the Generals Die?," *Indonesia* 43 (April 1987): 109–34.

92. For early examples of media reports on the alleged discovery of incriminating documents, see *Duta Masyarakat*, October 12, 13, 15, 1965; Sukanta, *Breaking the Silence*, 52.

93. Robinson, *Dark Side of Paradise*, 293.

94. Jenkins and Kammen, "Army Para-Commando Regiment," 88.

95. Melvin, "Mechanics of Mass Murder," 139.

96. Sunyoto and coauthors mention two such cases in East Java; in both cases, Ansor or Banser units reportedly used the holes as mass graves for the PKI members they killed. Sunyoto et al., *Banser Berjihad*, 119, 157. For additional references to the alleged discovery of holes, see *Angkatan Bersendjata*, October 8, 1965; Sukanta, *Breaking the Silence*, 26, 52; Kurniawan et al., *Massacres*, 13, 25, 31, 37, 52. A senior PSI figure told Kahin in 1967 that in his view, the holes "were pure fabrication to justify the later killing of communists." George Kahin interview with senior PSI figure, June 14, 1967, Jakarta, Kahin Papers.

97. For early examples of the alleged discovery of weapons, see *Duta Masjarakat*, October 12, 1965; *Angkatan Bersendjata*, October 14, 1965.

98. Van Langenberg, "Gestapu and State Power," 48–49. For examples of such rhetoric in the accounts of perpetrators, see Kurniawan et al., *Massacres*, 25, 31, 37.

99. As the US Embassy reported from Jakarta in mid-October, "Activities of Indo press and other information media here are almost certain to be continued bone of contention between Sukarno and his backers and Army leadership and other anti-communists. . . . Army still seems dissatisfied with activities of Indonesia's sole news agency, *Antara*, and continues to interrogate and harass its staff which, of course, was heavily communist infected." Embtel 1047, US Embassy Jakarta to Department of State, October 17, 1965, RG 59, POL 23-9 INDON, NARA.

100. Cited in Roosa, "September 30th Movement," 29.

101. British Embassy Jakarta (Gilchrist) to Foreign Office (Stewart), "Attempted Coup in Indonesia," October 19, 1965, DH 1015/215, FO 371/180320, UKNA.

102. For the operation of these teams in Bali, see Robinson, *Dark Side of Paradise*, 293–94. For Aceh, see Melvin, "Mechanics of Mass Murder," 155, 180.

103. "Orpol/Ormas PKI Bujar, Kekridan, Patjung dan Senganan Lempar Badju," *Suara Indonesia* (Denpasar), November 18, 1965.

104. "Kerambitan Bersih dari PKI," *Suara Indonesia* (Denpasar), December 1, 1965.

105. Cited in Melvin, "Mechanics of Mass Murder," 116. Similarly, in Meulaboh, Djuarsa reportedly told a crowd, "If you don't kill [the PKI] they will be the ones doing the killing." Cited in ibid., 118.

106. Presiden Republik Indonesia, *Keputusan Presiden/Panglima Tertinggi Angkatan Bersendjata Republik Indonesia/Panglima Besar Komando Operasi Tertinggi (KOTI), No. 179/KOTI/1965*, December 6, 1965, cited in van Langenberg, "Gestapu and State Power," 51 (emphasis added).

107. Dinas Sejarah TNI-AD, "Crushing the G30S/PKI in Central Java," 164.

108. *Duta Masjarakat*, October 7, 1965.

109. See Sunyoto et al., *Banser Berjihad*, 124, 136, 157.

110. Sunyoto cites many examples. See Sunyoto et al., *Banser Berjihad*, 128, 131, 133–35, 154. See also Sukanta, *Breaking the Silence*, 64.

111. Cited in Sunyoto et al., *Banser Berjihad*, 131–32.

112. Cited in ibid., 136.

113. Kiai Djalil, cited in ibid., 160.

114. Kurniawan et al., *Massacres*, 19.

115. Ibid., 31.

116. Ibid., 36.

117. Ibid., 37.

118. Donald Kirk, "Bali Exorcises an Evil Spirit," *Reporter*, December 15, 1966, 42.

119. Sukanta, *Breaking the Silence*, 39.

120. According to Soe Hok Gie, PNI leaders in Bali "incited people to violence by saying that God approved of the killing of PKI people, and that the law would not condemn those who did this." Soe Hok Gie, "The Mass Killings in Bali," in *The Indonesian Killings, 1965–1966: Studies from Java and Bali*, ed. Robert Cribb, no. 21 (Clayton, Victoria: Monash Papers on Southeast Asia, 1990), 255–56.

121. Ernst Utrecht, "Het Bloedbad op Bali," *De Groene Amsterdammer*, January 14, 1967. A similar explanation for the killing was provided by a Balinese informant in the 1967 NBC documentary *Indonesia: The Troubled Victory*.

122. *Suara Indonesia* (Denpasar), October 7, 1965.

123. Edelstam to Bergström (Utrikesdepartementet), "Likvidering av kommunister på norra Sumatra, Indonesien," June 16, 1966, National Archives of Sweden, U/HP 1/XI, Riksarkivet.

124. Cited in Prior, "Silent Scream," 133.

125. Cited in ibid., 134.

Chapter Seven: "A Gleam of Light in Asia"

1. Former CIA director Colby wrote in his memoirs that the "CIA provided a steady flow of reports on the process in Indonesia although we did not have any role in the course of events themselves." William Colby, *Honorable Men: My Life in the CIA* (New York: Simon and Schuster, 1978), 227. See also the denials by CIA officers Tovar and Collins, and former ambassador Green, noted in chapter 4.

2. That case has been convincingly argued by Bradley Simpson, *Economists with Guns: Authoritarian Development and U.S.-Indonesian Relations, 1960–1968* (Stanford, CA: Stanford University Press, 2008), especially chapters 7–8.

3. Cited in Richard Tanter, "The Great Killings in Indonesia through the Australian Mass Media," in *1965: Indonesia and the World, Indonesia dan Dunia*, ed. Bernd Schaefer and Baskara T. Wardaya, bilingual ed. (Jakarta: Gramedia Pustaka Utama, 2013), 140.

4. The officials of most other Western states did the same. Schaefer writes, for example, that the chain of events after October 1 "was enthusiastically welcomed by West German representatives in Jakarta." Bernd Schaefer, "The Two Germanys and

Indonesia," in *1965: Indonesia and the World, Indonesia dan Dunia*, ed. Bernd Schaefer and Baskara T. Wardaya, bilingual ed. (Jakarta: Gramedia Pustaka Utama, 2013), 101.

5. George Ball Telcon with Vice President, 9:18 a.m., October 8, 1965, Papers of George Ball, box 4, Indonesia (4/12/64–11/10/65), Lyndon Baines Johnson Library [LBJ Library]. Likewise on October 9, the US Embassy reported the following "encouraging developments" from Jakarta: "Communists are now on the run for the first time in many years in Indonesia.... [The] rallying call today among non-Communist elements is 'Hang Aidit.' ... PKI organizational apparatus has been disrupted and party documents dispersed.... The Army for its part is keeping up momentum of present campaign.... To date Army has arrested several thousand PKI activists." Embtel 923, US Embassy Jakarta to Department of State (DOS), October 9, 1965, Indonesia, vol. 5, Country file, NSF, box 247, LBJ Library.

6. CIA Report No. 14 to White House Situation Room, "The Indonesian Situation," October 5, 1965, Indonesia, vol. 5, Country file, NSF, box 247, LBJ Library.

7. Indonesian Working Group Situation Report No. 8, 5:00 a.m., October 5, 1965, Indonesia, vol. 5, Country file, NSF, box 247, LBJ Library.

8. CIA Report No. 21 to White House Situation Room, "The Indonesian Situation," October 7, 1965, Indonesia, vol. 5, Country file, NSF, box 247, LBJ Library.

9. Embtel 868, US Embassy Jakarta to DOS, October 5, 1965, US Department of State, *Foreign Relations of the United States* [*FRUS*], vol. 26, *Indonesia; Malaysia-Singapore, Philippines (1964–66)*, 309.

10. Embtel 1002, US Embassy Jakarta to DOS, October 14, 1965, Indonesia, vol. 5, Country file, NSF, box 247, LBJ Library (emphasis added). Likewise, in an October 23 cable to the State Department, the US Embassy wrote, "This is critical juncture for anti-communist forces and for US and free world causes in Indonesia. Central problem for US policy is how we can help right side win but without our help showing and thereby becoming handicap rather than asset." Embtel 1166, US Embassy Jakarta to DOS, October 23, 1965, Indonesia, vol. 5, Country file, NSF, box 247, LBJ Library.

11. DOS Report, "Indonesia," [May 1966?], US *Declassified Documents Catalog* [*DDC*], 1994, #3183. Walt Rostow, appointed national security adviser in April 1966, reportedly offered a similar assessment in a memorandum to the president. Simpson, *Economists with Guns*, 189. A later policy document noted that the United States had an interest in "refraining from any *apparent* interference events taking place in Indonesia" (emphasis added). Airgram A-263, US Embassy Jakarta to DOS, "Annual Report on Relations with Communist Countries," December 21, 1966, *DDC*, 1980, #85B.

12. Office of Political Advisor to Commander in Chief [C-in-C] Far East, Singapore, to Foreign Office (FO), Telegram No. 678, October 8, 1965, FO 371/18031, National Archives of the United Kingdom [UKNA].

13. Deptel 1918, DOS to US Embassy London, October 12, 1965, Indonesia, vol. 5, Country file, NSF, box 247, LBJ Library. This plan was discussed and approved by Ball and Secretary of State Rusk. See George Ball Telcon with Dean Rusk, 5:40 p.m., October 12, 1965, Papers of George Ball, box 4, Indonesia (4/12/64–11/10/65), LBJ Library.

14. Deptel 447, DOS to US Embassy Jakarta, October 13, 1965, Indonesia, vol. 5, Country file, NSF, box 247, LBJ Library.

15. Embtel 1006, US Embassy Jakarta to DOS, October 14, 1965, *FRUS*, vol. 26, 321. A later cable reported that "aide told Ethel last night that Nasution was very satisfied with our message and just hopes the British will lay off." Embtel 1017, US Embassy Jakarta to DOS, October 14, 1965, Indonesia, vol. 5, Country file, NSF, box 247, LBJ Library.

16. Embtel 1090, US Embassy Jakarta to DOS, October 20, 1965, cited in Simpson, *Economists with Guns*, 184.

17. Embtel 1255, US Embassy Jakarta to DOS, October 28, 1965, Indonesia, vol. 5, Country file, NSF, box 247, LBJ Library.

18. The report, based on a conversation with an Indonesian Army officer, said, "In Central Java, Army (RPKAD) is training Moslem youth and supplying them with weapons and will keep them out in front against the PKI. . . . With top PKI leadership most of whom are in Djakarta, Army is avoiding frontal attack. . . . Smaller fry being systematically arrested and jailed or executed. . . . [O]n Outer Islands local military commanders have free hand to take direct action against PKI and they are doing so." Embtel 1326, US Embassy Jakarta to DOS, November 4, 1965, *FRUS*, vol. 26, 354.

19. Department of External Affairs to Canadian Embassy Jakarta, January 26, 1966, 20-INDON-1-4, National Archives of Canada.

20. British Embassy Jakarta (Gilchrist) to FO (de la Mare), February 23, 1966, DH 1011/66, FO 371/186028, UKNA.

21. Embtel 2347, US Embassy Jakarta to DOS, February 21, 1966, Record Group [RG] 59, Central Files of the Department of State, 1964–66 [Central Files], POL 23-9 INDON, US National Archives and Records Administration [NARA].

22. See, for example, British Embassy Jakarta (Murray) to FO (de la Mare), January 13, 1966, FO 371/186027; Guidance No. 26 from FO and Commonwealth Relations Office (CRO) to Selected Missions, January 18, 1966, DH 1015/289, FO 371/186027; British Embassy Jakarta (Murray) to FO (Stewart), "Indonesia: Annual Review for 1965," February 7, 1966, DH 1011/1, FO 371/186025, UKNA.

23. British Embassy Jakarta (Gilchrist) to FO, Telegram No. 527, March 18, 1966, DH 1015/111, FO 371/186029, UKNA.

24. Airgram A-598, US Embassy Jakarta (Masters) to DOS, "A Political Assessment of Lt. General Suharto," April 6, 1966, RG 59, Central Files, 1964–1966, POL 15 INDON, NARA.

25. Taomo Zhou, "China and the Thirtieth of September Movement," *Indonesia* 98 (October 2014): 29–58.

26. UK Permanent Delegation NATO Paris to FO, Telegram No. 61, October 7, 1965, FO 317/180317, UKNA.

27. British Embassy in The Hague (Burrows) to FO (Hanbury-Tenison), October 14, 1965, DH 1015/216, FO 371/180320, UKNA.

28. Australian Department of External Affairs to Australian High Commission, London, AP118, October 14, 1965, UK Foreign Office archive, DH 1015/161(B), FO 317/180317, UKNA.

29. FO (Stanley) to FO (Brown and Cable), October 14, 1965, FO 371/180318, UKNA; replies from Brown and Cable, October 15, 1965, FO 371/180318, UKNA. See also British Embassy Jakarta (Gilchrist) to FO, Telegram No. 2134, October 11, 1965, DH 1015/179, FO 371/180318, UKNA.

30. Letter from FO (Cable) to UK Delegation NATO (Millard), November 16, 1965, DH 1015/288, FO 371/180323, UKNA.

31. See, for example, Edelstam to Nilsson (Foreign Minister), "Utrotningen av kommunist-partiet i Indonesien," February 21, 1966, National Archives of Sweden, Riksarkivet [UA/HP 1/XI, Riksarkivet]; Edelstam to Bergström, "Resa till centrala och östra Java," May 13, 1966, UA/HP 1/Mal XI, Riksarkivet; Edelstam to Bergström, "Likvidering av kommunister på norra Sumatra, Indonesien," June 16, 1966, UA/HP 1/Mal XI, Riksarkivet.

32. Edelstam to Bergström, "Resa till centrala och östra Java," May 13, 1966, UA/HP 1/Mal XI, Riksarkivet.

33. On Soviet-Indonesian relations before and after October 1965, see Ragna Boden, "Silence in the Slaughterhouse: Moscow and the Indonesian Massacres," in *1965: Indonesia and the World, Indonesia dan Dunia*, ed. Bernd Schaefer and Baskara T. Wardaya, bilingual ed. (Jakarta: Gramedia Pustaka Utama, 2013), 86–98. On East Germany, see Schaefer, "Two Germanys," 99–113.

34. See Boden, "Silence in the Slaughterhouse"; Schaefer, "Two Germanys"; Jovan Cavoski, "On the Road to the Coup: Indonesia between the Non-Aligned Movement and China," in *1965: Indonesia and the World, Indonesia dan Dunia*, ed. Bernd Schaefer and Baskara T. Wardaya, bilingual ed. (Jakarta: Gramedia Pustaka Utama, 2013), 66–81.

35. Cavoski, "On the Road," 80.

36. Boden, "Silence in the Slaughterhouse," 90–91.

37. US Embassy Jakarta, Joint Weekly Report No. 41, October 23, 1965, RG 59, Central Files, POL 2–1 INDON, NARA. Cavoski refers to "China's strong condemnations of the killing of so many communists." Cavoski, "On the Road," 77.

38. Indonesia Working Group, Situation Report No. 32, 5:00 a.m., October 18, 1965, Indonesia, vol. 5, Country file, NSF, box 247, LBJ Library. China also protested the search by Indonesian soldiers of the Chinese Embassy staff dormitory and residence of Chinese engineers. Zhou, "China and the Thirtieth of September Movement," 53.

39. US Embassy Jakarta, Joint Weekly Report No. 41, October 23, 1965, RG 59, Central Files, POL 2–1 INDON, NARA.

40. Cited in *Guardian*, October 26, 1965.

41. "Awas Neo-imperialisme Kuning," *Angkatan Bersendjata*, April 25, 1966, cited in Zhou, "China and the Thirtieth of September Movement," 55.

42. Zhou, "China and the Thirtieth of September Movement," 55–56. China also sent several ships to Indonesian port cities to pick up Chinese Indonesians seeking to flee.

43. The influential human rights and solidarity organization TAPOL, established by Carmel Budiardjo, was not founded until 1973. For an exploration of these examples of transnational human rights activism, see Katharine McGregor, "The World Was Silent? Global Communities of Resistance to the 1965 Repression in the Cold War Era" (paper presented at the annual meeting of the Association for Asian Studies, Chicago, March 28, 2015).

44. Schutte notes, however, that while criticizing the repression, *L'Humanité* never seriously questioned the mainstream account of events, as portrayed by the

army and Western press. See Heniz Schutte, "September 30, 1965, and Its Aftermath in the French Press," in *1965: Indonesia and the World, Indonesia dan Dunia*, ed. Bernd Schaefer and Baskara T. Wardaya, bilingual ed. (Jakarta: Gramedia Pustaka Utama, 2013), 128.

45. In a cable to Washington, for example, the US Embassy in Jakarta wrote that it was "still far from convinced that PKI leadership planned coup for October 5, 1965. PKI was doing too well for a coup to be necessary." Embtel 828, US Embassy Jakarta to DOS, October 3, 1965, Indonesia, vol. 5, Country file, NSF, box 247, LBJ Library.

46. Office of the Political Advisor to C-in-C Far East, Singapore, to FO, Telegram No. 671, October 5, 1965, FO 371/180313, UKNA. On the same day, Ambassador Gilchrist had called for "early and carefully [planned] propaganda and psychological war activity to exacerbate internal strife" and ensure "the destruction and putting to flight of the PKI by the Indonesian Army." Office of the Political Advisor to the C-in-C Far East, Singapore, Telegram 264, October 5, 1965, FO 1011–2, UKNA, cited in Simpson, *Economists with Guns*, 178.

47. FO to Office of the Political Advisor to the C-in-C Far East, Singapore, Telegram No. 1835, October 6, 1965, FO 317/180317, UKNA.

48. Embtel, 827, US Embassy Jakarta to DOS, October 3, 1965, RG 59, Central Files, POL 23–9 INDON, NARA.

49. It is likely that they also coordinated with their close allies, including Australia, New Zealand, Malaysia, and Germany. In any case, all these countries adopted similar psywar and propaganda strategies at this time. See, for example, Tanter, "Great Killings," 129–44.

50. US Cables Received by Stanley and Circulated to Cable, Peck, Tonkin, Hewitt, and others in the Foreign Office, October 5, 1965, FO 371–180319, UKNA.

51. Embtel 851, US Embassy Jakarta to DOS, October 5, 1965, RG 59, Central Files, POL 23–9 INDON, NARA. For further discussions of psywar plans and propaganda themes by British and US officials, see US Embassy Jakarta to DOS, Embtels 853, 855, 857, 858, October 5, 1965, RG 59, Central Files, POL 23–9 INDON, NARA; Embtel 1058, October 18, 1965, RG 59, Central Files, POL 23–9 INDON, NARA; British Embassy Jakarta to FO, Telegram No. 2224, October 16, 1965, DH 1015/203(A), FO 371/180319, UKNA.

52. Embtel 952, US Embassy Jakarta to DOS, October 11, 1965, RG 59, Central Files, POL 23–9 INDON, NARA.

53. Embtel 1184, US Embassy Jakarta to DOS, October 26, 1965, RG 59, Central Files, POL 23–9 INDON, NARA. As noted in chapter 4, allegations of China's role in the alleged coup attempt remain unproven. Zhou, "China and the Thirtieth of September Movement." As Cavoski writes, "The real scale of the Chinese involvement in these events is still a mystery. . . . Reading through all those declassified Chinese materials, it seems much more likely that . . . China came to the scene after the coup had failed in order to save its own political positions in Indonesia and defend its former allies." Cavoski, "On the Road," 77.

54. Contel 740, US Consul Hong Kong to DOS, October 27, 1965, RG 59, Central Files, POL 23–9 INDON, NARA.

55. Embtel 853, US Embassy Jakarta to VOA, October 5, 1965, RG 59, Central Files, POL 23–9 INDON, NARA.

56. Embtel 923, US Embassy Jakarta to DOS, October 9, 1965, Indonesia, vol. 5, Country file, NSF, box 247, LBJ Library.

57. As the US Embassy wrote on October 5, "Djakarta press … largely preoccupied with murder of Army generals. Both papers carry series of gruesome pictures of mutilated bodies." Embtel 857, US Embassy Jakarta to DOS, October 5, 1965, RG 59, Central Files, POL 23-9 INDON, NARA.

58. CIA Memorandum, "Covert Assistance to the Indonesian Armed Forces Leaders," November 9, 1965, *FRUS*, vol. 26, 362.

59. Other Western governments did the same. Schaefer writes, for example, that the West German Embassy in Jakarta "began to readily adopt army propaganda as truth, even when it received … dubious or outright fabricated army interrogation protocols." Schaefer, "Two Germanys," 104–5.

60. Embtel 903, US Embassy Jakarta to DOS, October 7, 1965, RG 59, Central Files, XR POL 23-9 INDON, NARA.

61. British Embassy Washington (Gilmore) to FO (Murray) October 5, 1965, DH 1015/163, FO 317/180317, UKNA.

62. CRO to British High Commission Canberra, Telegram No. 2679, October 13, 1965, FO 371/181455, UKNA; FO to Office of the Political Advisor to the C-in-C Far East, Singapore, Telegram No. 1835, October 6, 1965, FO 317/180317, UKNA.

63. British Embassy Jakarta (Gilchrist) to FO (Stewart), "A Further Report on the Attempted Coup d'État," November 22, 1965, DH 1015/311, FO 371/180324, UKNA.

64. FO (Tonkin) Cover Note to Dispatch No. 16 (November 18, 1965) from Gilchrist to Stewart, November 23, 1965, DH 1015/311, FO 371/180324, UKNA.

65. Embtel 903, US Embassy Jakarta to DOS, October 7, 1965, RG 59, Central Files, XR POL 23-9 INDON, NARA.

66. The French media also relied heavily on information gleaned from the army-controlled media. See Schutte, "September 30, 1965."

67. Tanter, "Great Killings," 138–40.

68. Schaefer, "Two Germanys," 105.

69. Sukendro had been dismissed and sent abroad by Sukarno, who accused him of initiating moves against the PKI in 1960. While in exile, he attended the University of Pittsburgh, where he is thought to have formed ties with the US intelligence community. He returned to Indonesia in late 1963, was appointed as minister of state for the Supreme Command of Economic Operations in 1964, and in 1965, was involved in the secret army negotiations with Malaysia. See Harold Crouch, *The Army and Politics in Indonesia* (Ithaca, NY: Cornell University Press, 1978), 49, 75, 81, 107. Simpson writes that he was "one of the CIA's highest level contacts in the army." Simpson, *Economists with Guns*, 186.

70. Finally, Sukendro "cautioned that GOI-GOM relationship through Army must now be clandestine because if PKI became aware they would use to discredit Army.… Army establishing special body [in] Bangkok for direct contact GOM-Army which would by-pass Indonesian Embassy there." Embtel 563, US Embassy Kuala Lumpur, November 17, 1965, RG 59, Central Files, POL 23-9 INDON, NARA.

71. Benedict Anderson, personal communication, October 1983, Ithaca, NY.

72. On November 6, the US Embassy in Jakarta cabled that "we have reliable report that Sukendro's pioneering anti-PKI/Subandrio/Chicom newspaper, *Api*, has

been banned [probably by pro-Sukarno information minister Achmadi] as of today but Djakarta War Administrator [Umar Wirahadikusumah] is fighting this action." Embtel 1360, US Embassy Jakarta to DOS, Joint Sitrep No. 47, November 6, 1965, Indonesia, vol. 5, Country file, NSF, box 247, LBJ Library.

73. CRO to British Embassy Canberra, Telegram No. 2679, October 13, 1965, FO 371/181455, UKNA.

74. Tanter, "Great Killings," 139.

75. George Ball Telcon with James Reston, 3:05 p.m., October 4, 1965, Papers of George Ball, box 4, Indonesia (4/12/64–11/10/65), LBJ Library.

76. James Reston, "A Gleam of Light in Asia," *New York Times*, June 19, 1966.

77. Embtel 2411, US Embassy Jakarta to DOS, February 26, 1966, RG 59, Central Files, POL 23-9 INDON, NARA.

78. Brian May, *The Indonesian Tragedy* (London: Routledge and Kegan Paul, 1978), 103. One exception to the rule was Seymour Topping of the *New York Times*. His stories accurately pointed out that most of the killings in Java and Bali had been committed or incited by the army. See Seymour Topping, "Indonesia Haunted by Mass Killing," *New York Times*, August 24, 1966.

79. For a detailed account of the logic and substance of US assistance in the period after October 1, 1965, see Simpson, *Economists with Guns*, chapters 7–8.

80. Confrontation was formally brought to an end with the signing of the Bangkok Accord in August 1966.

81. Thus Boden writes, "While Indonesian communists were being persecuted and slaughtered, Moscow was searching for an understanding with the military regime." On Soviet aid and investment policy at this time, see Boden, "Silence in the Slaughterhouse," 93–96. On East German policy, see Cavoski, "On the Road."

82. US Embassy Jakarta to DOS, December 3, 1965, *DDC*, 1977, #128E.

83. British Embassy Jakarta (Gilchrist) to FO, Telegram No. 2134, October 11, 1965, DH 1015/179, FO 371/180318, UKNA.

84. Deptel 508, DOS to US Embassy Jakarta, October 22, 1965, RG 59, Central Files, POL 23-9 INDON, NARA.

85. Embtel 1164, US Embassy Jakarta to DOS, October 23, 1965, Indonesia, vol. 5, Country file, NSF, box 247, LBJ Library.

86. Embtel 1511, US Embassy Jakarta to DOS, November 19, 1965, Indonesia, vol. 5, Country file, NSF, box 247, LBJ Library.

87. Deptel 434, DOS to US Embassy Jakarta, October 9, 1965, RG 59, Central Files, XR DEF 6 INDON, NARA. On US deliberations over providing rice aid during this period, see Simpson, *Economist with Guns*, 196.

88. *Duta Masjarakat*, October 13, 1965.

89. On October 12, Nasution's aide told Colonel Ethel, "On his return through Bangkok [about October 9], General Sukendro ... made arrangements to ship a lot of rice from Bangkok to Indonesia." Embtel 969, US Embassy Jakarta to DOS, October 12, 1965, RG 59, Central Files, POL 23-9 INDON, NARA.

90. Embtel 1113, US Embassy Jakarta to DOS, October 21, 1965, Indonesia, vol. 5, Country file, NSF, box 247, LBJ Library.

91. US Embassy Jakarta, Joint Weekly Report No. 41, October 23, 1965, RG 59, Central Files, POL 2-1 INDON, NARA

92. While the discussion here focuses on US military assistance, it seems apparent that other states were involved in similar activities. According to one account, for example, the West German intelligence service, the BND, "assisted Indonesia's military secret service to suppress a left-wing *putsch* in Djakarta, delivering submachine guns, radio equipment, and money to the value of 300,000 marks." Heinze Hoehne and Herman Zolling, *The General Was a Spy* (New York: Bantam, 1972), xxxiii.

93. Secretary of Defense (McNamara), Memorandum for the President, "Effectiveness of US Military Assistance to Indonesia," March 1, 1967, *FRUS*, vol. 26, 493–95. For a detailed discussion of the deliberations leading to the formal resumption of aid at this time, see Simpson, *Economists with Guns*, 222.

94. Embtel 1017, US Embassy Jakarta to DOS, October 14, 1965. Indonesia, vol. 5, Country file, NSF, box 247, LBJ Library. At about the same time, an Associated Press story datelined Jakarta quoted an "informed source" as saying that "General Suharto has sent [a] Colonel to [the] US for help in providing communications equipment to contain communist threat." Deptel 408, DOS to US Embassy Jakarta, October 13, 1965, Indonesia, vol. 5, Country file, NSF, box 247, LBJ Library.

95. Deptel 610, DOS to US Embassy Jakarta, November 12, 1965, Indonesia, vol. 5, Country file, NSF, box 247, LBJ Library. In all likelihood, Sukendro, whose repeated appeals for communications equipment are described in a number of documents, made the request. See *FRUS*, vol. 26, 364–66, 368–71, 440–43. On Sukendro's requests for various kinds of aid, see Simpson, *Economists with Guns*, 186.

96. Based on interviews with US government officials, the journalist Kathy Kadane has reported that by using US-supplied communications equipment tuned to frequencies known to the National Security Agency, US intelligence officials were able to monitor army communications, including "commands from Suharto's intelligence unit to kill particular persons at given locations." Kathy Kadane, Letter to the Editor, *New York Review of Books*, April 10, 1997.

97. Embtel 1970, US Embassy Jakarta to DOS, Roger Channel, January 5, 1966, RG 59, Central Files, DEF 21 INDON, NARA.

98. Embtel 1160, US Embassy Jakarta to DOS, October 22, 1965, Indonesia, vol. 5, Country file, NSF, box 247, LBJ Library.

99. Deptel 545, DOS to US Embassy Jakarta, October 29, 1965, Indonesia, vol. 5, Country file, NSF, box 247, LBJ Library.

100. Embtel 1304, US Embassy Jakarta to DOS, November 2, 1965, Indonesia, vol. 5, Country file, NSF, box 247, LBJ Library.

101. Deptel 610, DOS to US Embassy Jakarta, November 12, 1965, Indonesia, vol. 5, Country file, NSF, box 247, LBJ Library. Simpson writes that at about this time, "the White House also authorized the CIA station in Bangkok to provide small arms to Sukendro 'to arm Muslim and nationalist youth in Central Java for use against the PKI,'" Simpson, *Economists with Guns*, 186.

102. "We are informing Brit, Australia, and NZ Embs today that we have had request from Sukendro for medical supplies which we [are] supplying covertly." Deptel 610, DOS to US Embassy Jakarta, November 12, 1965, Indonesia, vol. 5, Country file, NSF, box 247, LBJ Library.

103. Gabriel Kolko, personal communication, October 1998.

104. Embtel 1333, US Embassy Jakarta to DOS, November 4, 1965, Indonesia, vol. 5, Country file, NSF, box 247, LBJ Library.

105. Embtel 1350, US Embassy Jakarta to DOS, November 5, 1965, Indonesia, vol. 5, Country file, NSF, box 247, LBJ Library.

106. Embtel 1353, US Embassy Jakarta to DOS, November 7, 1975, RG 59, Central Files, XR DEF 6 INDON, NARA. See also Simpson, *Economists with Guns*, 186.

107. Kathy Kadane, "US Officials' Lists Aided Indonesian Bloodbath in '60s," *Washington Post*, May 21, 1990.

108. Embtel 1628, US Embassy Jakarta to DOS, December 2, 1965, *FRUS*, vol. 26, 379–80.

109. Green had been the senior diplomat (chargé d'affaires) at the US Embassy in Seoul at the time of the May 16, 1961 military coup that brought Major General Park Chung Hee to power.

110. Embtel 2115, US Embassy Jakarta to DOS, January 20, 1966, RG 59, Central Files, XR POL INDON-US, NARA.

111. Embassy cables reported frequent requests for material assistance from a variety of civilian and military figures. See, for example, Embtel 1245, US Embassy Jakarta to DOS, October 28, 1965, RG 59, Central Files, POL 23–9 INDON, NARA; Embtel 1401, US Embassy Jakarta to DOS (Section 1 of 2), November 10, 1965, RG 59, Central Files, POL 23–9 INDON, NARA; Embtel 1408, US Embassy Jakarta to DOS, November 11, 1965, RG 59, Central Files, POL 23–9 INDON, NARA; Embtel 2115, US Embassy Jakarta to DOS, January 20, 1966, RG 59, Central Files, XR POL INDON-US, NARA.

112. Seda served as minister of plantations from 1964 until February 1966. After a brief stint as minister of agriculture in mid-1966, he served for two years (1966–68) as minister of finance. From 1961 to 1968, he aso served as chair of the Catholic Party. Embtel 2115, US Embassy Jakarta to DOS, January 20, 1966, RG 59, Central Files, POL 23–9 INDON, NARA; Embtel 1245, US Embassy Jakarta to DOS, October 28, 1965, RG 59, Central Files, POL 23–9 INDON, NARA.

113. US Embassy Jakarta to DOS, November 19, 1965, *DDC*, 1979, #435C.

114. As Simpson writes, "At every opportunity the embassy drove this point home to officials in Jakarta, making it clear that aid would march in tandem with Indonesia's efforts to reverse Sukarno's policies, restore its economic credibility, and stabilize the economy in accordance with policies approved by Western creditors and international institutions." Simpson, *Economists with Guns*, 213.

115. Deptel 959, DOS to US Embassy Jakarta, January 18, 1966, RG 59, Central Files, AID(US) INDON, NARA.

116. Deptel 1892, DOS to US Embassy Kuala Lumpur, March 29, 1966, RG 59, Central Files, XR POL 23–9 INDON, NARA.

117. Memorandum of Conversation, US Secretary of State and Others, March 31, 1966, RG 59, Central Files, AID(US) 15–6 INDON, NARA.

118. DOS Report "Indonesia," [May 1966?], *DDC*, 1994, #3183. The White House approved the sale in June 1966. Simpson, *Economists with Guns*, 217.

119. Simpson, *Economists with Guns*, 212.

120. British Embassy Jakarta (Murray) to FO, Telegram No. 24, May 10, 1966, IM 1051/74, FO 371/187573, UKNA.

121. Deptel 3970, DOS to US Embassy Jakarta, June 1, 1966, RG 59, Central Files, AID (US)–INDON, NARA. According to a State Department memo, $144 million of that $2.5 billion debt was owed to the United States, and $1 billion to the USSR, mostly for military equipment. Debt servicing in that year, it estimated, might amount to $450 million, which was more than the probable gross foreign exchange earnings for the year. DOS Report, "Indonesia," [May 1966?], *DDC*, 1994, #3183. See also Ropa to Rostow, July 9, 1966, *FRUS*, vol. 26, 444; Rusk to Johnson, August 1, 1966, *FRUS*, vol. 26, 452.

122. Embtel 144, US Embassy Jakarta to DOS, July 9, 1966, *DDC*, 1981, #368C.

123. Simpson, *Economists with Guns*, 225.

124. Embtel 1124, US Embassy Jakarta to DOS, September 7, 1966, RG 59, Central Files, POL 15 INDON, NARA.

125. The group was comprised of fourteen donor states and four international financial institutions. On its formation and early work, see Simpson, *Economists with Guns*, 238–39. See also *Administrative History: State Department*, vol. 1, chapter 7, section L–Indonesia [ND], *DDC*, 1994, #3184.

126. Embtel 2007, US Embassy Jakarta to DOS, October 27, 1966, RG 59, Central Files, DEF 19 US-INDON, NARA.

Chapter Eight: Mass Incarceration

1. For one of the few studies to analyze the connection between the detentions and killings, see Douglas Kammen and Faizah Zakaria, "Detention in Mass Violence: Policy and Practice in Indonesia, 1965–1966," *Critical Asian Studies* 44, no. 3 (2012): 441–66.

2. Cited in Justus M. van der Kroef, "Indonesia's Political Prisoners," *Pacific Affairs* 49 (1976): 626.

3. The figure of 106,000 was given in the report of the official Fact Finding Commission published in January 1966. See Komando Operasi Tertinggi (KOTI), *Fact Finding Commission Komando Operasi Tertinggi* (Jakarta, January 10, 1966), 3.

4. In April 1975, Foreign Minister Malik said that about 600,000 had been detained, and in October 1976, the Kopkamtib chief of staff Admiral Sudomo gave the figure of 750,000. Cited in Amnesty International, *Indonesia: An Amnesty International Report* (London: Amnesty International Publications, 1977), 41. For further discussion of the numbers, see Kammen and Zakaria, "Detention in Mass Violence," 451; van der Kroef, "Indonesia's Political Prisoners," 625–26, 635.

5. Amnesty International, *Amnesty International Report*, 23.

6. The official was Hari Sugiman, the director general of social and political affairs. *Tapol Bulletin* 70 (July 1985): 1. On the number of detainees, see Richard Tanter, "Intelligence Agencies and Third World Militarization: A Case Study of Indonesia, 1966–1989" (Ph.D. diss., Monash University, 1990), 299–300.

7. See, for example, John McBeth, "Prisoners of History," *Far Eastern Economic Review*, February 16, 1995, 27–28. The figure of 1.4 million may also represent an

army estimate of the number of "die-hard" Communists in the country. A Kopkamtib document from 1969, for example, notes that 1,396,173 PKI members had attended "party schools" up to the Kabupaten level. See Kopkamtib, Team Pemerika Pusat, *Partai Komunis Indonesia dan G.30.S/PKI* (Djakarta, April 1969), 55.

8. On the political trials, see Amnesty International, *Amnesty International Report*, 45–54; van der Kroef, "Indonesia's Political Prisoners," 639–40.

9. Sumiyarsi Siwirini C., *Plantungan: Pembuangan Tapol Perempuan* (Yogyakarta: Pusat Sejarah dan Etika Politik (Pusdep), Universitas Sanata Dharma, 2010), 44n7. See also Rachmi Diyah Larasati, *The Dance That Makes You Vanish: Cultural Reconstruction in Post-Genocide Indonesia* (Minneapolis: University of Minnesota Press, 2013).

10. See van der Kroef, "Indonesia's Political Prisoners," 630, 638–39.

11. The problem of informants and traitors is discussed in the memoirs of many former detainees. See, for example, Suwondo Budiardjo, "Salemba: Cuplikan Kecil Derita Nasional," unpublished typescript, 1979, 11–12; Carmel Budiardjo, *Surviving Indonesia's Gulag* (London: Cassell, 1996); Tan Swie Ling, *G30S 1965, Perang Dingin dan Kehancuran Nasionalisme: Pemikiran Cina Jelata Korban Orba* (Jakarta: Komunitas Bambu, 2010). See also the testimonies of former detainees in Baskara T. Wardaya, ed., *Truth Will Out: Indonesian Accounts of the 1965 Mass Violence*, trans. Jennifer Lindsay (Clayton, Victoria: Monash University Publishing, 2013), 90, 108–9, 155.

12. A former BTI leader, for example, described how a PKI official who had betrayed him to the authorities later took part in his interrogation: "Now there at [police] headquarters that same [PKI] cadre was doing the interrogation alongside the police, calling us names. He was even crueler than the police! There were quite a few PKI cadres who did this kind of thing. This was because they could not stand the terror and violence inflicted on them." Cited in Wardaya, *Truth Will Out*, 90.

13. Sudisman, "Analysis of Responsibility: Defense Speech of Sudisman, General Secretary of the Indonesian Communist Party at His Trial before the Special Military Tribunal, Jakarta, 21 July 1967," trans. Benedict Anderson (Melbourne, Victoria: Works Co-operative, 1975), 3.

14. See, for example, the accounts of survivors, witnesses, and perpetrators in Wardaya, *Truth Will Out*, 41, 90, 93–94; Putu Oka Sukanta, ed., *Breaking the Silence: Survivors Speak about the 1965–66 Violence in Indonesia*, trans. Jennifer Lindsay (Clayton, Victoria: Monash University Publishing, 2014), 64–65, 110, 117, 133–34, 151, 160, 163–64.

15. Willem Samuels, introduction to Pramoedya Ananta Toer, *The Mute's Soliloquy: A Memoir* (New York: Hyperion East, 1999), xviii. Describing his own arrest, Pramoedya wrote, "My hands were tied behind my back and the rope that bound my wrists was then looped around my neck. In the early days of the Indonesian revolution that kind of knot was a sure sign that the captive was to be killed." Ibid., 3–4.

16. Ibrahim Slamet, "Letter from Indonesia," *Index on Censorship* 3, no. 1 (1974): 61.

17. Cited in Sukanta, *Breaking the Silence*, 151.

18. Sumiyarsi, *Plantungan*, 37–38, 161. A Gerwani member, Rukiah, had a similar experience when a group of HMI members ransacked her house in Makassar in October 1965: "After an hour went by and they had not found Rukiah, they started

taking anything of value: watches, the radio, clothes, even crockery." Sukanta, *Breaking the Silence*, 160.

19. Pramoedya, *Mute's Soliloquy*, xix.

20. See Roy A. Medvedev, *Let History Judge: The Origins and Consequences of Stalinism* (New York: Knopf, 1971).

21. For a partial list of known detention sites, together with a map showing their approximate locations, see a report by the Dutch Section of Amnesty International, "Indonesia Special," *Wordt Vervolgd* (March 1973): 16–17. For a slightly different map, see Tapol, *Indonesia: The Prison State* (London: Tapol, 1976), 8–9.

22. General Suharto set up the army-controlled apparatus of investigation and prosecution in November 1965, acting in his capacity as Kopkamtib commander. For details, see Kammen and Zakaria, "Detention in Mass Violence," 445–48.

23. Sudisman, "Analysis of Responsibility," 1.

24. These are described in some detail in the memoirs and other accounts of former detainees. See, for example, Sumiyarsi, *Plantungan*, 58, 62, 63; Tan, *G30S 1965*, 19–37; C. Budiardjo, *Surviving Indonesia's Gulag*, chapter 10; Sulami, *Perempuan—Kebenaran dan Penjara* (Jakarta: Cipta Lestari, 1999); Sudjinah, *Terempas Gelombang Pasang* (Jakarta: Pustaka Utan Kayu, 2003); S. Budiardjo, "Salemba," 13; Wardaya, *Truth Will Out*, 91, 94; Sukanta, *Breaking the Silence*, 35, 37, 51–52, 55, 117, 136, 163–64.

25. See, for example, Pramoedya, *Mute's Soliloquy*, 4–5.

26. Sumiyarsi, *Plantungan*, 58.

27. C. Budiardjo, *Surviving Indonesia's Gulag*, 83.

28. On the problem of sexual violence against detainees, see Komnas Perempuan, *Kejahatan terhadap Kemanusiaan Berbasis Jender: Mendengarkan Suara Perempuan Korban Peristiwa 1965* (Jakarta: Komnas Perempuan, 2007); Annie Pohlman, *Women, Sexual Violence, and the Indonesian Killings of 1965–66* (New York: Routledge, 2015); Saskia Wieringa, *Sexual Politics in Indonesia* (New York: Palgrave, 2002); C. Budiardjo, *Surviving Indonesia's Gulag*.

29. See, for example, the case of Lambatu bin Lanasi in Sukanta, *Breaking the Silence*, 52–53.

30. Budiardjo recounts the story of Sri Ambar, who was repeatedly stripped naked and beaten while being interrogated at the Kalong detention center in Jakarta. C. Budiardjo, *Surviving Indonesia's Gulag*, 79–80. Tan notes that male prisoners too were sometimes made to strip naked before being interrogated. Tan, *G30S 1965*, 24.

31. Cited in Wardaya, *Truth Will Out*, 148.

32. Sumiyarsi, *Plantungan*, 70n8.

33. According to a former detainee, for example, the commander of the Plantungan women's prison kept one of the younger detainees as a "mistress." See Sumiyarsi, *Plantungan*, 96, 99, 152–53. Another inmate at the same prison recalled that "the military officers there had illicit sex [with the prisoners] so there were many fatherless babies born in Plantungan." Cited in Wardaya, *Truth Will Out*, 149. For additional accounts of rape by military and police authorities, see Sukanta, *Breaking the Silence*, 53, 155.

34. The film of the teenage girls reenacting their dance, mentioned above, was apparently presented as evidence in Subandrio's trial. Sumiyarsi, *Plantungan*, 70n8.

35. Slamet, "Letter from Indonesia," 61. One is reminded here of the prisoners at Tuol Sleng (S-21) prison in Pol Pot's Cambodia who were made to bow down to an image of Ho Chi Minh depicted as a dog. See David Chandler, *Voices from S-21: Terror and History in Pol Pot's Secret Prison* (Berkeley: University of California Press, 1999), 134.

36. Tan, *G30S 1965*, 31.

37. There was also a residual category X for prisoners who had not yet been classified. The following summary is drawn primarily from Amnesty International, *Amnesty International Report*; van der Kroef, "Indonesia's Political Prisoners."

38. Cited in "Indonesia Special," *Wordt Vervolgd* (March 1973): 12. Likewise, in July 1976, Admiral Sudomo said that category B prisoners "were indirectly involved" in the supposed coup, but "there is a lack of evidence that could be submitted to the court." *Sinar Harapan*, July 26, 1976.

39. In 1975, the C category was further divided into a number of subcategories (C1, C2, and C3) in an apparent effort to specify the different criteria of culpability. See van der Kroef, "Indonesia's Political Prisoners," 633.

40. Presiden Republik Indonesia, *Instruksi Presiden/Pangti ABRI/KOTI No. 22/KOTI/1965—Kepada Kompartimen2/Departemen2, Badan2/Lembaga2 Pemerintah—Untuk Laksanakan Penertiban/Pembersihan Personil Sipil dari Oknum "Gerakan 30 September,"* signed on president's behalf by Soeharto (Kepala Staf Komado Operasi Tertinggi/Panglima Operasi Pemulihan Keamanan dan Ketertiban), November 15, 1965, cited in Boerhan and Soebekti, *"Gerakan 30 September,"* 2nd ed. (Jakarta: Lembaga Pendidikan Ilmu Pengetahuan dan Kebudajaan Kosgoro, 1966), 238–48. This order was, in turn, based on instructions issued by General Nasution on November 12, and by General Suharto on October 10, 1965, that outlined procedures for cleansing G30S elements from the army. See Kammen and Zakaria, "Detention in Mass Violence," 443.

41. The classification system spelled out in the November 1965 decree "became the basis for the formal classification for long-term political prisoners outlined in Presidential Instruction No. 09/KOGAM/1966." Kammen and Zakaria, "Detention in Mass Violence," 460. The system was further amended by Kopkamtib, *KEP-028/KOPKAM/10/1968*, as amended by *KEP 010/KOPKAM/3/1969*, cited in Amnesty International, *Amnesty International Report*, 118–20.

42. Kammen and Zakaria argue, for example, that the extreme vagueness of the language in the relevant decrees gave military authorities "extraordinary discretionary powers." Kammen and Zakaria, "Detention in Mass Violence," 444, 450.

43. As Kammen and Zakaria write, they "show that the attack on the political Left was not a horizontal conflict but the result of strategic calculations made by Suharto and the Army high command and orders issued to and implemented by regional army commanders." Ibid., 445.

44. The official Kopkamtib figure for category B prisoners in 1976 was 29,470, in addition to 1,309 who had already been released. See Amnesty International, *Amnesty International Report*, 36.

45. In July 1967, the attorney general said there were about 4,700 category A prisoners. Van der Kroef, "Indonesia's Political Prisoners," 634. In December 1975, the Kopkamtib chief of staff Admiral Sudomo said that there were 1,200 category A pris-

oners, of whom 767 had been tried and convicted. *Kompas*, December 3, 1975. And in 1976, Sudomo told a Dutch church representative that 810 category A prisoners had been convicted, 220 were awaiting trial, and another 1,944 were being held without trial due to lack of evidence. Confidential memo on "Political Prisoners," July 30, 1976, by J. Bos, General Manager, Inter Church Coordination Committee for Development Projects (ICCO), The Netherlands. The order for the political trials was issued in Presiden Republik Indonesia, *Keputusan Presiden No. 370/1965 tentang Penunjukan Mahkamah Militer Luar Biasa untuk Perkara G30S/PKI*, December 4, 1965.

46. There were, of course, some exceptions to these general patterns. According to a journalist who visited six detention facilities in 1977, for example, the conditions in Nirbaya prison, which held some one hundred high-status category A detainees, were relatively good. See David Jenkins, "Inside Suharto's Prisons," *Far Eastern Economic Review* (October 28, 1977): 8–13. For a comprehensive overview of prison conditions, see Amnesty International, *Amnesty International Report*, 71–89.

47. Cited in Jenkins, "Inside Suharto's Prisons," 8.

48. See Tan, *G30S 1965*, 34, 53; Sumiyarsi, *Plantungan*, 48; S. Budiardjo, "Salemba," 15–16; Sukanta, *Breaking the Silence*, 151.

49. See Sukanta, *Breaking the Silence*, 53, 66, 92; Wardaya, *Truth Will Out*, 95, 129, 131; Pramoedya, *Mute's Soliloquy*. Between 1966 and 1972, official spending on food for prisoners was said to be just 2.5 rupiah per prisoner per day, or about US$1 for every eighty prisoners. Cited in van der Kroef, "Indonesia's Political Prisoners," 644.

50. Pramoedya, *Mute's Soliloquy*, 10–11.

51. Ibid., 9–10.

52. Ibid., 12–13.

53. Amnesty International, *Amnesty International Report*, 77.

54. Sumiyarsi recounts her efforts to assist patients and also the inadequacies of prison medical facilities. See Sumiyarsi, *Plantungan*, 93–94, 102–11. Between 1966 and 1972, official spending on medical service for prisoners was said to be 0.3 rupiah per prisoner per month, or about US$3 for every two thousand prisoners. Cited in van der Kroef, "Indonesia's Political Prisoners," 644.

55. S. Budiardjo, "Salemba," 16.

56. Together with reeducation and resettlement, forced labor for detainees was codified in a Kopkamtib instruction from October 1968. See Kopkamtib, *Petunjuk Pelaksanaan No. PELAK-002/KOPKAM/10/1968 tentang Kebijaksanaan Penyelesaian Tahanan/Tawanan G30S PKI.*

57. This is only a partial list of the resettlement camps that operated between 1965 and the late 1970s. Other camps are known to have existed in East Kalimantan, Central Kalimantan, and the vicinity of the rubber plantations in North Sumatra. On the camps in Central Sulawesi, see Nurlaela A. K. Lamasitudju, "Rekonsiliasi dan Pernyataan Maaf Pak Wali Kota," in *Luka Bangsa Luka Kita: Pelanggaran HAM Masa Lalu dan Tawaran Rekonsiliasi*, ed. Baskara T. Wardaya (Yogyakarta: Galang Press, 2014), 371–83. For South Sulawesi, see Taufik Ahmad, "South Sulawesi: The Military, Prison Camps, and Forced Labour," in *The Contours of Mass Violence in Indonesia, 1965–68*, ed. Douglas Kammen and Katharine McGregor (Singapore: NUS Press, 2012), 156–81. See also the accounts of former detainees in Sukanta, *Breaking*

the Silence, 14, 56–59, 149, 165; Kurniawan et al., eds., *The Massacres: Coming to Terms with the Trauma of 1965* (Jakarta: Tempo, 2015), 105–9, 112–14.

58. On forced labor in Tangerang and Nusa Kambangan, see Amnesty International, *Amnesty International Report*, 85–88; Hersri Setiawan, *Aku Eks Tapol* (Yogyakarta: Galang Press, 2003), 198. For Salemba prison, see S. Budiardjo, "Salemba," 18.

59. Tan, *G30S 1965*, 48.

60. Sumiyarsi, *Plantungan*, 49.

61. Jenkins, "Inside Suharto's Prisons," 10.

62. According to Tan, for example, the PKI figure Nyoto had been "loaned out" of military custody and was never seen again. Tan, *G30S 1965*, 55. See also S. Budiardjo, "Salemba," 15. For further references to the practice of "loaning out" in the accounts of former prisoners, see Sukanto, *Breaking the Silence*, 36; Wardaya, *Truth Will Out*, 24–25.

63. Budiardjo, who spent fourteen years in detention without charge or trial, later wrote that "it was this uncertainty that was the heaviest burden for us, the political detainees of the New Order." S. Budiardjo, "Salemba," 8.

64. Cited in Amnesty International, *Amnesty International Report*, 51.

65. For a unique audiovisual record of one such indoctrination session at a prison in North Sumatra, see the 1967 NBC documentary *Indonesia: The Troubled Victory*.

66. Cited in Jenkins, "Inside Suharto's Prisons," 8.

67. S. Budiardjo, "Salemba," 17.

68. For an account of this visit by one of the detainees, see Sumiyarsi, *Plantungan*, 124–27. The Major General Sumitro who joined this delegation was head of the armed forces mental development center, not the Kopkamtib chief. Tanter, "Intelligence Agencies," 298.

69. Jenkins, "Inside Suharto's Prisons," 11.

70. The Dutch institutions involved were the Radboud University of Nijmegen and University of Amsterdam; the Indonesian participants were the University of Indonesia, Gajah Mada University, and Pajajaran University. See Marnix de Bruyne, "Hoe Nederlandse psychologen collaboreerden met Soeharto," *Wordt Vervolgd* 12, no.1 (December 2016–January 2017): 34–35; Sebastiaan Broere, "The Gray Area of Indonesian Psychology: The KUN-2 Project, 1968–1976," draft paper, University of California at Los Angeles, November 2016; Dyah Ayu Kartika, "The Politicization of Psychology: The Role of Psychologists in Indonesia's Detention Camps During New Order Era" (MA thesis, International Institute of Social Studies, 2016).

71. See, for example, "Professor Jaspers besprak met mevr. Sadli 'afwijkend gedrag,'" *De Waarheid*, April 22, 1978.

72. Petteri Pietikainen, *Madness: A History* (London: Routledge, 2015), 281. Likewise, Tanter notes that the use of psychologists in interrogating political prisoners shows that "Indonesia's intelligence services have followed those of the industrial countries in attempts at scientizing their strategies of political dominance." Tanter, "Intelligence Agencies," 296.

73. In an insightful analysis, Kammen and Zakaria note significant variations in the *ratio* of killings to detentions, and offer a number of explanations for those different values. Kammen and Zakaria, "Detention in Mass Violence," 451–56.

74. There were, of course, some long-term detainees in these places. According to one source, there were forty-seven political prisoners in Aceh in 1974–75. Van der Kroef, "Indonesia's Political Prisoners," 635. In Bali, about a dozen were still in detention in the late 1970s. They included Pudjo Prasetio, who was sentenced to life imprisonment in 1979 and remained in detention in Bali until 1995, when he was transferred to a prison in Semarang. See Amnesty International, *Indonesia: 1965 Prisoners—A Briefing* (London: Amnesty International, 1995).

75. Kammen and Zakaria make a similar argument, noting that the responses of regional military commanders to Suharto's commands varied. Kammen and Zakaria, "Detention in Mass Violence," 453–54. See also van der Kroef, "Indonesia's Political Prisoners," 635.

76. Kammen and Zakaria suggest that beyond the political and personal preferences of commanders, a crucial factor in such outcomes was the nature of political party competition in a given region. Kammen and Zakaria, "Detention in Mass Violence," 454–56. That possibility warrants further research.

77. Yen-ling Tsai and Douglas Kammen, "Anti-Communist Violence and the Ethnic Chinese in Medan, North Sumatra," in *The Contours of Mass Violence, 1965–68*, ed. Douglas Kammen and Katharine McGregor (Singapore: NUS Press, 2012), 147.

78. British Embassy Jakarta (Gilchrist) to FO (de la Mare), February 23, 1966, DH 1011/66, FO 371/186028, National Archives of the United Kingdom.

79. Agus Sunyoto, Miftahul Ulum, H. Abu Muslih, and Imam Kusnin Ahmad, *Banser Berjihad Menumpas PKI* (Tulungagung: Lembaga Kajian dan Pengembangan Pimpinan Wilayah Gerakan Pemuda Ansor Jawa Timur and Pesulukan Thoriqoh Agung Tulungagung, 1996), 158.

80. David Jenkins and Douglas Kammen, "The Army Para-Commando Regiment and the Reign of Terror in Central Java and Bali," in *The Contours of Mass Violence in Indonesia, 1965–68*, ed. Douglas Kammen and Katharine McGregor (Singapore: NUS Press, 2012), 94.

81. Maskun Iskandar, "Purwodadi: Area of Death," in *The Indonesian Killings, 1965–1966: Studies from Java and Bali*, ed. Robert Cribb, no. 21 (Clayton, Victoria: Monash Papers on Southeast Asia, 1990), 204.

82. Cited in McBeth, "Prisoners of History." As a former army officer later clarified, "Many were arrested, but then that caused problems to do with the provision of food and so forth. It was difficult. So they had to be put in one place.... [T]his is where the idea arose of sending them to Buru Island." Cited in Wardaya, *Truth Will Out*, 19.

83. On Buru, see Amnesty International, *Amnesty International Report*, 90–100; Komisi Nasional Hak Asasi Manusia (Komnas HAM), "Laporan Akhir Tim Pengkajian Pelanggaran HAM Berat Soeharto (Sub-Tim Pengkajian Kasus 1965)," in *Luka Bangsa Luka Kita: Pelanggaran HAM Masa Lalu dan Tawaran Rekonsiliasi*, ed. Baskara T. Wardaya (Yogyakarta: Galang Press, 2014), 273–347; Asvi Warman Adam, "Pelanggaran HAM Berat Soeharto: Kasus Pulau Buru," in *Luka Bangsa Luka Kita: Pelanggaran HAM Masa Lalu dan Tawaran Rekonsiliasi*, ed. Baskara T. Wardaya (Yogyakarta: Galang Press, 2014), 349–59; I. G. Krisnadi, "Tahanan Politik Orde Baru di Pulau Buru 1969–1979," *Sejarah: Pemikiran, Rekonstruksi, Persepsi* 9 (n.d.): 47–58;

Sindhunata Hargyono, "Buru Island: A Prism of the Indonesian New Order," draft paper, Northwestern University, 2016.

84. The official Kopkamtib figure for 1976 was 11,085 detainees; Amnesty International estimated that the number was "about 14,000." Amnesty International, *Amnesty International Report*, 91.

85. Ibid., 95. In October 1972, for example, the attorney general said that the legal basis for sending political detainees to Buru was Kopkamtib Regulation No. 5 of 1969, which authorized the attorney general to "detain and exile prisoners considered to be disturbing society, without any limit of time and place." Cited in van der Kroef, "Indonesia's Political Prisoners," 631.

86. Cited in Krisnadi, "Tahanan Politik," 65.

87. Pramoedya claimed that those detained by the Dutch in Boven Digul were treated far better than those on Buru. The more apt comparison, he suggested, were Japanese, German, and Soviet death camps. Pramoedya, *Mute's Soliloquy*, 39, 25. Likewise, a former Buru prisoner, Leo, has written that the experience on Buru "was like the *romusha* [forced labor] during the Japanese occupation ... when people died with no rituals to mark their passing." Cited in Sukanta, *Breaking the Silence*, 72. Another former Buru prisoner, Setiawan, has written that Buru was "inspired" by Boven Digul, but that in almost every respect, it was far worse. See Setiawan, *Aku Eks Tapol*, 149–53.

88. These conditions are recounted in rich detail in the memoirs and accounts of former Buru detainees. See, for example, Pramoedya, *Mute's Soliloquy*; Setiawan, *Aku Eks Tapol*; H. Suparman, *Dari Pulau Buru Sampai ke Mekah: Sebuah Catatan Tragedi 1965* (Bandung: Nuansa, 2006); Wardaya, *Truth Will Out*, 92, 99–120, 123; Sukanta, *Breaking the Silence*, 72–77, 137–41.

89. On the program of forced labor and the regime's attempts to justify it, see Amnesty International, *Amnesty International Report*, 96–97.

90. For examples of such punishments, see Pramoedya, *Mute's Soliloquy*, 26, 38, 40, 43–45.

91. Ibid., 38.

92. Ibid., 46.

93. Setiawan, *Aku Eks Tapol*, 155–56. See also ibid., vi–vii, 183–84.

94. Being given permission to write in 1973, after being forbidden to do so for many years, offered Pramoedya a way back from the abyss: "Eventually, through this exercise, I rediscovered myself as an Indonesian, a person of respect, living and operating with a sense of values ... not powerless but, in fact, equipped with the will to define his own course in history." Pramoedya, *Mute's Soliloquy*, 36.

95. As Pramoedya writes, for example, "Four years of detention and uncertainty of my future had inflicted severe mental damage indeed." Ibid., 35.

96. On the problem of depression and suicide, see the accounts of former Buru prisoners in Sukanta, *Breaking the Silence*, 141; Wardaya, *Truth Will Out*, 117.

97. Sumiyarsi, *Plantungan*, 144–45. According to van der Kroef, mail privileges were suspended in May 1971 on the pretext that some Buru prisoners had been trying to contact the PKI underground in Java. Van der Kroef, "Indonesia's Political Prisoners," 645.

98. Cited in ibid., 645.

99. Setiawan, *Aku Eks Tapol*, x.

100. The documentary was *Blok aan het Ben, een Gevangenis in Indonesië*, which aired on the Dutch television show *Achter het Nieuws* in 1969.

101. Notably, however, some detainees found the program of religious instruction and worship to be oppressive. See, for example, Setiawan, *Aku Eks Tapol*, 43–63.

102. See Laurie J. Sears, *Situated Testimonies: Dread and Enchantment in an Indonesian Literary Archive* (Honolulu: University of Hawaii Press, 2013), 162–65. Even after the ban, students continued to sell the books, and as described in chapter 9, some of those students were themselves arrested and jailed.

103. Cited in Amnesty International, *Amnesty International Report*, 101.

104. *Newsweek*, February 14, 1972, cited in ibid., 97.

105. For accounts of ICRC visits, see Suparman, *Dari Pulau Buru*; Pramoedya, *Mute's Soliloquy*; Setiawan, *Aku Eks Tapol*; Amnesty International, *Amnesty International Report*, 71–74; Sukanto, *Breaking the Silence*, 73, 75; Wardaya, *Truth Will Out*, 118.

106. Sukanto, *Breaking the Silence*, 73, 75; Sumiyarsi, *Plantungan*, 140–42, 153.

107. Cited in Sukanta, *Breaking the Silence*, 75.

108. For a detailed account of this visit, see Pramoedya, *Mute's Soliloquy*, 46–64.

109. Cited in McBeth, "Prisoners of History," 27–28.

Chapter Nine: Release, Restrict, Discipline, and Punish

1. Benedict Anderson, "Seperti Minum Air Pegunungan," preface to Tan Swie Ling, *G30S 1965, Perang Dingin dan Kehancuran Nasionalisme: Pemikiran Cina Jelata Korban Orba* (Jakarta: Komunitas Bambu, 2010), xvii.

2. For a summary of Amnesty International's campaigning activities at this time, see Amnesty International, *Indonesia: An Amnesty International Report* (London: Amnesty International Publications, 1977), 144–46.

3. Moyn has made a largely convincing case that the 1970s marked a crucial turning point in the history of human rights. Samuel Moyn, *The Last Utopia: Human Rights in History* (Cambridge, MA: Harvard University Press, 2012).

4. During this period, for example, Indonesia's delegates to the annual meetings of the ILO in Geneva were routinely pressed to answer charges that political prisoners on Buru and elsewhere were subjected to forced labor. See "Statement of the Government Delegate of Indonesia," ILO meeting, Geneva, June 16, 1976.

5. The Carter administration's record in defending and promoting human rights did not always match its rhetoric. Notably, it turned a blind eye to widespread violations of human rights, possibly amounting to genocide, by Indonesian forces in East Timor.

6. The hearings were conducted in May 1976 by the Subcommittee on International Organizations of the House Committee on International Relations. Those invited to testify at the hearings included known critics of Indonesia's New Order, Professor Benedict Anderson of Cornell University, and Amnesty International.

7. H. Suparman, *Dari Pulau Buru Sampai ke Mekah: Sebuah Catatan Tragedi 1965* (Bandung: Nuansa, 2006), 243.

8. "A Call to Respect Human Rights," reprinted in *Indonesian News Selections: Bulletin of the Indonesian Action Group* (Australia) 4 (August 1977): 9–12.

9. DOS Memo, "Indonesia," [1976], US *Declassified Documents Catalog* [*DDC*], 1994, #2515. This document appears to have been prepared in connection with the congressional hearings on the question of human rights in Indonesia in May 1976. For a scathing critique of the department's testimony at those hearings, see Benedict R. O'G. Anderson, "Prepared Testimony on Human Rights in Indonesia," in *Human Rights in Indonesia and the Philippines* (Washington, DC: US Government Printing Office, 1976, hearings before the Subcommittee on International Organizations of the Committee on International Relations, House of Representatives, 94th Congress, December 18, 1975, and May 3, 1976), 72–80.

10. I. G. Krisnadi, "Tahanan Politik Orde Baru di Pulau Buru 1969–1979," *Sejarah: Pemikiran, Rekonstruksi, Persepsi* 9 (n.d.): 56.

11. On the Pertamina crisis, see Hamish McDonald, *Suharto's Indonesia* (Sydney: Fontana, 1981), 159–64.

12. Nugroho Notosusanto and Ismail Saleh, *The Coup Attempt of the "September 30 Movement" in Indonesia* (Jakarta: Pembimbing Massa, 1968). The official Indonesian-language version was not published until 1989. Nugroho Notosusanto and Ismail Saleh, *Tragedi Nasional Percobaan Kup G30S / PKI di Indonesia* (Jakarta: PT Intermasa, 1989).

13. Notosusanto and Saleh, *Coup Attempt*, ii–iii.

14. After a private meeting with Admiral Sudomo in mid-1976, a member of a Dutch church delegation wrote, "I may be wrong, but he seemed to be much more sensitive to world opinion than I had expected." Confidential Memo on "Political Prisoners," July 30, 1976, by J. Bos, General Manager, ICCO, Netherlands.

15. For international critiques of the political trials, see Amnesty International, *Amnesty International Report*, 45–54; Anderson, "Prepared Testimony on Human Rights in Indonesia," 9–10.

16. See Anderson, "Prepared Testimony on Human Rights in Indonesia."

17. "Statement of the Government Delegate of Indonesia," ILO meeting, Geneva, June 16, 1976, 3.

18. References to the "latent danger of Communism" appeared with some frequency in internal army documents starting in the late 1960s. See, for example, Kopkamtib, Team Pemeriksa Pusat, *Partai Komunis Indonesia dan G.30.S / PKI* (Djakarta, April 1969).

19. Cited in Amnesty International, *Amnesty International Report*, 95–96.

20. Anderson, "Prepared Testimony on Human Rights in Indonesia."

21. Amnesty International, *Amnesty International Report*, 115.

22. *ICJ Review*, no. 17, December 1976. More charitably, van der Kroef has suggested that by this time, foreign pressure was leading to some positive changes in government policy: "The Suharto regime, partly because of persistent probing by Amnesty International, the open criticism of Djakarta's prisoner policies by a few governments . . . and unfavorable publicity by private British, American and other foreign . . . campaigns, has moved in recent years to improve prison conditions and accelerate the release of 'C' category detainees." Justus M. van der Kroef, "Indonesia's Political Prisoners," *Pacific Affairs* 49 (1976): 646.

23. "Press Statement of the Kopkamtib Commander," December 1, 1976, reprinted in Amnesty International, *Amnesty International Report*, 121–23.

24. The construction of additional camps was reported in the Indonesian press around this time. One of these, described as a "New Buru," was set up in South Barito, Central Kalimantan, to house category A and B prisoners. *Kompas*, June 20, 1977. For a critique of the army's proposal, see Amnesty International, *Amnesty International Report*, 34, 100. For a somewhat more sympathetic account of the proposed program, see David Jenkins, "Inside Indonesia's Prisons," *Far Eastern Economic Review* (October 28, 1977): 8–13.

25. Sudomo, for example, expressed that view. Krisnadi, "Tahanan Politik," 54.

26. Department of Foreign Affairs, Republic of Indonesia, *Indonesian Government Policy in Dealing with the G-30-S / PKI (The 30th September Movement of the Indonesian Communist Party) Detainees* (Jakarta: Government Printing Office, January 1978), 17–18.

27. On the ever-changing official numbers and skepticism about them, see Amnesty International, *Amnesty International Report*, 31–44, 113–17; van der Kroef, "Indonesia's Political Prisoners," 626–27, 634–35.

28. Francis J. Galbraith and Martin Ennals, "What Happened in Indonesia? An Exchange," *New York Review of Books*, February 9, 1978.

29. Ibid.

30. Suparman, *Dari Pulau Buru*, 242.

31. Sumiyarsi Siwirini C., *Plantungan: Pembuangan Tapol Perempuan* (Yogyakarta: Pusat Sejarah dan Etika Politik (Pusdep), Universitas Sanata Dharma, 2010), 162.

32. See, for example, "Beberapa Perkembangan, Pemikiran dan Tindakan di Bidang Hak Hak Asasi Manusia 'ET,'" Jakarta, April 14, 1994, n.p.; Hardoyo, "Implikasi Penegasan Pangab Tentang Penghapusan Stigmatisasi 'ET' pada KTP eks-Tapol/ Napol," Jakarta, December 23, 1993, n.p.

33. Cited in Hardoyo, "Bersih Diri dan Bersih Lingkungan Khas Indonesia," April 18, 1990, n.p. On Yap Thiam Hien's life and work, see Daniel Lev, *No Concessions: The Life of Yap Thiam Hien, Indonesian Human Rights Lawyer* (Seattle: University of Washington Press, 2011).

34. Douglas Kammen and Faizah Zakaria, "Detention in Mass Violence: Policy and Practice in Indonesia, 1965–1968," *Critical Asian Studies* 44, no. 3 (2012): 462. In their memoirs, former detainees describe these oath-taking ceremonies with some bitterness. See Sumiyarsi, *Plantungan*, 160; Suparman, *Dari Pulau Buru*, 254.

35. Press Statement of Kopkamtib Chief of Staff, December 1, 1976, reprinted in Amnesty International, *Amnesty International Report*, 121–23.

36. Angkatan Bersendjata Republik Indonesia, "Operasi Ksatria 1974: Langkah Mendasar Untuk Penanggulangan dan Pencegahan Bahaya Latent Subversi Kiri," photocopy, n.d.

37. Presiden Republik Indonesia, *Keputusan Presiden No. 63 / 1985 tentang Tata Cara Penelitian dan Penilaian terhadap Warga Negara Republik Indonesia yang Terlibat G.30.S / PKI yang Dapat Dipertimbangkan Penggunaan Hak Memilihnya dalam Pemilihan Umum.*

38. Richard Tanter, "Intelligence Agencies and Third World Militarization: A Case Study of Indonesia, 1966–1989" (Ph.D. diss., Monash University, 1990), 300n53.

By one count, roughly 40,000 of those reviewed were disenfranchised in the 1987 elections. Liberation, "Intervention on the Question of Indonesia: Item 9 of the Agenda of the UN Sub-Commission on the Prevention of Discrimination and Protection of Minorities," London, August 1988, 2. Likewise, prior to national elections in 1992, the government announced that some 36,345 former PKI prisoners would not be permitted to vote. Amnesty International, *Power and Impunity: Human Rights under the New Order* (London: Amnesty International Publications, 1994), 94.

39. Cited in Putu Oka Sukanta, ed. *Breaking the Silence: Survivors Speak about the 1965–66 Violence in Indonesia*, trans. Jennifer Lindsay (Clayton, Victoria: Monash University Publishing, 2014), 101.

40. See "Oetojo Says Security Checks OK," *Jakarta Post*, January 11, 1995.

41. Tanter, "Intelligence Agencies," 291.

42. Van der Kroef, "Indonesia's Political Prisoners," 637.

43. Ibid.

44. Cited in an ABC broadcast, June 1, 1977, in *Indonesian News Selections: Bulletin of the Indonesian Action Group*, no. 3 (June 1977): 18. In advance of some elections, the army reportedly initiated campaigns encouraging citizens to find PKI symbols and report these to the authorities. Personal communication from Douglas Kammen, January 26, 2017.

45. Cited in "Bakorstanasda Jaya akan Data Ulang Mantan Narapidana," Jakarta, *Neraca*, September 5, 1994.

46. Cited in John McBeth, "Prisoners of History," *Far Eastern Economic Review*, February 16, 1995, 27–28.

47. Cited in Sukanta, *Breaking the Silence*, 79.

48. Ibid., 47.

49. The local authorities entrusted with this task included village and neighborhood Heads, but internal Kopkamtib documents make it clear that they acted under the orders and supervision of army authorities, such as the Koramil commander. See Kopkamtib, Daerah Djawa Timur, "Pokok-Pokok Kebidjaksanaan tentang Penjelesaian Tahanan/Tawanan G-30-S/PKI di Djawa Timur," Surabaya, November 6, 1969.

50. For a commentary on the fate of these exiles, see "Nasib 'ET' dan Anak-anaknya," *Surabaya Post*, April 3, 1995. On the blacklisting of former political detainees and others, see Amnesty International, *Power and Impunity*, 23.

51. These restrictions were spelled out in Kementerian Dalam Negeri, *Instruksi Mendagri No. 32/1981 tentang Pembinaan dan Pengawasan terhadap Eks Tapol/ Napol G30S/PKI.*

52. Tanter, "Intelligence Agencies," 295.

53. Hardoyo, "Bersih Diri," 2. See also Hardoyo, "The Effects of the 'Clean Environment' Campaign in Indonesia," May 1990, 5.

54. For example, see Suparman, *Dari Pulau Buru*, 270–81, 295–317; Marni, "I Am a Leaf in the Storm," trans. Anton Lucas, *Indonesia* 47 (April 1989): 49–60.

55. See Hardoyo, "Effects of the 'Clean Environment' Campaign," 5.

56. Kementerian Dalam Negeri, *Instruksi Mendagri No. 32 / 1981.*

57. Hardoyo, "Bersih Diri."

58. An internal Kopkamtib document summarizing government policy on political prisoners stipulated ominously that their families must be "monitored and guided

so that they do not become the target of G-30-S/PKI elements, and to ensure that they become good citizens (who embrace Pancasila and the 1945 Constitution.)" Kopkamtib, Daerah Djawa Timur, "Pokok-Pokok Kebidjaksanaan tentang Penjelesaian Tahanan."

59. On the emotional and psychological ramifications of the events of 1965 and the stigma, see Robert Lemelson, dir., *40 Years of Silence* (Los Angeles: Elemental Productions, 2009), DVD.

60. On the social stigma and other problems faced by former detainees and their families, see Andrew Marc Conroe, "Generating History: Violence and the Risks of Remembering for Families of Former Political Prisoners in Post–New Order Indonesia" (PhD diss., University of Michigan, 2012); Hardoyo, "Effects of the 'Clean Environment' Campaign"; Annie Pohlman, "A Fragment of a Story: Gerwani and Tapol Experiences," *Intersections: Gender, History, and Culture in the Asian Context* 10 (August 2004), http://intersections.anu.edu.au/issue10/pohlman.html. See also the accounts of former political detainees in Baskara T. Wardaya, ed., *Truth Will Out: Indonesian Accounts of the 1965 Mass Violence*, trans. Jennifer Lindsay (Clayton, Victoria: Monash University Publishing, 2013), 124–28, 136–46, 151–52; Sukanta, *Breaking the Silence*, 94, 105, 112, 121–22, 153–56.

61. For an incisive analysis of that system, see Tanter, "Intelligence Agencies," especially chapter 12.

62. One of the main decrees regulating the screening and removal of former PKI members from government bodies was Presiden Republik Indonesia, *Keputusan Presiden No. 300/1968 tentang Penertiban Personil Aparatur Negara/Pemerintah*. It authorized the powerful state security agency, Kopkamtib, to implement the policy.

63. Van der Kroef, "Indonesia's Political Prisoners," 643.

64. The key regulations before 1990 were Kementerian Dalam Negeri, *Instruksi Mendagri No. 32/1981*; Kopkamtib, *Petunjuk Pelaksanaan Kopkamtib No. JUKLAK 15/KOPKAM/V/1982* [May 27, 1982] *tentang Screening Mental Ideologis terhadap Pelamar untuk Menjadi Pegawai Negeri Sipil Karyawan Instansi Pemerintah/Perusahaan Swasta Vital*. See Hardoyo, "Bersih Diri."

65. See Hardoyo, "Implikasi."

66. "Pertanyaan-Pertanyaan Screening Pegawai Negeri/Swasta yang Masih Bekerja dan yang Akan Masuk (Test)," photocopy, November 1985. As Tanter has shown, the army also used questionnaires like this one as a technique of political surveillance and control in the course of its military campaign in East Timor, during industrial disputes, and in many other contexts. See Tanter, "Intelligence Agencies," 292–94.

67. The new system was spelled out in Presiden Republik Indonesia, *Keputusan Presiden No. 16/1990 tentang Penelitian Khusus Bagi Pegawai Negeri Republik Indonesia*, August 17, 1990. It replaced Presiden Republik Indonesia, *Keputusan Presiden No. 300/1968*. See Bakorstanas, "Coordinating Meeting of Special Review (Litsus) for the Republic of Indonesia Civil Servants, July 19, 1990: Clarification of Presidential Decree No. 16," trans. and reprinted in Asia Watch, "Indonesia: Curbs on Freedom of Opinion," September 4, 1990.

68. A Bakorstanas document explained that "loyalty and obedience" were "an absolute precondition for employment as a civil servant with the Republic of Indonesia,"

and "a special review to identify involvement in G30S/PKI comprises one way to determine the degree of loyalty and obedience." Bakorstanas, "Coordinating Meeting of Special Review," 5.

69. Bakorstanas, "Statement by the Head of the Coordinating Body for Securing National Stability to the Opening of the Coordinating Committee on Departmental and Agency Special Review Units," Jakarta, July 19, 1990, trans. and reproduced in Asia Watch, "Curbs on Freedom of Opinion," September 4, 1990.

70. Bakorstanas, "Coordinating Meeting of Special Review," 4.

71. Ibid., 5.

72. Ibid., 5. Or as General Sutrisno told state officials, "We use the term 'influence' because basically every interaction within the community will result in some degree of influence. No person is immune from the influence of his/her environment." Bakorstanas, "Statement by the Head of the Coordinating Body," 9.

73. On the problems of abuse and corruption in the implementation of political screening, see Hardoyo, "Effects of the 'Clean Environment' Campaign."

74. In 1994, a former political prisoner noted that the regulations on ex-tapols treat "guilt as genetically transmissible" and "revise the notion of collective punishment." Hardoyo, "Time to End the Cold War on Former Political Prisoners," *Inside Indonesia* (March 1994): 14–15. Tanter describes this approach as a "caste theory" in which "guilt spreads over generations and contemporary branches of a family and their affines." Tanter, "Intelligence Agencies," 296.

75. According to one report, in 1988 the coordinating minister for political and security affairs said that there were still some 175,000 category C ex-tapols in the civil service who would soon be dismissed. And in November 1985, some 1,700 oil workers from Caltex, Pertamina, and Tesoro were reportedly dismissed because of alleged family ties to the PKI. Liberation, "Intervention on the Question of Indonesia."

76. See, for example, "Membenahi Beberapa Kendala Pembangunan Hukum Moderen Indonesia Sesuai dengan Jiwa Pancasila/UUD 45," Jakarta, April 1, 1995, n.p. As in these other cases, the preoccupation with policing ideology "reminds us of the importance the Indonesian state places on thought control." Tanter, "Intelligence Agencies," 296.

77. Ariel Heryanto, "Where Communism Never Dies," *International Journal of Cultural Studies* 2, no. 2 (August 1999): 147–77.

78. Benedict Anderson and Ruth McVey, *A Preliminary Analysis of the October 1, 1965 "Coup" in Indonesia* (Ithaca, NY: Cornell Modern Indonesia Project, 1971), 132. Following a research trip to Indonesia in 1974, a group of Dutch physicians wrote about the psychological effects of this portrait and of the events of 1965 themselves: "Apart from the fact that the press cultivates such anxiety, a number of people still have an anxiety psychosis based on the events during the coup." Cited in van der Kroef, "Indonesia's Political Prisoners," 641.

79. Arifin C. Noer, dir., *Pengkhianatan Gerakan 30 September/PKI* (Jakarta: Perum Produksi Film Negara, 1984). *Pengkhianatan* was one of several films produced on the initiative of the "Kopkamtib Film Project," which was established in April 1969. On the New Order's use of film as propaganda and its legacies, see Ariel Heryanto, *Identity and Pleasure: The Politics of Indonesian Screen Culture* (Singapore: NUS Press, 2014), chapters 4–5.

80. All figures cited in Yosef Djakababa, "Narasi Resmi dan Alternatif Mengenai Tragedi '65," in *Luka Bangsa Luka Kita: Pelanggaran HAM Masa Lalu dan Tawaran Rekonsiliasi*, ed. Baskara T. Wardaya (Yogyakarta: Galang Press, 2014), 366. A *Tempo* poll of secondary school students conducted in 2000 found that 90 percent of respondents said they had learned the history of the events of 1965 primarily through film. Heryanto, *Identity and Pleasure*, 82.

81. In the early 2000s, new secondary school texts were introduced that downplayed the anticommunist message somewhat, but these were highly controversial. In 2007, they were banned by the attorney general, and replaced by texts that returned to the old narrative. Ibid., 83.

82. Cited in Joshua Oppenheimer, dir., *The Look of Silence* (Drafthouse Films, 2016).

83. See Katharine McGregor, *History in Uniform: Military Ideology and the Construction of Indonesia's Past* (Honolulu: University of Hawaii Press, 2007); Katharine McGregor, "Memory and Historical Justice for the Victims of Violence in 1965" (paper presented at the conference 1965 Today: Living with the Indonesian Massacres, Amsterdam, October 2, 2015); Djakababa, "Narasi Resmi dan Alternatif," 362.

84. "KSAD: Komunis Harus Tetap Diwaspadai," *Berita Yahoo*, September 30, 2011.

85. On the execution of political prisoners, see Amnesty International, *Indonesia: Four Political Prisoners Executed* (London: Amnesty International, February 1990); Amnesty International, Open Letter to President Suharto, March 9, 1990. For the angry official Indonesian reaction to Amnesty International's intervention, see "Pangab: Indonesia Tidak Mau Didikte," *Kompas*, March 11, 1990.

86. Amnesty International, *Indonesia: The 1965 Prisoners—A Briefing* (London: Amnesty International Publications, 1995).

87. In 1988, for example, two university students were arrested for possessing and distributing copies of literary works by the former Buru detainee Pramoedya. The students, Bambang Subono and Bambang Isti Nugroho, were found guilty of subversion, and sentenced to seven and eight years' imprisonment, respectively. See Amnesty International, *Indonesia: Subversion Trials in Yogyakarta* (London: Amnesty International Publications, 1989).

88. Anderson, "Prepared Testimony on Human Rights in Indonesia," 11.

89. As Heryanto writes, "Even at the height of the New Order's authoritarian rule, one could find audacious dissenting voices from within the population." Heryanto, *Identity and Pleasure*, 106.

90. Sudisman, "Analysis of Responsibility: Defense Speech of Sudisman, General Secretary of the Indonesian Communist Party at His Trial before the Special Military Tribunal, Jakarta, 21 July 1967," trans. Benedict Anderson (Melbourne, Victoria: Works Co-operative, 1975).

91. Cited in *Kompas*, July 28, 1975.

92. See Hardoyo, "Time to End the Cold War on Former Political Prisoners." A few months later, the former head of Kopkamtib, General Sumitro, reportedly said, "I don't see the PKI as a latent threat any more. Let's not keep making scapegoats of them." Cited in *Forum Keadilan*, no. 13–14 (October 1993).

93. *Kompas*, December 14, 1993.

94. The prominent citizens included H. Roeslan Abdulgani, Adnan Buyung Nasution, Franz Magnis Suseno, and T. Mulya Lubis. See "Amnesti, Menyembuhkan Luka Lama," *Surabaya Post*, April 3, 1995.

95. "Ideology Propagator Attacks Policy on Ex-Political Prisoners," *Jakarta Post*, March 15, 1995. Restrictions on the rights of ex-political detainees were the subject of a seminar in Jakarta in early 1995. See "50 Tahun Kemerdekaan RI dan Problem Tapol Napol di Indonesia," Jakarta, January 28, 1995, n.p. For reflections and conclusions from the seminar, see "Membenahi Beberapa Kendala."

96. The relevant decree was rescinded on August 18, 1995.

97. Cited in "Clement Times: Suharto Frees Prisoners, Lightens Coup-Era Blacklist," *Far Eastern Economic Review*, August 24, 1995.

98. Ibid. A high regional official declared that "the ideology of communism cannot be destroyed." Cited in "Membenahi Beberapa Kendala."

Chapter Ten: Truth and Justice?

1. For further details on this incident, see Katharine McGregor, "Mass Graves and Memories of the 1965 Indonesian Killings," in *The Contours of Mass Violence in Indonesia, 1965–68*, ed. Douglas Kammen and Katharine McGregor (Singapore: NUS Press, 2012), 234–62.

2. Mary Zurbuchen, "History, Memory, and the '1965 Incident' in Indonesia," *Asian Survey* 42, no. 4 (2002): 564–81.

3. Ibid., 569.

4. The two key laws were Republik Indonesia, *Undang-Undang Republik Indonesia Nomor 39 Tahun 1999 tentang Hak Asasi Manusia*; Republik Indonesia, *Undang-Undang Republik Indonesia Nomor 26 Tahun 2000 tentang Pengadilan Hak Asasi Manusia.*

5. Zurbuchen, "History, Memory," 571–72.

6. On the origins of the Truth and Reconciliation Commission, see ibid., 574.

7. In early 2000, for example, the commission released a hard-hitting report accusing Indonesian forces of widespread and systematic violations of human rights in East Timor. See Geoffrey Robinson, *"If You Leave Us Here, We Will Die": How Genocide Was Stopped in East Timor* (Princeton, NJ: Princeton University Press, 2010), 206–7.

8. See Komisi Nasional Hak Asasi Manusia (Komnas HAM), "Laporan Akhir Tim Pengkajian Pelanggaran HAM Berat Soeharto (Sub-Tim Pengkajian Kasus 1965)," in *Luka Bangsa Luka Kita: Pelanggaran HAM Masa Lalu dan Tawaran Rekonsiliasi*, ed. Baskara T. Wardaya (Yogyakarta: Galang Press, 2014), 273–47. For an account of the commission's investigation, see Asvi Warman Adam, "Penyelidikan Pelanggaran HAM Berat Soeharto," in *Luka Bangsa Luka Kita: Pelanggaran HAM Masa Lalu dan Tawaran Rekonsiliasi*, ed. Baskara T. Wardaya (Yogyakarta: Galang Press, 2014), 267–71.

9. On the history of the Komnas HAM's work on 1965, see Stanley Adi Prasetyo, "Jangan Biarkan Jalan Itu Kian Menyempit dan Berliku," in *Luka Bangsa Luka Kita: Pelanggaran HAM Masa Lalu dan Tawaran Rekonsiliasi*, ed. Baskara T. Wardaya (Yogyakarta: Galang Press, 2014), 259–65.

10. Komisi Nasional Hak Asasi Manusia (Komnas HAM), *Ringkasan Eksekutif Hasil Penyelidikan Tim Ad Hoc Penyelidikan Pelanggaran HAM yang Berat Peristiwa 1965–1966*, Jakarta, July 23, 2012), in *Luka Bangsa Luka Kita: Pelanggaran HAM Masa Lalu dan Tawaran Rekonsiliasi*, ed. Baskara T. Wardaya (Yogyakarta: Galang Press, 2014), 25–257. See also Komisi Nasional Hak Asasi Manusia (Komnas HAM), "Pernyataan Komnas HAM tentang Hasil Penyelidikan Pelanggaran HAM Berat Peristiwa 1965–1966," Jakarta, July 23, 2012.

11. For an account of the mayor's apology, and the history and work of the group Solidarity with the Victims of Human Rights Violations, see Nurlaela A. K. Lamasitudju, "Rekonsiliasi dan Pernyataan Maaf Pak Wali Kota," in *Luka Bangsa Luka Kita: Pelanggaran HAM Masa Lalu dan Tawaran Rekonsiliasi*, ed. Baskara T. Wardaya (Yogyakarta: Galang Press, 2014), 371–83.

12. See "Indonesia Urged to Hold Truth and Reconciliation Process over Massacres," *Guardian*, April 13, 2016; "HRW Calls on US Government to Reveal Truth about 1965 Massacre," *Jakarta Post*, April 14, 2016; "Pancasila Group Rejects 1965 Tragedy Symposium," *Tempo*, April 17, 2016.

13. "Wiranto Vows to Settle Historic Human Rights Abuses," *Jakarta Post*, September 15, 2016.

14. For a roundup of these nongovernmental initiatives, see Katharine McGregor, "Memory and Historical Justice for the Victims of Violence in 1965" (paper presented at the conference 1965 Today: Living with the Indonesian Massacres, Amsterdam, October 2, 2015); Anett Keller, "How to Deal with the Past? Approaches, Impact, and Challenges of Locally Driven Civil Society Initiatives" (paper presented at the conference 1965 Today: Living with the Indonesian Massacres, Amsterdam, October 2, 2015).

15. Yayasan Penelitian Korban Pembunuhan 1965–1966, accessed November 18, 2015, ypkp65.blogspot.com.

16. Apart from research and advocacy on 1965–66, ELSAM has assisted local groups doing the "work of truth-seeking through personal memory." Zurbuchen, "History, Memory," 578. See ELSAM, accessed November 18, 2015, http://elsam.or.id/beranda/. Over the years Kontras has campaigned actively on a wide range of human rights issues including 1965–66 and curated an exhibition in 2015 called Black September Campaign: Movement to Oppose Indifference. See Kontras, accessed November 18, 2015, http://www.kontras.org. Komnas Perempuan has conducted research into gender-based violence in 1965–66 and worked with other groups to build support systems for the victims of that violence. See Komnas Perempuan, *Kejahatan terhadap Kemanusiaan Berbasis Jender: Mendengarkan Suara Perempuan Korban Peristiwa 1965* (Jakarta: Komnas Perempuan, 2007).

17. The KKPK is a network of forty-seven national and local groups that has conducted hearings on human rights cases, including 1965–66, and published a major report on its findings. See KKPK, *Menemukan Kembali Indonesia*, accessed November 18, 2015, Kkpk.org/category/50-tahun-1965/. Asia Justice and Rights has undertaken human rights–related projects encompassing research, publication, film, and training on various cases, including 1965–66. See Asia Justice and Rights, *Surviving on Their Own: Women's Experiences of War, Peace, and Impunity* (Jakarta: Asia Justice and Rights, 2014); Asia Justice and Rights, *Enduring Impunity: Women Surviving Atrocities in the Absence of Justice* (Jakarta: Asia Justice and Rights, 2015).

18. For example, in its 2016 annual report, Amnesty International highlighted the problem of impunity for the crimes of 1965–66. See "Amnesty Slams RI's Rights Record," *Jakarta Post*, February 25, 2016. And in September 2016, it made all its documentation on 1965 available online. See "Indonesia 1965 Documents," Amnesty International, accessed June 12, 2017, www.indonesia1965.org. Meanwhile, echoing a Komnas HAM request to President Barack Obama, Human Rights Watch urged President Widodo to press the US government to release US documents about 1965–66. See "HRW Calls on US Government to Reveal Truth about 1965 Massacre," *Jakarta Post*, April 14, 2016; "Indonesian Rights Body Urges Obama to Open Secret US Files," *Jakarta Post*, March 11, 2016.

19. See, for example, the joint statement issued by Amnesty International in cooperation with Asia Justice and Rights, ETAN, La'o Hamutuk, Tapol, Watch Indonesia, and Yayasan Hak: "Close Gap between Rhetoric and Reality on 1965 Mass Human Rights Violations," October 1, 2016.

20. According to its organizers, IPT 1965 "was set up in 2013 by a group of victims in exile as well as in Indonesia, and an international group of human rights activists, artists, intellectuals, journalists, and academics. The initiative enjoys the support of a broad range of civil society groups in Indonesia and builds upon their actions in the past 15 years around the crimes [committed] in 1965–66." See International People's Tribunal 1965, accessed June 12, 2017, http://www.tribunal1965.org/en/.

21. IPT 1965 press statement, cited in *Jakarta Post*, November 5, 2015.

22. For a useful summary of the tribunal's proceedings and findings, see Aboeprijadi Santoso and Gerry van Klinken, "Genocide Finally Enters Public Discourse: The International People's Tribunal 1965," in *1965 Today: Living with the Indonesian Massacres*, ed. Martijn Eickhoff, Gerry van Klinken, and Geoffrey Robinson, Special Issue, *Journal of Genocide Research* 19, no. 3 (2017).

23. "Rights Group to Highlight RI Genocide at UN," *Jakarta Post*, September 19, 2016.

24. ELSAM, "Pembongkaran Kuburan Massal Peristiwa 1965 di Dusun Masaen, Jembrana," October 29, 2015.

25. See SKP-HAM, accessed November 18, 2015, www.skp-ham.org.

26. Ibid.

27. Baskara T. Wardaya, "Transitional Justice at the Grass-roots Level: The Case of Sekber '65" (paper presented at the conference 1965 Today: Living with the Indonesian Massacres, Amsterdam, October 2, 2015).

28. See Syarikat, accessed November 4, 2015, http://www.syarikat.org/. A similar spirit of reconciliation has been articulated by other religious figures with an anticommunist past. Franz Magnis-Suseno, a Jesuit scholar who was part of an ardently anticommunist youth group in Central Java in the 1960s, has advocated such an approach. The fact that the PKI was a hated and feared enemy, he has written, "cannot justify the systematic killing and destruction of millions of people who had been attracted to the PKI." Franz Magnis-Suseno, "Membersihkan Dosa Kolektif G30S," *Kompas*, September 29, 2015.

29. Chloe Olliver, "Reconciling NU and the PKI," *Inside Indonesia* (July 2007). See also Ariel Heryanto, *Identity and Pleasure: The Politics of Indonesian Screen Culture* (Singapore: NUS Press, 2014), 87, 97.

30. Ronnie Hatley, "Truth Takes a While, Justice a Little Longer," *Inside Indonesia* 112 (April–June 2013).

31. On the relatively greater influence of such media in Indonesia, see Heryanto, *Identity and Pleasure*, 90–91.

32. "Liputan Khusus: Pengakuan Algojo 1965," *Tempo*, October 1–7, 2012, 1–7, 50–125. Published in English as Kurniawan et al, eds., *The Massacres: Coming to Terms with the Trauma of 1965* (Jakarta: Tempo, 2015).

33. See, for example, Baskara T. Wardaya, *Bung Karno Menggugat! Dari Marhaen, CIA, Pembantaian Massal '65 hingga G30S*, 7th ed. (Yogyakarta: Galang Press, 2009); Baskara T. Wardaya, ed., *Luka Bangsa Luka Kita: Pelanggaran HAM Masa Lalu dan Tawaran Rekonsiliasi.* (Yogyakarta: Galang Press, 2014); Bernd Schaefer and Baskara T. Wardaya, eds., *1965: Indonesia and the World, Indonesia dan Dunia*, bilingual ed. (Jakarta: Gramedia Pustaka Utama, 2013); Baskara T. Wardaya, ed., *Truth Will Out: Indonesian Accounts of the 1965 Mass Violence*, trans. Jennifer Lindsay (Clayton, Victoria: Monash University Publishing, 2013).

34. Asvi Warman Adam, *1965: Orang-Orang di Balik Tragedi* (Yogyakarta: Galang Press, 2009).

35. See, for example, John Roosa, Ayu Ratih, and Hilmar Farid, eds., *Tahun yang Tak Pernah Berakhir: Pengalaman Korban 1965: Esai-Esai Sejarah Lisan* (Jakarta: Elsam, 2004); Hilmar Farid, "Indonesia's Original Sin: Mass Killings and Capitalist Expansion, 1965–66." *Inter-Asia Cultural Studies* 6, no. 1 (2005): 3–16.

36. Hermawan Sulistiyo, "The Forgotten Years: The Missing History of Indonesia's Mass Slaughter" (PhD diss., Arizona State University, 1997); Iwan Gardono Sudjatmiko, "The Destruction of the Indonesian Communist Party: A Comparative Analysis of East Java and Bali" (PhD diss., Harvard University, 1992); Yosef Djakababa, "The Construction of History under Indonesia's New Order: The Making of the Lubang Buaya Official Narrative" (PhD diss., University of Wisconsin at Madison, 2009).

37. Soebandrio, *Kesaksianku tentang G-30-S* (Jakarta: Forum Pendukung Reformasi Total, 2000); Sulami, *Perempuan—Kebenaran dan Penjara* (Jakarta: Cipta Lestari, 1999); Pramoedya Ananta Toer, *The Mute's Soliloquy: A Memoir*, trans. Willem Samuels. (New York: Hyperion East, 1999).

38. Zurbuchen, "History, Memory," 577. Pramoedya had not been permitted to travel abroad for some forty years. See "Pramoedya Ke Luar Negeri," *Tempo*, April 5, 1999; James Rush, "Pramoedya Ananta Toer," *The Ramon Magsaysay Awards* (Manila: Ramon Magsaysay Foundation, 2003), 12:229–53.

39. Some notable examples include Hersri Setiawan, *Aku Eks Tapol* (Yogyakarta: Galang Press, 2003); Tan Swie Ling, *G30S 1965, Perang Dingin dan Kehancuran Nasionalisme: Pemikiran Cina Jelata Korban Orba* (Jakarta: Komunitas Bambu, 2010); H. Suparman, *Dari Pulau Buru Sampai ke Mekah: Sebuah Catatan Tragedi 1965* (Bandung: Nuansa, 2006); Sumiyarsi Siwirini C., *Plantungan: Pembuangan Tapol Perempuan* (Yogyakarta: Pusat Sejarah dan Etika Politik (Pusdep), Universitas Sanata Dharma, 2010).

40. See, for example, Agus Sunyoto, Miftahul Ulum, H. Abu Muslih, and Imam Kusnin Ahmad, *Banser Berjihad Menumpas PKI* (Tulungagung: Lembaga Kajian dan Pengembangan Pimpinan Wilayah Gerakan Pemuda Ansor Jawa Timur and

Pesulukan Thoriqoh Agung Tulungagung, 1996); Tim PBNU, *Benturan NU-PKI, 1948–1965* (Jakarta, 2013).

41. Important examples include Wardaya, *Truth Will Out*; Putu Oka Sukanta, ed., *Breaking the Silence: Survivors Speak about the 1965–66 Violence in Indonesia*, trans. Jennifer Lindsay (Clayton, Victoria: Monash University Publishing, 2014); Mery Kolimon, Liliya Wetangterah, and Karen Campbell-Nelson, eds., *Forbidden Memories: Women's Experiences of 1965 in Eastern Indonesia*, trans. Jennifer Lindsay (Clayton, Victoria: Monash University Publishing, 2015); Kurniawan et al., *Massacres*; Roosa, Ratih, and Farid, *Tahun Yang Tak Pernah Berakhir*.

42. "Agatha Sumarni," cited in Wardaya, *Truth Will Out*, 152. Likewise, a survivor from Bali explained, "When I talk to someone and someone writes down my story, this is a victory for me. A victory that I am no longer silenced and can speak about things as they really are." I Ketut Sumarta, cited in Sukanta, *Breaking the Silence*, 48.

43. In 2016, the Komnas HAM called for a revision of official school texts: "We can't depend on the version of history that was provided by the New Order government." See "Rights Body Calls for Revision of History Books," *Jakarta Post*, March 31, 2016.

44. Sara Schonhardt, "Veil of Silence Lifted in Indonesia," *New York Times*, January 18, 2012.

45. "High School Teacher Introduces Alternative Narratives on 1965 Tragedy," *Jakarta Post*, April 17, 2016.

46. Others who have made important contributions include Eka Kurniawan, whose historial fiction has been compared to that of Pramoedya, and Ayu Utami, whose novels *Saman* (1998) and *Maya* (2013) offer stinging critiques of the New Order regime that emerged from the events of 1965–66.

47. Leila S. Chudori, *Pulang* (Jakarta: Kepustakaan Populer Gramedia, 2012).

48. Laksmi Pamuntjak, *Amba* (Jakarta: Gramedia Pustaka Utama, 2012).

49. These authors have challenged orthodoxies in other ways as well. Pamuntjak, for example, has written many opinion pieces that are openly critical of official government accounts. See Laksmi Pamuntjak, "Censorship Is Returning to Indonesia in the Name of the 1965 Purges," *Guardian*, October 27, 2015.

50. Chudori, Pamuntjak, and Utami were all special guests at the 2015 Frankfurt Book Fair, where their works were met with wide acclaim. Alex Flor, "In the Spotlight," *Watch Indonesia*, October 28, 2015.

51. For a review of some of these initiatives, see Keller, "How to Deal with the Past?" See also Anett Keller, *Indonesien 1965ff. Die Gegenwart eines Massenmordes. Ein Politische Lesebuch.* (Berlin: Regiospectra, 2015); Indonesien 1965ff, accessed June 13, 2017, http://indonesien1965ff.de/.

52. See Viola Lasamana, "Remixing Archives of Injustice and Genocide" (paper presented at the conference Memory, Media, and Technology: Exploring the Trajectories of Schindler's List, USC Shoah Foundation, Los Angeles, November 16–18, 2014.

53. Komunitas Taman 65, *Melawan Lupa: Narasi2 Komunitas Taman 65* (Denpasar: Taman 65 Press, 2012).

54. The CD was launched at Goethe Haus in Jakarta on August 21, 2015. See "Prison Songs," *Kompas*, August 22, 2015.

55. For a brief history of the song *Genjer-Genjer* and its banning, see Setiawan, *Aku Eks Tapol*, 203–16.

56. For Suryani's beautiful rendering of *Genjer-Genjer*, see https://www.youtube.com/watch?v=nof35Gjdusw. The song has also been used in a number of documentary and feature films about the events of 1965–66, including *40 Years of Silence*, *Putih Abu-Abu*, and *Gie*. For a discussion of the use of the song by the Indonesian Left since the fall of the New Order, see Heryanto, *Identity and Pleasure*, 85–86.

57. "The Act of Singing," *Exberliner*, August 24, 2015. For Simatupang's version of *Genjer-Genjer*, see https://www.youtube.com/watch?v=q8io8pd-NNQ.

58. On the role and significance of film in the post–New Order period, see Heryanto, *Identity and Pleasure*, chapters 4–5. Although Heryanto argues that younger Indonesians are generally not interested in the subject of 1965–66, he makes the case that film and other visual media have been more influential among them than works in print. Ibid., 91, 111, 117.

59. *Sang Penari* (Isfansyah, 2011) is based on Ahmad Tohari's trilogy *Ronggeng Dukuh Paruk*, published in the 1980s. Ifa Isfansyah, dir., *Sang Penari* (Jakarta: Salto Films, 2011), DVD. On *Sang Penari*, see Heryanto, *Identity and Pleasure*, 101–2. Another fictional film of note is the 1999 *Puisi Tak Terkuburkan*, directed by Garin Nugroho.

60. Syarikat also produced a short fiction film in 2007, *Sinengker: Sesuatu yang Dirahasiakan*.

61. On LKK and its films, see Heryanto, *Identity and Pleasure*, 94.

62. On *Mass Grave*, see Heryanto, *Identity and Pleasure*, 102–3. On *Tjidurian 19*, see ibid., 111–17. On *Buru Island My Homeland* and *On the Origin of Fear*, see "More Films on the Indonesian Tragedy," *Jakarta Post*, September 11, 2016.

63. As Heryanto writes, "More than about what happened in 1965–66, [*The Act of Killing*] is about present-day Indonesia, how the past was remembered in the present by some of the . . . executioners, and how these killers wished the world to remember them." Heryanto, *Identity and Pleasure*, 123.

64. For an extended reflection on the unique significance and qualities of *The Act of Killing*, see ibid., 118–32.

65. For details on public reaction to the screening of both films, see Joshua Oppenheimer, "The Release of *The Look of Silence* in Indonesia," press materials, Drafthouse Films and Participant Media, accessed June 13, 2017, http://thelookofsilence.com/press.

66. Zurbuchen noted in 2002, for example, that while Bakorstanas and the litsus regime were both closed down in March 2000, "regulations are still on the books that require former political prisoners to report to local authorities regularly and restrict their employment opportunities and civil rights. In some parts of Indonesia, these policies are still strongly applied." Zurbuchen, "History, Memory," 577n33.

67. The full title of Law No. 27/1999 is *Undang-Undang Nomor 27 Tahun 1999 tentang Perubahan Kitab Undang-Undang Hukum Pidana yang Berkaitan dengan Kejahatan Terhadap Keamanan Negara*, May 19, 1999.

68. Zurbuchen, "History, Memory," 572.

69. The operative regulations were Kementerian Pendidikan, *Peraturan Menteri Pendidikan Nasional Nos. 22/23/24, 2006*. In seeking to explain the new regulations,

the minister reportedly invoked MPRS Resolution XXV/1966. See Adam, *1965: Orang-Orang di Balik Tragedi*, 4–5. See also Schonhardt, "Veil of Silence Lifted in Indonesia."

70. John Roosa, "The September 30th Movement: The Aporias of the Official Narratives," in *The Contours of Mass Violence in Indonesia, 1965–68*, ed. Douglas Kammen and Katharine McGregor (Singapore: NUS Press, 2012), 26.

71. The attorney general's office banned the book in December 2009, but refused to disclose the reasons other than saying it contained 143 objectionable passages. Ibid., 49.

72. In October 2010, the Constitutional Court struck down a forty-seven-year-old law that had allowed the attorney general's office to unilaterally ban books. For details, see Lawan Pelarangan Buku, accessed December 21, 2015, http://lawanpelaranganbuku.blogspot.com/.

73. Hatley, "Truth Takes a While, Justice Even Longer."

74. According to a member of the Komnas HAM, that meeting marked a turning point in the president's position: "It was as though the voices of the victims and the members of the President's Advisory Council which until then the President had appeared ready to accommodate, were suddenly buried." Prasetyo, "Jangan Biarkan," 265.

75. Notably, the NU-affiliated NGO Syarikat accepted the Komas HAM report, and called for a presidential apology and community reconciliation. Its stance reflected a significant split within the NU between those who continued to support the military and those who sided with Wahid.

76. A member of the Komnas HAM described the attorney general's reasons for rejecting the report as "tired clichés." Ibid.

77. "PKI Purge Not a Gross Violation of Human Rights, Says AGO," *Jakarta Post*, November 11, 2012.

78. Prasetyo, "Jangan Biarkan," 265.

79. Cited in "No Justice in Sight for Rights Abuse Victims as President Touts Reconciliation over Prosecution," *Jakarta Globe*, August 14, 2015.

80. "Reconciliation Not Enough to Address the Painful Past: Activists," *Jakarta Globe*, August 23, 2015.

81. On the decision to ditch the Truth and Reconciliation Commission and establish a Reconciliation Committee, see Johannes Nugroho, "Indonesia Can Learn from Timor Leste on Human Rights," *Jakarta Globe*, July 21, 2015.

82. On the problem of justice and reconciliation in East Timor, see Robinson, *"If You Leave Us Here, We Will Die,"* chapter 10.

83. On Wiranto's indictment, see ibid., 212–14.

84. See, for example, "Government to Settle Past Human Rights Violations via a Non-Judicial Mechanism," *Jakarta Globe*, October 6, 2016.

85. Ibid.

86. According to one account, the task force was to include representatives from the attorney general's office, the national police, legal experts, the Komnas HAM, and unspecified public representatives. "Government to Form Task Force on Human Rights Abuses during 1965 Purge: Minister," *Jakarta Globe*, October 1, 2016.

87. Speaking in February 2017, for example, the commission's chair said, "Reconciliation has to meet some minimum conditions, such as truth finding, apologies,

acknowledgment of the violence that happened, rehabilitation of the victims and the relatives, and the guarantee of nonrecurrence." *Kompas*, February 6, 2017. See also "Mechanisms to Resolve Past Human Rights Abuses Remain in Place: State Commissioners," *Jakarta Globe*, February 2, 2017.

88. "Government to Form Task Force on Human Rights Abuses during 1965 Purge: Minister," *Jakarta Globe*, October 1, 2016. Writing in early 2017, Santoso and van Klinken noted that "Wiranto's initiatives virtually smothered any hopes victims might have had that the 1965 issue could be resolved judicially or perhaps by means of a presidential commission to investigate the events and rehabilitate the victims." Santoso and van Klinken, "Genocide Finally Enters Public Discourse."

89. "Apology for PKI: Sorry Is Not the Point," *Jakarta Post*, August 28, 2015.

90. "Menhan sebut PKI sudah bunuh 7 jenderal, permintaan maaf tak perlu," Merdeka.com, accessed August 19, 2015, http://www.merdeka.com/peristiwa/menhan-sebut-pki-sudah-bunuh-7-jenderal-permintaan-maaf-tak-perlu.html.

91. Ibid.

92. Cited in Jon Emont, "The Propaganda Precursor to 'The Act of Killing,'" *New Yorker*, October 24, 2015. And in November 2015, Vice President Jusuf Kalla said, "The first victims were our generals. They [the killers of our generals] should ask forgiveness from us." See "Kalla: Pemertintah Tidak Akan Minta Maaf untuk Kasus HAM 1965," *Kompas*, November 11, 2015.

93. "Apology for PKI: Sorry Is Not the Point," *Jakarta Post*, August 28, 2015.

94. For these and other official reactions to the IPT 1965, see Santoso and van Klinken, "Genocide Finally Enters Public Discourse."

95. On the "anti-PKI" symposium, see ibid.

96. Pengurus Besar Himpunan Mahasiswa Islam (PBHMI), "Awas Bahaya Laten Komunis," Jakarta, September 2006, reprinted in H. Firos Fauzan, *Pengkhianatan Biro Khusus PKI: Pelurusan Sejarah Tragedi Nasional 1 Oktober 1965*, 6th ed. (Jakarta: n.p., 2009), 172–73.

97. See Permak, "Organisasi Pendukung," n.d., reprinted in H. Firos Fauzan, *Pengkhianatan Biro Khusus PKI: Pelurusan Sejarah Tragedi Nasional 1 Oktober 1965*, 6th ed. (Jakarta: n.p., 2009), 183.

98. Dahlia G. Setiyawan, "The Cold War in the City of Heroes: U.S.-Indonesian Relations and Anti-Communist Operations in Surabaya, 1963–1965" (PhD diss., University of California at Los Angeles, 2014), 254.

99. See Permak, "Organisasi Pendukung."

100. Permak, "Pernyataan Sikap Terhadap Rencana Pengungkapan Pelanggaran HAM 1965," Jakarta, April 1, 2008, reprinted in H. Firos Fauzan, *Pengkhianatan Biro Khusus PKI: Pelurusan Sejarah Tragedi Nasional 1 Oktober 1965*, 6th ed. (Jakarta: n.p., 2009), 180–82.

101. Forum Komunikasi Purnawirawan TNI–POLRI, "Pernyataan Sikap," Jakarta, April 24, 2008, reprinted in H. Firos Fauzan, *Pengkhianatan Biro Khusus PKI: Pelurusan Sejarah Tragedi Nasional 1 Oktober 1965*, 6th ed. (Jakarta: n.p., 2009), 184–86.

102. GNPI, "Surat No. 011/Sekre/G.Patriot.Jatim/II/2009 kepada Bapak Kepala Polisi RI," February 2, 2009, reprinted in H. Firos Fauzan, *Pengkhianatan Biro Khusus PKI: Pelurusan Sejarah Tragedi Nasional 1 Oktober 1965*, 6th ed. (Jakarta: n.p., 2009), 189–90.

103. The head of YPKP later lodged a protest against the arrest with the Komnas HAM. According to his account, the group was just about to start its meeting "when three intelligence officers and one uniformed policeman arrived and ordered us to stop the meeting." See "YPKP Adukan Pembubaran Rapat ke Komnas HAM," *Kompas*, February 24, 2009.

104. "PKS Politician Wants 'Traitors' at IPT 1965 to Be Prosecuted," *Jakarta Globe*, November 22, 2015.

105. "Pancasila Front Group Rejects 1965 Tragedy Symposium," *Tempo*, April 17, 2016.

106. In one case, Pemuda Pancasila members stormed a radio station in Bogor because the station's review of *The Act of Killing* had referred to Pemuda Pancasila as "thugs."

107. Indonesian officials expressed their hostility to the films in other ways as well. Following the announcement that *The Act of Killing* had been nominated for an Academy Award in 2014, a presidential spokesperson warned that Indonesia would not be "pushed around by outside parties" to rush reconciliation. Josua Gantan, "Indonesia Reacts to 'Act of Killing' Academy Nomination," *Jakarta Globe*, January 23, 2014.

108. "Indonesia Faces Real Threats on Free Speech Rights," *Jakarta Post*, September 17, 2016.

109. Among the groups involved were the Islamic Defenders Front and Hizbullah Bulan Bintang. See Heryanto, *Identity and Pleasure*, 104.

110. Koalisi Masyarakat Anti Komunis Indonesia, "Latar Belakang Mengapa Produksi Film Lastri Ditolak," Jakarta, November 19, 2008, reprinted in H. Firos, Fauzan, *Pengkhianatan Biro Khusus PKI: Pelurusan Sejarah Tragedi Nasional 1 Oktober 1965*, 6th ed. (Jakarta: n.p., 2009), 198–200.

111. "A Poet Wanted by Mass Organization Pemuda Pancasila for Uploading PKI Photos on Facebook," accessed July 24, 2015, http://www.tribunal1965.org/en/.

112. "Dapat Ancaman FPI, Temu Nasional Korban 65 Dibatalkan," CNN Indonesia, August 6, 2015.

113. "Police Order Recall and Burning of Magazine on 1965 Communist Purge," *Tempo*, October 18, 2015. The issue of the magazine that was ordered burned was No. 3/2015 (October 9, 1965), of which five hundred copies had been printed. See "Student Magazine Withdrawn for Publishing about 1965 Massacre," *Jakarta Post*, October 20, 2015.

114. "1965 Purge Survivor in Search of Father's Grave Gets Deported, Blacklisted," *Jakarta Globe*, October 18, 2015.

115. The event was the Ubud Writers and Readers Festival. The canceled sessions included panels titled "1965, Bearing Witness," "1965, Writing On," and "1965, Bali." The canceled film was Oppenheimer's *The Look of Silence*. For details and commentary, see Ubud Writers and Readers Festival, accessed June 13, 2017, http://www.ubudwritersfestival.com/schedule-changes/. See also "At a Bali Festival, Indonesia Enforces Silence about Its Bloody Past," *New York Times*, November 6, 2015.

116. "Ubud Festival Banned from Discussing 1965 Massacre," *Jakarta Post*, October 23, 2015.

117. "Indonesia Threatens to Shut Down Bali's International Writers Festival," *Sydney Morning Herald*, October 24, 2015.

118. The film was ultimately screened at the offices of the Komas HAM. In February 2016, an arts festival called Left Turn (*Belok Kiri*) had to change venues for similar reasons. "Screening Packed Despite Threats," *Jakarta Post*, March 17, 2016.

119. The report was from the Southeast Asia Freedom of Expression Network. Of the cases of film bannings or disruptions noted, fully half were screenings of the *The Look of Silence*. See "Indonesia Faces Real Threats on Free Speech Rights," *Jakarta Post*, September 17, 2016.

120. Zurbuchen, "History, Memory," 577.

121. Heryanto, *Identity and Pleasure*, 111, 117.

Chapter Eleven: Violence, Legacies, Silence

1. Describing the system of privilege in North Korea, Nathan writes, "Personnel in the middle layers of privilege are afraid to question the system for fear of being demoted to layers suffering greater privation. This system generates an anxious conformity throughout society comparable to that generated by the Gulag in the Soviet Union and race exclusion in Nazi Germany." Andrew J. Nathan, "Who Is Kim Jong-un?" *New York Review of Books*, August 18, 2016.

2. We also know that genocides have often been preceeded by the violent persecution of politically defined enemies, such as German Social Democrats in the 1930s, before attacking racially or religiously defined groups. As Mazower writes, "The task the Nazis set themselves of nullifying the threat from the left—a threat that was seen as more urgent in the early days of the Third Reich than reactions by Jews—was an enormous one that involved targeting very large parts of German society, including millions who had belonged to the social democratic parties. We cannot understand the enormous violence unleashed beginning in the autumn of 1939 against Poles and Jews unless we bear in mind the degree to which the leadership had already sanctioned a brutal sadism—not only against the left but, in 1934, even against its own comrades on the right." Mark Mazower, "The Historian Who Was Not Baffled by the Nazis," *New York Review of Books*, December 22, 2016, 70–72.

3. On the psychological legacies of the violence, see Laurie J. Sears, *Situated Testimonies: Dread and Enchantment in an Indonesian Literary Archive* (Honolulu: University of Hawaii Press, 2013); Ariel Heryanto, *State Terrorism and Political Identity in Indonesia: Fatally Belonging* (New York: Routledge, 2006); Leslie Dwyer and Degung Santikarma, "'When the World Turned to Chaos': 1965 and Its Aftermath in Bali, Indonesia," in *The Specter of Genocide: Mass Murder in Historical Perspective*, ed. Robert Gellately and Ben Kiernan (Cambridge: Cambridge University Press, 2003), 289–305; Robert Lemelson, dir., *40 Years of Silence* (Los Angeles: Elemental Productions, 2009), DVD.

4. Mery Kolimon, cited in Willy van Rooijen, "Murdering Army, Silent Church," *Inside Indonesia* 124 (April–June 2016). Likewise, according to community members, the 2016 exhumation of a mass grave in Bali described in chapter 10 was undertaken to put an end to a troubling series events that had long plagued the community

and were understood to be the result of incorrect burial of the remains. ELSAM, "Pembongkaran Kuburan Massal Peristiwa 1965 di Dusun Masaen, Jembrana," October 29, 2015.

5. Heryanto writes that "the spectacular and rapid process of contemporary Islamization since the final decade of the past century has been made possible by, among other things, the slaughter of the Left." Ariel Heryanto, *Identity and Pleasure: The Politics of Indonesian Screen Culture* (Singapore: NUS Press, 2014), 75. See also Merle C. Ricklefs, *Islamisation and Its Opponents in Java: A Political, Social, Cultural, and Religious History, c. 1930 to the Present* (Honolulu: University of Hawaii Press, 2012).

6. On preman, especially in North Sumatra, see Loren Ryter, "Pemuda Pancasila: The Last Loyalist Free Men of Suharto's Order?," in *Violence and the State in Suharto's Indonesia*, ed. Benedict R. O'G. Anderson (Ithaca, NY: Cornell Southeast Asia Program), 124–55.

7. Cited in Heryanto, *Identity and Pleasure*, 129–30.

8. The National Commission on Violence against Women (Komnas Perempuan) established in 1998, for example, has been energetic in proposing solutions to persistent problems of gender discrimination and violence.

9. Peter Dale Scott, "The United States and the Overthrow of Sukarno, 1965–1967," *Pacific Affairs* 58, no. 2 (Summer 1985): 264.

10. On these features of the New Order state, see Benedict R. O'G. Anderson, ed., *Violence and the State in Suharto's Indonesia* (Ithaca, NY: Cornell Southeast Asia Program, 2001); Robinson, *"If You Leave Us Here, We Will Die": How Genocide Was Stopped in East Timor* (Princeton, NJ: Princeton University Press, 2010), especially chapter 3.

11. On the New Order's human rights record and reputation, see Amnesty International, *Power and Impunity: Human Rights under the New Order* (London: Amnesty International Publications, 1994); Amnesty International, *Indonesia: An Amnesty International Report* (London: Amnesty International Publications, 1977).

12. Mary Zurbuchen, ed., *Beginning to Remember: The Past in the Indonesian Present* (Seattle: University of Washington Press, 2005), 7.

13. Ibid., 6.

14. In March 2017, the US government's National Declassification Center announced that "in response to public comments," it had begun reviewing classified materials from the US Embassy in Jakarta for the period 1963–66. It was unclear, however, whether that process would yield anything new. Notably, there was no sign that the declassification would include files from the CIA or other intelligence agencies. "Declassification of Indonesia Files in Progress," National Declassification Center, March 6, 2017.

15. The collection of documents in question was US Department of State, *Foreign Relations of the United States*, vol. 26, *Indonesia; Malaysia-Singapore, Philippines (1964–66)*. See National Security Archive, "CIA Stalling State Department Histories," July 27, 2001, accessed August 27, 2015, http://nsarchive.gwu.edu/NSAEBB/NSAEBB52/.

16. United Nations, Convention on the Prevention and Punishment of the Crime of Genocide, December 9, 1948, Article II.

BIBLIOGRAPHY

Primary Sources

Angkatan Bersendjata Republik Indonesia. "Operasi Ksatria 1974: Langkah Mendasar Untuk Penanggulangan dan Pencegahan Bahaya Latent Subversi Kiri." Photocopy, n.d.

Anonymous. "Additional Data on Counter-Revolutionary Cruelty in Indonesia, Especially in East Java." In *The Indonesian Killings, 1965–1966: Studies from Java and Bali*, edited by Robert Cribb, 169–76. No. 21. Clayton, Victoria: Monash Papers on Southeast Asia, 1990.

Bakorstanas. "Coordinating Meeting of Special Review (Litsus) for the Republic of Indonesia Civil Servants, July 19, 1990: Clarification of Presidential Decree No. 16." Translated and reproduced in Asia Watch, "Indonesia: Curbs on Freedom of Opinion," September 4, 1990.

——. "Statement by the Head of the Coordinating Body for Securing National Stability to the Opening of the Coordinating Committee on Departmental and Agency Special Review Units." Jakarta, July 19, 1990. Translated and reproduced in Asia Watch, "Curbs on Freedom of Opinion," September 4, 1990.

Budiardjo, Suwondo. "Salemba: Cuplikan Kecil Derita Nasional." Unpublished typescript, 1979.

Departemen Angkatan Darat, Direktorat Kehakiman, Team Pemeriksa Pusat. "Laporan Team." Jakarta, January 19, 1967.

Dinas Sejarah TNI-AD. "Crushing the G30S/PKI in Central Java." In *The Indonesian Killings, 1965–1966: Studies from Java and Bali*, edited by Robert Cribb, 159–67. No. 21. Clayton, Victoria: Monash Papers on Southeast Asia, 1990.

"Gerakan 30 September" Dihadapan Mahmillub, Perkara Dr. Subandrio. Jakarta: Pusat Pendidikan Kehakiman A.D., 1967.

"Gerakan 30 September" Dihadapan Mahmillub, Perkara Njono. Jakarta: Pusat Pendidikan Kehakiman A.D., 1966.

"Gerakan 30 September" Dihadapan Mahmillub, Perkara Untung. Jakarta: Pusat Pendidikan Kehakiman A.D., 1966.

Kementerian Dalam Negeri. *Instruksi Mendagri No. 32/1981 tentang Pembinaan dan Pengawasan terhadap Eks Tapol/Napol G30S/PKI*.

Kementerian Pendidikan. *Peraturan Menteri Pendidikan Nasional Nos. 22/23/24, 2006*.

Komando Operasi Tertinggi (KOTI). Seksi Penerangan. *Tjatatan Kronologis Disekitar Peristiwa "Gerakan 30 September."* Jakarta, October 22, 1965.

——. *Fact Finding Commission Komando Operasi Tertinggi*. Jakarta, January 10, 1966.

Komisi Nasional Hak Asasi Manusia (Komnas HAM). "Pernyataan Komnas HAM tentang Hasil Penyelidikan Pelanggaran HAM Berat Peristiwa 1965–1966." Jakarta, July 23, 2012.

———. "Laporan Akhir Tim Pengkajian Pelanggaran HAM Berat Soeharto (Sub-Tim Pengkajian Kasus 1965)." In *Luka Bangsa Luka Kita: Pelanggaran HAM Masa Lalu dan Tawaran Rekonsiliasi*, edited by Baskara T. Wardaya, 273–347. Yogyakarta: Galang Press, 2014.

———. *Ringkasan Eksekutif Hasil Penyelidikan Tim Ad Hoc Penyelidikan Pelanggaran HAM yang Berat Peristiwa 1965–1966*. Jakarta, July 23, 2012. In *Luka Bangsa Luka Kita: Pelanggaran HAM Masa Lalu dan Tawaran Rekonsiliasi*, edited by Baskara T. Wardaya, 25–257. Yogyakarta: Galang Press, 2014.

Kopkamtib. *KEP-028/KOPKAM/10/68*, as amended by *KEP 010/KOPKAM/3/1969*.

———. *Petunjuk Pelaksanaan No. PELAK-002/KOPKAM/10/1968 tentang Kebijaksanaan Penyelesaian Tahanan/Tawanan G30S PKI.*

———. *Keputusan Pangkopkamtib No. KEP.06/KOPKAM/XI/1975 tentang Penyempurnaan Ketentuan Tata Cara Pemberian Surat Keterangan Tidak Terlibat G30S.PKI.*

———. *Petunjuk Pelaksanaan Kopkamtib No. JUKLAK 15/KOPKAM/V/1982* [May 27, 1982] *tentang Screening Mental Ideologis terhadap Pelamar untuk Menjadi Pegawai Negeri Sipil Karyawan Instansi Pemerintah/Perusahaan Swasta Vital.*

Kopkamtib, Daerah Djawa Timur. "Pokok-Pokok Kebidjaksanaan tentang Penjelesaian Tahanan/Tawanan G-30-S/PKI di Djawa Timur." Surabaya, November 6, 1969.

Kopkamtib, Team Pemerika Pusat. *Partai Komunis Indonesia dan G.30.S/PKI*. Djakarta, April 1969.

Majelis Permusyawaratan Rakyat Sementara (MPRS) Republik Indonesia. *Ketetapan MPRS Republik Indonesia No: XXV/MPRS/1966 tentang Pembubaran Partai Komunis Indonesia, Pernjataan Sebagai Organisasi Terlarang Diseluruh Wilajah Republik Indonesia bagi Partai Komunis Indonesia dan Larangan Setiap Kegiatan Untuk Menjebarkan Paham atau Adjaran Komunis/Marxisme-Leninisme*. July 5, 1966.

National Security Archive. "CIA Stalling State Department Histories." July 27, 2001, accessed August 27, 2015, http://nsarchive.gwu.edu/NSAEBB/NSAEBB52/.

"Pertanyaan-Pertanyaan Screening Pegawai Negeri/Swasta yang Masih Bekerja dan yang Akan Masuk (Test)." Photocopy, November 1985.

Presiden Republik Indonesia. *Instruksi Presiden/Pangti ABRI/KOTI No. 22/KOTI/1965—Kepada Kompartimen2/Departemen2, Badan2/Lembaga2 Pemerintah—Untuk Laksanakan Penertiban/Pembersihan Personil Sipil dari Oknum "Gerakan 30 September."* Signed on president's behalf by Soeharto (Kepala Staf Komado Operasi Tertinggi/Panglima Operasi Pemulihan Keamanan dan Ketertiban), November 15, 1965.

———. *Keputusan Presiden No. 370/1965 tentang Penunjukan Mahkamah Militer Luar Biasa untuk Perkara G30S/PKI*. December 4, 1965.

———. *Keputusan Presiden/Panglima Tertinggi Angkatan Bersendjata Republik Indonesia/Panglima Besar Komando Operasi Tertinggi (KOTI), No. 179/KOTI/1965*. December 6, 1965.

———. *Instruksi Presiden 09/KOGAM/1966.*

———. *Keputusan Presiden No. 300/1968 tentang Penertiban Personil Aparatur Negara/Pemerintah.*

——. *Keputusan Presiden No. 63/1985 tentang Tata Cara Penelitian dan Penilaian terhadap Warga Negara Republik Indonesia yang Terlibat G.30.S/PKI yang Dapat Dipertimbangkan Penggunaan Hak Memilihnya dalam Pemilihan Umum.*

——. *Keputusan Presiden No. 16/1990 tentang Penelitian Khusus Bagi Pegawai Negeri Republik Indonesia*, August 17, 1990.

Pusat Penerangan Angkatan Darat Republik Indonesia. *Fakta2 Persoalan Sekitar Gerakan 30 September*. Jakarta: Penerbitan Chusus nos. 1, 2, and 3, October–December 1965.

Republik Indonesia. *Undang-Undang Republik Indonesia Nomor 39 Tahun 1999 tentang Hak Asasi Manusia.*

——. *Undang-Undang Republik Indonesia Nomor 26 Tahun 2000 tentang Pengadilan Hak Asasi Manusia.*

Sekretariat Negara Republik Indonesia. *Gerakan 30 September: Pemberontakan Partai Komunis Indonesia. Latar Belakang, Aksi dan Penumpasannya.* Jakarta: Sekretariat Negara Republik Indonesia, 1994.

State Secretariat of the Republic of Indonesia. *The September 30th Movement: The Attempted Coup by the Indonesian Communist Party: Its Background, Actions, and Eradication.* Jakarta, State Secretariat of the Republic of Indonesia, 1994.

United Nations. Convention on the Prevention and Punishment of the Crime of Genocide. December 9, 1948.

US Department of State. *Foreign Relations of the United States* (*FRUS*). Vol. 12, *East Asia and the Pacific (1952–1954).*

——. *Foreign Relations of the United States* (*FRUS*). Vol. 22, *Southeast Asia (1955–1957).*

——. *Foreign Relations of the United States* (*FRUS*). Vol. 23, *Southeast Asia (1961–1963).*

——. *Foreign Relations of the United States* (*FRUS*). Vol. 26, *Indonesia; Malaysia-Singapore; Philippines (1964–66).*

Archival Collections Cited

Declassified Documents Catalog, United States (*DDC*)
Dwight D. Eisenhower Presidential Library
Hoover Institution Archives (Howard P. Jones Papers)
Lyndon Baines Johnson Library (LBJ Library)
National Archives and Records Administration, United States (NARA)
National Archives of Canada
National Archives of Sweden (Riksarkivet)
National Archives of the United Kingdom (UKNA)
Personal archive of George McT. Kahin (Kahin Papers)
Personal archive of Ruth T. McVey (McVey Papers)
Seeley G. Mudd Manuscript Library (Mudd Library)

Secondary Sources

Abdullah, Taufik, Sukri Abdurrachman, and Restu Gunawan, eds. *Malam Bencana 1965 Dalam Belitan Krisis Nasional: Bagian I, Rekonstruksi dalam Perdebatan*. Jakarta: Yayasan Pustaka Obor Indonesia, 2012.

——. *Malam Bencana 1965 Dalam Belitan Krisis Nasional: Bagian II, Konflik Lokal*. Jakarta: Yayasan Pustaka Obor Indonesia, 2012.

Adam, Asvi Warman. *1965: Orang-Orang di Balik Tragedi*. Yogyakarta: Galang Press, 2009.

——. "Pelanggaran HAM Berat Soeharto: Kasus Pulau Buru." In *Luka Bangsa Luka Kita: Pelanggaran HAM Masa Lalu dan Tawaran Rekonsiliasi*, edited by Baskara T. Wardaya, 349–59. Yogyakarta: Galang Press, 2014.

——. "Penyelidikan Pelanggaran HAM Berat Soeharto." In *Luka Bangsa Luka Kita: Pelanggaran HAM Masa Lalu dan Tawaran Rekonsiliasi*, edited by Baskara T. Wardaya, 267–71. Yogyakarta: Galang Press, 2014.

——. "Ben Anderson's Work on Indonesia Challenged Suharto's Military Rule," *Jakarta Globe*, December 18, 2015.

Ahmad, Taufik. "South Sulawesi: The Military, Prison Camps, and Forced Labour." In *The Contours of Mass Violence in Indonesia, 1965–68*, edited by Douglas Kammen and Katharine McGregor, 156–81. Singapore: NUS Press, 2012.

Alfian, M. Alfar. *HMI, 1963–1966: Menegakkan Pancasila di Tengah Prahara*. Jakarta: Kompas, 2013.

Amnesty International. *Indonesia: An Amnesty International Report*. London: Amnesty International Publications, 1977.

——. *Indonesia: Subversion Trials in Yogyakarta*. London: Amnesty International Publications, 1989.

——. *Indonesia: Four Political Prisoners Executed*. London: Amnesty International Publications, February 1990.

——. Open Letter to President Suharto. March 9, 1990.

——. *Power and Impunity: Human Rights under the New Order*. London: Amnesty International Publications, 1994.

——. *Indonesia: The 1965 Prisoners—A Briefing*. London: Amnesty International Publications, 1995.

Anderson, Benedict R. O'G. *Java in a Time of Revolution*. Ithaca, NY: Cornell University Press, 1972.

——. "The Idea of Power in Javanese Culture." In *Culture and Politics in Indonesia*, edited by Claire Holt, Benedict R. Anderson, and James T. Siegel, 1–69. Ithaca, NY: Cornell University Press, 1972.

——. "Prepared Testimony on Human Rights in Indonesia." In *Human Rights in Indonesia and the Philippines*, 72–80. Washington, DC: US Government Printing Office, 1976. Hearings before the Subcommittee on International Organizations of the Committee on International Relations, House of Representatives, 94th Congress, December 18, 1975, and May 3, 1976.

——. "How Did the Generals Die?" *Indonesia* 43 (April 1987): 109–34.

——. "Old State, New Society: Indonesia's New Order in Comparative Historical Perspective." In *Language and Power, Exploring Political Cultures in Indonesia*, edited by Benedict Anderson, 94–120. Ithaca, NY: Cornell University Press, 1990.

——. "Scholarship on Indonesia and Raison d'État: Personal Experience." *Indonesia* 62 (October 1996): 1–18.

——, ed. *Violence and the State in Suharto's Indonesia.* Ithaca, NY: Cornell Southeast Asia Program, 2001.

Anderson, Benedict, and Ruth McVey. *A Preliminary Analysis of the October 1, 1965 "Coup" in Indonesia.* Ithaca, NY: Cornell Modern Indonesia Project, 1971.

——. "What Happened in Indonesia?" *New York Review of Books*, June 1, 1978.

Angkatan Bersendjata Republik Indonesia. *40 Hari Kegagalan G-30-S.* Jakarta: Staf Pertahanan Keamanan, 1966.

Asia Justice and Rights. *Surviving on Their Own: Women's Experiences of War, Peace, and Impunity.* Jakarta: Asia Justice and Rights, 2014.

——. *Enduring Impunity: Women Surviving Atrocities in the Absence of Justice.* Jakarta: Asia Justice and Rights, 2015.

Bartov, Omar. "Seeking the Roots of Modern Genocide: On the Macro- and Microhistory of Mass Murder." In *The Specter of Genocide: Mass Murder in Historical Perspective*, edited by Robert Gellately and Ben Kiernan, 75–96. Cambridge: Cambridge University Press, 2003.

Benda, Harry J. *Crescent and the Rising Sun: Indonesian Islam under the Japanese Occupation.* The Hague: W. van Hoeve, 1958.

"Beberapa Perkembangan, Pemikiran dan Tindakan di Bidang Hak Hak Asasi Manusia 'ET.'" Jakarta, April 14, 1994, n.p.

Bergen, Doris L. *War and Genocide: A Concise History of the Holocaust.* Oxford: Rowman and Littlefield, 2003.

Bloxham, Donald. *The Final Solution: A Genocide* (Oxford: Oxford University Press, 2009).

Boden, Ragna. "Silence in the Slaughterhouse: Moscow and the Indonesian Massacres." In *1965: Indonesia and the World, Indonesia dan Dunia*, edited by Bernd Schaefer and Baskara T. Wardaya, 86–98. Bilingual ed. Jakarta: Gramedia Pustaka Utama, 2013.

Boerhan and Soebekti. *"Gerakan 30 September."* 2nd ed. Jakarta: Lembaga Pendidikan Ilmu Pengetahuan dan Kebudajaan Kosgoro, 1966.

Bourchier, David. "Crime, Law, and State Authority in Indonesia." In *State and Civil Society in Indonesia*, edited by Arief Budiman, 177–211. No. 22. Clayton, Victoria: Monash Papers on Southeast Asia, 1990.

Bowen, John. *Sumatran Politics and Poetics: Gayo History, 1900–1989.* New Haven, CT: Yale University Press, 1991.

Brands, H. W. "The Limits of Manipulation: How the United States Didn't Topple Sukarno." *Journal of American History* 76 (December 1989): 785–808.

Broere, Sebastiaan. "The Gray Area of Indonesian Psychology: The KUN-2 Project, 1968–1976." Draft paper, University of California at Los Angeles, November 2016.

Browning, Christopher R. *Ordinary Men: Reserve Police Battalion 101 and the Final Solution in Poland.* New York: HarperCollins, 1993.

Browning, Christopher, and Jürgen Matthäus. *The Origins of the Final Solution: The Evolution of Nazi Jewish Policy, September 1939–1942*. Lincoln: University of Nebraska Press, 2004.

Budiardjo, Carmel. *Surviving Indonesia's Gulag*. London: Cassell, 1996.

Bunnell, Frederick. "American 'Low Posture' Policy toward Indonesia in the Months Leading up to the 1965 'Coup.'" *Indonesia* 50 (October 1990): 29–60.

Cavoski, Jovan. "On the Road to the Coup: Indonesia between the Non-Aligned Movement and China." In *1965: Indonesia and the World, Indonesia dan Dunia*, edited by Bernd Schaefer and Baskara T. Wardaya, 66–81. Bilingual ed. Jakarta: Gramedia Pustaka Utama, 2013.

Chandler, David. *Voices from S-21: Terror and History in Pol Pot's Secret Prison*. Berkeley: University of California Press, 1999.

Chandra, Siddharth. "New Findings on the Indonesian Killings of 1965–66." *Journal of Asian Studies* 76, no. 4 (November 2017).

Chudori, Leila S. *Pulang*. Jakarta: Kepustakaan Populer Gramedia, 2012.

Colby, William. *Honorable Men: My Life in the CIA*. New York: Simon and Schuster, 1978.

Collins, J. Foster, and B. Hugh Tovar. "Sukarno's Apologists Write Again." *International Journal of Intelligence and Counterintelligence* 9, no. 3 (Fall 1996): 337–57.

Colombijn, Freek, and Thomas Lindblad, eds., *Roots of Violence in Indonesia: Contemporary Violence in Historical Perspective*. Leiden: KITLV Press, 2002.

Conroe, Andrew Marc. "Generating History: Violence and the Risks of Remembering for Families of Former Political Prisoners in Post–New Order Indonesia." PhD diss., University of Michigan, 2012.

Coppel, Charles A. *Indonesian Chinese in Crisis*. Kuala Lumpur: Oxford University Press, 1983.

Cribb, Robert. "Problems in the Historiography of the Killings in Indonesia." In *The Indonesian Killings, 1965–1966: Studies from Java and Bali*, edited by Robert Cribb, 1–44. No. 21. Clayton, Victoria: Monash Papers on Southeast Asia, 1990.

———, ed. *The Indonesian Killings, 1965–1966: Studies from Java and Bali*. No. 21. Clayton, Victoria: Monash Papers on Southeast Asia, 1990.

———. "Genocide in Indonesia, 1965–1966." *Journal of Genocide Research* 3, no. 2 (2001): 219–39.

———. "Unresolved Problems in the Indonesian Killings of 1965–66." *Asian Survey* 42, no. 4 (July–August 2002): 550–63.

———. "The Indonesian Massacres." In *Century of Genocide: Critical Essays and Eyewitness Accounts*, edited by Samuel Totten and William S. Parsons, 234–62. 3rd ed. New York: Routledge, 2009).

———. "Political Genocides in Postcolonial Asia." In *The Oxford Handbook of Genocide Studies*, edited by Donald Bloxham and A. Dirk Moses, 445–65. Oxford: Oxford University Press, 2010.

———. "On Victims Statistics." In *The Massacres: Coming to Terms with the Trauma of 1965*, edited by Kurniawan et al. Jakarta: Tempo, 2015.

Cribb, Robert, and Charles A. Coppel. "A Genocide That Never Was: Explaining the Myth of Anti-Chinese Massacres in Indonesia, 1965–66." *Journal of Genocide Research* 11, no. 4 (December 2009): 447–65.

Crouch, Harold. "Another Look at the Indonesian Coup." *Indonesia* 15 (April 1973): 1–20.

——. *The Army and Politics in Indonesia*. Ithaca, NY: Cornell University Press, 1978.

Curtis, Mark. "Democratic Genocide." *The Ecologist* 26, no. 5 (September–October 1996): 202–04.

Dake, Antonie. *The Sukarno File, 1965–1967: Chronology of a Defeat*. Leiden: Brill, 2006.

Davidson, Jamie, and Douglas Kammen. "Indonesia's Unknown War and the Lineages of Violence in West Kalimantan." *Indonesia* 73 (April 2002): 53–87.

de Bruyne, Marnix. "Hoe Nederlandse psychologen collaboreerden met Soeharto." *Wordt Vervolgd* 12, no. 1 (December 2016–January 2017): 34–35.

Demokrasono, A. Gumelar, and Harsutejo. *Dari Kalong Sampai Pulau Buru: 11 Tahun Dalam Sekapan, Penjara, Pembuangan dan Kerja Rodi (Kisah Tapol Dalam Sketsa)*. Yogyakarta: Pusat Sejarah dan Etika Politik, Universitas Sanata Dharma, 2006.

Department of Foreign Affairs, Republic of Indonesia. *Indonesian Government Policy in Dealing with the G-30-S/PKI (The 30th September Movement of the Indonesian Communist Party) Detainees*. Jakarta: Government Printing Office, 1978.

Djakababa, Yosef. "The Construction of History under Indonesia's New Order: The Making of the Lubang Buaya Official Narrative." PhD diss., University of Wisconsin at Madison, 2009.

——. "Narasi Resmi dan Alternatif Mengenai Tragedi '65." In *Luka Bangsa Luka Kita: Pelanggaran HAM Masa Lalu dan Tawaran Rekonsiliasi*, edited by Baskara T. Wardaya, 361–69. Yogyakarta: Galang Press, 2014.

Djie Siang Lan (Lani Anggawati). *Di Dalam Derita Manusia Membaja*. 2nd ed. Klaten: Wisma Sambodhi, 2004.

Dower, John W. *War without Mercy: Race and Power in the Pacific War*. New York: Random House, 1986.

Dwyer, Leslie. "The Intimacy of Terror: Gender and the Violence of 1965–66 in Bali." *Intersections: Gender, History, and Culture in the Asian Context* 10 (August 2004).

Dwyer, Leslie, and Degung Santikarma. "'When the World Turned to Chaos': 1965 and Its Aftermath in Bali, Indonesia." In *The Specter of Genocide: Mass Murder in Historical Perspective*, edited by Robert Gellately and Ben Kiernan, 289–305. Cambridge: Cambridge University Press, 2003.

Easter, David. "British and Malaysian Covert Support for Rebel Movements in Indonesia During the 'Confrontation,' 1963–1966." *Intelligence and National Security* 14, no. 4 (Winter 1999): 195–208.

Eickhof, Martijn, Donny Danardono, Tjahjono Rahardjo, and Hotmauli Sidabalok. "The Memory Landscapes of '1965' in Semarang," in *1965 Today: Living with the Indonesian Massacres*, edited by Martijn Eickhoff, Gerry van Klinken, and Geoffrey Robinson. Special Issue, *Journal of Genocide Research* 19, no. 3 (2017).

ELSAM. "Pembongkaran Kuburan Massal Peristiwa 1965 di Dusun Masaen, Jembrana." October 29, 2015.

Evans, Bryan, III. "The Influence of the United States Army on the Development of the Indonesian Army (1954–1964)." *Indonesia* 47 (April 1989): 25–48.

Farid, Hilmar. "Indonesia's Original Sin: Mass Killings and Capitalist Expansion, 1965–66." *Inter-Asia Cultural Studies* 6, no. 1 (2005): 3–16.

Farram, Steven. "The PKI in West Timor and Nusa Tenggara Timur, 1965 and Beyond." *Bijdragen tot de Taal-, Land- en Volkenkunde* 166, no. 4 (2010): 381–403.

Fauzan, H. Firos. *Pengkhianatan Biro Khusus PKI: Pelurusan Sejarah Tragedi Nasional 1 Oktober 1965*. 6th ed. Jakarta: n.p., 2009.

Fealy, Greg. *The Release of Indonesia's Political Prisoners: Domestic versus Foreign Policy, 1975–1979*. Working paper no. 94. Clayton, Victoria: Monash Centre for Southeast Asian Studies, 1995.

Fealy, Greg, and Katharine McGregor. "East Java and the Role of Nahdlatul Ulama in the 1965–66 Anti-Communist Violence." In *The Contours of Mass Violence in Indonesia, 1965–68*, edited by Douglas Kammen and Katharine McGregor, 104–30. Singapore: NUS Press, 2012.

Feillard, Andrée. *NU vis-à-vis Negara: Pencarian Isi, Bentuk dan Makna*. Yogkakarta: LKiS, 1999.

Feillard, Andrée, and Rémy Madinier. *The End of Innocence: Indonesian Islam and the Temptation of Radicalism*. Singapore: NUS Press, 2011.

Fein, Helen. *Accounting for Genocide: National Responses and Jewish Victimization during the Holocaust*. Chicago: University of Chicago Press, 1979.

———. "Genocide: A Sociological Perspective." *Current Sociology* 38 (Spring 1990): 1–126.

———. "Revolutionary and Anti-Revolutionary Genocides: A Comparison of State Murders in Democratic Kampuchea, 1975–1979, and in Indonesia, 1965–1966." *Comparative Studies in Society and History* 35, no. 4 (October 1993): 796–823.

Feith, Herbert. *The Indonesian Elections of 1955*. Ithaca, NY: Cornell Modern Indonesia Project, 1957.

———. *The Decline of Constitutional Democracy in Indonesia*. Ithaca, NY: Cornell University Press, 1962.

Fic, Victor. *Anatomy of the Jakarta Coup: October 1, 1965*. New Delhi: Abhinay Publications, 2004.

Field, Thomas C., Jr. *From Development to Dictatorship: Bolivia and the Alliance for Progress in the Kennedy Era*. Ithaca, NY: Cornell University Press, 2014.

"50 Tahun Kemerdekaan RI dan Problem Tapol/Napol di Indonesia." Jakarta, January 28, 1995.

Flor, Alex. "In the Spotlight." *Watch Indonesia*, October 28, 2015.

Friend, Theodore. *Indonesian Destinies*. Cambridge, MA: Harvard University Press, 2003.

Galbraith, Francis J., and Martin Ennals. "What Happened in Indonesia? An Exchange." *New York Review of Books*, February 9, 1978.

Gantan, Josua. "Indonesia Reacts to 'Act of Killing' Academy Nomination." *Jakarta Globe*, January 23, 2014.

Geertz, Clifford. *The Religion of Java*. Glencoe, IL: Free Press, 1960.

Gerlach, Christian. *Extremely Violent Societies: Mass Violence in the Twentieth-Century World*. Cambridge: Cambridge University Press, 2010.

Goscha, Christopher E., and Christian Osterman, eds. *Connecting Histories: Decolonization and the Cold War in Southeast Asia, 1945–1962*. Stanford, CA: Stanford University Press, 2009.

Grandin, Greg. *The Last Colonial Massacre: Latin America in the Cold War*. Updated ed. Chicago: University of Chicago Press, 2011.

Green, Marshall. *Indonesia: Crisis and Transformation, 1965–1968*. Washington, DC: Compass Press, 1990.

Hardoyo. "Bersih Diri dan Bersih Lingkungan Kas Indonesia." April 18, 1990, n.p.

———. "The Effects of the 'Clean Environment' Campaign in Indonesia." May 1990, n.p.

———. "Implikasi Penegasan Pangab Tentang Penghapusan Stigmatisasi 'ET' pada KTP eks-Tapol/Napol." Jakarta, December 23, 1993, n.p.

———. "Time to End the Cold War on Former Political Prisoners." *Inside Indonesia* (March 1994): 14–15.

Hargyono, Sindhunata. "Buru Island: A Prism of the Indonesian New Order." Draft paper, Northwestern University, 2016.

Harmer, Tanya. *Allende's Chile and the Inter-American Cold War*. Chapel Hill: University of North Carolina Press, 2011.

Harvey, Barbara. *Permesta: Half a Rebellion*. Ithaca, NY: Cornell Modern Indonesia Project, 1977.

Hatley, Ronnie. "'Truth Takes a While, Justice Even Longer.'" *Inside Indonesia* 112 (April–June 2013).

Hearman, Vannessa. "The Uses of Memoirs and Oral History Works in Researching the 1965–1966 Political Violence in Indonesia." *International Journal of Asia Pacific Studies* 5, no. 2 (July 2009): 21–42.

———. "Dismantling the Fortress: East Java and the Transition to Suharto's New Order Regime." PhD diss., University of Melbourne, 2012.

Hefner, Robert W. *The Political Economy of Mountain Java: An Interpretive History*. Berkeley: University of California Press, 1990.

Herlina, Nina. "'Tata Sunda' Digonceng Konflik Sosial Politik." In *Malam Bencana 1965 Dalam Belitan Krisis Nasional: Bagian II, Konflik Lokal*, edited by Taufik Abdullah, Sukri Abdurrachman, and Restu Gunawan, 51–78. Jakarta: Yayasan Pustaka Obor Indonesia, 2012.

Heryanto, Ariel. "Where Communism Never Dies." *International Journal of Cultural Studies* 2, no. 2 (August 1999): 147–77.

———. *State Terrorism and Political Identity in Indonesia: Fatally Belonging*. New York: Routledge, 2006.

———. *Identity and Pleasure: The Politics of Indonesian Screen Culture*. Singapore: NUS Press, 2014.

Hinton, Alexander L. "Why Did You Kill? The Cambodian Genocide and the Dark Side of Face and Honor." *Journal of Asian Studies* 57, no. 1 (February 1998): 93–118.

Hoehne, Heinze, and Herman Zolling. *The General Was a Spy*. New York: Bantam, 1972.

Hoek, Anne-Lot. "Wij gaan het hier nog heel moeilijk krijgen." *NRC Weekend*, January 9–10, 2016.

Holtzappel, Coen. "The 30 September Movement: A Political Movement of the Armed Forces or an Intelligence Operation?" *Journal of Contemporary Asia* 9, no. 2 (1979): 216–40.

Howland, Richard Cabot. "The Lessons of the September 30 Affair." *Studies in Intelligence* 14 (Fall 1970): 13–29.

Hughes, John. *Indonesian Upheaval*. New York: David McKay Co., Inc., 1967.

"Indonesia: Vengeance with a Smile." *Time*, July 15, 1966, 22–26.

Isa, Ibrahim. *Bui Tanpa Jerajak Besi: Pikiran Seorang Eksil Indonesia di Luar Negeri*. Jakarta: Klik Books, 2011.

Iskandar, Maskun. "Purwodadi: Area of Death." In *The Indonesian Killings, 1965–1966: Studies from Java and Bali*, edited by Robert Cribb, 203–13. No. 21. Clayton, Victoria: Monash Papers on Southeast Asia, 1990.

International Center for Transitional Justice and Kontras. *Derailed: Transitional Justice in Indonesia since the Fall of Soeharto*. Jakarta: International Center for Transitional Justice and Kontras, March 2011.

Jay, Robert R. *Religion and Politics in Rural Central Java*. New Haven, CT: Yale University Southeast Asia Studies Program, 1963.

Jeffreys-Jones, Rhodri. *The CIA and American Democracy*. New Haven, CT: Yale University Press, 1989.

Jenkins, David. "Inside Suharto's Prisons." *Far Eastern Economic Review* (October 28, 1977): 8–13.

Jenkins, David, and Douglas Kammen. "The Army Para-Commando Regiment and the Reign of Terror in Central Java and Bali." In *The Contours of Mass Violence in Indonesia, 1965–68*, edited by Douglas Kammen and Katharine McGregor, 75–103. Singapore: NUS Press, 2012.

Jetschke, Anja. *Human Rights and State Security: Indonesia and the Philippines*. Philadelphia: University of Pennsylvania Press, 2011.

Jones, Howard P. *Indonesia: The Possible Dream*. New York: Harcourt Brace Jovanovich, 1971.

Kadane, Kathy. "US Officials' Lists Aided Indonesian Bloodbath in '60s." *Washington Post*, May 21, 1990.

———. "Letter to the Editor." *New York Review of Books*, April 10, 1997.

Kahin, George McT. *Nationalism and Revolution in Indonesia*. Ithaca, NY: Cornell University Press, 1952.

———. *The Asian-African Conference, Bandung, Indonesia*. Ithaca, NY: Cornell University Press, 1956.

———. *Southeast Asia: A Testament*. New York: Routledge, 2003.

Kahin, George McT., and Audrey Kahin. *Subversion as Foreign Policy: The Secret Eisenhower and Dulles Debacle in Indonesia*. New York: New Press, 1995.

Kammen, Douglas, and Katharine McGregor, eds. *The Contours of Mass Violence in Indonesia, 1965–68*. Singapore: NUS Press, 2012.

Kammen, Douglas, and Faizah Zakaria. "Detention in Mass Violence: Policy and Practice in Indonesia, 1965–1968." *Critical Asian Studies* 44, no. 3 (2012): 441–66.

Kartika, Dyah Ayu. "The Politicization of Psychology: The Role of Psychologists in Indonesia's Detention Camps During New Order Era." MA thesis, International Institute of Social Studies, 2016.

Keck, Margaret, and Kathryn Sikkink. *Activists beyond Borders: Advocacy Networks in International Politics*. Ithaca, NY: Cornell University Press, 1998.

Keller, Anett. "How to Deal with the Past? Approaches, Impact, and Challenges of Locally Driven Civil Society Initiatives." Paper presented at the conference 1965 Today: Living with the Indonesian Massacres, Amsterdam, October 2, 2015.

———. *Indonesien 1965ff. Die Gegenwart eines Massenmordes. Ein Politische Lesebuch.* Berlin: Regiospectra, 2015.

Kiernan, Ben. "Twentieth Century Genocides: Underlying Ideological Themes from Armenia to East Timor." In *The Specter of Genocide: Mass Murder in Historical Perspective*, edited by Robert Gellately and Ben Kiernan, 29–52. Cambridge: Cambridge University Press, 2003.

Kirk, Donald. "Bali Exorcises an Evil Spirit." *Reporter*, December 15, 1966, 42–53.

Kolimon, Mery, Liliya Wetangterah, and Karen Campbell-Nelson, eds. *Forbidden Memories: Women's Experiences of 1965 in Eastern Indonesia.* Translated by Jennifer Lindsay. Clayton, Victoria: Monash University, 2015.

Komnas Perempuan. *Kejahatan terhadap Kemanusiaan Berbasis Jender: Mendengarkan Suara Perempuan Korban Peristiwa 1965.* Jakarta: Komnas Perempuan, 2007.

Komunitas Taman 65. *Melawan Lupa: Narasi2 Komunitas Taman 65.* Denpasar: Taman 65 Press, 2012.

Krisnadi, I. G. "Tahanan Politik Orde Baru di Pulau Buru 1969–1979." *Sejarah: Pemikiran, Rekonstruksi, Persepsi* 9 (n.d.): 47–58.

Kurniawan, et al., eds. *The Massacres: Coming to Terms with the Trauma of 1965.* Jakarta: Tempo, 2015.

Lamasitudju, Nurlaela A. K. "Rekonsiliasi dan Pernyataan Maaf Pak Wali Kota." In *Luka Bangsa Luka Kita: Pelanggaran HAM Masa Lalu dan Tawaran Rekonsiliasi*, edited by Baskara T. Wardaya, 371–83. Yogyakarta: Galang Press, 2014.

Larasati, Rachmi Diyah. *The Dance That Makes You Vanish: Cultural Reconstruction in Post-Genocide Indonesia.* Minneapolis: University of Minnesota Press, 2013.

Lasamana, Viola. "Remixing Archives of Injustice and Genocide." Paper presented at the conference Memory, Media, and Technology: Exploring the Trajectories of Schindler's List, USC Shoah Foundation, Los Angeles, November 16–18, 2014.

Lashman, Paul, and James Oliver. "How We Lied to Put a Killer in Power." *Independent*, April 16, 2000.

Latief, Abdul. "I, the Accused." In *Silenced Voices: New Writing from Indonesia*, edited by Frank Stewart and John McGlynn, 193–98. Honolulu: University of Hawaii Press, 2000.

———. *Pleidoi Kol. A Latief: Soeharto Terlibat G30S.* Jakarta: Institut Studi Arus Informasi, 2000.

Legge, J. D. *Central Authority and Regional Autonomy in Indonesia: A Study in Local Administration, 1950–1960.* Ithaca, NY: Cornell University Press, 1961.

———. *Sukarno: A Political Biography.* Sydney: Allen and Unwin, 1990.

Lemarchand, René. *The Dynamics of Violence in Central Africa.* Philadelphia: University of Pennsylvania Press, 2009.

Lestariningsih, Amurwani Dwi. *Gerwani: Kisah Tapol Wanita di Kamp Plantungan.* 2nd ed. Jakarta: Kompas, 2011.

Lev, Daniel. "Indonesia 1965: The Year of the Coup." *Asian Survey* 6, no. 2 (February 1966): 103–10.

——. *The Transition to Guided Democracy: Indonesian Politics, 1957–1959*. Ithaca, NY: Cornell Modern Indonesia Project, 1966.

——. "On the Fall of the Parliamentary System." In *Democracy in Indonesia: 1950s and 1990s*, edited by David Bourchier and John Legge, 39–42. No. 31. Melbourne: Monash Papers on Southeast Asia, 1994.

——. *No Concessions: The Life of Yap Thiam Hien, Indonesian Human Rights Lawyer*. Seattle: University of Washington Press, 2011.

Liberation. "Intervention on the Question of Indonesia: Item 9 of the Agenda of the UN Sub-Commission on the Prevention of Discrimination and Protection of Minorities." London, August 1988.

Limpach, Rémy. "Business as Usual: Dutch Mass Violence in the Indonesian War of Independence." In *Colonial Counterinsurgency and Mass Violence: The Dutch Empire in Indonesia*, edited by Bart Luttikhuis and A. Dirk Moses, 64–90. New York: Routledge, 2014.

——. *De Brandende Kampongs van General Spoor*. Amsterdam: Uitgeverij Boon, 2016.

Lipton, Sara. *Dark Mirror: The Medieval Origins of Anti-Jewish Iconography*. New York: Metropolitan, 2014.

"Liputan Khusus: Pengakuan Algojo 1965." *Tempo*, October 1–7, 2012.

Lubis, Firman. *Jakarta 1960an: Kenangan Semasa Mahasiswa*. Jakarta: Masup Jakarta, 2008.

Lyon, Margot. *Bases of Conflict in Rural Java*. Berkeley, CA: Center for South and Southeast Asia Studies Research Monograph No. 3, 1970.

Mackie, J.A.C. *Problems of the Indonesian Inflation*. Ithaca, NY: Cornell Modern Indonesia Project, 1967.

——. "Anti-Chinese Outbreaks in Indonesia, 1959–1968." In *The Chinese in Indonesia: Five Essays*, edited by J.A.C. Mackie. Honolulu: University of Hawaii Press, 1976.

Magnis-Suseno, Franz. "Membersihkan Dosa Kolektif G30S." *Kompas*, September 29, 2015.

Mann, Michael. *The Dark Side of Democracy: Explaining Ethnic Cleansing*. New York: Cambridge University Press, 2005.

Marni. "I Am a Leaf in the Storm." Translated by Anton Lucas. *Indonesia* 47 (April 1989): 49–60.

Maxwell, Neville. "CIA Involvement in the 1965 Military Coup: New Evidence from Neville Maxwell." *Journal of Contemporary Asia* 9, no. 2 (1979): 251–52.

May, Brian. *The Indonesian Tragedy*. London: Routledge and Kegan Paul, 1978.

Mazower, Mark. "The Historian Who Was Not Baffled by the Nazis." *New York Review of Books*, December 22, 2016, 70–72.

McBeth, John. "Prisoners of History." *Far Eastern Economic Review*, February 16, 1995, 27–28.

McClintock, Michael, *Instruments of Statecraft: U.S. Guerrilla Warfare, Counter-Insurgency, and Counter-Terrorism, 1940–1990*. New York: Pantheon Books, 1990.

McDonald, Hamish. *Suharto's Indonesia*. Sydney: Fontana, 1981.

McGehee, Ralph. "The CIA and the White Paper on El Salvador." *Nation*, April 11, 1981, 423–25.

McGregor, Katharine. *History in Uniform: Military Ideology and the Construction of Indonesia's Past*. Honolulu: University of Hawaii Press, 2007.

———. "Mass Graves and Memories of the 1965 Indonesian Killings." In *The Contours of Mass Violence in Indonesia, 1965–68*, edited by Douglas Kammen and Katharine McGregor, 234–62. Singapore: NUS Press, 2012.

———. "Memory and Historical Justice for the Victims of Violence in 1965." Paper presented at the conference 1965 Today: Living with the Indonesian Massacres, Amsterdam, October 2, 2015.

———. "The World Was Silent? Global Communities of Resistance to the 1965 Repression in the Cold War Era." Paper presented at the annual meeting of the Association for Asian Studies, Chicago, March 28, 2015.

McMahon, Patrice. *Taming Ethnic Hatred: Ethnic Cooperation and Transnational Networks in Eastern Europe*. Syracuse, NY: Syracuse University Press, 2007.

McVey, Ruth. *The Rise of Indonesian Communism*. Ithaca, NY: Cornell University Press, 1965.

———. "The Post-Revolutionary Transformation of the Indonesian Military." *Indonesia* 11 (April 1971): 133–42.

———. "Nationalism, Revolution, and Organization in Indonesian Communism." In *Making Indonesia: Essays on Modern Indonesia in Honor of George McT. Kahin*, edited by Daniel Lev and Ruth McVey, 96–117. Ithaca, NY: Cornell Southeast Asia Program, 1996.

———. "A Preliminary Excursion through the Small World of Lt. Col. Untung." Unpublished manuscript, n.d.

Medvedev, Roy A. *Let History Judge: The Origins and Consequences of Stalinism*. New York: Knopf, 1971.

Melson, Robert. *Revolution and Genocide: On the Origins of the Armenian Genocide and the Holocaust*. Chicago: University of Chicago Press, 1992.

Melvin, Jess. "Mechanics of Mass Murder: How the Indonesian Military Initiated and Implemented the Indonesian Genocide—The Case of Aceh." PhD diss., University of Melbourne, 2014.

———. "Documenting Genocide." *Inside Indonesia* 122 (October–December 2015).

"Membenahi Beberapa Kendala Pembangunan Hukum Moderen Indonesia Sesuai dengan Jiwa Pancasila/UUD 45." Jakarta, April 1, 1995.

Midlarsky, Manus. *The Killing Trap*. Cambridge: Cambridge University Press, 2005.

Mirajadi. "Tiga Tahun Provokasi Madiun." *Bintang Merah*, August–September 1951.

Mortimer, Rex. *The Indonesian Communist Party and Land Reform, 1954–1965*. Clayton, Victoria: Monash University Centre for Southeast Asian Studies, 1972.

———. *Indonesian Communism under Sukarno: Ideology and Politics, 1959–1965*. Ithaca, NY: Cornell University Press, 1974.

Moser, Don. "Where the Rivers Ran Crimson from Butchery." *Life*, July 1, 1966, 26–33.

Moyn, Samuel. *The Last Utopia: Human Rights in History*. Cambridge MA: Harvard University Press, 2012.

Mozingo, David. *Sino-Indonesian Relations: An Overview, 1955–1965*. Santa Monica, CA: Rand Corporation, 1965.

Mrázek, Rudolf. *The United States and the Indonesian Military, 1945–1966.* 2 vols. Prague: Czechoslovak Academy of Science, 1978.

Muldar, Niels. "Abangan Javanese Religious Thought and Practice." *Bijdragen tot de Taal-, Land- en Volkenkunde* 139 (1983): 260–67.

Nadia, Ita F. *Suara Perempuan Korban Tragedi '65.* 3rd ed. Yogyakarta: Galang Press, 2009.

Naimark, Norman. *Stalin's Genocides.* Princeton, NJ: Princeton University Press, 2007.

Nathan, Andrew J. "Who Is Kim Jong-un?" *New York Review of Books*, August 18, 2016.

Nishihara, Masashi. *The Japanese and Sukarno's Indonesia: Tokyo-Jakarta Relations, 1951–1966.* Honolulu: University Press of Hawaii, 1976.

Notosusanto, Nugroho, and Ismail Saleh. *The Coup Attempt of the "September 30 Movement" in Indonesia.* Jakarta: Pembimbing Massa, 1968.

———. *Tragedi Nasional Percobaan Kup G30S/PKI di Indonesia.* Jakarta: PT Intermasa, 1989.

Nugroho, Johannes. "Indonesia Can Learn from Timor Leste on Human Rights." *Jakarta Globe*, July 21, 2015.

Oei Tjoe Tat. *Memoar Oei Tjoe Tat: Pembantu Presiden Sukarno*, edited by Pramoedya Ananta Toer and Stanley Adi Prasetyo. Jakarta: Hasta Mitra, 1995.

Olliver, Chloe. "Reconciling NU and the PKI." *Inside Indonesia* (July 2007).

Oppenheimer, Joshua, and Michael Uwemedimo. "Show of Force: A Cinema-Séance of Power and Violence in Sumatra's Plantation Belt." *Critical Quarterly* 54, no. 1 (April 2009): 84–110.

Pamuntjak, Laksmi. *Amba.* Jakarta: Gramedia Pustaka Utama, 2012.

———. "Censorship Is Returning to Indonesia in the Name of the 1965 Purges." *Guardian*, October 27, 2015.

Pauker, Guy. "Political Consequences of Rural Development Programs in Indonesia." *Pacific Affairs* 41, no. 3 (Fall 1968): 386–402.

Peters, Robbie. *Surabaya, 1945–2010: Neighbourhood, State, and Economy in Indonesia's City of Struggle.* Singapore: NUS Press, 2013.

Pietikainen, Petteri. *Madness: A History.* London: Routledge, 2015.

Pizzicaro, John T. "The 30 September Movement in Indonesia." *Studies in Intelligence* 13 (Fall 1969): 97–111.

Poesponegoro, M. D., and N. Notosustanto. *Sejarah Nasional Indonesia.* Vol 6. 6th ed. Jakarta: Balai Pustaka, 1990.

Pohlman, Annie. "A Fragment of a Story: Gerwani and Tapol Experiences." *Intersections: Gender, History, and Culture in the Asian Context* 10 (August 2004).

———. *Women, Sexual Violence, and the Indonesian Killings of 1965–66.* New York: Routledge, 2015.

Pour, Julius P. *Benny Moerdani: Profil Prajurit Negarawan.* Jakarta: Yayasan Kejuangan Sudirman, 1993.

Power, Samantha. *A Problem from Hell: America and the Age of Genocide.* New York: Basic Books, 2002.

Pramoedya Ananta Toer. *This Earth of Mankind.* Translated by Max Lane. New York: Penguin Books, 1996.

——. *The Mute's Soliloquy: A Memoir*. Translated by Willem Samuels. New York: Hyperion East, 1999.

Prasetyo, Stanley Adi. "Jangan Biarkan Jalan Itu Kian Menyempit dan Berliku." In *Luka Bangsa Luka Kita: Pelanggaran HAM Masa Lalu dan Tawaran Rekonsiliasi*, edited by Baskara T. Wardaya, 259–65. Yogyakarta: Galang Press, 2014.

Prior, John M. "The Silent Scream of a Silenced History: Part One. The Maumere Massacre of 1966." *Exchange: Journal of Missiological and Ecumenical Research* 40, no. 2 (2011): 117–43.

Ransom, David. "The Berkeley Mafia and the Indonesian Massacres." *Ramparts*, October 9, 1970.

Reid, Anthony. *The Indonesian National Revolution*. Hawthorn, Victoria: Longman, 1974.

Reston, James. "A Gleam of Light in Asia." *New York Times*, June 19, 1966.

Ricklefs, Merle C. "The Birth of the Abangan." *Bijdragen tot de Taal-, Land- en Volkenkunde* 162, no. 1 (2006): 35–55.

——. *Islamisation and Its Opponents in Java: A Political, Social, Cultural, and Religious History, c. 1930 to the Present*. Honolulu: University of Hawaii Press, 2012.

Robben, Antonius C.G.M. *Political Violence and Trauma in Argentina*. Philadelphia: University of Pennsylvania Press, 2005.

Robin, Ron. *The Making of the Cold War Enemy: Culture and Politics in the Military-Intellectual Complex*. Princeton, NJ: Princeton University Press, 2001.

Robinson, Geoffrey. *The Dark Side of Paradise: Political Violence in Bali*. Ithaca, NY: Cornell University Press, 1995.

——. "*Rawan* Is as *Rawan* Does: The Origins of Disorder in New Order Aceh." *Indonesia* 66 (October 1998): 127–58.

——. "Indonesia—On a New Course?" In *Coercion and Governance: The Declining Political Role of the Military in Asia*, edited by Muthiah Alagappa, 226–56. Stanford, CA: Stanford University Press, 2001.

——. "People's War: Militias in Indonesia and East Timor." *South East Asia Research* 9, no. 3 (November 2001): 271–318.

——. *"If You Leave Us Here, We Will Die": How Genocide Was Stopped in East Timor*. Princeton, NJ: Princeton University Press, 2010.

——. "State-Sponsored Violence and Secessionist Rebellions in Asia." In *The Oxford Handbook of Genocide Studies*, edited by Donald Bloxham and Dirk Moses, 466–88. Oxford: Oxford University Press, 2010.

Rocamora, J. Eliseo. "Nationalism in Search of an Ideology: Indonesia's Nationalist Party, 1946–1965." PhD diss., Cornell University, 1974.

Rochijat, Pipit. "Am I PKI or Non-PKI?" Translated by Benedict Anderson. *Indonesia* 40 (October 1985): 37–56.

Roosa, John. *Pretext for Mass Murder: The September 30th Movement and Suharto's Coup d'Etat in Indonesia*. Madison: University of Wisconsin Press, 2006.

——. "The September 30th Movement: The Aporias of the Official Narratives." In *The Contours of Mass Violence in Indonesia, 1965–68*, edited by Douglas Kammen and Katharine McGregor, 25–49. Singapore: NUS Press, 2012.

——. "The State of Knowledge about an Open Secret: Indonesia's Mass Disappearances of 1965–66." *Journal of Asian Studies* 75, no. 2 (May 2016): 281–97.

Roosa, John, Ayu Ratih, and Hilmar Farid, eds. *Tahun yang Tak Pernah Berakhir: Pengalaman Korban 1965: Esai-Esai Sejarah Lisan*. Jakarta: Elsam, 2004.

Rush, James. "Pramoedya Ananta Toer." In *The Ramon Magsaysay Awards*, 12:229–53. Manila: Ramon Magsaysay Foundation, 2003.

Ryter, Loren. "Pemuda Pancasila: The Last Loyalist Free Men of Suharto's Order?" In *Violence and the State in Suharto's Indonesia*, edited by Benedict Anderson, 124–55. Ithaca, NY: Cornell Southeast Asia Program.

Said, Salim Haji. *Gestapu 65: PKI, Aidit, Sukarno, dan Soeharto*. Jakarta: Mizan Publishers, 2015.

Santoso, Aboeprijadi and Gerry van Klinken. "Genocide Finally Enters Public Discourse: The International People's Tribunal 1965." In *1965 Today: Living with the Indonesian Massacres*, edited by Martijn Eickhoff, Gerry van Klinken, and Geoffrey Robinson. Special Issue, *Journal of Genocide Research* 19, no. 3 (2017).

Schaefer, Bernd. "The Two Germanys and Indonesia." In *1965: Indonesia and the World, Indonesia dan Dunia*, edited by Bernd Schaefer and Baskara T. Wardaya, 93–113. Bilingual ed. Jakarta: Gramedia Pustaka Utama, 2013.

Schaefer, Bernd, and Baskara T. Wardaya, eds. *1965: Indonesia and the World, Indonesia dan Dunia*. Bilingual ed. Jakarta: Gramedia Pustaka Utama, 2013.

Schonhardt, Sara. "Veil of Silence Lifted in Indonesia." *New York Times*, January 18, 2012.

Schulte Nordholt, Henk. "A Genealogy of Violence." In *Roots of Violence in Indonesia: Contemporary Violence in Historical Perspective*, edited by Freek Colombijn and Thomas Lindblad, 33–61. Leiden: KITLV Press, 2002.

Schurmann, Franz. *The Logic of World Power: An Inquiry into the Origins, Currents, and Contradictions of World Politics*. New York: Random House, 1974.

Schutte, Heinz. "September 30, 1965, and Its Aftermath in the French Press." In *1965: Indonesia and the World, Indonesia dan Dunia*, edited by Bernd Schaefer and Baskara T. Wardaya, 114–28. Bilingual ed. Jakarta: Gramedia Pustaka Utama, 2013.

Scott, Peter Dale. "The United States and the Overthrow of Sukarno, 1965–1967." *Pacific Affairs* 58, no. 2 (Summer 1985): 239–64.

Sears, Laurie J. *Situated Testimonies: Dread and Enchantment in an Indonesian Literary Archive*. Honolulu: University of Hawaii Press, 2013.

Sémelin, Jacques. *Purify and Destroy: Political Uses of Massacres and Genocide*. New York: Columbia University Press, 2007.

Setiawan, Hersri. *Aku Eks Tapol*. Yogyakarta: Galang Press, 2003.

Setiyawan, Dahlia G. "The Cold War in the City of Heroes: U.S.-Indonesian Relations and Anti-Communist Operations in Surabaya, 1963–1965." PhD diss., University of California Los Angeles, 2014.

Setiyono, Budi, and Bonnie Triyana, eds. *Revolusi Belum Selesai: Kumpulan Pidato Presiden Sukarno 30 September 1965—Pelengkap Nawaksara*. 2 vols. Semarang: Masyarakat Indonesia Sadar Sejarah, 2003.

Sherman, Scott. "A Return to Java." *Lingua Franca* 11, no. 7 (October 2001): 38–49.

Sidel, John T. *Riots, Pogroms, and Jihad: Religious Violence in Indonesia*. Ithaca, NY: Cornell University Press, 2006.

Simpson, Bradley. *Economists with Guns: Authoritarian Development and U.S.-Indonesian Relations, 1960–1968*. Stanford, CA: Stanford University Press, 2008.

———. "International Dimensions of the 1965–68 Violence in Indonesia." In *The Contours of Mass Violence in Indonesia, 1965–68*, edited by Douglas Kammen and Katharine McGregor, 50–74. Singapore: NUS Press, 2012.

———. "The United States and the International Dimension of the Killings in Indonesia." In *1965: Indonesia and the World, Indonesia dan Dunia*, edited by Bernd Schaefer and Baskara T. Wardaya, 43–60. Bilingual ed. Jakarta: Gramedia Pustaka Utama, 2013.

Sjoekoer, Mohammad. "Death." In *Gestapu: Indonesian Short Stories on the Abortive Coup of 30th September 1965*, edited and translated by Harry Aveling, 23–26. Honolulu: University of Hawaii Press, 1975.

Slamet, Ibrahim. "Letter from Indonesia." *Index on Censorship* 3, no. 1 (1974): 60–64.

Smith, Joseph B. *Portrait of a Cold Warrior*. New York: Putnam, 1976.

Soe Hok Gie. "The Mass Killings in Bali." In *The Indonesian Killings, 1965–1966: Studies from Java and Bali*, edited by Robert Cribb, 252–58. No. 21. Clayton, Victoria: Monash Papers on Southeast Asia, 1990.

Soebandrio, H. *Kesaksianku tentang G-30-S*. Jakarta: Forum Pendukung Reformasi Total, 2000.

Soeharto. *My Thoughts, Words, and Deeds: An Autobiography*. Jakarta: Citra Lamtoro Gung Persada, 1991.

Sophiaan, Manai. *Kehormatan Bagi Yang Berhak: Bung Karno Tidak Terlibat G30S/PKI*. Jakarta: Yayasan Mencerdaskan Kehidupan Bangsa, 1994.

Spores, John C. *Running Amok: An Historical Inquiry*. Southeast Asia Series. No. 82. Athens, OH: Monographs in International Studies, 1988.

Staub, Ervin. *The Roots of Evil: The Origins of Genocide and Other Group Violence*. Cambridge: Cambridge University Press, 1989.

Stern. Steve J. *Battling for Hearts and Minds: Memory Struggles in Pinochet's Chile, 1973–1988*. Durham, NC: Duke University Press, 2006.

Stoler, Ann Laura. *Capitalism and Confrontation in Sumatra's Plantation Belt, 1870–1979*. New Haven, CT: Yale University Press, 1985.

Straus, Scott. *The Order of Genocide: Race, Power, and War in Rwanda*. Ithaca, NY: Cornell University Press, 2006.

———. "Destroy Them to Save Us: Theories of Genocide and the Logics of Political Violence." *Terrorism and Political Violence* 24, no. 4 (2012): 544–62.

———. *Making and Unmaking Nations: War, Leadership, and Genocide in Modern Africa*. Ithaca, NY: Cornell University Press, 2015.

Straus, Scott, and Evgeny Finkel. "Macro, Meso, and Micro Research on Genocide: Gains, Shortcomings, and Future Areas of Inquiry." *Genocide Studies and Prevention* 7, no. 1 (Spring 2012): 56–67.

Subritsky, John. *Confronting Sukarno: British, American, Australian, and New Zealand Diplomacy in the Malaysian-Indonesian Confrontation, 1961–1965*. New York: St. Martin's Press, 2000.

Sudisman. "Analysis of Responsibility: Defense Speech of Sudisman, General Secretary of the Indonesian Communist Party at His Trial before the Special Military

Tribunal, Jakarta, 21 July 1967." Translated by Benedict Anderson. Melbourne, Victoria: Works Co-operative, 1975.

Sudjatmiko, Iwan Gardono. "The Destruction of the Indonesian Communist Party: A Comparative Analysis of East Java and Bali." PhD diss., Harvard University, 1992.

Sudjinah. *Terempas Gelombang Pasang*. Jakarta: Pustaka Utan Kayu, 2003.

Sufi, Rusdi. *Pernak Pernik Sejarah Aceh*. Banda Aceh: Badan Arsip dan Perpustakaan Aceh, 2009.

Sugama, Yoga. *Memori Jenderal Yoga*. Jakarta: Bina Rena Pariwara, 1990.

Sukanta, Putu Oka. "Leftover Soul." In *Silenced Voices: New Writing from Indonesia*, edited by Frank Stewart and John McGlynn, 214–23. Honolulu: University of Hawaii Press, 2000.

——, ed. *Breaking the Silence: Survivors Speak about the 1965–66 Violence in Indonesia*. Translated by Jennifer Lindsay. Clayton, Victoria: Monash University Publishing, 2014.

Sukarno. *Nationalism, Islam, and Marxism*. Translated by Karel H. Warouw and Peter D. Weldon. Ithaca, NY: Modern Indonesia Project, Southeast Asia Program, Cornell University, 1970.

——. *"Indonesia Accuses!" Sukarno's Defense Oration in the Political Trial of 1930*. Edited and translated by Roger Paget. Kuala Lumpur: Oxford University Press, 1975.

Sulami. *Perempuan—Kebenaran dan Penjara*. Jakarta: Cipta Lestari, 1999.

Sulistyo, Hermawan. "The Forgotten Years: The Missing History of Indonesia's Mass Slaughter." PhD diss., Arizona State University, 1997.

——. *Palu Arit di Ladang Tebu: Sejarah Pembantaian Massal yang Terlupakan 1965–1966*. Jakarta: JKG, 2000.

——. "Mass Murder from 1965–1966: Vendetta and Jingiosm." In *The Massacres: Coming to Terms with the Trauma of 1965*, edited by Kurniawan et al., 83–87. Jakarta: Tempo, 2015.

Sulzberger, C. L. "Mass Murders Go on in Indonesia." *New York Times*, April 19, 1966.

Sumarwan, Antonius. *Menyeberangi Sungai Air Mata: Kisah Tragis Tapol '65 dan Upaya Rekonsiliasi*. Yogyakarta: Kanisius, 2007.

Sumiyarsi Siwirini C. *Plantungan: Pembuangan Tapol Perempuan*. Yogyakarta: Pusat Sejarah dan Etika Politik (Pusdep), Universitas Sanata Dharma, 2010.

Sundhaussen, Ulf. *The Road to Power: Indonesian Military Politics, 1945–1967*. Kuala Lumpur: Oxford University Press, 1982.

Sunyoto, Agus, Miftahul Ulum, H. Abu Muslih, and Imam Kusnin Ahmad. *Banser Berjihad Menumpas PKI*. Tulungagung: Lembaga Kajian dan Pengembangan Pimpinan Wilayah Gerakan Pemuda Ansor Jawa Timur and Pesulukan Thoriqoh Agung Tulungagung, 1996.

Suparman, H. *Dari Pulau Buru Sampai ke Mekah: Sebuah Catatan Tragedi 1965*. Bandung: Nuansa, 2006.

Supriatma, Made. "Kamerad Dalam Keyakinan: Pater Joop Beek, SJ dan Jaringan BA Santamaria di Asia Tenggara." *Harian Indoprogress*, September 29, 2016.

Suryawan, I Ngurah. *Ladang Hitam di Pulau Dewata: Pembantaian Massal di Bali 1965*. Yogyakarta: Galangpress, 2007.

Swift, Ruth Ann. *The Road to Madiun: The Indonesian Communist Uprising of 1948*. Ithaca, NY: Cornell Southeast Asia Program, 1989.

Tan Swie Ling. *G30S 1965, Perang Dingin dan Kehancuran Nasionalisme: Pemikiran Cina Jelata Korban Orba*. Jakarta: Komunitas Bambu, 2010.

Tanter, Richard. "Intelligence Agencies and Third World Militarization: A Case Study of Indonesia, 1966–1989." PhD diss., Monash University, 1990.

——. "The Great Killings in Indonesia through the Australian Mass Media." In *1965: Indonesia and the World, Indonesia dan Dunia*, edited by Bernd Schaefer and Baskara T. Wardaya, 129–44. Bilingual ed. Jakarta: Gramedia Pustaka Utama, 2013.

Tapol. "Women on Trial." *Tapol Bulletin* 9 (1975): 1–4.

——. *Indonesia: The Prison State*. London: Tapol, 1976.

——. *Treatment of Indonesian Political Prisoners: Forced Labour and Transmigration*. London: Tapol, 1978.

Tilly, Charles. *The Politics of Collective Violence*. Cambridge: Cambridge University Press, 2003.

Tim ISAI. *Bayang-Bayang PKI*. Jakarta: Institut Studi Arus Informasi, 1996.

Tim PBNU. *Benturan NU-PKI, 1948–1965*. Jakarta, 2013.

Tohari, Ahmed. "Village Dancer." In *Silenced Voices: New Writing from Indonesia*, edited by Frank Stewart and John McGlynn, 13–23. Honolulu: University of Hawaii Press, 2000.

Topping, Seymour. "Indonesia Haunted by Mass Killing." *New York Times*, August 24, 1966.

Törnquist, Olle. *Dilemmas of Third World Communism: The Destruction of the PKI in Indonesia*. London: Zed Books, 1985.

Totten, Samuel, and William S. Parsons, eds. *Century of Genocide: Critical Essays and Eyewitness Accounts*. 4th ed. New York: Routledge, 2013.

Tovar, B. Hugh. "The Indonesian Crisis of 1965–1966: A Retrospective." *International Journal of Intelligence and Counterintelligence* 7, no. 3 (Fall 1994): 313–38.

Tsai, Yen-ling, and Douglas Kammen. "Anti-Communist Violence and the Ethnic Chinese in Medan, North Sumatra." In *The Contours of Mass Violence in Indonesia, 1965–68*, edited by Douglas Kammen and Katharine McGregor, 131–55. Singapore: NUS Press, 2012.

Üngör, Uğur. "When Persecution Bleeds into Mass Murder: The Processive Nature of Genocide." *Genocide Studies and Prevention* 1, no. 2 (2006): 173–76.

US Central Intelligence Agency, Directorate of Intelligence. *Indonesia—1965: The Coup That Backfired*. Washington, DC: CIA, 1968.

Usamah. "War and Humanity." In *Gestapu: Indonesian Short Stories on the Abortive Coup of 30th September 1965*, edited and translated by Harry Aveling, 12–22. Honolulu: University of Hawaii Press, 1975.

Utrecht, Ernst. "Het Bloedbad op Bali." *De Groene Amsterdammer*, January 14, 1967.

Valentino, Benjamin. *Final Solutions: Mass Killing and Genocide in the Twentieth Century*. Ithaca, NY: Cornell University Press, 2004.

van der Kroef, Justus M. "Indonesia's Political Prisoners." *Pacific Affairs* 49 (1976): 625–47.

van Dijk, C. *Rebellion under the Banner of Islam: The Darul Islam in Indonesia*. The Hague: Martinus Nijhoff, 1981.

van Klinken, Gerry. *The Making of Middle Indonesia: Middle Classes in Kupang Town, 1930s–1980s*. Leiden: Brill, 2014.

van Langenberg, Michael. "Gestapu and State Power in Indonesia." In *The Indonesian Killings, 1965–1966: Studies from Java and Bali*, edited by Robert Cribb, 45–62. No. 21. Clayton, Victoria: Monash Papers on Southeast Asia, 1990.

van Rooijen, Willy. "Murdering Army, Silent Church." *Inside Indonesia* 124 (April–June 2016).

Wandita, Galuh, and Tati Krisnawaty. "The Act of Living: How Women Survivors of Indonesia's Genocide Organized Themselves to Create Change." Paper presented at the annual meeting of the Association for Asian Studies, Chicago, April 2015.

Wardaya, Baskara T. *Bung Karno Menggugat! Dari Marhaen, CIA, Pembantaian Massal '65 hingga G30S*. 7th ed. Yogyakarta: Galang Press, 2009.

——, ed. *Truth Will Out: Indonesian Accounts of the 1965 Mass Violence*. Translated by Jennifer Lindsay. Clayton, Victoria: Monash University Publishing, 2013.

——, ed. *Luka Bangsa Luka Kita: Pelanggaran HAM Masa Lalu dan Tawaran Rekonsiliasi*. 7th ed. Yogyakarta: Galang Press, 2014.

——. "Transitional Justice at the Grass-roots Level: The Case of Sekber '65." Paper presented at the conference 1965 Today: Living with the Indonesian Massacres, Amsterdam, October 2, 2015.

Webb, R.A.F. Paul. "The Sickle and the Cross: Christians and Communists in Bali, Flores, Sumba, and Timor, 1965–1967." *Journal of Southeast Asian Studies* 17, no. 1 (February 1986): 94–112.

Weinstein, Franklin B. "The Uses of Foreign Policy in Indonesia." PhD diss., Cornell University, 1972.

Weissman, Stephen R. "What Really Happened in Congo." *Foreign Affairs* 93, no. 4 (July–August 2014): 14–24.

Weitz, Eric D. *A Century of Genocide: Utopias of Race and Nation*. Princeton, NJ: Princeton University Press, 2003.

——. "The Modernity of Genocides: War, Race, and Revolution in the Twentieth Century." In *The Specter of Genocide: Mass Murder in Historical Perspective*, edited by Robert Gellately and Ben Kiernan, 53–74. Cambridge: Cambridge University Press, 2003.

Wertheim, W. F. "Suharto and the Untung Coup—the Missing Link." *Journal of Contemporary Asia* 1, no. 2 (Winter 1970): 50–57.

——. "Whose Plot? New Light on the 1965 Events." *Journal of Contemporary Asia* 9, no. 2 (1979): 197–215.

Wieringa, Saskia. *Sexual Politics in Indonesia*. New York: Palgrave, 2002.

Wise, David, and Thomas B. Ross. *The Invisible Government*. New York: Random House, 1964.

Young, Kenneth R. "Local and National Influences in the Violence of 1965." In *The Indonesian Killings, 1965–1966: Studies from Java and Bali*, edited by Robert Cribb, no. 21, 63–100. Clayton, Victoria: Monash Papers on Southeast Asia, 1990.

Zhou, Taomo. "China and the Thirtieth of September Movement." *Indonesia* 98 (October 2014): 29–58.

——. "Ambivalent Alliance: Chinese Policy towards Indonesia, 1960–1965," *China Quarterly* 221 (March 2015): 208–28.

Zurbuchen, Mary. "History, Memory, and the '1965 Incident' in Indonesia." *Asian Survey* 42, no. 4 (2002): 564–81.

——, ed. *Beginning to Remember: The Past in the Indonesian Present*. Seattle: University of Washington Press, 2005.

Film

40 Years of Silence. Directed by Robert Lemelson. Los Angeles: Elemental Productions, 2009. DVD.

Blok aan het Ben, een Gevangenis in Indonesie. The Netherlands, 1969.

Indonesia: The Troubled Victory. NBC, 1969.

Pengkhianatan Gerakan 30 September/PKI. Directed by Arifin C. Noer. Jakarta: Perum Produksi Film Negara, 1984.

Putih Abu-Abu: Masa Lalu Perempuan. Syarikat and Komnas Perempuan, 2016.

Sang Penari. Directed by Ifa Isfansyah. Jakarta: Salto Films, 2011. DVD.

The Act of Killing. Directed by Joshua Oppenheimer. Drafthouse Films, 2013. DVD.

The Look of Silence. Directed by Joshua Oppenheimer. Drafthouse Films, 2016. DVD.

Media

Agence France-Press

Angkatan Bersendjata

Australian Broadcasting Corporation

Berita Yudha

Duta Masyarakat

Editor

Far Eastern Economic Review

Guardian

Jakarta Globe

Jakarta Post

Kompas

Life

Los Angeles Times

New York Times

Reuters

Suara Indonesia

Surabaya Post

Tempo

Time

Washington Post

INDEX

Note: Page numbers in italic type indicate illustrations.

Human Rights and Crimes against Humanity

ERIC D. WEITZ, SERIES EDITOR

Echoes of Violence: Letters from a War Reporter by Carolin Emcke

Cannibal Island: Death in a Siberian Gulag by Nicolas Werth. Translated by Steven Rendall with a foreword by Jan T. Gross

Torture and the Twilight of Empire from Algiers to Baghdad by Marnia Lazreg

Terror in Chechnya: Russia and the Tragedy of Civilians in War by Emma Gilligan

"If You Leave Us Here, We Will Die": How Genocide Was Stopped in East Timor by Geoffrey Robinson

Stalin's Genocides by Norman Naimark

Against Massacre: Humanitarian Interventions in the Ottoman Empire, 1815–1914 by Davide Rodogno

All the Missing Souls: A Personal History of the War Crimes Tribunals by David Scheffer

The Young Turks' Crime against Humanity: The Armenian Genocide and Ethnic Cleansing in the Ottoman Empire by Taner Akçam

The International Human Rights Movement: A History by Aryeh Neier

Child Migration and Human Rights in a Global Age by Jacqueline Bhabha

"They Can Live in the Desert but Nowhere Else": A History of the Armenian Genocide by Ronald Grigor Suny

Evidence for Hope: Making Human Rights Work in the 21st Century by Kathryn Sikkink

The Killing Season: A History of the Indonesian Massacres, 1965–66 by Geoffrey B. Robinson